THE SOCRATES PRACTICAL LAW HANDBOOK:

Solutions for Everyday Legal Questions

BY THE EDITORS OF SOCRATES

SOCRATES™
KNOW HOW TO DO MORE
AND SAVE

Socrates Media, LLC
227 West Monroe, Suite 500
Chicago, IL 60606
www.socrates.com

This publication is designed to provide accurate and authoritative information in regard to the subject matter covered. It is sold with the understanding that the publisher is not engaged in rendering legal, accounting or other professional service. If legal advice or other expert assistance is required, the services of a competent professional person should be sought.

From a Declaration of Principles Jointly Adopted by a Committee of the American Bar Association and a Committee of Publishers and Associations

ISBN 1-59546-244-9

This product is not intended to provide legal or financial advice or substitute for the advice of an attorney or advisor.

PRINTING NUMBER 10 9 8 7 6 5 4 3 2 1

THE SOCRATES PRACTICAL LAW HANDBOOK:

Solutions for Everyday Legal Questions

Special acknowledgment to the following:

John J. Palmer, JD, Managing Editor; Amy Kruse, Associate Editor; Al Nicolini, Design & Production; Jeannie Staats, Product Manager; Derek Vander Laan, Cover Art; Lucas Otto, JD, Editor; Peri Hughes, Editor; Alison Somilleda, Copy Editor; Kristen Grant, Production Associate; Edgewater Editorial Services, Inc.

Get the most out of The Complete Law Handbook.

Take advantage of the enclosed CD and special access to the Legal resource section of Socrates.com that are included with this purchase.

The CD and legal resource section offer readers a unique opportunity both to build on the material contained in the book and to utilize tools such as forms, checklists, spreadsheets and appraisals that will save time and money. More than $100 worth of free forms and content are provided.

The CD bound into the back cover contains a read-only version of this book as well as a variety of fillable and savable forms, spreadsheets and checklists formatted in Microsoft Word and Excel.

Readers can access the dedicated legal resource section by registering their purchase at Socrates.com. A special eight-digit Registration Code is provided on the CD. Once registered, a variety of free forms, checklists, appraisals, research articles, government forms and other useful tools are available at:

www.socrates.com/books/law-handbook.aspx

From time to time, new material will be added and readers will be informed of changes in the law, as well as updates to the content of this book.

Finally, readers are offered discounts on selected Socrates products designed to help implement and manage their business and personal matters more efficiently.

TABLE OF CONTENTS

The following bonus sections, along with additional tools, checklists and valuable information are available at www.socrates.com/books/law-handbook.aspx when you register your purchase at Socrates.com.

Civil Rights

Consumer Finance

Criminal Law

Immigration, Naturalization & Citizenship

Intellectual Property

Internet, e-Commerce & Communications

Motor Vehicles

Names

Neighbors

Personal Property

Pets & Animals

Sports

Travel Law

INTRODUCTION

There is an enormous amount of legal information available these days. Unfortunately, most of it is written in legalese and directed specifically at lawyers. As a result, the law is indecipherable and remains a mystery to the average person. We just do not think that is right.

Our job at Socrates has been to make the law available to everyone. To do this, we have selected the most frequently asked questions that people may have an interest in or a need to know, and provided simple, clear answers–providing a basis for understanding legal and business issues that you will likely encounter in your everyday life.

While this resource may not have all the answers you are looking for, it is a great place to start. Beyond answers, we have offered Tips, Cautions, Sidebars and Examples, so that the material is more pertinent to your personal situation. Of equal importance, we have provided you with solutions on how to take the next step in resolving your dilemma. That is, once you understand the answer to the problem, you need to plot out a course of action. And quite often, that does not require a formal legal action, but a mere declaration that you know what your rights are and that you will not let them be infringed upon.

We have created this work to put information into the hands of the public–not to put lawyers out of business. By dispensing information, we are actually creating a greater demand for legal services. We hope that this resource will arm readers with enough information to pursue a solution on their own; and if they still feel they need a lawyer, we will have made it easier for them to pick up the phone, make an appointment, and speak with a lawyer without being intimidated. Knowledge is power–the power to create your own future–the power to direct your own life. We hope that you will use the knowledge of Socrates to become involved in the legal process and take control over your life.

1 ASSET PROTECTION

An asset is anything of value owned by an individual. Assets are either real property or personal property. For most people, their only real property asset is their home. Vehicles, furnishings, clothing, jewelry and tools are examples of personal property assets.

Assets have a fair market value—the price a willing seller would take from a willing buyer for the asset. Some assets, such as property, homes and vehicles have a value set by independent appraisers or experts in those fields. By law, assets belong to the owner and no one else has the right to dispose or sell those assets. However, in certain legal situations, the owner's assets can be seized and sold without his consent.

To protect assets from creditors, the owner must divest herself of ownership by transferring the asset or selling the asset and using the funds to purchase property that laws do not allow to be seized. For example, expensive jewelry can be sold and the cash used to buy a home, which is usually exempt.

> A creditor is a person or company that is owed money

LEGAL SEIZURE OF ASSETS

Laws allow assets to be seized by creditors and courts for a variety of reasons. The IRS can seize and sell assets to satisfy unpaid taxes. A bankruptcy court typically orders assets sold to raise cash to pay creditors. Bank accounts can be seized or garnished for unpaid child support.

In these cases, there is a court order or judgment in place setting out an amount owed. Unlike the typical collection efforts where a credit card company, for example, attempts to get voluntarily paid through calls and correspondence, the court judgment gives the creditor the immediate right to collect (without the debtor's cooperation) using any legal means.

Can a credit card company get a judgment against me? *Yes. Any person or business that claims you owe them money can, potentially, get a judgment against you.* However, it is unlikely a credit card company will invest the time, expense and trouble to litigate the manner, although they certainly have that right.

> **TIP:** Getting a judgment is not automatic or necessarily easy. The creditor must bring a lawsuit against you alleging that you owe a certain amount. At a trial of such a lawsuit, the creditor must prove the amount that you owe (through invoices, statements, contracts or notes you signed) and convince a judge or jury the money is, in fact, owed. Only then will a creditor be able to get a judgment against you.

Are any of my assets exempt? *Typically, assets are seized because a person has been sued, lost the case and a money judgment has been entered.* For example, an individual may be sued and found at fault in an automobile accident case and the jury awards the plaintiff $100,000 in damages. The person who was sued now has a $100,000 judgment entered against him, which he is required to pay. He is known as the judgment debtor and the plaintiff becomes the judgment creditor.

Because most people do not have large sums of money available to pay judgments, laws allow assets to be seized and sold to satisfy or pay the judgment. However, each state has enacted laws protecting certain assets from seizure. These assets are exempt from being used to satisfy a judgment. For instance, real property where a residence is located is almost always protected to some extent under state homestead laws. These homestead laws vary from almost total protection of real property to little or no protection.

> Florida and Texas provide the widest coverage of asset protection. In Texas, for example, up to 200 acres of land can be claimed under the state homestead exemption, no matter its value. Additionally, there are very few personal property assets that the typical person owns that can be seized to satisfy a judgment.

The easiest way to protect the largest number of assets is to reside in a state where laws offer wide protection.

> **TIP:** Moving simply to avoid paying a judgment or creditors is usually considered a fraudulent transfer of assets. The court in the state where the judgment was entered will rule the assets still "reside" in the original state and order their seizure.

Are my bank accounts exempt from seizure?

Although cash in a bank account is normally available to a judgment creditor, the account can be titled in such a way that the money may be protected and exempt.

EXAMPLE: Putting a bank account in the name of a separate corporation, rather than the name of the individual owing money, may block a creditor from seizing the funds.

Married persons should not have joint accounts with both their names on them if one of them owes a money judgment. Retirement accounts are exempt from payment on judgments as well.

What real property is exempt from seizure?

A debtor's personal residence is typically exempt from creditors. Debtors who do not own a home can sell assets and use the funds to buy a house, thus converting nonexempt assets into exempt assets, which are shielded from creditors. Likewise, selling a home can turn an exempt asset—the home—into seizable funds or assets. Generally, a person has 6 months to use funds from the sale of a home to buy another home. During that time period, the cash proceeds from the sale are exempt.

Can I transfer assets to avoid their seizure?

If an asset is not exempt, it can still be protected from a creditor by transferring the ownership from the judgment debtor. Transferring the ownership of assets is not illegal. However, the transfer cannot be done with the purpose of defrauding creditors.

EXAMPLE: Business owners routinely incorporate their business to protect its assets (such as the company truck) from the owner's personal creditors.

> Not only are fraudulent transfers illegal, in many cases the transfers are a criminal violation. A fraudulent transfer occurs whenever assets are transferred in an effort to obstruct a legitimate creditor from taking the asset.

> **TIP:** An attorney who participates in a fraudulent transfer scheme can be regarded as a coconspirator in the fraud, and can be subject to the same penalties as his client

What is a homestead purchase? *Because many states have laws that protect their residents' homes from judgments, bankruptcies and creditors, purchasing a home is one of the best and easiest ways to obtain a protected asset.*

Some laws protect the house from creditors regardless of its value, as well as a certain amount of land surrounding the home.

How does incorporation affect seizure of my assets? *A corporation is a legally formed company that is permitted to own assets (and owe debts).* Corporations are owned by shareholders and run by officers. However, neither the shareholders nor the officers personally own the company's assets. Therefore, if one of the shareholders owes child support, the corporate bank account cannot be garnished because she does not own the bank account.

Incorporating a business allows a person to place the ownership of assets in the corporation. Corporate assets become separate from personal assets and cannot be seized by the person's creditors.

> Laws look upon corporations as separate persons or entities from the owners or shareholders. Thus, the corporate assets belong to the corporation only, not the officers of the corporation. However, if the officers begin treating the corporate assets as if they personally owned them, laws allow creditors to seize company assets.

> Incorporation is a legal means to protect assets unless the company was formed with the intent to avoid potential creditors who have threatened or brought litigation. Corporations that are set up as an extension of the owner's personal transactions are not recognized by court. The "veil" that protects the corporation's assets from the owner's creditors will be "pierced" in those situations, and the creditors can seize the assets.

Can I avoid seizure through estate planning? *One of the best ways to protect assets is through estate planning.* It is essential that estate planning be discussed with an attorney; otherwise, the assets may not be shielded. Any individual can set up a trust, make annual gifts to family members or place money in a retirement account.

What is a domestic asset trust? *A trust is an excellent way to protect assets.* However, the trust cannot be managed or controlled in any way by the former owner of the assets. The trustee should not be a friend or family member. Debtors attempting to protect their assets by forming a trust are often unwilling to give complete control to a third-party trustee, in which case the assets will still be available to creditors.

What is a living trust? *During an individual's lifetime, ownership of his assets can be placed into a revocable trust.* At the time of death, the assets are not subject to probate as they are owned by the trust. However, a revocable trust is a poor asset protection technique. Because the debtor essentially controls the trust—he can revoke it at any time—the trust assets remain available to creditors.

The advantage to a living trust is the creditors will have more difficulty reaching the assets and might settle for less because of the expense and time it will take to break the trust.

What about a foreign trust? *Wealthy individuals often place assets in trusts that are located outside of the United States.* The individual transfers ownership of her assets to a trust with foreign trustees who manage the trust property from the foreign country. A foreign trust has no trust offices or agents in the United States. These offshore foreign trusts provide a great deal of asset protection because compelling a foreign nation to enforce a U.S. judgment on behalf of creditors is extremely difficult, time-consuming and costly. Additionally, courts in the United States have no jurisdiction over foreign trustees and cannot order the trustee to turn over assets.

> **TIP:** Countries with laws that protect foreign trusts include the Bahamas, Bermuda, the Turks and Caicos Islands and the Cayman Islands.

CAUTION: It may be nearly as difficult for your family to recover your money from a foreign trust as it would be for your creditors to do so.

What if I create a family limited partnership (FLP)? *A family limited partnership (FLP) is a limited partnership created to manage and*

control assets or property that is jointly owned among family members. The joint ownership of the assets is assigned or transferred to the FLP. The FLP then owns the assets, along with the right to manage and control them. Creditors are thus limited in their ability to recover assets to pay off judgments owed by one of the family members.

> Typically, parents become general partners of the FLP with a very small interest—generally 1 percent. The remainder of the interest in the FLP belongs to the limited partners, usually the children. Parents have limited exposure and almost no risk of losing property to creditors under an FLP arrangement.

Is my retirement plan exempt from seizure?

Pensions, IRAs, 401(k)s and other retirement plans are usually exempt from creditors. Income that is deposited into these plans is protected from any attempts by a creditor to seize it. However, once the plan begins to pay out or distribute the retirement money, the funds are no longer protected. For example, the cash in a retirement plan is protected; however, once monthly payments begin and cash is transferred to the beneficiary's bank account, it is subject to seizure by a creditor.

> **TIP:** Funds in health savings accounts are generally exempt under state laws.

Does bankruptcy help me avoid seizure of my assets?

Filing a petition for bankruptcy stops any creditor from attempting to collect a debt from the individual or company that filed. Even creditors that have judgments cannot continue to attempt to seize assets. At the conclusion of the bankruptcy, the debts are discharged and no longer have to be paid. Thus, many assets can be protected by using a bankruptcy strategy.

What if I buy foreign assets?

Debtors can convert assets owned in the United States into foreign assets. For example, real estate can be sold here and used to purchase a home in France. A creditor would then have to begin a new suit in the foreign country or countries in order to collect on the assets.

> **TIP:** Using this strategy as a way to avoid paying U.S. taxes is highly unadvisable.

BANKRUPTCY (CHAPTERS 7, 11 AND 13)

Bankruptcy is the legal process that allows a debtor to form a repayment plan or liquidate assets to pay off creditors with whatever assets he owns. Once the creditors are paid (if payment is possible), in full or in part, the debtor is free from liability on the debts. The debts are discharged and the person gets a financial "fresh start."

Bankruptcy proceedings are filed exclusively in federal bankruptcy courts. State courts have no jurisdiction over bankruptcy matters. Bankruptcy laws provide for several different options under which a debtor can file for bankruptcy. The options are referred to by their legal designations as a Chapter 7, Chapter 11 and Chapter 13 bankruptcy. Individuals file for either a Chapter 7 or Chapter 13 bankruptcy. Businesses may file for Chapter 11 bankruptcy.

> **TIP:** The U.S. Bankruptcy courts maintain a Web site at **www.uscourts. gov/bankruptcycourts.html** with useful information and links.

What is a debtor?

A debtor is an individual or business that has filed a petition for bankruptcy. The petition informs the court that the debtor has more liabilities than assets and, in essence, is unable to pay what she owes.

> **TIP:** Married couples should file jointly for bankruptcy or the debts will be extinguished as to only the filing spouse. Creditors may be able to continue to look for payment from the spouse that did not file.

When the debtor files for bankruptcy, the petition includes certain forms or schedules, listing all the debtor's assets and naming all the creditors. The court uses the schedules to send out notices of bankruptcy to any person or company listed on the debtor's schedule as a creditor.

Can anyone file for bankruptcy? *Yes. Any person or business may file for bankruptcy.* Depending on the type of business and the amount of the debtor's assets, if any, the debtor files under one of several bankruptcy provisions called chapters.

> **Municipal corporations, railroads, insurance companies and certain savings and loans institutions are prohibited from filing Chapter 7 bankruptcy.**

> **TIP:** Bankruptcy forms can be viewed online at **www.uscourts.gov/bkforms**.

What is a creditor? *A creditor is any person or entity to which the debtor owes money.* Typical creditors include mortgage companies, vehicle financing companies and banks that have issued credit cards or made loans to the debtor. However, anyone may be a creditor. For example, if the debtor owes his parents money, the parents are creditors in a bankruptcy.

Creditors are notified that the debtor has filed for bankruptcy shortly after the debtor files. Creditors have the right to contest the filing within 90 days by alleging that the debtor has the assets to pay or is attempting to defraud the creditor.

The filing puts in place an automatic stay to any and all collection activities. For instance, collection companies that have been calling the debtor's home must cease calling immediately or risk violating the automatic stay.

> **A frequently noted benefit of filing for bankruptcy is the halting of all collection calls, letters and other creditor activities common in the many months prior to filing.**

> **While the automatic stay halts most creditor activity, it does not stop or postpone the following:**
>
> - eviction proceedings
> - actions to withhold, suspend or restrict a driver's license
> - actions to withhold, suspend or restrict a professional, recreational or occupational license
> - lawsuits to establish paternity, child custody or visitation
> - lawsuits to establish, modify or collect domestic support
> - actions to intercept tax refunds
> - divorce proceedings (although proceedings to divide marital property are stayed)
> - the withholding of payments on pension, profit-sharing, stock bonus, or 401(k) loans from the debtor's pay
> - proceedings to enforce medical obligations
> - lawsuits related to domestic violence

Do some creditors have priority over other creditors? *Some creditors receive special, or priority, treatment from bankruptcy courts.* These creditors usually recoup some of what they are owed in preference to other creditors. The IRS is a priority creditor. Ex-spouses who are owed child support or alimony under a court order are also priority creditors.

What is the difference between a secured and unsecured creditor? *A secured creditor has collateral or security for her loan of money to the debtor.* For instance, a financed vehicle is the security for the car note. If the note is unpaid, the creditor may repossess the car. Likewise, a mortgage company has a lien on real estate that it can foreclose on if the debtor falls behind on house payments.

> **Vehicles and other property may not be repossessed while the automatic stay is in effect, even if payments are not being made.**

Most creditors involved in personal bankruptcies, however, are unsecured creditors, with credit card companies making up the majority of creditors. The unsecured creditor has loaned or allowed use of its money without any collateral. If the debtor does not pay, there is nothing for the creditor to take in lieu of payment. For example, MasterCard has no legal right to take clothing, furnishings or toys that were purchased with the card, and intangible items, such as dinners, trips and movies, can never be recovered.

> Large purchases, such as appliances and electronics that are financed by or through the store where the purchase was bought, can, in theory, be taken by the creditor to settle the debt.

> Hospitals and health care providers are also unsecured creditors. Any outstanding medical bills are completely discharged under a Chapter 7 bankruptcy.

What is a bankruptcy trustee? *Bankruptcy trustees are individuals appointed by bankruptcy courts to handle and supervise bankruptcies.* Because bankruptcy is often an ongoing process with a multiyear plan of repayment, the trustee is charged with supervising the plan and dealing with creditors' claims.

What is the 90-day rule? *Because bankruptcy discharges debts, leaving the creditor with little or nothing in payment for the items the debtor purchased, any purchases totaling more than $500 for luxury goods occurring within 90 days prior to the bankruptcy are generally considered fraudulent.* Similarly, cash advances totaling more than $750 and made within 70 days of filing are also not dischargeable in bankruptcy. The basis for the rule is the legal assumption that a debtor must have known how precarious her financial position was in the weeks prior to filing and made purchases knowing (or intending) never to pay. Those debts may not be discharged.

> **TIP:** Bankruptcy attorneys will not file a petition for client until 90 days have passed since the last credit card purchase. Anyone considering bankruptcy must cease using credit cards immediately, even the ones that are not past due.

Can the judge dismiss my bankruptcy petition? *Yes. At any time during the proceedings, the bankruptcy judge can dismiss the petition.* Typically, the trustee determines that the debtor does, in fact, have assets and is ineligible for bankruptcy. However, a debtor who is intentionally attempting to defraud creditors will not only have the petition dismissed but may also face criminal charges.

What is discharge? *The discharge is the final court order in a bankruptcy. The order discharges all the debtor's debts and releases him from further liability.* Under the law, the debts cease to exist and the creditors are permanently enjoined from pursuing collection. Discharges are automatically granted unless creditors object to the bankruptcy

> Chapter 7 discharges are granted once the time has passed for creditors to object to the bankruptcy, typically 60 days after the 341 meeting. Chapter 13 bankruptcies are discharged when the 3- to 5-year repayment plan has been completed.

> Under the new bankruptcy law, a debtor's case will be discharged only after he has completed an instructional course on personal financial management. This requirement applies to discharges under Chapter 7 and 13. However, this is currently a pilot project and may not apply to the district in which you file.

Can I be forced to file for bankruptcy involuntarily? *Yes. Creditors have the ability to force a debtor to declare bankruptcy.* Filing the bankruptcy protects the creditors from misuse of funds by the debtor and fraudulent payments to preferred creditors over other creditors.

> One creditor can force an individual into Chapter 7 bankruptcy only if he has fewer than 11 creditors. The creditor must be owed at least $12,300 of unsecured debt (such as a credit card account) to file an involuntary petition. Three creditors must join together to file if the debtor has more than 11 creditors.

CHAPTER 7 BANKRUPTCY

A Chapter 7 bankruptcy is a liquidation of all the debtor's assets. Anything of value owned by the debtor is sold and the cash is distributed among the creditors. Some items, however, are exempt and cannot be sold. Chapter 7 bankruptcies are frequently referred to as "no asset" cases as most Chapter 7 debtors have nothing that can be sold off to pay creditors.

> **TIP:** Persons without a regular income will generally be required to file under Chapter 7 because a repayment plan under Chapter 13 would be impossible.

Chapter 7 bankruptcies do not include a repayment plan that the debtor must adhere to for many months. Once the assets are liquidated, the bankruptcy is granted, the debts are discharged and the proceedings are finished. A typical Chapter 7 case takes approximately 6 months from start to finish.

> **TIP:** The administrative office of the U.S. courts published an online manual titled "Bankruptcy Basics" for debtors and creditors that can be downloaded at **www.uscourts.gov/library/bankbasic.pdf**

Chapter 7 bankruptcies make up the majority of individual bankruptcy filings. It is under Chapter 7 bankruptcies that state laws concerning exempt property and homestead exemptions become pivotal.

Some states, such as Texas, have generous exemption systems that let debtors keep nearly everything they own. In other states, very little property may be exempt. For example, some laws protect only one vehicle, with a value of up to $10,000.

> **Because the consequences of liquidation are so severe in states where little property is exempted, debtors residing in these states must file under Chapter 13 in order to keep their home, vehicles and other property.**

I know that I am going to file for bankruptcy this year. Is there anything I need to do financially to prepare? *Yes. The goal is to go into bankruptcy with as few nonexempt assets as possible—that is, assets that can be sold to pay creditors.* If you own jewelry or art, you can sell it and use the funds to pay off debts that will not be discharged and which you will always owe, such as child support, alimony and student loans. You can also use funds to purchase exempt property, which would be protected.

> **TIP:** Because transfers, sales and purchases that occur directly before bankruptcy are always looked at suspiciously by the courts, it is important to consult with a lawyer before you begin to convert nonexempt property into exempt property.

Is there a certain time that is better to file for bankruptcy than others? *Yes. One of the most important timing considerations involves determining when you are likely to receive any income tax refunds due to you.* If you file before the refund is received, the bankruptcy trustee can claim the funds to pay creditors. Your goal is to collect any money or assets that you have coming to you before you file for bankruptcy.

> **TIP:** Do not file for bankruptcy if you are expecting but have not yet received any of the following:
> - insurance proceeds
> - inheritances
> - lawsuit awards, including money and property received in a divorce settlement

Can I file for bankruptcy myself? *Yes. Debtors often handle their own bankruptcies because the filings are all on standard forms.* If you file yourself, then you are representing yourself pro se.

> **TIP:** The bankruptcy petition and schedules that must be attached are standard forms used by all bankruptcy courts. The forms are available at **www.uscourts.gov/bkforms**.

> **TIP:** All courts have local rules or procedures for filing in bankruptcy court. Call the bankruptcy court clerk and ask how you can obtain a copy of the local rules. It is possible the rules may be online, as well.

> **The debtor must swear that everything set out in the petition is true and correct when it is filed. There are criminal penalties for giving the court false information.**

How do I know in what court I should file my bankruptcy petition? You file in the federal judicial district where you live. Each state has one or more federal districts with a bankruptcy court. For example, debtors in Dallas, Texas, file in the Northern District of Texas.

> **You must have resided in the district at least 180 days before filing the petition.**

I am unable to pay the entire filing fee. Is there any way I can get the fee waived? *Yes. You may be able to fill out and file a pauper's affidavit requesting the court to waive the fees because of your dire financial circumstances.* However, it is more likely that the court will require installment payments if you have any means to pay.

> **TIP:** Chapter 7 and 13 bankruptcies cost $200 and $150, respectively, in filing fees. These fees must be paid in addition to your attorney's fees for representing you in court.

I am married and the debts I owe are mine alone. Can I file for bankruptcy without including my husband in the petition? *Yes.* However, filing separately is generally not recommended because creditors can look to the spouse who did not file and whose debts were not discharged in bankruptcy for payment.

> **TIP:** In community property states, both spouses are liable for debts incurred by one of them during the marriage. A single bankruptcy filing does not provide a "clean slate" in those cases because the nonfiling spouse is still liable on those same debts.

If my husband and I file jointly, can we both claim exemptions? *Yes. One of the main advantages to joint filing is that exemptions can be doubled.* For example, if one vehicle is exempt under your state laws, then you each can claim a vehicle.

Are there federal bankruptcy exemptions that I can choose to use instead of my state exemptions? *It depends. Not all states permit you to use the federal exemptions.* Some will allow you to choose between using federal or state exemptions, whereas others require you to use state exemptions only.

> **Currently, the states that permit you to choose between federal and state exemptions are Arkansas, Connecticut, Hawaii, Massachusetts, Michigan, Minnesota, New Hampshire, New Jersey, New Mexico, Pennsylvania, Rhode Island, South Carolina, Texas, Vermont, Washington and Wisconsin.**

In almost all cases, state exemptions are much broader than the federal exemptions. For example, the federal exemption protects homesteads up to $18,450 in value only. State exemptions typically exclude homesteads with a much higher value and allow a maximum limit of $125,000 for property acquired during the 1,215-day period before filling for bankruptcy (roughly, during the last 3 years, 4 months). .

If I represent myself, will I have to argue before or present evidence to a bankruptcy judge? *No.* Unless creditors object and litigation begins, debtors are only required to appear at the creditor's meeting, known as the "341 meeting."

> The "341 meeting" is an informal meeting between the debtor and the bankruptcy trustee. It is usually held in a conference room at the courthouse. The trustee asks for the debtor's identification and Social Security card, reviews the schedules of expenses, assets and exemptions and confirms with the debtor that the information is true and correct. Sometimes the trustee may ask for an explanation of the circumstances that led to filing bankruptcy.

TIP: The debtor must attend the creditor's meeting or the bankruptcy petition may be dismissed.

TIP: A debtor can request a time extension, or continuance, for the creditor's meeting. You must make the request in writing and state the reasons you cannot attend. The request should be filed with the bankruptcy clerk.

When I file for bankruptcy, will the court send my creditors a copy of my schedules and other documents? *No.* The court sends out only a notice that you filed for bankruptcy and reminds creditors that the automatic stay is in place, preventing them from further collection activities.

What are creditors allowed to do once the automatic stay has been issued? *Nothing. Creditors may not communicate with the debtor in any way.* Foreclosures, repossessions, garnishments and sheriff's sales must immediately cease until the bankruptcy is over.

What debts are not dischargeable in a bankruptcy? *Student loans, child support and alimony payments typically survive the bankruptcy.* The debtor will still owe or be obligated on these debts even though all other debts have been discharged.

TIP: Any debt that is not listed by the debtor in the bankruptcy schedules remains in effect. The debt must be listed in order to be discharged.

Are taxes ever dischargeable? *Yes.* Bankruptcy laws allow income taxes to be discharged in specific situations:

- more than 3 years have passed between the due date of the unfiled tax return at issue and the bankruptcy filing;
- more than 2 years have passed between the actual filing of the tax return at issue and the bankruptcy petition; and
- the taxes were assessed at least 240 days before filing for bankruptcy.

TIP: Always consult a board-certified tax attorney with experience in dealing with the IRS if tax issues arise. Bankruptcy attorneys may not be as familiar with the complexities of tax laws.

I want to continue to do business with the credit union. Is there any way I can avoid having my loan from them be discharged in bankruptcy? *Yes.* Debtors, with the approval of the court and before discharge, can reaffirm outstanding loans or debts by signing a reaffirmation agreement.

TIP: Mortgage companies sometimes require debtors to reaffirm their house note even if the debtors have not fallen behind in payments.

TIP: Do not reaffirm unsecured loans with creditors. Keeping the debt defeats the purpose of filing bankruptcy. Future loans are determined by your credit score, not by the fact that you reaffirmed the debt (which does not improve your credit score).

The adjustable rate mortgage on my home is due to change interest soon. Can I refinance although I just filed bankruptcy? *No.* Refinancing your mortgage is giving preference to one creditor over others. You can refinance once the bankruptcy is discharged.

Will I have to wait another 90 days to file bankruptcy if I had to use my credit card for emergency dental work? *No. Charges within 90 days of filing are only a problem if you purchased a luxury or unnecessary item* *and did not intend to repay.* In your case, a medical emergency arose and you had no intent to defraud the dentist when you went to her for dental work. However, an attorney may refuse to file for you until 90 days have passed.

> **TIP:** The 90-day time requirement starts when the purchase is made, not when the bill is received.

Are beer, wine and cigarettes legitimate expenses in a Chapter 7 bankruptcy?

Typically, liquor is not a legitimate expense and will not be allowed. Tobacco products are allowed in some districts; others do not let you add in expenses for cigarettes in calculating your total living expenses.

If I file for bankruptcy, will I get to keep my IRA?

Under the new bankruptcy law, up to $1 million in IRA accounts is exempt. However, IRA accounts that have been rolled over from qualified plans are protected without any dollar limitations.

> **TIP:** The bankruptcy law also exempts pension plans, 401(k) plans, and other ERISA-qualified plans.

One of my creditors has asked for relief from the automatic stay. What does this mean?

The creditor, typically a secured creditor, wants his collateral protected and needs relief from the automatic stay to continue to receive payments or repossess the item. For example, the bank that loaned money on a tractor may request relief allowing the debtor to continue to make payments on the note as the tractor's value is decreasing over time. Alternatively, the bank can ask for permission to repossess the tractor if you are behind on your payments.

Can a creditor fight my bankruptcy and try to keep what I owe from being discharged?

Yes. Creditors have the opportunity to object to the bankruptcy by filing a complaint with the court. The creditor can ask to have the entire bankruptcy dismissed or the court to exclude

a specific debt. The creditor must have "good cause" to object, such as charges for luxury items on credit cards a few days before filing.

> Once an objection is filed, an "adversary proceeding" or litigation is initiated. A pro se debtor should hire an attorney immediately if litigation starts.

What are the reasons the court can deny a bankruptcy?

If an objection has been filed, the court can deny the bankruptcy on the basis of the objection. Some bases of objection include:

- transfer or concealment of property with intent to hinder, delay or defraud creditors
- destruction or concealment of books or records
- perjury and other fraudulent acts
- failure to account for the loss of assets
- violation of a court order
- an earlier discharge in a Chapter 7 case within the last 8 years

I filed for bankruptcy. Can I get out of my apartment lease?

Yes. Housing and vehicle leases, plus equipment leases, can be terminated once you file for bankruptcy.

I overlooked some assets when I filed for bankruptcy. Can I add the assets to the schedules I already filed?

Yes. The petition, including the schedules can (and should) be amended to reflect any new information or changes. You can always add assets, expenses or even creditors you failed to list during the first filing.

Can I file for Chapter 7 bankruptcy more than once?

Yes. However, Chapter 7 bankruptcies must be filed at least 8 years apart.

CHAPTER 11 BANKRUPTCY

Businesses that wish to continue operating must file for bankruptcy under Chapter 11, which reorganizes the debtor company's finances. Businesses in bankruptcy are sometimes refereed to as being "in reorganization." The reorganization plan allows the company to repay creditors while it continues to operate.

> Family farmers file for bankruptcy under Chapter 12.

CHAPTER 13 BANKRUPTCY

Unlike a Chapter 7 bankruptcy, which permits the debtor to discharge her debts, a Chapter 13 proceeding does not discharge debts. Instead, a repayment plan is worked out where the debtor is required to pay the trustee a certain amount each month that the trustee then distributes among the creditors. Chapter 13 bankruptcies readjust the debts of individuals with regular incomes who have some money left over each month (after expenses) with which to repay their debts.

The repayment plans usually last approximately 3 to 5 years, and the debtor must report regularly to the trustee during that time regarding any income increases or windfalls. For example, a tax refund must be reported to the bankruptcy trustee who may then take it to pay creditors. There are strict rules in place with which a debtor must comply during the Chapter 13 process. Violating the rules or missing a payment means the bankruptcy can be dismissed and the debtor is still legally responsible for debts that were never discharged. Some debtors find that living under a Chapter 13 plan is extremely difficult and stressful; thus, discuss your decision to proceed under Chapter 13 with an attorney.

> **TIP:** A Chapter 13 debtor who has a bankruptcy dismissed may not refile. Additionally, the debtor is prohibited from filing for a Chapter 7 bankruptcy. Do not file for a Chapter 13 bankruptcy unless you have every intention of following through with the repayment plan.

Can anyone qualify for a Chapter 13 bankruptcy? *No. Debtors with extremely large debts do not qualify.* If you have more than $307,675 in unsecured debt (such as medical bills and credit card debt) and more than $922,975 in secured debt (such as real estate mortgages and car loans), you cannot file for a Chapter 13 bankruptcy.

I cannot keep up with the payments to the trustee. Can I convert my Chapter 13 bankruptcy into a Chapter 7? *Yes.* However, in order to convert to a Chapter 7, you will have to show a substantial decrease in income or increase in expenses that are beyond your control and involuntary, such as job loss or large medical expenses.

Can a creditor fight my bankruptcy plan and try to keep what I owe from being discharged? *Yes.* Creditors have the opportunity to dispute the plan at the time of the confirmation hearing.

> **TIP:** All creditors are notified of the debtor's confirmation hearing by the bankruptcy court, which mails out a "Trustees Notice of Confirmation and Plan Summary."

Are any debts discharged in Chapter 13 bankruptcies? *Typically, no. Debts in Chapter 13 bankruptcies are adjusted.* The amounts owing are generally reduced to an amount that is feasible for the debtor to pay back in 3 to 5 years.

> **TIP:** The advantage of a 3-year plan is that the repayment time is shorter, which requires a lesser amount to repay. If a debtor can only pay $100 a month under a 3-year plan, the adjusted amount of the debt could not exceed $3,600 ($100 x 36 months), even if it was originally $50,000.

> **Under the bankruptcy reform bill, discussed below, debtors whose income exceeds the state median and who can afford to repay some of their debts must use a 5-year plan, which allows for a greater amount to be repaid to creditors.**

Is it possible to have any debts discharged before the repayment plan is completed? *Yes. You can request a hardship discharge.* The discharge will be granted if the debtor cannot keep up with a portion of the plan payments because of circumstances beyond her control.

If my plan ends and I still owe money, are the debts discharged? *Yes.* Although most of your debts would have been reduced to allow for full repayment during the plan, any excess is discharged once the plan is completed. If you owed $50,000 on a credit card account and the amount was not adjusted, and you were placed on a 3-year plan paying $1,000 a month, at the end of the plan the amount still owed (over $45,000) is discharged.

BANKRUPTCY REFORM

In response to the increasing number of bankruptcies during the past decade, which has resulted in billions of dollars in losses to companies, Congress recently passed a sweeping set of bankruptcy reforms. Some of the important changes include:

- setting out specific amounts allowable for food, clothing, transportation and housing, and requiring the debtor to live within those guidelines unless he can show a reason to increase the allowed expenses;
- lengthening residency requirements in states before state exemptions can apply to the debtor;
- forcing the debtor to pay the full cost of an auto loan or lose the vehicle to repossession, even if the vehicle is not worth the outstanding balance on the loan;
- requiring debtors to attend courses in credit counseling and personal financial management as a condition for discharging debts;
- raising the priority of child-support and alimony payments;
- placing a $1 million maximum on the amount in Roth and regular IRAs that are exempt from creditors;
- requiring repayment of all credit card charges made in the 3 months before filing for bankruptcy; and
- allowing landlords, in some circumstances, to avoid the automatic stay and evict bankrupt tenants who are behind on their rent.

Additionally, the new law includes changes making filing for bankruptcy and liquidation under Chapter 7 much more difficult. Any person attempting to file bankruptcy must attend a credit-counseling program as well as pass a two-part "means test."

I have heard the new bankruptcy laws require me to get credit counseling. What is this? *Under the new law, anyone contemplating filing bankruptcy must attend a credit counseling class not more than 180*

days before filing bankruptcy. After completing the course, the agency will issue a certificate of compliance, which must be filed with the court along with a copy of the repayment plan created.

> **Failure to file proof of compliance may result in your case being dismissed. However, if no approved counseling services are available in your district, this requirement may be waived.**

What is a "means test"? *The means test is a formula applied to a debtor's income when that income is more than the state median.* (The national average median income is $60,000 for a family of four.)

> **Debtors earning less than the median income for their state will be able to file for Chapter 7 bankruptcy.**

Under the test, secured debts (e.g., mortgages and car notes) and necessities (alimony, child support and living expenses) are subtracted from the debtor's monthly income to determine what amount of money is left over for repayment of unsecured debts, such as credit cards. If there is enough left over so that the debtor can pay at least $10,000 toward unsecured debts over 5 years or $166 per month ($10,000 ÷ 60 months = $166 per month), the debtor must file Chapter 13 bankruptcy and make repayments.

> **Debtors (with an average median income) who can find at least $100 left over after expenses are prohibited from filing Chapter 7 bankruptcies. This "means test" will limit Chapter 7 filings to individuals and families with little or no cash flow. Under prior law, courts did not have any set formula to determine how much leftover cash tips the debtor out of Chapter 7 and into Chapter 13.**

> **Debtors are no longer able to include many items as necessary expenses that were previously allowed. For example, cell phone service, cable television, Internet services, movie rentals and some dining out can no longer be added to the debtor's expenses.**

The new law makes the means test inflexible. Previously, a bankruptcy court had great latitude in considering a debtor's personal circumstances in permitting her to file for bankruptcy. Under the new law, personal circumstances, no matter how sympathetic, are irrelevant.

> Historically, almost two-thirds of consumer bankruptcies have been filed under Chapter 7, which allows consumers to wipe out credit card debt.

> "Reasonable" living expenses for food and clothing, transportation and housing are determined by IRS guidelines. The guidelines take into account the region of the country where the debtor lives. A debtor is also allowed to deduct other reasonable living expenses, including:
>
> - up to $1,500 in expenses annually for grade and high school (per each minor child)
> - expenses of caring for elderly, chronically ill or disabled household family members, including children and grandchildren
> - a domestic support obligation that first becomes payable after the petition is filed
> - charitable contributions of up to 15 percent of gross income
> - payment of expenditures needed to continue, preserve and operate a business

Can I file under Chapter 7 if I pass the "means test"? *Individuals who pass the means test must file Chapter 13 bankruptcy and enter into a plan to repay creditors.* The means test requires a debtor whose income, based on the size of his family, is more than his state average to file under Chapter 13. Choice between chapters in filing for bankruptcy is virtually eliminated under the new law.

How do the new bankruptcy laws affect state exemptions? *Debtors who are eligible to file under Chapter 7 must have lived in the state for 2 years to use the state exemptions.* This provision prevents debtors from moving to big-exemption states (such as Florida and Texas) to avoid losing assets to liquidation.

We are in the middle of our Chapter 13 plan. Will the new bankruptcy law affect us? *No.* The law does not affect bankruptcies filed before its effective date.

What happens under the new law if we fail to complete our Chapter 13 bankruptcy plan? The court can dismiss the case and your creditors will resume collection activities against you.

Can a Chapter 13 bankruptcy be converted to a Chapter 7 under the new law? *Yes.* If you are unable to complete the repayment plan under Chapter 13 due to circumstances beyond your control, such as unemployment, illness or a decrease in income, you can petition the court to have your debts discharged completely.

> The court can revise the Chapter 13 repayment plan and require smaller payments because of a change in circumstances.

How can I avoid bankruptcy? *Although a bankruptcy does have an advantage in that it provides debtors with a fresh start, the damage to credit can have enormous consequences.* Individuals should seek to avoid bankruptcy when finances become tight by getting a clear picture of their current financial situation.

- Write down all your debts—the amounts, the interest rate and the monthly minimum payments.
- Calculate all the net income you have available.
- Add up your expenses and forego items such as cable TV, cell phone service, housekeepers and lawn services.
- Make a budget and stick to it.
- Sell any personal property and vehicles that you do not absolutely require.
- Cut up credit cards (except for an emergency card) and make purchases with a debit card only.
- Reduce late fees by signing up for direct debiting from your bank account on some bills.

Once you have a complete understanding of your financial situation, negotiate with creditors, primarily credit card companies, to lower interest rates and monthly payments. Do not tell the creditor you are thinking about filing bankruptcy—they will flag your file and close your credit line.

> **TIP:** Credit counseling services that negotiate with creditors on your behalf and pay them directly are not recommended. Typically, these services negotiate down your unsecured debts and have you pay the service one large payment, which is then distributed by the credit counselor to your creditors. Not only is your credit rating immediately damaged when the credit counselor contacts creditors, payments may be made late or not at all.

BUILDING CREDIT AFTER BANKRUPTCY

Rebuilding credit after bankruptcy has as much to do with making good financial decisions as working through your credit report to make sure it is accurate. All accounts following a bankruptcy are discharged and should be so noted on the credit report. However, it is common for accounts to remain "delinquent," "open" or "late." These comments are incorrect and must be removed when the consumer makes a dispute.

Although it was once almost impossible to obtain credit after a bankruptcy, many lenders, including credit card companies, make offers to debtors immediately after discharge. The credit card offers may have higher fees, interest rates and even require a security deposit, but you may want to consider opening an account in order to start rebuilding a positive credit rating.

Why is my bankruptcy listed in my credit report? *The bankruptcy is noted on the report because your creditors received notice that you filed and reported it to the credit bureau.* Additionally, a bankruptcy is a public record, and credit bureaus routinely search public records for judgments and bankruptcies to note on the credit report.

Is my bankruptcy always going to be part of my credit report? *No.* After 10 years, the bankruptcy must be dropped from the report.

Can I get a bankruptcy removed from my credit report before the 10 years is up? *Some consumers have been successful in getting bankruptcies removed because credit bureaus failed to timely verify the information with the court clerk.* (Of course, you must initially dispute the information as erroneous.) Under the Fair Credit Reporting Act (FCRA), unverified information must be deleted.

> **TIP:** Even if the credit bureau reports that they have verified the bankruptcy with the court, you should contact the court clerk to confirm. If the credit bureau did not actually contact the clerk, then they did not properly verify and the information must be removed.

> **Most credit bureaus verify public records information from services (going down to the courthouse is obviously inefficient). Under the FCRA, the court is the only entity that can verify court records.**

> **TIP:** If you suspect your public records have not been verified by the court, ask the credit bureau to provide you an explanation of how they verified. An improper verification means the information must be deleted.

My debts were discharged in bankruptcy. Should my credit report still show unpaid balances on my credit card accounts? *No. The balances must be deleted and the accounts should be noted as discharged.* If the credit bureau fails to make the corrections, they can be sued under the FCRA. The law requires a violating company to pay $1,000 in damages to the wronged consumer.

> **TIP:** If a credit card company is still showing a balance owing after a bankruptcy discharge, call customer service and request that you be sent a bill. At the same time, remind the person to whom you are speaking that they are attempting to illegally collect a debt that discharged under federal bankruptcy law. You will soon be speaking to a manager and it is probable the report to the credit bureau will be corrected to show a zero balance owing.

I see that a creditor that I had an account with years ago and closed before my bankruptcy pulled my credit report. Can the company access my account just because they received a notice that I filed for bankruptcy? *No. Many companies subscribe to services that routinely report bankruptcy filings.* The sole fact that you filed bankruptcy is not a permissible purpose for an old creditor to pull your file. The company has violated the law. You should write and demand that the hard inquiry be changed to a soft inquiry at once, or deleted all together. If they refuse, the company is liable for at least $1,000 in statutory damages.

Sometimes inquiries cannot be deleted completely, but impermissible hard inquiries can be changed to soft inquiries. The effect of the change can improve a credit score dramatically.

After bankruptcy, my credit card account shows a zero balance on my credit report but still includes prior late payments. Should the late payments be removed as well? *No.* The late payments prior to bankruptcy can remain on the credit report. If they have been reported in error, you can dispute them.

CREDIT

Without credit, it is impossible to purchase a vehicle, a home or even rent an apartment. Thus, building up a good credit history is essential for any adult. Build credit by starting small. College students are regularly offered credit cards with small credit lines. These cards are an excellent way to begin building credit. Additionally, local department stores may be willing to issue a credit card although the applicant has little or no credit history. By charging purchases and paying them off on time, a positive credit history begins to be built. It is important to have only one or two cards and to not spend up to (or over) your credit limit.

Other good ways to build credit include:

- residing at one location for several years, rather than changing apartments and addresses every couple of months
- getting telephone or utility service in your name, even if you have to pay a deposit (it will eventually be refunded)
- maintaining stable employment

CREDIT CARDS AND DEBIT CARDS

A credit card is issued by a bank to an individual and can be used to purchase items and services. Purchases are limited to a maximum amount or credit limit. A fee is typically charged by the bank for the use of a credit card; however, some cards are issued without requiring an annual fee. Banks issuing credit cards pay vendors for purchases, before the credit card holder has paid the bank.

A debit card basically allows a bank account holder to electronically transfer money to make a purchase. However, unlike an ATM (automatic teller machine) card, the debit card has a MasterCard or Visa logo, allowing a vendor to "charge" purchases to the debit card. The charge is really an automatic deduction from the debit cardholder's bank account.

TIP: Debit cards are also known as check cards because the holder is using it like a check without having to write one.

The Federal Reserve, which places limits on liability for fraudulent use of credit and debit cards, refers to debit cards as EFT (electronic fund transfer) cards.

> ATM cards cannot be used at stores to make purchases. They can only be used to withdraw money from the holder's account at automatic teller machines. Using an ATM requires a password or PIN (personal identification) number.

Can a credit card company refuse to issue a credit card for any reason? *No.* Laws prohibit credit card companies from refusing credit based solely on marital status or advanced age.

> The Equal Credit Opportunity Act requires that all credit applicants be considered on the basis of actual qualifications for credit (income, employment, credit history) and prohibits refusing credit because of certain personal characteristics.

What is the APR? *The APR is the annual percentage rate or interest a bank charges you on your outstanding debt.* By law, credit card companies must disclose the APR to consumers.

Is there a limit to the amount of interest credit card companies can charge consumers? Under federal law, no. However, some states have enacted laws that put a ceiling on allowable interest rates, typically 18 to 22 percent.

What are the disadvantages of debit cards? *Debit cards have two drawbacks: a PIN is often not required for store purchases and the holder is not automatically protected by the $50 fraudulent use limit.* A thief can use a debit card to charge purchases over the phone (no PIN required), for example, and drain the holder's bank account.

> The Federal Reserve has published the "Consumer Handbook to Credit Protection Laws" on their Web site at www.federalreserve.gov/pubs/consumerhdbk/default.htm.

Am I required to notify the bank if my debit card is stolen? Yes, if you want to limit your liability for any unauthorized purchases.

> **Your liability is:**
> - limited to $50 if the bank is notified within 2 business days of your learning of the loss or theft of your card or code
> - increases to $500 if the bank is notified after 2 business days
> - unlimited if you do not report an unauthorized transfer that appears on your statement within 60 days after the statement is mailed to you

Why am I not allowed to charge more than $50 worth of gas on my debit card? Banks have voluntarily limited an account holder's risk to $50 by not authorizing bigger purchases at convenience stores, gas stations and other business where identification may not be required when the debit card is used.

My debit card has a MasterCard logo on it. Does this mean I am protected as if it were a regular credit card? *Yes. Both MasterCard and Visa have increased liability protection.* MasterCard limits a customer's liability for losses incurred from a lost or stolen debit card to $50. Visa debit card customers pay nothing if the card is reported missing within 2 business days of the loss being discovered. After that, customer liability is capped at $50.

> **TIP:** Check with your financial institution about your liability. Many card issuers offer consumers better protection than what the government requires.

Why is my credit history important if I am applying for a credit card? *Banks issuing credit cards use your credit history to determine if you have paid previous loans or credit cards on time or late.* Credit histories show:

- current amount of outstanding debt (if you currently owe $100,000 on credit cards, it is unlikely you will be approved for another card even if your payment history is perfect
- stability in employment (shows you are likely to be continued to be employed in the future and able to make payments)
- home ownership (shows you were a good credit risk for a mortgage and that your

lifestyle is consistent, i.e., you are unlikely to skip town)

Can I get a credit card if I have a low credit score? *Yes. Many banks specialize in high–risk individuals.* Your fees and interest rates will be much higher because of your low score.

> **TIP:** Secured credit cards are also available. The credit cardholder deposits money on the card to be used for purchases. Although the secured credit card is essentially a debit card, it allows you to build up a good credit history and increase your score.

MAINTAINING YOUR CREDIT

All business, from banks to apartment complexes, request credit reports on new applicants. Although it can be time-consuming, it is important that you examine your credit report and have any false, misleading or incomplete information removed.

What is the Fair Credit Reporting Act (FCRA)?
The FCRA protects consumers against unfair and erroneous descriptions in credit reports. All consumers have basic rights that require that mistakes on credit reports be corrected in a timely manner.

What will I see on my credit report?
Information on credit reports is coded. However, the FCRA requires that symbols and coding be explained on the credit report. Before you begin to digest the information on your report, you must make yourself familiar with the coding, particularly the past due symbols.

> **TIP:** Accounts with late payments are marked according to the lateness of the payment. There are symbols for 30-, 60- or 90-day periods. For example, a credit card account might have some zeros (0) indicating no late payments, a one (1) indicating a payment made after 30 days, a two (2) for a 60-day late payment, i.e., two billing cycles went by without a payment and/or a three (3) for payments that are 90 days past due.

Credit reports also include comments, such as "judgment" or "bankruptcy." Obviously, these comments have a negative impact on your credit history and score. Some comments are coded and must be deciphered. For example, "charged to P&L" means a company has charged your account off to profit and loss, meaning your account has been classified as a bad debt that cannot be collected.

Negative, and positive, credit information does not stay on your credit report forever. Under the FCRA, certain information, such as charge-offs, must be dropped from the report after 7 years. For example, after 7 years, a Sears charge account with a balance of $1,000 that was never paid and charged off must be deleted from your report.

> **TIP:** Creditors often attempt to "re-age" the account so the 7-year time limit is extended. Re-aging is illegal. For example, an account that was charged off years ago may not be sent to a collection agency in the sixth year in order to restart the 7-year time limit. The 7-year timeline begins the date of the original charge-off.

What is a credit score? *Your credit score is currently the most important factor in obtaining credit.* Your score is a number assigned to you on the basis of your credit history and other factors (employment, income, home ownership) and is between 300 and 900. The higher the score, the better your chances are at obtaining credit.

> **TIP:** Do not apply for a bank loan, mortgage, personal line of credit or even a credit card without finding out your credit score. If you have a low score, you will be denied credit and your score may drop because of the inquiry.

> **Credit scores are based on information found in an individual's credit report. If it is not on the credit report, it will not be factored into the score.**

How is my credit score determined? The score is calculated by weighting specific items in the credit report, typically:

- 35 percent on payment history (late payments)

- 30 percent on the total amount currently owed
- 15 percent on the length of your credit history (young people have lower scores because their credit history is short)
- 10 percent on the number of new credit accounts opened or applied for (fewer accounts and applications is better)
- 10 percent on the credit account mix (mortgages, credit cards, installment loans)

How are credit scores ranked? Your credit is ranked, for the purposes of obtaining credit, loans and better interest rates, as follows:

EXCELLENT: Over 750

VERY GOOD: 720 or more

ACCEPTABLE: 660 to 770

UNCERTAIN: 620 to 660

RISKY: less than 620

What factors lower my credit score? *One reported late payment could lower your score 50 points; several late payments drop your score a 100 points or more.* Other reasons your score is lowered are:

- derogatory public record, such as a bankruptcy or outstanding judgment
- proportion of balances to credit limits is too high
- accounts referred to collection agencies
- accounts that have been charged off

> **TIP:** Your credit score is not a part of the credit report you can obtain from the credit bureaus.

> **The credit score or FICO score is calculated by Fair, Isaac and Co. You can access your credit score, for a fee, at www.myfico.com.**

Is it possible to improve my credit score? *Yes. Typically, you must clean up your credit report by having all erroneous information removed.* For example, a credit card account that has been closed should be corrected if it is shown as open on the report. Late payments that were never late can be removed. Additionally, your Social Security number or name could be wrong and it is possible your credit is being mixed up with another persons.

> **TIP:** The Federal Trade Commission publishes information on disputing credit report errors at **www.ftc.gov/bcp/conline/pubs/credit/crdtdis.htm**.

How do I go about cleaning up my credit report? You must follow certain steps:

1. Contact all three credit bureaus and obtain copies of your credit reports (you are entitled to one free report every year)

    EXPERIAN
    PO Box 2104
    Allen, TX 75013
    1.888.397.3742

    EQUIFAX
    PO Box 740241
    Atlanta, GA 30374
    1.800.997.2493

    TRANS UNION
    PO Box 1000
    Chester, PA 19022
    1.800.888.4213

> **TIP:** Free credit reports can be obtained through **www.annualcreditreport.com**, or Annual Credit Report Request Service, PO Box 105281, Atlanta, GA 30348.

2. Use the form that comes with each of the reports to dispute erroneous information with each credit bureau. Alternatively, you can write a letter to the agencies. A sample form letter is available on the FTC Web site at **www.ftc.gov/bcp/conline/pubs/credit/crdtdis.htm**.

> **TIP:** Try not to dispute more than three to five items at once; otherwise, your disputes may be deemed frivolous.

> **By law, the credit bureau must verify the information you are disputing is accurate. If the information is not verified, it must be removed. It is not uncommon for creditors to simply fail to respond, resulting in removal of the information.**

> **TIP:** Because it is common for the 30-day time frame for verification to expire, information that is not necessarily inaccurate can be disputed and possibly removed. Disputed information that cannot be verified must be deleted from your file.

3. Send in the dispute forms via certified mail so that you can track the running of the 30-day time period for verification.

> **TIP:** Credit repair can be complex, complicated and stressful. There are many Web sites devoted to helping consumers make their way through the credit bureau bureaucracy. A good site for information on how to plan a strategy is **http://creditboards.com**.

Can I just contact the department store that has mistakenly reported late payments and get it to correct the information on my report? *No. The actual creditor (in this case, a department store) is not required by law to fix its errors.* The store may or may not contact all three credit bureaus to correct the information.

> **TIP:** If the creditor agrees to make corrections, ask for something in writing to confirm their promise.

> **TIP:** Ask creditors who are correcting errors to provide you with a copy of the UDF (universal data form) that they send to the credit bureaus. The UDF should specify the changes the creditor wants made on the report (updated balance, deletion of late payments).

Do I dispute the inaccurate information with the creditor or the credit bureau? Although you can dispute the information with the original creditor (e.g., a department store), you should dispute with the credit bureau as only they must meet certain legal requirements for investigating errors.

My credit report has a serious error that the credit bureaus refuse to fix. What can I do? You must file a lawsuit. It is not uncommon for errors to go uncorrected.

I have a credit card account that was charged off over 7 years ago but it shows activity as recently as last year. The credit bureau refuses to drop the account. What do I do? *Your account has been re-aged. The creditor reported activity on the account in order to extend the 7-year drop-off time. This type of activity is prohibited by the FCRA.* You should write the credit bureau, inform them that the account has been impermissibly re-aged and remind them that they may be subject to a $2,500 fine if the account is not dropped from your credit report.

Why does the collection agency show up on my credit report instead of the creditor? *Creditors often turn over accounts to collection agencies. The transfer to a collection agency is noted on your report and is a negative entry.* The agencies then report information to credit bureaus. For example, Book-of-the-Month club could give your unpaid account to a collection agency. The fact that a collection agency is now attempting to collect is noted on the credit report.

You have the right to ask for verification from the collection agency of the alleged debt you owe. They must provide you with a copy of the original paperwork with your signature confirming that you do indeed owe the creditor. A computer printout from the creditor is not proof of the debt.

Collection agencies that are unable to verify the consumer's debt through proper paperwork are required to delete negative information provided to credit bureaus on that consumer.

Does applying for lots of credit cards improve my credit history? *No. In fact, excessive applications are a negative factor.* Every application is noted on your credit report—too many and creditors begin to think you are going to overextend yourself.

How many times a year can I dispute information on my credit report? *You can challenge the accuracy of your credit report at any time.* There is no limit on the number of times or items you can dispute; however, you must allow 90 days between each separate dispute letter.

Who corrects erroneous information on my credit report?

The credit bureaus that create the report make corrections by deleting incorrect information, removing expired information and making other changes that provide an accurate description of your credit history.

Is negative information on my credit report forever?

No. The FCRA requires that accounts that have been placed for collection or written off must be dropped from your credit report after 7 years. Creditors are required to report the actual month and year the account first became delinquent.

The charge- or write-off date is used by the credit bureaus to measure the maximum 7-year reporting period permitted under the FCRA.

How long does it take before a credit bureau looks into my dispute?

The credit bureau must investigate the dispute within 30 days of receiving your complaint.

How does the credit bureau determine if the information I am disputing is inaccurate?

The credit bureau asks the creditor that is reporting the information to verify it. For example, if Sears is reporting that you made your payments late six times 2 years ago, the credit bureau asks them to verify the payments were actually past due.

Are credit bureaus required to investigate all disputes?

Surprisingly, credit bureaus can determine that a dispute is "frivolous or irrelevant" and, under the law, do not have to investigate such disputes.

How does a credit bureau decide if my dispute is frivolous or irrelevant?

The fact checker looks for certain indications such as:

- disputing a large number of accounts (more than three or four), indicating you are attempting to have derogatory information removed by overwhelming the credit checker
- use of form letters derived from Internet sources
- failing to specifically point out the erroneous information

What happens to the inaccurate information if the credit bureau is unable to verify it with the creditor?

If the information you have disputed or challenged is not verified by the creditor within 30 days, it must be removed. It is common for creditors to miss the deadline, fail to reply altogether or simply be unable to verify old information.

Why does my credit report list companies that have made inquires about my credit?

Inquires typically mean that you are applying for credit. Too many inquiries indicate you are seeking excessive credit and may be in financial trouble. Credit bureaus use this information to help formulate a credit score.

My credit report lists a company I never heard of as making a credit inquiry. What is this about? *It appears that you applied for credit from that company so that they were authorized to pull your credit report.* If you did not apply for credit or authorize the company to look into your credit history, the company has made an illegal hard inquiry.

How do I get an illegal hard inquiry removed? Write to the credit bureaus that show the inquiry on their reports and inform them that the inquiry was never authorized.

I was denied credit because of an inquiry on my report I never authorized. Do have a legal recourse? *Yes. Companies that illegally, and without authorization, pull your credit history have broken the law.* The FCRA allows you to sue the company and recover damages.

A company can only make credit inquiries on a consumer for a permissible purpose. Permissible purposes include:

- credit transactions (applying for a loan)
- employment purposes
- insurance underwriting
- government financial responsibility laws
- court orders and/or subpoenas requiring the information
- written authorization of the consumer
- legitimate business needs

TIP: Collection agencies hired by creditors to collect a debt are permitted to access your credit report.

I never received a response from the credit bureau to a dispute letter I sent over 30 days ago. What do I do? *Document the fact that you did not receive a reply by sending another dispute letter and noting that your previous letter received no response.* The second letter should also be sent certified mail. Your goal is document the credit bureau's omissions.

CREDIT FRAUD

Anyone with a credit card can become a victim of credit card fraud or be saddled with a negative credit report because of fraud. There are numerous ways for thieves to obtain your credit card number and make thousands of dollars worth of purchases without your knowledge. Fortunately, laws limit the credit cardholder's liability to $50. If $1,000 is charged to a credit card account without authorization, the cardholder pays only $50 to the credit card company.

Federal law does not place a duty upon the cardholder to report the theft or fraudulent charge within any amount of time.

TIP: The $50 maximum liability amount is for each card. If seven credit cards are stolen and used, the cardholder's liability would be $450 total.

How can I decrease the risk that my credit card will be used without my authorization? You can do several things to prevent card theft as well as someone obtaining the credit card number.

1. Carry your credit cards only when you will be using them so that if your wallet or purse is lost or stolen the credit cards will not be stolen as well.

TIP: Instead of signing your name on a credit card, write "photo ID required" so that the store clerk asks for ID.

2. Sign your credit cards so that your signature can be compared.

3. Call your credit card company and ask them to put a computer notification on the card

that requires picture identification whenever a purchase is attempted.

4. Never sign a blank charge receipt. If you do, mark through all the blanks and keep your copy.

5. Have bills sent to your office if possible to avoid residential mail thefts.

6. Immediately review your credit card statement when it arrives.

7. Never give your credit card number to anyone over the phone.

8. Do not respond to e-mails that ask for credit card information.

9. Buy items over the Internet on secure sites only (symbolized by a lock icon on the bottom toolbar of the page).

What is a fraud alert? *It is a special notice placed on your credit report so that any company asked to give you credit will know your information has been stolen.* A thief who is attempting to obtain additional credit cards in your name will not be able to get credit if a fraud alert is in place. Companies must personally authorize credit with you over the telephone.

> **TIP:** You must notify the three credit bureaus that your credit cards have been stolen to obtain a fraud alert.
>
> Experian
> PO Box 2104
> Allen, TX 75013
> 1.888.397.3742
>
> Equifax
> PO Box 740241
> Atlanta, GA 30374
> 1.800.997.2493
>
> Trans Union
> PO Box 1000
> Chester, PA 19022
> 1.800.888.4213

If I believe my credit cards have been stolen, should I file a police report? *Yes.* The report will be useful in proving to the credit card company that you did not authorize any charges after the card was stolen.

IDENTITY THEFT

Identify theft is much more significant than theft of a credit card or credit card number. A thief who steals someone's identity typically has access to personal information that assures a lender or creditor the thief is you. For example, credit card companies typically ask for Social Security numbers, birth dates, mothers' maiden names and a previous address before a credit card is issued. Generally, this ensures that the person applying for the card is who she says she is. However, a thief who has that information can open credit cards accounts or write checks in that person's name, essentially destroying her credit rating and making her subject to criminal prosecution

> **The Federal Trade Commission operates a special Web site for victims of identity theft at www.consumer.gov/idtheft.**

How will I know if my identity has been stolen? Usually you will find unauthorized charges on a credit card bill; however, there are other signs your identity is being used:

- Credit card bills may cease to come to your address.
- You may receive a credit card that you did not apply for yourself.
- You may be denied credit suddenly.
- You may receive calls or bills from collections agencies concerning purchases you did not make.

CHECK FRAUD

Stolen checks and forged checks have always caused problems for anyone with a bank account. However, check fraud is becoming more common because anyone with a computer and a scanner can easily duplicate checks or replace the names on the checks while the account number remains. The increase in check fraud has led to changes in laws that previously placed most of the liability on the bank for failing to catch the forgery.

Laws prohibit banks from paying checks out of a customer's account if the check does not contain the customer's authorized signature. However, banks are not required to physically examine every check. The customer bears the responsibility of examining bank statements to determine if any unauthorized checks have been written.

New laws now require the customer to notify the bank of possible forgeries within a reasonable time after receiving her bank statement. The customer who fails to notify the bank in a timely manner, not exceeding 30 days, is precluded from asserting that the bank wrongfully paid the check. However, even if the bank did wrongfully pay the check, the customer may still be partly liable under the law.

My checks have been stolen. What do I do?
You must contact your bank immediately and notify them that your checks have been stolen. The bank will look for forgeries as the checks come in. Close the account as soon as any outstanding checks you have written have cleared.

> **TIP:** There is no federal law limiting the amount you are responsible for if your checks are stolen and forged. State laws require banks to make sure checks are not forged, to some extent. However, you must notify the bank that forgeries are a possibility.

> **TIP:** You can stop the stolen checks from being accepted at retailers who use a check verification company when your check is processed during a purchase by notifying the check companies. The store clerk will be unable to process the check. Warn the following companies that your checks are being forged and should not be accepted:
>
> - TeleCheck:
>   1.800.710.9898
>
> - Certegy, Inc.:
>   1.800.437.5120
>
> - International Check Services:
>   1.800.631.9656

What is an affidavit of forgery? *It is the document that is signed by you before a notary public in which you state you have not authorized use of your checks.* The bank will require you to make an affidavit.

Should I close my account? *Yes; however, forged checks that come in and "bounce" are reported to the check verification agencies.* You will then be reported to collection agencies or even pursued for prosecution. It is likely that your credit rating will decrease.

DEBT

FAIR DEBT COLLECTION

The federal Fair Debt Collection Practices Act (FDCPA) prohibits collection agencies and other debt collectors from taking certain offensive actions in trying to collect a debt. The FDCPA covers all personal, family and household debts, including car loans, medical fees owing, credit card payments and other bills. The actual creditor is not covered under the FDCPA. For example, a friend who loans another friend money does not have to follow the FDCPA in attempting to get paid back.

> **TIP:** The Federal Trade Commission's Web site at **www.ftc.gov/bcp/conline/pubs/ credit/fdc.htm** explains the act and answers consumers' questions.

What debt collection practices are prohibited under the FDCPA? *Collection agencies and even attorneys who are working on behalf of a creditor cannot contact a debtor before 8 a.m. or after 9 p.m.* Profane language, threats, constant calling and publishing your name are also prohibited. Additionally, phone calls to the debtor's place of employment are usually prohibited once the creditor is told not to call there.

Importantly, any false statements violate the FDCPA. Telling a debtor she will be arrested or implying she is talking to an attorney (rather than a collection agent) is prohibited.

> **Sending "fake" legal documents or documents that look like a legal filing and meant to convince a debtor she has been sued or a judgment was entered are prohibited.**

Does the FDCPA give me any rights as a debtor? *The FDCPA not only prohibits collectors from certain acts, it allows the debtor the right to sue a debt collector that violates the FDCPA.* The debtor may recover money for the damages suffered (plus additional damages up to $1,000) and recover court costs and attorneys' fees.

Is there any way to stop collection agencies from calling me and leaving messages on my answering machine? *Yes.* The FDCPA prohibits creditors from contacting you if you write a letter to the creditor (or collection agency) stating you want the phone calls to stop.

> **The letter should ask that all contact stop. Contact includes letters, bills and faxes.**

A collection agency sent me a letter telling me they were turning the matter over to an attorney and gave me her name. Have they violated the FDCPA because I wrote and told them to cease all contact? *No. Although a creditor must stop contacting you once you make the request in writing, the creditor is allowed to notify you that specific action is being taken.* In this case, you are being informed that an attorney is handling the collection matter. The notification does not violate the FDCPA.

Can a collection agency call my mother to get my phone number? *Yes. Creditors regularly contact friends, relatives, employers and former employers of debtors to get a current phone number or address of the debtor.* However, repeated phone calls or contacts to third parties may violate the law.

> **The creditor violates the FDCPA if the third party is informed that the creditors are trying to collect a debt.**

I received a collection letter stating that if I do not pay the debt, I will be reported to a credit bureau in 30 days. I will not be able to pay the debt. Is there any way to stop the collection agency from reporting me? *Yes. You have the right to dispute or contest the debt.* If you write a letter back to the agency stating

you do not owe the money, the amount is wrong or it was already paid, you cannot be reported to a credit bureau for failure to pay. Under the law, the collection agency must investigate your claims and verify you owe the debt.

> **The validation notice is a statement in a collection letter that the debtor has the right to dispute the debt within 30 days. Debt collectors must include the notice in their initial communication with the debtor.**

> **TIP:** Agencies do not violate any laws by failing to tell the debtor in letters sent after the initial communication that she can dispute the debt.

I was never billed (and never paid) for a sofa I purchased at a local department store, and after 6 years I am getting calls from the store trying to collect. Is the store violating the FDCPA? *No.* Although you can no longer be sued to collect the amount (since the statute of limitations has passed), the store can still attempt to collect.

> **The statue of limitations may be different depending on the type of debt. For example, a credit card account is an open account and has a shorter statute of limitations as opposed to a promissory note (a contract), which might have a 10-year time period.**

Is there a time limit as to how long a collection agency can pursue me for payment? *Yes. The time limit is called the statute of limitations.* After a period of years passes, the debt is no longer collectible and the collection agency (unlike the store) cannot continue to pursue you. The length of time depends upon the laws in the state where you live, but generally, a debt can legally be collected for 4 to 6 years after it first becomes delinquent.

> **A collection agency that falsely states the debtor will be sued when legally a lawsuit is not possible is violating the FDCPA.**

> **TIP:** A collection agency can allege "bona fide error" to defeat an unfair practices claim. If the collection agency was unaware of the statute of limitations and did not intend to mislead you, the FDCPA was not violated.

I hired an attorney and sued a collection agency for unfair debt collection practices. Can the agency continue to contact me about owing the debt? *No.* Once a lawyer represents you, it is a violation of the FDCPA to contact you (the debtor). The agency can only communicate with your attorney.

A major department store will not stop sending me bills for past due amounts on my credit card, even though I wrote and told them to stop contacting me. Is the store violating the FDCPA? *No. The department store is your actual creditor and the FDCPA does not apply to creditors.* The store can continue to bill you and contact you concerning your past due amounts.

The letter I received from the collection agency states I also owe "collection fees" and added $100 to my debt. Do I have to pay the fees? *No.* The agency is violating the FDCPA by unilaterally adding amounts to your debt that you do not owe and did not agree to.

DEBT COLLECTION

Debts that have been reduced to a court order or judgment can be collected under various legal methods. These remedies are available to judgment creditors only, not general creditors who have not yet obtained a court order or judgment against the debtor.

Garnishment

Garnishment is a legal process that allows a creditor to collect money awarded by a court that has not been paid. The award can result from a judgment against a person after a trial, or a court order such as a child support or alimony order. Typically, creditors file garnishment lawsuits to take money from a debtor's bank accounts. The bank is served with the lawsuit, along with the debtor.

Creditors can also garnish earnings directly from the creditor's employer. In child support situations, wage garnishment is a common method of obtaining child support from an unwilling parent. Usually, a form is served on the employer instructing it to take certain steps to direct the debtor's earnings to the creditor.

> **Garnishments can only be used by a judgment creditor. A creditor to whom you simply owe money cannot proceed with a garnishment suit against you.**

I have had my checking account garnished. Can I still use the account? *Yes. However, any money you deposit will be subject to the garnishment.* Additionally, any checks you write on the account will be returned.

Can my entire paycheck be garnished? *No. Laws limit the amount of money that can be garnished to a certain percentage of the debtor's net pay (gross pay minus state and federal taxes).* For example, the law may prohibit garnishing more than 20 percent of the debtor's net earnings.

> **TIP:** A child support garnishment can be as high as 50 to 60 percent of the debtor's net earnings.

My employer has been served with a garnishment for my wages. Is there any way I can prevent a portion of my salary from being garnished? *Yes. You can answer the garnishment.* Usually, a debtor's answer form is provided in the garnishment paperwork that you received. If you answer and assert a defense, your employer is prohibited from paying the creditor out of your earnings until there has been a hearing on the matter.

How long will my wages be garnished? *Depending on the laws of your states, several weeks' worth of paychecks could be affected.* A usual time period is 3 months. If the creditor is paid off before the garnishment period ends, the garnishment order terminates.

Can my bank account be garnished if my only income is Social Security disability payments? *No.* Social Security payments, pensions, unemployment and other state and federal aid payments are exempt from garnishment.

> **TIP:** You must file a garnishment exemption notice. The bank where you have your account usually provides the form.

If my wages are being garnished, can the same creditor garnish my bank accounts? *Yes.* If you want to avoid a bank account garnishment, cash your paycheck and pay bills with money orders and all other expenses in cash.

My mother's name is on my bank account because I was under 18 when I opened it many years ago. Can my mother's creditors garnish the funds although she has never deposited any money in the account? *Yes. If your mother's name is on the account, it is her account, too, and it is subject to a garnishment.* If garnishment papers were not served on you, get copies from the bank and file an answer appealing the garnishment order. The court will set a hearing and it is likely a judge will order the funds released because they belong to you alone.

Will the garnishment on my wages continue if I file bankruptcy? *No.* As soon as you file, the automatic stay goes into effect, stopping all collection efforts by your creditors, including those with judgments and court orders.

> **TIP:** Immediately provide the bank or employer and the creditor garnishing your wages with a copy of your bankruptcy petition. Do not wait on your lawyer (if you have hired one to file the bankruptcy) to send the petition; hand deliver it as soon as possible.

I filed suit in small claims court against my neighbor and was awarded $1,000. The neighbor refuses to pay. Can I garnish her bank account? *Yes.* You are a judgment creditor and can garnish up to $1,000 from her bank account. However, you must know the name of the bank and account number to pursue a garnishment.

> You must obtain a "Writ of Garnishment" from the small claims court. There will be a fee of approximately $50. Additionally, the court may require a sheriff's deputy to serve the writ on the debtor and the bank, which adds at least another $100 to the cost.

Repossession

A creditor with whom a debtor has a written contract, which includes an agreement to repay a loan for the purchase of certain property, has the right to take back, or repossess, the property when the debtor falls behind in the loan payments. Generally, repossessions occur where the purchaser of a vehicle fails to make payments on the car note. The contract gives the bank or company that financed the vehicle the right to seize it from the purchaser.

> The property is the collateral, and the creditor's right to take it is the security interest.

> **TIP:** Failing to make payments on a note or loan puts the debtor into default. When default occurs, the creditor can repossess the collateral.

How many payments do I have to miss before I have defaulted? Depending on the loan, one missed payment may be considered a default, although usually, the creditor does not act until the payments are several months overdue.

I have been making partial payments every month on my car note. Am I still in default? *Yes. Partial payments are equivalent to no payments at all under a default provision.* Although you will be credited for making the payments, you are still in default.

> **TIP:** Consistent late payments, although the full amount, can also put the debtor into default.

> **Creditors who consistently have accepted partial or late payments from a debtor may have waived their right to repossess because they ignored the default for a period of time.**

I have made all my car payments but my vehicle is still being repossessed because I never got auto insurance. Can the bank take my car? *Yes. You have defaulted on the loan by not taking out auto insurance.* Defaults can occur for reasons other than missed, late or partial payments. For example, most car financing companies and banks require purchasers to obtain auto insurance. If you fail to get the insurance, you defaulted under the contract.

I filed for bankruptcy because I cannot make my car payments. Can my car be repossessed? *No. The creditor is automatically stayed from repossessing the car.* Of course, the creditor may ask for relief from the stay because the collateral (the car) is diminishing in value. If you are unable to make the payments, it is likely that the court will allow the car to be repossessed.

I had equipment on my trailer when it was repossessed. Can the equipment be repossessed as well? *No. The creditor can only repossess the property described in your agreement.* In this case, the creditor has the right to repossess the trailer only. You have a legal right to have the equipment returned.

Can a credit card company repossess the bedroom furniture I charged? *No. The credit card company is loaning you money for purchases in general.* They have no right to repossess specific items. However, if you charged the furniture on the furniture or department store credit card, the furniture company may have the right to repossess, as credit was extended for a specific purpose and only in that store.

A creditor is threatening repossession. Is there anything I can do? *Yes. Typically, creditors want their money rather than the collateral.* You may be able to work out a different payment plan than is called for in the contract. You can also request an extension of time for payments.

> **TIP:** Filing bankruptcy will stop a creditor's repossession efforts immediately. Send the creditor a copy of the bankruptcy petition if the court has not yet notified it. Under the automatic stay, the creditor cannot repossess the property.

My vehicle is locked in the garage. Can the bank repossess it? *No. Although the bank has the right to "self-help" or repossessing the car on their own, they cannot do so if they "breach the peace."* Breaking into your garage or going in without your authority is a breach of the peace. The bank must get a court order and have a police officer reclaim, or replevy, the car.

> **TIP:** If your vehicle is in plain sight and accessible, it may be repossessed, even though it is on your property. For instance, a car sitting in the driveway can be towed.

What happens to my vehicle once it is repossessed? *The creditor can sell the vehicle and apply the money to the amount you still owe on it.* If the vehicle is worth the amount owing on it, the note may be cancelled.

> **If the vehicle is worth more than what you owe on it, you are due any funds from the sale that exceed the debt. You also have the right to force a sale if the creditor tries to simply cancel the debt when the vehicle is worth more than the amount owed. Forced sales should be discussed with an attorney.**

> **TIP:** The sale of repossessed property must be "commercially reasonable"; that is, the creditor is required to attempt to get a fair price. A vehicle, for instance, cannot be sold for $1; otherwise, the debtor would still owe the entire amount on the note plus be out a vehicle.

How will I know if my repossessed vehicle is going to be sold? *The creditor must give you notice of the time and place of a public sale or auction.* If the creditor intends to sell the vehicle to a private party (not offer it for auction), you are required to receive reasonable notice of a date when the vehicle will be sold.

Is there any way to get my car back once it has been repossessed? *Yes. Before the vehicle is sold, you are permitted to pay off the loan and repossession costs in order to have your car returned to you.* It is not uncommon to negotiate with your creditor after repossession and attempt to set up a new payment plan.

Is there any reason to let the bank repossess my car without trying to fight it? *Allowing the bank to take the vehicle may mean a bigger credit to your debt.* The bank will be able to sell the car more quickly and spend less money repossessing it (expenses that would be charged to your debt) if you voluntarily allow the bank to take it.

> **TIP:** Do not just give back the car without attempting to negotiate some reduction of the debt. Your actions are saving the bank money and time and it is reasonable for them to lower the amount you owe. If there is an agreement, get it in writing, signed by a bank officer and dated. Keep a copy.

My creditor repossessed my boat and sold it. Can I still be sued for the amount I still owe? *Yes. Because you still legally owe for the remaining debt (after credit for the sale), the creditor has the right to sue for recovery.* Laws in some states limit the creditor's ability to sue on the basis of the amount of the loan. You should consult a lawyer if you are sued because you may have some defenses to the suit.

Replevin

Replevin is a type of repossession. However, replevin is conducted by a sheriff with a court order. Repossession does not require a court order as the right to repossess is set out in the contract between the lender and the purchaser.

What happens if I refuse to comply with the sheriff's replevin attempts? You will probably be arrested for disobeying a court order and help in contempt.

Liens

A creditor may place a lien on a debtor's property if a court has entered a money judgment against the debtor. For example, the defendant who loses a car wreck case where the plaintiff is awarded $100,000 will have a judgment against the defendant in that amount. The creditor (in this case, the plaintiff) can attempt to collect by seizing the debtor's property and selling it or garnishing a bank account. However, because those options typically yield little or no money to pay off the judgment, judgment liens are commonly placed on a debtor's real property.

If I place a judgment lien on my neighbor's property for the $10,000 money judgment she owes me, can I force a sale of the property? *Probably not. Typically, homestead property is exempt from seizure and sale to pay a judgment.* Additionally, your lien is probably in second or even third place, after mortgage company liens.

How is a judgment lien ever paid if it is placed on exempt real property? The judgment is paid from the proceeds remaining after the mortgage is paid off when the house is sold.

EXAMPLE: A person who owns a home sells it for $100,000. She owes $75,000 on the mortgage so her profit is $25,000. However, you have a judgment lien on the property for $25,000. When the house sale closes, you will get a check for $25,000.

> **TIP:** Judgment liens "cloud" the title to property, making it almost impossible to sell until the judgment is paid off. No buyer wants to purchase a home that has a lien on it as the lien stays on the property until it is paid off. This situation often provides the impetus for the debtor to work out a settlement with the judgment creditor to have the lien removed so the property can be sold.

If I file bankruptcy, can I get a judgment lien on my home removed? *Yes.* If you have no equity in your home (once the amounts owing on it are deducted), the lien can be removed or "avoided."

Receivership

Appointment of a receiver is a traditional remedy available to creditors attempting to collect judgments. An individual, called a receiver (much like a bankruptcy trustee), is appointed by the court that entered the judgment to take control of all the debtor's nonexempt property. The receiver's job is to sell the property and pay the proceeds to the creditors.

> A receiver can also be appointed during pending litigation, before a judgment is entered, in order to prevent the debtor from wasting or transferring it.

UNIFORM FRAUDULENT TRANSFER ACT (UFTA)

In 1984, this Uniform Fraudulent Conveyances Act was revised and renamed the Uniform Fraudulent Transfer Act (UFTA). Under state and federal fraudulent transfer laws, a person who owes a debt cannot transfer or convey assets if the intent is to hinder, delay or defraud his creditors. The UFTA creates a right of action for any creditor against any debtor and any other person who has received property from the debtor in a fraudulent transfer. The UFTA has been adopted in many states, and others have enacted similar laws prohibiting a debtor from transferring assets in order to keep creditors from being paid.

Because it is difficult to prove intent to defraud, laws prohibiting fraudulent transfers are often assumed to be violated if a "badge of fraud" is present. Thus, the debtor is assumed to have made the transfer to defraud creditors in violation of the UFTA or other state fraudulent transfer laws if she:

- makes the transfer directly after being sued or threatened with litigation (suspicious timing);
- transfers property to a business partner, friend or relative (an insider);
- actually controls the property although it is no longer in her name;

- sells the asset for a price below its value; and/or
- transfers everything she owns, leaving no assets for herself.

> Conveying assets is more than transferring the title to a car or handing over a sum of cash. A conveyance, for purposes of determining fraud, is "every payment of money, assignment, release, transfer, lease, mortgage or pledge of tangible or intangible property, and also the creation of any lien or encumbrance."

I am involved in a lawsuit with my builder about payments I may owe him. Am I completely unable to transfer or convey any property or assets? *No. However, the transfers or sales you make cannot have a "badge of fraud." For example, you cannot sell your truck to your brother as he is a relative.* You may be able to sell the truck to a stranger who answered an ad in the paper, but even then the timing is suspicious because you are in the middle of litigation. You will have to prove to a court that you sold the truck without any intention to defraud a potential creditor.

> **TIP:** Transferring a small percentage of your assets, such as vehicle, tends to indicate there was no fraud. If the truck is the only thing you own in the world, the sale was probably fraudulent because you now have zero assets.

> Property that is exempt from seizure by a creditor, such as a homestead, can be transferred at any time. Fraudulent conveyances do not include exempt property because a creditor could not get to them anyway.

I owe my parents some money; however, I have been sued and will probably have a judgment entered against me. Can I go ahead and give my car to my parents to repay them before the judgment is entered? *No. If you transfer the car to your parents, you are making a fraudulent transfer.* You cannot pay off one debt in preference of another that will possibly arise in the future, such as a judgment.

The state wants to garnish my bank account for failure to pay child support to my ex-wife. Can my present wife and I enter into a postnuptial agreement, giving my earnings to her as her separate property? *No.* Any transfer of your earnings to a friend or relative is a conveyance to an insider and a "badge of fraud."

> **TIP:** Community property cannot be used to satisfy a debt one of the spouses incurred before marriage, such as an order to pay child support. In a community property state, the husband's earnings may be safe because income earned by spouses is community property.

> **Future earnings are property under the UFTA even though there is no present ownership in the money. For example, telling your employer to make out your paychecks to a friend is a fraudulent transfer even though the money has not yet been earned.**

I know my pension is safe from my creditors. However, in order to protect my monthly cash pension payments, can I have them directly deposited into an IRA instead of my checking account? *No. You are simply moving the funds to another account that you control.* In essence, you are making a transfer to an insider—yourself, which violates the UFTA.

> **TIP:** If there are no outstanding debts that creditors are currently trying to collect, placing funds in an IRA is not fraudulent. A fraudulent transfer is always a transfer that is suspiciously timed.

My house is my only asset and I am delinquent on the taxes. Can I sell it to my son at a discounted price? *No. Because you are selling the home to a family member and the transfer leaves you with no assets, the transfer looks fraudulent from the outset.* However, the sale would not violate the UFTA if he paid you fair market value for the house.

> **The house scenario could still be fraudulent (even if the son paid market price) if the selling parent continued to live in the home because this parent would be benefiting from and controlling a former asset.**

My former business partner has a large money judgment against me. Can I continue to make mortgage payments on my home? *Yes.* There is no "badge of fraud" in paying the mortgage because you have always made the payments, they are not suspiciously timed, the money is being paid to a third party and you are not attempting to hide the payments.

> **TIP:** Making extra mortgage payments or increasing the amount would be a fraudulent transfer.

My wife and I owe the IRS a large amount of back taxes and cannot afford to keep our home. If my parents assume our house note and we deed the property to them, will the IRS be able to prove the transfer was fraudulent? *Maybe not in the following circumstances: if the taxes are owed, but no tax lien has been filed; if your parents are unaware of the owed taxes; or if you and your wife no longer live on the property and the house's value is near the amount of the note.* In each of these cases, the transfer may not be fraudulent and the IRS could not put a lien on the property.

Can I sell my stocks and buy a house without violating the UFTA? *Yes. Because a homestead is exempt, the purchase (even if the money came from the sale of nonexempt property) is valid.* Creditors cannot "reverse" your purchase even though you may have intended to hinder their ability to collect by buying a home.

I owe my ex-business partner some money after he won a lawsuit against me. If I disclaim an inheritance under my parents' will, am I making a fraudulent transfer? *No.* Unless the law in your state makes disclaiming inheritances fraudulent, your refusal to accept your inheritance, with the intent that your ex-business partner will not be paid, does not violate the UFTA.

My ex-wife owes back taxes on some property that she sold to her brother to avoid a forced sale of the land. Now our children will not inherit the property. Can I bring a lawsuit against her based on her fraudulent transfer? *No. Only creditors can bring lawsuits based on fraudulent transfer laws.* Because neither you nor the children are creditors of your ex-wife, you cannot sue her on this basis.

2 CONSUMER PROTECTION

Almost every aspect of our lives is governed by some kind of contract. Imagine if there was no guarantee that the house you move into today would still belong to you in a week. Or if you went to work every day only to discover that your company decided not to pay you. When you write a check, you have a contract with your bank which says that you have the money to cover the check and will honor it. When you go to the dry cleaners, you have a contract which says that they will return your clothes clean and in one piece. Contracts give us piece of mind.

Because our lives are so entrenched in contractual matters, it is important to understand exactly what actions or inactions constitute a contract and how to get out of a bad one.

CONTRACTS

What is a contract? *A contract is a binding written or oral agreement that is enforceable by law between two or more competent parties to do or not to do certain things.* The elements of a valid contract are:

- an offer;
- acceptance of the offer; and
- sufficient consideration to support the offer.

What constitutes an offer? *An offer is a promise and a request for something in return.* Offers can be written or implied.

EXAMPLE: You drop your clothes off at the dry cleaners to be cleaned. By leaving your clothes, it is implied that you have accepted the cleaner's open offer to clean your clothes and that you will pay them for this service.

Is an advertisement an offer? *No.* An advertisement is generally considered an invitation to bargain.

Can an advertisement ever be an offer? Yes, any time a store advertises that it will give a free gift or special discount on the happening of a certain event (you buy $50 worth of merchandise; you are among the first 50 people at the store), they have made an enforceable offer.

Is an offer good forever? No, an offer ends when:

- the time to accept is over; either the stated deadline or, if no deadline is stated, a reasonable amount of time;
- the offeror cancels the offer;
- the offeree rejects the offer;
- the offeree dies or is incapacitated;
- a change in the law makes the contract illegal; or
- the subject matter of the contract is destroyed.

> An "option contract" is an agreement, made for consideration, to keep an offer open for a certain period of time. During this time period, the offer cannot be revoked.

Can I revoke my offer? *Yes, you can revoke an offer any time before it is accepted.* In order to revoke your offer, you must communicate the revocation to the other party. The revocation is effective once it is made.

What constitutes acceptance? *Acceptance is an assent by the party to whom the offer is made showing that the person agrees to all of the terms offered.* An offer is not binding unless the other party accepts it. Like an offer, acceptance can be express or implied. Generally, an affirmative action is necessary for acceptance of an offer; silence does not constitute assent.

To create a binding contract, both parties must give their assent. Their actions must lead the other people involved to believe that a contract is being formed. If one party is obviously not sincere in accepting an offer, chances are there is no contract. However, if a party has no intention of forming a contract but his or her actions lead others to believe that a contract has been formed, he or she may be held to the contract. It is the external appearance that determines whether you are held to a contract.

What is "consideration"? *Consideration is when one party gives up something or promises to give up something in exchange for something given up by the other party. Generally, a promise by one party without consideration in some form does not result in a contract.* Each party must extend consideration to the other; however, the value of the consideration does not have to be equal.

Consideration can be money, property, rights, services or the promise to do or not to do certain things. However, a duty that a party can refuse to perform is not considered consideration.

Who can enter into a contract? *Only competent parties can enter a contract. To be competent, a party must be able to understand what he or she is doing.* This requires both maturity and mental capacity.

What constitutes maturity? *Most states consider legal majority to be age 18.* Prior to that age, a person is legally incapable of entering into a contract. If a person or business enters into a contract with a minor, the minor is not responsible for keeping his or her end of the bargain.

> In some states, if a minor contracts for necessities (i.e., food or shelter) and is not under the care of a parent or guardian, then the minor is bound by the contract.

> **TIP:** No matter what your teenager says, a cell phone is not considered a necessity.

What is a "mental disability"? *A person suffers from a mental disability if they are intoxicated from drugs or liquor or if they are mentally ill or defective.* The important aspect concerning mental disability in regard to contracts is whether the person understands what he or she is doing.

Is an agreement to sell or do something illegal a contract? *No.* A court will not enforce a contract if its provisions are illegal. The courts will treat the contract as if it never existed.

However, if contract provisions were legal at the time they were made and later become illegal, the courts will generally consider the provisions in light of the law at the time the contract was formed.

Does a contract have to be in writing? *Not all contracts must be in writing.* Oral contracts are enforceable if they can be proven. An oral contract can be proven by showing that the circumstances would lead a reasonable person to believe that a contract existed. However, written contracts are easier to prove.

There are some contracts that must be in writing. These include:

- contracts to pay the debts of another person;
- contacts for the sale of land or any interest in real property;
- contracts which require more than 1 year to perform;
- prenuptial agreements;
- contracts for the sale of goods worth $500 or more; and
- contracts for the lease of goods worth more than $1,000.

Do written contracts have to be signed?

A written contract must be properly signed but generally does not have to be witnessed or notarized. It is sufficient that all the parties to the contract sign their names.

What qualifies as "signing"?

A contract may be signed in any manner that indicates an intention to be bound by it. A signature can be any mark, symbol or device chosen by the person signing to represent himself or herself. Electronic signatures are valid, and federal legislation has been enacted specifically to authorize them.

Can someone else sign a contract for me?

You cannot be bound by another person signing for you unless you have given that person legal authorization to do so—this is called a power of attorney. A "general power of attorney" permits almost any act; a "limited power of attorney" specifies the particular actions that can be done. You are called the "principal," and the person signing for you becomes your "agent."

If an agent exceeds the limits of his or her agency, the principal may or may not be liable depending on the particular case. If a third person dealing with the agent knows that the agent is exceeding the limitations of his or her agency, the principal is not liable.

However, if a principal knows that his or her agent has exceeded the limits of the agency in the past and has done nothing to rectify the situation, the principal may be liable for the actions of the agent.

I clicked a "YES" on the bottom of a computer Web site. Have I entered a contract?

Yes, most courts will hold that you have entered a contract in this instance.

What is a breach of contract?

A breach of contract is the failure of one party to perform his or her responsibilities under the contract. A breach of contract can occur by:

- failing to perform the contract terms as promised;

- making it impossible for the other party to perform; or
- announcing an intent not to perform. This is also known as "repudiation."

What is performance?

At one time, the law required exact compliance with all contract terms. A minor deviation would excuse total nonperformance by the other party or would be grounds for a breach of contract action.

Today, however, strict compliance is not necessary and "substantial performance" is sufficient. Under the doctrine of substantial performance, if one party to a contract performs the contract in large part, the other party cannot refuse to complete his or her part of the contract. The person giving substantial performance can recover damages from the other party for breach of contract. However, only the value of what was actually performed can be recovered.

What is partial performance?

Partial performance is anything less than substantial performance. A party who partially performs a contract cannot enforce it if the other party rejects the contract.

EXAMPLE: After getting estimates from a number of painting companies, Sue and Tom contract with Ace Painting Company to paint the outside of their home for $3,000. They chose Ace because its estimate was lower than the other companies by at least $500. Ace Painting begins to paint their home but leaves after painting only the eaves and never returns. Ace has only partially performed their part of the bargain. Sue and Tom then contract with Acme Painting Company to complete the job for $3,500. Ace cannot recover anything from Sue and Tom and, in fact, owe Sue and Tom $500 for the difference between the amount they agreed to do the job for and what Sue and Tom ultimately had to pay.

How can performance become impossible?

Performance becomes impossible when a party is unable to complete his or her part of the bargain, through no fault of his or her own, because of a fact which he or she has no reason to know and the nonexistence of which is a basic assumption under which the contract is made.

EXAMPLE: After getting estimates from a number of painting companies, Sue and Tom contract with Ace Painting Company to paint the outside of their home for $3,000. They chose Ace because their estimate was lower than the other companies by at least $500. Ace Painting shows up at Sue and Tom's house to begin painting, only to find that their pit bull is loose in the fenced yard and will not let them in. They call and leave a message for Sue and Tom saying they will return the next day and asking that they keep the dog in the house. Ace returns day after day, only to find the dog still in the yard. Sue and Tom never return their calls. Sue and Tom have "breached" the contract by making performance by Ace Painting impossible.

Will increased costs because of changing circumstances make a contract impossible to perform? The courts would most likely enforce the contract on the grounds that the changing circumstances were foreseeable at the time the contract was formed and that the possibility of rising costs should have been built into the contract terms.

What is "repudiation"? *Repudiation occurs when, before performance is due, one party clearly communicates to the other party that he or she cannot or will not perform a material part of his or her contractual obligations.* In this instance, the contract has been breached.

Are there any excuses for nonperformance of a contract? *Yes, there are certain situations in which a party may be excused from performing his or her part of the contract.* These include:

▸ **FRAUD:** A court will cancel a contract because of fraud when a person knowingly made a material misrepresentation that the other party reasonably relied on and was disadvantaged by.

▸ **DURESS:** A contract that a party agrees to under duress is void in most states. Duress is a threat or act that overcomes a party's free will.

▸ **IMPOSSIBILITY OF PERFORMANCE:** Performance will usually be excused and the contract terminated if an essential party to the contract dies, an essential item

or commodity has been destroyed or an intervening change of law has rendered performance of the contract illegal.

▸ **COMMERCIAL FRUSTRATION:** Nonperformance of a contract will be excused where performance would be virtually worthless or the objectives of the contract have become meaningless because of circumstances arising after the formation of the contract.

▸ **DELAY:** When the contract specifies that its duties or obligations must be performed by a specific time, a delay by one party can excuse performance by the other.

▸ **FAILURE OF CONSIDERATION:** A failure of consideration exists when a promise has been made to support a contract or good consideration existed when the contract was made, but that promise has not been performed and the other party is excused from further performance.

What are the remedies for breach of contract? *When a party breaches a contract by failing to perform his or her obligations, the usual remedy is a legal action for the damages caused by the breach.* However, under certain circumstances, the nonbreaching party can force specific performance of the contract, have the contract modified or canceled or obtain an injunction.

What types of damages are recoverable for a breach of contract? *A monetary damage judgment is the most common judicial remedy for breach of contract.* Depending on the circumstances of the case, you may receive nominal damages, punitive damages, compensatory damages, consequential damages and/or liquidated damages.

▸ **NOMINAL DAMAGES:** Nominal damages are awarded when a breach of a contract is proven, but the nonbreaching party is unable to prove any actual loss. The amount of nominal damages usually varies from between a few cents to a few dollars.

▸ **PUNITIVE DAMAGES:** Punitive damages punish a wrongdoer and set an example for others. While it is rare for a court to award punitive damages in a contract suit, if the breach is malicious, willful or physically injurious to the nonbreaching party, the court may award them.

- ▸ **COMPENSATORY DAMAGES:** Compensatory damages are those damages that flow from the wrongful conduct of the breaching party. The usual measure of compensatory damages is the amount of money necessary to compensate the nonbreaching party for the breach.

- ▸ **CONSEQUENTIAL DAMAGES:** Consequential damages (also known as special damages) are foreseeable damages that result from a party's breach. Consequential damages are granted in addition to compensatory damages when they are foreseeable to a reasonable person at the time the contract was entered.

- ▸ **LIQUIDATED DAMAGES:** A liquidated damages clause is a clause in a contract under which the parties agree in advance to the damages to be paid in the event of breach. The purpose of a liquidated damages clause is to ensure that a reasonable estimate of probable damages is available in case of breach. There are three elements to a valid liquidated damages clause. They are:

1. the clause must reasonably forecast the probable loss due to breach;
2. the loss anticipated by the breach is difficult to calculate; and
3. the clause must not be intended as a penalty.

> **If a contract provides that the nonbreaching party can choose between liquidated damages or actual damages, the liquidated damages clause is probably unenforceable.**

When a breach of contract occurs, the injured party must take reasonable steps to mitigate (meaning reduce or lessen) the damages that he or she sustains. The injured party may not recover damages for losses that he or she could have avoided without undue risk, burden or humiliation. In mitigating damages, the nonbreaching party must:

- refrain from piling up losses after notice of breach;
- avoid incurring further costs or expenditures; and

- make reasonable efforts to reduce his or her losses by obtaining a substitute at a reasonable price.

What is "specific performance"? *Specific performance is an equitable remedy that is available to the nonbreaching party when the remedy at law is not adequate.* In order to obtain specific performance, the nonbreaching party must prove that the subject matter of the contract is unique—for example, a rare painting. In this instance, the court will require the breaching party to comply with the contract.

> **Specific performance is never granted for breach of a personal service contract.**

When can a contract be canceled? The purpose of cancellation of a contract (also called "rescission") is to return the parties to the contract to the positions they would have occupied if the contract had never been made.

There are three general situations in which rescission is the appropriate remedy:

- when the contract involves a mutual mistake—for example, an agreement to sell a product that does not exist;
- when a contract involves a unilateral mistake due to fraud, duress or undue influence;
- when a material breach—for example, an unjustified failure to perform—occurs.

> **A party who substantially breaches the contract cannot receive rescission. Further, a fully executed contract cannot be rescinded.**

When can I get a contract modified? *Modification of a contract, also known as reformation, occurs when a court amends, modifies or rewrites the contract to reflect the parties' true intent.* This remedy is used when a party cannot perform the contract in the exact way it is written but can fulfill it in other ways.

Usually reformation will apply when fraud or mutual mistake—e.g., a typographical error—occurs. Generally, a court will only order reformation on a clear and convincing demonstration of mutual mistake. If only one party was mistaken, reformation will not be ordered unless the mistake on one side was caused by the other party's fraud.

Under what circumstances can I get an injunction? *An injunction is an equitable remedy which compels a party to act or not act in a certain way.* It is only granted when monetary damages are inadequate because irreparable injury will occur if the contract is not performed. An injunction would order a party to perform the contract.

EXAMPLE: You contract with a famous designer to create a one of a kind wedding dress. A week before your wedding, you find out that the designer is planning on selling your wedding dress to another person. You can go to court and ask the court to prevent the designer from selling the dress to the other person. If the designer violates the injunction, not only will he or she be responsible to you for monetary damages, but the designer may also be held in contempt of court for violating the injunction.

What is the FTC Cooling-Off Rule? *The FTC Cooling-Off Rule gives a consumer 3 days to cancel certain purchases of $25 or more that are made in his or her home or at a location that is not the seller's permanent place of business.* Under this rule, the consumer's right to cancel for a full refund extends until midnight of the third business day after the sale.

What kinds of sales or contracts are covered by the rule? The Cooling-Off Rule applies to:

- sales over $25;
- purchases of goods or negotiations of services made at the buyer's home, workplace or dormitory or at facilities rented by the seller on a temporary or short-term basis, such as hotel or motel rooms, convention centers, fairgrounds and restaurants; it also applies when you invite a salesperson to make a presentation in your home (for example, home sales parties);
- refinancing a real estate mortgage or purchasing an additional real estate mortgage.

What kinds of contracts are not covered by the rule? The Cooling-Off Rule does not cover sales:

- under $25;
- for goods or services not primarily intended for personal, family or household purposes;
- made entirely by mail or telephone;
- that are the result of prior negotiations at the seller's permanent business location where the goods are regularly sold;
- needed to meet an emergency;
- made as part of your request for the seller to do repairs or maintenance on your personal property (purchases made beyond the maintenance or repair request are covered);
- for real estate, insurance or securities;
- for automobiles, vans, trucks or other motor vehicles sold at temporary locations, provided the seller has at least one permanent place of business; and
- arts or crafts sold at fairs or locations such as shopping malls, civic centers and schools.

Does the salesperson have to tell me about my right to cancel? *Yes, the salesperson must tell you about your cancellation rights at the time of sale, as well as giving you two copies of a cancellation form (one to keep and one to send) and a copy of your contract or receipt.* The contract or receipt should be dated, show the name and address of the seller and explain your right to cancel.

> **TIP:** If you are not given a cancellation form, you have a continuing right to cancel beyond the 3 days. You may also have a continuing right to cancel if the seller misleads you about or interferes with your right to cancel.

How can I cancel a sale under the FTC Cooling-Off Rule? *To cancel an applicable sale, sign and date one copy of the cancellation form and mail it to the address given for cancellation, making sure the envelope is postmarked before midnight of the third business day after the contract date.* Keep the other copy of the cancellation form for your records.

If the seller did not give you a cancellation form, you can create your own. It must be postmarked within 3 business days of the sale.

> **TIP:** For purposes of the Cooling-Off Rule, Saturday is considered a business day; Sundays and federal holidays are not.

> **TIP:** Proof of the mailing date and receipt are important; therefore, consider sending the cancellation form by certified mail, return receipt requested.

What happens after I send in the cancellation form? Once you cancel your purchase, the seller has 10 days to:

- cancel and return any promissory note or other negotiable instrument you signed;
- refund all your money and tell you whether any product you still have will be picked up; and
- return any trade-in.

The seller has 20 days to either pick up the items left with you, or reimburse you for mailing expenses if you agree to send back the items.

If you do not make the items available to the seller or if you agree to return the items but fail to, you remain obligated under the contract.

WARRANTIES

What is a "warranty"? *A warranty is a promise by a manufacturer to stand behind its product.* Under federal law, warranties must be available for you to read before you buy, even when you are purchasing through a catalog or on the Internet. A warranty must be written in plain language and contain the following information:

- the name and address of the company making the warranty;
- the product or parts covered;
- whether replacement, repair or refund is covered and if there are any expenses you would have to pay;
- length of warranty;
- damages not covered by warranty;
- action to be taken if you need to take advantage of the warranty;
- whether the company requires you to use any specific methods to settle a dispute; and
- a description of your legal rights.

What types of warranties exist?

- Full warranties promise that the product will be fixed at no cost to the buyer within a reasonable time after the owner has complained; the owner will not have to undertake any unreasonable task to return the product for repair; and a defective product will be replaced with a new one or the buyer's money will be returned when the product cannot be fixed after a reasonable number of attempts.
- Limited warranties offer fewer benefits than a full warranty, most often offering only free parts, not labor.

> **It is possible that one part of a product could be covered by a full warranty and the rest covered by a limited warranty.**
>
> - Express warranties are those offered by the manufacture on a voluntary basis and are meant to encourage customers to buy a product. They can be both written and verbal.
> - Implied warranties guarantee that the product is suitable for sale. This means all parts work effectively, and the product does what it was designed to do, whether or not any other warranty exists. These warranties are required by state law, and in most states, you have up to 4 years to enforce an implied warranty after the transaction starts.

> **TIP:** If a seller states in writing that the product is sold "as is," implied warranties do not apply. This is true even if the salesperson makes a verbal promise to take care of any problems that may arise. Several states, including Kansas, Maine, Maryland, Massachusetts, Mississippi, Vermont, West Virginia and the District of Columbia, do not permit "as is" sales.

My warranty says that it does not cover "consequential damages." What are they? Consequential damages are losses resulting from failure of the product, including your time and expense in getting the damage repaired.

EXAMPLE: If your refrigerator breaks down, you may get a new refrigerator, but you will not be able to cover the cost of the food that spoils as a result.

Can I rely on an oral warranty? *There is no requirement that a company honor an oral warranty.* To protect yourself, if a salesperson makes an oral promise to you, get it in writing.

What is an extended warranty? *An extended warranty is actually a service contract, not a warranty.* Like a warranty, a service contract provides repair and/or maintenance of a product for a specific amount of time. Unlike a warranty, service contracts are not included in the price of the product; they will cost you extra money and are sold separately.

Should I pay for an extended warranty? *Whether or not you should purchase an extended warranty is up to you.* To determine whether you need a service contract, consider:

- whether the product warranty already covers the repairs that you would get under the service contract;
- whether the warranty already covers some of the time period of coverage that you would get under the service contract;
- whether the product is likely to need repairs and the potential costs of such repairs;
- the duration of the service contract;
- whether there is a deductible amount; and
- the reputation of the company offering the service contract.

I did not register my product after buying it. Can I still take advantage of its warranty? *Under federal law, the answer depends on whether it is a "full" or "limited" warranty.* Full warranties cannot be conditioned on the return of a registration card; limited warranties can.

How can I minimize problems?

- Always read the warranty before you buy a product. Understand exactly what protection is available under the warranty. When shopping online, look for hyperlinks leading you to the full warranty or to an address where you can write to get a free copy. If a copy of the warranty is available online, print it out and keep it with your records.
- Consider the reputation of the company offering the warranty. If you are not familiar with the company, ask your local or state consumer protection office or Better Business Bureau if they have any complaints against the company.

- Save your receipt through the warranty period and file it away with the warranty. It is your proof of when the warranty period started and that you are the original owner.
- Perform required maintenance and inspections. Any violation of the manufacturer's operating and service instructions may void the warranty.

CONDITIONAL AND INSTALLMENT SALES

In an ordinary buy and sell situation, the buyer owns the items he or she purchases and takes home. The purchase price of some items, however, is paid out over time to the seller, although the buyer is in possession of the goods. These transactions are called conditional or installment sales. For example, the buyer may have possession of the plasma screen TV he or she bought, but he or she does not own it if he or she is paying out installments toward the purchase price to the store where it was purchased.

> **An installment sale is not the same as charging a purchase on a credit card. There, the bank issuing the credit card pays the store the full purchase price of the plasma screen TV on your behalf. Since you are not paying out the purchase price to the seller directly, there is no installment sale.**

> **State laws typically regulate installment sales.**

If you are the seller, you legally own, or have title, to the item that is the subject of an installment sales contract. Under the contract, the seller is the creditor and the buyer is the debtor. If the buyer does not make his or her payments, the seller has the right to:

- retake the item and cancel the contract;
- retake the item, sell it, apply the proceeds to the amount owed under the contract and sue the buyer for the remainder; or
- sue the buyer for the total unpaid balance.

> **TIP:** If the seller prevails in court, he or she will recover the balance on the installment sales contract, interest on the balance for the entire time it was owed plus attorney's fees.

> A "sale on approval" allows the buyer to return the item if he or she chooses not to accept it after trying it out. The buyer does not own the item until he or she accepts it. For example, a copy machine delivered to an office to buy on approval is not paid for by the buyer until he or she accepts its condition and notifies the seller within a reasonable time.

Unlike installment sales contracts, which are generally regulated by state laws, rent-to-own agreements are often excluded from regulation. The weekly payments may be modest, but the interest rate charged can exceed 200 percent, making the final cost far beyond the original purchase price. Late payments can result in penalty fees and repossession of the item.

Never enter into a rent-to-own agreement without obtaining the following:

- a complete list of all fees;
- an explanation of penalties for late payments;
- the interest rate; and
- the total sales price of the item if the agreement is paid out.

I purchased a dining room set on installment and lost it in a fire. Do I have to keep paying for it? *Yes.* You must continue making the monthly payments; the dining room set was not returned—it was destroyed—and you must pay for it.

> **TIP:** Always take out insurance on items purchased on an installment plan. Typically, homeowner's insurance covers furnishings, but if you are renting, get renter's insurance. The proceeds you receive will allow you to pay off the purchase.

The amount I am paying off on a hot tub I purchased is more than the sales price. Why did the amount increase? *You are being charged interest and fees on the transaction.* The seller is obligated to provide you with an itemized list of interest charges and other fees. Ask for one immediately so you can understand the transaction.

> The seller is also required to provide you with a statement showing payments you made that have been credited to the purchase amount.

> **TIP:** Stores, particularly electronics stores, sell high-priced items (computers, wide-screen TVs, appliances, etc.) with "no payments or interest for 6 months" and other gimmicks. Do not purchase the item if you cannot make the payment due at the end of the time period (or an even number of payments to pay off the purchase during the no-interest period). If you miss the deadline, interest and other fees will be assessed—as much as 21 percent.

I missed a couple of payments on a computer purchase I was paying out and have now been billed for the entire amount left owing. Why can I not continue to make monthly payments as before? *You defaulted on the purchase contract.* Nearly all retail installment contracts (which is what you signed) provide that in the event of default the "entire unpaid balance of the total of payments" becomes immediately due and payable.

> **TIP:** When you buy an item at a store on an installment basis, a bank rather than the store itself finances the purchase. For instance, you do not owe the electronics store for the computer—you owe the bank that financed the transaction that is listed on the installment contract you signed.

I sold my friend some jewelry I owned for $2,000, and she is buying it on installments. Do I need to put our agreement in writing? *Yes.* Without a written agreement of some kind, the deal you made with your friend may be unenforceable, and you could be left without the money or the jewelry.

Your agreement should:

- identify the jewelry;
- set out the purchase price;
- set out the amount of the installment payments;
- list the dates the payments are due;

- give you the right to have the jewelry returned if payments are missed;
- permit you to refund payments if the jewelry must be returned; and
- give you the right to demand the entire purchase price if a payment is missed.

If you put the agreement in writing, laws make it much easier for you to collect the money she owes you in the case of default.

> It is common for retail installment contracts to contain arbitration clauses prohibiting the buyer from a filing a lawsuit based on the contract. Additionally, the buyer waives the right to a jury. You will not be able to litigate any dispute concerning the purchase in a court.

FRAUD

Fraud is an intentional deception resulting in an unfair or unlawful gain. Crimes utilizing fraud are widespread in today's world. It is estimated that consumers and businesses lose several hundred billion dollars each year to various fraudulent schemes.

When you are a victim of fraud, not only do you have to deal with the humiliation that comes with knowing that someone has taken advantage of you, but the financial costs can be enormous and long-lasting. What follows is a discussion of various types of fraudulent crimes and steps you can take to protect yourself.

What is "false advertising"? *Any advertising that is misleading in any material respect is considered to be false advertising.* Advertising that is misleading about a product's place of origin, nature, quality or make is prohibited under federal and most states' laws. To be found guilty of false advertising, it must be shown that the advertisement was deceptive in nature.

> Whether or not the advertiser intends to mislead you is not important; the overall impression of the advertisement is. Moreover, there is no requirement that the advertisement actually caused harm.

What is "palming off"? When an advertiser creates the impression that its products or services are those of a competitor, the advertiser is guilty of palming off.

What is "product disparagement"? Product disparagement is when an advertiser intentionally makes false or misleading negative remarks about competing goods or services, causing its competitor to lose sales.

What is "bait and switch" advertising? *Bait and switch advertising occurs when a particular item is priced so low that you are lured into the store to buy it.* This is known as the "bait." However, once you try to buy the item, you are told that it is sold out or you are discouraged from buying it by the salesperson. The store employee may tell you that the product is actually inferior and try to convince you to buy a more expensive product. This is the "switch." This type of advertising is illegal in most states if the advertised product is not available in reasonable quantities.

Do not confuse bait and switch tactics with a salesperson who is merely aggressive. Depending on your needs, a reputable salesperson may try to persuade you to buy a better quality item or a different brand at a higher price. There is nothing unethical or illegal about this practice, as long as you are given a choice without undue pressure.

How can I protect myself against bait and switch advertising?

- Be cautious of ads that offer low, low prices and salespeople who try to steer you away from advertised specials.
- Deal only with reputable firms. Check with the Better Business Bureau for a reliability report.
- Ask for a "rain check" when advertised products are not available for sale.
- Remember that you do not have to fall for high-pressure sales tactics. Take your time and think about what it is you are getting for your money. Comparison shop at other stores.
- When in doubt, walk away.

What federal laws protect a consumer against false and deceptive advertising?

Congress has enacted two statutes that have the greatest effect on advertising: the Federal Trade Commission Act and the Lanham Act.

Under the FTC Act, the FTC is given broad authority to regulate advertising. Within this power, the FTC has issued regulations barring advertisements that could be misleading, even if they are true.

EXAMPLE: At one time, advertisements for Anacin® (a brand of aspirin) claimed that clinical tests proved that it provided the same headache relief as the leading pain relief medicine. Unfortunately, the ad did not mention that the leading pain relief medicine was, in fact, aspirin. According to the FTC, this advertisement was misleading.

The FTC also has the power to order corrective ads. These are ads a business will be required to run that alert future consumers to certain unfavorable facts about a product that were not revealed in past advertising campaigns.

EXAMPLE: For many years, advertisements for Listerine® promoted its use as a cold and sore throat remedy. Under its power to order corrective ads, Listerine was forced to run ads stating that Listerine would not cure colds or relieve sore throats.

In addition to these measures, the FTC can:

- try to bring the violator into voluntary compliance through informal means;
- issue a cease and desist order;
- bring a civil lawsuit on behalf of people who have been harmed; and/or
- seek a court injunction to stop a false ad.

Only the FTC has the authority to enforce the FTC Act; it does not provide a cause of action for consumers. However, consumers and competitors can bring a legal action for false advertising under the Lanham Act.

To establish a violation under the Lanham Act, a plaintiff must prove:

- the advertiser made false statements of fact about its product;

- the false advertisements actually deceived or had the capacity to deceive a substantial segment of the target population;
- the deception was material;
- the falsely advertised product was sold in interstate commerce; and
- the plaintiff was injured as a result of the deception.

> **TIP:** Actual loss is not required to show an injury; only a reasonable basis for the belief that the plaintiff is likely to be damaged as a result of the advertising.

The penalties for a Lanham Act violation include the plaintiff's lost profits, the additional profits to the advertiser resulting from the deceptive ad, treble damages and attorneys' fees.

Are door-to-door sales safe or not? *That depends. While some door-to-door salespeople are honest, many are not.* Unfortunately, there is no guaranteed way to tell the difference. Door-to-door con artists are charming and friendly; they are successful because they seem so honest.

How can I protect myself from an unscrupulous door-to-door salesperson?

- If you do not know the salesperson, do not let them into your house.
- Do not buy on impulse or feel pressured to make a purchase.
- Ask to see the salesperson's credentials. Look up the phone number for your local business permit office yourself and call to check the door-to-door salesperson's permit. Do not use a phone number provided by the salesperson—it could connect you with someone involved in the scam.
- Never buy right away. Take the salesperson's telephone number and tell him or her that you will be in touch after you have had a chance to read all the material given to you. This gives you time to comparison shop and to check with the Better Business Bureau about the company.

I have done all that and decided to sign a contract. What should I know?

- Understand all the contract terms; ask for clarification if necessary.
- Make sure the contract is complete, signed and dated.

- Get every promise the salesperson makes in writing. If they are not, you cannot enforce them later.
- Never sign a contract with blank spaces. Cross out any blanks.
- Get all terms of the sale in writing, including the total price, warranties, return policy, financing and all conditions of sale.
- Be sure you have an address and phone number (not a post office box number) so that you can get in touch with the company.

Is there any way I can get out of a contract I made with a door-to-door salesperson? Yes, the FTC Cooling-Off Rule gives a consumer 3 days to cancel purchases of $25 or more that are made at the buyer's home.

MAIL-ORDER SHOPPING

Mail order can be a convenient way to make a purchase, and there are many legitimate companies who sell by mail order. However, as with any type of transaction, there are still things that you should keep in mind.

What should I know before ordering by mail? Before ordering a product through the mail, keep the following things in mind:

- Is the item you want to buy described well in words, not just pictures? Know what you are actually getting before you order.
- Are there handling and shipping charges in addition to the price of the item? If so, is it still a good buy?
- Can you trust the company you are buying from?
- Does the company offer a written, money-back guarantee if you are not happy with the product?
- Does the company provide a street address and contact phone number? Never buy from a company that just gives a P.O. Box number.
- Beware of exaggerated claims for products or unrealistically low prices for merchandise.
- Check the Better Business Bureau for a reliability report on the company with whom you are thinking of doing business.

How should I pay for my mail-order purchase? *Never send cash when paying for a mail-order purchase.* If a problem arises, it will be easier to solve if you have paid by credit card.

I have decided to make a mail-order purchase. Are there any steps I can take to protect myself?

Keep a copy of the advertisement, a record of the name and address of the company, exactly what you ordered, the date you placed the order, the amount you paid for the item and your method of payment. Keep a record of any delivery period that was promised.

Check what you ordered as soon as it arrives. If you are dissatisfied, immediately get in touch with the company.

When should I receive my merchandise? *Under FTC rules, if an advertisement states that your merchandise will be "rushed" to you within a certain time period, you must receive it within that time frame.* If no date is given, the manufacturer must make the shipment within 30 days.

If the company is unable to ship within the promised time, they must give you an "option notice." This notice gives you the choice of agreeing to the delay or canceling your order.

If you decide to cancel, the seller must refund all of your money within 7 days of your cancellation.

There is one exception to the 30-day rule: if a company does not promise a shipping time, and you are applying for credit to pay for your purchase, the company has 50 days to ship after receiving your order.

Can a mail-order company send me substitute merchandise? *They can send you anything they want, but that does not mean that you have to keep it.* If you do not want the substituted merchandise, send it back and ask for a refund. If you do not return the merchandise, the company can assume that you are accepting the substitute and bill you accordingly.

Is shopping on the Internet safe? *For the most part, the information found above regarding mail-order shopping applies to Internet shopping.* However, there are few points that are unique to the Internet. These are:

- Confirm the online seller's physical address and phone number in case you have questions or problems.

- If you get an e-mail or pop-up message while you are browsing that asks for personal or financial information, do not reply or click on the link in the message. Legitimate companies do not ask for this information via e-mail.
- Print and save records of your online transactions, including the product description and price, the online receipt and copies of every e-mail you send to or receive from the seller.
- Check the company's privacy policy. It should tell you what personal information the Web site is collecting, why and how they are going to use the information. If you do not like their policy, consider shopping elsewhere.

> **TIP:** If you initiate a transaction and are charging your purchase, make sure the site is secure. Look for a lock icon on the browser's status bar or make sure the company's URL address begins with "https:" (the "s" stands for "secure").

Do I have to pay for merchandise I did not order? No, you can treat it as a gift. Federal laws prohibit mailing unordered merchandise to consumers and then demanding payment.

Do I have to notify the seller that I am keeping the merchandise without paying for it? *While you are not legally bound to notify the seller, it will not hurt to write the company a letter stating that you did not order the item and that you have a legal right to keep it without paying for it.* A letter may prevent the seller from sending you repeated bills or dunning notices. It may also clear up a shipping error.

> **TIP:** You should make a copy of the letter and send the original by certified mail, return receipt requested. Keep the return receipt and the copy of the letter. You may need them at a later date to establish that you did not order the merchandise.

I received merchandise as a result of a shipping error. What should I do? *In this situation, write the company and tell them of the error, offering to return the merchandise if they pay for postage and handling.* Give them a specific yet reasonable amount of time to pick up the merchandise or arrange to have it returned

at no expense to you. Inform the seller that you reserve the right to keep the merchandise or dispose of it after that date.

Once again, you should make a copy of the letter, and send the original by certified mail, return receipt requested. Keep the return receipt and the copy of the letter. You may need them at a later date to establish that you tried to return the merchandise.

What merchandise can legally be sent to me without my consent? *You may legally be sent free samples that are clearly and plainly marked as such and merchandise mailed by charitable organizations asking for contributions.* In both of these instances, you may keep the merchandise without paying for it.

How can I protect myself against receiving unordered merchandise? *Be cautious when participating in sweepstakes or placing an order for goods advertised as "free," "trial" or "unusually low-priced."* Read all of the fine print to ensure that you are not joining a "club," with regular purchasing or notification obligations.

Where can I go for help in dealing with this problem? *You should always try to resolve your dispute with the company first.* However, if the company is unresponsive, contact your state or local consumer protection office, local U.S. Postal Inspector or the Better Business Bureau in your area for help.

HOME IMPROVEMENT SCAMS

What should I do before hiring a contractor to work on my home? *Before hiring a contractor to work on your home, you should interview each potential candidate to find out how long they have been in business, whether they are licensed and registered with your state, how many projects similar to yours the contractor has completed within the previous year (ask for a list of references and then check them out), whether your home improvement project will require permits and what types of insurance they carry.* The contractor should have personal liability, worker's compensation and property damage coverage.

Thoroughly check the contractor's references; these past customers can help you decide if the contractor is right for you. Ask the references if you can visit their home to see the contractor's work. Find out whether or not they were satisfied with the work and whether it was completed on time. Where there any unexpected costs? Did the contractor show up on time? Most importantly, would they use the contractor again?

Get written estimates from several different contractors. Make sure the estimates are based on identical project specifications.

CAUTION: Do not hire a contractor merely because you share an ethnic or cultural background. Coming from the same part of the world as your ancestors does not make a contractor competent or trustworthy. Many contractors use such influences to secure work and then fail to adequately deliver.

Are there any warning signs of a potential home improvement scam? *Yes.* Certain things should set off alarm bells when dealing with home improvement businesses. For example:

- door-to-door salespeople who do not have local connections and who offer to do work for substantially less than market price
- companies that list only a telephone number or post office box as contact information (This is especially true if it is an out-of-state company.)
- contractors who will not provide references
- salespeople who offer to inspect your house for free (Never let anyone into your house unless they can present authentic identification that establishes their business status. Look up the employer's phone number yourself and call to verify the salesperson's identity.)
- contractors demanding cash payment for a job or who ask you to make a check payable to a person other than the owner or company name
- contractors who offer to drive you to the bank to withdraw funds to pay for the work
- contractors who offer you discounts for finding other customers
- contractors who ask you to get the building permits

What should be included in a home improvement contract? *Remember that contract requirements vary from state to state.* Before signing any contract, check the laws of your particular state. Moreover, even if your state does not require a written contract in this instance, demand one.

The contract should be clear, concise and complete. Do not sign a contract that contains blank spaces; cross them out.

Before you sign, make sure the contract contains:

- the name, address, phone number and license number of the contractor;
- a detailed description of the work to be performed;
- a detailed list of all materials including color, model, size, brand name and product;
- a schedule and method of payment, including down payment, subsequent payments and final payment;
- any oral promises made by the contractor;
- the start and completion dates;
- the contractor's obligation to obtain all necessary permits;
- a list of warranties covering materials and workmanship with the names and addresses of the parties honoring the warranties and the length of the warranty periods;
- a provision stating the grounds for termination of the contract by either party—remember, you have 3 business days to cancel the contract if you signed it in your home or at a location other than the seller's permanent place of business; and
- total cost of work to be performed.

My contractor never finished the job. What do I do now? *You must pay the contractor for the work he or she completed.* However, do not make the final payment until you are satisfied with the work and all subcontractors have been paid. Or, you can cancel the contract and may be entitled to a refund of any down payment or other payments made towards the work, once you have sent the contractor a written demand by certified mail.

TRAVEL

What is travel fraud? *Travel fraud schemes come in all shapes and sizes. One example involves vacation travel packages in which the consumer pays hundreds of dollars to receive a travel package that includes round-trip air transportation for one person and lodging for two people in a specified location.* However, you must purchase a high-priced, round-trip ticket for the second person from the fraudulent travel operation, or you must pay for costly accommodations in less-than-ideal timeshares or resorts. In the end, you may pay more for this vacation package than if you had purchased your own tickets in advance or bought them through an airline or reputable travel agency.

How can I avoid becoming a victim of a travel scam? *First and foremost, use your common sense.* Any offer that seems too good to be true is most likely too good to be true. Nobody gives away something for nothing.

EXAMPLE: If you are told that you have been awarded a prize, but you have not entered a contest, you are being scammed.

Do not be pressured into buying right now. If the offer is legitimate, you will not be expected to make an immediate decision.

Do not be afraid to ask questions. Know exactly what the price covers and what it does not. Find out if there will be any additional charges later. Find out the names of the hotels and airlines that are included in your package and double-check arrangements with them. Ask about cancellation policies and refunds. If the salesperson cannot answer your questions, you do not want the package.

Before you purchase a travel package, ask for detailed written information. Once you receive the information, make sure the written material confirms everything you were told by phone.

Never give your credit card number to unsolicited telephone salespeople, even if they say that they need the number for verification purposes. Once they have your credit card number, all the scam artists have to do is charge your account.

> **TIP:** When in doubt, say no.

Does the airline have to compensate me if it bumps me off a flight because of overbooking? *Overbooking is not illegal, and most airlines overbook their scheduled flights to a certain extent in order to compensate for "no-shows."* As a result, passengers are sometimes left behind or "bumped."

When a flight is overbooked, the Department of Transportation requires airlines to ask people who are not in a hurry to give up their seats voluntarily in exchange for compensation. Those passengers bumped against their will are, with a few exceptions, entitled to compensation.

The DOT rules require that:

- Your original ticket can be used another time or be fully refunded.
- You get a free seat on the next available flight leaving from any airline. Your original carrier will arrange it.
- You get immediate cash compensation, based on how long the delay will be from your original planned arrival time.
  - Compensation is equal to twice the cost of a one-way fare to your destination or $400, whichever is less.
  - Compensation is equal to the cost of a one-way fare or $200, whichever is less, if the next available flight arrives within 2 hours of the original flight, if it is a domestic trip, or within 4 hours for international flights.
  - There is no compensation if the alternative flight is scheduled to arrive within an hour of your original flight.
- You must be at the gate at least 10 minutes before your departure time or you forfeit your reservation and the DOT compensation does not apply.

What is a "vacation timeshare"? Under a timeshare, you pay a one-time price plus annual maintenance fees, and in turn, you buy the right to use a given vacation property for a certain amount of time each year.

Is a timeshare a good investment? *Not necessarily. Some timeshares require you to decide up to 2 years in advance which week you want to use it.* You are often restricted to one location, although some timeshares allow you to trade your week for one at another location. Moreover, sometimes annual fees rise to equal the amount you would spend renting for a week at the facility, so you actually are not saving any money.

If I buy a timeshare, will I have trouble selling it later? *Studies show that there is a very small resale market for timeshares.* This is because there are more owners looking to sell than there are people wanting to buy timeshares.

If you are able to sell your timeshare, it is likely that you will lose money on your investment. In most instances, the original price of the timeshare may have included premiums of up to 40 percent to cover sales costs. You will also have to pay a commission to the broker who sells the property for you.

Can I get out of my timeshare contract? *Most states have "cooling-off" laws that allow you to get out of a timeshare contract if you act within a few days after signing the contract.* Check the laws of your state and the state of the timeshare location. If there is no such law or if you change your mind after the time has passed, your only recourse may be a formal lawsuit.

INVESTMENTS

Are online investment newsletters legitimate? *There are many online investment newsletters that offer investors unbiased information, free of charge, about featured companies or recommend stock picks of the month.* However, while legitimate online newsletters help investors gather valuable information, others are tools for fraud.

Some fraudulent online newsletters claim to independently research the stocks they profile, while they are actually being paid by the profiled company. Others spread false information or promote worthless stocks. Still others drive up the price of the stock with baseless recommendations and then sell their own holdings at high prices and high profits.

How can I tell if an online investment newsletter is fraudulent? Be cautious of any investment newsletter that promises quick profits,

offers to share inside information and pressures you to invest before you have an opportunity to investigate.

Remember that no financial investment is risk free. Therefore, no investment newsletter can "guarantee" a high return on your investment. Also remember that a high rate of return means a greater risk.

Think twice before investing in investment opportunities in other countries. When you send your money abroad, if something goes wrong, it will be more difficult to find out what happened and to locate your money than if you invested locally.

I keep receiving e-mails telling me about a hot stock. Because I have gotten so many, I assume that the investment company is here to stay and that the offer is legitimate—do you? *Because junk e-mail is cheap and easy to create, it is increasingly used by con artists to find investors for bogus investment schemes or to spread false information about a company.* By using a bulk e-mail program, a con artist can send personalized messages to thousands of Internet users at one time.

The simple answer to this question is "no." If you are solicited through e-mail, remember this: no one does legitimate business though unsolicited e-mail.

What is a "Ponzi scheme"? *A Ponzi (or pyramid) scheme is an investment fraud in which the fraudulent operator promises incredible returns on nontraditional investments. Investors are strongly urged to bring family and friends into the investment group.* The problem is that the dividends paid to the initial investors are comprised of the money invested by new victims of the scam—sometimes your friends and relatives. The scheme goes south when the scammer takes off with all the money, or when new investors cannot be brought into the scheme. Without the money from new investors to pay for the older members, the cash flow will dry up.

What does "pump and dump" mean? *Pump and dump refers to investment schemes (often found on Internet bulletin boards) that urge* investors to buy a stock quickly or tell investors to sell before the price goes down. Quite often, the proponents of this information will claim to have "inside" information about an upcoming development with the company in question. However, they are most often paid promoters who stand to gain by selling their shares after the stock price is pumped up by gullible investors. Once these promoters sell their shares and stop hyping the stock, the price falls and investors lose their money.

How do I know whether or not it is safe to invest in a company? *Although the information in this section has dealt with Internet investment frauds, it is important to recognize that online investment fraud mirrors frauds which are perpetrated over the phone or through the mail.* Therefore, the following information should be taken into consideration when thinking about any investment —regardless of how you received the information.

Before investing in any company, ask the following questions:

- Is the investment registered with the Securities and Exchange Commission and the state securities agency in the state where you live, or is it subject to an exemption?
- Is the person recommending this investment registered with your state securities agency? Is there a record of any complaints about this person?
- How does the investment match your investment objectives?
- What are the costs to buy, hold and sell this investment? How easily will you be able to sell?
- Who is managing the investment? What experience do they have?
- How great is the risk of losing money?
- What return can be expected on your investment? When can you expect to receive a return?
- How long has the company been in business? Are they making money? What other companies are in the same business, and how are they doing financially?
- How can you get more information about the investment, such as audited financial statements?

What can I do if I have fallen for an investment scam? If you have reason to believe that you have been the victim of a securities-related fraud, whether through the Internet or otherwise, or if you believe that any person or entity may have violated or is currently violating the federal securities laws, you can submit a complaint using the SEC's online complaint form found at: **www.sec.gov/complaint.shtml** or e-mail the SEC at **enforcement@sec.gov**.

CAR REPAIR FRAUD

Anyone who owns a car will eventually find themselves in need of car repair. The National Highway Traffic Safety Administration estimates that consumers lose tens of billions of dollars due to car repair fraud each year. While most repair shops are honest, because the average car owner does not know enough about auto mechanics to protect himself or herself, it is not difficult for unethical mechanics to convince a car owner that unneeded repairs are necessary.

How can I protect myself against car repair fraud?

Before you choose a mechanic, ask your friends, family members or co-workers to recommend repair shops they trust. In addition, check with the Better Business Bureau to see if there are any complaints against the shop you choose.

If you are a member of the American Automobile Association, use a repair shop they endorse. These shops must meet rigorous standards and guarantee their work for AAA members. Moreover, AAA will arbitrate any disputes between its members and approved shops.

Look for shops that display an Automotive Service Excellence Seal. This indicates that some or all of the technicians have met basic standards of knowledge and competence in specific technical areas.

If your car needs major repairs, find a dealer or repair shop that specializes in the type of repair needed.

If your car is still under warranty, follow the manufacturer's requirements. In some cases, you must have the repair work done at an authorized, franchised dealership to keep your warranty in effect.

Write down a complete description of your car's problems and give it directly to the mechanic. Do not diagnose the problem yourself.

Make sure that the repair shop is qualified to make the necessary repair. Verify that the shop has experience working on the same type of vehicle as yours and whether they have done this type of repair before.

Insist on a written estimate that includes work orders, part prices, labor rates and warranty information.

Ask the mechanic to contact you before performing any repair that you have not already agreed to in a work order.

If you are not satisfied with the estimated cost of a car repair, get a second opinion.

Find out about the repair shop's guarantee policy and any warranty on the repair. Get a copy of the warranty in writing before you authorize the repair. Ask that your bill itemize all the repairs completed so that if a problem occurs later, you can prove that it is covered by the warranty or guarantee.

Ask for old parts back; then you do not have to worry about the mechanic charging you for a replacement part and not putting it on your car.

When you pick up your car, ask the service manager to explain all work completed and all replacements made.

TIP: Before you have a problem, follow the maintenance guidelines found in your owner's manual. Many car repairs can be avoided by simply taking better care of your car.

What is a repair order? A repair order is actually a contract which describes the work that will be done on your car and authorizes the mechanic to make the repairs outlined.

It should include:

- the make, model and year of your car;
- the mileage on your car;
- the date of the repair;
- a description of the problem;
- a listing of the parts to be used and the charges for the parts;
- an estimate of the amount of labor necessary to fix your car;
- the rate to be charged for the work—either hourly or a flat rate;
- your name, address and telephone number.

In some states, if you have not signed the repair order, you do not have to pay for the repairs.

How can I prevent unnecessary repairs? *One way to avoid this problem is to let the mechanic know that you want to see old parts replaced during the repair.* This puts the mechanic on notice that you are watching what they are doing.

> **TIP:** Some states require mechanics to give you any parts they have removed from your car unless the warranty requires they be sent back to the manufacturer.

Another way to avoid unnecessary repairs is pay $30 or $40 to have your car checked at a diagnostic center that is not affiliated with the repair shop. These shops have no reason to recommend unnecessary repairs.

When I picked up my car, I was charged more than the estimate. What do I do? *First of all, question the bill. Find out why the final charge was more.* Have the repair shop write out the reasons for the increased cost and keep this record with the work estimate, final bill and other paperwork.

Next, pay the bill, but make it clear that you are doing so under protest. Then, file a complaint with your state attorney general's office and the local branch of the Better Business Bureau. If the repair shop is endorsed by the AAA, be sure to contact the organization. If your complaint is egregious enough or joined by others, the garage may lose the AAA's seal of approval. You can also file suit against the mechanic. State consumer laws prohibit unfair and deceptive practices in auto repair. Mechanics who mislead, deceive or make misrepresentations to consumers may be subject to penalties.

I feel that I have been ripped off. Why should I bother to pay the bill? *In most states, if you refuse to pay the bill, even if you disagree with it, the repair shop has the right to keep your car until they are paid.* If you choose not to pay, the repair shop may ultimately sell your car to recover the costs of repair.

CAUTION: Do not pay by check just to get your car back and then stop payment on the check. The mechanic may then have a right to repossess your car.

TELEMARKETING FRAUD

According to the FBI, Americans lose over $40 billion per year by becoming victims of fraudulent marketing of goods and services over the telephone or through the mail. While there are many legitimate telemarketing firms, there are also numerous fraudulent ones. Taking the time to learn how to tell the difference can save you time and money.

How do I know whether a magazine solicitation is legitimate? *If a telephone caller or a postcard you receive through the mail offers you a "free," "prepaid" or "special deal" on magazine subscriptions, think twice before you take advantage of this offer.* You may become obligated to years of monthly payments for magazines you do not want or could purchase elsewhere for less.

Listen to the sales presentation. If you are not interested, simply hang up. If you are interested but are too busy to listen to the entire sales pitch, ask the salesperson to call back when you have more time to focus on the conversation. Saying "yes" without getting all the facts can obligate you to more than you want.

> **TIP:** The best way to protect yourself from unscrupulous sales presentations is to be suspicious when anyone tries to sell you a "bargain" or give you something for "free." Do not take advantage of the offer until you know exactly what is being sold and all the costs involved.

What type of questions should I ask a magazine solicitor? *Find out the name, address and phone number of the company the salesperson represents.* Then call the company yourself for verification before you place an order.

Find out the total annual cost for each magazine and then do the math. Is the "bargain" price really less expensive than the regular subscription price?

Ask the salesperson to send you a written copy of the sales terms offered over the telephone before you agree to buy anything. Read the sales agreement carefully and make sure you understand what you will be receiving and what it will cost.

The salesperson told me that they need my credit card number or bank account number for verification. Should I give it to them? *Never give out this information unless you have initiated the call or are familiar with the company with whom you are doing business.* Giving out this information may result in unwanted charges to your account or debits to your checking account.

How can I get out of a magazine subscription I ordered by phone? *Once you order magazines by phone, you cannot simply call the company to cancel your agreement; oral cancellations will not be honored by the company.*

In order to cancel your agreement, look for the provision allowing you to cancel your subscription when your sales agreement comes in the mail. Generally, cancellation must be made within 3 days of receipt of the agreement.

CAUTION: Remember, the FTC Cooling-Off Rule does not apply to sales made by telephone or mail.

Sign and return the cancellation notice to the proper address, which may be different from the company sending you the information. This information may be hard to find; read the agreement until you find the correct address.

Send the cancellation by certified or registered mail. This will provide you with proof of the mailing date. Photocopy the signed and dated notice and keep it for your records.

Once you have mailed the cancellation form, contact your bank or credit card company to stop any unauthorized payments.

I received a postcard telling me that I have won a fabulous prize. How can I win if I did not even enter? *If someone calls or sends you a post card saying that you have won a valuable prize in a sweepstakes, proceed with caution.*

Do not pay anything to receive your prize. If it is a legitimate sweepstakes, you do not have to pay anything to collect your prize. If you have won merchandise, the sweepstakes promoter will pay the delivery charges. If you win cash, the sweepstakes promoter either will withhold taxes from the cash award or report the winnings to the Internal Revenue Service.

Do not give your credit card number for verification purposes. Again, legitimate sweepstakes do not need this information.

If you have to attend a sales presentation before you can receive your prize, be wary. Your chances of winning a valuable prize are doubtful, and you may end up the recipient of a high-pressure sales pitch.

How do I know if a solicitor calling on behalf of a charity is legitimate? *This is probably one of the most despicable fraudulent practices.* You may be asked to buy tickets to send a handicapped child to the circus or buy light bulbs at inflated prices to help veterans.

Before donating any money based on one of these calls, ask for written information about how much of your donation will go to the charity and how much will be spent on administrative costs.

If the "charity" refuses to send you information (often telling you that the cost of printing and mailing this information will reduce the amount of money going to the charity), do not send them any money. Reputable charities will always send you information.

What is a "sucker list"? *A sucker list contains the names, addresses and telephone numbers of people who have fallen for telemarketing scams.* This list may also contain your name, income, hobbies, marital status and other information that helps the telemarketer personalize the call. They are created, bought and sold by unscrupulous telemarketers. These lists provide the telemarketers with an easy target for their scams.

What are "reloaders"? *Reloaders are con artists who use various schemes to target consumers who have already fallen for a telemarketing scam.* They may purport to be a representative of a consumer organization that will help you recover the money you lost due to telemarketing fraud. However, they require a fee for their services. If you take them up on the offer, you have been scammed again.

National, state and local consumer enforcement agencies and nonprofit organizations do not charge for their services.

I have heard that it is not a good idea to call a 900 telephone number. Is this true? *Using a 900 number can be a good way to do business, but you should be aware that you will be charged for the call. A 900 telephone number is not a toll-free number.* You will either be charged a flat fee for the call, or you may be charged per minute. These charges can add up. Some states have enacted laws regulating the telephone providers of information services.

EXAMPLE: Under the provisions of Illinois law, in any advertising for these services, the provider must:

- accurately and clearly describe the content of the message and the terms, conditions and price of the service; and
- state that any callers under age 12 must get parental or adult guardian permission before calling.

You cannot be billed for any call unless the sponsor gives you a certain message during a 12-second "delayed timing period." The message must accurately give you a description of the service and a summary of its cost and tell you that you will not be charged for the call if you hang up the phone during the message and that when the message is over, you still have 3 seconds to hang up to avoid being charged.

My son will be going to college next year and received a postcard in the mail from a scholarship search company guaranteeing him $2,000 in scholarships. Is this legitimate? *No.* No company can guarantee that your son will get a scholarship; that is entirely up to your son.

Before you take advantage of any "scholarship" offer, here are some things to keep in mind:

- Beware of any scholarship that requires an application fee, even one as low as a few dollars. If enough people take them up on the offer, those few dollars add up. Legitimate scholarship programs do not require an application fee.
- You should never have to give credit card or bank account information to award providers.
- No one can guarantee that you will win a scholarship, because no one can control scholarship judges' decisions.

- Look for contact information. Legitimate sponsors will provide contact information on request. If the sponsor does not supply a valid e-mail address, phone number and mailing address (not a P.O. Box) after you have asked for one, it could be the sign of a scam.
- If you are notified that you have received a scholarship for which you never applied, be careful. It is most likely a scam.
- Be aware that con artists often use official-sounding words like "national," "education" or "federal," or they display an official-looking seal to fool you into thinking they are legitimate. Check with your school if you question a scholarship provider's legitimacy.
- If you cannot get a straight answer from a sponsor regarding their application, what will be done with your information or other questions, do not take them up on their offer.

> **TIP:** There is no reason to pay a scholarship search service when the same information is available at the public library and the financial aid office of your school free of charge.

How can I stop telemarketing calls? *The FTC has created the National Do Not Call Registry to give Americans a choice about getting telemarketing calls at home.* You can register online at www.donotcall.gov or call toll-free 888.382.1222. Registration is free.

Once your number has been on the registry for 3 months, most telemarketing calls will stop. However, not all calls are covered by the registry. You may continue to get calls from, or on behalf of, political organizations, charities and telephone surveyors, as well as calls from companies with whom you have an existing business relationship.

I put my name on the FTC's "Do Not Call" list, and I am still getting telemarketing calls. What do I do? *First, make sure that your number is actually on the registry. You can verify that your number is on the registry online at* **www.donotcall.gov** *(click on "Verify a Registration"), or by calling 888.382.1222 from the phone number you wish to verify.*

If your number has been on the registry for at least 3 months and you are still receiving telemarketing calls, file a complaint with the FTC by going to **www.donotcall.gov** or calling

888.382.1222. You will need to provide the date of the call and the phone number or name of the company that called you.

I received a call from someone saying they were confirming my registry on the "Do Not Call" registry. Why would the government do that? *The government would not do that, but a con artist would.* Under this scam, the phony registry "official" asks for your personal information to verify that you want to be on the "Do Not Call" list. They then use this information to run up debts in your name or otherwise steal your identity.

IDENTITY THEFT

Each and every day, Americans share personal information about themselves with others without even realizing it. We write checks at department and grocery stores, charge purchases online or over the phone, rent a car, book a hotel room, mail our tax returns, use our cell phones and apply for credit cards. Each of these transactions requires you to share personal information: your bank and credit card account numbers; your income; your Social Security number; or your name, address and phone numbers.

Unscrupulous individuals can use this personal information to commit identity theft. Identity theft is one of the fastest growing white-collar crimes in the United States. In fact, surveys show that there are 7 to 10 million victims of identity theft per year. If your identity is stolen, it can take months or years, not to mention thousands of dollars, to clear your name and your credit record. According to the FTC, the average victim of identity theft is unaware of the problem for 12 months. By the time it is detected, it is already too late. Victims of identity theft may be denied credit and refused loans, lose job opportunities or even be suspected of crimes they did not commit.

What is identity theft? *Using a variety of methods, criminals steal their victims' Social Security numbers, driver's license numbers, bank account numbers, credit card numbers, ATM cards, telephone calling cards and other pieces of individual's identities such as names, addresses, telephone numbers and dates of birth.*

They then use this information to impersonate their victims and apply for additional credit cards or bank loans, open new bank accounts, set up telephone services and purchase merchandise.

There are four kinds of identity theft:

- ► **FINANCIAL IDENTITY THEF**t focuses on your name and Social Security number. Using this information, the imposter may apply for telephone service, credit cards or loans, buy merchandise and lease cars or apartments.

- ► **CRIMINAL IDENTITY THEFT** occurs when an imposter provides the victim's information instead of his or her own when stopped by the police. Eventually, when a warrant for arrest is issued, it is in the name of the person issued the citation—the victim.

- ► **IDENTITY CLONING** is when the imposter uses the victim's information to establish a new life. They work and live as you.

- ► **BUSINESS OR COMMERCIAL IDENTITY THEFT** occurs when the imposter gets credit cards or checking accounts in the name of the business. The business finds out when unpaid suppliers send collection notices, or their business rating score is affected.

How can my identity be stolen? Thieves can get your personal information in the following ways:

- stealing wallets and purses containing your identification and credit and bank cards;

- stealing your mail, including your bank and credit card statements, preapproved credit offers, investment reports, insurance statements, benefits documents, new checks and tax information;

- completing a "change of address form" to divert your mail to another location;

- rummaging through your trash or the trash of businesses, a practice known as "dumpster diving," for unshredded credit card and loan applications, copies of checks, credit card or bank statements or other records that bear your name, address, telephone number and sometimes even your Social Security number;

- Fraudulently obtaining your credit report by posing as a landlord, employer or someone else who may have a legitimate need for, and legal right to, the information;

- using personal information you share on the Internet;

- posing as legitimate companies or government agencies you do business with, often through e-mail;
- stealing files out of offices where you are a customer, employee, patient or student; bribing an employee who has access to your files; or "hacking" into electronic files;
- hacking into your computer, especially those without firewalls;
- looking over your shoulder at ATMs to steal your PINs;
- using phony telemarketing schemes to convince you to give them your personal data;
- purchasing your identifying information at one of the identity search companies found on the Internet; for a nominal fee, these companies will sell people's Social Security number, their mother's maiden name, their home and employment address, their previous addresses, their credit history and more.

If my identity is stolen, what can the imposter do with the information? *Given enough personal information, an imposter can literally take over your identity and commit an array of crimes—all in your name.* They can:

- cash a check or, using their own personal computer, print fraudulent checks bearing your name but a different address and then drain your account;
- get a loan;
- open a bank account with a line of credit;
- open new credit accounts or call your credit card issuer pretending to be you and request a change of address and then run up a multitude of charges; because the bills are sent to a different address, it could be months before you realize there is a problem;
- rent an apartment;
- buy a car;
- purchase a cell phone;
- commit a crime and give your name to the police; if they are released from custody and do not show up for their court date, an arrest warrant will be issued in your name.

Will I be held responsible if an imposter uses my identity to commit a crime?
From a financial perspective, if an imposter fraudulently uses your credit card, the Consumer Credit Protection Act limits your liability for unauthorized credit card charges to $50 per card.

The Electronic Fund Transfer Act provides protection for transactions involving an ATM or debit card or another electronic way to debit or credit an account. It also limits your liability for unauthorized electronic fund transfers.

It is important to note that the extent of your financial liability may depend on the length of time it takes you to report the fraud. However, VISA® and MasterCard® have voluntarily agreed to limit consumers' liability for unauthorized use of their debit cards in most instances to $50 per card, no matter how much time has elapsed since the discovery of the loss or theft of the card.

Although no federal law limits your liability if someone steals your checks and forges your signature, you may be protected under state law. However, while most states hold the bank responsible for losses from a forged check, they also require you to take reasonable care of your account. Therefore, you may be held responsible for the forgery if you fail to notify the bank in a timely manner that a check was lost or stolen.

What do I do if I believe I have been a victim of identity theft? *Contact your bank and all credit card companies by telephone immediately. Follow up with an e-mail and faxed letter summarizing your phone conversation.* You will probably be asked to sign an affidavit attesting to the fact that purchases and account withdrawals were made without your consent.

Next, contact the FTC, the agency that enforces the Identity Theft and Assumption Deterrence Act, at 877.ID.THEFT/877.438.4338 and make an official complaint.

Report the theft by contacting the fraud sections of the three major credit-reporting agencies on the Internet, or call:

- ▶ **EQUIFAX:** 1.800.525.6285 or write to P.O. Box 740250, Atlanta, GA 30374
- ▶ **EXPERIAN:** (formerly TRW): 1.888.EXPERIAN or 1.888.397.3742, fax to 1.800.301.7196 or write to P.O. Box 1017, Allen, TX 75013
- **TRANSUNION:** 1.800.680.7289 or write to P.O. Box 6790, Fullerton, CA 92634

Lastly, where checking accounts and stolen checks are involved you must contact the major check verification companies, which retain data on unpaid checks, to report any fraudulent use of your checks. You will no longer be able to use checks for purchases if these companies are not made aware of your situation.

- **CHECKRITE:** 1.800.766.2748

- **CHEXSYSTEMS:** 1.800.428.9623

- **CHECKCENTER/CROSSCHECK:** 1.800.843.0760

- **CERTIGY/EQUIFAX:** 1.800.437.5120

- **INTERNATIONAL CHECK SERVICES:** 1.800.526.5380

- **SCAN:** 1.800.262.7771

- **TELECHECK:** 1.800.710.9898

> **TIP:** For more information, a comprehensive Web site that has been set up to aid victims of identity fraud is located at **www.privacyrights.org**.

How can I prevent identity theft? *While there is no definitive way to prevent identity theft, diligence in guarding your personal information minimizes the threat.* Following are some steps you can take to keep your personal information secure:

- Carry only the personal identification, credit cards and debit cards that you need. Store infrequently used identification and cards in a secure location.

- Keep a list of all credit cards, account numbers, expiration dates and the customer service phone numbers in a secure place so that you can quickly contact your creditors in case your cards are lost or stolen.

- Cancel all inactive credit and debit cards; even though you do not use them, the accounts appear on your credit report, which can in turn be used by thieves.

- Never carry your Social Security card in your wallet; keep it in a secure place.

- Do not have your Social Security number or your driver's license number pre-printed on your checks.

- Only give out your Social Security number when absolutely necessary. Ask if it is possible to use other types of identifiers. If a company refuses to use another identifier to complete a transaction, consider taking your business elsewhere.

- Deposit your mail, especially bill payments, directly at the post office rather than leaving it in your mailbox for the postal carrier to pick up. If you are going to be out of town, request a vacation hold from the post office.

- Review all credit card statements, telephone and utility bills. If you do not recognize a charge or phone call, report it immediately.

- Pay attention to your billing cycles. If your bills do not arrive when expected, contact the creditor; a missing credit card bill could mean an identity thief has taken over your account and changed your billing address.

- Order your credit report every year. This report contains information on where you work and live, credit accounts opened in your name, how you pay your bills and whether you have been sued, arrested or have filed for bankruptcy.

- Immediately report any inaccurate information. To review a copy of your credit report, contact the following credit bureaus:

- **EQUIFAX:** 1.800.685.1111

- **EXPERIAN:** 1.888.397.3742

- **TRANS UNION:** 1.800.916.8800

- Place passwords on your credit cards, bank and telephone accounts. Do not use obvious passwords such as your mother's maiden name, the last four digits of your Social Security number, birthdays or anniversaries.

- Change your passwords and PIN numbers regularly.

- Memorize passwords and PIN numbers and destroy any paper on which they are written.

- Never throw away credit card receipts in public; shred them once you are home.

- Shred or tear up any offers of preapproved credit cards you do not intend to use and beware of offers from companies you do not recognize. Identity thieves can easily create an official-looking credit application offering you preapproved credit if you provide your Social Security number, mother's maiden name and signature.

- To cut down on the number of unsolicited credit card applications you receive and thereby reduce the chance of these applications being stolen, call 888.5OPT.OUT to have your name removed from marketing lists sold by credit bureaus.

- Protect your trash by tearing up or shredding sensitive materials: credit applications or preapproved credit offers, insurance forms, medical statements, charge receipts, checks and bank statements, bank receipts, canceled or expired credit and ATM cards and any other papers that include your personal information, identification and account numbers.

- Do not give personal information over the phone, through the mail or over the Internet unless absolutely necessary and only if you initiated the phone call. If someone calls claiming they are from your bank or credit company, ask for a number to call them back and then check to ensure that it is the actual phone number. Similarly, if contacted through a telephone solicitation, ask that they mail you information so you can research their company, products and services.

- When shopping on the Internet, only shop at secure Web sites. These are sites that use encryption technology to transfer information from your computer to the online merchant's computer. Encryption scrambles the information you send, such as your credit card number, in order to prevent computer hackers from obtaining it. The only people who can unscramble the code are those with legitimate access privileges. There are several ways to determine whether you are using a secure web site:

  - Verify that the Web site's URL address begins with "https://". The "s" that is displayed after "http" indicates that the Web site is secure.

  - Look for a closed padlock displayed at the bottom of your screen. If that lock is open, you should assume it is not a secure site.

  - Look for an unbroken key.

- Pick up your new checks from the bank instead of having them sent to your home.

- Store canceled checks in a safe place. If they are stolen, the thief has access to your checking account number, your phone number and driver's license number.

- If you find your personal information posted somewhere on the Internet, demand that it be removed.

- Ask about information security procedures in your workplace. Identify who has access to your personal information and verify that records are kept in a secure location. Ask about disposal procedures for sensitive records.

- Do not put personal information on a computer home page or personal computer profile.

- Protect personal information stored on your computer. Use a firewall and secure browser; maintain current virus protection; never download files or click on hyperlinks from strangers; and avoid automatic login processes that store your account name and password. Moreover, when disposing of your computer, delete all personal information and completely overwrite the hard drive.

- Be wary of promotional scams. Identity thieves may use phony offers to get you to give them your personal information.

What should I do if I discover that my identity has been stolen? *If you find that your credit cards, driver's license, Social Security number or any other type of identifying information is stolen, your identity may be stolen as well.* As soon as you are aware of the theft, you should proceed as follows:

CONTACT THE FEDERAL TRADE COMMISSION: Call the FTC's Identity Theft Hotline toll-free at 877.ID.THEFT/877.438.4338 to report the theft. The FTC's counselors will take your complaint and give you advice on how to deal with credit-related problems that may result from the theft. The hotline also provides you with one place to report the theft to the federal government. Once notified, the FTC will put your information into a secure consumer fraud database where it can be used to help other law enforcement agencies and private entities in their investigations and victim assistance.

CREATE AN IDENTITY THEFT AFFIDAVIT: Create an identity theft affidavit and have it notarized. The FTC has an official identity theft affidavit that you can use to alert different companies, including the major credit bureaus, your credit card companies, your banks and so on. You can use this form for each company. This affidavit can be found at **www.consumer.gov/idtheft**.

CONTACT THE CREDIT BUREAUS: Contact the fraud departments of any of the three major credit bureaus to place a fraud alert on your credit file. This alert requests creditors to contact you before opening any new accounts or making any changes to your existing accounts. When the credit bureau verifies your fraud alert, the other two credit bureaus will be notified to also place fraud alerts on your accounts, and all three credit reports will be sent to you free of charge. To report fraud, contact the credit bureaus at:

► **EQUIFAX:** 1.800.525.6285 and write: P.O. Box 740241, Atlanta, GA 30374

► **EXPERIAN:** 1.888.397.3742 and write: P.O. Box 9532, Allen, TX 75013

► **TRANS UNION:** 1.800.680.7289 and write: Fraud Victim Assistance Division, P.O. Box 6790, Fullerton, CA 92834

Once you receive your reports, review them carefully and pay close attention to inquiries you did not initiate, accounts you did not open and unexplained debts on your accounts. If you find anything out of order, notify the credit company immediately. It is important to note that credit issuers are not required by law to observe fraud alerts. Therefore, it is important to request copies of your credit report every few months so you can ensure no new fraudulent activity has occurred. The automated "one-call" fraud alert process only works for the initial placement of your fraud alert. Orders for additional credit reports or renewals of your fraud alerts must be made separately at each of the three credit bureaus.

FILE A POLICE REPORT: File a police report with your local police department or the police department in the location where the theft took place, and keep a copy of the report to submit to your creditors and other entities that may require proof of the identity theft. Know the telephone number of your investigator so that you can give it to creditors and others who require verification of your case.

When filing out a police report, provide as much documentation as possible. This may include debt collection letters, credit reports, your notarized Identity Theft Affidavit and any other evidence of fraudulent activity.

Do not take "no" for an answer. If the police department tells you that identity theft is not a crime in your state, ask to file a Miscellaneous Incident Report instead. Remind the police of the importance of a police report—many creditors may require one to resolve your dispute.

CANCEL/CLOSE ACCOUNTS: Cancel all of your credit cards, ATM cards and phone cards. Notify your utility company. Call your bank and have them close all existing bank accounts. Put stop payment orders on any outstanding check of which you are unsure. Open new accounts with new passwords. Do not use obvious passwords like your mother's maiden name, birthdays or anniversaries.

You have 60 days from the date your bank account statement is sent to you to report in writing any money withdrawn from your account without your permission. If your ATM or debit card is lost or stolen, report it immediately because the amount you can be held responsible for depends on how quickly you report the loss. If you report the loss or theft within 2 business days of discovery, your losses are limited to $50. If you report the loss or theft after 2 business days, but within 60 days after the unauthorized electronic fund transfer appears on your statement, you could lose up to $500. If you wait more than 60 days to report the loss or theft, you could lose all the money that was taken from your account.

REPORT STOLEN CHECKS: Report stolen checks to your bank as well as the following agencies:

► **CERTEGY, INC.:** 1.800.437.5120

► **TELECHECK:** 1.800.710.9898

► **CHEXSYSTEMS:** 1.800.428.9623

► **INTERNATIONAL CHECK SERVICES:** 1.800.526.5380

► **SCAN:** 1.800.262.7771.

NOTIFY THE POST OFFICE: If you have reason to believe that the thief has filed a change of address form in your name, notify the local Postal Inspector. Call the U. S. Postal Service at 800.275.8777 to get the phone number. The change of address form will be an important piece of evidence for the police to follow.

Find out where fraudulent credit cards were sent. Notify your local post office to forward all mail in your name to your address.

CONTACT THE DMV: If your driver's license is stolen, call the state office of the Department of Motor Vehicles to see if another license has been issued in your name. If your state DMV provides a fraud alert process, place a fraud alert on your license. Be prepared to show proof of theft and damage. Go to your local DMV to request a new driver's license number. Fill out the DMV's complaint form to begin the investigation process. Send supporting documents with the completed form to the nearest DMV investigation office.

DEBT COLLECTION: Do not pay bills for which you are not responsible. If debt collectors attempt to force you to pay unpaid bills on fraudulent accounts, ask for the name of the company, the person contacting you, their telephone number and address. Request the name and contact information for the referring credit issuer, the amount of the debt, account number and the date of all charges.

Inform the collector that you are a victim of identity theft and are not responsible for the account. Ask the debt collector if their company has a specific fraud affidavit form or if you can use the form provided by the FTC.

Send the debt collector a follow-up letter explaining your situation, including copies of documents that support your claim and asking them to confirm in writing that you do not owe the debt and that the account has been closed.

CRIMINAL IDENTITY THEFT: If a civil judgment is entered in your name for your identity thief's actions, contact the court where the judgment was entered and report that you are a victim of identity theft.

If you are wrongfully arrested or prosecuted for criminal charges, contact the police department and the court in the jurisdiction of the arrest, as well as the state Department of Justice and the FBI. File an impersonation report with the police department or the court and confirm your identity. Ask the police department to take your fingerprints, photograph you and make copies of your photo identification documents. To establish your innocence, ask the police to compare the prints and photographs with those of the identity thief. If the arrest warrant is from a state or county other than where you live, ask your local police department to send the impersonation report to the police department in the jurisdiction where the arrest warrant, traffic citation or criminal conviction originated.

This action should cause the police department to recall any warrants and issue a "clearance letter" or "certificate of release" (if you were arrested or booked). It is important that you keep this document with you at all times in case you are wrongfully accused again. Ask the police department to file the record of the follow-up investigation establishing your innocence with the district attorney's office and/or court where the crime took place. This will result in an amended complaint.

> **TIP:** Once your name is recorded in a criminal database, it is unlikely that it will be completely removed from the official record. Therefore, request that the primary name in the database be changed from your name to the imposter's name, with your name listed as an alias.

Maintain Thorough Records: Keep records of all conversations and correspondence with everyone you notify regarding the identity theft, including dates, names and telephone numbers. Keep track of the time spent and expenses incurred in case you are able to seek restitution in a later judgment or conviction against the thief or if you itemize tax deductions for theft-related expenses (consult your accountant). Confirm conversations in writing. Send correspondence by certified mail, return receipt requested.

Are there any laws that prohibit identity theft? *Under the provisions of the Identity Theft and Assumption Deterrence Act (18 U.S.C.A Section 1028), using another person's identification with the intent to commit any unlawful activity is a federal crime.* Federal agencies, including the U.S. Secret Service, the FBI and the U.S. Postal Inspection Service investigate suspected violations of the Act. Prosecutions are handled by the U.S. Department of Justice.

Identity theft may also involve violations of other statutes such as:

- credit card fraud (18 U.S.C.A. Section 1029)
- computer fraud (18 U.S.C.A. Section 1030)
- mail fraud (18 U.S.C.A. Section 1341)
- wire fraud (18 U.S.C.A. Section 1343)
- financial institution fraud (18 U.S.C.A. Section 1344)

Each of these federal offenses is a felony and carries substantial penalties, which in some cases can be as high as 30 years imprisonment, fines and criminal forfeiture.

Many states have passed or are considering laws related to identity theft. If your state does not have an identity theft law, it is likely that the issue is covered under other state laws. Contact your state attorney general's office or local consumer protection agency for laws related to identity theft.

CREDIT CARDS

What is a credit card? *Credit is a contract between a consumer and a credit issuer. A credit issuer may be a bank, a credit card company or other lender.* A credit card is an indication to merchants that the person holding the card has a satisfactory credit rating and that, if credit is extended by the merchant, the credit issuer will pay or insure that the merchant will receive payment for his or her merchandise.

By using a credit card, a cardholder is making an implied representation that he or she intends to pay the credit issuer for the charges made.

Who is a cardholder?

The Truth in Lending Act defines "cardholder" as "any person to whom a credit card is issued or any person who has agreed with the card issuer to pay obligations arising from the issuance of a credit card to another person."

What is authorized use of a credit card? *Authorized use of a credit card is when a cardholder freely allows someone else to use his or her credit card.* There is no fraud, theft or duress involved. In this situation, the cardholder is liable for the charges, even if the person charges more than they were told they could.

What is unauthorized use of a credit card? Unauthorized use of a credit card is use of the card by any person other than the cardholder who does not have actual, implied or apparent authority for its use.

I bought something with a credit card and I am not satisfied. What do I do? The Fair Credit Billing Act allows you to withhold payment for inferior or damaged goods or poor quality services. However, you must first make a real attempt to solve the problem with the merchant or service provider. You should then notify the card issuer of your claim.

> **TIP:** If you made the purchase with a bank credit card as opposed to a store card, your right to withhold payment is limited to purchases that are more than $50 and that were made in your home state or within 100 miles of your home address.

If you refuse to pay for defective goods or services, the creditor may sue you for payment. If the court finds that the goods or services were defective, you will not have to pay for them.

I have been receiving bills for a credit card that I do not own. What do I do? Under the Truth in Lending Act, a cardholder is liable for the unauthorized use of a credit card only if:

- the card is an accepted credit card;
- the liability is not in excess of $50;
- the card issuer gives adequate notice to the cardholder of the potential liability;

- the issuer provided the cardholder with a description of means by which the issuer may be notified of the loss or theft of the card;

- the unauthorized use occurs before the card issuer has been notified that an unauthorized use of the credit card has occurred or may occur as the result of loss, theft or otherwise; and

- the card issuer has provided a method through which the user of the card can be identified as the person authorized to use it.

Should I notify the credit card company that my card has been lost?

Yes, if someone steals, borrows or otherwise uses your credit card without permission, you should immediately make a report to your credit card company. You do not have to pay any unauthorized charges made after you notify the credit issuer. Under the Truth in Lending Act, the most you will have to pay for charges made before you notify the credit issuer is $50 on each card.

What do I do if I think there is a mistake in charges on my credit card?

To dispute the amount you owe on you credit card, look at the back of your bill. It contains information about how to go about raising a dispute, including the proper address to use. You must raise a dispute in writing within 60 days of the first bill with the improper charge and include your name and account number, the dollar amount in dispute and the reason for the dispute.

Once you raise a dispute, the credit card company must investigate and report back to you in writing. Until the dispute is resolved, you do not need to pay the disputed portion of the bill.

What does a credit repair company do?

A credit repair company charges anywhere from $50 to $1,000 to "fix" your credit report. Often, these companies take your money and do nothing to improve your credit.

Should I use a credit repair company?

Probably not. The FTC and a number of state attorneys general have sued credit repair companies for falsely promising to remove bad information from credit reports.

Keep in mind the following:

- Your credit history is maintained by private companies called credit bureaus that collect information reported to them by banks, mortgage companies, department stores and other creditors.

- These credit bureaus can legally report accurate negative credit information for 7 years and bankruptcy information for 10 years.

- Accurate items that are within the 7-year (or 10- year) reporting period cannot be erased from your credit record by companies advertising "credit repair" services.

- The only information in your credit report that can be changed are items that are actually wrong or beyond the 7-year (or 10-year) reporting period.

> **TIP:** The only things that a credit repair company can legitimately do—remove genuine mistakes or outdated items in your credit report—you can do yourself for free.

What is in my credit report?

A standard credit report contains personal information, account information and public record data, as well as a listing of credit inquiries and credit scoring. Credit scoring is the credit bureau's numerical assessment of you as a credit risk.

Companies examine your credit report before deciding whether to give you credit. When a company denies your request for credit because of your credit report, it must tell you so and identify the credit bureau that supplied the report.

Where can I get my credit report?

To receive a copy of your credit report, contact the following credit bureaus:

- ▶ **EQUIFAX:** 1.800.685.1111
- ▶ **EXPERIAN:** 1.888.397.3742
- ▶ **TRANS UNION:** 1.800.916.8800

I got a copy of my credit report. Now what do I do?

Once you receive your credit report, carefully analyze it, checking for these common problems:

- inquiries made without your approval;
- errors in personal information listed on the report;
- credit or collection accounts you did not create;

- negative ratings on accounts which do belong to you;
- information more than 7 years old (10 years for bankruptcy); and
- public records information which is erroneous.

If there is information in your credit report more than 7 (or 10 for bankruptcy) years old, contact the credit bureau and ask them to delete it.

If there are mistakes, notify the credit bureau of the problem. The bureau must reinvestigate the disputed information at no charge to you. It then must correct any mistake or delete any information it cannot verify. Request that the bureau send a corrected copy of your report to anyone who received the incorrect version within the past 6 months.

You should also contact the creditor directly to notify them of the mistake and ask them to correct their records.

If you are unable to resolve the problem, you can file a written statement of up to 100 words with the credit bureau explaining your side of the story. This explanation will be included in your credit report.

> **TIP:** If you do not understand something in your credit report, ask. The credit bureau is required by law to explain your report to you.

DEFECTIVE PRODUCTS

What are "lemon laws"? *Lemon laws are one of the federal consumer protection laws created to prevent fraud and the misrepresentation of the condition of cars, trucks, vans, SUVs, boats and other consumer products at the time of sale.* While the lemon laws actually cover many types of products, most people refer to the lemon laws when they talk about either new or used vehicles still under warranty that cannot be properly repaired.

Lemon laws vary from state to state; therefore, you will need to know the laws in the jurisdiction in which you purchased the product you wish to return. Lemon laws will define what constitutes a product as being a "lemon" and will usually mandate that the manufacturer, not the dealer, assume responsibility.

What qualifies as a "lemon"? In most states, in order to be categorized as a "lemon," the vehicle must have a substantial defect that occurred within a certain period of time after you bought it and that cannot be fixed after a reasonable number of repair attempts.

What is a "substantial defect"? *A substantial defect is a problem that impairs the vehicle's use, value or safety.* Depending on the state law, the substantial defect must occur within a certain period of time (usually 1 or 2 years) or within a certain number of miles (usually 12,000 or 24,000).

What are "reasonable repair attempts"? *If the defect is a serious safety defect involving brakes or steering, it must remain unfixed after one repair attempt to qualify as a lemon.* If the defect is not a serious safety defect, it must remain unfixed after three or four repair attempts depending on the particular law of the state. If the vehicle is in the shop a certain number of days (usually 30 days in a 1-year period), it may fit the definition of a lemon.

Do lemon laws apply to used cars? *All states have lemon laws that apply to new cars, but only a few states have lemon laws covering used cars.* Under most of these laws, it is the dealer's responsibility to repair the car or refund the buyer's money if repair is unsuccessful.

My car is a lemon! What do I do now? *Every state gives the consumer a right to obtain a refund or replacement vehicle from the manufacturer if they are sold a lemon. How you go about receiving this relief will be dependent on the laws of your state.* However, in all states, the consumer must first notify the manufacturer of the defect. If you are not offered a satisfactory settlement, most states require you to go to arbitration before going to court. The arbitrator will hear both sides of the dispute and make a decision, usually within 60 days after the hearing. If the arbitrator decides that your car is a lemon, you will be entitled to a refund or replacement.

Is there any way to prepare for arbitration?
Absolutely. Studies show that consumers who bring documentation and evidence to the arbitration hearing tend to do better than those who do not. The following types of documentation can help:

- brochures and ads about the vehicle (the arbitration panel will likely make the manufacturer live up to its claims);
- vehicle service records showing how often you took the car into the shop; and
- other documents you may have that illustrate your attempts to get the dealer to repair your car, including old calendars and phone records.

I did not like the results of my arbitration. Can I sue? *Yes. The results of arbitration are often binding only on the manufacturer.* If you do not like the result, you can always go to court.

What other laws protect car owners?
- The Federal Anti-Tampering Odometer Law prohibits anyone from falsifying mileage readings in a car.
- The Federal Used Car Law requires used car dealers to post buyers guides on used cars.
- The Federal Automobile Information Disclosure Act requires new car dealerships to put a sticker on the windshield or side window of the car, listing the base price of the car, the options added and their costs, as well as the dealer's cost for transportation and the number of miles per gallon the car gets.

What is "strict liability"? *Strict liability is a legal doctrine that makes a person or persons responsible for damages their actions or products cause, regardless of any "fault" on their part.* In strict product liability, anyone who is engaged in the stream of commerce of the product (from the manufacturer to the wholesaler to the retailer or all of them) can be held responsible if the product was defective and someone was injured. There is no need to prove negligence; the injured party must prove that the product was defective.

Can a product be defective because of an inadequate instruction manual? *If the manual failed to adequately warn the consumer of a hazard involved in the foreseeable use of the product, the product is defective.* However,

the manufacturer will not be held responsible when injury results from an unforeseeable use of its product.

Can a manufacturer disclaim liability for a defective product? *Disclaimers and waivers of liability for products are often invalidated by courts as against public policy. This is due to the belief that courts should not condone the manufacture and distribution of defective products.* Moreover, courts find complete disclaimers unfair because the consumer is not in an equal bargaining position to the manufacturer.

What should I do if I am injured by a product?
- Keep evidence of the defective product and the incident. This can include the parts of the product and pictures of the injury and the injury site.
- Get the manufacturer's name and the serial number and model of the product
- Keep a copy of the user's manual or other instructions that came with the product.
- Document when the injury occurred and under what circumstances.
- Keep a list of the names and addresses of all the doctors and hospitals treating you.
- Call a lawyer.

CONSUMER PROTECTION LAWS

There are various federal laws protecting consumers in credit situations. Most of these laws have state law counterparts. What follows is a brief discussion of the federal laws.

THE TRUTH IN LENDING ACT helps customers know exactly what they are getting into. The Act requires creditors to disclose their exact credit terms to credit applicants. It also regulates how creditors advertise.

The information which must be disclosed to a consumer buying on credit includes:

- the monthly finance charge;
- the annual interest rate;
- when payments are due;
- the total sale price; and
- the amount of any late payment charges and when they will be assessed.

If a creditor fails to disclose the required information or gives inaccurate information, you can sue for actual damages. In the case of some credit disclosures, you may also sue for twice the finance charge. If you win, the least amount you can be awarded is $100 and the most is $1,000. You are also entitled to recover the costs of your action as well as attorney's fees.

THE FAIR CREDIT BILLING ACT protects consumers who believe there is a mistake on their credit card bill. Under the Act, the customer must notify the creditor within 60 days after the first bill containing the error was mailed. If the dispute is not resolved, the creditor must respond within 30 days. The creditor must also conduct a reasonable investigation and, within 90 days of receiving the letter, explain why the bill is correct or correct the error.

> **TIP:** During the time that the bill is in dispute, you do not have to pay the disputed amount.

If a creditor fails to follow this procedure, the consumer will receive a $50 credit toward the disputed bill. You can also sue for actual damages as well as twice the amount of any finance charges; if successful, the least you can recover is $100 and the most is $1,000. In addition, a successful plaintiff can recover court costs and attorney's fees.

If a state law dealing with billing disputes conflicts with the federal statute, the federal statute will control unless the state law gives a consumer more time to notify the creditor about a billing error.

THE EQUAL CREDIT OPPORTUNITY ACT prohibits a creditor from discriminating against a credit applicant on the basis of race, color, religion, national origin, sex or marital status.

Under the Act, a creditor can look at legitimate factors, such as the applicant's financial status and credit record, before granting credit.

A consumer who has been discriminated against in applying for credit can sue the creditor. If successful, the consumer can recover actual damages as well as punitive damages of up to $10,000 and court costs and attorney's fees.

> Although the Act prohibits age discrimination, a consumer can be refused credit if he or she has not reached the legal age for entering contracts.

THE FAIR CREDIT REPORTING ACT covers credit reports issued by credit reporting agencies. The intent of the Act is to protect consumers from being refused credit based on incomplete or incorrect credit report information.

The Act gives consumers the right to receive a copy of their credit report, and ask to have inaccurate entries removed. If the business reporting the credit problem does not agree to the change or deletion or if the credit reporting agency does not make a change or deletion, the consumer is entitled to add a 100-word statement to his or her credit report explaining his or her side of the issue. The statement will then become part of future credit reports.

A consumer may sue any creditor or credit reporting agency that violates the Act. If successful, the consumer is entitled to actual damages as well as punitive damages if the violation is proven to be intentional. A successful litigant can also recover court costs and attorney's fees.

In addition, any officer or employee of a consumer reporting agency who knowingly and willfully gives credit information to a person who is not authorized to receive the information can be fined, imprisoned for up to 2 years or both.

THE FAIR DEBT COLLECTION PRACTICES ACT prohibits certain methods of debt collection. Personal, family and household debts are covered under the Act.

Under the Act, in the collection of a debt, a debt collector may not:

- harass, oppress or abuse any person in the collection of a debt;
- Use any false, deceptive or misleading representation or means in the collection of a debt; or
- Use unfair or unconscionable means to collect or attempt to collect any debt.

A debt collector found guilty of violating the Act is liable to the consumer for any actual damages sustained by the consumer, additional damages allowed by the court not to exceed $1,000, court costs and attorney's fees.

THE ELECTRONIC FUND TRANSFER ACT limits a consumer's liability for the unauthorized use of an ATM card, debit card or other device used in the handling of an electronic deposit, payment or withdrawal.

The Act limits your liability for lost or stolen ATM or debit cards to $50 if you notify your financial institution within 2 business days of discovering the loss or theft. If you wait more than 2 business days to report a lost or stolen card but notify the card issuer about an unauthorized transaction within 60 days of the date the bank mails the statement containing the error, you could lose as much as $500. If you wait longer than that, you may be liable for $500 plus the amount of any unauthorized transactions after the 60-day period.

If your financial institution does not comply with the provisions of the Electronic Fund Transfer Act, you can sue for actual damages as well as punitive damages of at least $100 but not more than $1,000. If you are successful in your suit, you can also recover court costs and attorney's fees.

THE FAIR CREDIT AND CHARGE CARD DISCLOSURE ACT requires new disclosures on credit and charge cards, regardless of whether they were issued by a financial institution, retail store or private company. Information such as APRs, annual fees and grace periods must be provided in tabular form along with applications and preapproved solicitations for cards. Card issuers that impose an annual fee must provide disclosures before annual renewal. Card issuers that offer credit insurance must inform customers of any increase in rate or substantial decrease in coverage should the issuer decide to change insurance providers.

Any creditor who fails to comply with the requirements of the Act will be liable for actual damages the consumer sustained as a result of noncompliance, twice the amount of any finance charge assessed as a result of the transaction and, in an action relating to a credit transaction not under an open-end credit plan secured by real property or dwelling, not less than $200 or greater than $2,000. A consumer bringing a successful suit can also recover costs of the action and attorney's fees.

THE CREDIT REPAIR ORGANIZATIONS ACT prohibits false or misleading representations by a credit repair company and requires certain disclosures on the part of these companies. The Act forbids credit repair companies from demanding advance payments, requires that credit repair contracts be in writing and allows consumers certain contract cancellation rights.

A consumer can bring an action against a credit repair company for violation of the Act and, if successful, recover actual damages which are the greater the amount of any actual damages sustained by the consumer as a result of the violation or any amount paid by the consumer to the credit repair organization. A successful litigant may also recover punitive damages in an amount determined by the court as well as court costs and attorney's fees.

THE MAGNUSON MOSS WARRANTY-FEDERAL TRADE COMMISSION IMPROVEMENTS ACT (TITLE I) authorizes the FTC to develop regulations for written and implied warranties. The Act directs the Commission to establish disclosure and designation standards for written warranties, specifies standards for full warranties and establishes consumer remedies for breach of warranty or service contract obligations.

THE POSTAL REORGANIZATION ACT makes the mailing of unordered merchandise an unfair or deceptive practice in violation of the FTC Act. The Act allows any recipient of such mail to treat the merchandise as a gift.

THE TELEPHONE DISCLOSURE AND DISPUTE RESOLUTION ACT requires the FTC to promulgate regulations respecting advertising for, operation of and billing and collection procedures for pay-per-call or "900 number" telephone services. The regulations must include certain provisions, such as price disclosure requirements, mandatory warnings on services directed to children and required disclosures in billing statements.

CONSUMER PROTECTION Chapter 2 |

THE TELEMARKETING AND CONSUMER FRAUD AND ABUSE PREVENTION ACT prohibits deceptive or abusive telemarketing acts or practices and prohibits telemarketers from engaging in a pattern of unsolicited telephone calls that a reasonable consumer would consider coercive or an invasion of privacy. The act also restricts the hours of the day and night when unsolicited telephone calls may be made to consumers and requires disclosure of the nature of the call at the start of an unsolicited call made to sell goods or services.

RESOLVING DISPUTES

The first place to start when trying to resolve any consumer dispute is with the business with which you have the dispute. Send a letter to the business (return receipt requested) explaining what the problem is and asking for your money back. Many of the procedures discussed above require this as a first step in the dispute resolution process.

> **TIP:** Do not think that just because the business was not responsive when taking your telephone complaint, it will be equally unresponsive to a letter. A letter has far less emotion than an angry telephone call to customer service and allows you to rationally present the reasons for your dispute.

Your demand letter should outline the reasons why the business owes you money and inform the business of the steps you plan to take if you do not receive satisfaction, including filing suit.

> **TIP:** Be sure to keep copies of your letter in the event that you are forced to sue the business. This letter can then be used in evidence at your trial.

What can a state consumer protection agency do for me? *State consumer protection agencies are valuable resources for consumers.* These agencies provide a variety of services, including:

- educating consumers about their rights;
- publishing pamphlets on state consumer protection laws;
- advising consumers on how to avoid scams;
- maintaining consumer complaint phone lines;
- conducting investigations into scams;
- enforcing consumer protection laws;
- bringing civil lawsuits to stop scammers;
- prosecuting scammers under criminal laws; and
- licensing and regulating various professions, such as real estate brokers or insurance agents.

> **TIP:** You can find your state's consumer protection by visiting the federal Consumer Action Web site at **http://consumeraction. gov/caw_state_resources.shtml**.

I have heard about "alternative dispute resolution." What is this? *Many businesses and private organizations, as well as public agencies, offer dispute resolution programs. These programs are quicker, less expensive and less stressful than going to court.* Moreover, many courts encourage the use of these programs before suit is filed.

To determine whether dispute resolution programs are available in your area, contact your state or local consumer protection agency, state attorney general, local court, Better Business Bureau or the local bar association.

> **TIP:** If the dispute resolution program is unable to solve your problem, you may still be able to file suit against the business. Two things to remember: some programs are binding on both parties and, therefore, you will be precluded from filing suit. Moreover, if you are able to file suit, some jurisdictions limit the timeframe in which you may bring suit. Make sure to check the laws in your state.

What are some other government agencies that can help me?

- **THE FEDERAL TRADE COMMISSION** works for the consumer to prevent fraudulent, deceptive and unfair business practices in the marketplace and to provide information to help consumers identify, stop and avoid them.

  To file a complaint or to get free information on consumer issues, visit **www.ftc.gov** or call toll-free: 877.FTC.HELP/877.382.4357; TTY: 866.653.4261. The FTC enters Internet, telemarketing, identity theft and other fraud-related complaints into Consumer Sentinel, a secure, online database available to hundreds of civil and criminal law enforcement agencies in the United States and abroad.

- **THE FEDERAL CITIZEN INFORMATION CENTER WEB SITE** can be found at www. pueblo.gsa.gov. The Web site provides directions on how to file a consumer complaint as well as information on the latest scams, frauds and consumer abuse items in the news.

- **FEDERAL RESERVE.** If you have a complaint about a bank regarding any federal credit law, you can get advice from the Federal Reserve. Submit your written complaint describing the questionable bank practice, including the name and address of the bank involved to:

  > The Division of Consumer and Community Affairs
  >
  > Board of Governors of the Federal Reserve System
  >
  > Washington, D.C. 20551

> **The Board supervises only state chartered banks that are members of the Federal Reserve System. Complaints about other institutions will be referred to the appropriate federal regulatory agency, and a notice will be sent to you notifying you as to where your complaint has been referred.**

- **THE NATIONAL FRAUD INFORMATION CENTER** can help you if you have been defrauded. The Center has an online form you can use to report suspected telemarketing or Internet fraud. The information provided on the form will be transmitted to the appropriate law enforcement agencies. The Center also provides information on current fraud schemes and advice on avoiding fraud.

  You can contact the NFIC at 800.876.7060 or visit its Web site at **www.fraud.org**.

- **THE BETTER BUSINESS BUREAU** has an online complaint form. After filling out the form, the BBB will contact the business or organization to attempt to resolve the issue. You can reach the BBB at www.bbb.org.

- **PROSECUTORS.** Call your district attorney or state attorney general's office and ask whether there is a consumer fraud division.

- **MEDIA.** Contact your local newspaper, radio station or television station and ask if they have an action line. Often, these entities have volunteers ready to pursue consumer complaints.

- **SMALL CLAIMS COURTS.** If the amount of money in question is relatively small, you can file a lawsuit in small claims court. The costs of doing so are low, the procedures are straightforward, and you probably will not need to hire an attorney.

- **CONTACT AN ATTORNEY** about filing suit. When all else fails, make an appointment with an attorney and present your case. If the attorney believes that it is warranted, he or she can file suit on your behalf. The various types of recovery available to you have been discussed throughout this chapter.

3 ELDER LAW ISSUES

Elder law has become one of the fastest growing segments of the legal industry. This is mainly due to the fact that America's baby boomers are reaching the age of retirement in numbers never seen before. The World War II generation was the first to take full benefit of Social Security, Medicare and Medicaid. These programs have changed over the years to adjust to seniors' needs and will continue to do so as an ever-increasing strain is put on these systems with the retirement of baby boomers.

Reaching your "golden years" means an introduction into programs and benefits that you may not have given much thought to earlier. There will be challenges both financially and medically. Families are more spread out than in previous generations and may not be close by to help out as they were in your parents' and grandparents' day.

Seniors have many legal rights and a number of services to help them enjoy their retirement years. But you must plan ahead. Make yourself aware of the laws and benefits available. Most importantly, do not be afraid to take charge and ask questions when you do not feel comfortable.

MANAGING YOUR MONEY

BANKING AND FINANCE

Keeping your money safe and accounted for is important as you head into your retirement. You will be living on the savings from your years of work and probably from some form of government payments. Know how to handle this money and what to do with it in the event of your death.

I am concerned about what will happen to my bank account after I pass away. Which type of account is best for my situation?
Your bank account may pass under your will or not, depending on the type of bank account you have.

> **TIP:** Different states have different rules. Be sure to check with your bank.

There are several different ways you can hold your bank account, and each will affect how the funds pass after your death:

► **JOINT ACCOUNT.** This is a bank account in two or more names. You own the portion that you contribute. The biggest drawback is that any named account holder can withdraw all the money in the account— even if he or she did not contribute all the money. At your death, the money in the account that can be attributed to your contributions passes under the terms of your will. If you do not have a will, state law will determine who receives your property, including the money in your bank accounts. These laws generally favor your surviving spouse and children.

- **TENANTS IN COMMON.** This is also a bank account in two or more names, and again, you own only that portion that you contribute. As with a joint account, any named account holder can withdraw all the money in the account–even if he or she did not contribute all the money. At your death, the money in the account that can be attributed to your contributions passes under the terms of your will. If you do not have a will, state law will determine who receives your property, including the money in your bank accounts. These laws generally favor your surviving spouse and children.

- **JOINT TENANCY.** This type of account passes the same as a joint account.

- **JOINT TENANTS WITH RIGHTS OF SURVIVORSHIP.** This type of account does not pass through your will. You can establish the account with two or more people. When the account is opened, you must sign a survivorship agreement, which allows the survivor or survivors to take all the money in the account at the death of one of the joint tenants.

- **PAYABLE ON DEATH (POD) ACCOUNT.** In this type of account, the money is payable to you during your lifetime, but funds in your bank account at your death are paid to someone else. In this case, the money does not pass through your will, but instead goes directly to the person you designate. You must designate this person when opening the account.

- **TRUST ACCOUNT.** This is much like a POD account, except that you are the trustee of the money in the account and you hold the money in trust for designated beneficiaries. The trust can only hold the money in the trust account. During your lifetime, the money belongs to you as trustee. At your death, the money passes to your designated beneficiary or beneficiaries.

> **TIP:** Most people go to the bank to open a checking or savings account without much thought as to how the money is distributed at death. It is important to know which type you are opening when you sign the signature card at the bank. If you do not know which type of account you have, check with your bank. They should be able to quickly tell you—and help you change your account to one that may better suit your overall estate plan.

Who can open my safe-deposit box after I die? *If you open a safe-deposit box with your spouse, you most likely opened it jointly.* This means your surviving spouse has the right to open the safe-deposit box and remove any or all of its contents. If the safe-deposit box is held in your name only, state laws vary. Some states allow spouses, parents, adult children and executors access to your safe-deposit box after your death if they provide proper identification of their relationship. In other states, your safe-deposit box is "sealed" and your will and other important documents (life insurance and deeds) cannot be removed without a court order. This takes time and money.

> **TIP:** Be sure to ask your bank representative what the law is in your state. If your safe-deposit box will be sealed in the event of your death, consider opening a safe-deposit box jointly with your spouse or other trusted family member and make sure your attorney has an original, signed copy of your will.

My bank is cutting back on all its services. Are there any banking programs addressing the problems of seniors? *While some banks are cutting back on services, many realize that seniors make up a large percentage of their customers and are updating services to help them.* This may include accounts specifically designed for seniors with higher interest rates for larger accounts. They also may be able to give you one monthly statement that includes your checking and savings accounts, your retirement accounts and mortgage information.

Larger banks will often offer asset management services. These may include professionally managed investment services and trust services, including helping to create living trusts and serving as estate executors.

Some banks offer newsletters with specific community information relating to seniors. Banks often host seminars on financial issues relevant to seniors. Contact several of your local banks to see if they have any of these services.

I am ill and need money now. My friend said to get a "viatical settlement" on my life insurance. Can you explain what that is? *A viatical settlement occurs when you sell the rights to your life insurance to a company.* They pay you a lump sum amount that represents the payout of your life insurance policy, usually a percentage of your policy's face value. This can be anywhere from 50 percent to 75 percent of the policy's value. The purchasing company then pays the premiums on the policy, and when you die, the proceeds are paid to that company. Many elderly people with a terminal illness and large medical bills may find that a viatical settlement agreement offers a way to pay for their medical costs. But these are not without risk—there are both legal and tax consequences, including affecting your participation in public assistance programs such as Supplemental Social Security and Medicaid.

> **You can change you mind anywhere from 15 to 30 days after you receive the money, depending on your state, by giving the purchaser of your life insurance policy written notice.**

> **TIP:** Viatical settlements are not the only answer. Consider contacting your life insurance company to see if they will allow you to surrender the policy for its cash value. Or they may offer accelerated death benefits or offer loans against the policy amount. Also, if your policy covers other family members such as your spouse, be sure that you are not surrendering that portion of the policy. As with any financial decision, check with several companies to compare prices and contracts and do not let any company pressure you into a contract. Call the Better Business Bureau to find out more about the companies you contact. State insurance commissioners also should have information about companies that purchase insurance policies.

What are "subprime loans" and "predatory loans"? *Unfortunately, many elderly Americans are targets for unscrupulous financial institutions.* These lenders will target elderly homeowners needing money to pay real estate taxes, make needed home repairs or who may have less than perfect credit histories.

Subprime loans are generally extended to consumers with low incomes and flawed credit history. These loans are not themselves illegal. But they do become illegal, predatory loans when vulnerable consumers, such as the elderly, are the subject of aggressive sales techniques. This may include exorbitant fees and interest rates and the use of misleading and fraudulent sales pitches. Lenders may even try to get you to "flip" a loan—that is, encourage you to pay off an existing loan with a second, more expensive loan. Each time you flip a loan, you have to pay costs and fees associated with the loan—more money out of your pocket and into the lender's.

People claiming to be creditors are contacting me both by phone and mail. Is this legal? *Unfortunately some debt collectors use abusive and deceptive practices to try to recover debt.* To help stop this, the government has passed the Fair Debt Collection Practices Act. Most states also have state laws forbidding this practice. Most basically, debt collectors cannot contact you before 8 a.m. and after 9 p.m. or at your place of business if the collector has reason to know that your employer forbids such communication. You can notify the collector in writing that you refuse to pay the debt and to stop further contact. In this case, they can only contact you to let you know of their specific remedies being sought.

> **The Act specifically forbids the collectors from making false or misleading representations, from threatening you or using profanity.**

CONSUMER FRAUD ISSUES

Almost any consumer transaction can be wrought with peril and senior citizens are particularly susceptible to consumer scams. Professional salespeople can make even the most unnecessary item seem indispensable. Be cautious and know when to say no. Never feel pressured to buy something from an unsolicited salesperson.

Almost every transaction you enter into involves a contract. When you extend payments over time, make sure you know what the total cost will be including interest payments.

> **The Federal Truth in Lending Act requires the seller to inform you of the finance charge and interest rate on your purchase. The Act also allows you to cancel certain contracts within 3 days of purchase.**

> **TIP:** Make sure to read through any contract before signing it. Keep copies of the contract and all payments.

What financial plans or consumer scams should I watch out for? *Deceptive practices are not limited to predatory loans.* The Federal Trade Commission warns homeowners—especially the elderly–to be aware of other fraudulent practices. These include:

▶ **HOME IMPROVEMENT SCHEMES.** Be wary of any door-to-door salespeople that try to sell you unsolicited home improvements. These contractors may want your money up front to "buy" the needed supplies. Chances are they will disappear with your money.

▶ **DEBT CONSOLIDATION.** An unsolicited mortgage broker or other lender may pressure you to consolidate all of your existing debt into one mortgage. In reality, this consolidated loan will generate fees for the broker and you will be no better off—in some cases even worse off.

▶ **FORECLOSURE ASSISTANCE.** In these schemes, someone will approach you after you have missed a couple of house payments. You sign papers after being told they will give you enough money to pay off the loan, but in reality the papers sign over the title to your home to the unsolicited lender for the price of your outstanding mortgage. Then, not only are you short on cash, but now someone else owns your home.

▶ **EQUITY STRIPPING.** These loans sound great because they are based on the equity you have in your home. The more equity you have, the more the lender will let you borrow. But they do not take into consideration your income and your ability to pay back the loan. You may end up in foreclosure if you cannot make your monthly payments.

▶ **BAIT AND SWITCH.** The lender may offer you what seem like rates that are too good to pass up. Then when you go to sign the papers, there will be reasoning as to why the fees and interest rate is more. They will pressure you in to signing the agreement with the higher rates.

▶ **DOOR-TO-DOOR SALES.** Most cities require door-to-door salespeople to get a permit before hitting the streets. Ask anyone who appears at your home to sell something to see his or her permit. Do not buy anything on the spot. Take a few days to think about it.

▶ **IDENTITY THEFT.** People can use your driver's license and Social Security card to open credit card accounts in your name. Give out this information sparingly.

▶ **TELEMARKETING.** While most telemarketers are legitimate, some are not. You may be told that you have won a sweepstakes but need to pay a small fee to collect your winnings. If you have to pay for something you "won," chances are you will never hear from the telemarketer after they receive your fee. Never give out your financial information over the phone unless you know and trust the requesting person.

CAUTION: If you do not understand exactly how much you are borrowing, the interest rate and the costs associated with the loan, do not sign any paperwork. Be completely satisfied with all the answers given by the lender. If you do not feel comfortable, get a second offer from another financial institution to see if the rates compare favorably. Use only established banks, credit unions or other financial institutions. Any reputable lender will not call you on the phone to solicit you or approach you as a door-to-door salesperson.

I need to repair my roof quickly. What should I do? *Home repairs can involve a number of people. Get at least two references, preferably three or four.* Check references and the local Better Business Bureau. Make sure you have a contract for the work and that it is in writing. Never agree to pay the full amount in advance. It is best to pay a good faith amount to start the project, with installments during the project and a final payment at completion. Make sure the amount of work agreed on is done before paying the installments and do not pay until all work is completed according to the contract.

CAUTION: Contractors can file a mechanic's lien on your property if you do not pay the full amount. This places a lien on your property for the amount owed. Be sure that the contractor removes all liens on your property as part of any dispute settlement.

My car is in the repair shop, and the cost of the repairs is more than the estimate the repair shop quoted me. Do I have to pay the amount above the estimate? *Most states require automobile repair shops to provide you with an estimate for repairs over a certain amount and to disclose the hourly labor rate.* You may have to pay for amounts over the quoted estimate if the repairs are unforeseen but necessary and the amount is within a specific percentage of the estimate.

I get a lot of telephone calls trying to sell me different products. Some seem like a great deal, and the telemarketer seems

really excited for me to buy. How do I know if these deals are too good to be true? *Be very cautious of telemarketers calling to sell you something. If something seems too good to be true, it probably is.* New laws give you the right to tell them to put you on their "do not call" list, and they can be fined if they fail to do so. Telemarketers must identify themselves and their product, tell you the total costs involved and whether you can be refunded your money or the sale is final.

> **TIP:** Never send money to any salesperson demanding immediate payment. If they tell you that you have to pay a nominal fee for a prize or access to information, hang up. You should never pay for a prize.

I received some unordered merchandise in the mail. Do I have to pay for it? *This is one time you do not have to pay for something. If merchandise that you did not order is sent to you, you do not have to pay for it.* The company cannot force you to pay for the product or pressure you to send it back to them.

I ordered something over the phone and have not received it yet, even though I paid for it. What can I do? *A seller must ship ordered products within 30 days if not otherwise stated.* If it does not do so, you have the right to cancel your order and get a refund within 7 days. But the law does not apply to all mail-order transactions.

EXAMPLE: Magazine subscriptions and plants or seeds do not have to meet the 30-day requirement.

I bought a camera from a door-to-door salesperson and now do not want it. Can I get my money back? *Yes—if you act quickly and your purchase was over $25. Federal law requires the seller to give you a "Notice of Cancellation."* This gives you 3 days to cancel a purchase. Fill out the cancellation notice and mail it within 3 days of the purchase.

I just received a notice that I won a sweepstakes contest and all I have to do is mail in a processing fee. Should I do

this? *The law does not allow sweepstakes to require you to pay for any "prize."* This includes purchasing any product, such as magazines, to increase your chances of winning.

My neighbor said to be aware of a scam called the "pigeon-drop." What is this? *This scam is especially targeted towards seniors and is used to steal your savings.* The scam typically begins with someone approaching you and telling you that he or she has "found" a large amount of money. They will offer to share the money with you, but only in exchange for you giving them some money as a "good faith" gesture. The person will then give you back an envelope with no money in it. Or the scam artist may tell you that he or she has hidden the money and will bring it to you later or even the next day. The person then disappears with your money.

> **TIP:** A variation of this scam has recently been updated, using e-mail to ask for your "investment." Delete or block all such messages.

> **TIP:** Never give money to someone you do not know. If the person wants the money right away, chances are he or she is not legitimate. If you have any reservations about the person, call the police.

After I left the bank, a man approached me and said he was a bank examiner and needed my help. I had an appointment and had to leave. Should I call him and help him? *No. This is a common scheme to defraud seniors and others.* The so-called "bank examiner" will try to tell you that he or she works for the bank and is trying to determine if a bank employee is stealing money from the bank. The scam artist will then ask you to withdraw money from your own account so that he or she can check the serial numbers on the bills you receive. Once the money is in the hands of the bank examiner, chances are you will never see your money or the bank examiner again.

How can I know that I am giving my donation to a real charity? *It can be hard to tell if some "charities" are really just businesses looking for* a way to make money. To avoid giving your money to a sham, only donate to charities that you know. Some charities will adopt a name that is very similar to a reputable and established charity. Have the person asking you for a donation leave information about the charity that includes a phone number or Web site. Call the charity and the Better Business Bureau to learn more about the organization. Never feel pressured to give money immediately. Any reputable charity will understand that donating is a personal decision that should not be rushed. If the charity only takes cash donations, do not give any money.

> **TIP:** If you have any questions about the legitimacy of a charity, contact:
>
> BBB Wise Giving Alliance
>
> 4200 Wilson Blvd., Suite 800
>
> Arlington, VA 22203
>
> You can also call them at 703.276.0100 or visit their Web site at **www.give.org**.

What can I do if a store is out of an advertised special and wants to sell me a higher priced item? *This is the classic bait-and-switch scam. A store will advertise an item at a bargain price, but when you arrive to buy it, the store will be out of the item and try to pressure you to buy a "better," more expensive item.* You should be very wary about buying the higher priced item. This scam works often because you are led to believe the less expensive item was not all that good and that the more expensive item is right for you.

> **TIP:** If you are the subject of this scam, you can file a complaint with the Better Business Bureau.

HOUSING

What is a "reverse mortgage"? *A reverse mortgage allows older Americans to receive cash for the equity in their homes.* Instead of paying money to a lender as in a traditional mortgage, the lender would pay you monthly installments that reflect the equity in your home. You can continue to live in your home and the proceeds paid to you are tax-free, although you cannot deduct the interest on the reverse mortgage on your income taxes. The lender, in turn, then owns that portion of your home's equity that you contract for. The loan usually becomes due when you die or sell your home. You can choose the way you want to receive the money: monthly payments, a lump sum distribution or line of credit.

> **You generally have 3 days to cancel a reverse mortgage after you have signed it. The cancellation must be in writing.**

Will a reverse mortgage help me or hurt me? *The most attractive feature of a reverse mortgage is the ability to stay in your home. But reverse mortgages are more expensive than other traditional loans.* A reverse mortgage will lessen the amount of equity you own in your home, so there will be less to pass on to your heirs. You are still responsible for taxes and insurance on your home. Be aware of unscrupulous lenders. They may charge extra fees that drive up the cost of the mortgage. Also, be aware of mortgages with adjustable rates (they may rise, costing you more in interest) and acceleration clauses that allow the lender to declare the loan due immediately.

Is a reverse mortgage available to anyone? *No.* You must be at least 62 years old and have very little left to pay on your existing mortgage. You also must own your home free and clear.

> **The Department of Housing and Urban Development administers the federally insured Home Equity Conversion Mortgage (HECM) program. This program is insured by the federal government and tells lenders how much they can lend to you based on the value of your home and your age. The HECM limits the costs associated with the loan and guarantees that your lender will meet its obligations.**

> **TIP:** The AARP's Web site offers extensive details on reverse mortgages in general and HECM requirements. Visit **www.aarp.org/revmort** for more information.

I am afraid the bank is going to foreclose on my home. Is there any way out of this? *Yes. Work with the bank that owns your mortgage. You may be able to have your monthly payments lowered or even possibly suspended for a short time.* Another option is to refinance your home. This may result in lower monthly payments. But you will most likely have to pay some fees for the refinancing process, so be sure the amount of your monthly savings offsets these costs.

I have missed some mortgage payments because of unexpected medical bills, and now the bank is threatening to foreclose. What can I do? *Failure to pay your mortgage can happen for many reasons.* Maybe your spouse recently died, and that income stream is gone. Increased medical bills and higher utility bills in the winter can also put a strain on your ability to pay your mortgage.

In some states, the creditor (the bank holding your mortgage) has to file a foreclosure action in the court where the property is located. You must answer the foreclosure complaint in court or risk losing your home.

> **TIP:** Contact your local housing authority to find out more information on what to do if you are the subject of a foreclosure.

Other states have what is known as nonjudicial foreclosures. In these states, the creditor can simply advertise your property for sale. The onus is then on you to file a lawsuit in court to stop a sale.

> **TIP:** Always pay your mortgage before other bills. Call your lender if you have any trouble making payments—most will work with you to find a solution rather than missing payments. Also, contact your local social services office to see what kind of assistance is available in your area. By lowering other costs, you will free up money to pay your mortgage.

The apartment manager says I do not need to sign any paperwork to rent an apartment, but I think I should. Who is right? *Although you can rent an apartment with just an oral agreement, it is much safer to sign a written lease agreement.* The written document lists all of the landlord's rights and duties as well as your rights and duties as a tenant.

> **TIP:** Read your lease carefully. If you do not understand something, ask the landlord to clarify.

Do I have to give the landlord a security deposit? *Seniors on a tight budget may not want to pay money that does not go directly to their monthly overhead.* But it is normal for a landlord to require one. The landlord is only trying to ensure that you will care for the property during the term of your lease. Generally, the amount of the security deposit cannot exceed more than 2 months' rent.

> **The landlord must give you a written document listing any damages and the amount of the security deposit kept for those damages. He can only keep that portion of the security deposit that does not cover owed rent, damages and cleaning costs after you move out.**

I am having trouble paying rent to my landlord each month. Are there any programs that can help me with this? *Yes. Renters over the age of 62 qualify for the federal government's Rental Assistance Program.* You may qualify at a lower age if you are blind or disabled. To qualify, you cannot exceed a certain maximum annual income. The program only requires that you pay (up to) 30 percent of your income towards your rent.

> **TIP:** Contact your local Franchise Tax Board or Area Agency on Aging office for more information.

It is December and the utility company is going to shut my heat off for nonpayment. What can I do? *First, call your utility company and explain the situation to them. Many*

companies are willing to work with customers to find a satisfactory solution for both you and the company. For low-income seniors, the Energy Assistance Program may help. To qualify, you cannot exceed a maximum annual income. Call the National Energy Assistance Referral at 800.674.6327 or contact them at **www.acf.hhs. gov/programs/liheap/states.htm** for help in applying for assistance.

Can I install modifications, such as grab-bars in my shower, without my landlord's consent? *Usually you can make modifications that are necessary for your full enjoyment of the apartment.* You normally must agree to return the property to its original condition at your own cost when you move out.

HEALTH CARE ISSUES

COMPETENCY AND GUARDIANSHIP

Each state has specific laws dealing with incapacitated persons and the appointment of guardians.

> **TIP:** Check with your local library for specific materials. The library may even be able to direct you to local nonprofit organizations with specific familiarity in this field.

What does it mean to be "incompetent" or "incapacitated"? *An incapacitated person is someone who cannot receive or evaluate information or communicate decisions regarding his or her physical or mental well-being.* This means the person cannot make decisions about his or her housing and dietary needs, care for physical needs or manage finances.

What procedures are needed to declare a person incompetent? *You will first have to file a petition in court. The petition should state a relationship to the alleged incapacitated person, the name and address of the person with the alleged incapacity and the nature of the incapacity.* Provide the court with names of people who are familiar with the person and the alleged incapacity. Generally, the court will then appear an attorney to represent the person with the alleged incapacity and a person or committee to examine the person.

> **TIP:** In some jurisdictions, it may be up to the party seeking the finding of incapacity to locate professionals to make the examination. Call the clerk of the court to see if you are responsible for finding and paying for these professionals.
>
> The examining person or committee will then file a report with the court and the court will rule whether the person is incapacitated.

What is a "guardian"?
A guardian is a person entrusted with the duty to take care of another person (the "ward") and that person's property. The guardian can be either "general" or "specific" (also known as "unlimited" and "limited" guardianship, respectively). A general guardian cares for the ward and his or her property. A specific guardian cares for only specific or limited aspects of the person's well-being or the person's estate.

EXAMPLE: A specific guardian may take care of only the ward's health care decisions or, alternatively, only the ward's estate.

How is a guardian appointed?
A person becomes a guardian of an incapacitated person by a parental or spousal appointment or upon appointment by the court. An individual or a person interested in the senior's welfare may petition for a determination of incapacity, in whole or in part, and for the appointment of a limited or unlimited guardian for the individual. The petition must set forth the petitioner's name, residence, current address (if different), relationship to the respondent and interest in the appointment. To the extent known, state the senior's alleged incapacity, his or her next of kin and any caretakers or legal representatives and the proposed guardian. The court generally looks for a general statement of the respondent's property with an estimate of its value, including any insurance or pension, and the source and amount of any other anticipated income or receipts.

How are guardians chosen?
Once the court receives a petition to establish a guardianship, the court sets a date and time for a hearing and appoints someone to visit and examine the senior, usually a social worker or someone with training or experience in the type of incapacity alleged. The court can also appoint a lawyer if it determines there is a need for one. The social worker then files a report with the court about the alleged incapacitated person's abilities and those of the proposed guardian.

Courts normally consider proposed guardians by priority. Considered first is a person nominated by the alleged incapacitated person before the incapacity affected him or her. The court also considers a guardian under a durable power of attorney for health care decisions. The next in line are spouses and adult children.

> The court, acting in the best interest of the respondent, may decline to appoint a person having priority and appoint a person having a lower priority or no priority.

> In most situations, an owner, operator or employee of a long-term-care institution at which the alleged incapacitated person is receiving care cannot be appointed guardian unless he or she is related by blood, marriage or adoption.

What powers does a guardian have?
Unless a court places specific limitations on the guardianship, a guardian may apply for and receive money payable to the ward or the ward's guardian for the ward's support. The guardian can take custody of the ward and establish the ward's domicile. Normally, this has to be in the state where the guardian is appointed and the ward resides. The guardian can consent to medical treatment, marriage or divorce and other decisions affecting the ward's well-being.

Is a conservator the same as a guardian?
Technically, no, but the terms are often used interchangeably. A guardian is responsible for the custody of the incapacitated person (the "ward") and makes personal and health-related decisions. A conservator only controls the ward's

property, either real estate or finances or both. Sometimes a conservator is called a "guardian of the estate." One person can serve as both guardian and conservator. A successor guardian or conservator succeeds to the predecessor's powers, and a successor conservator succeeds to the predecessor's title to the protected person's assets.

Who pays for the guardian's services? *As approved by order of the court, a guardian is entitled to reasonable compensation for services as guardian and to reimbursement for services and goods, such as clothing, provided to the ward.* The money is paid out of the ward's estate. If a conservator other than the guardian or person who is affiliated with the guardian's custody has been appointed for the estate of the ward, reasonable compensation and reimbursement to the guardian may be approved and paid by the conservator without order of the court.

Does a guardian have to make periodic reports to the court? *Yes. In most states, a court-appointed guardian must file a report within a specified number of days of being appointed.* This report will include all of the assets owned and debts owed by the incapacitated person. Then the guardian must file an annual report stating the account balances and physical and mental condition of the incapacitated person.

Can a guardian be replaced? *Yes.* The appointment of a guardian terminates on the death, resignation or removal of the guardian. A resignation of a guardian is effective when approved by the court.

> **Termination of the appointment of a guardian does not affect the guardian's liability for previous acts or the obligation to account for money and other assets of the ward.**

A ward or a person interested in the welfare of a ward can petition for removal of a guardian on the ground that removal is in the best interest of the ward. A guardian may petition for permission to resign. A petition for removal or permission to resign may include a request for appointment of a successor guardian or conservator.

The court may appoint an additional guardian at any time. The successor guardian becomes eligible to act when the vacancy occurs, on a designated event, or when the acceptance of appointment is filed.

What are some alternatives to guardianship? *Petitioning for and having a guardian appointed is a complex and relatively expensive process.* If you can accomplish the same goal— while protecting the person's best interest —in another manner, it may be the better alternative. Any alternative will depend on the type and extent of the incapacity. Also, most alternatives require the consent of the incapacitated person before the onset of any mental incapacity.

Alternatives, sometimes referred to as "advance directives," include:

- Power of attorney
  - Durable power of attorney for health care decisions.

    This allows a competent adult to designate another competent adult to carry out his or her medical wishes. This may include CPR and artificial feeding. It should include a statement that the declarant wishes for it to continue in the event of mental incapacity, not just physical incapacity.

  - Financial power of attorney

    This power of attorney appoints someone to make financial decisions for the grantor in the event he or she becomes incapacitated. It should include a statement that the grantor wishes for it to continue in the event of mental incapacity, not just physical incapacity.

- Living wills

  A living will allows a competent adult to state whether he or she wants to be kept alive by artificial means.

> **TIP:** You can revoke any of these as you would other documents. Destroy any written documents. Make a separate written document stating that you expressly revoke any earlier written directives.

MEDICARE AND MEDICAID

Medicare and Medicaid have been in existence since the 1960s. These programs have helped millions of elderly citizens live in comfort and will continue to do so for many millions more. But the programs differ substantially, and you should not count on either of them to pay for all of your needs.

CAUTION: Both programs have undergone substantial revisions in recent years and will continue to evolve as the "baby boom" generation takes full advantage of them.

Understanding all of your options for private health benefits and public assistance is a huge undertaking. Be sure to consult with your physician and local Social Security Administration office for more information about Medicare and Medicaid.

> **TIP:** The Social Security Administration has many brochures to help you better understand what the programs offer and what programs you are eligible for. The Administration also has counselors that can explain the benefits you are entitled to.

Here are some important contact phone numbers and Web sites:

- Centers for Medicare and Medicaid Services. The Centers for Medicare and Medicaid Services (CMS) administer the Medicare and Medicaid programs. Call 877.267.2323 or visit **www.cms.hhs.gov**.
- Medicare. Call 800.MEDICARE for direct questions about Medicare, or visit **www.medicare.gov**. TTY users should call 877.486.2048.
- Medicaid: For questions about your state's Medicaid program, visit **www.cms.hhs.gov/medicaid/statemap.asp**.
- State Health Insurance Assistance Programs. These state programs help the federal government administer health benefits. For a list of state Web sites and phone numbers, visit **http://hiicap.state.ny.us/home/linko8.htm#links**.
- Social Security Administration. For the nearest Social Security office, look in your yellow pages in the government pages. To reach the Social Security Administration, call 800.772.1213 or visit **www.ssa.gov**.

Medicare offers many publications about its programs. You can order free publications online at **www.medicare.gov** or by calling 800. MEDICARE (800.633.4227). Some booklets are available in Spanish, in Braille, on audio cassette and large print (English and Spanish). TTY users should call 877.486.2048.

- Medicare & You gives basic information about Medicare coverage, benefits, health plan choices and more (CMS Pub. No. 10050).
- Medicare Coverage of Skilled Nursing Facility Care explains when and how much Medicare covers skilled nursing facility care (CMS Pub. No. 10153).
- Medicare Hospice Benefits explains Medicare coverage of hospice care for people with terminal illnesses (CMS Pub. No. 02154).

Medicare

What is Medicare and who is it for? *Medicare is federally funded health insurance. It is for Americans over age 65.* You may qualify if you are under age 65 if you have certain disabilities or you have permanent kidney failure.

> **Medicare does not take your income into consideration—Medicaid does.**

What is Medicare Part A and what does it do? *Medicare Part A is hospital insurance. It pays for inpatient hospital care, skilled nursing facilities, hospice care and limited home health care.* Most participants do not have to pay for Part A coverage and are automatically eligible when they turn 65. You will have to pay for Part A coverage if you or your spouse never paid Medicare taxes while working. Your Medicare card should state "Hospital Part A" on it if you are covered under Part A.

> **TIP:** If you are unsure whether you have to pay for Medicare Part A, call your local Social Security Administration office to find out.

What is Medicare Part B and what does it do? *Medicare Part B is medical insurance.* It covers doctor visits, outpatient hospital treatment, physical and occupational therapy and limited home health care. The services must be medically necessary to be covered. You must pay a monthly premium for Part B coverage and enrolling in Part B is optional. Your premium will usually be paid out of your Social Security or other government retirement benefits, such as Railroad Retirement benefits or Civil Service benefits.

Is Medicare free? *No. As mentioned above, Medicare Part A (hospital insurance) is free if you have paid into it, but Part B (medical insurance) requires a monthly premium.* It is either paid out of Social Security benefits, or you must pay the premium on your own.

What is a Medicare-approved drug discount card and where can I get one? *Most Medicare participants are eligible to receive a Medicare-approved discount drug card.* This new program helps seniors with prescription drug costs. If you signed up in 2004 when this benefit was introduced, you received a $600 credit towards the purchase of prescription drugs. This credit is prorated if you sign up in 2005. By 2006, Medicare's new prescription drug program will take full effect, and all Medicare recipients will be eligible for prescription drug benefits. You can get a card through one of the many private insurance companies that have contracted with Medicare to provide this service.

> **TIP:** Call Medicare at 800.633.4227 or visit their Web site at **www.medicare.gov** for a list of Medicare-approved providers. Approved discount cards will have a Medicare logo on them that says "Medicare Approved."

CAUTION: If you have Medicaid-provided prescription drug benefits, you are not eligible for a Medicare-approved drug discount card.

Can I get a Medicare prescription drug card if I am in a nursing home? *You must meet certain specific conditions. You must have Medicare Part A and/or Part B, and you cannot have outpatient prescription drug benefits from Medicaid.* Medicaid cannot pay for your nursing home stay. You also must receive your prescription drugs through the nursing home

pharmacy—not from an outside source such as a community pharmacy or mail order. There are also income limitations.

How do I apply for Medicare? *If you currently receive Social Security or Railroad Retirement benefits, you will be automatically enrolled in Medicare.* The Social Security Administration will mail your enrollment package to you.

> **TIP:** If you do not receive your enrollment information by your 65th birthday, contact your local Social Security Administration.

If you do not currently receive Social Security or Railroad Retirement benefits, you will need to apply by yourself. Call the nearest Social Security Administration to obtain the application. If you do choose to participate, you must do so within a very specific time frame—the 3 months before and the 3 months after your 65th birthday.

> **TIP:** It is best to sign up for Medicare before you turn 65. Mark your calendar 3 months before you turn 65 to be sure you sign up within the short period.

You may not want to pay for Part B coverage if you are covered under another medical insurance policy. But if you do not sign up while you are covered under another policy or within a specific time period from the end of medical coverage, you will have to pay a penalty on application.

> **TIP:** Contact your local Social Security Administration office or State Health Insurance Assistance Program (SHIP) if you have questions about whether and when to sign up for coverage.

Does Medicare pay for hospice care? *Yes. It pays for certain hospice and home health care services.* Medicare covers physician and nursing services, pain medication, medical supplies, physical and occupational therapy and social services counseling.

CAUTION: Only "medically necessary" home health services are covered. The Medicare program must approve the agency making home visits and your physician must certify that you are terminally ill.

Does Medicare pay for nursing home care?

Medicare will pay some nursing home costs under limited conditions. Medicare beneficiaries must require skilled nursing or rehabilitation services and receive them from a Medicare-approved skilled nursing home after a qualifying hospital stay of at least 3 days. Your physician must certify that you require skilled nursing care. Medicare will pay up to a set number of days of skilled nursing care per illness. It will pay for all covered service for a short period, and then you will be billed a daily fee for the remainder of your stay.

What are "approved" charges? *Medicare determines on a yearly basis what it will pay for specific medical services.* Your physician may actually bill you more or less than the Medicare-approved amount. You will be billed for a portion of those services that are above the percentage that Medicare pays for.

What is Medicare+Choice/Medicare Advantage? *Medicare+Choice was renamed Medicare Advantage in 2004.* It is private insurance that is subsidized by the federal government. It is sometimes referred to as "Part C." It allows enrolled Medicare participants to choose plans similar to health maintenance organizations (HMOs) or fee-for-service plans. Under this plan, you must have Part A and Part B coverage and still pay Medicare Part B premiums in addition to any premiums required by the private insurer.

CAUTION: This option is not available in all areas.

What kinds of plans are available under Medicare+Choice/Medicare Advantage?

These "managed care" private insurance plans can be fee-for-service, health maintenance organizations (HMOs) and preferred provider organizations (PPOs).

- **FEE-FOR-SERVICE PLANS.** This allows you to choose any physician or hospital. Medicare will then pay a share of the fees for covered Medicare services. You have to pay a monthly premium to the insurance company plus any deductibles or copayments.

- **HMOS.** These plans have a network of physicians, hospitals and other medical service providers from which you can choose. You must use the doctors or hospitals in this network. You will normally pay a small monthly premium plus copayments for some services.

- **PPOS.** Under these plans, you can choose your doctor and are encouraged to use him or her as your primary care doctor. But you usually do not need to get a referral from your primary care doctor to see a specialist.

- **MEDICAL SAVINGS ACCOUNTS (MSAS).** This is basically a Medicare-sponsored health care plan with a high deductible. You establish the MSA, and Medicare makes a deposit into your account. You can use these funds to pay for noncovered services and costs you incur before you meet your deductible.

CAUTION: Each of these plans varies widely. Contact your nearest SHIP to see if one of these plans is right for you.

What is Medigap insurance? *Like Medicare+Choice, private companies, not the government, sell Medigap. It is intended to fill in the "gaps" in Medicare coverage. You must be enrolled in Part A and Part B. If you enroll in Part B after age 65, you must apply for MediGap within 6 months of your enrollment in Part B.* Plans generally start at "A" for the least amount of coverage to "J" for the most comprehensive coverage. They cover such things as deductibles, coinsurance payments and may even cover dental and vision care.

What can I do if I think Medicare denied a claim that is covered? *You can generally appeal claims that involve medical necessity, reasonableness and inpatient versus outpatient issues.* You must make a written appeal within 60 days of the denial to your local Social Security office. Medicare will notify you of its decision. If you are not happy with Medicare's reconsideration, you have the right to a hearing. You must request a hearing within 60 days of Medicare's reconsideration decision. From this point, you can still make appeals to the Social

Security Appeals Council and the federal district court in your jurisdiction if you meet specific requirements.

Medicaid

What is Medicaid and how does it differ from Medicare? *Medicaid is a joint insurance program between the federal government and states for low-income people of all ages.* Whereas Medicare is for elderly people, Medicaid is available to low-income children and adults. Medicaid programs vary by state and have different restrictions.

> **TIP:** Individual state agencies and the Health Care Financing Administration (HCFA) oversee the program. Contact your state agency to see if you qualify.

Who is eligible for Medicaid? *Medicaid is generally for people that are determined to be low-income, have a disability and are eligible for federal aid.* In some states, you are automatically eligible for Medicaid if you receive Supplemental Security Income (SSI).

CAUTION: The eligibility requirements differ in each state. Contact your state's program to see if you qualify.

How much will Medicaid cost? *Depending on your state's rules, you may have to pay a small deductible or copayment.* But Medicaid beneficiaries who are hospital or nursing home patients and are expected to contribute most of their income to institutional care are exempted from this requirement. And you do not have to pay a copayment for emergency services.

Can I make a salary and still get Medicaid? *Because Medicaid is directed toward low-income citizens as opposed to just the elderly, income is a factor to consider.* Generally, if you receive SSI, you will be eligible to receive Medicaid benefits. Medicaid categorizes resources as either countable or noncountable; it uses countable assets to determine eligibility. These assets include those that can be converted to cash, such as bank accounts, retirement benefits and property. Noncountable assets do not affect

eligibility and include such assets as your home, one car, personal belongings and household furnishings and appliances.

A friend says I have too much money in assets to be eligible for Medicaid and that I should sell some off to qualify. Can I do this? *No. Medicaid has strict rules about transferring your assets to be eligible for the program.* State programs vary, but generally, any transfers made for up to 60 months (5 years) before you apply for Medicaid may be considered assets for eligibility purposes. Before trying to sell any of your assets, check to see what your state's transfer limit is.

Someone told me I can still apply for Medicaid even though my income exceeds the limit, but I will have to "spend down" some of my assets. What does this mean? *A "spend-down" is like an insurance deductible.* If your income or assets are above the Medicaid limit, you will have to incur bills in the amount of your spend-down to be eligible. You will receive a Medicaid card after you prove your spend-down.

EXAMPLE: Joe has $1,000 in assets over the Medicaid limit. Once Joe spends $1,000 on medical bills and submits copies to his local Medicaid office, Medicaid will provide Joe with a Medicaid card.

What requirements are there for getting Medicaid? *Medicaid is offered to several categories of people, included the aged.* As mentioned above, you must also meet your state's income and asset limits to be eligible. Medicaid also requires that you be a United States citizen and a resident of the state in which you apply. Some legal immigrants may also qualify.

How do I apply for Medicaid? *You can apply for Medicaid at your local social services office. Look in the government pages of your phone book.* If you cannot find it, call your local Social Security office, and they can direct you to the closest Medicaid office. Or visit **www.cms.hhs. gov/medicaid/statemap.asp** to locate your state's program.

What does Medicaid pay for? *Medicaid requires all states to provide some basic medical services.* After these basics, the states can offer— or not offer—services of their choosing. Required medical services include inpatient and outpatient hospital services, physicians' services, some home health care services and nursing home services in Medicaid-approved facilities.

LIVING WILLS

A living will is one form of an "advance directive," meaning you are telling your loved ones and others in advance how you wish to be treated in the event of a terminal or life-threatening illness. They are recognized in all 50 states.

What is a "living will"? *A living will is a written and signed document by you stating whether you wish to be kept alive using artificial means in the event a doctor declares your death to be imminent.* Doctors are legally bound to follow this directive. Some states require you to use specific language. For example, North Carolina requires you to state that you do not want doctors to use artificial means, including feeding and hydrating, to keep you alive in the event of a terminal illness or if you are in a persistent vegetative state, and that you know that your living will means that your doctor can withhold or stop medical treatment, including food and water.

> **Many states also require that the document be signed by a specific number of witnesses and notarized or certified.**

What is a "durable power of attorney for health care"? *A durable power of attorney for health care designates someone to make health care decisions for you in the event that you become incapacitated.* About half of the states allow this person to make a decision concerning ending life support treatment. Other states will not allow this person to make this decision unless you have previously clearly and convincingly indicated your wish not to receive artificial support to prolong your life.

> **TIP:** Make sure the person to whom you give this power is trustworthy and will carry out your wishes. He or she may have to deal with doctors and family members who disagree with your choices.

Should I have both a living will and a durable power of attorney for health care? *You can have both.* The living will is directed to the doctors and the durable power of attorney for health care gives another person the power to make health care decisions in the event of your incapacity.

TIP: To make your decision clear, it is best to have both. You may want to outline all of your particular desires in order to avoid any misunderstandings.

What is the difference between a power of attorney and a durable power of attorney? *A power of attorney lasts only as long as you remain competent. In the event you become incapacitated or disabled, a power of attorney is no longer effective.* On the other hand, a durable power of attorney survives through your incapacity or disability. So, a durable power of attorney lasts longer. For elderly Americans, durable powers of attorney will most of the time be a better choice.

Can my family members or I change or revoke these documents? *You always have the right to change your mind.* Tear up the old living will and create a new one stating that you do (or do not) wish to be kept alive by artificial means. Be sure to give the new document to the same people you gave the first one to.

Someone acting on your behalf, such as a guardian, can also revoke your living will or durable power of attorney for health care. This does not mean an adult child can revoke the documents because he or she does not agree with the decisions you made. Make sure all or your family members know your wishes before you become incapacitated.

Who should I tell about these documents, and where should they be kept? *Give one signed copy to your doctor. This way he or she will know your wishes beforehand.* Provide another copy to the person you have designated to serve as the executor of your estate. Also give copies to family members and your pastor or rabbi. Keep the original in a safe place with your other important documents such as your will..

LONG-TERM CARE, NURSING HOMES AND RESIDENTIAL PROGRAMS

No longer being able to live independently is one of the hardest challenges facing the elderly. But it is important to look at your options while you can still decide for yourself what is best for you. There are a range of services available to help senior citizens with their day-to-day tasks. For those who require more help, long-term care facilities range from assisted living to full-scale 24-hour nursing facilities.

> **TIP:** Your local Administration on Aging can be a great resource in helping locate and evaluate long-term care alternatives in your geographic region. Contact them at **www.aoa.gov** or call their Eldercare Locater at 800.677.1116.

What are alternatives to a nursing home?
Many elderly people may not want or need the services of a full-scale nursing home. There are many alternatives:

▶ **COMMUNITY SERVICES.** This may include adult day care facilities where seniors may stay during certain times of the day or home health caregivers. Programs such as Meals-on-Wheels may help with cooking needs. Look in your local phone book to see what other community services may assist with elder needs.

▶ **ASSISTED LIVING FACILITIES.** These facilities allow seniors to live independently within a larger complex. They generally focus on elderly citizens who need some help with their daily activities, but who do not need the specialized care of a nursing home. The facility may help with tasks such as bathing, meals and prescription drug medication reminders.

▶ **GOVERNMENT-SUBSIDIZED SENIOR HOUSING.** This housing allows low-income seniors with no major medical conditions to live independently in a large housing complex. You will need to fill out an application and meet your state's income limits. Many of these programs have waiting lists. You generally have to pay a percentage of your income for rent.

▶ **RETIREMENT COMMUNITIES.** These communities serve elderly people who can live independently through skilled nursing facilities. The largest, most extensive communities provide housing, meals and medical care for the rest of the retiree's life. You normally pay an entrance fee along with a monthly fee. For more information on the accreditation of retirement communities, contact the Continuing Care Accreditation Commission at 202.783.7286 or online at **www.ccaconline.org**.

How can we determine what the best long-term care is for our situation? *That will depend on many factors. You may be able to live independently for many years, or you may need specialized medical care that is best suited to a skilled nursing facility.* Discuss this with your spouse and adult children. Also talk with your doctor about facilities in the area and how they meet your specific needs. Your financial condition will also play a role in determining which long-term care option is best for you. Contact your local Agency on Aging for information on facilities in your area.

What is the difference between skilled nursing care and intermediate care? *The terms are not interchangeable.* They were created along with the creation of Medicare and Medicaid.

• Skilled nursing facility. This facility has 24-hour nursing services available to residents.

• Intermediate nursing facility. These facilities provide health services and some nursing supervision. They also provide help with eating, dressing and other personal needs. Medicaid may pay for intermediate care but Medicare never does.

What should I consider when I tour nursing home facilities? There are many things you need to remember when touring nursing home facilities. Many social services groups can provide checklists. Some things to keep in mind include:

- Does the facility have a current license?
- What are the different levels of care provided by the facility?
- What kind of social activities does the facility provide?
- Are the meals nutritious and good? Can they meet any dietary restrictions you have?
- What are basic charges and what are extra charges?
- How often are fees increased?
- What kind of payment does the facility accept?
- Does your physician have a good relationship with the facility?
- Under what circumstances can the facility discharge you?
- Is the facility clean?
- Are staff members courteous to each other and residents?
- What kind of weekly religious services are held at the facility?
- How do the current residents look—happy, content and well-cared for?
- What are the emergency and evacuation policies of the facility?
- Is there a pharmacy in the facility?
- What kind of physical and occupational therapy is available onsite?
- What is the size and condition of each room and how many roommates will you have?
- What are the visiting hours?

If we choose a nursing home, what issues should influence our selection? *Many factors go into deciding which nursing home suits your needs.* First, consider all the alternatives. You may not need a full nursing home, but instead may enjoy the independence of an assisted living facility. Your ability to finance nursing care, both through your own assets and public aid, should be a strong factor in your decision. Find out which programs you qualify for and which facilities are approved by and accept Medicare and Medicaid funds.

What should I know about long-term care insurance? *Long-term care insurance is relatively new but gaining in popularity.* These policies can cover home care and nursing home care. Some may only cover stays in Medicare-approved facilities. The best policies cover all levels of nursing care: skilled, intermediate and

custodial. Some policies may require a hospital stay before entering a nursing home. The policy should last your lifetime and guarantee your ability to renew. Contact your nearest SHIP to see if one of these policies is right for you.

> **TIP:** For more information about long-term care insurance, get a copy of *A Shopper's Guide to Long-Term Care Insurance* from the National Association of Insurance Commissioners, 2301 McGee Street, Suite 800, Kansas City, MO 64108-3600.

Will Medicare help pay for nursing home expenses? For a caregiver? *Medicare will pay some nursing home costs under limited conditions but generally does not pay for long-term nursing care.* Medicare beneficiaries must require skilled nursing or rehabilitation services and receive them from a Medicare-approved skilled nursing home after a qualifying hospital stay of at least 3 days. It pays for certain hospice and home health care services. Medicare covers physician and nursing services, pain medication, medical supplies, physical and occupational therapy and social services counseling. Only "medically necessary" home health services are also covered. The Medicare program must approve the agency making home visits.

The facility we chose wants us to submit a full financial disclosure of our assets. Should we refuse? *No. Most long-term care facilities require full financial disclosure from prospective residents who will be paying privately.* Many nursing home residents start paying with their own funds but eventually must rely on Medicaid. The facility wants to know how long you can pay using your own funds and when you will need to apply for Medicaid.

Will I give up any of my personal rights if I enter a long-term care facility? *No. Nursing homes are subject to both state and federal government regulation.* They can require you to abide by its facility rules, and you must respect the rights of other residents and staff as you would in any other living arrangement. But you do not relinquish your civil rights by living in a nursing home. Many states have adopted a nursing home residents' bill of rights. The facilities must generally inform residents of their rights both in writing and orally.

What rights do I have as a resident of a nursing home? *The Nursing Home Reform Act of 1997 provides nursing home residents with minimum basic rights.* The nursing home must provide you written information about your funds, how to file a complaint with the state, any room changes, health care advance directives and Medicare and Medicaid eligibility.

As a nursing home resident, you have the right to choose your own doctor, participate in your care and file complaints about your care. The nursing home must allow your doctor to have access to you at all times.

I am worried about my privacy in a nursing home. What are my privacy rights? *States require that facilities maintain their residents' right to privacy.* This means that you have a right to choose and maintain your own physician, manage your financial assets, be medically treated in private, keep confidential records, have private visitation with any visitor, send and receive mail unopened and make telephone calls unmonitored.

My nursing home wants to move me to another room on the other side of the nursing home. Can I stop this? *You have the right to not be arbitrarily moved to another room within a licensed nursing home.* The nursing home, however, does have the right to move you involuntarily if the move is due to an incompatibility with your current roommate, if the move is in your best interest or if medical reasons exist.

Generally, the nursing home must give you written advanced notice stating the reason for the transfer. This notification requirement may be waived in an emergency situation.

My nursing home said it was transferring me to another facility. Can I object? *A nursing home can only transfer or discharge you for specific reasons.*

EXAMPLE: You can be transferred if you have not paid your fees or the nursing home is closing or no longer providing the kind of care you require. Your doctor may indicate that a transfer to another facility is in your best interest, or a Medicare or Medicaid review may conclude that you no longer require the services of the nursing home you are in.

A nursing home cannot discharge you because you are a Medicaid recipient. If the nursing home indicates that it will be transferring you or discharging you, talk to them and make sure you understand the specific reasons. You can also appeal a facility's decision to transfer you through your state's appeals process.

> **TIP:** Contact your state's Long-Term Care Ombudsman for assistance in this situation.

How do I file a complaint against a long-term care facility? *First, try to resolve the matter with the facility's staff and management.* If you cannot come to an agreement that suits both parties, contact your SHIP for information on how to file a complaint and start an investigation in your area.

What is the "Ombudsman Program" for long-term care? *The Older Americans Act created the Long-Term Care Ombudsman Program.* Each state is required to have an ombudsman program to receive and investigate complaints. The program also seeks to educate consumers about long-term care options and facilities. Contact your local Agency on Aging to learn more about your state's program.

ALZHEIMER'S DISEASE

Alzheimer's disease has become more prevalent as medical technology has improved and the population ages. Many seniors suffer from one form of dementia or another. Living day-to-day with dementia or Alzheimer's can put a strain on any family. The Alzheimer's Association estimates that 14 million people will develop Alzheimer's by the middle of this century.

Will Medicare cover the cost of my spouse's Alzheimer's care? *Medicare will cover some, but not all of the services required to care for Alzheimer's.* For example, it does not cover the cost of long-term nursing home care.

TIP: The Alzheimer's Association and the American Bar Association have started the Medicare Advocacy Project to help Medicare beneficiaries who have Alzheimer's disease. For information on this program, see **www.alz. org/Advocacy/priorities/medicare/MAP.asp**.

Medicare denied my claims for some of my Alzheimer's treatment. What can I do? *Make sure your treatment of Alzheimer's is billed under the correct billing code. If treatment is billed under an older dementia code, you may have to pay more.* Medicare can also no longer automatically deny you coverage for rehabilitative services based on a dementia diagnosis. It now has to determine coverage on a case-by-case basis.

Can I receive home health care benefits from Medicare for the treatment of my spouse's Alzheimer's? *Yes.* Medicare should cover home health care services for "homebound" Medicare beneficiaries.

CAUTION: Medicare's definition of homebound is very strict, so be sure to check with your physician as to the most current definition.

My spouse was diagnosed with Alzheimer's disease. Can I still purchase long-term care insurance? *Once a person is diagnosed with Alzheimer's disease, it is generally too late to apply for long-term care insurance.* That is why it is important for you and your spouse to make informed decisions about your long-term care options before the choice is made for you.

I am the primary caregiver for my husband who has Alzheimer's, and I am exhausted. What kind of help can I get? *As the primary caregiver, you need to take a break and have some time to rest. Families, friends and your spiritual advisor can help on a daily basis, but you may need more time than that. Contact home health providers.* They can send someone to your house on a regular basis to allow you some free time. Other services may help you with your shopping or cooking. Another option is an adult day care facility. These facilities can provide your spouse with activities geared toward Alzheimer's patients. Some facilities even provide "respite care"—they will provide full-time care for the Alzheimer sufferer for a short period of time, usually a few days.

TIP: Call your local chapter of the Alzheimer's Association for more information on services in your area.

ORGAN DONATION

Donating your organs can be your last charitable act. The National Transplant Act governs many aspects of the process, and each state allows for you to register your wishes in some manner.

How can I donate my organs to others when I die? *Some states allow you to register as an organ donor when you register for your driver's license.* In this case, there will be some sort of symbol on your driver's license to indicate your wish to be an organ donor. You can also obtain a form from one of the national organ banks. This is called a "Uniform Organ Card." You can also indicate your wishes in your living will and/or durable power of attorney for health care.

TIP: Give a copy of these documents to your family, doctor and the person you gave your durable power of attorney to. That way there will be no question as to your intent.

Who will receive my organs? *The National Transplant Act determines who will receive your organs based on need.* Your organs will go to a person who matches your blood type and tissue type.

If I donate my organs, will my family still be able to have an open casket at my funeral?
Yes. Your body is still treated with dignity by the doctors and nurses who perform anatomical gift surgeries. Any normal service will still be able to be performed with organ donation.

Does my estate have to pay for the procedure?
No. It is considered a donation and your family will not have to pay for any costs of the procedure. Laws also forbid families from receiving payment for organ donations made by deceased family members.

Can I change my mind about organ donation?
Yes. Tear up any written documents that you have signed in the past. Tell your family, physician and the person designated to act as your durable power of attorney to do the same. If you have signed the back or your driver's license, you can usually write "VOID" over your signature. In this instance, also call your state's organ donation hotline to tell them of your change of mind.

DEATH OF YOUR SPOUSE

My spouse recently passed away, and there are so many loose ends to tie up. What should I do next?
Give yourself some time after the funeral or other service. You will need to make sure that you have a copy of the death certificate. Financial institutions and others you may deal with may request a copy before they disperse funds or property.

> **TIP:** Make sure you locate the original will so it can be entered into the probate court in the county where your spouse lived.

Who should I contact if my spouse dies?
First, contact relatives and friends. They can be of great comfort and assistance during this time. Contact the deceased's employer so the proper paperwork can be started. The employer can take care of final wage or salary payments and any retirement savings accounts set up through the employer. Also, notify your local Social Security office. You will receive a one-time death benefit from Social Security. Also, check with your bank and any other financial institution where accounts are held in order to ensure proper distribution of assets.

I am not sure what benefits I am eligible for after my spouse's death. How can I find out?
First, check with your spouse's employer to determine if your spouse had any retirement benefits that are payable to you as the beneficiary. Also, call your local Social Security office to inquire about a death benefit you may be eligible for as a surviving spouse. If your spouse was a member of the military, you may be eligible for military veterans' benefits. Contact your local Veterans' Administration office if you think you qualify.

Hopefully, you and your spouse talked about what would happen in the event of either of your deaths. Talking ahead of time about how you will be supported after your spouse's death can be difficult, but it will save you a lot of time, stress and uncertainty and provide a needed level of security.

ELDER RIGHTS

DISCRIMINATION

Seniors are often the target of discrimination— some intentional and some not. Either way, know when you are being discriminated against and demand your rights.

> Both federal and state laws forbid discrimination based on age. This applies to employment, housing and participation in federal aid programs.

What is the Age Discrimination in Employment Act (ADEA)?
The Age Discrimination in Employment Act forbids employers from discriminating against an employee based on his or her age. The law applies to employees and applicants over the age of 40.

Most states have also enacted similar laws.

> **TIP:** Check with your local librarian to see whether any community service groups have information available about age discrimination in your area. Also, contact the nearest Equal Employment Opportunity Commission (EEOC) office for more information.

Some of my benefits have been cut back at work since they cost more for older workers. Is that okay? *No. The Older Workers Benefit Protection Act of 1990 forbids employers from denying benefits to older employees.* The only way for an employer to lower benefits is if the cost of providing reduced benefits to older workers is the same as the cost of providing reduced benefits to younger workers.

I am disabled. What protections do I have under the law? *The Americans With Disabilities Act (ADA) prohibits employers from discriminating based on a disability. Many states have enacted similar laws.* The law applies to private employers with more than 15 employees and prohibits discrimination based on both actual and perceived disabilities. This means that your employer cannot fire you because he or she thinks you cannot perform your essential job functions based on a mistaken belief as to your "disability."

To qualify for protection under the ADA, you must be able to perform the job's essential functions with or without accommodation. This means that your employer is not discriminating against you by demoting you because you cannot lift more than 15 pounds when the job requires lifting 20 pound boxes on a regular basis.

> **TIP:** If you think you have been a victim of discrimination, talk with your employer. Chances are you can figure out a solution that fits both of your needs. If no solution is reached, you must file a complaint within a specific amount of time, depending on whether you file under the ADA or state statute.

How does the Fair Housing Act protect older people? *The Fair Housing Act prohibits discrimination in any activities relating to the sale, rental or financing of dwellings because of race, color, religion, sex, handicap, family status or national origin. This Act protects older, handicapped Americans. If you have a disability, a realtor or landlord cannot discriminate against you based on that handicap.*

> **TIP:** If you think you have been the subject of discrimination, contact the nearest Equal Employment Opportunity Commission (EEOC) office for more information.

> **TIP:** Many states have enacted state laws and regulations forbidding age discrimination in housing contracts. Check with your local library or social services office to find out about the laws in your state.

How can the Equal Credit Opportunity Act assist me? *The Equal Credit Opportunity Act (ECOA) prohibits creditors from denying you credit based on your age.* A creditor will normally ask questions about your income, expenses and may ask your age if relevant to your ability to repay a loan. The use of your age is strictly regulated under the Act.

> **TIP:** If you are denied credit, make a written request for the reasons. If the problem continues, you may sue the creditor and recover damages, including attorney's fees and punitive damages.

What other discrimination issues should older people be aware of? *The Age Discrimination Act forbids discrimination based on your age in any federally funded program.* This includes federally funded housing, welfare and health and rehabilitation programs.

> **TIP:** Contact your regional Office for Civil Rights in person or in writing if you feel you have been discriminated against because of your age. Or you can write to:
>
> Director
> Office for Civil Rights
> U.S. Dept. of Health and Human Services
> 200 Independence Ave. S.W.—Room 506-F
> Washington, D.C. 20201

DOMESTIC VIOLENCE

What is elder abuse? *Abuse is intentional hurting of another person. The hurt can be in many forms: physical, mental or financial.* Abuse can also involve physical and medical neglect. A caregiver may confine an elderly person and allow minimal or no contact with the person.

> Some states have laws making it a crime to mistreat or exploit people 65 and older. Criminals may face harsher penalties for acts against seniors than for the same act against younger citizens.

My caretaker has become abusive. What can I do? *If you feel you are in immediate danger, call 911. Tell the responding officers of your situation and the concern for your own safety.* If there is no immediate danger, check with your local adult protective services agency. A call to your library or city hall should help you locate resources in your area. These agencies can investigate suspected abuse and help families find proper support and care.

> **TIP:** Call the National Center for Elder Abuse at 800.677.1116 for a list of state elder abuse hotlines. Or check their Web site (www.elderabusecenter.org) for your hotline number.

If I report my abuser, who will take care of me? *There are many options available to seniors who need extra help. The federal Administration on Aging is a good starting point.* The Administration works with the National Center for Elder Abuse and has created an "Eldercare Locator." The phone number is 800.677.1116, or you can visit their Web site at **www.eldercare.gov/Eldercare/Public/Home.asp**. They can provide you with information and referrals for resources in your area. Services may include in-home care with day-to-day tasks, home health care workers to help with medical needs and delivery of meals. The Administration can also help you locate area adult day care facilities, senior centers and nursing homes.

What else can I do? *Always report any suspected elder abuse. If you have been the victim of abuse, see your doctor.* The doctor can check you for injuries and provide you with elder resources in your community.

> **TIP:** Call 911 if there is an immediate danger or your local Adult Protective Service program for guidance.

DRIVING

Driving can be difficult at any age. Seniors in particular need to be aware that they can lose their driving privileges based on medical conditions, traffic violations and failed driving tests.

I am afraid my elderly father could endanger himself and others because of his driving abilities. What can I do about it? *Many states offer "refresher" courses for seniors. Some insurance companies even offer discounts to seniors who complete these courses.* States such as California also allow concerned people to fill out requests for driver re-examinations at their local department of motor vehicles (DMV). This will notify the DMV about a possibly unsafe driver. Other states, such as Texas, allow doctors and family members to notify the DMV of any disability that may affect the driving qualifications of a driver.

My daughter wants to have my driver's license revoked. Do I have any options? *Some states allow for partial or complete retesting, restrictions to driving privileges or complete cancellation of driving privileges.* See if your state issues driver's licenses for a shorter period of time than a regular license. Or you may qualify for a restricted license. This may allow you to drive only during daylight hours or restrict you from highway and freeway driving. Another possible restriction is allowing you to drive only within a short distance from your home, for example 20 miles.

My insurance company revoked my auto insurance after I had an accident. Can they do that? *An insurance company can revoke your car insurance if your license is suspended or revoked as a result of an accident.* In most cases, you must receive written notification of the company's intent to cancel at least 30 days before cancellation.

Do I really need auto insurance? *Yes. All states require that each driver operating an automobile in their state have liability insurance.* Proof of insurance must be in your car at all times. Failure to have car insurance can result in a costly fine.

> **TIP:** Although monthly car insurance premiums may seem like an added strain on elderly people's fixed incomes, you cannot afford to be without it. If you are in an accident and have no insurance, you may have to personally pay for any damages to other cars or property as well as medical bills for any person injured as a result of an accident. The cost of this far exceeds the monthly premiums.

GRANDPARENT RIGHTS

My daughter says she will not let me visit with my granddaughter. Can she do this? *Laws regarding grandparent visitation varies with each state.* Some states may allow you to go to court and petition for visitation rights. Your right to visitation is usually determined on different circumstances. Your child may have died or divorced, leaving you with limited access to your grandchildren.

Courts will consider whether someone else has adopted the grandchild when determining your right to visitation. For example, adoption terminates the legal relationship between the child and his blood parent. Courts have generally held that this parental termination carries over to your rights as a biological grandparent. This means that if another family adopts your grandchild, you may have no legal relationship with the grandchild—and thus no legal right to visitation. But courts have not been this strict when a stepparent or another relative adopts the child.

> **TIP:** For more information on your rights as a grandparent, contact:
>
> The Grandparent Information Center
> c/o AARP
> 601 E Street N.W.
> Washington D.C., 20049

BENEFITS

SOCIAL SECURITY

Social Security was started in the late 1930s to guarantee that each retired worker over the age of 65 had a guaranteed source of income. Social Security has undergone many changes since then, but it still guarantees the right to receive payments after retirement. Both workers and employers fund the program and pay a percentage of the worker's salary into Social Security. However, those payments are not held in a separate account for you to use at your retirement. Funds collected today are used to fund current Social Security beneficiary payments.

Social Security has become an integral part of our society. Almost all workers are in jobs that are covered (taxed) by Social Security. Almost every current retiree receives Social Security benefit payments each month. For two-thirds of senior citizens, Social Security is their major source of income. There are three major components of Social Security: retirement benefits, disability benefits and Supplemental Security Income.

> **TIP:** The Social Security Administration has numerous pamphlets and brochures to help seniors navigate the complex maze that is Social Security. Call their toll-free telephone number, 800.772.1213. The TYY telephone number is 800.325.0778. Or check their Web site for information and forms: **www.ssa. gov**. Either a phone call to the Social Security Administration or a visit to their Web site can lead you to your nearest Social Security office where you can speak to a representative in person.

Who is eligible for Social Security benefits?

You are generally eligible for Social Security benefits after you have worked a total of 10 years in work covered by Social Security. The work is "covered" by Social Security if both the employee and employer pay a tax to the Social Security Administration. You do not have to work for a continuous 10-year period. Your work time can accumulate over your life.

The Social Security Administration has different eligibility requirements for different types of employment. These different types include federal government employees, state government employees, self-employed persons, military personnel, farmers, nonprofit employees and overseas workers.

> **TIP:** Visit your local Social Security office or go online at **www.ssa.gov/retire2/qualify** for more detailed information.

I am self-employed. Am I still eligible for Social Security benefits?

Yes. Instead of an employer reporting your Social Security taxes to the government, you must make these payments yourself when you file your federal income tax return. Report your yearly earnings on a Schedule SE along with your other tax return documents.

Can I work after retiring and still receive Social Security benefits?

After you reach your full retirement age, you can collect retirement benefits and still continue to work without any reduction in your benefits. Delayed retirement credit is generally given for retirement after the full retirement age. But no credit is given after age 70. To receive full credit, you must be insured at your full retirement age. You will receive increased benefits for each year you delay retirement.

When should I retire so that I can collect maximum benefits under Social Security?

This depends on you current age. Social Security currently has a graduated retirement age between ages 65 and 67. For anyone born before 1938, full retirement age is 65. Between 1938 and 1960, the age is graduated upwards every 2 months until those born in 1960 or later will reach full retirement age at 67.

You can also take early retirement benefits starting at age 62. But you will receive less money if you chose to begin these early payments. Further, receiving maximum benefits is complicated by how long you will live after you start receiving your benefits, and if you plan on working after you start to collect benefits.

> **TIP:** These issues are highly complex—the Social Security Administration suggests exploring your options with one of their representatives at 800.772.1213. Contact your local Social Security office to discuss the best option for you.

I am divorced. Can my ex-spouse collect Social Security on my record?

In some cases, yes. He or she can collect Social Security disability benefits. You must have been married for at least 10 years. Your ex-spouse must be at least 62 years old and currently unmarried. He or she cannot be eligible for equal or higher benefits on his or her own Social Security record.

> **The amount of benefits paid to your ex-spouse has no effect on the amount of your benefits or your current spouse's benefits.**

What are "survivor's benefits"?

If you are a fully insured worker, meaning you have met the Social Security eligibility requirements, your Social Security benefits can be paid to a surviving family member at your death. Eligible family members include a surviving spouse over age 60 and an ex-spouse over age 60 if you were married more than 10 years.

What are "disability benefits"?

Social Security pays disability benefits to insured applicants—meaning the applicant meets Social Security eligibility requirements—who also meet the Administration's definition of "disabled." "Disability" under Social Security is based on a person's inability to work because of a medical condition. You are considered disabled if:

- you cannot do work that you did before and the Administration decides that you cannot adjust to other work because of a medical condition;
- your disability lasts or is expected to last for at least 1 year or result in death.

What if the Social Security Administration reduces or terminates my benefits? *The Social Security Administration can reduce or terminate your benefits based on a finding that your income exceeds a threshold limit, you are no longer fully disabled or a partial disability no longer exists.* You have 60 days to appeal the Social Security Administration's decision, starting the day after you receive notice of the change in your status. If you want to receive benefits during the appeals process, you must ask for an appeal within 10 days of receiving the reduction or termination letter.

> **TIP:** Your appeal must be in writing. The Social Security Administration has forms you can use.

What is a "representative payee"? *A representative payee is someone else who has the right to collect your Social Security payments.* You may elect to do this when you are no longer able to manage your funds by yourself. These are generally family members or nursing homes responsible for your day-to-day care. You must notify the Social Security Administration that you are incapable of handling your funds. The Social Security Administration can appoint a representative payee, or you can indicate who you would like to serve.

How can I get a copy of my Social Security Statement? *Each year, the Social Security Administration sends each worker an annual statement of the estimated future Social Security benefits based on their reported income.* If you do not receive this statement, contact your local Social Security office. You can also request a statement online at **www.ssa.gov.**

I received a "Notice of Overpayment" from the Social Security Administration. What is it and what should I do? *You may get a "Notice of Overpayment" if the Social Security Administration sends you more money than you are entitled to.* The notice will usually tell you that you were overpaid and the overpayment amount will be deducted from your next payment. You have the right to appeal this notice, but must do so within 30 days of receiving

the notice. You can ask the Social Security Administration to reconsider the overpayment or to waive its rights to the overpayment.

How do I apply for benefits? The Social Security Administration suggests that you apply for your benefits at least 3 months before you want to start receiving them.

> **TIP:** ou can apply for benefits online at **www.ssa.gov**, or you can call 800.772.1213. You will need to supply your Social Security number, your birth certificate, your previous year's tax return and W-2 forms, and your bank account information so your benefits can be deposited directly into your bank account.

Can my dependents receive my Social Security benefits? *Yes.* Retirement or disability payments can be made to spouses over age 62 and spouses under age 62 if the spouse is caring for a minor or disabled child.

Do I have to pay tax on my Social Security income? You may have to pay federal income tax on up to one-half of your Social Security benefits for any year in which your adjusted gross income plus nontaxable interest income and one-half of your Social Security benefits exceed a base amount.

> **TIP:** Contact your local Social Security office if you have additional income to find out more.

What is Social Security Disability Insurance? *This pays benefits to you and certain members of your family if you are "insured," meaning that you worked long enough and paid Social Security taxes.* You must meet the Social Security Administration's strict definition of disabled. If you do, you will receive a monthly payment. The program does not pay for partial or temporary disability. Call or visit your local Social Security office to find out if you qualify for this program.

What is Supplemental Security Income? *Supplemental Security Income pays benefits to the elderly and disabled based on financial need.* This program does not require that you have worked and paid into the Social Security system. The Social Security Administration will count some assets and not others towards their determination of your need.

EXAMPLE: Your home and one automobile do not count.

> **Some states supplement the benefit amount with a state program.**

VETERAN'S BENEFITS

The Department of Veterans Affairs (VA) is responsible for providing benefits to veterans and their families. It has a nationwide system of health benefits, financial assistance and burial benefits. The most well-known component of the VA is its medical care program. Most veterans must enroll in the program to receive benefits.

> **TIP:** The types and ranges of veterans' benefits are complex. It is important to contact your local VA office to find out whether you qualify for benefits and if so, for what types of benefits. Call the VA's Health Benefits Service Center Monday through Friday between 8 a.m. and 8 p.m. (Eastern Time) at 877.222.VETS to learn more.

What are some of the benefit programs for veterans? As a U.S. veteran, you may be eligible for various benefits, including:

- medical care and insurance
- dental insurance
- prescription drug assistance
- retirement pensions
- alcohol and drug addiction treatment
- some burial benefits

How do I find out if I am eligible for benefits? *First, the VA will determine if you qualify for "veteran status." This generally means you were an active-duty member of the Army, Navy, Air Force or Marines and you were not dishonorably discharged.* Some veterans must have served active duty for 24-continuous months. Once your veteran status is verified, the VA will place you in a "priority group," with some groups having a higher priority for enrollment. For example, a veteran who has a "service-connected" disability of more than 50

percent has the highest priority for enrollment. Service-connected means the veteran was disabled while in active service in the line of duty.

Do I have to pay for veteran medical benefits? *This will depend on which "priority group" you qualify for.* Some veterans have to pay minimal copayments.

> **TIP:** To find out more, call the VA's Health Benefits Service Center, Monday through Friday between 8 a.m. and 8 p.m. (Eastern Time) at 1.877.222.VETS.

Who else beside veterans may be eligible for benefits from the VA? *A disabled veteran's spouse, widow, children or dependent parents may also receive VA benefits.* These benefits may include medical care, pensions and death benefits.

My spouse recently died. Can the Department of Veterans' Affairs help with providing a marker? *Yes. As long as your spouse was not dishonorably discharged, he or she is eligible to receive a headstone and marker.* If the burial is in a national cemetery, the cemetery can order the headstone or marker. Otherwise, you will have to order it through your local VA office. You can also receive an American flag.

PENSIONS

For many elderly workers, pensions will help pay for many of the costs associated with their retirement. You should fully understand your pension program both before and after you retire. While still working, be sure to ask the administrator of your company's pension plan any questions you may have about the plan and your savings in it.

> **TIP:** Many complicated rules govern pension plans. The Department of Labor's Employee Benefits Security Administration (EBSA) oversees pension plans. Contact your local EBSA office if you have any questions.

What is a pension plan and who can participate? *Pension plans allow workers to defer a portion of their salary into a financial account.* The worker then receives these benefits at retirement. Companies do not have to offer pension plans to their employees. If they do offer a pension plan, it does not have to offer the plan to all employees.

If your employer offers a pension plan, you will have to meet certain eligibility requirements. These generally consist of an age requirement and a minimum length of employment.

EXAMPLE: Most plans require that participants be at least 21 years old and have worked for the company for at least 1 year. You generally also have to work a certain number of years to become "vested" in the plan. You do not have a legal right to collect money in your pension until you are vested.

What are the different types of pension plans?
Pension plans can be divided into two general categories: defined contribution plans and defined benefit plans.

- ▸ **DEFINED CONTRIBUTION PLANS.** In these plans, a separate account is set up for each participant. Generally, both the employer and employee pay in a specific amount. Employers will normally "match" contributions up to a certain percentage of the employee's pay. Common defined contribution plans include 401(k) plans, profit-sharing plans and employee stock ownership plans. The contributions by both the employer and the employee, along with any profits made by the company, determine your benefits at retirement.

- ▸ **DEFINED BENEFIT PLANS.** These are plans that pay a specific amount to the participant at retirement. The plan sets the amount of each participant's benefit, as opposed to each participant's contribution in a defined contribution plan.

How can I be sure that my pension fund is safe?
Both defined contribution plans and defined benefit plans are subject to fund mismanagement. Poor management can reduce the amount of money in the plan and affect your payout at retirement. Federal pension insurance applies to some, but not all, pension plans.

> **TIP:** It is up to you to review your pension plan statements and ask your plan administrator questions about any discrepancies you may find.

What is ERISA and how does it affect me?
The Employee Retirement Income Security Act (ERISA) protects worker's retirement funds. It sets minimum standards and guarantees employees' rights under pension plans. It also governs plans' fiduciary responsibilities to manage the fund. The fiduciary, usually your plan administrator, must manage the fund with the participants' best interest in mind. The fiduciary must act prudently in managing the fund and must diversify investments in the fund to minimize losses.

What is a Summary Plan Description?
Private employers that offer pension plans must provide a Summary Plan Description (SPD) to each participant. The SPD must state who can participate in the plan, how the plan determines benefits, how old you have to be to receive benefits under the plan, any vesting schedule, who the plan administrator is and all procedures relating to claims against the pension plan.

What is a Summary Annual Report?
Every pension plan is required to provide each participant with a Summary Annual Report (SAR). This SAR will summarize the financial reporting that each plan is required to file each year with the federal government. It will show you the amount of gain or loss in the plan's investments and plan expenses. You can also request (in writing) the actual forms that the plan filed with the Internal Revenue Service.

My employer told me I would not be receiving as much in benefits as I thought because I had a "break in service." What is this?
A break in service can affect the amount of pension "credits" you earn. Under ERISA, a plan may provide that an employee incurs a break in service if he or she fails to complete more than 500 hours of service in a 1-year period. On returning to work more than 500 hours in a 1-year period, you lose those benefits

that were not vested if the number of years of your break is greater than the number of years credited before your break.

CAUTION: Breaks in service are governed by very complex rules. In some cases, when you return to employment, you have the immediate right to rejoin the pension plan, and in other situations, you must wait to enroll. Read your SPD to find out about your plan's specific break in service rules. Contact your plan administrator and your local Employee Benefits Security Administration office if you have any questions.

When can I start receiving my benefits?
ERISA rules govern when you can start to receive benefits under a pension plan. Plans normally define a retirement age at which time you can start to receive benefits. Some plans will allow early payment of benefits if you terminate your employment, become disabled or die.

> **TIP:** Rules vary according to the type of plan—defined contribution plan or defined benefit plan—so be sure to consult your SPD or contact your plan administrator.

How do I claim my benefits? *Each plan will set the rules on how benefits are received.*
ERISA does, however, require that each plan have a written procedure in place for claims and any appeals of claim benefits. Check with your SPD or plan administrator to find out what steps you need to take.

What if I die before I receive my pension benefits? Can my spouse receive them?
ERISA allows some surviving spouses to receive benefits if the participant was vested in the plan before his or her death. The amount of benefits will depend on what type of plan the employee participated in and whether benefits had already begun to be paid out.

> **TIP:** Check with your SPD or plan administrator to find out whether survivor benefits exist.

My pension plan has a "joint and survivor annuity." What does this mean? This means that your spouse will receive a portion of your benefit payments even if you die.

EXAMPLE: In a defined benefit plan, you will receive monthly installments for the rest of your life. On your death, your spouse will receive continued benefits. The payment does not have to be for the full amount paid to you during your lifetime, but it must be at least 50 percent of the amount paid to you. You and your spouse can waive the right to these payments and choose to receive payment in another form.

I was recently fired. What happens to my pension plan account? *Most defined contribution plans allow for a lump-sum payment in the amount of your accrued benefits.*
This is not always the best solution. You will have to pay substantial taxes on this lump-sum amount. It is best to "roll over" these funds into another retirement savings vehicle.

> **TIP:** You generally have 60 days to roll over your funds into another account, such as an Individual Retirement Account (IRA).

Defined benefit plans, on the other hand, will most likely still pay benefits when you reach the retirement age specified in the plan. If you are fired, be sure you have a copy of the SPD. This will explain your rights regarding accrued benefit money for this situation.

My employer terminated its pension plan. Can it do this? *Yes. ERISA governs all pension plan terminations and provides some protection to participants.* Thus, in most cases, you will become 100 percent vested in all accrued benefits at the time your employer terminates the plan.

WILLS AND TRUSTS

WILLS

Having a will enables you to control where your property—both personal and real estate—goes after your death. Without out a will, your property will go to people based on your state's priority laws.

A will is just one tool that can be used to distribute your property upon death.

Is a will really necessary? *Yes. You want to make sure the people you care about receive your property.* With a will, you can leave your real estate, financial assets and personal belongings to whomever you wish, even to charities.

CAUTION: Remember that retirement benefits, insurance policies and any bank account held in joint tenancy passes to your designated beneficiary under those policies. If you want to change the beneficiary in any of the policies, you must do so through the policy, not your will.

Do I need a lawyer to draft a will? *A lawyer can be helpful in drafting a will that meets your state's legal requirements, but you do not have to use an attorney to create a will.* If you are not using an attorney, carefully review your state's laws governing wills. If you do not follow the laws, your will may be invalid.

> **TIP:** Always follow two major rules when executing a will: first, sign the will at the end; second, sign it preferably before three witnesses—always before two—and ask them to add their names to the attestation clause at the end, along with their addresses. The people who sign as witnesses cannot also be beneficiaries in your will.

What other options do I have to distribute my property besides a will? *Wills must go through what is called probate. This can cause delays and cost money.* Instead of a will, you can establish a living trust. You can also hold your assets jointly with rights of survivorship. Property held jointly passes to the survivor. You can set up your bank accounts as "payable on death" and that person will be paid any assets in the account on your death.

> **TIP:** You may hold and distribute your property in numerous ways, but it is always best to have a will to cover any property that already has a designated beneficiary or passes outside your will.

What if I die without a will? *Dying without a will is known as "intestate."* State laws, which are substantially the same, will provide for the distribution of your property, and this may not be how you want your property distributed. Generally, your surviving spouse and children receive the majority of your property.

Can I give everything to my grandchildren instead of my spouse or children? *With a will, you can give your property to whomever you want. But most states do not allow you to leave absolutely nothing to your spouse.* A surviving spouse can "renounce" your will and the state will then give the spouse a share of your estate, depending on whether you have children or not. But if you die without a will, your property will go to your surviving spouse first, then to surviving children. So, if you want to make sure your grandchildren receive your property, you will need to make a valid will that complies with your state's laws.

Now that I am getting older, I have changed my mind about some of my beneficiaries in my will. How can I change my will? *You can make changes to a valid will with a "codicil."* A codicil is a clause added to a will to change, confirm or explain provisions of the will. The codicil must be executed and witnessed in the same manner as the original will.

TRUSTS

A trust is an arrangement in which you transfer property to a second person for the benefit of a third person. The person creating the trust is called the "grantor." The person holding legal title to the trust property is the "trustee." The person to whose benefit the trust is created is the "beneficiary." All three of the people—the grantor, trustee and beneficiary—can be the same person.

Living trusts are one important tool in distributing your property upon death.

CAUTION: Living trusts can be the subject of consumer fraud. Be very cautious if someone approaches you with a living trust scenario that sounds too good to be true. Get advice from someone you trust and never feel pressured to sign any documents immediately.

What is a living trust, and how can it assist me? A living trust is created during your lifetime. A revocable living trust—meaning you can revoke it during your lifetime—is an increasingly popular way to avoid probate. You place property in the trust. To do so, you will have to give the trust legal ownership of the property.

EXAMPLE: You register all new assets in the name of the trust. You can name yourself or someone else as trustee. You then reserve the right to revoke the trust so the property can be returned to you.

Generally, the trust will designate who is to receive the property at your death. This typically avoids probate of the property.

What advantages does a living trust have that a will does not? *A living trust avoids the inefficient and expensive probate system. It usually avoids the delays and costs involved with probate courts.* You can enjoy all the income from the trust assets during your lifetime. You do not lose control of your property because you can always terminate, modify or revoke the trust and reclaim the assets.

> **TIP:** Trusts also ensure privacy. Unlike trusts, property going through probate is a public record. Anyone can gain access to this personal information in probate.

How do I create a living trust? A *living trust is established by creating a trust document.* The trust document provides instructions for managing the trust property during your lifetime. It also directs the distribution of the trust property at your death.

If I put all my property in a living trust, do I still need a will? *It is best to have both. Although you may place all your property in a living trust, there may be assets outside the trust that require probate.* This may include someone owing you money or a legal claim you have against someone. You also want a will to name a personal guardian of any minor children.

Will I save taxes by using a living trust? *No. Assets in your living trust are included in your estate for estate tax purposes.* But you can include in the trust document any tax-saving provisions that you could include in a will.

Can my creditors reach the assets in my living trust? *Yes. Because living trusts are fully revocable, your creditors can reach the assets held in the living trust.* Under some circumstances, an irrevocable trust offers protection against creditors.

What if I become incapacitated while I am the trustee? *Living trusts generally provide for successor trustees.* Therefore, if you become incapacitated before your death, the successor trustee can manage the trust for your benefit.

TAXES

As it has been said, nothing is certain but death and taxes. Federal income tax law is complicated and always changing. You need to be sure your tax information is current, or you could face penalties for filing incorrectly. And do not forget that the majority of states also have state income taxes that you need to pay.

> **TIP:** Contact your local IRS Taxpayer Assistance Center for the most detailed and up-to-date information. You can locate the nearest location by looking in your yellow pages under the federal government pages, by calling 800.829.1040 or by visiting **www.irs.gov**.

> **TIP:** The Tax Counseling for the Elderly (TCE) Program offers free tax help to individuals who are age 60 or older. As part of this program, AARP offers tax-counseling programs at more than 9,000 sites nationwide during the filing season. Trained AARP volunteers help people of low to middle income with special attention to those ages 60 and older. For more information on AARP's Tax-Aide Program or for the location of their sites, call 888.227.7669 or visit **www.aarp.org**. To find your nearest TCE location, call the IRS at 800.829.1040.

Are my Social Security benefits taxable? *It depends on whether your income is greater than a threshold level.* The IRS Form 1040 includes instructions on how to calculate whether your Social Security benefits are subject to the federal income tax.

I just retired and received my first pension benefit this month. Do I have to pay taxes on this benefit? *Pension or annuity payments received as retirement benefits may be taxable—fully or partially—in the year you receive them.* Your pension distributions are taxed depending on whether they are periodic payments, such as an annuity, that are paid regularly over several years or nonperiodic payments.

Will I be taxed on withdrawals from my Individual Retirement Account? *Traditional IRA distributions are generally taxable in the year you receive them.* Plus, you must include on your tax return—and will be taxed on—any distributions made to you from a traditional IRA before age 59_. You will also incur a penalty tax on early distributions unless they meet specific exceptions.

What are some of the exemptions available to seniors? There are numerous exemptions or credits that may help lighten your taxes:

- **PERSONAL EXEMPTION.** If you are not eligible to be claimed as a dependent by someone else, you are eligible to file a personal exemption for yourself.

- **DEPENDENTS.** You may have additional exemptions, depending on whether you have other dependents as defined by the IRS.

- **FEDERAL INCOME TAX CREDIT.** You may also qualify for a tax credit if your income does not exceed a threshold limit, you are disabled and over 65.

- **EARNED INCOME CREDIT.** The IRS allows an earned income credit if you work and you have a child under a certain age or who is a student or disabled.

- **STANDARD DEDUCTION FOR AGE AND BLINDNESS.** You can claim a second standard deduction if you do not file an itemized tax return and you are over 65 years old or blind.

- **MEDICAL EXPENSES.** Some medical expenses may be deducted if they total more than a certain percentage of your adjusted gross income.

> **TIP:** It is best to contact your local IRS if you think you may qualify for a tax exemption or credit. The IRS can explain how the exemption or credit applies to your situation.

Property taxes in my neighborhood are skyrocketing along with all the new construction. Is there any relief for an older person? *Many states offer a property tax exemption to seniors over a specific age or if you are disabled.* Renters may also qualify for an exemption or reduction in their rent payments. Contact your state's department of revenue for more information.

I heard that the federal estate tax has been done away with. Is that true? *Not yet. While there is always talk about ending the federal estate tax, it is not gone yet.* The estate and gift tax exemption amount has steadily increased since 1998 and will top out at $1 million in 2006.

> **TIP:** As with all tax issues, be sure to consult with your local IRS office before filling out your tax return. Changes to the tax laws are made continuously.

My eyesight is not what it used to be. Does the IRS have forms in large print? *Yes, you can order large-print tax forms from the IRS.* You can use these forms to help you figure your taxes, but you will need to file your taxes on a regular form. Call 800.829.3676.

4 EMPLOYMENT LAW

Employment is a fact of life for most Americans. You will be an employee, an employer or both at some point in your lifetime. And as you might imagine, employment involves many laws for both the employee and the employer. In this chapter, we take a look at some of the larger issues in employment: recruitment and hiring; wages and hours; benefits; employee rights; time off; safety and security in the workplace; unions; and separation from employment.

RECRUITMENT AND HIRING

Whether you are an employer looking to add or replace staff or an individual seeking a new opportunity, the hiring and recruitment process is the first step in determining if a match exists. Both parties should be looking at "fit." What is the likelihood that this individual will be comfortable in the company's culture? Are the responsibilities of the position sufficient enough to challenge the applicant or are they more rigorous than what this person has done in the past? Does this individual or this position provide the ability to grow with the company?

For the employer, hiring the wrong employee can result in wasted time in training and start-up costs, as well as disrupting the organization as a whole. From the candidate's perspective, the wrong decision can make going to work frustrating and unrewarding.

FILLING AN OPEN POSITION

Do I need a job description? *Though job descriptions are not required, they prove helpful in identifying the characteristics and experiences you would like to see the candidate possess.* The job description normally includes the duties and tasks of the job; it may describe what tools the applicant may use to be successful, (e.g., "must know Excel"); and often lists the skills, education, requirements and abilities that the candidate should have.

Having a job description also makes it easer to screen resumes and applications that you may receive. If applicants do not meet the requirements of the position, then they need not be considered further.

The job description also benefits the candidate, serving as a tool to prepare for a successful interview and as a roadmap regarding what will be expected of him should the position be offered.

CAUTION: Be aware that all requirements for a job carry the same weight. You need to remember that under the Americans with Disabilities Act (ADA), an applicant cannot be rejected if a reasonable accommodation can be made for the individual's disability.

How do I advertise an open position? *There are a number of methods by which you can get the word out about your position.* These include:

- word of mouth
- employee referral
- newspaper advertising
- Internet posting
- employment agency

Word of Mouth

This is the least expensive means to find applicants. It usually entails getting word out to friends that a position is available and asking if they know anyone who would be qualified. The plus side is that you will often receive candidates that are a known entity. The downside is that often the position may not get enough exposure, limiting the applicant pool.

Employee Referral

This method is similar in scope to word of mouth. Here, employees are asked to refer people they know for the job. They are often paid a bounty for recommending good people. Employees usually recommend good employees because they feel their reputation is at stake if they recommend someone.

CAUTION: In both of these methods the employer needs to be aware of the demographics of its workforce and the people from whom they seek recommendations. If the group is too similar in background, the Equal Employment Opportunity Commission (EEOC) may say that the recruitment process implicitly discriminates against women or minorities.

Newspaper Advertising

This method works well, particularly if you are looking for local candidates. The cost is relatively small.

Internet Posting

This method is the most likely to bring in the greatest number of applications. The most common Web sites that are used are **www.monster.com, www.hotjobs.com** and **www.careerbuilder.com**. The cost to post is relatively low.

Employment Agency

These firms charge a fee, typically 20 to 33 percent of the employee's salary. They will locate and screen applicants for you, and will present only those that best meet the criteria of the job. This source is the most costly.

Is there any law that requires the posting of a job? *There are no federal laws that have such a requirement.* You do need to be aware that posting can help in the event of an EEOC discrimination claim.

> **TIP:** It is beneficial to place at the bottom of any employment posting that "ABC Company is an Equal Opportunity Employer."

Am I required to use a formal job application? *There is no formal requirement that you have an application.* Many companies use them because it standardizes the information the candidate is giving you, such as past employers, specific skills and contact information. The application also puts the candidate on notice and seeks consent that:

- you may verify the information on the form;
- the individual may be subject to drug testing if it is the company policy to do so;
- if hired, the individual understands he is an "at will" employee;
- references can be checked; and
- should any information prove false, the individual may be subject to discharge.

Can I take notes on the application? *Notes of any kind should not be made on employment applications or resumes.* Anything that is recorded may be discoverable if there is a lawsuit in the future.

How long must I keep applications if I use them? *Keep solicited applications at least 1 year.* Unsolicited applications can be discarded immediately; however, it is a better practice to hold on to them for a year as well.

CAUTION: Should you elect to discard unsolicited applications and resumes, you should discard all that are received. Picking and choosing can result in a disparate treatment claim by a human rights agency.

What is an "at will" employee? *An "at will" employee is one who can be let go for any reason, provided it is not discriminatory.* This individual may also resign for any reason.

CAUTION: An employer needs to be careful in the representations made to employees so as not to alter this "at will" status. Statements such as "you can expect a long career with our company" can potentially alter "at will" status.

May I ask whether someone is an alien to the country? *The proper question should be, "Are you legally allowed to work in the United States?"* If the person responds in the affirmative either verbally or in writing, it is not necessary to verify this information until after an offer of employment has been made.

Is drug testing of job applicants permissible? *Drug testing does not fall under the ADA and is permissible. It is important to note that if testing is done, it be done for all applicants.* Confidentiality is also essential. The results of the test should only be shared on a need-to-know basis. Some states will allow testing only to ensure the safety of workers and others.

Can a potential employer require medical examinations? *The ADA does not permit medical exams before a tentative offer of employment is extended. As with drug testing, if the exams are given, they must be given to everyone.* Medical questions should be directly related to the key functions of the job for which the individual is applying.

> **The ADA only applies to companies that have at least 15 employees.**

May applicants be required to submit to a lie detector test? *No.* Both the federal government and many states strictly prohibit polygraph testing, except under very limited circumstances involving national security, private sector security firms and the pharmaceutical industry, or if there is reasonable suspicion of someone being involved in a workplace incident.

INTERVIEWING

> **TIP:** Before asking an applicant any question, first ask yourself "Why do I need to know this information?" "How is it related to the requirements of the position?" Unless there is a direct relationship, do not ask the question.

Recently, I heard that there is a new type of interviewing called behavioral interviewing. What is this? *Behavioral interviewers ask questions in a different style than the typical interviewer.* They ask questions about what specifically you did in the past to try to predict what you would do in the future. They also ask questions regarding how you felt. Some examples of behavioral questions might include:

> "Tell me about a time you had difficulty with a fellow employee. What was the problem and how did you resolve the issue?"
>
> "Give me an example of a situation where you had to abruptly change what you were doing. What did you do? How did it affect you?"

How do I respond to someone who has called to follow up on a job interview but who did not get the job? *Responding to this question requires a balance. The candidate is looking for feedback and the company is looking to ensure it does not create a legal issue.* In responding, thank the candidate for her time and interest in the company, adding that someone who better met the qualifications of the job was chosen. Do not get into specifics as to what skills the selected applicant possessed.

CAUTION: Do not say that the candidate's salary requirements were too high or that they are overqualified for the position. Both statements can be indicative of age discrimination.

Is there any value to reference checking? *Reference checking is a two-edged sword. When you check references it is highly likely that you will not receive any information other than name, title and dates of employment. And this in turn is all the information you should give out, provided you have received a signed release from the former employee.* This is because companies fear being sued for slander by a former employee if they release negative information or, conversely, a misleading reference suit by a hiring company dissatisfied with their hire.

Failure to check references can also be problematic because it can leave an employer open to a negligent hiring claim.

CAUTION: Do not give a former employee who was discharged for cause a false or misleading reference. Doing so can open you individually and your company to a damage award.

SALARY NEGOTIATIONS

How can I determine if the offer I am making (or have received) is competitive? *One of the best ways to check is to go to* **www.salary.com**. This site lists hundreds of positions and gives a range for the position based on your geographic location.

CAUTION: Employers often base their salary offer on what the last salary the candidate was earning. In cases where this figure is significantly below what other employees are making, a potential discrimination claim may exist. In constructing an offer, look at both the internal and external market for the appropriate rate and verify that men, women and minorities are paid comparably.

WAGES AND HOURS

Whether you are an employer or an employee, compensation is critical. Employers have a number of laws and regulations that must be followed to properly pay their staff. Both parties are also concerned that they are being paid equitably, compared with the external and internal (in comparison to their peers) market.

If a company has money to spare, it may elect to contract a firm to do a salary survey. Firms such as Hewitt Associates, Mercer and Towers Perrin all do this type of work. For the smaller company, jobs may be benchmarked by going to **www.monster.com** and looking at what similar jobs pay, or to **www.salary.com**, which gives salaries for hundreds of positions in cities all over the country.

MINIMUM WAGE

What is the minimum wage I can receive? *The current federal minimum wage is $5.15 per hour. However, many states have set their own minimum wage, which may be higher.* An employee who is eligible for both the state and federal minimum wage must be paid the higher of the two.

TIP: The federal government provides extensive information on this issue on its Web site at **www.dol.gov/dol/topic/wages/minimumwage.htm**.

Does the minimum wage apply to teenagers? *The Fair Labor Standards Act (FLSA), the law that regulates wages, provides that if someone is less than 20 years old, the minimum wage is $4.25 per hour for the first 90 days of consecutive employment.* The one proviso is that the person who is paid this rate cannot displace other workers. After the 90 days or when the person reaches age 20, whichever comes first, the employee must be brought up to the federal minimum of $5.15.

TIP: The above is the federal rule; your state may have a different practice. Check with your local Department of Labor.

Are the rules different if my compensation includes tips? *Most likely. Under the FLSA, a tipped employee may be paid $2.13 per hour if that amount plus tips exceeds the federal minimum wage.* The employee must regularly receive at least $30 per month in tips and be entitled to keep all of it.

EXAMPLE: John has a part-time job shining shoes. He shines seven pairs of shoes an hour and normally gets tipped $1.00 a pair. He would be entitled under federal law to a minimum hourly wage of $2.13. If, however, he shined only two pairs an hour, his employer would be required to make up the difference of $1.02. It would be computed as follows:

Minimum wage to tipped employee:	**$2.13**
Tips received	2.00
Total	**$4.13**
Shortfall made up by employer	**$1.02**
Federal minimum wage	**$5.15**

Again, it must be remembered that each state may have different rules regarding tipped employees.

If I am a full-time student who works in a store, in agriculture or for my college or university, am I entitled to the minimum wage? *The answer depends on how many hours that you work.* Under the FLSA, if you work no more than 8 hours per day and 20 hours per week when school is in session (40 hours when it is out of session), you can be paid less than the minimum wage but in no case less than 85 percent of that minimum.

Are there other any other exceptions to the minimum wage rules? *An exception exists for disability if the disability impairs the worker's productive capacity for the work being performed. Just because an individual may have a disability does not mean she may be paid less.* Employers who wish to take advantage of this exception must first receive a certificate from the Wage and Hour Division of the Department of Labor.

THE WORKWEEK

Officially, the workweek is 40 hours per week. It is comprised of any 7 consecutive days with seven 24-hour periods. For many people, it extends from Monday through Friday, but this need not be the case.

Do I get paid more for working at night?
No. There is no requirement to give a shift premium or overtime to any employee unless it is provided for by agreement. Many employers however, elect to pay extra for the second and third shifts in recognition of the inconvenience of working these hours.

> There is no requirement for extra pay or overtime for someone who works on a Sunday.

What if I work more than 40 hours per week?
Nonexempt employees (those employees who are entitled to overtime) are entitled to one and one-half times their regular rate of pay after 40 hours of work per week. For an exempt employee, such as an executive, salaried administrator or a professional, it is likely that no additional compensation is due.

How do I know if I am an exempt employee?
In 2004, the government modified its rules with respect to what constitutes an executive, administrative and professional employee for purposes of overtime eligibility. The following criteria must be met to consider an employee exempt from overtime.

Executives

a. The employee's primary duty must be management of the enterprise, or of a customarily recognized department or subdivision.

   i. The government will look at how much time the person is spending performing exempt work; generally 50 percent or more will satisfy this requirement.

   ii. The individual regularly exercises discretionary powers.

b. The executive customarily and regularly directs the work of two or more other employees.

c. The employee has the authority to hire, fire, or his or her recommendations on hiring or firing, advancement, promotion or other changes affecting employees are given particular weight.

d. The employee must be paid on a salary basis at a rate of at least $155 a week.

Some examples of managerial duties include:

- interviewing, selecting and training employees
- setting and adjusting pay rates and work hours
- handling employee complaints and grievances
- planning and apportioning work among employees
- preparing payrolls

Administrative Employees

a. Primarily performs office or nonmanual work directly related to the management or general business operations of the employer or its customers.

b. Customarily and regularly exercises discretion and independent judgment with respect to matters of significance.

   i. Regularly assists a proprietor or bona fide executive.

   ii. Performs under only general supervision along specialized or technical lines requiring special training or executes special assignments under general supervision.

c. The employee must not spend more than 20 percent on nonexempt work.

d. The employee must be paid on a salary of not less than $155 a week.

Professional Employees

a. Employee's primary duty must be one of the following:

   i. Work requiring advanced knowledge in science or learning customarily obtained by prolonged study.

   ii. Work that is original or creative in character in a recognized field or artistic endeavor.

   iii. Work as a certified teacher.

b. The employee must consistently exercise discretion and judgment.

c. The employee must do work that is predominately intellectual and varied as distinguished from routine and mechanical.

d. The employee must not spend more than 20 percent of the time working on activities incidental to the professional duties.

e. The employee must be paid a salary of not less than $170 per week.

The interpretation of the terminology of these criteria can be difficult. It is recommended that you seek a professional where there are questions regarding overtime eligibility.

Further information is also available at: www.dol.gov/asp/programs/flsa/report-neweconomy/Appendix.htm and at www.dol.gov/elaws/esa/flsa/screen75.asp.

Is overtime required if I work more than 8 hours in a day? *Under federal law the answer is no. Many states however do provide for payment after 8 hours work in a day, even where the 40 hours in the week have not been exceeded.* Please check with your state Department of Labor to see its overtime requirements.

Is there a maximum number of hours I can work in a week? *If you are over age 16 the answer is no.* However, it is not in the best interest of either the employer or employee to

work an excess amount of overtime in a week. Excessive overtime results in both an increase in accident rates and a decline in productivity.

Can an overtime-eligible employee waive their right to receive overtime? *It is illegal for an employer not to pay a nonexempt employee overtime, even if the employee agrees to this.* If you are asked to waive this right or are not being paid for the overtime hours you work, contact your local Department of Labor Wages and Hours division.

Do I have to work overtime if I do not want to? *Unfortunately, yes. A reasonable amount of overtime can be expected of you or from your employees.* Failure to work required overtime can result in disciplinary action.

What if my company requires that I work 9 hours per day, but only allows me to bill for 8? *The answer depends on whether you are an exempt or nonexempt employee and the type of work you may be performing. If you are doing billable work and you are nonexempt, you are due money for all hours worked.* If you are exempt and on a salary, your payment should not vary based on the hours billed, and overtime will not apply.

I work from 7:00 a.m. to 3:00 p.m. My company has a mandatory meeting once a month at 4:00 p.m. Should I be paid to attend? *Yes.* If you are a nonexempt employee, your company must pay you for time spent at business functions or meetings where you are subject to the company's discretion and control.

My company is looking to save cash. Can I be given "comp time" in lieu of overtime pay? *If you are a nonexempt employee the answer is no.* For exempt employees the practice is acceptable.

> **TIP:** A simple rule to follow is that if an employee is nonexempt, they need to be paid for all hours worked.

When am I entitled to double-time pay? *Under the FLSA, you are not. There are no provisions for double-time compensation.* However, many employers, and some states, require double-time after 12 consecutive hours of work. Some companies also pay double-time for work on a holiday. A union will often negotiate this payment in collective bargaining agreements.

I carry a beeper as part of my job. Am I entitled to additional pay for wearing it on the weekend? *In most cases, you will not be entitled to additional compensation. The FLSA does not require any payments for merely being "on-call" or carrying a beeper.* The determining factor turns on whether the employee is free to use their time as they like. As long as you are not required to sit at home, but simply have to be reachable, no pay is required.

> **TIP:** If an employee is paged and then responds, compensation will be due.

EQUAL PAY

In 1963, Congress passed the Equal Pay Act. This law requires that men and women be given equal pay for equal work when the jobs require equal skill, effort and responsibility and are performed under similar working conditions within the same place of business. Under the act, a person's job title is not as important as the job content.

What is meant by the terms "skill," "effort," "responsibility" and "working conditions"?

- ▶ **EFFORT.** The amount of physical or mental exertion needed to perform a job.

- ▶ **SKILL.** Factors such as experience, ability, education and training required to do the job.

- ▶ **RESPONSIBILITY.** The degree of accountability required in the performance of the job.

- ▶ **WORKING CONDITIONS.** the environmental surroundings and physical hazards of the job.

Are there any pay differences between men and women that are legal under the EPA? Yes, if the compensation is based upon a seniority system, a merit system, a system that measures earnings by quality and quantity of production or where the differential is based on a factor other than sex.

Can I pay a woman with more education more than a man for the same job? *The answer depends on whether the additional education is required to do the job.* If it is nice to have but not required, a distinction cannot be drawn with respect to compensation.

I think a coworker is making more than I am for doing the same job. What can I do? *Before taking any action, it is important to determine if the work that you are doing is actually the same.* Are the same amounts of hours being worked? Does one person work in the office and the other out on the factory floor? Is there a higher level of skill required for one job over the other? If there truly is a difference, then a pay differential may be warranted. If not, contact the Equal Employment Opportunity Commission (EEOC) regarding your equal pay concerns.

My employer says that I get paid less than my coworker because he has a family, whereas I am single. Should this affect my salary? *No. If you believe you have been treated differently because of your gender, race, national origin or marital status, you can file a complaint with the EEOC for equal pay.* You do not need a lawyer; the EEOC will help you prepare the case and advise you of additional rights you may have or steps you should take (including any requirements for filing complaints with state agencies).

CHILD LABOR

The child labor laws are designed to protect the health and welfare of workers who are under 16 years of age. The law establishes minimum wage, overtime pay and working standards. It also is designed to protect the educational opportunities of minors, in part, by restricting the hours they may work when school is in session.

My child is 15; can she work 30 hours a week for a local merchant when school is in session? *No. The maximum she could be employed under the federal child labor laws is 3 hours per day and 18 hours per week.* In addition, she cannot work before 7:00 a.m. or after 7:00 p.m. When school is not in session, she could work a maximum of 8 hours per day and up to 40 hours per week. During the summer, work may continue until 9:00 p.m.

I want to employ a 17-year-old neighbor to work with me as a roofer for the summer. Is this permissible? *No.* In general, the federal child labor provisions prohibit those under 18 from working in or with the following:

- liquor
- hazardous materials, such as chemicals, explosives or substances under pressure
- hazardous operations, such as logging, lumber, construction and mining
- transportation, such as driving boats, buses or cabs
- machinery, such as power-driven, erecting, dismantling, lift or hoisting equipment

Check with your local Department of Labor to see if any additional restrictions exist within your state.

PAYROLL DEDUCTIONS

In most cases, there are only four conditions under which an employer may take deductions from an employee's paycheck. These include:

- The employer is required to do so by law for federal and state income taxes, Social Security and Medicare payments, workers compensation or a garnishment order from a court.
- The employee has authorized the deduction voluntarily and it is for the employee's benefit (e.g. medical deductions, 401(k) contributions or daycare costs).
- The employee has voluntarily given the company permission for other items, such as savings bonds through a local bank or money directed to another account.
- Deductions pursuant to a collective bargaining agreement, typically called "check-off."

Can my employer deduct money from my check for the purchase of uniforms or tools that are required for the job? *In many states the answer is no. Payroll deductions may not be made for an item that is required to do the job.* Check with your local Department of Labor to see what the rules are in your jurisdiction.

Can my employer make deductions for meals and lodging? *Again, the answer varies by state.* Most states allow this deduction, provided that the meals and/or lodging are for the private benefit of the employee.

CAUTION: Any deductions that an employer takes from an employee's check that is not authorized by law must be in writing.

If I break a work rule or negligently destroy company property, can the company deduct from my paycheck? *No. In the great majority of states, payroll deductions may not be made for these purposes.* Though the company may have a right under certain circumstances to fine you, it cannot collect by deducting from your paycheck.

Can my employer require me to use direct deposit? *No. Direct deposit benefits both the employer and the employee. The employer does not have to write checks or have cash at the work site. It also makes tracking and recovery easier.* For the employee, it avoids having to wait for a check to clear to receive payment. Under most direct deposit programs, the money is in the employee's account on payday, so that there is no need to go to the bank. Despite the convenience, if an employee wishes to receive a check, the employer must comply.

GARNISHMENT

A wage garnishment occurs where a portion of the wages of an employee are withheld for the payment of an outstanding debt. More often than not, the garnishment is a result of a court order.

The Consumer Credit Protection Act—the law governing garnishments—limits the amount that may be deducted in any workweek or pay period to the lesser of 25 percent of the person's disposable earnings, or the amount of the employee's disposable income that is greater than 30 times the federal minimum wage.

EXAMPLE: "Disposable income" is your paycheck minus taxes and minimum living expenses.

Can I be fired if my employer receives a garnishment notice? *Federal law prohibits you being let go for any one debt.* If you have multiple notices, however, you lose this protection.

CAUTION: It is a criminal offense to fire an employee whose wages have been attached for child support.

My employee owes child support and alimony. Are the rules regarding garnishment different? *Yes. An employee can have up to 60 percent of their disposable income deducted if he is not supporting a second spouse or child. If he is supporting a second household, the law allows a 50 percent deduction.* Payments that are in arrears for more than 12 weeks can also result in an additional 5 percent being subject to garnishment.

Child support payments also take priority over other garnishment deductions.

Are there any other exceptions? *Yes.* There are no restrictions on the amount that can be deducted or garnished by order of a bankruptcy court or debts owed for federal or state taxes.

FILING A WAGE CLAIM

Each state has its own procedures for the filing of an unpaid wages or FLSA claim. Check with your state Department of Labor Wages and Hours division. There is no cost to you should you elect to file a claim. It is also illegal for an employer to fire an individual who brings a claim.

More often than not an incorrect payment may be a mistake, and can easily be resolved through a discussion with the payroll or human resources department.

BENEFITS

In today's economy, employees look beyond just salary in determining which jobs to apply for and which positions they will remain in. Often the determining factor will be the benefits that go along with the job. Benefits can help protect employees from economic loss, assist in dealing with illness, disability or death and can help employees plan for the future. Benefits also help

with employee retention and are important for employers to get an edge on the competition. However, benefits do not come cheap. Employers often spend over 30 percent of an employee's annual wages in order to offer a competitive program.

Most benefits are just that, they are not required by law. There are three areas, however, in which benefits are mandatory:

- Social Security;
- workers' compensation; and
- unemployment insurance.

SOCIAL SECURITY BENEFITS

What is Social Security? Social Security is a federal program that is intended to provide assistance to people who would otherwise exhaust their savings as a result of retirement, disability or death.

Who pays for Social Security? *We all do. Funding comes from payroll taxes paid by you and your employer.* Each year you pay a percentage of your salary up to a maximum. Part of this money is directed for retirement benefits and the other portion is directed for Medicare.

At what age can I start collecting retirement benefits? *Benefits are available at age 62 but at a reduced rate. The normal retirement age for Social Security purposes is currently 65.* Should you elect to defer retirement until age 70, you will be entitled to a higher rate.

Where can I get more information, such as how to file a claim, learn more about disability or get a statement of what is in my account? *All of this information is available at the Social Security Web site, Social Security Online.* The Web address is: www.ssa.gov.

WORKERS' COMPENSATION

Why were workers' compensation laws put into effect? *Workers' compensation laws were enacted in the 1930s to give economic protection to employees who got injured on the job.* Today, all 50 states have laws providing these protections.

How does workers' compensation help the employer? *Workers' compensation is one of the earlier forms of "no-fault insurance."* In return for paying for the program, employees give up their right to sue the company for injuries or illnesses incurred while working.

UNEMPLOYMENT INSURANCE

What is unemployment insurance? Unemployment insurance is a jointly run program by the federal government and the states that provide payments, typically 26 weeks, for individuals who have lost their jobs through no fault of their own.

I work in one state but live in another. In which state do I file for benefits? *You should file benefits with the state in which you reside.* Each unemployment office has an interstate unit that works out the payments due where employees have crossed state lines to work.

How do I file a claim for unemployment benefits? *Contact your state Department of Labor. Many states now allow for you to file a claim over the phone.* Once you have filed, you will have to call in weekly and answer a series of questions. These questions almost always include the following: "Have you looked for work during the past week?" A requirement to collect unemployment is that you must be actively seeking to return to the workplace.

HEALTH CARE PLANS

I am considering offering my employees a group health care plan. What options do I have? *There are three typical types of plans that are offered by employers.* These are:

1. **INDEMNITY PLANS.** This type of plan allows an employee to pick her own doctors without restriction. These plans, like the others below, often have deductibles and copays. Depending on the level of coverage, this type of plan is usually the most costly.

2. **PREFERRED PROVIDER ORGANIZATIONS (PPOS).** This type of plan offers a network of hospitals and doctors to provide coverage to employees at an established rate.

3. **HEALTH MAINTENANCE ORGANIZATIONS (HMOS).** This is the most limited of the options. Normally, an employee has a primary care physician that serves as a gatekeeper. Employees are not allowed to seek services outside the network.

What happens to my health care insurance if I change jobs? *In the past, it is likely that you were left without insurance. However, in 1996, the federal government passed the Health Insurance Portability and Accountability Act (HIPAA).* The intent of this law is to make sure you do not lose benefits while you may be in transition or between jobs.

HIPAA also provides that group health care insurance at your new job:

- limits the exclusions for preexisting conditions;
- prohibits you and your dependents from being discriminated against based on their health status; and
- allows a special opportunity to enroll in a new plan to individuals in certain circumstances.

Further, HIPAA may also give you a right to purchase individual coverage if you have no group health care insurance available and have exhausted COBRA or other continuation coverage.

What preexisting conditions may be excluded from coverage under my new employer's health care plan? A preexisting condition is a condition or illness that you had prior to coming to a new employer.

The only preexisting conditions that may be excluded under HIPAA are those for which medical advice, diagnosis, care or treatment was recommended or received within the 6-month period before your first day of coverage in the new plan.

I am changing jobs and am 6 months pregnant. Do I qualify for health care insurance with my new employer? *Under HIPAA, pregnancy may not be considered a preexisting condition.* Therefore, you cannot be denied maternity coverage if the new plan provides for these benefits.

How do I prove that I had health care coverage with my old employer? *Your former employer's group health plan or insurance company is required to provide you with a statement certifying that you had coverage.* You should have received it automatically when you received your COBRA paperwork. Under the law, you have up to 2 years from the time your coverage ended to request a certificate of credibility coverage.

Why would I need such a certificate? *HIPAA deals with health care portability. In essence, this means the ability to move your coverage from one employer to the other.* Under the rules, you get credit for your previous coverage that occurred without a break of 63 days or more. This 63-day break can be extended if you elected COBRA.

I have just been diagnosed with a chronic heart condition. Can I lose my coverage or be charged more under my employer's health care plan? *Your company's health insurer or health plan provider may not establish rules for eligibility, or continuation of coverage for any person in the plan based on health status related factors.* These include:

- health status
- physical or mental medical condition
- claims experience
- receipt of health care
- medical history
- genetic information
- evidence of insurability
- disability

Plans are expected to charge the same premiums for those similarly situated.

Then why do smokers have to pay more than nonsmokers for coverage? *Though it appears to be in violation to do so, HIPAA provides an exception to the above in the case of a bona fide wellness program.* To qualify:

- the total reward that may be given is limited (no more than 10 to 20 percent of the cost to the employee);
- the program must be designed to foster good health or prevent disease;

- the reward must be made available to all similarly situated individuals and must allow any individual who cannot reasonably meet the wellness standard be given an opportunity to satisfy a reasonably alternative standard; and
- all plan materials explaining the terms of the program disclose the availability of a reasonable alternative standard.

I was hired after "open enrollment." Do I have to pass a physical to enroll in my employer's health care plan? *No.* You do not have to take a physical in order to be eligible for coverage.

> **TIP:** More information is provided regarding other HIPAA issues at the U.S. Department of Labor's Web sites. The addresses are: **www.dol.gov/ebsa/faqs/faq_hipaa_ND.html** and **www.dol.gov/ebsa/faqs/faq_consumer_hipaa.html**.

EMPLOYEE RETIREMENT INCOME SECURITY ACT (ERISA)

ERISA is a law established to set uniform minimum standards to ensure that employee benefit plans are set up and maintained in a fair and financially prudent manner. Employee benefit plans include pension and welfare benefit plans. The rules require that the persons or entities that manage and control the funds do the following:

- Manage the plans for the exclusive benefit of the participants and beneficiaries;
- Carry out their duties in a prudent manner and refrain from conflict-of-interest transactions;
- Comply with limitations on certain plans' investments in employer securities and properties;
- Fund benefits in accordance with the law and plan rules;
- Report and disclose information on the operations and financial condition of plans to the government and participants; and
- Provide documents required in the conduct of investigations to assure compliance with the law.

Sound daunting? These rules essentially say that the plans: (1) have to be for the benefit of the employees, (2) must follow the law, (3) have to tell the employees what they have in the plans, and (4) must act in a nondiscriminatory manner.

Why should I offer a retirement plan to my employees? *Offering retirement benefits is critical to stay competitive in the labor market.* These plans help build loyalty and create an incentive for an employee to stay with an organization. Many of us will spend as much as a quarter of our lives in retirement. It is essential that employees start making plans early in their careers.

What types of plans typically fall under ERISA regulation? In general, there are two types of plans:

DEFINED BENEFIT PLANS. This type of plan sets a fixed preestablished benefit for the employees. It is typically tied to employee's earnings, length of service or both. It is the company's responsibility to ensure that the plan is adequately funded so that the money is there when the employee retires. Because of the costs, these types of plans are used less frequently than they had been in the past.

DEFINED CONTRIBUTION PLANS. There are a number of different plans that fall within this group. They include:

- ▸ **401(K)S.** These plans allow an employee to put a percentage of pretax income into a retirement savings account. No tax is paid until the money is withdrawn. The maximum an employee can put into this account for 2005 is $14,000, rising to $15,000 in 2006.

- ▸ **PROFIT SHARING.** These plans allow the flexibility of making contributions based on the existence of profits. Under these plans an employer may make a contribution to the employee up to 15 percent of salary, but no more than $30,000.

- ▸ **MONEY PURCHASE PLANS.** Here, the company commits to making annual contributions equal to a certain percentage of the employees salary up to 25 percent of earned income. Like the profit-sharing plan, the maximum contribution is $30,000. The rules for these plans require

that all employees must receive the same percentage of salary. The plan also is paid even in years when there are no profits.

- ▸ **SIMPLIFIED EMPLOYEE PENSION (SEP).** This is the only defined contribution plan that requires no filings, IRS approvals and no annual reporting. SEPs work like IRAs; however, rather than a $2,000 limit, you can defer up to $30,000 or 15 percent of annual earnings, whichever is less.

ADDITIONAL BENEFITS

What other benefits can I offer my employees? The basics include:

- ▸ **DENTAL.** Cleanings, x-rays and some coverage for dental services.

- ▸ **LIFE INSURANCE.** Typically, a multiple of an employee's annual salary to provide for an employee's survivors.

- ▸ **LONG-TERM DISABILITY INSURANCE.** This pays a percentage of the employee's salary if she should become disabled and unable to work.

- ▸ **EDUCATIONAL REIMBURSEMENT.** Providing employees an annual dollar amount for continuing their education. It is often required that the class be job related.

What other benefits can the company offer to attract employees? The list here is almost endless. It includes:

- Fitness memberships
- Magazine subscriptions
- Legal services
- End-of-year bonuses
- Annual physicals
- Club memberships
- Company cars
- Estate planning
- Child care
- Scholarships

The only limitation is your imagination.

EMPLOYEE RIGHTS IN THE WORKPLACE

Many of our workplace rights are protected under Title VII. Title VII is a federal law passed in 1964 that prohibits discrimination in employment based on race, color, religion, sex or national origin.

In 1967, additional legislation was passed prohibiting discrimination on the basis of age. This law was called the Age Discrimination in Employment Act (ADEA), and it protects individuals who are age 40 or older.

TITLE VII AND ADEA

What types of employment actions does Title VII protect?

- Hiring and firing
- Promotions
- Benefits
- Transfers and layoffs
- Training
- Compensation
- Retirement plans
- Any other terms or conditions of employment

I work for a small company. Am I covered by Title VII? *If your company has 15 or more employees, Title VII covers you.* If your company has less than 15 employees, there may be similar protections provided by state law.

> **The ADEA covers employees with 20 or more employees.**

I have an employee who works for me who is turning 65 next month. Can I make him take retirement? *No.* Under the ADEA, mandatory retirement was outlawed with the exception of a few positions (airline pilots and some public-safety officers).

Federal laws always seem to have exceptions. Are there any exceptions to the ADEA? *Yes.* Generally speaking there are three:

1. Law enforcement, firefighters and certain other public-safety employees (air traffic controllers);

2. Executives in "high policy-making positions," provided their annual retirement benefit to be paid them is $44,000 or more; and

3. If the employer can prove that age is a bona fide occupational qualification (e.g., airline pilots). This is a difficult burden for employers to meet.

I want to replace a 55-year-old worker with a 41-year old. Is this allowed because both employees are in the protected class?

Though the facts would have to be looked at more carefully, it is likely that it would not be acceptable. The intent of the ADEA is to protect older workers, and that can be viewed in relative terms. Replacing a 43-year old with a 41-year old, however, would most likely not be a problem.

CAUTION: Employers need to be careful what they say in the workplace. Even if there is no age animus, statements to an older employee that "both of us have been around a long time and make a lot of money" or "you're a war horse" have been found by the courts to be indicative of age discrimination.

May I ask an employee to waive their rights under the ADEA? *An employer may ask an employee to waive his rights.* However, there are some specific requirements which must be met in order for the waiver to be enforceable. The waiver must:

- be in writing and understandable, and clearly present the agreement and waiver;
- specifically refer to the ADEA rights or claims;
- may not refer to rights or claims that arise in the future;
- be in exchange for valuable consideration beyond what the employee would normally be entitled;
- advise the employee in writing that he consult an attorney before signing the waiver;
- provide at least 21 days to consider the agreement;
- provide 7 days to revoke acceptance of the agreement; and
- for employment termination or exit incentive programs, the employee must be given certain information that is easily understood as to what groups or class of individuals are entitled to participate in the program, as well as the titles and ages of all those eligible or selected for the program.

My hiring manager is a light-skinned African-American. Is it discriminatory if he does not hire dark-skinned African-Americans? *The law provides that it is discriminatory to make an employment determination based on skin color or based on any characteristic associated with a particular race.* The fact that the hiring manger is African-American is not relevant.

Is it okay to assign my minority employees to handle most of my minority accounts or minority locales? *This type of action is illegal if it will deprive the employee of an employment benefit.* If the nonminority territories or accounts provide for greater commissions or opportunities for advancement, this could raise a race discrimination claim.

My company has a no-beard policy. Is there any problem with this? *It is possible that the policy could be discriminatory.* Some African-American men suffer from pseudofolliculitis barbae (severe shaving bumps). You may wish to rethink the policy unless it is in place as a result of business necessity.

I have a number of employees for whom English is a second language. Can I require them to speak only English when they are on the job? *The EEOC has taken the position that "English only" rules are presumed to be discriminatory.* They are usually allowed only if the employer can show a business necessity: for example, a job that requires interacting with customers who only speak English.

My employee refuses to work on Saturday because of her religious beliefs. All of my employees are required to work on the weekends. Do I have to give her Saturday off? *The law requires that an accommodation be made so employees can follow their religious beliefs.* The tricky part is that the accommodations sought must be reasonable. If they would result in extra costs for overtime or create problems with other employees, the courts may find that the accommodations are not necessary.

> **TIP:** It is best to try to work out an accommodation with the employee. Using the above question, if your business is open on Sunday as well as Saturday, an accommodation may be to have this employee work on Sundays.

An employee says that he belongs to the Red Sox Nation. They believe that all followers must attend every Red Sox game. Does Title VII protect this type of claim? *No.* The belief has to be a bona fide religious belief. In looking at what is bona fide, the courts will look to see if:

- the practices are actually mandated by the religion;
- the belief occupies a place in the believer's life similar to that filled by the idea of "God;" and
- it is more than someone's personal moral code.

We have a number of women working in our factory who say that wearing a dress is required by their religion. I am concerned about safety; can I make them comply with our dress code and require that they wear pants instead? If safety is truly the issue, then yes you can require them to comply.

CAUTION: You cannot require an employee to wear something different than what may be required by their religion if the reason for the request is a concern that it will make customers or coworkers feel uncomfortable.

What is sex discrimination? Sex discrimination occurs when someone is treated differently because of his or her sex. It takes a number of forms.

May an employer make it a requirement that all secretaries be women? *No. This would be sex discrimination based on gender.* The situation would be no different if a woman applied for a position in the shipping department and was turned down because the manager believed that women could not handle manual labor. The only time an employer can specify gender is where it is a bona fide occupational qualification.

I recently applied for a job that a male friend applied for as well. He was not asked, as I was, whether I had preschool age children. Is this fair? This is an example of "sex-plus" discrimination and it is illegal.

An opening recently came up in my company for an outside salesperson. When I applied, the boss said he wanted a man because it was not safe for women to travel. Is this a valid reason to deny me the position? *No. Whether it is safe for you to travel is a determination that you need to make, not your boss.* Denying you this opportunity may constitute sex discrimination.

DISABILITY

In 1990, the federal government passed the Americans with Disability Act (ADA), which prohibits employers from discriminating against qualified individuals with disabilities when hiring, firing, promoting, training, allowing advancement opportunities and other terms and conditions of employment.

Are all companies subject to the ADA? *No.* Like Title VII, an employer must have at least 15 employees.

What is a "qualified individual" under the ADA? *A qualified individual with a disability is someone who can perform the essential functions of the position with or without reasonable accommodation.* What this means is that the person must:

- satisfy the job requirements from an educational perspective, experience, skills and any other standard that may be job related; and
- be able to perform the essential duties of the job.

I am concerned that my employer will say all the functions of my job are essential. Are there any guidelines that I can turn to? *The Equal Employment Opportunity Commission, which enforces the ADA, has developed some factors to determine if a function is essential.* They include:

- whether the reason the position exists is to perform that function;

- how many other employees are available to perform the function; and
- the degree of skill or expertise required to perform the function.

How is a disability defined? An individual is considered to have a disability if she:

- has a physical or mental impairment that substantially limits one or more major life activities;
- has a record of such an impairment; and
- is regarded as having such an impairment.

Does the ADA cover people with AIDS? *Yes.* The law protects individuals with AIDS and HIV disease from discrimination.

Is illegal drug use covered by the ADA? *No.* Applicants and employees who currently use illegal drugs are specifically excluded from coverage.

I understand that as an employer I must make a reasonable accommodation for someone with a disability. What types of accommodations may this include? Reasonable accommodation may include:

- making existing facilities more readily accessible;
- restructuring jobs, modifying work schedules or reassigning to a vacant position; and
- modifying equipment, providing training, materials or policies that assist the disabled.

What can I do if the reasonable accommodation creates an undue hardship? *The EEOC recognizes that in cases where the accommodation would be unduly expensive, substantial or disruptive, or would fundamentally alter the nature of the business, a hardship would be created.* If this is the case, the employer is expected to try to identify another accommodation that would not impose such a hardship.

SEXUAL HARASSMENT

Sexual harassment is a form of sex discrimination. It is defined by the EEOC as:

"Unwelcome sexual advances, requests for sexual favors and other verbal or physical conduct of a sexual nature when submission

to or rejection of this conduct explicitly or implicitly affects an individual's work performance, or creates an intimidating, hostile or offensive work environment."

I applied for a job and the hiring manager said he would give me the job if I went out with him. Is this legal? *Whenever there is either a promise or threat made in exchange for sex as a term or condition of employment, sexual harassment exists.* This type of sexual harassment is called quid pro quo (Latin for "this for that"). If the threat or promise is made by a supervisor or agent of the company, both the company and the person making the threat are liable.

Is it sexual harassment if someone makes an inappropriate comment to me? *A single comment is usually not sufficient to create a claim for harassment.* If the comment or comments are repetitive, they could create what the courts refer to as a "hostile work environment."

What other types of behaviors can create a hostile work environment? *There are a number of behaviors that, if pervasive, can create a hostile work environment.* They can best be grouped into three categories: Verbal, nonverbal and physical.

VERBAL

- Whistling, cat calling
- Using so-called terms of endearment, such as "honey," "babe," "sweetheart," "stud," or "chick."
- Making sexual comments or innuendos
- Telling sexual jokes or stories
- Making comments about a person's body
- Repeatedly asking a person out for a date who is not interested

NONVERBAL

- Inappropriate e-mails and screensavers
- Making sexual gestures
- Staring at someone
- Throwing kisses or licking lips
- Calendars
- Eating in a provocative manner

PHYSICAL

- Touching a person's clothing, hair or body
- Hugging, kissing, patting or stroking
- Touching or rubbing oneself sexually around another person
- Standing or brushing up against a person

Is it still harassment even if I do not mind the off-color jokes? *One of the requirements for sexual harassment to exist is that the conduct or behavior is unwelcome. If this condition is not met, then harassment may not be present.* An issue may be created for others, however. Though you may not be offended, someone else who hears the joke may be. It is best not to engage in this type of behavior at work.

Do some people just ask for suggestive comments by their dress or provocative behavior? *Within reason, individuals have the right to determine what they wear.* One's personal opinion of whether a coworker's appearance is provocative does not provide the right to sexually harass that person.

I work with someone that I am attracted to. If I ask her out could I be subject to a claim of harassment? *It is highly unlikely. Some statistics show that as many as 40 percent of all individuals meet their spouse at work.* Harassment rules were not implemented to inhibit dating. The most likely situation where a problem could arise is if the person asking for the date is told there is no interest and they continue to make requests.

CAUTION: Supervisors should not ask subordinates out. The nature of their role in having a say on promotions, transfers, work hours and other terms and conditions of employment greatly increases the risk of a harassment claim being lodged against them.

My supervisor is the same sex as me and has been making unwelcome suggestive comments. I am not gay and he is making me feel very uncomfortable. Is this harassment? *Sexual harassment need not be between opposite sexes.* It is possible for a man to harass a man or a woman to harass a woman. What is required is that the basis of the harassment be sex.

How does sexism tie in with the issue of sexual harassment? *Sexism occurs when attitudes promote stereotyping of roles based on gender.* If an individual takes actions toward someone else based on a stereotype, and the actions are unwelcome, sexual harassment may exist.

Does a comment or conduct have to be sexual to be considered harassment? *No.* If a supervisor yells only at his female staff and not his male staff, this could be considered sexual harassment.

What is the best way to deal with a harasser? *The best way to deal with someone who is harassing you is to confront him. More often than not an individual is not aware that they are engaging in unwelcome behavior and need only to be told.* In cases where confronting is not appropriate, tell your supervisor, the human resources head or the person designated in your company to receive sexual harassment complaints.

If a coworker harasses me, what should I do? *You should report the harassment to your supervisor or the designated employer representative as soon as possible. It is important that you document the evidence in your complaint.* This includes keeping copies of any offensive material as well as detailed notes of instances, witnesses and frequency of occurrences. Your company then has an obligation to take action to stop the harassment. If the company fails to act on your complaint, you can file a complaint with the EEOC.

Must the harasser be another employee? *No. The harasser can be the delivery person, a vendor, a client or anyone else who comes into the workplace.* You must give notice to your employer so that the company can remedy the situation.

What are my employer's responsibilities with respect to sexual harassment? Employers have a number of responsibilities:

- They must establish a sexual harassment prevention policy.
- The policy must be communicated to all staff.

- There should be a procedure spelled out for filing a complaint.
- They must investigate any complaint that is received.

> **TIP:** It is good practice to investigate complaints as soon as possible. Doing so will show the company's willingness to act decisively and eliminate undesirable behavior.

What steps can I take to ensure that I am not harassing someone else? The best way is to ask yourself the following questions:

1. Would you say the same thing in front of your mate?
2. Would you say it if it would be quoted in the newspaper?
3. Would you say it to a member of the same sex in exactly the same way?
4. Why does this need to be said? What business purpose is being advanced?
5. Is there an unfair use of power between you and the person you are interacting with?

Do I have any responsibilities with respect to dealing with harassment? *Yes. It is important that you support your coworkers and friends. If you see harassment take place, encourage the person who is being harassed to report it.* If they are unwilling, you may wish to do so. What is important to remember is that harassment is not about sex but about power, so it is likely that not only is your friend is being harassed but others are as well.

When can I file a complaint with the EEOC? *A complaint may be filed at any time with the EEOC or your State Division of Human Rights. The numbers for both should be in the Blue Pages of your phone book. The EEOC will begin investigating once it receives your complaint.* Usually, they send an information request to your employer. They will try to determine if there were other complaints, how pervasive the problem, is if it all, and what appropriate actions should be taken.

What steps are normally followed in a sexual harassment investigation? *Once the company receives a complaint, it is under an obligation to investigate.* The steps are as follows:

1. Interview the target. The target is the person who is bringing the complaint. Questions should include when, where, how often the inappropriate behavior has taken place, whether or not there are any witnesses, if the offender was confronted and the relationship between the two parties.

2. Interview the witnesses. See if anyone has firsthand knowledge of what occurred. Also establish what their relationship is to the parties to help eliminate bias. After speaking with firsthand witnesses, speak with those who may have indirect knowledge.

3. Adjust the workplace if necessary. If the harassment is ongoing or if the parties work together, find ways to diffuse the situation.

4. Interview the alleged harasser. Get this individual's perspective of what happened. Be objective when interviewing. Ask questions based on the information obtained from the target and the witnesses.

5. Make a determination. Evaluate all the facts and balance the weight of the evidence.

6. Severity of discipline. If harassment is found to have taken place, take the appropriate action. This will be determined by the severity of the offense, your company policy, whether the alleged harasser is a repeat offender and what your company may have done in similar situations.

7. Inform the parties. Get back to the target and let that person know that action has been taken. Have the supervisor institute any discipline or corrective changes recommended for the harasser.

CAUTION: An accusation alone of sexual harassment can harm a person's reputation. Therefore, it is absolutely essential that all parties maintain confidentiality throughout the entire investigative process.

What happens if the investigation has no definitive result? The parties should be told that the company was unable to substantiate the complaint one way or the other, but that in the event there is a subsequent complaint against the alleged harasser, it will be treated as a second offense.

PREGNANCY DISCRIMINATION

The Pregnancy Discrimination Act (PDA) is an amendment to Title VII. It prohibits employers from discriminating on the basis of pregnancy, childbirth or related medical conditions. As with Title VII, it provides protection in the case of hiring, firing, promotions, leaves, benefits, pay increases and other terms and conditions of employment.

Can my supervisor force me to take pregnancy leave? *No. As long as you are able to perform your job you can remain at work.* In addition, your employer may not mandate when you may return to work. Pregnancy is treated as a disability and you should be allowed to return to work as soon as you are able.

May my employer charge me a larger health insurance premium because I am pregnant? *Here again, the answer is no.* Any health insurance provided by the employer must be provided to you on the same basis as for other medical conditions.

I have to reduce my workforce and I have an employee out on pregnancy leave, must I guarantee her position? *The law does not provide this type of protection. Had the pregnant employee been at work, she would have been subject to the staff reduction.* As long as the reduction is based on business necessity and not the pregnancy, her position could be subject to being cut.

Does the Pregnancy Discrimination Act cover breastfeeding? *The law does not address breastfeeding.* However, check with your state, as a number of jurisdictions do have laws which allow for breastfeeding in public areas.

POLYGRAPH (LIE DETECTOR) TESTS

In 1988, Congress passed the Employee Polygraph Protection Act (EPPA), which prohibits most private employers from using lie detector tests for either preemployment screening or during the course of regular employment.

The act does allow an employer to request an employee to submit to a test in connection with an ongoing investigation if it has a reasonable suspicion that the employee was involved. However, this is only permitted if the employer provides the employee with a written statement describing the basis of the reasonable suspicion.

Are there any exemptions from this act?
Yes, but they are limited. In addition to "reasonable suspicion," security firm and drug manufacturers may have the right to test. However, they cannot deny employment or discharge or discriminate against employees based solely on the test.

What are my rights if I am subject to a test?
If you are subject to the test, you are entitled to reasonable notice as to when and where the test will take place. You also have the right to consult with an attorney or an employee representative before the test is given.

Can my employer ask me to waive my rights under the EPPA? *No.* An employee cannot waive these rights.

WHISTLE-BLOWER PROTECTION

What is a "whistle-blower"? A whistle-blower is an employee who reports his employer for a reasonable belief that a law has been broken.

What laws generally have whistle-blowing protections? *There are many laws that provide this type of protection.* The Occupational and Safety Health Administration (OSHA) administers provisions of the following laws as well as others:

- Clean Air Act
- Sarbanes-Oxley Act
- Asbestos Hazard Removal Act
- Occupational Safety and Health Act

In addition, the EEOC enforces the nonretaliation provisions of Title VII.

Federal employees also fall under the Whistle-blower Protection Act, which is enforced by the U.S. Office of Special Counsel.

What discriminatory actions do whistle-blower provisions prohibit?

- Assignment to undesirable shifts
- Blacklisting
- Demotions
- Denying overtime or promotion
- Transfer
- Layoff or discharge
- Reduction in pay

Can an employee be penalized for bringing a frivolous whistle-blower discrimination claim? An employee that files a frivolous or bad faith complaint may be ordered to pay the first $1,000 of the company's attorney's fees in defending against the claim.

Are there whistle-blower protections on the state level? Yes. Not only do most states provide this protection, there are a number of cities that have enacted this type of legislation as well.

PERSONNEL FILES

Do I have a right to view my personnel file?
The answer to this question depends on the state in which you work. The states of Alaska, California, Connecticut, Delaware, Illinois, Iowa, Maine, Massachusetts, Michigan, Minnesota, Nevada, New Hampshire, Oregon, Pennsylvania, Rhode Island, Washington and Wisconsin allow at least limited access to your files. In the other states, reviewing your file is at the discretion of the employer.

CAUTION: Never take information from your personnel file without permission from your employer. Doing so may be illegal and create additional problems.

What should I expect to find in my file?
Typically, documents will fall under the following categories:

- Employment documents
- Payroll information
- Performance appraisals
- Training
- Separation information
- Benefits
- Wage and salary data

- Employee communications
- Discipline

Are there certain documents that should not be kept in the personnel file? *Yes. Medical records should be kept separate, as well as Employment Eligibility Verification forms (Form I-9).* Any investigative records, security clearances and credit reports should also be kept out of the file.

> **TIP:** It is good policy to audit your employee's personnel files on a regular basis. Remove items that are no longer relevant, such as performance reviews more than 3 years old.

Is my electronic mail (e-mail) private?
Though there is an expectation of privacy, the answer is no. The company owns the equipment and the e-mail software, and is entitled to monitor its use. This extends to Web-based e-mail as well, whether it is Yahoo, AOL, AIM, or any other. The same rules hold true for voice mail.

> **TIP:** Employers are advised to inform employees that they maintain the right to monitor e-mail. The best way to do this is by having an e-mail and Internet policy in which the employee consents to any monitoring.

Can my boss listen to my phone calls at work? *It depends. Companies often monitor calls for quality-control purposes. If they are monitoring for business reasons, there is generally no issue.* In cases where the call is personal, the employer, under the Electronic Communications Privacy Act (ECPA), is supposed to immediately stop monitoring. There is an exception to this, where the employees are told not to make personal calls from business phones.

> **A number of states, most notably California, have state wiretap laws that provide employees with additional protection.**

Is my employer entitled to see what is on my computer at work? *Again, because the employer owns the equipment, it is entitled to monitor that equipment to ensure its use is for business purposes.* This monitoring can be done with the use of software that will monitor network and Internet usage.

Another type of computer monitoring is called "keystroke monitoring." Here the system counts how many keystrokes per hour each employee is making. It is typically used in industries where people spend most of their time inputting data. Some systems can monitor exactly what is being typed and deleted.

What restrictions, if any, are there on my company videotaping me without my permission? *For video monitoring to be permissible, the company must generally show a legitimate business purpose to do it, such as to protect inventory.* Monitoring should not be done in private areas such as restrooms or locker rooms.

May my employer search my desk? *The answer to this varies by state. In some cases where you can lock the desk, the answer is no. In other jurisdictions, the desk is treated as employer property and therefore the employer maintains the right to inspect.* Check with your local Department of Labor for the regulations in your state.

FILING A DISCRIMINATION CLAIM

Who investigates claims of discrimination?
The EEOC is the federal agency that receives and processes complaints in regard to Title VII and sexual harassment. There will be times when the agency will coordinate with state authorities in handling a complaint.

Who may file a claim of discrimination? Any individual who believes that her employment rights have been violated can file with the EEOC.

Where do I file a charge? *Charges may be filed by mail, in person or over the phone.* The local EEOC office may be reached by calling 800.669.4000.

How long do I file a discrimination claim?
In most cases the claim must be brought within 180 days of the discriminatory act. If your state has an antidiscrimination law, this deadline

may be extended to 300 days. Check with your state Human Rights Commission to see if your jurisdiction has extended the filing deadline.

What happens after the charge is filed with the EEOC? *Your company will be told that a charge has been filed. At that point the agency may ask the employer to respond in writing to the allegations that have been made.* The EEOC also has the right to investigate and may request documents, interview employees and visit the work site. The agency may also suggest mediation.

Do I lose my right to sue if the EEOC dismisses my claim? *No. Upon notice of dismissal, the EEOC will issue you a "right to sue" letter.* You will then have 90 days in which to file a lawsuit on your own behalf.

What remedies exist should the EEOC find that discrimination did occur? *There are a number of remedies available, including front and back pay, hiring, promotion, reinstatement or other reasonable accommodations.* In addition, the EEOC can order attorney's fees, expert witness costs and court costs be paid.

TIME OFF

As with benefits, most time granted away from the job is at the discretion of the company. Time off is often granted because it allows an employee to "recharge their batteries" (vacations), carry out civic responsibilities (jury duty) or deal with health or childcare issues. Payment for this time off is not required, although most companies do pay for time away from the job as an employee benefit.

IN GENERAL

Does my boss have to give me a rest break? *Under federal law the answer is no.* However, the federal Fair Labor Standards Act (FLSA) does provide that when breaks are granted and they last between 5 and 20 minutes, they must be considered work time and therefore must be paid.

Breaks on the state level vary greatly. A number of states mandate a 10-minute break for every 4 hours worked. Some have special rules for specific industries. Check with your local Department of Labor for the rules that apply to your location.

My boss has me eat lunch at my desk so I can answer the phone. Should I be paid for this time? The answer is most likely yes. Meal periods are generally not compensable where:

- they are at least 30 minutes long;
- the employee is not required to perform work duties; and
- the employee can walk around and leave the work area.

> **TIP:** To avoid questions being raised about whether these standards are being met, it may be advisable not to allow employees to eat at their desks.

Does my company have to offer sick leave? *Sick leave is granted at the discretion of the employer.* Most companies offer a limited amount of sick days or personal time off (PTO) days in recognition that illnesses and emergencies arise.

CAUTION: Companies that provide sick leave or PTO days often closely monitor the amount of time being taken off. An employee who takes an excessive amount of days may be subject to disciplinary action up to and including separation from employment.

> **TIP:** It makes sense to have a written sick leave policy. The policy should include such things as:
>
> - Number of days allotted and when and how they are earned
> - Whether they may be carried over into following years
> - Who should be called and notified of the absence
> - Whether the illness has to be the employee's or a member of the immediate family
> - Disciplinary action that may be taken if leave is exceeded

Does my employer have to pay me for federal holidays? *No. Payment of holidays is up to employer.* The 10 federal holidays are:

- New Years Day
- Martin Luther King's birthday
- Presidents' Day
- Memorial Day
- Independence Day
- Labor Day
- Columbus Day
- Veterans' Day
- Thanksgiving Day
- Christmas Day

Many employers give only 8 or 9 of these days off.

What does it mean to accrue vacation time? *Many employers have policies stating that vacation time "accrues." What this means is for every month you work, you accrue (or earn) time for vacations.* If your company policy is that employees can take 2 weeks (10 days) of earned vacation per year, you would be accruing the time at a rate of .833 days per month (10 days/12 months = .833).

If I have earned vacation time and have not taken it, must my employer pay me for that time? *Most likely. Twenty-nine states have rules dealing with "use it or lose it" policies.* The most stringent is California. Check with your state Department of Labor to see if your state has such a restriction.

Can my boss tell me when to use my vacation time? *Yes.* A company can designate an annual time when the facility is closed or restrict employees from taking time off during their busy season.

> **TIP:** To avoid problems, it makes sense to tell your employer as far in advance when you plan to take vacation so coverage or other alternative arrangements can be made.

Must my employer pay me if I take time off to vote? *It depends. Federal law protects an employee's right to vote, but it does not require that private employers give their employees time off to do so.* On the state level however, the rules are different. Twenty states require that employees be paid at least for the time spent voting. A number of others require that employees give notice to their employer that they are going to take time off. Check with your state Department of Labor to see what rules apply for your location.

I just received a summons to appear for jury duty. Does my employer have to give me time off? *Yes. Both federal and state laws require that employers give their employees time off in order to meet their civic duty of sitting on a jury.* In fact, if you are called to serve in a federal court, your employer cannot fire or threaten you for attending federal jury service. Most states also have similar types of protections for potential jurors.

Does this mean my employer has to pay me for my jury service? *The answer to this depends.* If you are an exempt employee and the jury service lasts less than a week, you must be paid your full salary under the FLSA.

If you are nonexempt, no such requirement exists. However, if you live in New York, Massachusetts or Connecticut, you may be entitled to pay from your employer for a limited period of time. Check with your state Department of Labor.

> **TIP:** No state provides for paid leave in the case of inclement weather. Check with your employer to see what the company's notice and closing procedures may be.

An employee just informed me that her brother passed away. Do I have to give her leave to attend the funeral? *There are no state or federal requirements that require an employer to provide funeral or bereavement leave.* From a practical perspective, an employer would be viewed as cold-hearted if it did not allow this time off. Depending on the economics of your company, this leave, which is typically 2 to 5 days, can be with or without pay.

FAMILY AND MEDICAL LEAVE ACT (FMLA)

In 1993, in an effort to provide employees an opportunity to take care of certain family and medical needs including early child-rearing, Congress passed the Family and Medical Leave Act (FMLA). A number of states have also enacted similar laws, which in some cases provide more coverage than the federal regulations.

I work for a small company, with only 10 employees. Am I covered under the FMLA? *If you work for a public employer, yes.* If you work for a private business, you will be covered if the following criteria are met:

- The employer has at least 50 employees at its location, or within a 75-mile radius.
- You worked for that employer for at least 1 year.
- You worked at least 1,250 hours during the 12 months prior to the start of the leave.

What does the FMLA do for me? If you meet the criteria above, the FMLA will allow you up to a total of 12 workweeks of unpaid leave in a 12-month period:

- for the birth, adoption or placement of a child;
- to care for an immediate family member (spouse, parent or child who has a serious health condition; or
- to handle your own serious health condition that leaves you unable to work.

Under FMLA, do I have to take the 12 weeks granted to me in a row? *No. The time can be broken up on an intermittent basis.* It is possible to take a few hours of leave every week for medical treatment.

My mother-in-law is ill. Can I take FMLA leave to care for her? *No.* The law specifically states that "parent" does not include a parent-in-law.

What constitutes a "serious health condition"? A serious health condition is an illness, injury or condition or impairment that involves:

- hospital care (includes hospice or residential medical facility);
- absence from work for 3 or more days, plus continuing treatment;
- pregnancy or prenatal care;
- treatment for a chronic serious health condition that requires periodic visits to a health care provider;
- permanent or long-term condition for which treatment may not be effective; or
- absence to receive multiple treatments (e.g., chemotherapy).

Do I have to let my employer know I want to take FMLA leave? *Yes, provided the leave is not in response to an unexpected medical emergency.* The law requires 30 days notice of an intention to take leave and the reasons for the leave.

May my employer require my medical records to prove a serious illness? *Medical records do not have to be provided.* The employer however, can ask that you provide medical certification that the condition exists. The certification must include:

- A description of the serious health condition.
- The date the condition began or treatment became necessary.
- The expected duration of the condition or treatment.

Does my health care insurance continue while I am on leave? *Yes.* If you share the cost of this coverage with your employer, you will have to arrange to continue to pay your portion of the insurance premiums.

What position will I return to at the end of my leave? Under the FMLA, you have to be reinstated into the same or equivalent job that you left, with the same pay and benefits.

Will taking FMLA leave affect my gaining a bonus, promotion or raise? *No. The leave cannot be held against an employee.* If you were eligible for a bonus prior to the leave, you will be entitled to that bonus on your return.

Is my job at risk for raising a complaint about the handling of an FMLA claim? An employer may not in any way interfere with, deny or take any adverse action with your rights provided under the FMLA.

Where do I go if I need to file a complaint regarding my rights under the FMLA? *The federal Wage and Hour Division of the Department of Labor (DOL) investigates and enforces the FMLA. Contact them at 866.4USWAGE (866.487.9243).* If your state has its own family medical leave legislation you may also contact your state DOL.

I am expecting to have a baby shortly. Does my company have to grant me maternity leave? *The answer to this question is yes; however, the leave will either be called "pregnancy leave" or "parental leave."* "Maternity leave" is a term that is normally reserved for women; using that reference can run afoul of the antidiscrimination laws.

Pregnancy leave is a type of medical leave that allows a woman time off from work during the period of time she is disabled as a result of having a baby. Parental leave applies to men as well as women and relates to leave for the care of a child, including a child who may have been adopted.

If your company has 15 or more employees, the federal Pregnancy Discrimination Act (PDA) protects a pregnant woman against being fired, refused a new job, or denied a promotion. Further, leave for pregnancy would be treated the same as any other disability that someone in your company may incur. Also, many states have pregnancy discrimination protection for women.

My wife and I are adopting a child. Can I take parental leave? *If your company has at least 50 employees, you are eligible for unpaid leave under the Family and Medical Leave Act (FMLA).* You may also be able to take sick, personal or vacation days. Some companies allow for unpaid leave. Check with your human resources department or supervisor about your company policy.

This type of leave is becoming more common. In 2004, California became the first state to offer paid family leave, giving eligible employees up to 6 weeks at partial pay to care for a new child.

MILITARY LEAVE

In 1994, the federal government passed the Uniformed Services Employment and Reemployment Rights Act (USERRA). The act states that anyone in the "uniformed services" (Army, Air Force, Marines, Navy, Coast Guard, Air and Army National Guard and the Commissioned Corps of the Public Health Service) is eligible for military leave.

The law then defines military service as including the performance of duty whether it be voluntarily or involuntarily, which can include active duty, active or inactive duty for training and full-time National Guard duty.

If my employee goes on military leave, do I have to continue paying his health care coverage? *The answer depends upon how long the leave lasts. If the military leave is less than 31 days, coverage must continue and the employee may not be required to pay more.* Employees whose service goes beyond 31 days may elect COBRA coverage.

> **TIP:** Employees returning from military service are exempt from any waiting periods to reestablish health care coverage, and any preexisting condition that is a result of their military service may not be excluded from coverage.

What rights do employees returning from military duty have with respect to their position? *If the leave from work was for 90 days or less, the employee has to be given back her position as if her employment had been continuous.* If the position has changed, the returning employee must be given a reasonable amount of time to upgrade her skills in order to qualify for reemployment. "Reasonable efforts" must be made by the employer to assist the employee in upgrading those skills.

If the leave was more than 90 days, the employee has to be reinstated into his or her prior position or into a position of like seniority, status and pay, so long as the employee is qualified. As in the prior scenario, the employer must make reasonable efforts to ensure the returning employee qualifies for the position.

I need to schedule my workforce in advance. Are employees required to give notice when leaving for or returning from military service? *Employees must provide their employer with advance notice of their upcoming military service, either orally or in writing.* There are exceptions if it would be impossible or unreasonable to give notice, or military necessity prevents giving notice.

Further, an employee must report back to work or apply to return to work under the following requirements:

Length of Leave	Period When Employee Must Return to Work or Apply for Reemployment
1-30 days (or to take a fitness exam)	Report back to work at the next scheduled shift after returning home and 8 hours of rest.
31-180 days	Apply for reemployment within 14 days after release from service.
181 days or more	Apply for reemployment within 90 days after release from service.

Am I allowed to discharge anyone who has returned from military leave? *If the employee served for more than 6 months, he cannot be let go for 1 year after reemployment except for cause.* For those who served less than 6 months but more than 30 days, they must be retained (except for cause) for 6 months. Service of 30 days or less does not carry any protection.

SAFETY AND SECURITY

In 1970, the federal government passed the Occupational Safety and Health Act in an effort to get both employers and employees to reduce hazards and injuries in the workplace. The act also encouraged companies to put safety and health programs into place. It is beneficial to everyone that the workplace be a safe and healthful.

OCCUPATIONAL SAFETY AND HEALTH ACT

Who is responsible for administering this act? *When Congress passed the Occupational Safety and Health Act, they also created within the Department of Labor a new agency called the Occupational Safety and Health Administration (OSHA).* OSHA is responsible for ensuring worker safety and issuing safety guidelines.

> **Twenty-three states have their own OSHA programs. These programs offer protections similar to the federal plan. The states can conduct inspections, set standards and respond to employee complaints.**

Does OSHA protect me? *If you work for a company, whether it is publicly or privately held, the answer is yes.* You have OSHA coverage either under the federal or state run programs, or both. Public-sector workers are not covered in states under federal OSHA jurisdiction but may have state protection if their state runs an OSHA program.

What rights, if any, does OSHA grant me as an employee? Some of the rights granted to you include the right to:

- review standards and regulations;
- request information from your company on safety and hazards that may exist in the workplace;
- request an OSHA inspection if you believe there is a violation;
- ask for written information as to whether any substance in the workplace has potentially toxic effects; and
- file a complaint if you are disciplined or are discriminated against for "whistle-blowing."

Can I refuse to do a job if I think it is too dangerous or it is harmful to my health? *This is a sticky area. Ordinarily, you do not have the right to refuse to do work.* In most cases you are expected to perform your assigned tasks and then file a complaint later. However,

OSHA regulations state that if you have a good faith belief that doing the job will put you in imminent danger, you can refuse to do the job.

> **TIP:** Prior to refusing to do a job, make sure that all of these conditions are met:
>
> 1. You have asked the employer to eliminate the risk and the company failed to do so.
>
> 2. You truly believe that a danger exists.
>
> 3. A reasonable person would agree that the danger is real or there is a strong likelihood of serious injury.
>
> 4. There is not enough time to get the problem corrected through regular channels.

I am worried about safety conditions at work. How do I know whether to ask my employer to correct the situation or call OSHA? *In most situations you will want to give your employer the opportunity to correct the unsafe or unhealthy situation.* The company then may wish to decide to call OSHA or another consultant to get advice on correcting the problem. OSHA may be contacted at any time, but should be called as a first resort only if your company has a history of ignoring safety concerns or if it is a serious safety or health hazard.

Can my employer fire me because I filed an OSHA complaint? *No.* You cannot be fired, transferred, denied a raise or promotion, or have any other term or condition of employment changed as a result of raising an issue to OSHA.

> **TIP:** Complaints about reprisals have a short filing period. You must notify OSHA within 30 days of the alleged action.

Does my employer have to provide safety training specific to my job? *Generally speaking, the answer is no.* While there are a number of OSHA standards that specifically require training, most make it the employer's responsibility to train employees in the safety and health aspects of their jobs.

OSHA has developed voluntary training guidelines to help companies provide the needed health and safety information. The guidelines help employers to determine if a work-site problem can be resolved by training, help determine what training if any is needed, establish goals for the training, create learning activities, assist in conducting the training and give feedback on the effectiveness of the training. Employers interested in learning more should contact their local OSHA office.

Does my employer have to provide me with protective equipment, or do I have to buy it myself? *At present, it is not clear who has to pay. OSHA has proposed legislation that will require employers to pay for Personal Protective Equipment (PPE) at no cost to employees.* But there are a few exceptions: the employer would not need to pay for safety-toe protective footwear or prescription safety eyewear if all three of the following conditions are met: (1) the employer permits such footwear or eyewear to be worn off the job site; (2) the footwear or eyewear is not used in a manner that renders it unsafe for use off the job site (e.g., contaminated safety-toe footwear would not be permitted to be worn off a job site); and (3) such footwear or eyewear is not designed for special use on the job.

What is an OSHA "standard"? *A "standard" is a rule that OSHA puts into effect to protect workers.* It could be the amount of time an employee can spend in a noisy area, the amount of hazardous chemicals a worker may be exposed to or a specification regarding safety equipment. If your company does not comply with an established standard, it could receive a fine from OSHA.

As an employer, I do my best to comply with OSHA standards, but I am confused. What are the differences between OSHA "guidelines" and OSHA "standards"? *Simply, a standard is a requirement. Standards specify the minimum conditions that the employer must provide to ensure its employees' safety.* Guidelines are voluntary. They are there to give employees suggestions for resolving a health or safety concern, but allow the employer to come up with its own method of resolving a potential problem situation.

If OSHA enacts a new standard that I cannot meet, do I have any recourse? *Employers who cannot comply with new standards or disagree with the standard have three options.* They have the following three options:

1. Petition the court for review.
2. Request a permanent, temporary, or experimental variance from the standard.
3. Apply for an interim order to continue working under existing conditions while OSHA reviews a variance request.

What is an OSHA "variance"? *A variance is permission given by OSHA that allows an employer to deviate from a standard or a time frame in which to comply.* OSHA has three types of variances:

- ▸ **TEMPORARY.** Granted if there is not enough time to comply, or if the technical personnel, material or equipment are not available.

- ▸ **PERMANENT.** Granted if the employer can show that its methods of providing safety are as safe and healthful had it complied with the standard.

- ▸ **EXPERIMENTA .** Granted if the employer is involved in a study to show or prove a new safety or health technique.

Is an employer required to keep records for OSHA? *If you have less than 10 employees, you are exempt from having to keep an OSHA log of injuries and illnesses, unless specifically directed to do so by the government.* OSHA also exempts certain low hazard industries from having to report.

CAUTION: All employers must report to OSHA within 8 hours of the following:

- the death of any employee from a work-related accident; or
- the in-patient hospitalization of three or more employees as a result of a work-related incident.

> **TIP:** All employers must also post the OSHA "Job Safety and Health Protection" poster.

What types of companies are subject to OSHA inspections? *Any business may be subject to an OSHA inspection.* However, because there are so many businesses, OSHA normally inspects only the most hazardous. To determine where they will go first, the agency follows these priorities: (a) imminent danger— conditions or dangers that are likely to cause death or serious harm; (b) catastrophes and fatal accidents; (c) employee complaints regarding imminent danger; (d) referrals; (e) planned inspections; and (f) follow-up review businesses that have been previously inspected.

What happens during an OSHA inspection? *In general, most inspections follow the same pattern. An inspector will arrive and show his credentials.* The inspector will then explain the reason for the inspection and discuss the scope of the visit. He may request that an employee accompany him when walking around the plant. During the walk around, the inspector will be looking for hazards and make corrective action suggestions. Following the walk around, the inspector will meet with the employer again and discuss any violations that may have been found. Citations may be issued. He will then inform the employer of the right to contest the citations.

> **OSHA does not allow the employer to select the employee representative for the walk around.**

What kind of penalties can be assessed? *The amount of the penalty varies. An amount of up to $7,000 may be assessed for violations that relate to job safety and health, but would not cause serious physical harm or injury.* For willful violations, penalties range from $5,000 to $70,000. Criminal convictions and higher dollar penalties are also possible for willful violations where the death of an employee has occurred.

What type of information and training material if any is available from OSHA? *OSHA has made great strides in the last few years to make as much information accessible to employers and employees.* Their Web site, **www.osha.gov**, is replete with information, posters and publications. A list of OSHA publications may be found at **www.osha.gov/pls/publications/pubindex.list**.

VIOLENCE IN THE WORKPLACE

Violence in the workplace is a growing and serious problem. Homicide is the second leading cause of death on the job after motor vehicle accidents and is the leading cause of workplace death among women. However, workplace violence goes beyond physical assault. It can include acts by which a person is abused, threatened, intimidated or assaulted.

Are there factors that increase the risk of work related violence? Some of the working conditions or factors that increase an employee's risk to violence include:

- Handling money, valuables or prescription drugs
- Providing service, education or advice
- Working with individuals who may be unstable
- Working alone
- Working where alcohol is served

Does my employer have a duty to protect me or to make changes to make my job safer? *An employer is not under a specific obligation or standard to protect you.* However, under OSHA's "General Duty Clause," an employer is responsible for providing its employees "employment and a place of employment which are free of recognized hazards that are causing or are likely to cause death or serious physical harm to … employees."

I work in the health care industry where violence is on the rise. How can OSHA make my job safer? OSHA has issued guidelines for employers outlining the factors needed for a Workforce Violence Protection Program. The general elements of such a program include:

- A written company workplace violence policy
- The establishment of a threat assessment team
- Hazard assessment
- Hazard control and prevention
- Training and education
- Reporting, investigating and follow-up procedures
- Record keeping

What elements should be included in a workplace violence policy? The policy should include the following:

- A clear definition of what is meant by workplace violence
- Definitive examples of behaviors that are not acceptable
- The company's commitment to prevention of workplace violence
- The specific consequences of making threats or committing violence (zero tolerance)
- A mechanism for reporting all incidents of violence, which provides for confidentiality
- A description of investigation procedures and assurance of no reprisals

As an employer, how do I respond to a threat in the workplace? *If a threat appears to be imminent, law enforcement officials should be notified.* Where the threats are against a certain employee, such as "I know which car is yours," it may be best to provide the employee who was threatened with options such as alternate parking, a change in work hours or the use of an escort to their vehicle. The threatening employee should be dealt with in a manner consistent with your violence prevention policy.

UNIONS

The National Labor Relations Act (NLRA) is the primary law that governs an employee's right to organize and bargain collectively. The National Labor Relations Board (NLRB) enforces the act. The NLRA guarantees covered employees the right to form, join or assist labor organizations, bargain collectively through a representative of their choosing, engage in concerted activities for the purpose of collective bargaining, strike and to refrain from union activity.

Are all employees covered by the NLRA? *No.* The act sets out a number of exclusions. These include:

- Supervisors
- Agricultural workers
- Individuals employed by a parent or spouse
- Those employed in domestic service in a home
- Those employed subject to the Railway Labor Act

- Those employed by state, local or federal government
- Those employed by any person who is not defined as an employer under the NLRA

How does a union organize within a company?

Workers form unions in their company by organizing a majority of their coworkers. If 30 percent or more of eligible employees sign a petition to recognize a union, the NLRB will schedule an election. If the union receives more than half of the votes from those eligible to vote, they then have the right to bargain collectively with the employer. It is also possible that the company will voluntarily recognize the union. This, however, is unusual.

If my employees wish to organize a union, are there things I am prohibited from doing when convincing them they are making a mistake?

A company has the right to present the facts as they see them as to why a union would be inappropriate for its workforce. Though they are generally free to have meetings to express these views or send out communications, they may not engage in the following behaviors. These behaviors can be remembered as TIPS.

T　An employer may not make threats against its employees;

I　The employer may not interrogate employees with respect to union activity;

P　Promises cannot be made, (e.g., vote against the union and I will give you a raise); and

S　An employer may not engage in surveillance.

Can I ban my employees from using e-mail to organize a union?

You can if the policy is uniformly adopted. If you allow your employees to solicit for Girl Scout cookies, or collections for birthdays or weddings over the e-mail system, you would have a hard time enforcing such a ban.

Are there any practices that the union cannot engage in?

Yes. The union may not:

- threaten employees with a loss of job or benefits if they fail to support the union;
- refuse to process a grievance because of a personal bias;
- fine an employee for engaging in protected activity after resigning from the union;

- seek the discharge of an employee for not complying with a union shop agreement when the employee has paid or offered to pay a lawful initiation fee and dues; and
- refuse referral or give preference in a hiring hall on the basis of union activity.

What are the benefits of belonging to a union?

The greatest benefit derived by union membership is the ability to bargain collectively over wages, benefits, safety, job security and other terms and conditions of employment. By acting in concert, the workforce has far greater economic power to bear over the employer than does an employee standing alone.

Are there drawbacks to belonging to a union?

Many of the pluses of belonging to a union can also be seen as drawbacks. They bring a loss of individuality, so if someone is an outstanding performer, they may not get recognized for promotion due to someone else's seniority, or may be limited in earnings due to wage rules.

Do I have to join the union or pay union dues?

You may not be required to join the union but you may have to pay union fees unless you work in one of the 29 right-to-work states. In non-right-to-work states, the collective bargaining agreement between your employer and the union will provide for one of the following:

Open Shop	You do not have to join the union or pay dues.
Agency Shop	You do not have to join the union but you do have to pay dues.
Union Shop	You do not have to be a union member before accepting the job, but must join the union within a certain period of time.

How do the union and my employer resolve disputes?

Almost every collective bargaining agreement has a grievance procedure. This procedure spells out the steps to be followed to resolve workplace disputes. The grievance procedure is typically multistepped, with more senior management involved in the later steps.

In cases where the dispute cannot be resolved between the parties, there is often a provision that requires arbitration. Here, a third-party neutral, called an arbitrator, is called in to listen to the facts and make a ruling. The arbitrator's decision is final and binding upon the parties.

What happens if the union goes on strike?

When employees have a dispute with their employer, they have the right to declare a strike. More often than not, this takes place when the collective bargaining agreement is up for renewal. If the strike is for economic reasons, the company may hire replacement workers. These employees may remain even when the strike ends, until there are new job openings. If the strike is a result of an unfair labor practice by the employer, workers can demand reinstatement when the strike is over.

EMPLOYMENT PRACTICES AND POLICIES

EMPLOYEE HANDBOOKS

Many companies create employee handbooks to help communicate their policies, provide a consistent standard of operation and to set the appropriate level of expectations. Creating a handbook helps cut down on misunderstandings and avert claims of discrimination. Creating a handbook need not be an expensive undertaking; it could just be a number of pages stapled together. Its form is not as important as its substance.

What should be included in my employee handbook? Most handbooks include the following topics:

- Company rules and procedures
- Holidays and paid time off
- Leave provisions
- Information on working hours
- Pay practices and procedures
- Performance review and promotion practices
- Benefits
- Vacation
- Safety
- Dress code

- Sexual harassment and non-discrimination policy
- Discipline and discharge practices
- Drug and alcohol policy
- Employment at will statement
- An acknowledgment page stating that the employee agrees to comply with the policies within the handbook

> **TIP:** You can write the handbook yourself and then send it to an attorney for review.

EMPLOYEE DISCIPLINE

Despite their best efforts, there are times when employees do not perform up to expectations. This could be due to a family situation that is distracting them, a lack of training, an inability to keep up with the work or a myriad of other reasons. It is unusual for employees to perform poorly on purpose, and this should be kept in mind when you initiate any disciplinary action.

What is progressive discipline and how does it differ from a corrective action program? *A progressive discipline program is one where the penalty increases for continued violation of the rules or poor performance.* A corrective action program is similar in that the discipline increases during each step, but in this type of program the focus is more on correcting the behavior rather than punishing for it.

What are the typical steps in a corrective action program? Generally, there are four steps:

1. **VERBAL WARNING.** As with all corrective actions, this should be given in private away from other staff and interruptions. The employee should be told what they are doing incorrectly and asked how they are going to correct it. A note should be made to the employee's personnel file indicating the date the discussion took place and actions agreed upon.

> **TIP:** Employees who are subject to corrective action should also document when meetings take place and what was discussed.

2. **WRITTEN WARNING.** This is a second warning to an employee. It is more formal than an oral warning, as it is a formal

document that is handed to the employee. Typically it includes the date of the warning, a description of the misconduct, a personal improvement plan (PIP), specific items the employee must improve upon and an open-ended time frame in which to improve, a signature by the manager and a line for the signature of the employee. This signing acknowledges receipt, not necessarily agreement.

> **TIP:** It is beneficial to have another management representative present for this and any subsequent steps to serve as a witness for what is discussed.

3. SUSPENSION. Depending on the severity of the offense, this can be from 1 day to 2 weeks. In almost all cases it is unpaid. Along with the suspension should be another written warning. The suspension may include a statement that says "Should there be a repetition of this action, you will be subject to separation from employment."

4. TERMINATION. The employee is released.

> **TIP:** In designing your corrective action program, the company should maintain the right to skip any step if the situation so warrants. Then, if there is a serious violation of policy, such as theft, violence or insubordination, the company may terminate the individual immediately.

As an employee, am I entitled to have someone present during a corrective action discussion?

Yes. In what has become the Weingarten Rule, the U.S. Supreme Court ruled that an employee may be represented by the union at an investigatory interview with his supervisor if the employee reasonably believes that the interview may lead to disciplinary action. The National Labor Relations Board has expanded this right to nonunion employees who can request that a coworker be present.

> **TIP:** For this rule to apply, the employee must make a clear request for union representation or to have a fellow coworker present.

Is my employer required to give me a performance review?

There are no federal or state requirements that employers review their employees. However, performance reviews are valuable to both the company and the employee for the following reasons:

- They help set objectives and review accomplishments.
- They can provide a basis for compensation decisions.
- They provide a forum for communication and problem solving.
- They help identify training needs.
- They clarify employees' career aspirations.
- They improve supervisor/subordinate relationships.

> **TIP:** For performance appraisals to be effective, they need to be viewed as fair and equitable. It is important that managers be trained in how to review staff and learn to focus on objective rather than subjective factors of performance.

I just took a new position with a company that has a probationary period. What does this mean? *Many companies have such a practice. In general, for the first 30, 60, or 90 days or 6 months of employment, you are considered on probation.* As such, you may not be subject to the progressive discipline program or entitled to certain benefits. The company uses this period to determine if it made the right hiring decision.

> **TIP:** Employers who wish to engage in such a practice are far better off calling this an introductory period. A number of courts have held that when an employee completes probation, she become a permanent employee. This type of ruling can invalidate an employee's "at will" status. By using an introductory period upon completion, an employee becomes a "regular employee and "employment at will" status is maintained.

I am a supervisor with my company and want to date one of my subordinates. My boss said this violates the company dating policy.

Is this legal? *There are no federal or state laws that prohibit an employer from establishing a dating policy in the workplace.* Dating a subordinate is always a risky proposition due to the potential of sexual harassment. Even if the relationship is initially welcome, if it ends badly, problems can arise. In addition, if a company has a number of supervisors dating subordinates, it may be perceived as the only way to get ahead in the company and create a hostile work environment.

> **TIP:** When drafting a dating policy, make sure that the policy is gender neutral and does not have a discriminatory impact. Policies that require the employee in the lesser job to transfer have often been found to violate sex discrimination statutes.

Can my employer prohibit me from wearing controversial T-shirts or buttons in the workplace? *If the company can show a valid business reason for not allowing the T-shirt, it may do so. These reasons can include not wanting to alienate customers or coworkers, safety or avoiding confrontation.* What an employer cannot prohibit in almost all cases is protected activity. Therefore, wearing a T-shirt saying "Vote yes for the union" or a button stating "I am a member of XYZ union" is permissible.

How do I identify employees who may have a substance abuse problem? *Substance abuse issues usually show themselves through a change in the employee's behavior and in a diminishing of performance.* Some of the telltale signs include the following:

PERFORMANCE

- Inconsistent work quality
- Poor concentration
- Lowered productivity
- Increased absenteeism
- Unexplained disappearances from the job site
- Careless mistakes
- Errors in judgment
- Needless risk-taking

BEHAVIORAL INDICATORS

- Financial problems
- Avoidance of friends and colleagues
- Blaming others for own problems and shortcomings
- Complaints about problems at home
- Deterioration in personal appearance

Can I require one of my employee's to take a drug test? *You should first have a drug test policy that spells out under what conditions the company may test, usually for cause or following an accident.* To ensure that it complies with local regulations, an attorney should review your policy. If the policy is valid, there should be no problem in testing.

What should I do if one of my employees has a substance abuse problem? *It is important to keep your observations job related. Look at performance and document what you see. Next, reaffirm the company's position on substance abuse.* Explain the policy and reiterate the company's expectations. Finally, be supportive and help identify resources the employee can turn to if they have a problem. If the company has an Employee Assistance Program, you could suggest that the employee make a call.

SEPARATION FROM EMPLOYMENT

It is not uncommon to hear that a friend or relative has lost his job. Maybe you have personally experienced a recent job loss. The likelihood that an individual will be let go sometime in their career is extremely high. Often the separation will be due to no fault of your own. Companies get acquired, downsized, have economic hardships or just elect to close their doors.

In other situations an employee may have brought the separation upon themselves through excessive absenteeism, theft, insubordination, breaking work rules or by failing to perform the requirements of the job. Whatever the reason for the job loss, it is important that you put it behind you and get ready to move on to the next opportunity.

IN GENERAL

Should I quit if I think I am about to be fired?
In general, this is not a good idea. Many states deny unemployment benefits to employees who resign their position. Further, it is also often easier to find another job when you are working than when you are unemployed.

Does the company have to grant me severance pay?
There is no legal obligation to provide severance pay to an employee who has been laid off or fired. However, an employer can create a severance obligation if it has paid severance in the past to employees in similar positions or the company's handbook states that the company pays severance.

Do I have to be warned by the company prior to them letting me go?
In most cases the answer is no. If your company has a progressive discipline procedure or corrective action procedure, it may require that certain steps be followed prior to a termination. Many companies provide for a performance improvement plan before an employee is released. However, in almost all of these policies there is a provision that states in cases of "just cause" an employee may be let go immediately.

My company has offered to pay me severance if I waive my right to sue them. Can they do this?
A company can do this, but the courts look to ensure that the employee has received adequate consideration for the release. This means that the company has to give you more than what they give other employees who do not waive their rights.

For employers who wish to secure such a release it is necessary to show the following:

- The release was secured voluntarily.
- It is written in easily understood language.
- The employee was encouraged to consult an attorney before signing it.
- Adequate consideration was provided.
- The employee was given an opportunity to negotiate the terms.
- Enough time was given for the employee to think about signing (The Age Discrimination in Employment Act requires 21 days).
- The employee was given the ability to repudiate (usually 7 days).

I have an employee who I need to let go. What factors should I keep in mind in deciding whether to terminate?
Prior to any termination, you should ask yourself the following questions:

1. Did the employee have notice of the requirements of the job or the policies and procedures?
2. Have the policies been applied consistently?
3. Was the employee warned that his actions could lead to termination?
4. Did you listen to the employee's position?
5. Were there any extenuating circumstances?
6. Have others who performed similarly been let go?
7. Have you checked to ensure that no discriminatory issues exist or that the employee did not engage in protected activity?
8. Have you documented your case?

What is "wrongful discharge"?
Wrongful discharge is an exception to the employment at-will rule. It occurs when the employee is fired for violating a public policy, such as whistle-blowing or refusing to do something illegal. It may also occur where the employer violates the employment contract.

"AT WILL" EMPLOYEES

What is an "at will" employee?
Most of us are "employees at will." This means that we work at the discretion of the employer. At-will employees can be let go at any time and for any reason, provided the action is not discriminatory or for whistle-blowing.

CAUTION: An employer can create an implied contract of employment if it makes verbal or written statements that are contrary to employment at will.

> **TIP:** Employers should review their employee handbook to ensure that there are no statements or policies that may be construed as changing the at-will relationship. Also, they should avoid making such statements such as "We only let go employees for good reason."

I have only been working 2 weeks. Can I be terminated in my new job? *Yes.* In at-will employment situations, you do not have the right to a certain amount of time on the job before you can be terminated.

I do not have an employment contract, but I signed the agreement at the back of the company handbook to follow the procedures in it. Can I still be terminated? *Yes. The law is clear that signing an employee or company handbook is not the same as having a job contract.* You are an employee at will and can be terminated at any time for no reason at all.

> **If the handbook varies the terms of employment and is signed, then a job contract may exist. For example, if the handbook states that "employees can only be terminated for just cause," the employer has limited his right to fire an employee for any or no reason.**

Are there employees who do not work at will? *Yes, there are some employees who work under an employment contract.* The contract defines the terms of employment including the duties of the job, compensation, language regarding separation and often a confidentiality and noncompete clause. It is highly unusual for employers to offer employment contracts to any employee other than the senior managers or to individuals with special skills.

EMPLOYEES WITH RIGHTS TO A JOB

I am a civil service employee and have been notified that I am being terminated. What happens next? *Because of your employment classification, your employer is required to follow certain procedures.* If the requirements are not fulfilled and you are still terminated, you have a cause of action against your employer.

Typically, the procedure for terminating a civil service employee requires:

- providing the employee with a written notice giving the reasons for termination;
- allowing the employee a reasonable time period (10 days, for example) to respond or file an appeal;
- permitting the employee to take the appeal to a higher authority (a state personnel board of review, for example);
- setting a hearing within a reasonable amount of time (30 days, for example);
- allowing the employee to give his side of the story, including presenting evidence at the hearing;
- allowing the employee to have a legal or union representative at the hearing; and
- permitting the employee the right to appeal a hearing decision to a court.

During this time period, the employee remains on the job (unless there has been alleged criminal activity) and continues to be paid.

> **TIP:** Civil service employees generally work under a probationary status when they first begin a job. During a probationary period, the employee is an employee at will and has no property interest in the job. Once the probationary period ends, if the employee stays on or is offered the job, she has a property interest in it.

I work in the state transportation office. Am I a civil service employee? *Not necessarily.* Some employees, such as those who work for elected officials, are at-will employees.

Can I sue my employer for firing me when I was told I would always have a job at the company until I retired? *Yes. If you employer made a clear and unequivocal promise that you had lifetime employment, you may have been wrongfully terminated.* However, some state courts require you to show that you gave some additional consideration (something beyond your agreement to do your job) to the employer in exchange for the lifetime job. For example, if you had to move to accept the job, you gave the employer additional consideration.

If the agreement was for lifetime employment as long as the employee performed satisfactorily, the agreement may be unenforceable. In such a situation, either party can terminate the employment at will because the employee has a duty to perform satisfactorily regardless of the duration of the job. In that case, it seems unlikely than an employer would offer lifetime employment.

An oral promise that cannot be performed within 1 year must be in writing. If you were promised a job until age 65 when you were hired at age 55, the promise must be in writing. Without a written agreement, the court will not even consider if it is enforceable or not.

TIP: If the employer promised that the job would last "until retirement," the agreement may not have to be in writing. It is conceivable the employee could retire within the year, making a written agreement unnecessary.

I have a teaching contract for a year. Does that mean I cannot be terminated during the year? *No. The contract means certain procedures must be followed by the school district before it can terminate you.* Typically, you have the right to notice of the termination and an opportunity to a hearing before the school board before a final decision is made. If the school district fails to follow its procedures, you will have a cause of action for wrongful termination.

There is no inherent constitutional right to public employment. The constitutional right that does exist is the right to be heard before termination. These due process rights exist because of an employment contract or a specific law that protects that job (a postal employee, for example).

My employer refuses to tell me why I am being terminated. Am I entitled to an explanation? You are if you have a property interest in your job. In that situation, the law requires that you be furnished with:

- an oral or written notice explaining why you are being terminated, including any allegations or charges against you;
- an explanation of your employer's evidence; and
- an opportunity to present your side of the story.

You are not owed an explanation if you are an employee at will.

My employment contract does not state how long I have a job but it does include a 6-year bonus schedule. Am I guaranteed a job for 6 years? *No.* Bonus schedules do not alter the duration of an employment contract. If your contract does not state how long you will be employed, you can be terminated at any time.

TIP: An offer of employment at "an annual salary of $40,000" is not an employment contract for 1 year. The term "annual" does not limit the employer's right to terminate the employee at any time.

"JUST CAUSE" DISMISSALS

I was terminated for no reason even though I have an employment contract requiring "just cause." Can I file a lawsuit against my former employer? *Yes. You can sue for wrongful discharge based on the breach of your employment contract.* If your employer wrongfully discharged you, you can recover the wages, bonuses and other amounts you would have received if you had not lost your job, plus attorneys' fees and court costs.

What constitutes "just cause"?
- Theft
- Violence
- Insubordination
- Lying on the employment application
- Excessive absenteeism or lateness
- Other similar causes

If you believe that you may be terminated and wish to challenge it, you should create a paper trail. This includes keeping documents of work-related events such as performance reviews, salary increases, reprimands and letters of commendation. You should also keep a copy of the employee handbook, if there is one, and, if permitted by your state, request to make a copy of your personnel file.

PLANT CLOSINGS AND MASS LAYOFFS

In 1988, the federal government passed the Worker Adjustment and Retraining Act (WARN). This act protects workers and their families by requiring employers to provide notice 60 days in advance of a plant closing or mass layoff.

Who is covered by WARN? *WARN generally covers employers with 100 or more employees.* All employees are entitled to notice, including managers and supervisors as well as hourly and salaried workers.

What constitutes a "plant closing"? A covered plant closing occurs when a facility or operation is closed down and the shutdown results in a loss of employment for 50 or more employees during any 30-day period.

What is a "mass layoff"? A mass layoff is defined as an employment loss at the employment site during any 30-day period for 500 or more employees, or 33 percent of the workforce, whichever is larger.

> **The layoff needs to be at one site, not the company as a whole.**

Who must receive notice? If a union represents the employees, the union must be notified of the plant closing or the mass layoff. If unrepresented, any worker who may expect to lose her job needs to be notified.

Are there specific requirements of what has to be in the notice? The notice needs to be written in language easy to understand and must contain the following elements:

1. A statement as to whether the planned action is expected to be permanent or temporary.

2. The expected date when the plant closing or mass layoff will begin and the expected date the individual will be separated.

3. An indication if seniority (bumping) rights exist.

4. The name and telephone number of a company official to contact for further information.

What if there is a failure to give notice to employees? *Failing to notify can be costly.* Damages include back pay and benefits to each affected employee who did not receive notice for the period of violation up to 60 days. There is also a civil penalty of up to $500 per day.

What do I do if I get laid off? *Confusion, anger, disappointment and embarrassment are all normal emotions after being laid off. People often try to keep their job loss a secret, even from their family. Fight this feeling.* Unemployment can be a stressful time and you need the support of family and friends. They will be the people who will support you while you look for a new opportunity. Keeping up a routine will help keep you on the right path. Treat yourself well. Eat right, exercise, get enough sleep and go about looking for a job as a job itself.

> **TIP:** Although you may be angry, remember to leave the employer on good terms. You may need to go back to them for references, and you want them to remember you as being a professional even as you walk out the door.

First steps to take after a layoff:

In the short term, plan to do the following:

1. **SPEAK TO YOUR FORMER EMPLOYER ABOUT COBRA.** COBRA is a federal program that requires employers in most cases to allow you to continue your medical insurance at the group rate for the next 18 months. For more on your COBRA rights, see below.

2. **FILE FOR UNEMPLOYMENT.** Each state has a program that gives assistance to those employees who have lost their jobs through no fault of their own. While you were working, you paid into the fund. It is there for your use so take advantage of it. Most states' employment offices also offer out-of-

work individuals training, Internet assistance and job leads. Check with your local employment services agency.

3. **UPDATE YOUR RESUME.** Add skills and responsibilities that you have learned in your last position. Put in any training or other skills that you may have acquired.

4. **NETWORK.** Make a list of everyone you know. Friends, family and old work acquaintances. All these people can help in making you aware of new opportunities to consider.

> **TIP:** If you were fired from your last position, the worst thing that you can do is lie about it. Bad situations are often the best learning experiences. Speak about what you gained at your last job rather than focusing on the negative.

PROVIDING A REFERENCE

Prior to your former employee being rehired, it is likely that you will be called to give a reference. Providing a reference is not required, but failing to meet the request often raises negative connotations for the former employee and for your company. The number one rule in providing references is to be honest and objective. Supply only facts that can be documented and avoid giving your opinion regarding work performance. Care must be taken in order to avoid law suits alleging defamation or invasion of privacy.

> **TIP:** Prior to issuing a reference, get a release in writing from the former employee that gives you permission to release employment-related information.

> **TIP:** Responsibility for employment verification should rest only with the human resources department or a designated person trained in giving public responses.

UNEMPLOYMENT COMPENSATION

To provide temporary wage replacement to those people involuntarily let go and to help stabilize the economy during recessions, the federal government created a program for unemployment compensation within the Social Security Act. Both employers and employees pay to support this fund.

Am I automatically eligible because I paid into the fund when I was working?
No. Each state determines its own eligibility requirements and has different rules as to what constitutes unemployment "due to no fault of your own." There are also requirements for wage credits earned during an established base period. These vary state by state, so check your local rules through the state unemployment service.

How do I file a claim for unemployment?
Again, this varies by state. Many require you to apply in person. Others allow filing via the telephone.

How long am I eligible for benefits?
In general, your eligibility will be for 26 weeks, which may be extended under certain circumstances. However, each week you will be asked a series of questions. These include whether you have been looking for work, turned down an offer for work, if you worked temporarily for yourself or others, or if you returned to school. If you do not satisfy all the state's criteria, you may be denied benefits for a week or longer.

What is the unemployment benefit rate? In
most instances, the rate is based on a percentage of your earnings over the past year up to the state's maximum amount.

CONSOLIDATED OMNIBUS BUDGET RECONCILIATION ACT (COBRA)

In 1986, Congress passed COBRA to provide continuation of group health coverage for employees and their families in certain situations, such as when there is a voluntary or involuntary job loss, reduction in the number of hours worked, transition between jobs, death, divorce or other life changing events. Under COBRA, employee family members may also continue coverage. If you qualify for COBRA, you have 60 days in which to opt to continue your benefits. COBRA is not free. An employer may charge you up to 102 percent of what it is paying for the group level of coverage you elect.

Are all group plans covered by COBRA?
No. COBRA applies only to plans where the employer has 20 or more employees. However, the government does require that part-time employees count as a fraction of an employee based upon the number of hours worked.

Who is entitled to benefits?
There are three requirements to be eligible for benefits:

1. You belonged to a group health plan with at least 20 employees.
2. You are a qualified beneficiary.
3. You lost your group health insurance as a result of a qualifying event.

What does it mean to be a "qualified beneficiary"?
A qualified beneficiary is usually a person who had coverage on the day before the qualifying event took place. It could be an employee, their spouse or dependent child.

What are "qualifying events" under COBRA?
These are the circumstances under which COBRA allows an individual to continue health care coverage. The qualifying event does not have to just happen to the employee; it can happen for a spouse or dependent child as well. Qualifying events are as follows:

For employees:
- Voluntary or involuntary separation from employment except in cases of gross misconduct; or
- Reduction in the number of hours of employment.

For spouses:
In addition to the two reasons given above for the employee:

- The covered employee becomes entitled to Medicare;
- Divorce or legal separation from the covered employee; or
- Death of the covered employee.

For dependent children:
All of the items listed for spouses with the addition of:

- Loss of dependent child status.

I recently quit my job. Can I still receive health benefits under my former employer's health care plan?
If you meet the criteria above, your company had 20 or more employees, you were covered by an employer plan and you left under circumstances other than gross misconduct, the answer is yes.

Why should I bother to stay under my former employer's health care plan if I have to pay full price?
While it may seem expensive, your former employer is most likely getting a group rate discount for the health care coverage it provides. If you purchased an equivalent plan on your own, it is unlikely that you would be able to do so at a rate as competitive as the employer's group rate.

What benefits are covered under COBRA?
The benefits offered have to be the same as for all others in the health care plan (i.e., those not under COBRA). So unless the employer changed the plan benefits, you should receive the same benefits you received when you were still an employee.

My divorce will be finalized soon. Can I still get health coverage under my spouse's group plan?
Yes. Under COBRA, you and any covered dependent children can continue your plan coverage. Under the law you can continue coverage up to a maximum of 36 months. However, you must notify the plan administrator within 60 days of the divorce or separation that you wish to elect COBRA coverage.

> **TIP:** Anyone who is eligible for COBRA coverage has 60 days to decide whether to elect coverage.

My company went out of business. Can I still get health care coverage?
If there is no longer a health care plan, then there will be no coverage available under COBRA.

How long does COBRA coverage last?

Beneficiary	Qualifying Event	Coverage
Employee Spouse Dependent child	Termination Reduction in hours	18 months
Spouse Dependent child	Employee enrolled in Medicare Divorce or legal separation Death of covered employee	36 months
Dependent child	Loss of dependent child status	36 months

TIP: For more information see the U.S. Department of Labor Web site **www.dol. gov/ebsa**.

APPENDIX

POSTERS

Throughout this chapter are references to federal laws that provide workplace protections. Many of these laws are enforced by agencies within the Department of Labor and require employers to post a notice informing its employee of their rights. Each state also has posting requirements.

Posters	Who Must Post	Coverage they Provide	Display Requirements	Penalty for Failure to Posting
Occupational Safety and Health Act	Private employers engaged in a business affecting commerce	Gives workers the right to safety inspections and provides protections for reporting unsafe conditions	Poster must be displayed where it can be readily observed by employees and applicants.	Citation. Fines are also possible.
Equal Employment Opportunity Laws	Employers with three or more employees Labor unions Employment agencies	Title VII protections from being discriminated based race, color, religion, sex, age, national origin, disability or military service.	Post in a conspicuous place available to employees, and representatives of labor unions.	Fines up to $100. Extension of time in which complainants may file. Sanctions to federal contractors.
Family and Medical Leave Act	Businesses with 50 or more employees. Public agencies	On Federal level, up to 12 weeks of unpaid leave to care for newborn or adopted children, health issues and other family matters.	Poster must be displayed where it can be readily observed by employees and applicants. If workforce is not primarily English speaking, posting must also be in Spanish.	Fines up to $100.
Fair Labor Standards Act	All Businesses	Notice of minimum wage	Poster must be displayed prominently.	No fines
Uniformed Services Employment and Reemployment Rights Act	Businesses with employees entitled to rights and benefits under USERRA.	Reemployment, discrimination, and health insurance rights under USERRA.	Posting notice where employee notices are customarily placed; handing or mailing the notice to affected individuals, or distributing the notice via e-mail.	No citations or penalties for failure to notify.
Employee Polygraph Protection Act	Any employer engaged in or affecting commerce or in the production of goods for commerce.		Poster must be displayed where it can be readily observed by employees and applicants.	Secretary of Labor can bring court actions and assess civil penalties.

If I have less than 50 employees, am I required to post a notice regarding the Family and Medical Leave Act? *The federal government does not require employers to post notices if the applicable statute does not cover their employees.* Employers do need to be aware, particularly as their organizations grow, that they will have to comply once they meet an act's eligibility requirements.

Are there requirements as to where I have to place these posters? *In each instance, the posters need to be posted in a conspicuous place. They must be able to be clearly seen, unaltered and not defaced.* They are also supposed to be placed where an employee is likely to see them, such as a lunch or break room, locker room or a bulletin board near the water cooler.

If I put up the required federal posters, am I fully compliant with the law? *No. Virtually every state has its own posting requirements.* These include state OSHA requirements, Department of Human Rights postings, and State Department of Labor requirements. Please check with you local state government to see what requirements apply to you.

DEPARTMENT OF LABOR CONTACT INFORMATION

STATE	PHONE	WEB ADDRESS
Alabama	334.242.3460	www.dir.state.al.us
Alaska	907.465.5980	www.labor.state.ak.us
Arizona	602.542.4515	www.ica.state.az.us
Arkansas	501.682.4500	www.state.ar.us/labor
California	415.703.4810	www.dir.ca.gov
Colorado	303.318.8000	www.coworkforce.com
Connecticut	860.263.6505	www.ctdol.state.ct.us
Delaware	302.761.8000	www.delawareworks.com
Dist. of Columbia	202.671.1900	http://does.ci.washington.dc.us
Florida	850.488.3131	www.state.fl.us/dbpr/ or www.MyFlorida.com
Georgia	404.656.3011	www.dol.state.ga.us
Hawaii	808.586.8865/8844	www.dlir.state.hi.us
Idaho	208.334.6112	www.labor.state.id.us
Illinois	312.793.1808	www.state.il.us/agency/idol
Indiana	317.232.2378	www.state.in.us/labor or teenworker.org
Iowa	515.281.3447	www.iowaworkforce.org/labor
Kansas	785.296.7474	www2.hr.state.ks.us
Kentucky	502.564.3070	www.kylabor.net
Louisiana	225.342.3011	www.ldol.state.la.us
Maine	207.287.3787	www.state.me.us/labor
Maryland	410.767.2999	www.dllr.state.md.us
Massachusetts	617.727.6573	www.mass.gov/dlwd or www.state.ma.us
Michigan	517.373.3034	www.michigan.gov/bwuc
Minnesota	651.284.5010	www.doli.state.mn.us
Mississippi	601.961.7400	www.mesc.state.ms.us
Missouri	573.751.9691	www.dolir.state.mo.us
Montana	406.444.9091	http://dli.state.mt.us
Nebraska	402.471.3405	www.dol.state.ne.us/
Nevada	702.486.2650	www.LaborCommissioner.com or http://dbi.state.nv.us
New Hampshire	603.271.3171	www.labor.state.nh.us
New Jersey	609.292.2323	www.state.nj.us/labor/index.html
New Mexico	505.841.8409	www3.state.nm.us/dol/dol_home.html
New York	518.457.2741/212.352.6000	www.labor.state.ny.us
North Carolina	919.733.0359	www.nclabor.com
North Dakota	701.328.2660	www.state.nd.us/labor/
Ohio	614.644.2239	www.state.oh.us/ohio/agency.htm
Oklahoma	405.528.1500, ext. 200	www.state.ok.us/~okdol
Oregon	503.731.4070	www.boli.state.or.us
Pennsylvania	717.787.3756	www.dli.state.pa.us
Rhode Island	401.462.8870	www.det.state.ri.us
South Carolina	803.896.4300	www.llr.state.sc.us
South Dakota	605.773.3101	www.state.sd.us/dol/dol.htm
Tennessee	615.741.6642	www.state.tn.us/labor.wfd/
Texas	512.463.0735	www.twc.state.tx.us
Utah	801.530.6880	www.labor.state.ut.us
Vermont	802.828.2288	www.state.vt.us/labind
Virginia	804.786.2377	www.dli.state.va.us
Washington	360.902.4203	www.lni.wa.gov
West Virginia	304.558.7890	www.state.wv.us/labor
Wisconsin	608.267.9692	www.dwd.state.wi.us
Wyoming	307.777.7261	http://wydoe.state.wy.us/

5 ESTATE PLANNING

Throughout our lives, we plan for one thing after another: education–career–family. But surprisingly few of us plan for our deaths. Maybe we think we are too young to die, not realizing that sometimes things happen unexpectedly. Or perhaps we feel that we don't own much, not understanding that estate plans are important for even the smallest of estates. An estate plan is important because it speaks of your wishes after you have departed, regardless of what you own. It will give you control over decisions such as who receives your property, who will take care of your children, how your business will be run, can help to reduce estate taxes, and can even plan for your care in the event you become incapacitated and unable to make decisions for yourself. Failure to properly plan for your death gives rise to many risks–your property could end up in the hands of distant relatives, or worse, the state; or it may be given to someone who will squander it; or your children may be forced to live with someone you don't favor. So why not do what you can now and live with peace of mind that at least if the unexpected does happen, you have the final word on what happens with your estate.

WILLS

A will is the most commonly used estate-planning tool, though it is often used in conjunction with other devices, such as a trust. It is a legal document and, through it, you can accomplish many things–you can give away your belongings, name a guardian for your children, cancel any debts owed to you by another person, transfer property into an existing trust, or designate a trusted person to administer your estate (called an "executor"). If you care about what happens with your property when you die, even if you own only a small amount of cash and few belongings, then a will can reflect your wishes after you die.

CREATING YOUR WILL – THE BASICS

Why should I create a will? *You should have a will because it is an effective way to control what happens when you die.* Without one, you are said to have died "intestate" and your property passes pursuant to "intestate succession," which is a statutorily prescribed method of distributing your belongings. In other words, the state will decide who receives your property, without any regard as to what you would have preferred. Your house may fall in the hands of a relative you have never met, when you would have given it to your unmarried partner. Perhaps you would have given your property to a good friend or a charity, but without a will it would go to your family. Or maybe you don't want your children to share your estate equally, as they would if you die without a will. To avoid these types of situations, it would be to your benefit to create a will to guarantee that your property passes to the people that you select in the manner that you desire.

Can anyone make a will? *Generally, yes. But there are requirements set forth by state law that must be met for it to be valid.* The person making the will (called the "testator") must be of a certain age (usually 18) at the time the will is made. If the will is created while the person is a minor, it is invalid regardless of when death occurs. He must also have testamentary intent (i.e., he wants that particular document to be his will). Additionally, the testator must have testamentary capacity. This means that he is of sound mind (i.e., mentally competent and not suffering from any mental illness) and understands that he is creating a will, knows the extent of the property he owns, knows the people that are related to him, and understands the estate plan that he is creating. If any of these requirements are not met, the will is invalid and the property passes as if it were never created.

The above requirements must be satisfied at the time the will is made. Anything before or after that point in time will not cause the will to be invalid. For example, if you become afflicted with a mind-disabling illness between the time you make your will and die, it does not matter–as long as you were mentally competent when you made your will. Or if you were 14 when you made your will, but you die at age 21, your will is invalid because you were not of the minimum age when you made your will.

I'm only 25. Am I too young to worry about a will? *No. You need to plan for the unexpected, and having a will prepared in the event of your untimely death is crucial.* Regardless of your age, you probably own property and care about what happens to it if you die unexpectedly. Or you may have young children who need to be cared for if you die. You need to decide what you want to happen in these types of situations, or you leave the task up to the state and the results may not be to your liking.

Can I create a will even though I have a serious illness? *Yes; in fact, it is advisable that you do so provided you are capable of understanding the nature of your act.* If your illness in any way affects your mental capacity, the will can be invalidated because you lack testamentary capacity.

What is required for the will to be valid? *Every state sets forth a few general criteria for the will to be valid, commonly known as "requirements for due execution."* Generally, the will must be written (handwritten or typed), signed by the person making it, and signed by at least two (and sometimes three) competent witnesses. You must sign in the presence of your witnesses and they have to sign in your presence. Remember that the testator also has to be a certain age and of sound mind.

Can I sign my name anywhere on the will? It depends on the law in your state–some require that you sign at the end of the will, while others allow you to sign anywhere on the will.

My hands shake very badly. Is my will valid if someone else signs my name for me? *Yes.* This is called a "proxy signature" and is valid as your signature as long as it is done pursuant to your request and the person signs your name in your presence.

Do I have to sign my full name for the will to be valid? *Technically, no. For purposes of meeting the signature requirement, any mark, scribble or initial made by you on the signature line is acceptable as your signature as long as you intended the mark to be your signature.* That said, it is highly recommended that you sign your full legal name in order to avoid any problems when the will is offered for probate.

During my will signing ceremony, my attorney asked the witnesses to sign the will before I signed it. Do I have to redo the will since I did not sign first? *No. The will and the signatures to it are valid as long as they were done during the same execution ceremony.* The law does not require that you actually sign your name before the witnesses sign theirs, as long as you do so within a reasonable time after they sign theirs.

My neighbor asked me to be a witness to her will. I signed a folded copy, which showed only her signature; she did not show me any of the contents of the will to prove that I was in fact signing her will. Is my signature valid? *Yes. In most states, your purpose as a witness is to attest to the testator's signature, not to the document itself. Therefore, the signature is all you need to see. You do not need to know the contents of the will for your* *signature as a witness to be valid.* In fact, you do not even need to know that you are signing her will. Your signature is valid even if she told you that you were witnessing the deed to her house. (But check your state's specific laws–a few do require that the testator declare the document to be her will.)

My neighbor had already signed her will before the other witness and I arrived. Doesn't she have to sign it in front of us? *Generally, yes. But if she already signed the will, she can "acknowledge her signature" in front of both witnesses, and the result is the same as if she had signed her name in the presence of the witnesses.* To acknowledge the signature simply means that she claims that the signature is her own.

I executed my will 10 years ago, and at that time both of my witnesses were sane and healthy. However, one of my witnesses now has been diagnosed with dementia. Will her current condition cause my will to be invalid when I die? *No. The signature of your witness is valid as long as she was competent when she signed the will.* Her mental condition at any time before or after she signs the will does not affect your will's validity.

What information should my will contain? *At a minimum, your will should include your full name and address, your signature and the signatures of your witnesses. It should also list all of your assets and the name and address of the beneficiary who is to own each particular asset.* If you have any minor children, it should designate a guardian to care for them. You should also name an executor who will help settle your estate during the probate process.

> **TIP:** Do not include funeral instructions in your will. It may not be found for days or weeks after your death.

How do I name a guardian for my minor children in my will? *It is very simple. You just insert a clause in the will that states who you choose to raise your children if you die. Be sure to name a guardian for each minor child (you should choose the same person for all of them),*

and you should consider naming an alternate guardian in case your first choice refuses or is unable to accept the responsibility. In selecting the guardian, be sure to consider, among other things, the age and health of the guardian, whether your child will have to move to a new state, and whether the guardian can financially care for your child.

My attorney wants me to include a "self-proving affidavit" with my will. What is that? *A "self-proving affidavit" is a notarized document signed by you and your witnesses (usually during the will execution ceremony) that verifies that you signed your will in the presence of your witnesses and that they in turn signed in your presence, and that they believed you to be competent to execute your will.* The affidavit allows your will to stand on its own based on the signatures of you and your witnesses. What this means is that your witnesses will not have to testify as to your will's validity when you die–the affidavit sufficiently speaks to the will's validity.

What kind of property can I give away through my will? *You can give away any property that you own when you die or in which you have an interest at death. This property is said to comprise your estate and includes land, homes, cars, bank accounts, stocks, any debts owed to you, personal belongings (such as jewelry, furniture, books, etc.) and any interest you own in property as a tenant in common.* However, you cannot give away "nonprobate property," which is defined as property that passes on your death by some means other than your will or intestacy. The following are common forms of nonprobate property that cannot be given away in your will.

▸ **JOINT TENANCY PROPERTY WITH RIGHT OF SURVIVORSHIP**

   When you die, your share automatically passes to the surviving joint owner. If you try to give it away in your will the gift is ineffective.

▸ **TENANCY BY THE ENTIRETY PROPERTY**

   This is property given to a husband and wife and carries with it a right of survivorship and automatically passes to the surviving spouse.

- ▶ **PROCEEDS FROM LIFE INSURANCE POLICIES, IRAS, PENSIONS AND EMPLOYEE BENEFIT PLANS**

  These are governed by your contract with the insurance or financial company and descend to the beneficiary that you named in that contract. If you attempt to give it to someone else in your will, it is ineffective.

- ▶ **LIFETIME GIFT TO ANOTHER (CALLED "INTER VIVOS GIFT")**

  Since you gave the property away when you were alive, you cannot give it away again on your death—you no longer own it so it is not in your estate.

- ▶ **PROPERTY PLACED IN A TRUST**

  The terms of the trust control how the property is to be distributed.

- ▶ **COMMUNITY PROPERTY**

  You can give away only the one-half share that you own; the other one-half belongs to your spouse.

- ▶ **PAY-ON-DEATH ACCOUNTS (ALSO CALLED "TOTTEN TRUST ACCOUNTS")**

  When you die, the proceeds pass to the person in whose favor you created the account.

Who can be a beneficiary in my will? *A beneficiary is a person or organization to whom you leave property in your will and can be anyone you want. You can name as beneficiary your mother, next door neighbor, employee, favorite charity or a person you have never even met. It is your property and you can leave it to whomever you like.* Note that from a legal standpoint, a beneficiary is not the same as an heir. A beneficiary is a person you name in your will to receive property and can be anybody. An heir is a person who takes your property under intestate succession if you die without a will (or without having disposed of all your property) and usually is a member of your family, however remote.

> **TIP:** Be sure that you clearly identify the beneficiaries to avoid any confusion. For example, if you have two nieces named Sarah, specify which Sarah you are referring to in your will. The court does not like to guess as to your intentions.

I want to leave a sum of money to my pet poodle? Can I do that? *No. You cannot leave property to a pet because a pet is considered to be property itself.* But that does not mean that you cannot provide for your pet's care beyond your death. One option is to leave a sum of money to a trusted individual with the requirement that the money be used for your pet's care. Another option is to set up an honorary trust in favor of your pet (see Trusts section in this chapter).

Can one of the beneficiaries in my will also be a witness to the will? *Yes; your will is still valid if a beneficiary acts as a witness. However, by acting as a witness that beneficiary will lose all or part of the gift in the will, subject to two exceptions.* If there were more witnesses to the will than required by law (three witnesses when only two were required), she will receive her entire gift. If she would have taken a portion of your estate if you had died without the will (by intestacy), she is entitled to either the gift in the current will or her intestate share, whichever is smaller.

> **TIP:** It is best if you choose witnesses who are "disinterested," meaning that they have no stake in your estate when you die. Good choices for witnesses include your attorney's secretary, a trusted friend or neighbor (of course, provided they are not left anything in your will), or perhaps an employee.

What do I need to consider when writing out the gifts in my will? *First, take time to think about who you want to include in your will and what property you want to give them. When it comes time to write out the gifts, describe each beneficiary and item of property with exact specificity.* You do not want any confusion when the will is being probated. For real property, state the address and any other descriptive information. For personal property, describe the item and state where it can be found. Your beneficiaries should be identified by full name and you should include their addresses. It might also be a good idea to name a contingent beneficiary for each gift in the event the original beneficiary dies before you or rejects the gift, in which case the gift either fails and passes under intestacy or passes to the beneficiary's descendants under the anti-lapse statute (if she is related to you).

> **TIP:** Before drafting your will or consulting an attorney, make a list of everything you own along with the name of the person to whom you want it to belong. Doing so will help prevent you from forgetting to make any gifts.

What types of gifts can I make? *You can make four types of gifts: specific, demonstrative, general or residuary. The gift will be either real property or personal property.* Real property includes any land that you own, including any structures on the land, such as your home and garage, and any interest you own in gas, oil or minerals. Personal property is everything else—both tangible and intangibles. Examples of personal property are: cash, stocks, bonds, clothes, furniture, jewelry, automobiles and bank accounts.

> **Type of gift:** Specific gift:
> A gift of a specific item of property.
> "My vacation home in Aruba to my daughter."
>
> **Type of gift:** Demonstrative gift:
> A gift of money to be paid from a specific source.
> "$25,000 to my sister, to be paid from the proceeds of the sale of my business."
>
> **Type of gift:** General gift:
> A gift of money paid out of your estate (but not necessarily from a specific source).
> "$15,000 to my brother."
>
> **Type of gift:** Residuary gift
> A gift of the balance of your estate that is not otherwise disposed of.
> "The rest and residue of my estate to my next door neighbor."

Can you explain how a residuary clause operates? *A residuary clause devises the remainder of your estate after all claims have been paid and all other gifts in the will have been distributed.* It is a "catch-all" clause because it includes anything you own (other than nonprobate property) that is not specifically given to someone else in your will, including any property you acquired after the will was written and any gifts that fail for some reason. Some examples are:

- You have clauses in your will giving away your house, car, jewelry and clothing. However, you did not have specific clauses with respect to your computer or furniture. The computer and furniture fall into the residuary clause and pass to the beneficiary of your residuary clause.
- After you write your will, you inherit $50,000 from your aunt. You place the money in a bank account and leave it there until you die. The money falls into the residuary estate and passes to the beneficiary.
- You leave your extensive book collection to your college buddy, but he dies several years before you. The gift to him fails and you don't revise your will to give the books to someone else, so they fall into the residuary clause and pass to the beneficiary.

> **TIP:** Be sure to include a residuary clause in your will because it avoids any partial intestacy. If there were no residuary clause in any of the above examples, the property would have to pass according to your state's intestate laws because it was not disposed of by any other means.

Where should my will be kept? *You should keep your will in a safe place where it won't be subject to damage and won't be lost, such as a safe deposit box.* It is a good idea to keep a copy, if not the original, with your attorney.

If your executor or relatives have to search for your will, it will cause problems and delays in probating your will and your beneficiaries will have to wait before receiving their gifts.

CHECKLIST: What you need to consider when making your will.

- Did you sign your will?
- Does it contain the signatures of the appropriate number of witnesses required by your state?
- Did you clearly identify all the property and all the beneficiaries so there is no confusion?
- Did you remember to dispose of everything that you own in order to avoid any partial intestacy?

- Are you anticipating any change in a family relationship? If so, be sure to provide for your new spouse or child, or remove a soon-to-be ex-spouse.
- Did you name contingent beneficiaries in case the original beneficiaries cannot take their gifts?
- Did you include a residuary clause?
- Did you name a guardian for any minor children? If you did not, the court will appoint one.
- Did you name an executor? If you did not, the court will appoint one.

TYPES OF WILLS

What is a holographic will? *A holographic will is one that is handwritten and signed by the testator but is not signed by any attesting witnesses.* Most states require that wills be witnessed by at least two other persons, often making holographic wills ineffective.

> **Although most states do not allow holographic wills, the will might still be valid if it was executed in another state and meets that other state's legal requirements. For example, assume you wrote your will when you lived in California, but later died in Illinois (which does not permit holographic wills). The will can still be admitted to probate in Illinois because it was written in a state that allows holographic wills and is valid pursuant to California law.**

Is an oral will valid? *Oral wills are valid in about 20 states under certain limited circumstances.* The states that permit oral wills consider it to be valid only if it was "uttered," or made, in front of two or three witnesses and during the testator's most recent illness, at a time when he expected to die, or while he was in the armed forces. Some states even require that it be put in writing at some time after it is spoken. The oral will can be used to give away only personal property (e.g., furniture, clothing, or jewelry).

My husband and I want to prepare an estate plan for when we die and heard that we should have a joint will. Is it the same as a reciprocal will? *No, but the difference is minor. A joint will is one single will or property distribution for more than one*

person. *It is single will that disposes your and your husband's estate.* Reciprocal wills are two separate wills, one for you and one for your husband, which contain the same provisions for distributing your estate. For example, the wills provide that you both leave your estate to each other in the event one of you dies before the other, and then to your children in equal shares when the last of you dies. If you and your husband agree to one plan for devising your joint estate, then a joint will or reciprocal wills would serve that purpose.

What is a living will? *A living will is not a will in the sense that it disposes of your property or names an executor.* Rather it is a document that states your wishes in the event you become terminally ill or in a permanent unconscious state and is effective while you are still alive.

CHANGING OR REVOKING YOUR WILL

Why should I change my will? *You should review and change your will on a regular basis in order to keep it current. Many people these days make wills, but not all of them realize that it needs to be modified whenever something changes in their life, most often with their finances or relationships.* It is wise to update or revoke your will in light of any new circumstances, that way your family and friends avoid any unnecessary problems when your estate is being settled.

When should I change my will? *Other than a simple change of mind, there are many events that may prompt you to change your will.* Common reasons for changing are will are:

Life-changing events
- Marriage
- Divorce
- Birth or adoption of a child
- Relocation to a new state or country (you should change the will so it conforms to that region's laws to avoid delays in probating it)

Changes in your financial situation or assets
- Inheritance of a large amount of money or other asset

- Purchase or acquisition of a new home or car, or other asset
- Purchase or sale of a business
- Sale or destruction of an asset that was included in your will

Changes in your original beneficiaries

- Death of a spouse or other beneficiary
- Relationship with a beneficiary takes a turn for the worse
- Desire to include new beneficiaries

In the event of a divorce, the law automatically revokes any provisions in your will that favor your ex-spouse. Regardless, you still need to update your will because if you do not redirect the property originally devised to your ex-spouse to another beneficiary, then that property will either fall into the residuary clause, or if there is none, it will pass to your intestate heirs.

How can I change my will? *You can change your will in one of two ways. You can revoke your current will and write a new one. Or you can amend your existing will by creating a codicil.* A codicil is a formal supplement to your will and must conform to the same requirements for executing a will (must be written and signed by you and your witnesses).

> **TIP:** If you execute a codicil to your will, make sure that you store it with your will. If the changes in your codicil are extensive, you should consider revoking the old will and starting over with a new one. This will avoid any confusion when it is offered for probate and will insure that you do not make any mistakes.

How do I revoke my will? *If you revoke your will, it is legally dead—as if you never created it.* You can revoke your will by a later writing (e.g., a new will or codicil that is totally inconsistent with your previous will or that includes a statement that you intend to revoke your previous will) or by physically destroying it (burning, canceling, tearing, or obliterating it). If you physically destroy your will, make sure you destroy the entire will; otherwise you risk an ineffective revocation. For example, if you want to write "void" on your will, write it across the face of every page, not just the first page.

> **TIP:** Make sure that your new will includes a statement indicating your intent to revoke the old will. It is usually sufficient to state something to effect that you "revoke all prior wills and codicils." This will protect your intentions in the event that you forgot to destroy any originals or copies of prior wills or codicils.

My attorney keeps my will in his office for safekeeping. Can I call him and ask him to rip it up since I want to create a new one? *You can have your attorney destroy the will for you, but he must do it in your presence.* If you are on the phone with him when he does it, the revocation is ineffective and the will is still valid.

What happens if my revocation is ineffective? *If you do not properly revoke your old will, it remains alive and it will be admitted to probate along with your new will.* In that event, the court will try to dispose of your estate pursuant to the terms of both wills, and if there is an inconsistency between the two, the terms of the most recent will take precedence. All the remaining provisions of the old will are still given effect, provided they do not conflict with the new will!

EXAMPLE: Assume you have a will that, among other gifts, devises your car to your mother and your home to your sister. You later write a new will that devises the car to your father, but you do not mention the home and you never revoke the old will. Both wills are valid and both will be probated. Because there is an inconsistency between the two wills with respect to who gets your car, the most recent will controls and it passes to your father. The home will pass to your sister under the first will even if you did not want her to receive it.

> **TIP:** If your new will is completely inconsistent with the prior will, then you do not need to worry about this happening—the prior will is considered to be revoked. This makes sense if you think about it—the second will controls any inconsistencies between the two wills, so if the two wills are entirely inconsistent, then the second one controls, revoking the prior will! However, it is best to err on side of caution and destroy any unwanted wills.

Writing a new will seems like too much work. Can I just cross out the provision I do not like and insert a new one on my existing will? *This is called a "partial revocation by physical act," and although it is permitted in some states, it is not recommended.* What if you have so many changes that you are left with a will with a lot of crossed-out provisions? How is the court to know whether you intended to revoke the entire will or just portions of it? And what if your new clauses are hard to read or understand? At a minimum, you should make the change by executing a codicil to the will. And if your changes are significant, then you would do your beneficiaries a favor by rewriting your will. It is more time-consuming but you ensure that there will be no problems when the will is probated.

After having executed my will, I realized that I forgot to give away my new computer. Can I just add that clause to the end of the will? *No. This type of change will be ineffective because it was not present when the will was executed.* If you add anything new to the will, you must re-execute it for the new material to be valid. In other words, it must again be signed by you and your witnesses.

My mother used to keep her will in her desk drawer, but after her death we could not find it there. How can we admit its contents to probate? *You cannot. If the will cannot be found and it was last seen in your mother's possession, then the court will assume that she revoked it. Also, if it is found in a damaged condition (e.g., torn into pieces), it is presumed that she damaged it with the intent to revoke it; so again, it will be invalid.* However, if you can prove that the will was not revoked by your mother, then the court will accept proof of the will's contents by carbon copy or photocopy, or by the testimony of a person who knew its contents. One way to prove this is if you have evidence that a third party (perhaps someone who was left out of the will) had access to the will and destroyed or damaged it.

I revoked my 2000 will through a clause in the will that I executed in 2005. Now I have decided to revoke my 2005 will because I want to reinstate the terms of the 2000 will. Can I just tear up the 2005 will and do nothing more? *No. The 2000 will was revoked and remains revoked. You must take affirmative action if you want to revive its terms, and you have three options. You can create a new will that contains the same terms as the 2000 will.* You can properly re-execute the 2000 will (re-date it and have it signed by you and your witnesses). Or you can execute a codicil that states your intent to revive the 2000 will. Be sure to completely revoke the 2005 will!

A few years ago, I executed a codicil to my will that changed my executor. I have now decided that I feel more comfortable with my original choice, so I want to revoke the codicil. Does this revalidate my original designation? *Yes.* If you create a codicil to your will and then later revoke the codicil, the will is still valid and the clauses in the will that were changed by the codicil now take their original effect.

I executed a will a few years ago, and then subsequently executed a codicil that amended a portion of the will. As I am reviewing my documents, I realized that I forgot to sign the will. Is it valid? *Standing alone, the will is invalid because without your signature it is not properly executed.* However, if your codicil was properly executed (in writing and signed by you and two witnesses), then it validates your previously invalid will as of the date of the codicil. Therefore, your will is considered to be valid.

YOUR FAMILY: THEIR RIGHTS TO YOUR ESTATE

I'm afraid that my large estate will be tied up in probate for a long time after my death. Will my family be entitled to any allowances to provide for their living expenses before my estate is settled? *Yes. Your family will be entitled to a family allowance, homestead exemption and personal property exemption.* These allowances are mutually exclusive—your family can receive all three—and they are in addition to gifts in the will, the elective share or an intestate share.

Type of Allowance	Purpose	Application
Family Allowance	Provides the spouse and minor children with a monetary allowance for living expenses during the estate's administration.	Amount varies by state law.
Homestead Allowance	Protects the family home from any claims by the estate's creditors.	Some states provide that the spouse and children can live in the home for up to a specific period of time, while others will grant a sum of money to cover housing expenses.
Personal Property Exemption	Protects tangible personal property items for the family's use.	Usually applies to items such as furniture, household items, jewelry and vehicles.

My husband left me only a very small share of his substantial estate in his will. Do I have any recourse? *Yes. You have the right to renounce or reject the will and file for an "elective share" (provided by statute) of your husband's estate, which is usually one-half or one-third of his estate.* This right protects surviving spouses from being disinherited or from being left with minimal gifts. For purposes of determining what property makes up your husband's estate, most states even include any nonprobate transfers in which he retained an ownership interest when he died (e.g., joint bank accounts or joint tenancies). Including nonprobate property prevents a spouse from transferring all of his property into nonprobate transfers, thereby effectively defeating the elective share. If you decide to take your elective share, you must file for it within a certain amount of time (ranging from 4 to 9 months) after your husband's death. To make up your share, all the gifts in the will are proportionately reduced so that each beneficiary contributes to your share of the estate.

The amount to which you are entitled varies by state law, so check your state's statutes to find out what the elective share amounts to. Some states condition the amount you receive on the length of your marriage.

I live in a "community property" state. What does that mean with respect to the property that I own? *Community property is defined as all property acquired by you and your spouse while you are married. Property that each of you owned before your marriage and anything that was given to either of you (e.g., by will) during your marriage is not community property.* The community property states are Arizona, California, Idaho, Louisiana, Nebraska, New Mexico, Texas, Washington and Wisconsin. If you live in one of these states, then you own 50 percent of your community property, and your spouse owns the other 50 percent. This means that you can give away only your one-half share of the property, and your spouse can do as he pleases with respect to his share. For example, if you and your spouse bought a vacation house after you got married, the house is community property. When you die, you can only give away your one-half share in the house, and the beneficiary of that share will then own the house as a tenant in common with your spouse.

I executed a will a few years ago and now am getting married. What rights will my new spouse have in my estate if I die before changing the will? *Your spouse has several options depending on the law of your state. First and foremost, she can file for her elective share and receive up to one-third or one-half of your estate.* If your state has a "pretermitted spouse" statute, she may be entitled to an intestate share of your estate, which in most states is one-half if you are survived by any descendants. Additionally, your spouse will receive the allowances allowed by law—family, homestead and exempt personal property.

> **TIP:** The event of a remarriage is a good time to revise your will, especially if you want your spouse to receive more than what she is entitled to under the law.

How will a prenuptial agreement affect my spouse's rights to my estate? *Depending on the terms of the agreement, it can limit, and in some cases even waive, your spouse's right to share in your estate.* For the agreement to be valid, it must have been entered into voluntarily and your spouse must have understood the meaning of the agreement (e.g., that she was forfeiting any rights to your estate).

My partner and I never married. How can I make sure that he will receive my property when I die? *To protect your partner, you must execute a carefully thought-out estate plan; otherwise, he will be left with nothing. Some ideas are to make lifetime gifts to him, set up joint accounts with him; name him as beneficiary of any trust, life insurance policy, or otherwise; and provide for him in your will.* If you fail to take these important steps, your partner will not receive any of your property—not even under your state's intestate succession laws. Nor will he be entitled to an elective share or any of the family allowances.

> **TIP:** Nonprobate transfers are best in this instance because the transfer on death is automatic. There will be no delay in the event your will is contested or your estate is tied up in probate.

I never changed my will after my divorce and it names my ex-spouse as a beneficiary. Will she have any rights to my property when I die? *No. Any gifts or appointments that are in favor of your ex-spouse are invalid.* The property that was left to your ex-spouse will pass as if your spouse died before you: it will fall into your residuary clause or pass under intestate succession.

> **TIP:** If you go through a divorce, then you should protect your property by writing a codicil to your will with respect to the property that was devised to your ex-spouse. Your ex-spouse will not receive the property if you fail to do this, but you might want to control who the beneficiary will be.

What about any property that I left to my ex-spouse's children from her previous marriage? Are those gifts invalid too? *No. The divorce revokes only the gifts to your ex-spouse. Any gifts to her family members are still valid.* If you do not want her children to share in your estate, then you need to adjust your will accordingly.

What if my ex-spouse and I remarried a few years before my death? Is the gift still invalid? *No. In many states, remarriage will revalidate those portions of the will that were revoked by the divorce.* Your spouse will still receive the property that you originally devised to her.

I gave birth to a child after executing my will. Will he be left with nothing? *No. Most states allow a child who is born or adopted after a will is executed to receive a share in the estate, usually equal to what he would have received under intestacy.* Some states do limit this right if the will indicates a clear intent to disinherit the testator's children, or if the child is provided for by some nonprobate transfer.

Is there a limit on how much I can leave to my minor children? *No. You can leave as much as you like to your children.* However, if you choose to leave gifts of over a certain amount, which varies by state law but is typically $2,500, then you need to designate a responsible adult (called a "property guardian") who can manage that property for your child until he reaches the age of majority, and at that point the child gains full control over the property.

> **TIP:** Keep in mind that in some states the age of majority is 18, and at that age, many kids are not yet responsible with large sums of money. Consider leaving the property to your child in a trust or custodial account instead, as you can better control, and even delay, his receipt of it.

I do not want to leave anything to my oldest child. Can I put something in the will that states that she is disinherited? *A disinheritance clause in a will is called a "negative bequest clause" and is ineffective in some states. The best way to make sure that* *your daughter does not receive anything is to completely dispose of all your belongings.* If you die without having disposed of all your belongings, she will have rights to them under intestate distribution.

I had a very close relationship with my mother, and although she provided for me in her will, she left me only a small share of her substantial estate. She left the remainder of her estate to a friend she has not seen in 10 years. What are my rights? *Unfortunately, you cannot claim a larger share in your mother's estate than what she gave you in her will, unless you can prove that she was mentally incompetent or that there was some type of fraud by her friend. Given that she has not seen her in 10 years, that is unlikely.* The mere fact that the disposition seems unfair is not enough motivation for a court to risk altering your mother's wishes. Thus, you are stuck with what she left to you, and nothing more.

I inherited a generous portion of my friend's estate, but I do not want to accept it because I recently had a judgment entered against me and fear that I may lose it to my creditor. Can I reject the gift? *Yes. You can reject all or part of a gift if you file a valid disclaimer with the court within 9 months after your friend's death.* The disclaimer must be in a writing signed by you and must describe the property that you are rejecting. The gift that you reject will then pass under your friend's residuary clause or to her intestate heirs (if she did not have a residuary clause).

Before my father's death, he promised me that he would leave me $20,000 in his will. When the will was probated, the gift that he promised me was not included and the executor is refusing to pay it. Can I sue the estate for the $20,000? *No. The mere fact that your father promised to leave you something in his will is not sufficient grounds for suing the estate.* To win, you would have to prove not only that there was a contract between you and your father that he would leave the gift (and you would have to show more than the fact that he orally promised the gift), but also that the gift

was in exchange for some type of service that you provided him, such as taking care of him during his final illness.

My grandfather's will devises his artwork to me, but when the executor was inventorying his estate, he learned that my grandfather sold the artwork to an art gallery before he died. Can I get it back from the gallery? *No.* The bequest to you is ineffective because your grandfather no longer owned the artwork when he died.

I was named a beneficiary in my boyfriend's will, but the court found the will to be invalid because it was signed by only one witness, so now I get nothing. Can I sue the attorney who prepared the will? *It depends on the law of your state, but most states will allow you to sue the attorney for his negligence.* A few states allow only the client to sue the attorney, which leaves you with no recourse because the client is now dead.

My brother left his entire estate to a local charity. Can he do that? Yes, as long as your state does not place any monetary limit on gifts to charities.

DEATH OF A BENEFICIARY – WHAT HAPPENS TO THE GIFT?

In my will, I devised my car to my granddaughter, Sheila, but she died last month. What happens to the car? *Generally, a gift to a beneficiary is invalid if the beneficiary dies before you.* The property will pass under your residuary clause or, if none, under intestacy. However, every state has what is called an "anti-lapse statute," which is designed to save the gift of a beneficiary who dies before you for that beneficiary's descendants. For the statute to apply, the beneficiary must have been related to you in a specified manner (grandchildren are normally included; friends and remote relatives are not) and must have left surviving descendants. Since Sheila is your granddaughter, she will probably fall within the scope of your state's statute, and if she left any surviving descendants (e.g., children or grandchildren), then the gift will pass to them.

> Now would be a good time to change your will, especially if you are not fond of the person who will receive the property under the anti-lapse statute.

In my will, I left a gift to "my employees for all their hard work over the years." If one of my employees dies before me, what happens to her share? *Assuming the anti-lapse statute does not apply, her share will pass to the remaining employees.* A gift to "my employees," or any other group of people that is not individually named, is called a "class gift." If a member of that particular class dies, then her share passes to the remaining class members (unless the anti-lapse statute applies).

Understand that these anti-lapse rules apply only if the beneficiary dies before you. If you die first, then the beneficiary obviously receives her gift, and when she dies it will pass to her heirs or beneficiaries.

How is this different from my having left the gift to "Mark, Caroline, and Dan, my trusted employees, for all their hard work over the years"? *In this instance, the gift is to three individually-named persons so it is not a class gift.* If one of them dies before you, that share will not pass to the other two persons. Instead, it will either pass to her descendants under the anti-lapse statute (if it applies) or it will pass through your estate under your residuary clause or under intestacy.

SUMMARY: UNDERSTANDING THE ANTI-LAPSE STATUTE

If a beneficiary dies before you, change your will to designate a new beneficiary to receive the property. If you do not change your will, then the gift will either fail, or if there is an anti-lapse statute in effect, will be saved for the descendants of the beneficiary who died. If the beneficiary who died was related to you within the degree required by your state's law and is survived by descendants, the property will pass to those descendants. If the beneficiary who died is not related as specified by your state's law, or if she did not leave surviving descendants, then the gift fails—it will then pass under your residuary clause (if there is one) or under intestacy.

Contesting the Will

What does it mean to contest a will? *A will contest is a challenge to a will, usually initiated by a family member or a beneficiary who feels slighted by the testator's choice of property distribution.* Valid grounds for a will contest include claims that it was improperly executed (e.g., the testator did not sign it), the testator lacked testamentary capacity (e.g., he did not understand what he was doing), it contains a mistake, or it is the result of fraud, undue influence, duress or insane delusion.

What happens if a challenge to a will is successful? *It depends on the reason for the will contest. If the will is found to be invalid because it does not conform to the state's requirements or because the testator was not mentally competent when it was made, then the property will pass under intestacy as if the will never existed.* But sometimes only part of the will is found to be invalid. For example, if a beneficiary is found to have coerced the testator into leaving her part of his estate, then only the gift to that beneficiary is invalid and the property falls into the residuary estate (if there is one) or under intestacy; the rest of the will remains valid.

I do not want my family to fight over my will. Can I insert something in my will that causes anyone who challenges the will to lose his gift? *Yes. This is called a "no-contest clause," and has the effect of causing the beneficiary to forfeit his gift if he challenges the will.* But beware—many states will allow the beneficiary to challenge the will and still keep his gift as long as his challenge is based on probable cause (i.e., an allegation of fraud or mistake).

I left my will on my desk and my family saw it. They are not happy with how I divided my belongings and want to formally contest the will in court. Can they do that? *No. Your will has no effect until you die; therefore, your family (and any other named beneficiaries) has no interest in it until then.* They will have to wait until the will is probated on your death before they can contest any of the provisions. And they may have problems contesting it on your death if they have no valid grounds to do so–they cannot contest it merely because they are unhappy with the distribution.

I am not happy with the way my mother distributed her estate. Can I contest the will? *Not if your mere dissatisfaction is the sole ground for contesting it.* A court will not entertain a will contest unless it is based on an assertion of improper execution, lack of testamentary capacity or insane delusion, lack of knowledge of the will's contents by the testator, mistake, or some type of wrongdoing by a third party, such as fraud or undue influence.

My friend's will left her diamond ring to her "good friend, Mary." I believe that she meant me, but she has another friend Mary who claims that she is entitled to the ring. If I contest the will, who will win? *It depends on how persuasive you are in proving to the court that your friend intended that the ring belong to you.* The will is ambiguous in that it does not specify which Mary your friend meant, so the court will consider any evidence as to whom she meant, including anything she may have said to you or anyone else regarding the ring.

My daughter suspects that her children unduly influence her husband to leave his entire estate to them, attempting to disinherit her. She is too upset to take the matter to court. Can I do it for her? *No. Only a person who has a financial interest in the estate can file a will contest.* This usually means only the persons named in the will and anyone who would have inherited if the person had died without a will. Since you do not qualify under either scenario (you are not named in the will and would not have been an intestate heir), you cannot file the contest for her; she will have to do it herself. Note that if she chooses not to file the contest she can still renounce the will and claim her elective share.

There is a time limit for filing a will contest, which varies by state law. If she is uncertain as to whether she wants to take action, she should at least research the state's specific law to find out how long she has to make up her mind.

PROBATE AND ESTATE ADMINISTRATION

What are "probate" and "estate administration"? *In a nutshell, probate is the winding up of your affairs after you die. It is the process of determining the validity of your will or establishing the identity of your intestate heirs.* A personal representative is appointed to administer your estate–to act on your behalf and manage your estate, collect your assets, pay your debts, and distribute your remaining property to your beneficiaries or heirs.

How long does the probate process take? *It generally takes a few months to a year, but it depends on the size of your estate and whether there are any complications (such as a relative contesting the will).* The process usually requires court supervision in order to protect your family, beneficiaries, and creditors, so it may take a long time if your estate is large.

> **TIP:** To avoid making your beneficiaries wait too long before receiving their inheritances, you should consider gifting the property through nonprobate alternatives (e.g., trusts, joint bank accounts and lifetime gifts). Also, remember that your spouse and minor children are entitled to statutory allowances to provide for their living expenses while your estate is in probate.

What is a "personal representative"? *A personal representative is the person responsible for managing your estate after you die and making sure that your wishes are carried out.* He usually acts as a liaison between your estate and the court, your heirs/beneficiaries, and your creditors. It is someone who is designated by you in your will (called an "executor"), or appointed by the court if you did not name one or if you have no will (called an "administrator"). The person must usually be of legal age, competent and a U.S. citizen; he cannot be a convicted felon.

> **TIP:** Before you name an executor in your will, make sure that person will accept the appointment on your death. Also, you should name a successor executor in case the person of your choice is unable or unwilling to serve.

What happens to my will when I die? *When you die, your will is offered to the court for probate. This is usually done by your personal representative or someone who has possession of it, and must usually occur within a certain amount of time after your death.* The court then verifies the will's validity, which sometimes requires the testimony of witnesses who either verify that the signatures on the will are yours and theirs or that the handwriting is yours (this testimony is not necessary if the will is accompanied by a self-proving affidavit). If all is compliant, the court declares the will valid and the process of settling your estate begins.

What if the court rules that my will is not valid? *Sometimes the court may determine that the will is invalid. This might happen if it was not signed by you, if it is not signed by the appropriate number of witnesses, or if it is the result of someone else's coercion.* If it is declared invalid, the will is denied probate and your property passes as if you had no will to begin with, pursuant to your state's intestate succession statutes.

If I create a will in one state, but die in another, is the will still valid? *Yes. The will can be probated in the state in which you die as long as it is valid pursuant to the laws of either the state in which it was created or the state in which you lived before your death.* For example, if you executed your will when you lived in Minnesota, but you lived in Illinois when you died, then your will is valid in Illinois–even if it does not conform to Illinois law–as long as it was valid in Minnesota when you created it. Similarly, if your will was not valid in Minnesota when you created it, but is valid under Illinois law, then it is admissible to probate in Illinois. Note that this does not apply to oral wills–they are valid only in the state in which they were created.

I am named executor in my mother's will. What are my responsibilities? As executor of your mother's estate, it is your duty to perform the duties required of executors by law and to make sure that the wishes in your mother's will are carried out.

Generally, you are responsible for performing the following tasks with respect to your mother's estate:

- Present her will to the probate court.
- Make a list of all her probate assets (called an "inventory") and submit it to the court.
- Publish a notice of her death in a local newspaper (to provide notice to her creditors that she has died).
- Collect all her assets and sell those that are needed to pay any claims against the estate (if there is not enough money to pay all debts).
- Pay all her debts (i.e., funeral expenses, estate taxes, hospital bills).
- Pay any allowances to her husband or minor children.
- Distribute any remaining assets to the people named in her will as beneficiaries.

> **TIP:** These duties can seem overwhelming and you can certainly hire an attorney to assist you. But keep in mind that any fees will be charged to the estate.

Do I get paid for my services as an executor? *Yes. You are entitled to payment out of the estate.* Your fee will either be set forth in the terms of the will or by state law (usually a percentage of the estate's value). If the decedent is a family member, you might want to consider waiving your fee.

My mother left a will but did not name an executor. Who will be appointed? *It depends on your state's particular statute, but the surviving spouse usually is first in the order of priority.* If there is no surviving spouse, the court might appoint a child, parent, or other beneficiary in the will.

The laws of the state where I live require that my executor be "bonded." What does that mean? *The bond serves as a type of insurance that your estate is managed in a way that is not detrimental to the interests of your beneficiaries.* The executor must act in good faith in managing your assets, and if he acts in any way which results in harm to a beneficiary, the bonding agency will compensate the beneficiary.

> Most states require executors to be bonded. However, if you trust that the person you name will act according to your wishes and in the best interest of your beneficiaries, then you can insert a clause in your will requesting that the court waive the bonding requirement.

My mother left so many bills when she died that the assets in her estate are not sufficient to pay all the bills and still make all the gifts. As her executor, what do I do? *You will have to apply some of the gifts towards her debts, which might involve selling some items.* This is referred to as the process of "abatement," which means that payment of the debts is made out of the property that is left to the beneficiaries or heirs. Property generally abates in the following order of priority:

- First, any property passing by intestate succession is used.
- Second, any property that falls in the residuary estate is used.
- Third, any general gifts (gifts of cash) are used.
- Finally, any specific gifts (gifts of a specific item of property) are used.

You begin in the first category and if that property is exhausted, then you continue onto the next category, and so on until all the debts are paid. If you only need part of the property in one category, then the property in that category abates on a pro rata basis, so that all of the beneficiaries in that category contribute towards the debts. Any remaining property after the debts are paid is then distributed to the appropriate beneficiary or heir.

EXAMPLE: Assume your mother dies with debts totaling $250,000 and leaves an estate valued at $500,000, which contains the following items of property:

- $100,000 cash left to her granddaughter. This is a general gift.
- Home worth $200,000 left to her mother. This is a specific gift.
- Boat worth $75,000 left to her son. This is a specific gift.
- Residue worth $125,000 left to her neighbor. This is the residuary gift.

First, you start with the residuary estate because there is no intestate property. The residuary estate is worth $125,000, leaving $125,000 in debt. Next, you move onto the general gifts. This is only $75,000, leaving $50,000 in debt. Next, you move on to the specific gifts. These are worth $275,000, but you need only $50,000 so both gifts make a pro rata contribution to make up the $50,000. The remaining property is then distributed to the mother and son. The neighbor and granddaughter take nothing because the full value of their gifts was exhausted in paying the debts.

What if I am forced to sell all the assets and still am not left with enough to pay all her debts? If the estate is not large enough to pay all of her bills, then all the assets must be sold and applied towards her debts in the following order of priority:

- administration expenses;
- funeral expenses and medical expense from the last illness;
- family allowances;
- claims of the U.S. government (e.g., taxes);
- secured claims;
- judgments against her; and
- all other claims.

My aunt's estate is very small. What alternatives are there to a formal probate process? Some states allow a small estate to be administered in one of the following manners:

▸ **INDEPENDENT ADMINISTRATION**

The court approves the appointment of the personal representative, who then files an estate inventory with the court. After that, the personal representative can act on behalf of the estate without any court supervision or approval.

▸ **MUNIMENT OF TITLE**

Purpose is to simply clear title to certain real property. Can be used when the estate has no debts and there is no need for a personal representative.

▸ **SMALL ESTATE AFFIDAVIT**

Heirs file an affidavit with the court stating they are entitled to outright distribution if the value of the estate is less than an amount specified by state statute (usually $50,000), excluding nonprobate assets, homestead and family allowances.

▶ **INFORMAL FAMILY SETTLEMENT**

Can be used for small estates that contain only tangible personal property (not bank accounts or stocks).

My uncle executed a will before he died but now we cannot find it. What can we do? *The will can be probated as a "lost will" after a few requirements have been satisfied. First, it must be established that he executed a valid will and that it is lost (as opposed to him having destroyed it before he died).* Then the contents of the will have to proven. This is usually accomplished by either submitting an acceptable copy of the will or through the testimony of anybody who knew the contents of the will, such as the attorney who prepared it.

These days I hear a lot about avoiding probate. Why would I want to do that? *There are many benefits to avoiding probate, chief among them are to reduce or avoid the payment of death taxes and to accomplish the speedy of delivery of your belongings to your heirs or beneficiaries.* Probate is a costly process, and sometimes a lengthy one. If you can transfer your property without having to go through the court, your family, friends and loved ones will reap the benefits.

How can I avoid the probate process? *You can avoid probate by planning your estate so that some, or all, of your belongings pass through nonprobate transfers (also called "will substitutes").* There are many types of will substitutes, each designed to offer a particular type of benefit. Some options are to place your property in a living trust (by far the most common type), change ownership of your property to joint tenancy or tenancy by the entirety, or give property away during your lifetime.

> **TIP:** You should have a will even if you decide to transfer property in one of these ways. You can use it to name a guardian for your children, name an executor, and state your wishes in the event you become incapacitated.

ESTATE TAXES

How does an estate plan reduce taxes? *Payment of estate taxes can significantly diminish the size of a person's estate, and therefore greatly reduce the value of each beneficiary's gifts.* A well-thought out estate plan serves to minimize estate taxes by reducing the value of the assets that pass through probate (by will or under intestacy) in order to avoid the assessment of taxes.

Will my estate be subject to federal taxes? *Your estate is subject to federal taxes if it is worth more than a specific amount, which is based on the year of your death (see chart below).* For example, if you die in 2009, then the first $3,500,000 (or $7,000,000 if you are married) of your estate is exempt from federal death taxes; anything over that amount will be taxed. This exemption amount is referred to as the "unified credit."

If your estate is worth more than $3,500,000, you can avoid or reduce the assessment of taxes by reducing the estate's probate value before your death. This is done through nonprobate transfers– e.g., lifetime gifts, tax-saving trusts and taking advantage of the unlimited marital tax deduction. It is best to consult an attorney experienced in estate planning to help you in this respect.

Year of Death	Exempt Amount
2005	$1,500,000
2006, 2007 and 2008	$2,000,000
2009	$3,500,000
2010	No estate tax
2011	$1,000,000 (unless Congress extends repeal)
The amount doubles if you are married	

What is the "unlimited marital tax deduction"? *The unlimited marital tax deduction provides that any property left to your spouse is exempt from federal death taxes as long as she is a U.S. citizen.* There is no limit on the amount you can leave to your spouse to avoid the assessment of taxes–you can leave your entire estate. The deduction applies even if your estate is worth more than the tax-exempt amount.

Although it is tempting to leave everything to your spouse to avoid payment of the taxes, it may only have the effect of deferring payment of the taxes if your spouse does not remarry (because she will not be able to take advantage of the deduction on her death). This means that she will probably die owning all of the property, and then it is subject to taxes on her death. This is especially of concern if you are both elderly. To find out how to avoid this result, consult a tax attorney who will help you understand other estate planning options.

What is the rate at which my nonexempt property is taxed? *The federal estate tax rate is high, and ranges from 39 to 48 percent. This means that nearly one-half of your nonexempt estate will go towards the payment of taxes—a huge loss for your beneficiaries!* To avoid this result, and to maximize the amount that your beneficiaries receive on your death, plan ahead. There are many ways to avoid being hit by federal estate taxes:

- Leave property to your spouse–if he is a U.S. citizen the gift will be tax-free.
- Give cash gifts before you die–up to $11,000 (or $22,000 if it is a joint gift with your spouse) per recipient per year is tax-free.
- Make lifetime gifts of your property.
- Set up tax-saving trusts and place your assets in the trusts to shield them from taxes.
- Donate money to an IRS-approved charity–the gift will be tax-free.

How is the federal estate tax computed? The government will tax any portion of your estate that exceeds the exemption amount, based on its current fair market value.

What property is included in the taxable estate? *The taxable estate includes your probate estate (whatever passes under your will or by intestate succession) plus certain nonprobate transfers, such as the value of any life insurance or 401k plan or property in a revocable trust.* Examples of property that may be taxed are the family home, any cars, jewelry, stocks and bank accounts.

A good estate plan is one that minimizes the effects of taxes. Be sure to make the most of the unified credit and the unlimited marital deduction–doing so will preserve the value of the property so it transfers to your beneficiaries instead of to the government.

Will I have to pay death taxes to my state as well? *Most likely, but it depends on the state in which you live.* There are three types of death taxes that a state can charge:

- **ESTATE TAXES**–paid by your estate before it is distributed to the beneficiaries.
- **INHERITANCE TAXES**–paid by your beneficiaries after they receive the property (there are exemptions for gifts to spouses and other family members).
- **PICK-UP TAXES**–comes out of the share you pay under the federal estate tax and is equal to the state death tax credit provided under the federal estate tax.

Will my estate have to pay taxes on gifts that I leave to a charity? No. The IRS (and most states) provides an exemption from federal estate taxes on charitable gifts made to an approved charity.

> **TIP:** You can find a comprehensive list of charities that qualify for tax-exempt donations in Publication 78, Cumulative List of Organizations. This is an IRS publication and can be found at your local library or can be downloaded from the IRS Web site: **www.irs. gov**.

Will the recipients of my lifetime gifts have to pay any taxes? *Yes, depending on the state in which you live. A few states impose a gift tax, and the rate will vary depending on state law.* The tax is usually limited to property that you give away during a specified time before your death (e.g., 2 years before your death). However, under the "gift tax annual exclusion," the first $11,000 made to any person is tax-free every year. That means that you can give $11,000 to as many people as you like every year and the gift will not be subject to the gift tax. And if you and your spouse make the gift together, the exemption amount is $22,000.

What if I give my daughter $15,000 during my life, and before my death she invests it so that it has increased to $20,000. If the

first $11,000 is tax-exempt, then does she pay gift tax on the remaining $9,000? *No. That is the beauty of the lifetime gift. The tax is levied only against the value of the property at the time the gift was made, not against any increase in value.* Therefore, at the time you made the gift, it was $15,000. The first $11,000 is exempt from tax, so she will have to pay gift tax on only $4,000. The $5,000 increase in value is not subject to the gift tax! (Note: She will have to pay income tax on the increase.)

To understand the advantage of making this type of lifetime gift, consider what would happen if you had kept and invested the money yourself. If you took $15,000 and invested it during your life, so that when you died the amount had earned $5,000 in interest, the full $20,000 would be a part of your probate estate and your estate would pay taxes on the full $20,000. The lifetime gift to your daughter protected $16,000 from taxes–the $11,000 that was exempt under the gift tax annual exclusion and the $5,000 increase in value.

Will my estate have to pay income taxes? *Yes, if any of the property in your estate generates any income (usually in the form of interest) before the estate is closed.* Some sources subject to income tax include deferred compensation, dividends declared before death, royalties and proceeds from a sale that was entered into before you died.

INTESTACY–DYING WITHOUT A WILL

What does "dying intestate" mean? If you die intestate, it means that you die without having executed a valid will.

What will happen to my property if I die without a will? *When this happens, your belongings are distributed to your "heirs," as defined by your state's law, and in shares pursuant to your state's law.* Basically, the state will decide who gets your property, without any regard as to your feelings toward family members, nor any special relationships you may have formed outside of your family. The law assumes, sometimes incorrectly, that you would have devised everything to your family. You have

no control over the disposition of your property, so if you care about who owns your property, have a will prepared before you die. Also, if your will is invalid or if you do not dispose of all of your property under your will, and you have no residuary clause, then the undisposed-of property will pass under intestacy.

> If you want to disinherit a family member or next of kin, then you need to create a will and dispose of all of your property. It is the best way to make sure that your property does not end up in the hands of someone you disfavor.

Who are my heirs? *Your heirs are the people who receive your property when you die without a will, as determined by your state's intestacy laws.* They generally include your relatives, sometimes even remote next of kin. The statutes vary from state to state, but the order of priority might look like this:

- If there is a surviving spouse and no descendants, then your surviving spouse takes the entire estate.
- If there are descendants but no surviving spouse, then your descendants take the entire estate.
- If there are descendants and a surviving spouse, then they will share the estate (usually one-half to your spouse and the other one-half is divided among your descendants).
- If there is no surviving spouse or descendants, then your parents take the estate.
- If there are no parents, then your siblings and their descendants take the estate.
- If there are no siblings or their descendants, then your grandparents and their descendants take the estate.
- If there are no grandparents or their descendants, then your estate goes to the state.

What if I die without any heirs – will my property pass to my friends? *No—your estate "escheats."* This means that it passes to the state. All the more reason to plan for your death by planning your estate!

According to which state's laws does my property pass? *Real property is governed by the laws of the state in which it is located, while personal property is governed by the law of the state in which you lived when you died.* This is important for intestate succession purposes because sometimes people die owning land in other states. To determine who the land passes to under intestacy, the intestate succession laws of the state in which the land is located control.

I am married and have no children. I want my spouse to receive everything when I die so I do not really need a will. Is that what happens under intestacy? *Not necessarily. It depends on your state's intestate succession laws—some provide that your spouse will have to share your estate with your parents.* It would be in your spouse's best interest for you to leave a will; or at the very least, check your state's law before deciding against one.

What if I want to disinherit some of my relatives? How can I do that without a will? *You cannot! That is why it is so important to have a will.* If you die owning any property that is not mentioned in your will or given away by some other means, it will pass under intestacy, possibly to relatives that you do not like. The best way to disinherit someone is to make a will and dispose of all of your property!

My half-sister recently passed away. Am I entitled to any part of her estate? *It depends on the law of your state.* Some states allow half-bloods to share in an estate equally as whole bloods, while most others provide that half-bloods take only half as much as whole bloods.

My daughter is adopted. Will she be entitled to my property since she is not my natural child? *Your daughter can inherit from you and will be treated as your natural child for purposes of distributing your intestate estate or that of your relatives.* That means that if you have any other children, she will share your estate equally with them.

What about her birth parents – can she inherit from them as well? Generally, she will not be able to inherit from her birth parents (unless they include her in their wills), though some states do make exceptions to this rule if she is adopted by a relative or if her birth parent died before she was adopted.

I don't get along with my stepchildren. Will they be entitled to my property when I die? *No, as long as you did not adopt them or make any type of agreement to adopt them before you died.* Unless you provide for them in your will, they will not share in your estate.

My girlfriend and I recently had a son. Will he be able to inherit from us if we are not married? Your son will be able to inherit from his mother, but he can inherit from you only if you and his mother get married or if he is legally proven to be your son by the establishment of paternity.

WILL SUBSTITUTES

A will substitute (also called "nonprobate transfer") is a method of transferring property outside of your will with the purpose of avoiding the probate process. These methods help to put your property in the hands of your beneficiaries faster than they would receive it through probate, and they offer a more diversified estate plan than you would have if you executed only a will. There are many types of will substitutes, and this section describes the most popular.

Trusts – In General

What is a trust, and what is its purpose? *A trust is a legal instrument where you name a person ("trustee") to hold and manage property for the benefit of another ("beneficiary"). You then transfer property into the trust by changing its ownership so that it is owned in the name of the trustee instead of in your name.* It is a versatile estate-planning tool and is a commonly-used alternative to a will for giving away your property, because it allows you to control the circumstances under which the beneficiaries receive the trust's property. For example, you can set up a trust for your minor children and state that they are not to receive the property until they are age 30 (whereas under a general property guardianship they would receive it when they reached the age of majority). You can put your son's inheritance in trust to protect it from the claims of his creditors or from his own irresponsibility with money. You can even place your property in trust and name yourself as beneficiary in the event you become unable to manage your own financial affairs.

The trust cannot be used for an illegal purpose or one that is contrary to public policy.

I already have a will. Why should I create a trust? *A trust allows you to do many things that you cannot accomplish with a will. You can protect assets from creditors, possibly minimize the effects of estate taxes, or provide for the support and maintenance of beneficiaries over a period of time.* For example, if you leave money to your child under your will, he will receive it when you die. But if you put the money in a trust and name your son as beneficiary, you can control the amount he receives on a regular basis and can prevent him from squandering away large sums of money by spreading the payments out over a period of time.

> **TIP:** It is a good idea to have a will even if you decide to create a trust, because the will can accomplish things that cannot be done with a trust (e.g., naming a guardian or an executor). Also, if you die owning any property that was not transferred into a trust, then it can pass under the will (usually through a specific provision or under the residuary clause) and avoid any intestacy.

What types of trusts are there? There are too many types to name here, but the most common are:

- ▸ **TESTAMENTARY:** A testamentary trust is set up through your will and becomes effective on your death. Basically, you designate certain property in your will to be held in trust after your death. The trust can be revoked or modified while you are alive, but becomes irrevocable after your death. It passes through probate because it is created by your will.

- ▸ **LIVING:** A living trust is created and is effective while you are alive, and may or may not be revoked or modified. It is usually not subject to probate.

- ▸ **DISCRETIONARY:** A discretionary trust is one that gives the trustee power to decide how much and when to pay out to a beneficiary. The trust's property is protected from the beneficiary's creditors until the trustee decides

to pay out any money, but then he must pay it directly to the beneficiary's creditors.

- ▸ **SUPPORT:** A support trust requires the trustee to disburse payments to (or on behalf of) the beneficiary as is necessary to provide for her support. The right to the payments cannot be assigned to others and is not subject to the beneficiary's creditors.

- ▸ **HONORARY:** This is a trust that does not name a beneficiary and the trustee is "on her honor" to carry out her duties. It is usually established to provide for the care of a pet or plot of land.

- ▸ **CHARITABLE:** A charitable trust is in favor of a specific charity or group of unnamed beneficiaries. It must be created to accomplish a charitable purpose that benefits the public.

- ▸ **Q-TIP:** This is a "Qualified Terminable Interest Property Trust," and provides that the income from the trust is to be paid to your spouse during her life and then is to be distributed to the beneficiary when she dies. This type of trust delays paying estate taxes until your spouse dies.

Who should I name as trustee? *The creator of a living trust generally names himself as the only trustee so he can have complete control over its management.* However, you can name anyone that you want as long as the person is competent. Be sure the person you select is someone that you trust with your personal affairs. Common designations are in favor of family members, though some people choose to hire a professional trustee, such as a bank (which usually charges a fee).

I forgot to name a trustee. Is my trust invalid? No. If you forgot to name a trustee, or if the one that you named is unable or unwilling to serve, the court will appoint one for you and the trust remains valid.

I am named trustee of a trust. What do I need to do? *Your duty is to administer the trust in good faith and as a reasonably prudent person.* You must act in the best interests of the beneficiaries and according to the directions set forth in the trust instrument. You are required to protect and preserve the trust's assets, invest them in a manner that will increase their value, and make timely distributions to the beneficiaries.

You may not mix the trust's assets with your own, loan to or borrow money from the trust, or use your position as trustee in an improper manner.

> **TIP:** The administration of a trust can be a time-consuming task. If you feel you need help, you can hire a professional (i.e., attorney or accountant) to perform some of the duties, but you cannot delegate the entire administration of the trust; you can delegate only some of the functions.

Does a named trustee have to serve? *No. The trustee can refuse the appointment as long as he has not assumed any of the trustee's duties.* If the trustee accepts the appointment but subsequently decides that she no longer wants the responsibility, she can resign with the court's approval.

When can a trustee be removed from office? *The court will remove a trustee from office whenever it feels that the trustee could jeopardize the trust.* Common grounds for removal are commission of a serious breach of trust (e.g., he failed to properly invest the trust's assets), inability to carry out his responsibilities (e.g., he is imprisoned), or he does not get along with the beneficiaries.

What issues should I consider when designating beneficiaries? *You can select as beneficiary any person or organization capable of taking title to property (charities and unborn individuals are acceptable beneficiaries; pets and unincorporated associations are not).* The beneficiary does not have to identified by name, but must be capable of being identified when it is time to distribute the interest. For example, if you want to leave property in trust for your sister's future children, you can do so even if you do not name them because it is possible to determine who the children are when it is time to distribute their interests.

Can I be a beneficiary of a trust that I create? Why would I bother doing that? *Yes. But you cannot be the only beneficiary and the only trustee. In that case, the title is said to "merge" and there really is no trust.* One reason for placing your assets in trust for yourself is so you can appoint a co-trustee who will manage your affairs in the event you become sick and unable to do so yourself. In that event, the trustee can invest your assets, sell them if necessary, and make regular interest payments to you or on your behalf.

Can a beneficiary transfer his interest in the trust to another person? *Yes, unless the trust contains a "spendthrift clause." A spendthrift clause prohibits the beneficiary from transferring his interest to another, and it also protects his interest from the claims of his creditors (unless the creditor is a dependent or the government).* However, once the property is distributed to the beneficiary it loses its protection and the beneficiary can do whatever he wants with it (and his creditors can get it).

> **TIP:** If the beneficiary of your trust is someone who is incapable of handling his financial affairs, is irresponsible with money or has a lot of debt, a spendthrift clause is crucial. Without one, the trust property could disappear quickly.

LIVING TRUSTS

What is a living trust? *A living trust is one that is created and becomes effective while you are still alive (as distinguished from a testamentary trust, which is created in your will and does not become effective until you die). It can be revocable, meaning that you can change it or revoke it; or it can be irrevocable, which means that you cannot change it without the court's permission. It is usually created by you, for your benefit, and names you as trustee.* This means that you continue to have control over the trust property while you are alive, even though it is now owned by the trust–you can sell it, mortgage it, or do whatever else you want with it. On your death, the principal is distributed to the beneficiaries named in the trust and the trust ends.

What is the benefit of having a living trust? *A living trust can help avoid probate by transferring your property into the trust so it is not owned by you on your death. Your beneficiaries do not have to deal with the aggravation of going through probate and* *waiting up to a year before they receive the property.* It gives you great flexibility with respect to managing your property–if you have a large estate, you can delegate the task of managing certain types of property to a named trustee while you simply collect any income off the property. In addition, you can name a successor or co-trustee who will take over the management of the trust in the event you ever became incapacitated.

How does a living trust avoid probate? *A living trust avoids probate because the property is owned by the trust, not by you, so it is not in your estate when you die.* But to avoid probate, the property must be placed into the trust before you die, if it does not happen until your death (done through a pour-over will), the property must pass through probate.

How do I create it? *You execute a written trust document (called a "declaration of trust"), which states your intention to hold specific property in trust for yourself or other named beneficiaries.* The document usually contains the following information:

- ▸ **TRUSTEE:** It most often will be you, but you can name a co-trustee to help you;
- ▸ **BENEFICIARY:** You are usually the income beneficiary; you also need to name a principal beneficiary, who will receive the trust property when you die;
- ▸ **ASSETS:** Include a list of the assets that will be placed in the trust.

You should also name a successor trustee who will distribute the property to the beneficiaries when you die. The trust also should set forth the trustee's responsibilities, including instructions regarding payment of income and principal to the beneficiaries.

How do I fund my trust? *To fund the trust means that you transfer property into it. If you are creating a living trust, you fund it by depositing money into the trust and transferring property into it.* The trust's assets must be formally transferred into the trust so that they are owned by the trustee and not by you. To transfer the property to the trust, you have to change the property's ownership registration so that it is in the name of the trustee and no longer in your name. For example, if you want to put

your stock account in trust, you need to change its ownership registration from "Mary Baker" to "Mary Baker, Trustee of the Mary Baker Trust." Personal property is usually transferred by a bill of sale and real property is transferred by deed.

> **TIP:** To change the ownership registration to trust property, you will have to contact whichever company or agency issued the original title and ask for a new one in the name of the trustee. For example, if you are placing your bank account in the trust, give a copy of the trust instrument to the bank and ask it to change ownership of the account to yourself as trustee of the trust.

When do I fund the trust? *The trust can be funded during your lifetime, or through a pour-over will, which devises your property to the trust when you die.* You can transfer assets through a pour-over will only to a trust that is created before or concurrently with your will. If you fund the trust during your lifetime, you avoid probate. But if you fund it through a pour-over will, that property is subject to probate.

What kind of property can I put into the trust? *You can include anything that you own and have the power to give away, including your interest in property that you own as a tenant in common with others.* Examples include artwork, copyrights, real estate and cash.

What duties do I have as trustee of my living trust? Basically, you need to keep records regarding which property is placed into the trust; keep an accounting of income earned by the trust and expenses or payments made by the trust; maintain a separate checking account for the trust; and obtain insurance on the trust's assets.

What happens if I devise trust property to someone through my will? *Nothing.* The property already belongs to the trust so you cannot give it away in your will.

When will my trust end? *Your trust will terminate on the date, or upon the happening of an event, that is specified by you in the trust instrument.* For example, you may simply state that the trust is to continue until January 1,

2010. Or you may state that it is to terminate when your child turns 30. When the trust ends, the principal is distributed to the beneficiaries.

Can my creditors reach the trust's assets?

Yes. If the trust is revocable then you maintain a sufficient amount of control over the assets and therefore it is subject to your creditors' claims. To avoid this, you would have to make the trust irrevocable, because you would then retain little or no control over the trust property.

Can I change the terms of my trust? *Yes. You can amend or revoke your trust as long as the trust instrument states that it is revocable–this is important: you need to reserve a right of revocation in the trust instrument or it is presumed to be irrevocable.* If the trust is revocable, you can change it however you like. You can add or remove property from it, change the beneficiaries, add a trustee, or change the terms–and you can make these changes for no reason other than a simple change of heart. If the trust is irrevocable, you will have to request the court's permission based on a change in circumstances.

> **TIP:** If your changes are extensive, you should revoke the trust and start over.

Why would I make the trust irrevocable?

Whether you decide to make your trust irrevocable will depend on the purpose for creating the trust. Irrevocability leaves you with little control over the property after you place it in the trust, but it does have benefits that are not associated with a revocable living trust, which is usually designed to avoid probate and nothing more. For example, if the purpose for creating a trust is simply to avoid probate or relieve you of the task of managing substantial assets, then a revocable trust will accomplish that purpose. But if your estate is large, you might want to minimize federal estate taxes, or you might want to protect the assets from the claims of your creditors. To accomplish these purposes, an irrevocable trust will better suit your needs.

Does a living trust provide more privacy than a will? *Yes. The trust does not have to be filed so it never becomes a public record. You are insured privacy with respect to the identities of your beneficiaries, the assets of the trust, and the terms for distribution.* A will, on the other hand, becomes a public record when it is filed with the probate court and can be viewed by anyone who goes through the trouble of looking it up.

Will my living trust help avoid estate taxes?

It depends on how the trust is set up. If it is a basic revocable living trust, it is still subject to estate taxes. If it is a tax-saving trust (such as an "AB trust"), it will provide federal estate tax savings.

LIFE INSURANCE AND OTHER PROPERTY PASSING BY CONTRACT

What happens to the proceeds of my life insurance policy when I die? If you named a beneficiary in your policy, the proceeds will pass to that beneficiary without going through probate.

I do not want the beneficiary to receive the proceeds. Can I devise it to someone else in my will? *No.* If you want to name a new beneficiary before you die, you must change the designation on the contract or the property will pass to the original beneficiary.

What happens if the beneficiary dies before I do? *If you named a contingent beneficiary, she will receive the proceeds.* If you did not name one, the proceeds will pass with your probate estate–either through your will's residuary clause or under intestacy.

Are there any alternatives to naming a person as my beneficiary? *Yes. You can name your estate as beneficiary or you can set up a trust so that the proceeds are transferred into the trust instead of directly to a beneficiary (called a "life insurance trust").* The benefit of doing this is so you can specify how the proceeds are to be used: e.g., to support your family, pay for someone's education, or be applied towards expenses related to your death.

What about the proceeds from my IRA or 401k plan? The proceeds pass to the beneficiary immediately on your death without passing through probate.

JOINT TENANCY WITH RIGHT OF SURVIVORSHIP

What is the difference between property owned in "joint tenancy with right of survivorship" and property owned in "tenancy in common"? *Joint tenancy property cannot go to anyone other than to the surviving joint tenant; tenancy in common property can be devised by your will or inherited by your heirs.* In a joint tenancy with right of survivorship, the property passes to the surviving joint tenant on your death without passing through probate. In a tenancy in common, the property falls into your probate estate and passes to your heirs or beneficiaries.

Are there any disadvantages to owning property as joint tenants with right of survivorship? *Yes. You could lose the property to the other joint tenant's creditors.* Or maybe she has plans for the property that you do not agree with (she may want to sell when you would prefer to preserve property). To avoid these types of scenarios, be sure that the person is someone you trust before making her a joint tenant to your property.

TOTTEN TRUST BANK ACCOUNTS

What is a "Totten trust" account? *It is a bank account that you hold as trustee for another person (the beneficiary) selected by you.* You have complete control over the money during your life, and when you die, the balance remaining in the account passes to the beneficiary without going through probate.

What if the beneficiary dies before me? *If she dies before you, the trust terminates.* On your death the balance passes through your probate estate.

What if I spend all the money before I die? If there is nothing in the account when you die, the beneficiary gets nothing.

How is this different from a joint bank account? *In a joint bank account, the joint tenant has rights to access the account while you are alive.* The beneficiary of a Totten trust account has no rights to the account until you die, so she cannot access it while you are still alive. A joint bank account cannot be devised to another person in your will. A Totten trust account, however, can be devised under your will to a person other than the named beneficiary.

CUSTODIAL ACCOUNTS/UNIFORM TRANSFERS TO MINORS

What is a "custodial account"? *It is a method of transferring property to a minor child pursuant to the Uniform Gifts to Minors Act or Uniform Transfers to Minors Act (depending on which is adopted by your state).* Basically, you leave a gift to the minor by transferring the property to another (the "custodian") who manages the property until the minor turns 21, at which point the property is distributed to the child.

> **TIP:** Remember that under the annual gift tax exclusion, the first $11,000 of the gift is tax-free.

INTER VIVOS GIFTS

What is an inter vivos gift? *An inter vivos gift is one that is made while you are still alive.* It is a great way to reduce your taxable estate–if you no longer own the property when you die, it cannot be taxed (though it may be subject to tax if it is made during the 2 years before your death). These gifts also avoid probate and allow your beneficiaries to enjoy the property much sooner.

> **TIP:** For cash gifts, remember that the first $11,000, or $22,000 if it is a joint gift from you and your spouse, will be tax-free.

PLANNING FOR YOUR INCAPACITY: LIVING WILLS AND DURABLE POWERS

An important part of estate planning is determining what you want to happen in the event you become terminally ill or incapacitated to the extent that you are unable to care for yourself. To make your wishes known, you should have ready a living will and a durable power of attorney for health care and for your financial matters.

What is a "living will"? *A living will is not really a will and does not dispose of your property, but instead is an instrument that states your wishes for your care in the event that you become terminally ill or permanently unconscious.* Through a living will you can state whether you want any type of treatment to prolong your life, reduce pain or provide nourishment.

What is a "durable power of attorney for health care"? *A durable power of attorney for health care names a person (called an "agent") who will be responsible for making decisions on your behalf if you become incapacitated and unable to care for yourself.* The power becomes effective when you are determined to be incapacitated.

I do not understand how the two differ—are they really the same? *No. A living will does not name an agent and applies only if you become terminally ill.* A durable power of attorney for health care is much broader and gives the agent full decision-making authority with respect to a wide variety of situations involving your medical, surgical, hospital and related care.

What about my financial affairs—who manages those if I become ill or incapacitated? *You should execute a power of attorney for financial matters, which will designate a certain person of your choice to handle your financial affairs in the event you become ill or incapacitated.* The person you name will then be able to perform many duties such as paying your bills, managing your bank accounts and investing your assets.

How are these instruments created? *Generally, they must be in writing, signed by you, and witnessed by two people.* Although you can fill out a generic form for a power of attorney or living will, you should still have it reviewed by an attorney to make sure it meets your state's requirements.

> **TIP:** It is a good idea to give a copy of the document to your doctor, a family member or the person you name as agent.

Can I ever revoke the living will or power of attorney? *Yes.* Either document can be revoked in much the same way that you would revoke an ordinary will (i.e., destruction, written revocation). Many states even permit oral revocations.

Who can be my agent under a durable power of attorney for health care? You can name almost anyone to be your agent, though some states prohibit you from naming family members or your doctor.

What types of decisions regarding my care will the agent be able to make? *You have the power to limit or specifically name the powers given to your agent in the instrument that creates the durable power, but the agent's decision-making authority is generally quite broad.* It includes any decision that is related to your care, such as whether to decline or consent to medical care, access your medical records, select your doctors, or admit you to a hospital.

6 FAMILY LAW

The legal issues relating to families are as simple as applying for a marriage license and as complicated as a child custody case. Family laws run the gamut from the happiest moments in a person's life to the most despairing. Because of the great emotion involved, decisions are sometimes made hurriedly and without considering the legal ramifications. If you are unable to consult with an attorney, it is imperative that you at least familiarize yourself with the laws of your state before embarking on marriage, divorce, adoption and other matters concerning personal relationships.

COHABITATION

Until recently, two people "living together" or cohabitating had no legal relationship and thus no claim on each other's property or assets. When the relationship terminated, property and income belonged to the owner. Any rights and duties that did exist between the couple were purely self-imposed. The status of the couple's relationship was inconsequential to any legal dispute that might arise.

In 1976, the California courts recognized a cause of action one partner might have against another based on an implied agreement or understanding while the two were cohabitating. As a result of famous "palimony" cases tried in California, the concept of living together began to have legal consequences. Rights that once only a spouse had, such as money owed for support to one person by another after the relationship dissolved, are now commonly considered in relationships where no marriage existed.

PROPERTY RIGHTS

Unmarried people living together have no rights to the other person's property unless they have entered into a cohabitation agreement, which can be either written or implied. The built-in protections that a spouse has as a married person do not exist when two people live together. The fact that two people are living together or cohabitating is irrelevant to property rights between the two. The obligation one person has to another is strictly a contract question with no consideration of their cohabitation arrangement.

For example, the length of time the parties lived together is of no consequence to the amount of support, if any, that is awarded after the relationship terminates. The amount awarded depends on the agreement that existed between the couple. On the other hand, the length of a marriage is a determining factor in awarding support and dividing property. The relevant question in cohabitation arrangements is whether the two people had an agreement to divide property, own assets together or support one another. A claim based on that agreement is known as a Marvin claim (based on a 1976 lawsuit involving actor Lee Marvin).

> The judgment your ex-partner owes on a Marvin claim can be discharged if he or she files bankruptcy. However, awards for spousal support are not dischargeable and must be paid.

> **TIP:** Only spousal support payments are tax deductible.

My partner and I were never officially married but we have always acted and considered ourselves married. If we break up, do I have to file a Marvin claim to get my half of our property? It depends. In states where common law marriages are recognized, you are treated as a spouse. However, if you live in a state that does not recognize common law marriages, you must file a Marvin claim to obtain your share of the property.

> A common law marriage is a relationship where two people hold themselves out to the public as a married couple. Common law marriages are discussed below.

Why should my partner and I have a cohabitation agreement? A cohabitation agreement protects your interests by clearly spelling out your obligations to one another. If one of you is supporting the other person (for example, paying bills and mortgage, buying food, clothing and vehicles), the agreement can provide that support will not continue if the relationship ends.

> If a death occurs without a valid will, your partner inherits nothing.

> **TIP:** If you want to be responsible for decisions about your partner's health care if he or she becomes incapacitated, you must have a durable power of attorney for health care.

Do we need a lawyer to draft the cohabitation agreement? *No.* However, to avoid messy financial entanglements, it is advisable that an attorney draft the cohabitation agreement.

> **TIP:** Each person should consult their own attorney.

What should the cohabitation agreement include? The agreement needs to cover how you and your partner wish to be treated during the relationship and when it terminates. Some points to include are:

- directions for distribution of property (what and to whom) if one or both of the partners die;
- provisions that one partner is supporting the other (if that is the case) and a listing of specific elements of support (e.g., housing, food, vehicle, amount of cash per month);
- provisions that neither partner has the obligation to support the other (if that is the case) and that all expenses are shared equally;
- specification of the expenses for which each partner is responsible;
- specification of the debts for which each partner is responsible;
- specification of whether a joint bank account will exist and the amount of contribution each partner will make;
- waiver of any claims of support after the relationship is terminated;
- amount and number of payments, if any, to be made by one partner to the other after the relationship is terminated;
- directions for the disposition of jointly owned property and distribution of the proceeds;
- provisions revoking the agreement if cohabitation is ended on mutual agreement;
- provisions voiding the agreement should one partner be unfaithful (or other applicable event); and
- recitation that each partner consulted their own attorney.

What do we leave out of the agreement? The cohabitation agreement should never refer to a promise to divorce or provide sexual favors.

We do not have a written cohabitation agreement, but I have quit my job because my partner promised to always support me. Can I hold my partner to the promise? Yes; however the matter will most likely have to be litigated in court. In order to enforce your partner's promise, the jury or judge must believe that the two of you had a clear understanding regarding support.

If I left my partner because she was unfaithful, is my promise to support her still enforceable? *No.* You can argue that your ex-partner breached the cohabitation agreement. As with any contract, her breach may extinguish any duties you had towards her.

Is my ex-girlfriend entitled to monthly support while we are litigating her Marvin claim against me? *No.* She is suing you based on a contract and she has no right to support or any type of recovery on her contract claim until the matter is decided.

Can an ex-partner sue for support and property if the relationship was a same-sex one? *Yes.* Gender is irrelevant in determining if a cohabitation agreement exists between two unmarried persons.

My partner and I were married for less than a year after living together for a decade. Can I still make a claim for support based on a cohabitation agreement that we had while living together? *Yes.* Marriage does not extinguish your Marvin claim.

I was awarded a sum of money after I sued my ex-partner for support. I have since lost may job. Can the amount of the award be increased? *No.* Unlike spousal support judgments, a judgment on a Marvin claim cannot be modified or changed.

How is the cohabitation agreement enforced? The agreement is generally enforced through litigation. The Marvin claim is either settled or the parties go to trial. Once a judgment has been entered, it can be enforced through several means, including contempt of court, if a party disobeys the court's orders.

> The agreement does not have to be written or express to be enforceable. Instead, if one of the partners in a cohabitation arrangement can prove that an implied partnership (i.e., contract) existed, that party may be owed compensation.

> Cohabitation is not a prerequisite to the finding of an implied agreement between unmarried persons concerning their property.

What is "palimony"? Palimony is the term for monetary support paid to an ex-partner through a Marvin claim. Your right to palimony is never automatic. Unlike alimony, which is a right granted on the basis of your status as a married person, palimony is based on an agreement or understanding between partners. If no agreement exists, palimony is not a remedy.

CIVIL UNIONS

Vermont currently issues certificates of civil unions to same sex couples who are unable to legally obtain a marriage license. Although a civil union is not a marriage, laws allowing couples to form civil unions give those couples the same rights and benefits of spouses. However, no other state is required to recognize the civil union and the federal government does not give same-sex couples any of the benefits, protections and responsibilities that are granted to married spouses. For example, a couple that is in a civil union may not file a joint federal tax return as a married couple or receive Social Security benefits if one partner dies. Dissolution of civil unions also follows the same procedures for divorce.

REQUIREMENTS FOR CIVIL UNION

- A civil union is only available to same-sex couples since they are ineligible for marriage.
- Both parties must be at least 18 years of age, of sound mind, and not already in a marriage or in another civil union.

There is no residency requirement, and any eligible couple can obtain a civil union in Vermont.

As with marriage, a person may not enter into a civil union with a parent, grandparent, sister, brother, child, grandchild, niece, nephew, aunt or uncle.

Additional information on civil unions is available on the Vermont Secretary of State Web site at **www.sec.state.vt.us/otherprg/ civilunions/civilunions.html**.

PROPERTY RIGHTS

In Vermont, couples in a civil union have the same property rights as spouses. Laws concerning inheritance (such as homestead rights of a surviving spouse), ownership of real property, title to assets and causes of actions a person may have that typically are only available to a spouse (such as wrongful death) apply to couples in certified civil unions. Additionally, civil unions give the couple the right to claim insurance benefits and proceeds, retirement and worker's compensations benefits and family leave benefits.

> **By virtue of a civil union, the parties are automatically included in terms such as "spouse" or "next of kin" for any legal purpose that may arise. For example, one member of a civil union can authorize medical care for his partner since he is considered a spouse or next of kin under the law.**

Who issues a civil union license? Any town clerk in the state of Vermont will issue a civil union license to eligible couples.

Is any type of ceremony required? *Yes*. Until an authorized person certifies the civil union it does not come into existence.

Does the civil union license expire? *Yes*. The union must be certified within 60 days or the license expires.

Can we apply for a civil union license by mail? *No*. You must apply in person and sign the application in the presence of the clerk. Additionally, a proxy is not permitted to stand in for one member of the union.

Who is authorized to certify the civil union? Any judge or clergy member residing in the state issuing the license can certify the union.

What do we do with the civil union license once we find someone to certify it? The judge or clergy member must sign and date the license at which time it becomes a civil union certificate. The certificate must be filed with the town clerk that originally issued it (as a license) within 10 days after the date it was signed by the person who certified it.

DOMESTIC PARTNERSHIPS

Certain state and cities are allowing committed couples that live together to document their relationship by registering as domestic partners.

A domestic partnership is a living arrangement between two unmarried persons where one partner supports the other in return for the other performing domestic duties (housekeeping, travel companion, taking care of children and home, participating in household decisions, etc.). The courts treat domestic partners just as they would any unmarried persons living together.

> **TIP:** Agreements based on one person providing sexual favors to another (a man and his mistress, for example) are always invalid. This is known as "meretricious consideration"– where sexual acts form an inseparable part of the consideration for the agreement.

REQUIREMENTS

Anyone who meets the eligibility requirements for marriage may register a domestic partnership. Thus, at a minimum, the partners must be 18 years of age, unmarried and unrelated. Additionally, the persons wishing to register must state that they:

- intend to live together;
- are each other's sole domestic partner; and
- are in a committed and mutual relationship.

What are the benefits to registering a domestic partnership? While domestic partner status does not convey the same rights and benefits as those given to a spouse, a domestic partner may be named as a beneficiary in a health insurance policy and may qualify for family leave benefits.

> **TIP:** For an updated list of cities and employers that recognize domestic partnerships, check the Worklife section of the Human Rights Campaign Organization at **www.hrc.org**.

> **TIP:** Some employers require a signed affidavit and proof of a joint residence before benefits can be obtained.

Where do we register a domestic partnership? In cities that permit domestic partnerships, registration takes place at the county or city clerk's office.

Do we both have to be present to register? *Yes.* As with marriage license applications, you are both required to be present before the clerk and sign an affidavit or certification that you meet the requirements for a domestic partnership.

What documents do we need to bring with us? You are required to bring picture identification, such as a driver's license, along with a birth certificate.

Is there any way to keep our domestic partnership confidential? *Yes.* You may not be required to actually file the certification with the clerk. Instead, you will retain the original certificate that has been signed and notarized by the clerk.

> **TIP:** If your domestic partnership is filed with the clerk, it becomes public record. Any member of the public will be able to access your names, dates of birth, date of registering and certificate number.

How do we dissolve a domestic partnership? You must complete and file a termination form stating the partnership has ended. If a domestic partnership certification was filed with the clerk, the termination form should be filed with clerk as well.

Do both partners have to sign the termination form? *No.* One of you may complete and sign the form. The signed form should be given or mailed to your partner.

> **If the non-signing partner is uncooperative, the partner terminating the relationship must show that he or she attempted to notify the ex-partner of the termination.**

> **TIP:** A copy of the signed and file-marked, if applicable, termination notice should be sent to your ex-partner by United States certified mail, return receipt requested. Your return receipt card will be evidence that you notified or attempted to notify your ex-partner that you terminated the domestic partnership.

If we register our domestic partnership, have we created a common law marriage? No, a common law marriage is not created unless all the requirements are met in a state that recognizes such marriages.

> A same-sex domestic partnership cannot become a common law marriage since same-sex marriages are typically not recognized and even banned in some states.

CALIFORNIA "DOMESTIC PARTNER RIGHTS AND RESPONSIBILITIES ACT OF 2003"

A law giving registered domestic partners "spousal" status was recently enacted in California and became effective on January 1, 2005. The Domestic Partner Rights and Responsibilities Act applies to domestic partners who are prohibited from marrying. Since same sex couples are prohibited from marrying in California, gay couples are covered under the Act and have the same rights and duties as married couples. (Marriage is defined under California law as being solely between a man and a woman.)

> Hawaii allows any two adults who are legally prohibited from marrying to enter into a "reciprocal beneficiary" relationship which gives the couple selective rights and benefits.

We are registered domestic partners in California. Can we enter into an agreement so we are not covered under the Domestic Partner Rights and Responsibilities Act?
Yes. Just as married couples can enter into prenuptial agreements that supersede California law regarding spousal rights, the two of you can enter into a pre-partnership agreement. Your agreement can direct distribution of property, right to and the amount of support, and provide for "step-ups" in support and property rights. If the agreement is validly executed, the provisions of the Act will not control property and support issues (or anything else you cover in the agreement) when the relationship ends.

Does a pre-partnership agreement have different requirements than a prenuptial agreement? *No.* The pre-partnership agreement must be in writing and signed by both partners who, ideally, have consulted with their own attorneys. The agreement must be fair and not place one of the partners in circumstances where he or she must rely on public assistance at the termination of the relationship.

PRENUPTIAL AGREEMENTS

A prenuptial or premarital agreement is a written contract that a couple enters into before they are married. The prenuptial agreement typically sets the "rules" for property division that apply when and if the marriage ends. However, a prenuptial agreement can address any subject, including payment of household expenses and bills, ownership of property acquired or location of the marital residence.

NECESSITY

Formerly utilized by persons of wealth and property, prenuptial agreements are becoming more common as marriages occur later in life, when careers have been established and significant assets have been accumulated. Additionally, prenuptial agreements may be vital in determining inheritance rights of children from a previous marriage. By entering into a prenuptial agreement, the couple is directing that property rights are determined by the contract rather than the usual rights afforded to a spouse under the law. Under the agreement, the less wealthy spouse may receive a significantly reduced distribution of property on divorce or death.

> Spouses residing in a community property state have their assets divided equally on divorce. In other states, courts divide property based on equity and fairness. The prenuptial agreement supersedes laws concerning the division and distribution of property when the marriage terminates.

The prenuptial agreement generally protects the spouse with the greatest wealth on termination of the marriage. Property, cash, assets and family businesses owned by either or both of the spouses are protected against a claim by the other spouse if the marriage ends. The agreement directs the distribution of property when the marriage ends, either by death or divorce, along with the amount of support payments a spouse is entitled to receive. By entering into the prenuptial agreement, the couple is removing the court from the determination of how a couple's property will be divided in a divorce, or in an estate matter should one spouse die. Some prenuptial agreements expire after a period of time. For instance, after 10 years of marriage the agreement may expire and the spouse's legal rights will be determined under the law of the state where they reside.

REQUIREMENTS

The requirements for a prenuptial agreement are the same as for any contract—it must be executed voluntarily, freely and knowingly. Moreover, laws require the agreement to be in writing. Parties should consult an attorney before signing a prenuptial agreement. Further, a party is required to have a reasonable opportunity to consider the ramifications of the agreement. For instance, an agreement presented to the bride on her wedding day does not give her reasonable time to speak with an attorney and will probably not be enforced.

Uniform Premarital Agreement Act (UPAA)

The Uniform Premarital Agreement Act ("UPAA") is recognized by many states and simplifies the creation and requirements of prenuptial agreements. The Act:

- defines a premarital agreement;
- requires that the agreement be in writing and signed by both parties; and
- makes the agreement effective upon marriage.

Under the UPAA, a premarital agreement is defined as "an agreement between prospective spouses made in contemplation of marriage and to be effective upon marriage."

> **The provisions of the UPAA do not apply to cohabitation or post-nuptial agreements.**

Invalid Prenuptial Agreements

The UPAA sets out several circumstances that can occur during the process of executing a prenuptial agreement that can make the agreement invalid and unenforceable against one of the parties. An agreement will be invalid if the agreement:

- is not executed voluntarily;
- was unconscionable when it was executed;
- was signed without a full financial disclosure or waiver of disclosure and the party did not

have adequate knowledge of the other party's finances; or

- provided so little support that a spouse is eligible for welfare or public assistance when the marriage terminates.

Provisions Included in a Prenuptial Agreement

The UPAA gives a long list of issues which should be addressed in a prenuptial agreement in order to fully resolve problems that arise when a marriage ends. The parties may agree:

- to their rights as to each other's property owned at the time of the marriage or acquired during it;
- how each spouse controls their property, i.e., limits on their ability to buy, sell, transfer or mortgage the property;
- to the disposition of the property when the marriage ends;
- to an amount of spousal support or the elimination of spousal support;
- to execute a will or trust to carry out the provision of the prenuptial agreement;
- on rights in insurance proceeds and benefits;
- on which state's laws will apply to interpret and enforce the agreement; and
- to any personal obligations one party has to another.

Can I refuse to sign a prenuptial agreement? *Yes.* You will have to weigh the detriment of signing an agreement against the possibility that the marriage may not occur unless you do sign.

> **TIP:** Agreements presented immediately prior to the marriage are generally found to have been signed under duress and are invalidated by the courts.

Do I have to disclose my net worth and income to my fiancé if we enter into a prenuptial agreement? *Yes.* Both of you must disclose the value of the assets you own and your income as well as your debts for the agreement to be valid.

> **TIP:** To avoid any confusion as to what assets are covered by the agreement, make a list of all your assets and debts and attach them to the prenuptial agreement as exhibits.

Should I have my own attorney review the agreement? *Yes.* Your own attorney can walk you through the agreement and explain the consequences of entering into it.

> **TIP:** If the bride, for example, is the one presenting the agreement, she should require her fiancé to consult an attorney. If he does not, he can later argue that he signed the agreement without knowing what it meant.

Consultation with an attorney is not a requirement unless required by the law in the state in which the parties live. The prenuptial agreement will be enforced if it is valid even though it was signed without talking to a lawyer.

We have a cohabitation agreement. Do we still need a prenuptial agreement? *Yes.* Prenuptial agreements become effective when you marry; cohabitation agreements do not.

How long before the wedding do I have to sign the agreement? *You may sign the agreement at any time before you marry.* However, a greater amount of time between signing the agreement and the actual wedding tends to show that the agreement was entered into voluntarily after considering the ramifications.

My spouse demanded that I sign a prenuptial agreement the night before our wedding. All of our friends and family had already arrived, and I felt that I had to sign it. Is the agreement still enforceable? *Possibly not.* Because you were presented with the prenuptial agreement immediately prior to the wedding, you can argue that you were pressured to sign the agreement and that it is not valid.

My husband told me that I would get certain property and cash payments if we divorced. Do I have a valid prenuptial agreement? *No.* Laws generally require a prenuptial agreement to be in writing and signed by both of the parties.

My prenuptial agreement states that I am entitled to no support if I divorce my husband. Is this valid? *Yes.* However, a judge will not look favorably on the agreement and may decide that the provision denying support is unconscionable, especially if you have no other means of support.

"Unconscionable" means unreasonable or morally unacceptable. Contracts that are found to be unconscionable are not valid and cannot be enforced.

My fiancé presented me with a prenuptial agreement with "phased-in" support provisions. What does this mean? Phased-in support or distribution of property provides that the longer the marriage lasts, the more money or property a spouse is entitled to receive. For instance, if a marriage ends before 1 year, the agreement may not give you a share in any property. As each year passes, your share increases until at 10 years of marriage you get 50 percent of the property your fiancé owns.

> **TIP:** Phased-in increases can also be based on increases in a spouse's income, assets or property.

Can a prenuptial agreement limit child support payments? *No.* Child support payments are based on legal guidelines.

Does the prenuptial agreement cover property and assets my husband and I acquire during marriage in a community property state? *Yes.* Your prenuptial agreement will supersede laws that would normally divide marital property between the spouses. In your case, the agreement will be enforced rather than state law.

Can we modify our prenuptial agreement during the course of our marriage? *Yes.* In fact, if circumstances change, the agreement should be modified. For instance, if one of you has suffered a financial setback, the support payments provided for in the agreement may need to be reduced.

> Both parties must agree to and sign off on any amendments or modifications to the agreement. For example, one spouse cannot unilaterally decide to decrease the support payments provided for in the agreement. Modifications and amendments to the prenuptial agreement must be in writing to be enforceable.

REVOCATION

If both parties consent, a prenuptial agreement may be cancelled or revoked at any time. Without mutual consent, the agreement continues to exist and can be enforced when the marriage terminates.

> **TIP:** The agreement should contain a provision requiring any change, including revocation, to be in writing and signed by both parties.

> The UPAA requires a signed, written agreement if there is any amendment or revocation of a premarital agreement after marriage.

During the year we were married, my now-deceased husband told me that he wanted to terminate our prenuptial agreement. Did his statement to me terminate the agreement? *No.* Your husband must have put his wish to terminate the agreement in writing in order for it to be effective. His oral statement to you does not change the agreement and it can be enforced against you.

Our prenuptial agreement states that all of our property is separate, including income we earn during the marriage. By depositing all our money in one account, have we revoked the agreement? *No.* Although you have commingled property that is separate under the terms of the agreement, the agreement itself is still in full force. The two of you have simply made a choice to share your income with each other.

> It is possible to abandon the prenuptial agreement by acting in a way that is inconsistent with its terms. However, the abandonment must be clear and decisive. For example, if the agreement provides that the husband's cattle ranch and any income from it remains his separate property but the wife consistently contributes her income to make mortgage payments on it, the husband has abandoned his right to keep the ranch separate property.

Does our separation agreement agreed upon during our divorce revoke the prenuptial agreement we signed before marriage? *Yes.* When the separation agreement sets out the property each of you will receive, the support to be paid and other spousal rights that become issues when a marriage ends, it has been substituted for the prenuptial agreement.

> **TIP:** To incorporate the terms of a prenuptial agreement into a separation agreement, the separation agreement should clearly refer to the provisions of the "prenup" the parties wish to include.

My husband, who insisted on a prenuptial agreement before we were married, tore it up. Has it been revoked? The agreement is revoked only if both of you intended it to be revoked at the time it was torn up.

> Physically destroying a prenuptial agreement is a positive act of revocation. For instance, tossing the agreement into the fire is inconsistent with wanting the agreement to continue to be in force.

ENFORCEMENT

Courts routinely enforce prenuptial agreements if the parties executed the agreement voluntarily and knowingly. Just like any other contract, the agreement is presumed to be legally executed and valid unless proved otherwise. The agreement may be unfair and unreasonable as to one party, but it will be enforced unless fraud, duress or undue influence is shown.

> **The agreement is likely to not be enforced if it is so unfair as to make one spouse destitute.**

Can the prenuptial agreement be enforced against me if I did not talk to a lawyer before signing it? *Yes.* Hiring an attorney to review the agreement is not necessary (although highly recommended). The agreement will be enforced if a reasonably intelligent adult could understand the terms of the agreement and had an opportunity to consult with a lawyer.

> **For example, if one of the couple has the agreement several weeks or days before signing, she has had the opportunity to talk with an attorney. The person's choice to forego legal advice will not make the agreement unenforceable against her.**

> **TIP:** Choosing to purposefully forego consulting with an attorney in order to argue later that the prenuptial agreement cannot be enforced against you will not work in your favor.

Is the prenuptial agreement I signed on our wedding day enforceable? *Not if it was the first time you saw or heard of it.* In that case, you did not have an opportunity to consult with an attorney. Further, you were placed in a position where you signed the agreement unknowingly, involuntarily and under duress.

An attorney advised me before I signed our prenuptial agreement. Can I still challenge the agreement in court? *Yes.* If you executed the agreement under duress, the agreement may not be enforceable against you. For example, if your attorney advised you to make some changes to the agreement and on the day of the wedding your husband refused and threatened to cancel the wedding, you can argue that you signed under duress.

> **TIP:** Courts routinely enforce agreements signed immediately prior to the wedding where the person is educated, experienced and reasonably intelligent yet failed to take their attorney's advice.

> **A prenuptial agreement will not be enforced if the attorney for one of the parties was not acting in his client's best interest. For instance, if the attorney failed to fully explain the agreement, especially where the provisions are heavily tilted toward the husband's interest, the court may not enforce it.**

When I signed my prenuptial agreement, I was employed, and I agreed to a certain amount of support payments. Now that I am out of work due to a disability do I still have to pay that amount? *No.* An agreement will not be enforced where the circumstances of one or both of the parties have drastically changed.

I signed a prenuptial agreement in which I waived support payments because my wife's financial statement showed no assets even though she owned valuable stocks. Can my agreement to forego support payments be enforced? *No.* Your wife misrepresented and concealed her true financial situation. The agreement will not be enforced against you.

> **Misrepresentation and concealment of relevant facts (fraud) concerning one of the party's finances is a major reason courts refuse to enforce a prenuptial agreement.**

I signed a prenuptial agreement when we married 10 years ago. Now that we are divorcing, I have discovered that my wife concealed her true financial worth. Can I allege fraud to make the agreement unenforceable? *Probably not.* The agreement is a contract, and certain allegations must be brought within a specified time to successfully challenge it.

> **TIP:** Statutes of limitations apply to prenuptial agreements. Thus, allegations that fraud, duress or undue influence were present at the time you entered into a prenuptial agreement must be brought within a certain time period. For example, in a state with a 6-year statute of limitations on fraud actions based on a contract, a husband cannot complain of fraud 10 years after the marriage occurred. However, many states have adopted laws that begin the time period for making allegations of fraud, etc. when the parties separate, rather than beginning it on the date they were married.

We have been married for 10 years and have two small children. Is our prenuptial agreement giving me $100 support per month for a year enforceable now that we are getting divorced? *No.* Not only have the circumstances changed (you now have two children), the agreement is unconscionable. The court will not enforce an agreement, i.e., include it as part of the divorce decree, if it is grossly unfair and unequal.

> **TIP:** There is no statute of limitations on alleging unconscionability.

My husband was unfaithful and filed for divorce. Do I still have to pay him the $10,000 that I agreed to in our prenuptial agreement? *Yes.* Typically, infidelity does not change the circumstances so as to make the prenuptial agreement unenforceable.

Can a prenuptial agreement be enforced after it expires? *No.* However, the agreement can be extended so that it will not expire.

> **TIP:** The extension must be in writing, dated and signed by both parties.

My ex-husband refuses to pay me the money owed under our prenuptial agreement. What can I do to enforce the agreement? *You can sue your husband for breach of contract.* By refusing to make the payment as required by the terms of the agreement, your husband has violated the contract (your prenuptial agreement).

MARRIAGE

Marriage places two people into a legal relationship with one another. Beyond any societal implications, marrying conveys rights and liabilities to a spouse that are far-reaching. Once married, you have the right to share in your spouse's income and property, be responsible for his or her debts, have sole authority over your spouse's medical care should he or she become incapacitated and have the right to inherit in the case of his or her death. Under the law, none of these rights require additional agreements between the spouses. The marriage is the agreement.

The important legal implications of marriage mean that certain requirements must be met in order to become a married person. Laws generally require that the person be of a certain age (usually 18 years of age or over), and that a license be obtained from a government agency, such as a county clerk. The requirements are simple; however, the obstacles are many. As discussed below, marriages may be invalid or voidable, for many reasons, including incapacity, age and a current marriage to another person.

REQUIREMENTS

The requirements for entering into a valid marriage are determined according to state law. The laws set out different requirements, but once married and having met the requirements, the marriage is recognized in all states. If a marriage is valid in the place it was performed, it is valid wherever the couple resides.

Marriage License

A license is generally required before a couple is allowed to marry. The couple applies at the county marriage license office and pays a fee to have the license issued. The official marrying the couple signs the license and it is then filed with the county clerk's office.

It is difficult for me to leave work. Do we both have to be present to get the marriage license? *Yes.* Laws require that both parties applying for a marriage license appear in person. The application must be signed by both of you in the presence of a city or county clerk.

I gave my mother a power of attorney allowing her to apply for my marriage license on my behalf since I'm overseas. Can the clerk issue the license? *No.* You must be present with your fiancé in order to obtain a marriage license. The clerk will not accept a power of attorney.

Do we have to live in the state where we are applying for a marriage license? *No.* If you meet the state law requirements, you will be issued a license.

Can we obtain a marriage license if we are the same sex? Only the state of Massachusetts currently issues marriage licenses to same sex couples. Laws will not allow the marriage to be recognized in most states and although there is no clear prohibition in others, no state has the obligation to recognize your marriage under the Defense of Marriage Act (DOMA).

> **TIP:** For information on how to get married in Massachusetts if you are a same sex couple, go to **www.glad.org/marriage/howtogetmarried.html**.

> Laws concerning the issuance of marriage licenses routinely prohibit issuing a marriage license for people of the same sex.

> The Defense of Marriage Act (DOMA) permits one state to refuse to recognize a same-sex marriage that occurred in another state even if the marriage was legal. Additionally, DOMA denies federal recognition of same-sex marriages by recognizing marriage between a man and a woman only.

> **TIP:** DOMA does not outlaw same-sex marriages; however, many states are adopting constitutional amendments prohibiting marriage between couples of the same sex.

> The Federal Marriage Amendment (FMA) has been proposed as an amendment to the U.S. Constitution, creating a definition of marriage as between a man and a woman. The proposed amendment states:
>
> "Marriage in the United States shall consist only of the union of a man and a woman. Neither this Constitution or the constitution of any State, nor state or federal law, shall be construed to require that marital status or the legal incidents thereof be conferred upon unmarried couples or groups."

What do we need to bring with us when we apply for a marriage license? At a minimum, you must bring a driver's license or passport (proving your identity) and a birth or baptismal certificate (proving your age).

> **TIP:** Always call the clerk in the marriage license office to determine what documentation is required before a marriage license will be issued. Ask if you need a notarized copy of your birth certificate. Copies are sometimes not accepted.

How much is the fee? Fees vary widely depending on the state in which you live. Some marriage license offices charge as little as $4 and some as much as $80. Typically, the fee is approximately $50.

> **TIP:** Call ahead to find out the fee and ask what form of payment is accepted. In some cases, you may need to bring cash.

Can the fee be waived? *No.* Most counties do not have a provision for waiving the fee. However, if you are unable to afford the fee, it is advisable that you call the clerk's office and ask what the policy is.

Can we get married without a license? *No.* Laws generally make it a misdemeanor for an authorized official to marry a couple without a license.

Can we use our marriage license in any state? *No.* The license can only be used in the state in which it was issued. For example, an official in New Jersey will not marry you if you have a New York marriage license.

We want to get married in Mexico. Where do we get a license? *Couples marrying in a foreign country must meet the marriage requirements of that country.* You should contact the Mexican embassy in the United States to determine what is required.

> **TIP:** Once in the foreign county, immediately contact the U.S. Embassy there to confirm that you meet the requirements allowing your foreign marriage to be recognized in the United States.

> **TIP:** Some countries require couples to have resided there for a period of time before a marriage can take place. For example, France requires that couples wishing to get married there live in the country at least 40 consecutive days before the marriage occurs.

> **An American's marriage to a foreign citizen in no way guarantees that the foreigner will be able to obtain American citizenship.**

Do marriage licenses expire? *Yes.* Once the license expires, you must reapply in order to be married.

The pastor did not sign our license. Can we still file it? *No.* The license must be signed and dated by the pastor before it can be returned to the clerk's office for filing.

When does our marriage license have to be filed? The license must usually be filed within a matter of days after the marriage occurs. Laws vary from state to state, but a 30-day time period is typical.

My husband did not give his real age on our marriage license. Are we legally married? *Yes.* A benign fraudulent statement made in obtaining a marriage license typically does not affect the validity of the marriage.

My husband and I never obtained a marriage license although we have been married for 10 years. Is our marriage valid? *Yes, in states that recognize common law marriage.* However, if you live in a state where the law provides that a marriage is void unless you have obtained a marriage license, you and your husband are not legally married.

> **TIP:** States that recognize common law marriages include Alabama, Colorado, the District of Columbia, Georgia, Iowa, Kansas, Montana, Oklahoma, Pennsylvania, Rhode Island, South Carolina and Texas. The requirements for a common law marriage are discussed below.

Legal Age

Persons who have not reached a certain age are prohibited from marrying. An under-age applicant will not be issued a license unless they obtain parental consent. Laws in all states except for Mississippi (21 years old) and Nebraska (19 years old) require that those wishing to marry be at least 18 years of age.

Does it matter how old I am if my parents consent to my marriage? *Yes.* Laws generally prohibit the issuance of a marriage license if the person is under 14 years of age; it is irrelevant if a parent consents or not.

Can my 16-year-old daughter get married without my consent? *No.* Your consent is necessary for a marriage license to be issued.

> **TIP:** Often the written consent of both parents is required.

> **TIP:** Parents giving consent must accompany their child when applying for a marriage license.

My 16 year old daughter has my permission to marry but I have no idea how to get in touch with her father. Is his written consent necessary? *Yes; however, an exception to this rule is sometimes allowed.* While laws vary, generally one parent's consent is sufficient if:

- the consenting parent was given sole custody of the child at the time of a divorce;
- the other parent's whereabouts have been unknown for 1 year prior to applying for a marriage license; or
- the other parent is deceased or has been judged incompetent

Waiting Period

In the past, a couple had to wait a matter of days or hours after obtaining the marriage license before they could actually marry. Currently, waiting periods exist in only a handful of states. For example, Texas law requires a 72-hour waiting period while Wisconsin requires 6 days. Where one is required, the typical waiting period is 2-3 days after the license is issued.

Because my fiancé is being shipped to Iraq tomorrow, we don't have time to wait. Can the waiting period be waived? *Yes.* Military personnel on active duty are typically exempt from waiting periods.

How do we get the waiting period waived? *You must request a waiver from a judge.* Typically, the clerk in the marriage license office will have a waiver form. You must find a judge and explain the reasons for needing the waiver. Once he signs the form, you can be married.

Blood Test

Laws requiring a blood test to be performed on couples wishing to marry exist in only a few states. In those states, a marriage license will not be issued until a blood test is performed.

Why do we have to have blood tests? *The blood test screens for syphilis and/or rubella (German measles).* Laws requiring blood tests were enacted to prevent persons with venereal and other sexually transmitted diseases from obtaining a marriage license and passing the disease to a spouse or children of the marriage.

In most states, blood tests can be waived for people over 50 and for other reasons, including pregnancy or sterility.

If the test is positive, what happens next depends on the state in which the marriage will take place. Some states may refuse to give you a marriage license while other states will allow you to marry as long as you are both notified that the disease is present.

> **Currently, blood tests are required in Connecticut, the District of Columbia, Georgia, Indiana, Massachusetts, Mississippi, Montana and Oklahoma.**

Do we both have to be tested before getting a marriage license? *Yes.* Both marriage license applicants must have a blood test performed.

I had a blood test last year during my annual physical. Is that sufficient? *No.* Laws require the blood test to be done within a matter of days before or after applying for the marriage license. Typically, the blood test must be performed within 30 days of the application.

Is there a fee? *Yes.* The county health department will charge approximately $25. Lab and physician fees vary.

Who has to perform the blood test? *The test can be given by your own doctor, any physician or an authorized lab.* Additionally, county heath departments typically perform blood tests in states where the test is required to obtain a marriage license.

Are you tested for AIDS? *No.* The blood tests do not screen for HIV, AIDS or sexually transmitted diseases other than syphilis. However, in some states, the person who tests you will provide you with information about HIV and AIDS.

> **TIP:** If you want your blood tested for HIV or other factors, such as cholesterol, those tests can be added to the screening.

We had our blood tests done. Can we get our marriage license now? *No.* You must wait until a medical or health certificate has been issued by either the county or your doctor.

Ceremony

A marriage is not completed until a ceremony is performed. The issuance of a marriage license is written permission from the state allowing a couple to marry. However, until the ceremony takes place, a legal marriage does not exist.

Can only a judge or pastor/priest marry us? *No.* Laws allow for several types of officials to perform marriages, including:

- the mayor of a city;
- military chaplains (if one member of the couple is in the military);
- the city clerk in very large cities; and
- a marriage "officer" appointed by a city council.

We belong to a religion that is not generally recognized. Can our minister marry us? *Yes.* Generally, a spiritual leader chosen by a spiritual group to preside over the congregation is recognized by the law as someone with the authority to conduct a marriage ceremony.

Our yoga teacher conducts marriages during class. If he marries us, is our marriage valid? Not unless the yoga teacher is authorized to marry people, i.e., he meets the criteria for officials entitled to perform marriages.

We were married by a person whom we have since found out did not have the authority to marry us. Is our marriage valid? *Not unless you live in a state that recognizes common law marriages.* Laws require that authorized persons must conduct the ceremony in order for the marriage to be valid.

Can a ship's captain marry us? *No.* Unless the ship's captain is a judge or a minister, he or she does not have the authority to marry at sea. In fact, U.S. Navy regulations specifically forbid commanding officers from performing marriages.

TIP: If you were married on a ship by the captain and believe the marriage is valid, you may have a common law marriage in states that recognize them.

Are there any requirements as to what must be said or recited during a marriage ceremony? *No.* Laws generally do not require any specific oaths, recitals, vows or responses during the ceremony.

Can a marriage ceremony be performed if one of the parties is unable to be present? *Yes.* The absent party can appear through a proxy—a person he or she has authorized to take his or her place. The marriage is presumed valid if it is valid in the country that performs the ceremony. However, before the ceremony can be conducted with a proxy, the absent party must execute a power of attorney naming a person as his or her proxy for the purposes of a marriage ceremony.

TIP: Only a few states in the United States allow marriage by proxy. Before attempting to enter into one, research the laws of the state in which you plan to be married.

Can we be legally married without witnesses? *Yes.* The absence of witnesses to the ceremony does not make your marriage illegal or invalid.

COMMON LAW MARRIAGE

In some states, laws convey marital status to couples who live together as man and wife without ever having obtained a marriage license or participated in a marriage ceremony. Even if the laws of one state do not recognize common law marriages, the marriage will usually be recognized if it was formed in a state that does permit them.

A common law marriage is no different from a ceremonial marriage—it is simply a marriage without the formalities. However, since formalities are absent, certain requirements must be met to prove the existence of a common law marriage.

Requirements

A valid common law marriage must meet the basic requirements of a licensed marriage–the person must be of age and not already married. Additionally, the couple must:

- openly cohabitate or live together;
- hold themselves out or conduct themselves in public as man and wife, so that they are believed to be married by others in the community; and
- have an intent or agreement that they are in a marital relationship, i.e., are man and wife.

How long do we have to live together before a common law marriage is formed? *There is no specific time period required.* You must have an agreement that the two of you are married and have held yourself out as man and wife.

> **Common law marriages can be "verified" by the parties by making and registering a "declaration of informal marriage" in the county in which they reside.**

Can I just tell a few friends that I am married in order for a common law marriage to exist? *No.* Holding yourself out as married to the public means letting more than a few close friends know that you consider yourself married. However, actually announcing a marriage is not required. Actions such as living together for a period of time and referring to each other as "husband" or "wife" prove the intent to be married.

We have never talked about marriage but I used my partner's name when we rented apartments and on utility bills. Do we have a common law marriage? *No.* Although you can argue that you have held yourself out to the public as married, the two of you have no agreement or intent to be married. Without an agreement, a common law marriage is not formed.

For years, my partner has introduced me as his "wife" although we were never actually married. Do we have a common law marriage? *Yes, assuming you are cohabitating and the public believes you are married.* By not contradicting your "husband" when you were introduced as his "wife," it appears that you had an agreement or intent to be married over the course of several years.

I have lived with my girlfriend for many years and everyone believes we are married. We plan to get married in the future but in the meantime have we established a common law marriage? *No.* An agreement to marry in the future means you do not have a present intent to be married. Although the two of you are living together and apparently are holding yourself out as married, there is no present agreement between the two of you that you are currently married.

My husband and I were divorced but are now living together again and our family believes we are married. Have we established a common law marriage? *Yes.* If you meet the requirements, you can create a common law marriage even though you are legally divorced.

I am 17. Can I establish a common law marriage? *No.* You must be at least 18 to enter into a common law marriage.

I have been living with my girlfriend for 4 years (since I was 17). We refer to each other as husband and wife, and our family believes we are married. Do we have a common law marriage? *Yes.* At the age of 17, the law does not permit you to be in a common law marriage, but once you turn 18 years old, a common law marriage comes into existence if all the other requirements are present.

If we split up, do we need an actual divorce? *Yes.* Although common law marriage exists, common law divorce does not. The marriage ends only through death, divorce or an annulment.

RESTRICTIONS TO MARRIAGE

Even if all the basic requirements are met, a marriage license cannot be issued if certain factors are present. These impediments make the marriage void under the law.

Can I marry someone who is not an American citizen? *Yes.* There are no restrictions as to the citizenship, nationality or race of the person you wish to marry.

Can I marry someone who is incarcerated in prison? *Yes.* Inmates are permitted to marry. However, you must comply with the regulations of the prison where the person is serving his sentence. Prisons have visitor or family coordinators who will be able to provide you with information.

> **TIP:** If you are marrying a federal prisoner, the U.S. Department of Justice's Bureau of Prison's Web site at **www.bop.gov** is a good source of information.

Void versus voidable marriages

Marriages may occur even though all the legal requirements are not fulfilled. The marriage will still be valid unless its basis is challenged; thus resulting in a voidable marriage. For instance, a minor may be able to obtain a marriage license by lying about her age. If she does marry, the marriage is valid unless the minor, a parent or guardian petitions the court for an annulment. Additionally, if the challenge to the marriage does not occur before the minor turns of age, the marriage can never be challenged on that basis.

On the other hand, some marriages are so against public policy that they are null and void automatically under the law. In those circumstances, an annulment resolves any legal issues between the parties and dissolves the purported marriage. Void marriages are those where the "spouses" are:

- closely related (laws do not allow marriages between parents and their children, brothers and sisters (including half-siblings), aunts and uncles); or
- already married to someone else.

Couples in void marriages have no rights to their spouse's property, income or assets. For example, if one person passes away, no inheritance rights vest in the living spouse. In that situation, even in a community property state, no community property could exist since the marriage did not legally exist.

My wife was already married when she married me. Is it necessary to get an annulment? *Yes.* Although the marriage is null and void, your relationship should be legally severed by obtaining an annulment.

My husband and I never obtained formal divorces from our ex-spouses. Now that he has passed away, will I get the benefits from his retirement plan that generally pass to a spouse? *No.* You are not a spouse and therefore have no legal right to the benefits. However, if you were named as the beneficiary of his retirement plan, your marital status is irrelevant and you would be entitled to receive payments.

My wife and I had several joint bank accounts. I knew she was married to someone else when we married. Do I inherit her share of the money? *No.* The marriage is void, since at the time of the marriage your wife was legally married to another person and you were aware of that fact. Unless you were specifically named in a will, the law typically gives the right to inherit to her children or parents.

Can I marry my adopted daughter? *No.* Laws prohibit marriages between a parent and a child, even where the child was adopted.

> **TIP:** A marriage to an adopted child is also a criminal act because the relationship is incestuous. Incest is a crime.

> **In blended families, parents may legally marry their step-children if no adoption has occurred.**

Capacity

A marriage is voidable if a person marries without the capacity or understanding that a marriage is occurring. A mental illness may incapacitate a person. Intoxication often results in a voidable marriage, as well. In these situations, the incapacitated person is entitled to an annulment. Additionally, a person who cannot perform sexually is considered incapacitated and an annulment can be granted on those grounds.

My elderly mother just married a much younger man. Is she incapacitated and unable to marry? *No.* Age alone does not incapacitate a person so he or she cannot marry. You have to show that your mother was not capable of understanding what she was doing when she married the younger man.

> Eccentricity is not incapacity.

Minors

In the United States, a person must be at least 18 years old to marry (some states require the parties to be older than 18) without parental consent. However, minors who do marry have a valid marriage until it is annulled or voided. Additionally, a married person or spouse, regardless of age, is generally given adult status under the law. For example, a married minor can enter into contracts.

I lied about my age and used altered documents to obtain a marriage license. Is my marriage valid? Yes, if you have since turned the legal age for marriage in your state.

> Underage marriages are valid marriages until they have been voided or annulled by a court order.

> Once married, the minor becomes "emancipated" and remains emancipated until the marriage is voided or annulled.

I am a minor. Can I have a common law marriage? *No.* Although common law marriages are recognized in some states, a common law marriage is void for someone who is a minor.

> **TIP:** A spouse cannot inherit from his common law wife who was a minor at the time of her death.

My underage daughter got married in Mexico. Can I have the marriage annulled? *Yes.* Since your daughter is underage, her marriage is voidable. As her parent, you can file a petition with the court requesting an annulment.

My son was married in another country when he was 16 years old. He has since died and I want the marriage declared void. Can I have it annulled? *No.* You could only file your petition for annulment while your son was alive. The death of a spouse means the marriage can no longer be challenged.

DUTIES

Spouses are required to support one another by law. Additionally, a spouse who fails to fulfill that duty is liable to the person who does provide necessary support. The duty to support is limited to providing the necessities of life and no more. Housing, food, transportation and medical care are necessities. Additionally, a spouse has a duty to pay the debts of his or her spouse that relate to those necessities. A husband, for example, is liable for his wife's medical bills even if he had no agreement with the hospital to pay.

According to the couple's lifestyle, necessities may be more extravagant. For instance, it might be necessary for a wife to purchase designer clothing because of social commitments that are customary in the household.

> In community property states, if there is no community income, a spouse must use separate property to support the other spouse. For instance, where neither the husband nor the wife has a job and the sole income is from the wife's parents who give her gifts of cash, that cash must be used to support the husband.

Are charitable donations a necessity? *No.* Charitable donations do not constitute a basic need nor are they necessary to maintain a particular standard of living.

Is a housecleaning service a necessity? *No.* Paying someone to clean your house is not a necessity of life.

Are therapy sessions a necessity? *Yes.* Therapy and psychiatric care are medical necessities.

Do I have a legal duty to have sex with my spouse? *No, and forcing sexual relations may be a sexual assault under some state laws.* However, refusal to engage in sexual intercourse with a spouse is grounds for an annulment.

CHARACTERIZATION OF PROPERTY

Once married, a couple's property is either characterized as marital, separate or community property. Marital property is the property and debt that a husband and wife acquire during marriage for the benefit of the marriage. Everything a married couple acquires during the marriage is owned by the two of them, regardless of in whose name the acquisition was made or whose money was used to purchase it. As a general rule, property and debt acquired after the date of separation is not marital, unless a marital resource was used to acquire it.

Property that is not marital is called non-marital or separate property. This property belongs to only one of the individuals in the marriage, not to both. The property that each spouse brings into the marriage is considered to be separate or non-marital property. In addition, inheritances, including bequests and devises, and gifts from third parties, are the separate property of the acquiring spouse, even if they are acquired during marriage. In order for the property to remain separate, the spouse must keep it entirely in her own name. Once the separate property has been commingled (mixed) with marital or community property, it becomes part of the marital property.

In addition to marital property and separate property, there are nine community property states: Arizona, California, Idaho, Louisiana, Nevada, New Mexico, Texas, Washington and Wisconsin. In addition, Puerto Rico is a community property jurisdiction.

In these states, the income earned and the property acquired during a marriage is shared equally by the spouses. This is true even if one spouse earns all the money used to acquire the property. While there are differences in each state, all states have special laws that operate on the theory that both spouses contribute equally to the marriage. Therefore, all property acquired during the marriage is the result of the combined efforts of both spouses.

By virtue of community ownership, each spouse has an equal right of management and control of the community property; however, the property cannot be bought, sold or mortgaged without the other spouse's consent.

EXAMPLE: If John buys a vehicle with his earnings, Mary owns it as well, even though her name is not on the title. John cannot secretly buy property during the marriage with his earnings and claim that it is separate–the property belongs to Mary, too.

As stated, in community property states, income earned by one spouse is treated as if the other spouse had earned half of it. This treatment has important tax consequences. For example, spouses filing separate returns must report half of the income the other spouse earned.

> **TIP:** More information on tax liability in community property states can be found in IRS Publication 555, or online at **www.irs.ustreas. gov/pub/irs-pdf/p555.pdf**.

Not only are assets community property, one spouse's debts also belong to the other spouse. For example, a wife is liable on her husband's credit card debt. However, community property cannot be used to satisfy a separate debt of either spouse. For instance, if a couple pays off the wife's student loan during their marriage, the husband is entitled to a reimbursement should the marriage end.

Marriage in community property states does not completely obliterate all separate property. The property and assets a spouse brings to the marriage remain her separate property as long as they are not commingled with community assets. Inheritances and gifts are also the separate property of the spouse who received them. Additionally, spouses can make written agreements dividing, or partitioning, the property acquired during marriage.

I have $10,000 in a bank account. Will the cash belong to my husband as well if I continue to keep the money separate from our joint accounts? *No.* The $10,000 remains your separate property as long as you keep it separate. The money must remain in an account that marital earnings (such as your and your husband's income) are not deposited into.

I have an IRA that I plan to continue to contribute to after I get married. Will it still be my separate property? *No.* If you add money to the IRA with your earnings after you marry, the IRA will become marital property. Your earnings are marital property and by using those earnings to increase the IRA, you have commingled separate and marital property.

> Once separate property assets are commingled with marital property, the assets become marital property. In some cases, the separate property can be traced or followed, but typically monetary assets become so commingled they are characterized as marital property.

My husband had a lot of money in our bank account when we got married. Now that we are divorcing, he wants to be reimbursed. Does he get back the original amount he had in the account at the time of our marriage? *No.* Since the bank account became both of your account, the money has been commingled and all the cash in the account is now marital property.

My parents are giving me $5,000. Is this my separate property? *Yes.* Gifts given to one spouse are that spouse's separate property. However, if you deposit the money in your joint account, it will become commingled with martial property.

I have inherited an office building from my grandparents. Does it belong to my husband as well? *No.* Your inheritance remains your separate property. If you sell the building, that amount remains your separate property as well if you are careful not to commingle it.

> **TIP:** Rental payments from leasing the building are income and count as marital property.

I receive gas royalty payments every month on some mineral interests I owned before marriage. Are the payments community property? *Yes.* Royalty payments earned during marriage are characterized as income. Income in a community property state belongs to both spouses. However, the mineral interests themselves (which produce the gas for which you are being paid) are not community property since you owned them before you were married.

I live in a community property state. My husband took out an equity loan on our house and cannot make the payments. Do I have to make them? *Yes.* The bank that made the loan can sue you, as well as your husband, to recover the money. Because you live in a community property state, even though you did not sign off on the documents you are liable for all of your husband's debts (and vice versa).

We are moving from a community property state to a non-community property state. Will our assets become separate property when we move? *No.* The assets you and your spouse acquired remain community property. For instance, the money you receive from selling your house in Texas (a community property state) is community property. When you use the money to buy a new home in Oklahoma (a non-community property state), that house is community property.

My wife and I are divorcing. Can she sell the jewelry she acquired with our money while were married and keep the money? *No.* Unless you agreed otherwise, the jewelry belongs to both of you and you are entitled to split the proceeds.

Converting Marital Property to Separate Property

Marital property can only be converted to separate property by a written agreement, such as a postnuptial or partition agreement (see below). Oral agreements to convert marital property into separate property are not valid and will not be enforced by the courts. For example, a verbal agreement that each spouse's income belongs to the earning spouse is not enforceable.

Marital property that can be converted includes income from separate property that is typically owned by both spouses. For instance, in a community property state, rent a wife receives on a duplex she owns separately is characterized as community property under the law. However, the spouses can agree in writing that those rental payments will remain her separate property.

Converting Separate Property to Marital Property

At any time during marriage, spouses can agree that all or part of their separate property is converted to community property. However, the agreement must:

- be in writing;
- be signed by both spouses;
- identify the property being converted; and
- specify that the property is now community property.

POSTNUPTIAL AGREEMENTS

After marriage, spouses are free to enter into an agreement dividing property and assets both during the marriage and in the event it terminates. This martial contract is sometimes referred to as marital property agreement or postnuptial agreement.

A postnuptial agreement can be useful when the circumstance of one spouse's financial situation changes. For instance, if a wife stands to inherit a large amount of property and assets from her parents, a postnuptial agreement can clearly define her property as separate and make provisions for its disposal, if any, when the marriage ends.

UNIFORM MARITAL PROPERTY ACT

The Uniform Marital Property Act (UMPA) sets out the requirements for making a marital property agreement or postnuptial agreement. The Act provides that spouses can vary the characterization of their property from state laws. The agreement must be in writing and signed by both spouses. The agreement cannot attempt to change any duty to support children of the marriage.

PROVISIONS OF POSTNUPTIAL AGREEMENTS

The UMPA lists several issues that spouses can cover in the agreement. These rights include:

- the rights in any of their property;
- the management and control of any of their property;
- the disposition of any of their property on divorce, death or any other occurrence they choose;
- the modification or elimination of spousal support; and
- the obligation to make a will or trust to carry out the agreement.

ENFORCEMENT OF POSTNUPTIAL AGREEMENTS

A postnuptial agreement is valid and will be enforced by the court if:

- each spouse made fair and reasonable disclosure to the other of his or her financial status;
- each spouse has entered into the agreement voluntarily and freely; and
- the division of the property in the agreement at the time of divorce is fair to each party.

Although currently adopted only in Wisconsin, the principles of the UMPA are mirrored in state laws that include most of the same requirements under their statutes.

At what point during our marriage is it too late to enter into a postnuptial agreement? It is never too late for you and your spouse to enter into a postnuptial agreement.

Why do we need a postnuptial agreement? *A postnuptial agreement will supersede state laws if you divorce.* Without an agreement, state law controls the division of property and spousal rights and benefits. By entering into a postnuptial agreement, you and your spouse will control those issues.

What items should we cover in our postnuptial agreement? The agreement should set out:

- how marital debts will be paid;
- a determination of the ownership of your home (separate property or jointly owned);
- a determination of the ownership of all other property (furniture, jewelry, art, real estate, etc.);
- what amount will be paid for alimony or spousal support; and

- a determination of the status (marital or separate) of property either spouse comes into by gift, inheritance, windfall, etc.

> **TIP:** Each spouse should attach a list of his or her assets and debts to the agreement.

Can we change our postnuptial agreement?
Yes. The agreement can be changed, modified or revoked at any time as long as the changes are in writing and signed by both parties.

Can we have more than one postnuptial agreement?
Yes. Spouses can execute as many agreements as they want. Several different agreements can cover different issues without making any other agreement invalid. For instance, if the first agreement covers debts and expenses and the second covers inheritances, the agreements can be enforced together.

> **TIP:** If the second agreement changes or modifies provisions in the first agreement, the second agreement is controlling.

I signed a postnuptial agreement because my husband threatened to divorce me and take our children if I did not sign. Is the agreement valid?
No. You entered into the agreement under duress. It cannot be enforced against you if your marriage ends.

> **A postnuptial agreement is only valid if each spouse entered into it voluntarily and freely.**

My husband wants us to enter into a postnuptial agreement. Do I have to disclose my financial worth?
Yes. Both parties must disclose their net worth in order for the agreement to be valid.

If I know my husband is wealthy, do I have an approximate knowledge of his net worth?
No. Your husband's reputation of wealth is not the same as having a general knowledge of his finances. For instance, you should have an approximate idea of his annual income and the kind and amount of property he owns. Unless you generally know what you are potentially giving up by signing the postnuptial agreement, the agreement is invalid.

According to our postnuptial agreement, my husband gets twice as much cash as I do if we divorce. Is this so unfair that the agreement is invalid?
No. Although a postnuptial agreement must be fair and equitable, an unequal division of property does not automatically invalidate the agreement.

According to our postnuptial agreement, a lake house that my husband inherited, and any increase in its value, is his separate property. However, its value has tripled during our marriage due to our remodeling efforts. Is the agreement regarding the lake house still fair?
No. An agreement might be considered fair at the time it was executed but if circumstances have changed, it might be unfair when the marriage ends. In this situation, your remodeling efforts (along with your husband's) resulted in the large increase in the lake house's value. The agreement is no longer fair in this regard and that portion of the postnuptial agreement will not be enforced against you.

PARTITION AGREEMENTS

A partition agreement between spouses divides property they jointly own between them.

In community property states, property acquired after marriage belongs equally to both spouses. However, when a partition agreement is executed, each spouse owns one-half of the community property as his or her own separate property. Future earnings and income arising from the separate property during the marriage remain the separate property of the owning spouse under the partition agreement.

The agreement can be in the form of a postnuptial agreement covering income and property or it can be a deed transferring one spouse's interest in the property to the other. For instance, a husband and wife can buy a house together and the husband can execute a deed conveying his interest in the house to the wife as her separate property. Consequently, the entire house belongs to the wife, including any proceeds she might receive from selling it.

> **TIP:** A partition agreement must be in writing and signed by both the parties.

> **TIP:** The spouses can partition existing property but agree that future earnings and income will be community property after the partition.

We are separated. Is it too late to enter into an agreement dividing our property? *No.* Partition agreements are commonly executed when spouses separate. The agreement can divide the marital property you own into separate property as you see fit.

Our partition agreement divides our interest in a piece of property equally between us and specifies that it is to be considered our separate property. Can I sell my half? *Yes.* Once the property has been partitioned, it is your separate property and you have the right to sell and manage it as you desire.

> **If marital property is not partitioned, neither the husband nor the wife can sell or dispose of their interest in it. For instance, a wife cannot sell or convey her half interest in the vacant lot she and her husband own together as community property unless there is a written and signed partition agreement transferring that interest in the lot to her as her separate property.**

Can the judge divide our marital property when we divorce without any regard to our partition agreement? *No.* If the agreement is valid, the division of marital property set out in the partition agreement controls. For example, if the partition agreement gives all the cash in joint bank accounts to you, it will be awarded to you in the divorce decree (assuming the agreement is valid).

SEPARATION

When spouses begin to live apart with the intent to end their marriage sometime in the future, they have separated. Separation can mean several things. Most states require a couple

to live separate and apart for a period of time, usually 6 months, before a divorce action can be filed. Additionally, divorce is complicated and expensive and the couple may want to delay the process for a time beyond the waiting period with a prolonged separation. Some couples may have intertwined business interests that make an immediate divorce difficult to obtain. In all these situations, a separation agreement can provide a measure of security to the couple concerning their rights and obligations to each other in the interim before a divorce is filed.

A permanent separation between a married couple who does not intend to divorce and that is sanctioned by a court is a legal separation. In that case, the separation agreement divides and settles the ownership of property, right to income and issues concerning children without the spouses losing their marital status. Typically, however, separation agreements are "made in contemplation" of divorce rather than as permanent legal separations.

LEGAL SEPARATION

Most states have laws recognizing legal separations. While legal separation is not a divorce, it is obtained through a court action. Unlike a divorce, obtaining a legal separation does not require a waiting period. The parties can fix their rights and obligations to each other immediately via the courts rather than waiting several months. A couple may want to avoid divorce and seek a legal separation because of religious reasons, tax and insurance considerations or in order to continue to receive state or federal benefits.

Grounds

The grounds for obtaining a legal separation from the court vary among state laws but typically a legal separation is granted if the court finds that:

- the parties are incompatible;
- there are irreconcilable differences causing the breakdown of the marriage;
- one of the spouses has abandoned the other for at least a year;
- one of the spouses has committed a felony and is incarcerated in prison; or
- there is evidence of ongoing domestic abuse and violence.

Some laws require a finding that continuing their status as married persons protects the parties' financial, legal, social or religious interest. Either the husband or wife may file for a legal separation.

Effect

A legal separation does not return the parties to an unmarried status. Any rights and obligations that married couples have to each other continue to exist unless they were modified by a decree of legal separation.

A legal separation gives the court the power to make decisions concerning children of the marriage. Additionally, if a divorce action is filed, the court that issued the decree of legal separation has jurisdiction over the divorce as well.

SEPARATION AGREEMENTS

When a marriage dissolves, issues surrounding the division of property, temporary support payments, and the support and custody of children can be decided by the court, or preferably, by the spouses themselves. If the divorcing spouses can agree on major points, then a separation or settlement agreement avoids expensive legal maneuvers and inevitable delays that result when the parties must go to court. The UMPA approves separation agreements as a way of promoting the amicable settlement of disputes between the spouses.

Because laws specify that a divorce action cannot be filed until the spouses have lived apart for several months, the separation agreement can provide direction for basic financial support, payment of expenses and other matters in the interim. Additionally, the court can approve the separation agreement once the waiting period is over and the divorce action is filed, so that the couple can continue to operate under their agreement.

Generally, however, the separation agreement addresses more permanent matters: division and ownership of property, right to benefits and insurance and medical coverage. Separation agreements that include provisions for issues typically decided by the court are also known as marital separation agreements or MSAs.

TIP: The agreement is also termed a "property settlement agreement" (or PSA) where the spouses have come to a final agreement on the division of their marital property.

Effect On Legal Rights to Property

A separation agreement supersedes any legal rights a spouse normally has to certain property. The parties can agree to any division or ownership of property that suits them. As long as the agreement is valid, the provisions are enforceable. For instance, a spouse generally shares in retirement benefits accrued by the other spouse. However, the right to a portion of the benefits can be waived by agreement. Likewise, marital property can be converted to separate property under a separation agreement. One spouse can assume the entire responsibility for debts even though the other would be liable under the law. The separation agreement can even require a spouse to make certain provisions in her will.

Valid agreements will be overturned if the provisions are completely inequitable and unconscionable. For instance, if the agreement leaves the wife destitute without any property, it is invalid.

Effect On Legal Rights Regarding Children

The rights of children are not affected by their parents' separation agreement unless the court approves the terms of the agreement and incorporates them into the final divorce decree. Additionally, a court always has the ability to modify support, custody, visitation and any other issues concerning children while they are minors. For instance, the court can agree to the amount of child support set out in the separation agreement and make it part of the final decree, but that amount can be modified at any time without regard to the agreement.

TIP: If the court-approved separation agreement provides for additional support amounts beyond what the court orders, that amount is a debt the ex-spouse owes under the terms of the agreement.

What should be included in a separation agreement? The agreement can cover:

- a spouse's right to alimony and support;
- who resides in the home;
- the ownership and use of vehicles and other property;
- the ownership of personal property;
- a division of household goods and furnishings;
- a division of cash, bank accounts, IRA's, etc.;
- insurance coverage;
- the custody and visitation of the children;
- the support of the children (including clothing, activities, school fees, etc.);
- the payment of medical expenses;
- the payment of credit cards;
- the payment of mortgage, utility and household bills; and
- whether joint or separate tax returns will be filed.

Does a separation agreement have to be in writing? *Yes.* Laws require that separation agreements be in writing.

> **TIP:** A written agreement is not required if you and your spouse made your agreements in open court before the judge. By speaking in court, your separation agreement is "on the record."

Is a separation agreement valid if I signed without consulting an attorney? *Yes.* The fact that you did not speak with a lawyer before you entered into the agreement does not make it invalid as long as you signed it freely and voluntarily. You must be able to show that you signed the agreement free of fraud, duress or undue influence.

I finally signed off on a separation agreement because my husband called me repeatedly at work asking me to sign. Did I sign under duress? *No.* The pressure you received from your husband to sign is not necessarily duress. If you could have continued to refuse to sign but signed anyway, then you entered into the agreement freely and voluntarily.

My husband threatened to make our divorce expensive and protracted if I did not sign the separation agreement. Is this duress? *No.* Your husband's threat is really a promise to do what he has a right to do–file for divorce and litigate against you.

> **TIP:** For a threat to constitute duress there must be a promise to do an unlawful act unless the threatened person does something they have a legal right not to do. For instance, the wife has a legal right to refuse to sign the separation agreement. If the husband says he will kidnap their children unless she signs, his threat amounts to duress. The agreement is invalid if the wife signs it.

What happens if one spouse breaches the separation agreement? If it has approved it, the court will enforce the agreement. The breaching spouse can be held in contempt of court and fined or sent to jail. If the separation agreement is not yet part of a court proceeding, the spouse can file for divorce and ask the court to enforce the provision that has been breached.

> **TIP:** The separation agreement should include a penalty clause providing for restitution or payment if one of the parties breaches the agreement.

Do we have to file for divorce to enter into a separation agreement? *No.* At the time you file for divorce, the separation agreement can be approved by the court and eventually incorporated into the final divorce decree.

Does the court have to approve the separation agreement? *No.* Your separation agreement is not binding on the court until and unless the judge finds that the agreement is fair and voluntary.

Can the court change the separation agreement or order a different division of property than that to which we agreed? *No.* The court can only approve or reject the agreement. If the agreement is rejected, the court will divide the property in a just and equitable manner as required by law.

Can we change the separation agreement? *Yes.* The agreement can be changed or modified just like any other contract. However, the changes must be in writing and signed off on by both parties.

> **The agreement is always a contract between the parties. The fact that it becomes part of a judgment does not change its contractual nature. The division of property was made pursuant to a contract between the parties rather than a judicial determination.**

Our separation agreement sets up the child support my husband must pay me. Can the court change the amount? *Yes.* Provisions in the agreement concerning support, custody, visitation and other matters concerning the children are not binding on the court. The judge makes her decisions based on legal child support guidelines and the best interest of the children.

In the state in which we live, ex-spouses do not have the right to alimony. Can our separation agreement provide that alimony will be paid after divorce? *Yes.* Your agreement can provide for contractual alimony.

My husband and I never went through with a divorce and are living together again. Is our separation agreement still valid? *Yes.* Your reconciliation only revokes the separation agreement if you both have the express intention to abandon the agreement. Merely living together or cohabitating does not terminate the agreement.

> **Resumption of sexual relations, joint management of the household, commingling of money, along with cohabitation, are facts that tend to show that the parties mean to terminate their separation agreement.**

ANNULMENT

An annulment is a judicial declaration that a marriage never occurred, as opposed to a divorce, which declares that a marriage is dissolved. The grounds for obtaining an annulment range from violating the waiting period after a marriage license was obtained to being under the influence of alcohol or drugs at the time of the marriage ceremony. A marriage cannot be annulled after the death of one of the spouses.

> **An annulment that has been granted by a church or religious entity is not a legal annulment. A legal annulment requires a judicial decree. The parties to an annulment granted by a religious entity are not free to legally remarry until they obtain an annulment through the court.**

My wife and I have been married only a month. Because of the duration of our marriage, can I get an annulment instead of a divorce? *No.* The brief length of your marriage is not a recognized ground for obtaining an annulment. Unless you have a legal basis for an annulment, you and your wife must seek a divorce.

Can I get my marriage annulled if I am pregnant? *Yes.* The fact that you are pregnant does not prohibit you from obtaining an annulment if the requisite grounds exist.

> **TIP:** Courts generally do not grant annulments where children have been born of the marriage or are expected, because that indicates that the couple lived together voluntarily at some point. Obtaining an annulment generally requires that the couple not cohabitate once the basis for an annulment is discovered.

Can I receive alimony after getting an annulment? *Yes.* However, the alimony will be temporary. Permanent alimony or support payments are ordered when a marriage is dissolved only. The annulment is a declaration that the marriage never existed and therefore such payments are not available.

Is there a waiting period after an annulment is granted before I can remarry? *No.* Typically laws only require parties to a divorce to wait a period of time before remarrying.

Grounds

There are many different grounds for annulment. The length of the parties' marriage is not relevant as to whether or not an annulment will be granted. The pivotal question is whether the spouses continued to voluntarily live together after a basis for an annulment was discovered.

Duress or force

To prove that a person was under duress or forced into a marriage (as a basis for an annulment) there must be a wrongful act or unlawful threat which overcomes the will of a person.

EXAMPLE: A man that threatens to injure a woman unless she marries him is acting wrongfully. If she is in such fear of great bodily harm that she feels she must marry him, then her free will is "overcome" and the marriage may be annulled.

> If the party seeking the annulment is voluntarily living with her spouse, she cannot claim duress or force. She will have to obtain a divorce instead.

> If you were forced into a marriage yet decided to stay and live with your spouse, you have ratified the marriage and it cannot be annulled on the grounds of duress.

My elderly grandfather's girlfriend convinced him to marry her. Can I have the marriage annulled on the grounds of duress? *No.* Duress or force must be proved by clear and convincing evidence. Unless you have facts that tend to show your grandfather was threatened or his girlfriend committed a wrongful act, duress is not a ground for annulment.

> **TIP:** Persuasion or pressure is not duress.

My girlfriend's mother threatened to go the police and file charges of statutory rape unless I married my girlfriend. Can the marriage be annulled on the grounds of duress? *No.* If you had the opportunity to consult with an attorney after the mother's threat and before the marriage, you could have received some guidance and avoided the marriage. In other words, you were not being compelled against your will to marry the girl. Additionally, the mother's threat is not unlawful if your girlfriend was underage and the two of you engaged in sexual relations.

I am pregnant and told my boyfriend that the baby was his child in order to get him to marry me. Can he get our marriage annulled on the grounds that I used duress and forced him to marry me? *No.* Because of your lie, your boyfriend may have felt he had a moral duty to marry you, but he was not forced to marry you. Your statement was untruthful, but it was not necessarily unlawful.

Capacity

The more common ground for annulment is lack of legal capacity to marry. Lack of capacity comes in many forms, including:

- **AGE**–persons who are under 18 and who are marrying without the consent of their parents do not have the capacity to legally marry.

- **CURRENT MARRIAGE**–persons who are married to someone else when they marry again do not have the capacity to enter into another marriage.

> **TIP:** Remarriage after divorce cannot occur until after a certain time period (typically 30 days). A person who marries before the waiting period does not have the capacity to marry and an annulment can be obtained by the spouse who was unaware of the divorce.

- **BLOOD RELATIONSHIP**–immediate family members may not marry one another (parents, grandparents, siblings, aunts and uncles). The marriage is illegal and an annulment can be obtained at anytime.

- **MENTAL INCAPACITY**–a person who has a mental defect which makes him incapable of consenting to marriage or understanding the nature of marriage can obtain an annulment.

> **Mental incapacity to marry takes two forms. The person who cannot consent suffers from such an extreme mental disease or defect that his guardian must file for the annulment on his behalf.**
>
> **On the other hand, a person can suffer from a mental defect at the time of the marriage only and later return to his normal state of awareness. For example, if you can show that you were unaware of your mental illness at the time of your marriage, you can request an annulment from the court. Some laws refer to this ground as "temporary insanity." This is similar to seeking an annulment because of intoxication at the time the marriage took place.**

- **INTOXICATION**–couples that marry when one or both of them are under the influence of alcohol or drugs can obtain an annulment

as long as they did not live together after the intoxicating effects wore off.

My father has Alzheimer's disease. Can his recent marriage be annulled? *Yes.* If the disease has progressed to the extent that his physicians believe that, at the time of the marriage, he was no longer able to properly care for himself, that his memory was failing and that he was becoming unaware of his surroundings, then your father did not have the mental capacity to marry.

My sister has Down's syndrome. Can her marriage be annulled on the grounds of mental incapacity? *No.* The fact that she has Down's syndrome does not automatically make her mentally incapable of entering into a marriage. Unless you can show that she did not understand that she was getting married and the consequences of marriage, mental incapacity is not a ground for annulling her marriage.

My son has been hospitalized many times for mental illness, is under the care of a psychiatrist and I am his court-appointed guardian. Are there grounds for annulling his recent marriage? *Yes.* If you were able to obtain a guardianship based on his incompetency, then your son does not have the mental capacity to consent to marriage and you can seek an annulment.

> **TIP:** To serve as a basis for an annulment, the mental incapacity must exist at the time the marriage took place. Prior or subsequent mental illness is not a valid basis.

During a state of deep depression, I agreed to marry my boyfriend. I am now on anti-depressant medication and realize I made a terrible mistake. Can I have the marriage annulled? *Yes.* If you did not know you were chronically depressed or have reason to believe that you were, the marriage can be annulled on the basis of your mental incapacity at the time of the marriage.

How intoxicated do I have to have been at the ceremony to have a marriage annulled? You must have been so intoxicated at the ceremony that you were incapable of understanding that a marriage took place.

> The courts often look for evidence of intoxication in the events that occurred after the marriage. For example, a person who wakes up the next day without any memory of where she is or that she got married can obtain an annulment. A person who was in a "drunken stupor" when he got married is intoxicated enough to receive an annulment. Additionally, attempts by the person to immediately investigate, rectify and "cancel" (calling a lawyer, for instance) the marriage indicate that he was so intoxicated that he was not capable of deciding to enter into a marriage.

Fraud

In order to establish fraud as basis for annulment, there must be a:

- a false representation made by the spouse;
- that is material to the marriage;
- to induce a marriage;
- which the other spouse relied on as the truth; and,
- acted on by entering into the marriage.

The person making the representation must know that his representation is false. For example, there is no fraud if a man promises to have children but did not know he was sterile.

Additionally, the statement has to be made with the intent to get the other person to enter into a marriage. A man's false statement about his wish to have children is not fraudulent unless he made it with the intent to convince a woman to marry him. False statements that are made on a date or in casual conversation cannot be later characterized as fraud. However, that same false statement made during premarital counseling is fraudulent.

False statements that are not material to a marriage, i.e. that do not go to the heart of the marriage, are not fraudulent. For instance, claims of famous ancestors, a college education that does not exist, or even lack of sexual experience do not impact the core of a marriage.

My wife did not tell me before we got married 5 years ago that she had been married and divorced several times. Can I have our marriage annulled on the grounds of fraud? *No.* Annulments are typically not granted on the basis of fraud when you have lived with your spouse for some time and consummated the relationship. You might have obtained an annulment when you first married, but at this point a court would be reluctant to find that her prior marriages are enough to declare that your marriage never existed.

My husband married me when he was still married to his first wife. She has since died, some years after my discovery. Can I get an annulment? *No.* If you continued to live with your husband as man and wife after the first wife's death, then your marriage is no longer subject to annulment. By continuing to live with your husband, your void marriage "ripened" or evolved into a valid common law marriage.

> Void marriages, i.e., marriages that can be annulled, can be converted into common law marriages that must be dissolved by divorce. For example, while it is possible to obtain an annulment at 17 years of age, once the spouse turns 18, she must file for divorce.

I work overseas and my wife married me with the understanding that she would live overseas with me. She has since decided to move back to the United States. Can I have our marriage annulled because of fraud? *No.* Your wife's decision to return home is not fraudulent unless you can prove that, at the time of your marriage, she married you with no intention of living overseas. Her later decision to live in the United States rather than overseas is not grounds for an annulment.

I am a physician and my husband promised to do all the housework, cooking and shopping because he works from home. Can I get an annulment now that he refuses to do any of the things he promised? *No.* Although your husband broke his promises, his failure to do as he said does not amount to fraud.

> **Fraud, when used as grounds for an annulment, must go to the "heart" of the marriage. For example, a husband's agreement before marriage to have children and his later refusal, go the heart or essence of a marriage so that he has committed fraud. Failing to do chores or pay bills are not acts of fraud.**

My wife did not tell me that she was an alcoholic before our marriage. Can I get an annulment because she concealed her alcoholism? *No.* Unlike drug addiction, your wife's alcoholism is not a crime, and her concealment of her problem is not fraud. You must seek a divorce instead.

> **Courts do not grant annulments merely because a person fails to disclose their bad temper, extravagant or miserly spending, drinking habits, bad hygiene or other unattractive and annoying traits.**

My husband concealed the fact that he has a debilitating disease when we married. Can I obtain an annulment? *Yes.* Your husband's disease has increased your duties to him as a spouse without any prior knowledge on your part. This failure to tell you about his disease goes to the heart of the marriage, and he defrauded you. Household income and expenses, your ability to be employed full-time, and ability to take care of your children have been directly affected by the disease which he concealed.

> **Fraud is only available as a ground for annulment to the innocent spouse. Once the innocent spouse learns of the fraud, she must cease cohabiting with her husband. If she continues to live with him, she is no longer an innocent spouse because she is now aware of the nature and facts of the fraud.**

My husband married me with no intention of consummating the marriage. Is this grounds for an annulment? *Yes.* Your husband deceived you regarding a basic part of marriage. You can obtain an annulment because of his refusal to consummate the marriage.

> **TIP:** Concealment of sexual preference from a spouse is fraud that goes to the heart of a marriage and is grounds for an annulment.

> **TIP:** Concealment or misrepresentation of religious views can usually be a ground for annulment.

Untimely Marriage

Laws prohibit marriage within 72 hours after a marriage license was issued. Annulment on these grounds permits parties who have married hurriedly and without thought, but who have no other grounds, to obtain an annulment rather than a divorce. A request for annulment based on untimeliness typically is required to be filed within 30 days of the marriage.

> **TIP:** Marrying before the waiting period is up does not automatically invalidate your marriage.

The marriage can also be annulled for untimeliness if one of the parties married within the waiting period after a divorce is granted (typically 30 days) and the new spouse was unaware of the recent divorce.

> **TIP:** Concealed divorce, as a basis for an annulment, must be alleged within a year after the marriage ceremony. After a year, it is assumed that the new spouse became aware of the divorce at some point in time.

Impotency

If one of the spouses was permanently impotent (for physical or mental reasons) at the time of the marriage and the other spouse was unaware of the impotency, an annulment will be granted. The spouses cannot have lived together once the impotency was discovered. A couple that continues to cohabit after discovery of impotency will have to seek a divorce instead of an annulment.

Desertion

Desertion is not a ground for annulment unless the spouse abandoned the marriage immediately after it occurred. For instance, a wife's desertion of her husband after a year of marriage is a ground for divorce rather than annulment. However, in the situation where the wife abandoned the husband immediately after the marriage took place, the husband can ask for an annulment on the basis of fraud since it appears the wife never intended to live with him.

EFFECT OF ANNULMENT

In annulment cases, the court may decide issues concerning the custody of children of the marriage and require the payment of child support and spousal support. An annulment can also have unexpected consequences with regard to taxes and alimony.

Taxes

The IRS has concluded that couples who have their marriage annulled do not have the right to file a joint tax return for the years they were married. The IRS follows the logic that since the marriage never existed the parties incorrectly filed joint returns. The couple must refile any joint tax returns under the rules for unmarried (single) persons.

Support Payments

After an annulment, a spouse may be entitled to support payments (spousal maintenance) for a period of time.

Alimony

By law, alimony paid to an ex-spouse terminates if the ex-spouse remarries. In cases where that second marriage is annulled, there is an issue of whether alimony should be reinstated.

The person paying alimony no longer has an obligation to his ex-spouse when she marries. However, in extenuating circumstances, alimony has been reinstated when the ex-spouse's marriage

is annulled. Reinstatement of alimony depends on the facts of each case that led up to the annulment. For instance, a woman receiving alimony from her ex-husband may have the alimony reinstated after her second marriage was annulled where she married the man after knowing him only a few weeks, then he drained her bank accounts and disappeared.

If our marriage is annulled, are our children illegitimate? *No.* The law clearly provides that children of an annulled marriage are legitimate.

VOID/ILLEGAL MARRIAGES

Void or illegal marriages are marriages that do not exist in the eyes of the law. Spouses in a void marriage do not have any spousal rights. For example, the wife of a man already married cannot claim her husband's estate when he dies. Since he was married at the time of their marriage, the marriage is void.

Theoretically, these "non-existent" marriages would not require a judicial decree dissolving the marriage, but obtaining an annulment resolves any legal issues that might arise regarding whether or not the parties are single and free to marry again.

> Same sex marriages are void in some states. For instance, the California Supreme Court has declared marriages invalid that occurred because a license was issued in San Francisco.

DISSOLUTION

In order to end the marital relationship, the marriage must be dissolved. The dissolution proceeding can be in the form of a declaration that the marriage is void, an annulment or a divorce. Until the marriage is formally dissolved through a court judgment, it continues to exist.

The dissolution of a marriage begins with a lawsuit. One of the spouses (or a parent in cases other than divorce) files a petition with the court requesting that the marriage be dissolved and property be divided. The filing spouse is known as the petitioner; the other spouse is the respondent. Issues concerning child custody and child support are decided separately.

VENUE AND JURISDICTION

Laws require that a spouse reside in the state (and county) for a period of time before a suit for dissolution can be filed in that location. Residency requirements vary according to the state. For instance, a spouse who has moved to another state may be required to live there at least 6 months before fulfilling the residency requirement. The place the lawsuit is filed is the venue.

Jurisdiction allows the court to decide matters concerning a person's obligations during the divorce proceeding. For instance, if the court does not have jurisdiction over one of the spouses, the judge cannot order that spouse to pay alimony. Typically, the court gets jurisdiction over a person because she lives or works in the state or county. In divorce actions, laws give the court jurisdiction over the non-resident respondent for a period of time after the spouses stopped living together as man and wife. For example, a husband who moved out and left the state a year ago is still under the court's jurisdiction when the wife files for divorce. The judge can make any orders concerning division of property, payment of support and issues concerning child custody and the husband must follow them.

Can I file for divorce from my husband if he has been living in another state for 5 years? *Yes.* Since you are the party who is filing the lawsuit, you are the one who must meet the residency requirements. However, the divorce will not be granted until your husband is notified, or served, with the lawsuit.

I have been living in California for 6 months and was served with a suit for divorce my husband filed in Texas. Can he obtain a divorce? *Yes.* Now that you have been served, you must reply to the lawsuit or risk a default judgment. Since you recently moved, the Texas court still has jurisdiction over you.

> **TIP:** Once you reply or answer the lawsuit, the Texas court has jurisdiction over you and the judge can decide any matters pertaining to you in the divorce action.

> Laws generally give courts jurisdiction over the nonresident spouse if the last place she lived during the marriage was in the state where the divorce was filed. However, the filing must occur within a certain time period–e.g., 1 year after the spouses stopped living together.

I visited my sister during the month prior to filing for a divorce. Can my wife claim I am no longer a resident of the county in which I filed? *No.* Temporary absences from your normal place of residence do not cause you to lose residence in the county. Your wife would have to prove that you intended to establish a new residence elsewhere.

> Absences due to military service or public service, such as an elected official moving to Washington, D.C., from the usual place of residence do not end the residency.

I have been living and working in Europe for several years with only occasional visits to my husband in the states. In a divorce action, will the state court have jurisdiction over me? *Yes.* Although, it has been many years since you actually resided in the state or with your husband, your separation is a work separation, not a marital one. Courts do not consider spouses that are living apart due to job responsibilities or to pursue careers as having ended their marital cohabitation. For purposes of jurisdiction, you still have a martial residence with your husband.

DIVORCE

Marriages are dissolved through divorce actions filed with the court. Additionally, the court sets the perimeters for the spouse's future dealings with each other, especially where children are involved.

Because public policy favors continuation of marriage, a divorce cannot be obtained unless the parties are separated for a period of time. The time required varies from state to state but generally, a 6-month separation is required before a spouse can file for divorce. Another waiting period occurs after the divorce is filed and before it can be granted. Typically, a divorce can be granted no earlier than 90 days after filing the petition.

A divorce is a legal action. Like any lawsuit, it can be set for trial and heard by a jury. However, due to the expense of litigation, most divorces are handled without the need for a trial. Additionally, many states have laws requiring the spouses to mediate the issues on which they disagree before setting the case for trial.

Can I handle my own divorce? *Yes.* However, if you and your spouse have children, large assets and others complicated matters to decide, you should have an attorney handle the divorce.

> **TIP:** Do not attempt to represent yourself if your spouse has an attorney. Family law courts have their own peculiar rules and operating procedures that can overwhelm and confuse the nonattorney. Simple procedural errors, such as missing a filing deadline, can lead to tragic outcomes, such as losing custody of your children.

Where do I file a divorce petition? *The petition is filed in the state and county in which you or your spouse live.* There are residency requirements that you must fulfill before you can file for divorce.

I filed for divorce but I cannot find my husband to have him served. Can I still get a divorce? *Yes.* If the sheriff is unable to find your husband to serve him with the divorce papers, you can "serve" him with the pending lawsuit by putting a notification in the local newspaper.

> **TIP:** Large urban counties typically rely on specialized newspapers that print notices, filings, registrations, etc. for those in the legal profession. It will be less expensive to publish a notice in this type of paper than the city newspaper.

My wife was served with divorce papers but has never answered the lawsuit. Can I obtain a divorce? *Yes.* The court can grant the divorce through a default judgment. You will simply go to court and testify before the judge to the facts surrounding your divorce petition.

> **TIP:** Courts set aside a day or part of a day each week to hear defaults. If you are handling your own divorce and you can obtain a default decree of divorce, find out from the court clerk when default hearings are set. You will able to appear at that time and prove up the divorce.

I am handling my own divorce and need to "prove it up." What do I do? *"Proving up" a divorce means testifying to the judge that all the legal requirements have been met, allowing her to grant the divorce.* The requirements vary by state, and laws require testimony concerning many different facts and events. However, your testimony basically follows the allegations in your petition. You will need to testify as to:

- your name, age, Social Security number and address;
- your spouse's name, age, Social Security number and address;
- your place of residence and how long you have lived in the county and state;
- the date of your marriage;
- the date you and your spouse separated;
- the date you filed the divorce petition; and
- the fact that the marriage is insupportable or irreconcilable.

> **Do not go before the judge unless you are prepared to testify to all the necessary requirements. The judge will not grant the divorce if you leave out an important fact.**

REQUIREMENTS FOR FILING A DIVORCE

Any married person may file for divorce. However, all states have enacted residency requirements that prohibit temporary residents from filing for a divorce in their state.

Residency requirements make a "quickie" divorce impossible. The shortest residency requirement is in Nevada, which requires a 6-week stay, plus a witness who can testify to your residency before you are allowed to file for a divorce.

GROUNDS FOR OBTAINING A DIVORCE

In the past, a divorce was granted only if one of the parties could show some fault on the part of his or her spouse. For example, a husband that abused his wife was at fault for cruelty and the wife could obtain a divorce. In modern times, finding fault is no longer necessary and "no-fault divorces" are routinely granted. A no-fault divorce avoids the necessity of presenting sordid details of a couple's private life to the public.

A no-fault divorce is not the same as an uncontested divorce. In an uncontested divorce the spouses are in agreement on all the issues—neither one is contesting or challenging the other's point of view. On the other hand, no-fault divorces routinely include many contested issues, such as alimony payments and child custody.

Additionally, a spouse who pleads grounds for divorce that place the fault on the other party, such as adultery, is generally in no better position because of the infidelity. At one time, a wife, for example, may have received a larger share of property when the divorce was granted if she proved her husband had been unfaithful. Currently, however, grounds for divorce based on the fault of one of the spouses do not affect the outcome to a great degree.

Incompatibility

When a couple can no longer live together because of their differences, laws in most states permit a divorce to be granted based on incompatibility, insupportablity or irreconcilable differences. Divorces granted on these grounds are known as no-fault divorces. No specific event needs to occur or be shown in order to prove the couple's incompatibility. The filing spouse simply has to allege that there is a discord or conflict of personalities that has destroyed the marital relationship and that prevents any reasonable expectation of reconciliation. The laws in most states specifically provide that fault need not be proved.

Laws may utilize terms such as "general indignities" instead of "incompatibility." In these cases, the parties are required to show a series of events and occurrences that humiliated one of the spouses. Arkansas, for instance, requires a showing of habitual, continuous and permanent hate, alienation, and estrangement on the part of one spouse that makes life for the other spouse intolerable.

It is not necessary that both the husband and wife feel that the marriage has become intolerable. For instance, if the wife testifies that she believes there is no chance of reconciliation, then the divorce may be granted, even where the husband has a different opinion.

My husband and I are still living together. Can I get a no-fault divorce? *Yes.* The fact that your marriage is intolerable is not necessarily disproved because you and your husband are cohabitating. The court will look at other facts to which you can testify to show incompatibility. For instance, if your husband is consistently drunk, then the marriage may be intolerable because you are living with him and have no where else to go. (Note that a physical separation may be required under state law before the divorce is granted.)

I do not have any facts to show that my husband and I are no longer compatible–I just know that our marriage is over. Can I get a no-fault divorce? *Yes.* It is not necessary to recite a list of events or occurrences that make your marriage intolerable. You only need to testify that there is no chance of reconciliation and that the marriage is over in your mind.

> In legal terms, when a marriage is "over," there has been an "irretrievable breakdown of the marriage."

My husband is going to testify that he believes we have a chance of reconciling. Will the judge refuse to grant a divorce even though I will testify that I believe reconciliation is impossible? *No.* It is not necessary that both of you believe the marriage is over. Your testimony is sufficient to permit the judge to grant a divorce.

I filed for a no-fault divorce. However, my wife is alleging adultery and cruelty. Can the judge grant a no-fault divorce? *Yes.* The court does not have to grant the divorce based on fault simply because that is your wife's testimony. You can still obtain a divorce based on the breakdown of the marriage alone.

Cruelty

Cruelty by one spouse toward the other spouse is a ground for divorce. The cruelty can be emotional or physical, but there must be proof that the actions were extreme and inhumane. Although in general the cruel behavior must be continuous and habitual, a single act can be the basis for a cruelty allegation in a divorce suit.

Is physical violence toward a spouse considered to be "cruelty" for the purposes of obtaining a divorce? *Yes.* Anytime you are in bodily danger and believe that you are unsafe, your spouse is engaging in cruel treatment.

My wife is constantly drunk and is impossible to deal with on a daily basis. Can I prove cruelty as grounds for divorce? *Yes.* Habitual and excessive drinking is generally viewed as cruel behavior by the courts.

My husband recorded my phone conversations. Does this rise to the level of cruelty? *No.* Recording your conversations is not inhumane treatment.

Am I being subjected to cruelty because my husband constantly calls me rude names? *No.* Rudeness alone does not rise to the level of cruel and inhumane treatment. However, verbal abuse is different from rudeness and does rise to the level of cruelty. If your mental well-being is so affected by the verbal abuse that you can no longer live in the house with your spouse, then cruelty exists.

My wife has gambled away our life savings. Can I get a divorce based on cruelty? *No.* You are not in physical danger; she has not verbally abused you or acted inhumanely. The fact that she has caused you worry and anxiety is not enough to obtain a divorce on cruelty grounds alone.

Adultery

An individual who has engaged in sexual relations with a person other than her or his husband or wife has committed adultery. Laws allow the court to grant a divorce based on a single act of adultery by either the husband or wife–and nothing more. For instance, a wife can obtain a divorce based on her husband's one-time infidelity without showing that any other problems or issues exist in the marriage.

I think my wife is cheating. Do I need actual proof of adultery to obtain a divorce on that basis? *Yes.* You must show the court either direct or circumstantial evidence of her infidelity. A feeling or belief is not enough proof.

My husband is involved in a homosexual relationship. Has he committed adultery? *Maybe not.* Although, for purposes of divorce, laws typically do not limit adultery to sex outside marriage between only a man and a woman, some courts have ruled that a homosexual relationship is not adulterous.

> A New Hampshire court reasoned that adultery requires sexual intercourse, which it found to mean sexual relations between a man and woman.

My wife and I were separated when she had an affair with her boss. Can I allege adultery in my divorce petition? *Yes.* The fact that you and your wife were separated does not change the legal definition of adultery: sex with another person outside of marriage. Since you were still married when she had her affair, you can allege adultery in your petition.

Abandonment

Laws allow a spouse to obtain a divorce when their husband or wife has deserted or abandoned them for a period of time. Time periods vary according the state in which the petitioner resides, but generally range from 1-2 years.

Abandonment, as a ground for divorce, requires that the petitioner show that:

- the abandoning spouse left without consent;
- the abandoning spouse left without any justifiable reason; and
- the petitioner does not know where the abandoning spouse is living.

My wife has refused to sleep with me, eat meals with me or talk to me for over a year. Do her actions "constitute abandonment"? *Yes, your wife's actions amount to constructive abandonment.* In other words, she may have been physically present in the home, but in all other ways she abandoned the marriage.

During an argument, I told my husband to leave. He has been gone for over a year. Can I get a divorce based on abandonment? *No.* He not only left with your consent, he left at your request. Under these circumstances, you cannot allege abandonment.

If my spouse left because of my inability to stop drinking, can I allege abandonment in my divorce petition? *No.* Desertion or abandonment requires a spouse to leave without any reason or justification. Since you have a

drinking problem, you spouse can argue that he had no other choice but to leave, or that his leaving was justified.

My wife moved out, and I'm glad she is gone. Can I use abandonment as grounds for divorce? *No.* Courts typically grant divorces on abandonment grounds when the spouse who is "abandoned" wants the husband or wife to return. In your case, you have no desire for your wife's return.

My husband went to work overseas against my wishes. Can I divorce him because he abandoned me? *No.* Your husband had a good reason for leaving–work. Since he had a justifiable reason for being away, he has not abandoned you.

Living Apart

Spouses who have not lived together for several years may obtain a divorce. Laws require a separation as long as 7 years in some states, if used as a ground for divorce. Couples who have gone their separate ways and have not seen each other for many years are able to obtain a divorce in this way without any other allegations.

Neglect of Marital Duties

Laws permit a spouse to divorce his wife or her husband for gross neglect or dereliction of marital duties. Spouses have certain obligations to one another under the law. Failing to perform those obligations, or neglecting a duty, is a ground for divorce.

Marital duties include fidelity toward one another, engaging in sexual relations and participating in the care and raising of children. For example, a husband will be granted a divorce on these grounds where his wife abused credit cards, took out a second mortgage on the house to pay them off, and refused to cook or clean, because, taken as a whole, the wife was grossly neglectful.

My husband has filled our house with so much junk, newspapers and other items that it is practically unlivable. Is he neglecting a marital duty? *No.* The duty to keep a home clean is minimal. Bad housekeeping is not gross neglect of a marital duty.

> The home's condition, due to neglected housekeeping, must be "flagrant, heinous, odious, atrocious, shameful or despicable," for a finding of gross neglect.

> **TIP:** Filling the home you share with your spouse with dozens of cats, for example, is a gross neglect of a marital duty, because the house would meet the atrocious and odious standard.

Confinement in Mental Facility

A husband or wife whose spouse has been confined to a mental hospital or facility can petition for divorce. Laws typically require some amount of time to pass before the divorce petition can be filed. Additionally, the mentally ill spouse must be diagnosed with a condition from which there is little chance of improvement.

> **TIP:** An attorney ad litem must be appointed by the court to represent the mentally ill spouse in a divorce proceeding.

Although my wife has been living in the state mental hospital for several years, she sometimes returns home to visit. Can I get a divorce based on her confinement in the mental hospital? *Yes.* Your wife's home visits do not change the fact that she has been committed to a mental hospital. Unless she has been finally discharged, your wife is confined because of her mental illness and you can seek a divorce on these grounds.

My husband has severe bipolar disorder and has been in and out of mental hospitals. Is this grounds for divorce? *No.* Mental illness alone is not a basis for divorce. Your husband must have a prolonged confinement in a mental hospital in order for you to get a divorce.

> **TIP:** Where one spouse's mental illness is not a ground for divorce, other grounds, such as incompatibility, can be alleged.

Conviction of Felony or Incarceration

Laws in some states permit divorce where one of the spouses has been convicted of a felony crime, or has been imprisoned for a period of time. For instance, the wife of a corporate CEO convicted of a white-collar felony crime may obtain a divorce based on her husband's conviction.

My wife is on trial for felony theft. Can I get a divorce because she committed a felony? *No.* A criminal charge alone is not enough. Your wife must be convicted or imprisoned before you can obtain a divorce on these grounds.

> **TIP:** A guilty plea is the same as a conviction.

TEMPORARY ORDERS

Temporary, or interim orders, are put in place to fix the rights and obligations of the divorcing couple before their divorce is finalized. Divorce petitions typically contain requests for certain judicial orders to preserve the spouse's property and protect the parties. Additionally, the payment of the bills, maintenance payments to a spouse and establishment of child visitation are all matters handled through temporary orders.

Temporary orders provide a measure of stability for one or both of the spouses. For instance, a stay-at-home mother without an income could not continue to live in the house with the children unless the husband continued to pay the mortgage. The court's orders requiring that the mortgage payments be made allow the wife and children to stay in the home without further anxiety or disruption.

Can the judge enter a temporary order requiring my husband and me to attend counseling? *Yes.* A court can make any orders it believes are in the best interests of the parties.

Temporary Spousal Support

If a spouse qualifies, she may receive support payments from her husband until the divorce is finalized. Laws refer to these payments as "temporary alimony," "temporary support" or "spousal maintenance." In general, the spouse with the greater income makes some sort of monthly payment to the other spouse. The purpose of temporary support is to keep the parties at approximately the same financial level they were in before the divorce was filed until a divorce is granted.

Eligibility for spousal support payments depends on:

- the length of the marriage;
- the couple's standard of living;
- the lack of employment or sufficient income;
- physical or mental disability; and
- the age and health of the spouse.

The court also weighs how much one spouse contributed to the other's education or training. For example, a wife who worked while her husband went to medical school may get a larger support payment to compensate her for her past contributions. Additionally, women who have taken a hiatus from their careers to have and raise children may be due more support because their skills are not as marketable.

I have always been a stay-at-home mom. Can I continue to stay at home and receive spousal support during our divorce? *No.* If you have the education or skills to find employment, you must go back to work and earn some income. Your husband is not under a duty to completely support you during the divorce.

> Laws do not favor spousal support, and unless the spouse requesting support can show that he has sought out employment or is acquiring the skills, through schooling or training, necessary to find a job, the court will not award full support.

My wife has supported us while I have been working on getting a college degree. Do I have to stop going to school and get a job? *No.* Your degree substantially increases your ability to support yourself. You may be required to find part-time employment, but the court will probably order your wife to make some payments so you can continue your education.

Can temporary support be extended after the divorce is granted? *No.* After the divorce is final, the spouse will either receive permanent spousal support (known as alimony) or the payments will be terminated completely.

> The laws in some states limit the duration of spousal support once the divorce is granted to a period of 2-3 years, unless the spouse has a physical disability.

Temporary Restraining Orders

Because divorce is acrimonious, laws have been enacted prohibiting or restraining divorcing spouses from taking certain actions during litigation. The parties may not:

- use vulgar, obscene or profane language when communicating with each other;
- threaten unlawful actions;
- place repeated telephone calls with the intention of annoying or alarming the other spouse;
- cause, either by intent or recklessness, a child of the marriage to be physically harmed;
- conceal or hide property belonging the spouses;
- damage either person's property; or
- falsify or destroy records or other documents.

Most divorce petitions include a "laundry list" of prohibitions that eventually become part of the court's temporary orders even where the spouses are cooperative.

My wife keeps calling me in violation of the temporary restraining order. What can I do? *You must notify your lawyer or the court.* Your wife is violating the temporary orders and, by doing so, she is in contempt of court. The judge has the authority to place her in jail unless she stops making the calls.

Temporary Injunction

An injunction is a judicial order prohibiting a specific action by one of the parties. During a divorce action, the injunction serves to preserve the couple's property and keep one spouse from wasting or disposing of it. For example, the husband may be enjoined from withdrawing money from the spouse's savings account.

A protective order is a type of temporary injunction. It is used to restrain one spouse from committing or threatening to commit violent acts when there is a history of family violence.

> **A protective order is available any time violence has occurred or is likely to occur. Filing for divorce is not necessary.**

> **TIP:** A protective order can be obtained after a divorce is finalized.

> **TIP:** A protective order can direct that the spouse's gun license be suspended.

INVENTORY AND APPRAISEMENT

Parties to a divorce are generally required to file a sworn statement with the court listing and valuing their assets. The statement is called an "inventory and appraisement" or "financial statement." The temporary orders issued by a court when a divorce petition is filed typically require the spouses to produce the inventory by a certain date and set out the form of the inventory.

Each spouse files his or her own inventory with the court, which is signed under oath. The value a spouse places on the property may be based on opinion or fair market value, if known. The spouse's inventory also includes a list of any debts owed. It is not necessary that an independent appraiser be hired to value the property.

> **TIP:** If there is a dispute in the inventories as to the value of a piece of property, hire an appraiser to settle the dispute.

The inventory is not binding on the court. In fact, the court is required to hear evidence that the property listed is valued correctly. Evidence of property value can be in the form of testimony, receipts, deeds, notes, tax appraisals and other documents.

Marital Property

In the inventory, the spouse must identify "marital property" (or "community property" in community property states), owned jointly by the couple. Marital property consists of both real estate and personal items, and generally includes:

- the family home;
- real estate purchased during the marriage;
- vehicles;
- tools and equipment; and
- bank accounts, certificates of deposits, stocks, bonds and IRAs.

> **TIP:** If any of the property is mortgaged, the amount of the mortgage must be included along with the value of the property.

> **Benefits should be listed as marital property. A value must be placed on the benefit. Typical benefits include employment benefits (profit-sharing plans, retirement plans, pension plans) and union membership benefits (insurance, pensions, retirement benefits)**

Separate Property

Not all property is necessarily marital or community property and spouses should include any and all property that they believe is separately owned.

In a community property state, a spouse's separate property is typically limited to:

- property received through gift or inheritance;
- property owned before the marriage (which was not commingled);
- property that is partitioned by written agreement; and
- bank accounts, certificates of deposits, stocks, bonds and IRAs owned before marriage and kept separate.

In non-community property states, separate property may also include items the spouse purchased with their own income.

> **TIP:** Separate property includes any claims for reimbursement one spouse has against the other. For instance, if the couple's joint income was used to pay off the husband's car loan (purchased before marriage), the wife should list a claim of reimbursement for a portion of the payments.

> **TIP:** Property that has been lost or destroyed should be included on the inventory. For instance, a valuable painting that was purchased by the husband and wife during the marriage but which was destroyed in a fire since the separation must be listed, along with a statement explaining its loss or destruction.

Debts

Spouses are required to list their debts in the inventory. Both the husband and wife, or only one of the spouses, can owe the debt. The debt is listed as either a marital debt or as a separate debt. In community property states, both spouses are liable for all debts incurred during marriage.

The debt must be identified by setting out:

- a description of the property;
- the date the debt was created;
- the amount of the debt;
- the name of the person or company that is owed the debt;
- the date the debt is due; and
- the amount of monthly payments required, if any.

> **TIP:** Credit cards must be listed as well. The person or persons on the account must be identified, along with the total amount owed. It is also wise to include the amount of monthly payments and interest rate.

> **TIP:** Attorney's fees owed or that will be owed as a result of the divorce litigation must be listed.

Can I change the inventory once it is filed? *Yes.* In fact, you must correct the inventory if you have made a mistake or error.

What happens if I forget to list a piece of property? You can file a new inventory with the court listing the property you forgot. The inventory is called the "Amended" or "Corrected Inventory and Appraisement."

My spouse did not list one of his stock portfolios on purpose. What do I do? *Notify your attorney or the court.* If your spouse is fraudulently concealing property, he is in contempt of the court's temporary orders and could be jailed or fined.

> The inventory and appraisement is a type of discovery (a document that must be furnished in litigation), and failing to provide discovery can result in a monetary fine.

PROPERTY DISTRIBUTION

Depending on how the parties work together, and the length of the marriage, the determination of which spouse gets what property can be extremely easy or difficult and acrimonious. Couples who have been married a short time and have not acquired much property together usually take what they brought to the marriage and go their separate ways. Even if a home was purchased, it can be sold and the proceeds divided or one spouse can pay the other for her half.

On the other hand, couples in lengthy marriages have typically acquired a large amount of property and debt. One or both may have a vested interest in staying in the family home. Substantial employment and retirement benefits have usually accrued. The wife may have stopped working to raise the children and have no retirement benefits. Furniture, art and jewelry may have been purchased throughout the marriage. Gifts have been exchanged between the spouses; one or both may have received an inheritance.

Standard of Equitable Division

"Equitable" is a term often used in the law. It refers to a fair result when the law in question is applied. Laws concerning the division of property when a divorce occurs require an equitable, or fair, result.

There is no set formula for the division of property when couples divorce. In order to achieve an equitable or fair result, the court divides the property among the spouses in a just and right manner. "Just and right" does not mean an equal division of property. Courts divide the spouses' property according to the rights each spouse has in the property and considering the needs of any children born during the marriage. For instance, if the wife used her inheritance to purchase the family home, the court may determine she has a larger interest in it than the husband (it is not automatically her separate property since she contributed it to the marriage as the family home).

Factors in Determining Distribution

If the couple can agree as to how their property should be divided, they enter into a marital settlement agreement or property settlement agreement, file it with the court and distribute the property according to the agreement. However, if there is a dispute, the judge decides what property each spouse receives when the divorce is finalized.

Generally, property owned jointly by the couple is valued and divided equally. However, one spouse may be entitled to a larger share based on several factors the court considers, including:

- the disparity in earning capacities or incomes;
- the spouses' abilities and education;
- the spouses' relative financial conditions (debts owed and future expenses);
- the difference in spouse's ages;
- the value of separate property;
- the type of property being divided;
- the fault of one spouse in causing the divorce; and
- the waste by one spouse of money or property.

Based on these factors, the more dependent and less financially well-off spouse generally will receive a larger share of the property.

Spouse's Fault in Divorce

One spouse's fault in causing the divorce is usually irrelevant because divorces are typically granted on "no-fault" grounds. However, the court can find fault with one of the spouses and grant the divorce on that basis. In those instances (and even in no-fault divorces), the wrongful actions by one of the spouses may be a factor in determining that the innocent spouse is awarded a larger share of the property.

> Because the judge has broad discretion in dividing marital property, even where a no-fault divorce is granted, the fault of one spouse can be taken into consideration by the judge.

> In community property states, the courts overwhelmingly find "fault" when highly disproportionate property divisions are ordered. Since all income earned and property acquired during the marriage belongs equally to both spouses, it is not typical to give one of the spouses little or no property unless his behavior was egregious.

> **TIP:** A finding of fault is not required to divide the property unequally.

Does an equitable division of property mean that the judge will order a 50/50 split of our assets? *No.* To the contrary, a 50/50 split is never presumed. Under some fact patterns, an equitable division can be an award of all property to one spouse.

Who determines the value of the property that is going to be divided? *The judge makes the final determination of the property's value.* Evidence is presented that establishes what certain property may be worth and, based on this evidence, the court places a value on it.

Who gets the keep the house in a divorce? *The parent with custody of the children is generally entitled to keep the house.* The court may order the spouse with the greater income to make all or a portion of the mortgage payments for a time. However, if the spouse living in the house cannot afford its upkeep and mortgage payments, the home will likely have to be sold at some point in the future.

> **TIP:** The spouse who wants the family home often "buys out" her ex-spouse's interest in the house, rather than selling it and dividing the proceeds.

Can I testify as to the value of my stamp collection? *Yes.* You are not required to hire an expert. Your testimony is evidence on which the judge can rely in determining the value of the stamp collection. However, your spouse, or an expert he or she hires, may dispute your testimony regarding the value of the collection.

> **TIP:** Do not assume that the court will agree with the value that you place on the property.

Can the judge punish my husband for his cruelty by requiring him to donate all the money in his bank account to charity? *No.* The court may not punish your husband for his behavior. However, the judge may compensate you by awarding the cash in the account to you.

During our marriage, my husband bought his mistress many expensive gifts and gave her large sums of cash. Will I get a larger share of our property? *Most likely.* The court will generally consider your husband's spending on his mistress as a frivolous and unjustified use of marital assets. However, if the expenses were paid out of your husband's separate property, they may not factor into the division of property.

> **In a community property state, any income spent on extravagances, especially on another person, without the other spouse's knowledge and consent is considered to be a waste of the community's assets. The innocent spouse will get a larger portion of community property to compensate for the other spouse's waste. If the expenses were paid out of the husband's separate property, they may not factor into the division of property.**

I am not happy with the way that the court divided our property during the divorce. Can I appeal the judge's order? *Yes—but you will probably be unsuccessful.* The court has broad discretion in the way property is divided among the spouses. Unless the judge acted without any regard to the facts, a higher court will not overturn her order.

> **The judge also has discretion in the monetary value she places on the property.**

> **TIP:** You must offer any and all evidence you have to the judge in support of how you want the property divided. If you fail to present relevant facts in your favor, you cannot later complain that the property was divided unfairly. For instance, if you have been informed that your company is going to lay you off, testify to the situation.

My attorney's fees are enormous. Will the court consider the fees when making the property division? *Yes.* The judge can factor in your attorney's fee and award you a larger portion of the property to offset your expenses.

> **TIP:** Attorney's fees that have been increased due to any failure on your part to cooperate with the court or follow the judge's order will likely not be considered.

Since we separated, my husband received a $10,000 bonus from his employment. Will the bonus be considered when the court divides our property? *Yes.* Increases or decreases in income or to the value of property since you separated can be considered by the court.

I lied to my wife about my prior divorces before we married. Will my lies affect the property division? *Yes.* Since the judge has broad discretion, she can factor in the misrepresentations you made to your wife before you married when she makes a property division. Depending on the judge, your lies may have a little, a lot, or nothing at all to do with the court's final decision.

> Courts are not limited by the time frame in which certain events occurred. In other words, your actions before the marriage may be considered along with your behavior during the marriage.

My wife lied to get me to marry her. Since there wouldn't have been a marriage but for her lies, can she be awarded any property? *Yes.* Although the marriage might not have occurred except for her fraud, she is not legally barred from receiving a portion of the property. It will be up to the judge to decide what weight, if any, to give to the fact that your wife fraudulently induced you to marry her.

> **TIP:** Even where a marriage is annulled because of one spouse's fraud, the judge is not required to award all the property to the innocent spouse.

My wife and I, and our respective attorneys, have agreed to a property settlement dividing our property. Will the judge change it? *Probably not.* Although the court has the authority to change the agreement, the court does not have the time or any reason to upset an agreement between the parties. It is not the place of the judge to insert herself into issues that have already been resolved.

> **TIP:** A party that is not represented by an attorney should not expect the judge to review the agreement. Even if the agreement is one-sided in favor of the party with legal representation, a red flag will not go up with the court.

However, the judge will review, and may refuse to accept, settlement agreements if there are children and one of the parties does not have an attorney. The court's view is that the children's interest must be represented by an attorney before any issues concerning them are settled.

My wife and I came to a marital settlement agreement but the judge is awarding her a larger share of the assets than we agreed on. Can the court change our agreement? *Yes.*

Theoretically and legally, the judge can change your agreement in any way she believes will be fair to both parties. However, it is unusual for the court to change it. It is simply not practical for the court to refuse agreements when there are cases with disputed issues waiting to be heard.

> Generally, the court would need to find that the agreement is unconscionable to one of the spouses, i.e., completely unfair, before setting it aside and entering her own order dividing the assets.

Does the amount of alimony I may be ordered to pay have any bearing on the property division? *Yes.* The amount of alimony is considered, together with the property division. In other words, you may get "credit" for the alimony you are paying and your spouse may be awarded a lesser portion of the property.

Currently, my wife and I have approximately the same amount of income. However, she just received a major industry award. Will the award effect the property division? *Yes.* Since courts consider the potential for earnings or income and your wife's award has a great impact on her future earnings, you may receive a larger share of the property.

We do not have any assets, just a lot of debt. How will the court divide our liabilities? *Debts are divided the same way assets and property are allocated to the spouses—in an equitable manner.* In this case, a spouse who is responsible for running up the credit cards bills to buy expensive but unneeded items may end up owing most of the debt, since an equal split would not be fair.

Some of our property was overlooked and not included in the divorce decree. Who gets it now that the divorce is final? *Both spouses are entitled to a half-interest in the property because it is owned jointly.* Since the divorce is final, one or both of you must file a suit to partition or divide the property, so that it can be sold or distributed without impinging on the other spouse's rights.

QUALIFIED DOMESTIC RELATIONS ORDER (QDRO)

Retirement or pension benefits typically must be distributed to the employee only. However, a QDRO (pronounced "quadro") is a special court order directing the retirement plan to distribute the benefits, or a portion of them, to someone other than the employee. Since retirement benefits that accrued during a marriage are often divided among the divorcing spouses, a QDRO is necessary. It is a separate order from the final divorce decree.

The QDRO must meet certain federal requirements. The U.S. Department of Labor has more information about QDROs on its Web site at **www.dol.gov/ebsa/faqs/faq_qdro3.html**.

> **TIP:** Social Security benefits are automatically distributed to divorced spouses under different rules, and a QDRO is not necessary.

> **TIP:** QDROs are routine for retirement and pension plan administrators. Most plans have QDRO specialists. Contact their office for forms and information relating to the retirement plan from which you will be receiving benefits.

> **Until the plan administrator approves the QDRO, the retirement benefits cannot be distributed to the employee's former spouse. Under federal law, a divorce decree from the court that orders a division of retirement benefits is not authority for paying out the benefits to the ex-spouse.**

AWARD OF ALIMONY, MAINTENANCE OR SPOUSAL SUPPORT

Alimony is an amount of money one spouse must pay to the other after a divorce to meet the needs of the more dependent spouse and permit that spouse to become self-supporting. It is now commonly referred to as "spousal support" or "maintenance" in divorce law. In some cases, courts also award alimony to maintain the status quo of the spouses and allow the less affluent spouse to continue a certain standard of living.

Alimony, maintenance or spousal support payments are awarded as a substitute to the support regularly provided by one spouse to another during marriage. Spousal support may not be available if the marriage lasted less than 10 years.

> **Laws in some states specifically prohibit an award of "alimony."**

> **Alimony is not a lifetime pension for one of the spouses; its purpose is to ease the transition to the time the spouse can support him or herself in a reasonable manner.**

There are several different types of spousal support that can be ordered by the court.

"Pendente lite alimony" is the temporary spousal support the court orders one spouse to pay before the divorce becomes final. The payments are typically part of the court's temporary orders that the parties must abide by until the final divorce decree.

"Permanent alimony" is support that is paid until the death of the spouse receiving the payments, or until her remarriage. Permanent alimony paid on a month-to-month basis is sometimes referred to as "periodic alimony." It is awarded to a spouse who does not have the capacity to support himself because of advanced age or disability.

In some cases, the court periodically reviews an award of permanent alimony. If the spouse receiving the payments regains the ability to work, remarries or begins living with someone else on a permanent basis, the court may terminate the payments.

> **Alimony is not awarded in community property states because it is regarded as an allowance that is the personal debt of the spouse. In those states, one spouse cannot owe another spouse support after a divorce. Instead, the payments are based on the rights the spouse receiving support has in the community property, which is owned by both.**

EXAMPLE: A husband may be ordered to pay a wife $1,000 per month for 3 years after the divorce. The wife spent several years staying home with the children and her time is an asset she contributed to the community property. The support payments allow her to share in the assets since her time cannot be recovered.

"Rehabilitative support" or temporary alimony is routinely awarded by courts for the purpose of getting a spouse on his feet until such time as he is able to support himself. In most states, the payments are referred to as "spousal maintenance" and the law often limits the duration of the payments. Typically, the payments last for 1 to 5 years. Spouses with a decreased earning capacity, lesser education, fewer skills and fewer business opportunities generally receive some amount of payments for a time.

A lump sum payment is a one-time payment to an ex-spouse that fulfills any future support obligations. The payment can be calculated based on the number of alimony payments that would be due in the future, or may be based be a "cash-out" of one spouse's interest in the marital property.

If my ex-husband dies, is his new wife responsible for continuing my alimony payments? *No.* Alimony payments end when the person paying dies. You have no further claim for alimony from your ex-husband's wife or his estate.

> **TIP:** Take out a life insurance policy on your ex-spouse. The benefits will compensate you and replace the alimony payments in case of his death.

Do I have a right to alimony? *No.* There is no legal right to alimony or post-divorce support. You must show the court that you qualify for spousal support after the divorce is granted.

How does the court determine if I will receive spousal support payments after the divorce? The judge considers:

- the length of your marriage;
- your education and earning capacity;
- the age difference between you and your spouse, if any;
- your financial prospects or business opportunity available in the future;

- your health;
- the fault in causing breakdown of the marriage;
- your contributions as a homemaker; and
- your contributions to the other spouse's education, training or increased earning power.

I stopped practicing law to stay home and raise our children. Will my husband be ordered to pay support? *Probably not.* Your education, skills and earning capacity most likely do not qualify you for support payments.

Do I have to work while I am receiving support payments? *Not necessarily.* If you are unable to work because of a disability, or if you are in the process of getting an education and training to obtain employment skills, you are not required to get a job. However, if you are able to work, you must be actively seeking employment to remain eligible for support payments.

I am quite wealthy. Is there a limit to the amount of maintenance my ex-spouse can receive after our divorce is final? *Yes.* Laws generally set a ceiling on the amount of maintenance that the court can award. For instance, the law in your state may prohibit payments that exceed 20 percent of your gross income.

> Laws may set a maximum amount on spousal support payments, regardless of the paying spouse's income. For example, Texas law prohibits the court from ordering monthly support payments in excess of $2,500.

Can I have the amount of spousal support I receive increased? *Yes.* You can ask the court to modify the support or maintenance payments any time there is a change in circumstances.

I have lost my job since our divorce. I was not awarded spousal support when the divorce was granted. Can I ask for it now? *No.* The change in your circumstance does not "reopen" the issue of whether you are due spousal support. If you have been receiving some support, the court may increase the amount. However, the court will not begin instituting support payments.

Can my ex-husband have my alimony payments stopped if I am living with my boyfriend? *Yes.* Although you are not married, the court may have the authority to terminate the payments if you are cohabiting with your boyfriend on a permanent basis.

> **TIP:** A platonic roommate will not affect your support payments. The payments typically terminate only if you have a sexual relationship with the person.

> **Mere allegations that an ex-spouse is living with a person on a permanent basis are not enough to terminate support payments. There must be actual evidence to support the allegations. For instance, testimony from someone other than you that your ex-spouse moved her furniture to her boyfriend's house is evidence of the living arrangement.**

I may be laid off in 6 months. Should the support payments that the court awards take this into account? *No.* The court cannot base support payments on the possibility that an event may occur in the future.

> **TIP:** Increases in property taxes, health insurance and other expenses that have increased in the past and will increase in the future may be taken into account in determining the amount of spousal support. Those events are not purely speculative.

During the 2 years it took to obtain a divorce, my husband provided me with only the bare minimum in support although he could have afforded much more. Will my alimony be increased as a result? *No.* However, you may be entitled to retroactive alimony in the form of increased payments.

> **Courts award retroactive alimony dating back to the date the divorce was filed.**

My wife has refused several promotions to keep her income down as well as her support payments to me. Is there anything I can do?
Yes. The court will assign or impute income to your wife if she is refusing to use her best efforts to earn more money.

INTERVENTION IN DIVORCE BY CREDITORS

Certain persons with a legitimate interest in a lawsuit to which they are not an original party can intervene in the lawsuit. Creditors intervene to protect their interest in property that is going to be distributed and divided in the divorce. For instance, the wife's former divorce attorney who is owed legal fees can intervene in the divorce as a creditor. Since he is a party, the court must consider his interests when allocating the spouse's property.

On the other hand, while the court may have ordered the wife to pay all the credit card bills, if the account was in both spouses' names, the bank can go after the husband for payment. The divorce decree does not take the husband's name off the account or relieve him of his liability to the bank.

MEDIATION

Mediation, also referred to as "alternative dispute resolution," allows the spouses to resolve the issues themselves rather than have the court resolve the issues. The mediator does not decide issues; she simply facilitates a process that allows the spouses to create their own settlement agreement. A settlement agreement reached during mediation is referred to as a "mediated settlement agreement" or MSA.

In some cases, the spouses choose mediation as the sole method of determining property, maintenance and custody issues. After a successful mediation, a marital settlement agreement can be created and filed with the petition for divorce. In most instances, however, mediation occurs because the court has ordered it after a divorce has been filed. Laws in some states require the court to order mediation before a final divorce decree is entered. When mediation is ordered, the parties must attend and attempt to resolve their differences in good faith.

> Divorcing spouses can agree to go to arbitration. Unlike the mediator, the arbitrator does make the final decision on the issues in dispute. Arbitration has been likened to a mini-trial and like a judge, the arbitrator's decision is generally binding on the parties (unless they agreed otherwise.)

Is mediation required by law before a divorce will be granted? *In some states.* In others, mediation is ordered by the court if the parties request it or as part of the judge's selected procedure.

CAUTION: Once mediation is ordered, you must attend.

> In cases where there is family violence or domestic abuse, mediation typically cannot be ordered.

Who picks the mediator? *Both parties must agree on the mediator.* If the mediation process is court ordered and no person is acceptable to both spouses, the court will appoint a mediator.

> **TIP:** Once the court appoints a mediator, you must use that person and pay his fee. However, by choosing your own mediator, you have the ability to control the expense.

What requirements should our mediator have? *In some states, mediators may be required to obtain a license.* However, most states do not require licensing and anyone "can hang out their shingle" advertising his mediating services. It is important that the mediator you choose:

- be trained in mediation;
- have experience in divorce mediation (at least 10 prior mediations); and
- a working knowledge of family law in your state.

How long does mediation take? Typically the parties spend most the day resolving their differences and putting the agreements in written form.

> Some mediators practice ongoing mediation with divorcing spouses where the parties attend mediation meetings on a regular weekly basis until a settlement is worked out.

> **TIP:** If you and your spouse agree that a divorce is inevitable, consider hiring a mediator from the outset to help negotiate the entire process. The divorce will be much friendlier if the two of you "mediate" the fact that one of you must move out, rather than having one person feel as if they were forced to leave.

Is the mediator a lawyer? *Not always.* Some mediators are retired judges; others are therapists, religious leaders and sometimes accountants.

Can the mediator give me legal advice? *No.* Only your attorney can you give you legal advice.

How much does it cost to use a mediator? The mediator usually bills by the hour. The fee can be anywhere from $50 - $250 an hour or more.

> **TIP:** A lawyer or retired judge will be on the high end of mediation fees.

What is a mediation agreement? A mediation agreement is the contract that all of the participants sign before mediation begins. The agreement sets the ground rules for the mediation, such as the maximum length the parties can be required to mediate with each other. The agreement also includes a confidentiality clause prohibiting the parties from revealing to third parties what was said during mediation.

Can I refuse to sign the mediation agreement? *Yes.* You cannot be forced to sign the agreement even if you previously consented to its terms. However, once you sign the agreement, or some variation of it, you are contractually bound by it.

Who attends the mediation? *The spouses and their attorneys, if they have attorneys, participate in the mediation.* While children of the marriage can be involved, especially when they are old enough to voice an opinion, they usually are not present.

Can I bring my best friend to the mediation as moral support? *No.* Because the discussions during the course of mediation are confidential settlement talks, outside parties will not be allowed to attend or participate in the mediation.

If we have successfully mediated, do we still have to go to court? *Yes.* A divorce is a legal decree. You must file a lawsuit in order to obtain a final decree of divorce, or you remain married.

> **TIP:** Since all the issues have been resolved where there is a mediation settlement agreement, the divorce is uncontested, and it will be granted as soon as the waiting period has passed.

Can the mediator represent me in court? *No.* Only a licensed attorney, or you yourself, may represent you in court. If you are handling the divorce, the mediator can advise you and attend court proceedings, but she cannot speak to the judge on your behalf.

Can what we say during mediation be used at a trial or hearing before the judge? *No.* Settlement talks are confidential and cannot be used later as evidence in court.

> **The signed agreement may be presented to the court if one of the parties is refusing to abide by its terms.**

If the court orders mediation, do we have to enter into a settlement agreement? *No.* You always have the option to litigate your differences before the judge or jury.

Can I withdraw my consent to an agreement reached in mediation? *Yes.* However, if you signed an agreement, your spouse can attempt to enforce the agreement as a contract between the two of you. The judge may be inclined to grant a divorce decree based on the terms of the signed agreement because of your consent.

> **TIP:** Some mediation agreements include a provision that they are binding and cannot be revoked once signed. If you sign such an agreement, it is likely the court will enforce it and make it part of the final decree over your objections.

My spouse lied about her assets during mediation. Can the agreement we reached and filed with the court be set aside? *Yes.* Agreements that are reached because of fraud, such as your wife's failure to disclose assets, will be set aside by the court.

TRIAL

A divorce is set for trial when the spouses are unable to come to an agreement on an issue. The parties can request a bench trial or a jury trial. A bench trial is one that is held before a judge only; no jury is present.

When the trial is completed, the judge or jury makes a final determination on the issues in dispute, and the court enters a final decree of divorce.

A divorce trial proceeds like any other trial: a jury is picked if it is a jury trial, lawyers make opening statements, witnesses testify, evidence is presented to the court, closing statements are made and a final ruling is announced by the court.

What issues are decided at trial? The judge determines:

- whether the parties are entitled, i.e., meet the legal requirements to a divorce;
- to whom the divorce is awarded;
- the custody and visitation of minor children;
- the identification of separate property;
- the value of marital property;
- an equitable division of marital property;
- an award of child support;
- an award of spousal support (amount and duration); and
- an award of attorney's fees.

Do I have to testify at my divorce trial? *Yes.* If you want the judge or jury to hear your side of the story, you must testify. Additionally, if your spouse does not appear at trial, you must testify to "prove up" or recite the relevant facts in order to obtain a final divorce decree.

What questions will I be asked on the witness stand? You will be asked to give:

- your name and address;
- the date of your marriage;
- the names and ages of your children; and
- the facts supporting or grounds for a divorce.

Once the trial has begun, is it too late for my spouse and me to come to an agreement? No, cases are routinely settled during the trial. Since you are already before the judge, your attorneys will read the agreement to the court and each of you will testify that you have consented to settle the case.

Appeal

Once a final divorce decree is entered after the trial, either party can appeal the ruling. The first appeal is to the trial court in the form of a motion for new trial (generally not granted). The party then files an appeal with the appellate court. In an appeal, one of the parties is asking the appellate court to overrule or reverse the rulings of the trial court judge. The appeal can be confined to one issue or cover several different matters the party believes were incorrectly determined.

Appeals have extraordinarily short deadlines. The timeline in an appeal consists of many different deadlines that must be met. The failure to meet any of these deadlines means that the appeal is waived. Because they are so complicated, appeals are usually handled by appellate lawyers–lawyers who specialize in this field.

> **TIP:** Once a final divorce decree is entered, it cannot be modified unless the trial court orders a new trial or an appeals court reverses the trial court's order.

NAME CHANGE

A spouse, almost always the wife, has the right to have her name changed back to the one she used prior to the marriage. The name change is ordered in the final divorce decree and is accomplished by filing a name change certificate or other documents with the court clerk. The fact that any children of the marriage and their mother will have different last names is not a basis for opposing a name change.

My husband wanted the divorce and now has requested that the court change my name back to my maiden name. Can my name be changed over my objection? *No.* The court does not have the authority to change your name on your husband's, or anyone else's, request. Only you can request the name change.

If I change my name, am I still liable for the debts I incurred under my married name? *Yes, your name change does not extinguish any money you owe.* Your liabilities follow you, even with a different name.

REMARRIAGE

Persons who obtain a divorce return to their status as unmarried and single. They are free to remarry after the final divorce decree is entered and a short waiting period has passed. The waiting period can date from the date of the divorce decree or relate back to when the respondent was served with the lawsuit.

> Texas law, for example, prohibits remarriage within 30 days after the judge signs the divorce degree. In California, however, a party may remarry as soon as the divorce is final, as long as at least 6 months have passed since the ex-spouse was served with the divorce papers.

POST-DIVORCE ISSUES

Although a divorce has been granted and a final decree has been entered, the issues between the parties do not dissipate. After the divorce, the court continues to have authority over the parties with regard to any obligations they were ordered to perform under the divorce decree. If the parties do not proceed according to the decree, the court can enforce the order by placing one of the ex-spouses in contempt or fining him or her.

ENFORCEMENT OF DIVORCE DECREE

The court that issued the final divorce decree has the continuing authority to enforce its provisions. Either party can bring a suit to enforce the decree with the court at any time. After hearing evidence, the court may hold the non-complying party in contempt for refusing to follow the provisions in the decree.

Typically, issues arise as to property division (identity of property, time and manner of delivery) and the decree may need to be clarified. Rather than hold one party in contempt, the court can issue a "clarification order" setting out further instructions for the division of property.

> The judge cannot amend or change a final divorce decree. Clarifying the decree simply clears up any ambiguity; it cannot change the original terms. For instance, if the decree ordered the husband to put all the household furnishings in storage for the wife and he did not include the china or silver, the judge can clarify that "furnishings" in the original decree included china and silver. Broadening "furnishings" to encompass additional items is not considered to be a change; it is a clarification of what the judge meant by the term.

My husband quit paying my support payments. How do I get the decree enforced so he will make the payments as ordered?
You must file a suit to enforce the decree. The court can then convert the past due payments into a money judgment. The judgment is just like any other judgment that a person could obtain against your husband, and he becomes a judgment debtor.

> **TIP:** Judgments are enforced by first filing with the county clerk, and then by seeking certain legal actions. For instance, once you have a judgment, you can obtain a writ of garnishment. A writ of garnishment is a legal summons concerning the taking of wages of a debtor to satisfy a debt. As an example, the writ can be served on the husband's bank, and any money in the debtor's account is taken, or garnished, to satisfy the judgment.

CHILD CUSTODY

The issue of who retains custody of the children in a divorce and the amount of child support to be paid remains problematic for the courts.

At the time of the divorce, the court determines which parent has custody of the children. Custody is commonly referred to as "conservatorship." Anyone with an interest in the child can be appointed as the conservator, but typically the parents are appointed (unless both are deceased, or their parental rights have been terminated). The goal of the court is to provide the child with a day-to-day caretaker who has the authority to make all of the decisions that affect the child.

The judge in a divorce case has the authority to make determinations regarding all of the issues affecting the children. These include custody, visitation, support, school and holiday schedules. The spouses and the children themselves can voice their opinions, but the final authority rests with the court, who must consider the best interests of the child.

> **"Best interests of the child"** is a phrase that is frequently used in child custody matters. It is the standard used by the court to determine what arrangements are to a child's greatest benefit.

CONSERVATORSHIP

Where one parent has primary control and care over the child, that parent is the sole managing conservator or primary custodian. When both parents have equal control and care over their children pursuant to the court's order, they are joint managing conservators or joint custodians.

The typical parental rights that the parents had when they were married are converted into their rights as the child's conservator or custodian. The rights are specified in the court order that appoints one or both parents as conservator of the child.

Determination of Conservatorship

The judge's decision to appoint a conservator is based on the "best interests of the child." However, the court also takes into consideration:

- the child's ability to have frequent and continuing contact with her parents;
- the availability of a safe, stable and nonviolent environment for the child; and
- the goal of encouraging parents to share in the rights and duties of raising their child after a divorce.

Best Interests of the Child

Since the court is charged with considering the best interest of the child in all its decisions relating to possession of and access to the child, it is generally assumed that the judge is in the unenviable position of choosing the "best" parent. The court does consider the parent's incomes, their housing situations, their personal habits, their mental stability, and the time they have available for the child. However, in deciding what is best for the child, the court examines many factors that are not related to parenting at all.

In order to determine what type of conservatorship is best for the child, the judge considers:

- the potential separation from siblings;
- the child's preference;
- the child's religious beliefs and habits;
- the child's current school situation;
- the child's access to other family members, such as grandparents;
- the access to activities in which the child is involved;
- the physical and emotional needs of the child, based on their gender;
- the child's age;
- the emotional tie between the child and the potential custodial parent;
- the ability of the parent to provide the necessities for the child;
- the current living arrangement between the parent and child; and
- the ability of the potential custodial parent to foster a healthy relationship between the child and the other parent.

I have been appointed the sole managing conservator of my children. What are my rights and duties? As the primary custodian, you have the sole right to:

- determine your child's residence;
- consent to medical, dental and surgical treatment, including psychiatric and psychological treatment;
- make decisions concerning your child's education;
- receive child support payments and spend the money for your child's benefit; and
- make legal decisions concerning your child.

> **TIP:** The custodial parent can also consent to marriage and enlistment in the military.

Is a mother always awarded custody of very young children? *No.* If it is not in the child's best interest to be with their mother, the court will not appoint the mother as conservator, regardless of the child's age. However, all other things being equal, young children are typically placed in their mother's care.

> The judge is prohibited from deciding custody on the basis of sex alone. The court cannot discriminate against the father simply because he is a man. However, the judge can make a finding that the child's needs are best managed by the mother. In other words, the gender of the parent can be factored in; it just cannot be the only consideration.

My ex-husband remarried and I am still single. Will he be awarded custody of the children because he can offer a two-parent home? *No.* Laws generally prohibit courts from factoring in either parent's marital status.

My ex-husband is a homosexual. Isn't he prohibited from being appointed our son's primary custodian? *No.* The law does not prohibit homosexual parents from having custody of their children. However, your husband's sexual preference may be taken into consideration. Whether it weighs against him will depend on the judge.

If my children live with me, they will attend church and Sunday school regularly, participate in the church choir and go on a mission trip to Mexico. Should the court place the children with me because they will be exposed to religion? *No.* The court may consider your faith in deciding which parents gets custody, but the judge is prohibited from favoring one religion over another, or favoring one parent with religious exposure to one with no religious exposure. The court may find, however, that the church activities are in the children's best interests.

My ex-wife is very bitter since our divorce and insists on running me down constantly in front of the children. Can the judge consider this when deciding custody of the children? *Yes.* Since the best interests of the children are paramount, the court will not look favorably on placing them in a negative atmosphere. Additionally, if your wife is attempting to interfere or undermine your ability to parent the children, the judge can find that their best interests are not served with her as the primary custodian.

Can the judge change custody from one parent to another? *Yes.* The court always has the authority to modify or change any orders that affect the children. If it is in their best interests to live with another parent, the court will terminate the current custodian and appoint a new one.

VISITATION

Where one parent has been appointed sole managing conservator or primary custodian, the other parent is allowed to visit with the child on a regular and periodic basis. However, it is not the parent that has the right to visitation; it is the child. It is presumed that allowing a child access to both parents is always in his or her best interest. Therefore, prohibiting or decreasing visitation requires a finding that the child's best interests are no longer being served under the current visitation schedule.

With regard to visitation, the judge can decide:

- the place of visitation;
- the time of the visit;
- the duration of the visit;
- the frequency of the visit;
- the persons permitted to visit; and
- prohibitions during the visit.

Standard Visitation Rights

Because divorce and child custody issues are so common, most states have enacted laws that set out a standard visitation schedule. Unless the circumstances warrant a change, the judge will enter a standard custody order that sets out the visitation schedule to which the parents must adhere.

Can visitation between a parent and child be completely denied? *Yes.* If visitation with a parent will endanger the child, physically or emotionally, the court can prohibit visitation entirely. However, the court must find that the facts contributing to the adverse impact on the child are an extraordinary circumstance

As a result of my re-marriage, my son now has a half-brother. Is that a consideration in setting up a visitation schedule? *Yes.* Courts favor visitation that fosters a relationship between siblings.

My ex-husband chose to work in a different state. Will he get longer visitation with the children as a result of his living far away? *Yes.* The court takes geographic proximity of the children and a parent into consideration. Since visits are necessarily less frequent due to the distance involved, the court has the discretion to order longer visitation time periods. For instance, the children's visit during summer vacation may be extended from 2 weeks to 6 weeks, since their father is unable to see them much during the school year.

My ex-wife lives 8 hours away and she wants me to drive the children to her home every weekend. Will the court approve that visitation schedule? *No.* If the court orders weekend visits, the schedule might be modified to require the two of you to meet halfway. Alternatively, the court may order visits every other weekend, or require your ex-wife to pay for your gas. The judge will do whatever is in the best interests of the children.

EXAMPLE: It is not in the best interests of the children to require them to visit with their father who lives 2 hours away every Wednesday after school. The visits will have a negative impact on their schoolwork.

My ex-husband refuses to make support payments on time. Should his visitation with the children be curtailed? *No.* The court cannot use visitation as a "stick" to punish a parent. Visitation is a benefit to the child, not the parent, and it will only be curtailed if it is in the best interests of the children.

> The judge can and will decrease or terminate visitation when the parent's behavior becomes so outrageous that the physical, mental, economic and/or social well-being of a child is affected. For example, a wife who yells and argues with her ex-husband when he picks up the children after weekend visits with their mother, locks the door and attempts to block him from entering the house and taking the children, is acting in outrageous manner.

My ex-husband's girlfriend lives with him. Should the children get to stay at his house overnight? *Yes.* The court cannot base a visitation decision on the fact that your ex-husband's girlfriend is in the house. However, if her presence (and the resulting sexual relationship with your ex-husband) affects the children's emotional well-being, overnight visits may be prohibited. Additionally, the court is within its rights to limit visitation if it finds that the children are too young, and it is not in their best interests to be exposed to their father's sexual relationship with his girlfriend.

> A parent's illegal drug use always has an adverse impact on the visiting child.

Can the court order visitation between my daughter and her mother, who is in prison? *Yes.* Incarceration alone does not warrant denying visitation entirely. It's presumed that it is in your daughter's best interest to see her mother.

> Parents convicted of a felony relating to sexual abuse or assault can be denied visitation because the crime constitutes an extraordinary circumstance.

My 11-year-old son wants longer visitation periods with his father. Is his preference going to mean the court will change the visitation schedule? *No.* The court may consider your son's wishes; but children typically do not base their preferences on what is in their best interests. By itself, your son's preference is not enough to change the visitation schedule. By the same token, the child who prefers not to visit a parent will not be allowed to "skip" visitation.

MODIFICATION OF CHILD CUSTODY ORDERS

Courts are loath to disrupt the status of a child's custody situation. Laws typically prohibit any modification within a year of the divorce unless the child's health is in danger or the custodial parent has let the child live with the other parent for most of the year.

Custody orders can be modified if there is a substantial change in the life of the parents or the child. A substantial change of circumstance means that new facts have arisen that would have changed the court's previous custody decision.

Additionally, laws often allow children of a certain age to choose where they want to live (which, in essence, determines the custodian).

My son's grades have dropped ever since he has lived with my ex-wife. Can I get custody changed? *Not on that basis alone.* You must be able to show the court some facts that would have persuaded the judge to place the child with you, if they existed at the time of your divorce.

My former husband has started drinking again. Will the judge let the children come live with me? *Yes.* Based on changes in your husband's lifestyle, the court may decide that it is in the best interest of the children to have you appointed as the new primary custodian. Your husband's excessive drinking poses a physical and emotional danger to the children.

My ex-wife has not established regular mealtimes for my son, he is constantly ill, was injured on the playground while he was unsupervised, and he is left with teen-aged baby sitters routinely during the week. Can I get primary custody? *Yes.* While each fact alone may not be enough to warrant a modification in the custody order, as a whole the situation equates to a change of circumstance.

> Although modifications require a change in circumstance, sometimes the usual living arrangement is so inadequate and harmful to the child, he or she may be placed with the other parent.

My ex-husband spanks our daughter. Is this enough to allow me to get primary custody? *No.* Unless your child is in physical danger, your husband's disciplinary methods alone are not enough for a modification. However, spankings or any other type of discipline that leave a permanent injury on a child, such as bruising, rise to the level of "physical danger."

I was arrested for drunk driving. Am I going to lose custody of my children? *No.* A parent does not automatically lose custody if he or she is arrested or even convicted of a crime. To obtain a modification, your ex-spouse must prove your children's physical and emotional health has been adversely impacted or that they are in danger. For example, if they were in the car with you when you were driving under the influence and if there is evidence that this was not an isolated occurrence, the judge may modify custody.

The court modified our custody order and now my ex-husband is the primary custodian of our daughter. Does this mean I have been found to be an unfit mother? *No.* The court does not necessarily make a finding that the parent who did not receive custody, or even loses custody, is unfit. The court's determination is based on the best interests of the child. The facts may show you in a bad light; however there has been no official adjudication that you are an unfit mother.

My husband has adopted a religion that does not celebrate birthdays or holidays. Can I change custody so that I am the primary custodian? *No.* You may not agree with your husband's religious practices, and you may even think they are "weird," but his new religion does not substantially change the circumstances. The children can always celebrate birthdays and holidays at your home.

My son turned 12 and wants to live with his father. Will the court abide by his wishes and modify custody? *Yes.* Laws permit the court to give a preference to a child's wishes when the child reaches a certain age, can articulate his reasons, and his best interests will be not be adversely impacted.

> **TIP:** The child must officially contact the court in writing, notifying the judge of his preference.

I have sobered up, obtained a great job and just purchased a new home. On the other hand, my ex-wife, who has custody of the children, has grown depressed, reclusive and uncommunicative. Can I get custody modified? *Yes.* The combination of the improvements made in your life and your ex-wife's decline has created a substantial change in circumstances permitting the court to give you primary custody of the children.

Moving out of State

Child custody orders routinely prohibit the custodial parent from removing the child from the state. Since the move greatly affects the child's relationship with his other parent, under some laws the court has the authority to prohibit the move.

Courts typically rely on four factors before allowing the child to be moved:

1. whether the move will improve the quality of life for the child, as well as that of the custodial parent;

2. evidence of the absence (versus a presence) of the desire to defeat or undermine the child's relationship with the noncustodial parent by moving away (in other words, the custodial parent is not moving to another state just to get back at the other parent);

3. the objections, if any, of the noncustodial parent (who may not object since his support obligation will lessen if the financial prospects of the ex-spouse improve); and

4. the ability to compensate for the move with extended visitation periods.

Can the court really prevent me from moving out of state with my child if I have been transferred? *Yes.* The court is concerned with the best interests of the child, which include an ongoing relationship with the noncustodial parent. Unless the four factors listed above are present, you may not be allowed to move with the child. You can, of course, pursue your job, if you agree to leave the child in your ex-spouse's custody.

ENFORCEMENT OF CHILD CUSTODY ORDERS

A party whose ex-spouse is not obeying the custody order can file a motion to enforce the order with the court, which specifically points out the provisions of the custody order that have been violated. Parents who violate the order can be held in contempt by the court.

Custody orders issued in one state are enforced in all the states under the Uniform Child Custody Jurisdiction and Enforcement Act (UCCJEA).

The Act facilitates enforcement when a child sent for visitation out of state is not returned to the custodial parent.

> **TIP:** A parent with primary custody, whose child regularly goes to another state to visit the other parent, should register the custody order with that state. Call the district or county clerk's office where you ex-spouse lives and find out the process for registering out-of-state custody orders.

PARENTAL ABDUCTION OF CHILD

Rather than use the court system to work out custody disputes, a parent may resort to abducting or kidnapping her child. By abducting the child, she is assured of never obtaining legal custody of her child.

> **The Parental Kidnapping Prevention Act, a federal law, prevents an abducting parent from ever obtaining legal custody in another state where the court might be unaware that the child has been kidnapped. Under the Act, the court's order would be invalid.**

Parental abduction of a child is a grave matter, and any parent who believes his child is at risk should take certain precautions, including:

- notifying local law enforcement if your ex-spouse has threatened to abduct the child;

- notifying school administrators and teachers, bus drivers, day care providers, neighbors and friends that your child may be at risk;

- keeping recent photographs of your child, along with a current physical description;

- maintaining current information on your ex-spouse: addresses and telephone numbers of friends, employers, former employers and places he or she frequents;

- knowing your ex-spouses driver's license number and Social Security number (these are on the divorce decree); and

- teaching your child his full name, address and telephone number and showing him how to use the phone (he should be aware he can dial 911 from any pay phone or cell phone).

My ex-husband refused to return our children to me after a weekend visit. Is this an abduction even though I know the children's whereabouts? *Yes.* Abduction is any act that keeps a child from her lawful custodian or a person with a legal right to visitation. It is not necessary that the child be hidden or concealed.

My husband and I are living apart and I want to take the children with me to another state. Since I am their mother and there is no custody order in place, is this an abduction? *Yes.* Although you and your husband are not yet divorced, it is a crime to deny your husband access to the children. The fact that you are the mother of the children does not give you the right to obstruct their father's legal right to see them.

I believe allowing my son to return to his mother after his weekend visit to me would put him in danger. Can I be charged with abduction if I refuse to return him? *Yes.* If you believe your son is in physical danger, you should contact the local police. Depending on the situation (for example, if criminal activities are ongoing at your ex-wife's home), the police may permit you to keep your son.

My ex-husband refuses to allow our children to visit me as required by the court. What do I do? You must go to court and ask for a contempt hearing. If your husband refuses to follow the court's order, he will be held in contempt and could face time in jail.

Additionally, you can insist local law enforcement arrest your ex-husband for abducting the children. If your ex-husband has fled with the children, a felony warrant will be issued for his arrest.

GRANDPARENTS' RIGHTS

In some states, laws allow grandparents to sue for access to a grandchild. Grandparents typically have the right to request that the court allow them access to their grandchild if:

- the parent who is the child of the grandparents is in jail;
- the grandchild's parents are divorced or living apart;
- the grandchild was abused by one of her parents; or
- the grandchild lived with the grandparents for a period of time before the suit was filed.

The court will grant the grandparents' request if they are eligible and access is in the best interests of the grandchild.

Where both of the parent's rights are terminated, the grandparent generally has no right to request to see the child. Grandparents may not sue for access when the grandchild's parents are married and living together. While the parents are married, they have the right to limit or deny grandparents' access to the grandchildren.

> **Grandparents can be granted custody of a grandchild if neither parent is able to raise the child. The court factors in the grandparents' ages, health and ability to care for a young child. If placing the child with his grandparents is in the child's best interest, they will be awarded custody.**

Can I get custody of my grandchildren? *Yes.* If the children have been living with you for an extended period of time and you have had actual care, custody and control over them, the court may grant you custody.

> The grandparent must file a petition requesting custody of the grandchildren with the court. If there is an ongoing divorce, the petition would be filed in the same court that is considering the divorce.

> **TIP:** Legal custody is important because a formal custody order allows the grandparent to enroll a child in school, provide health insurance, make medical treatment decisions and apply for aid such as food stamps. Unless the grandparent has legal custody, he is unable to do any of these things.

If I get custody of my grandchildren, have my daughter's parental rights been terminated? *No.* Your daughter and the children's father are still the legal parents of the children. However, because you have custody, the parents no longer have the right to make decisions affecting the children. You have authority over their education, medical care and treatment and any other aspects of the children's life.

My 16-year-old daughter has had a baby. Am I legally required to care for and support the baby? *Yes.* Some states have enacted "Grandparent Liability" laws, which require the parents of teenaged mothers and fathers to support their grandchild. The laws require both sets of grandparents to financially support and provide medical care to the grandchild born to the minor(s).

> The grandparents' financial responsibility to the grandchild lasts until the mother or father is 18 years old.

> The court can order grandparent support at the request of the mother, father or the state agency involved in obtaining assistance for new mother and baby.

Do I have a constitutional right to see my grandchildren? *No.* The only rights you have are those given to you under state laws. All states have laws allowing for grandparent visitation, but the circumstances that permit the court to order

visitation vary from state to state. For instance, you may have no rights to visitation if the grandchild's parents are not divorced.

Can relatives (other than grandparents) petition for visitation with a child? *Yes.* Laws may allow aunts, uncles and siblings access to a child in certain situations.

> **TIP:** Where the law allows, nonrelatives with close ties to a child can petition for visitation if the child's emotional well-being would be enhanced by seeing the relative.

My daughter's parental rights were terminated and my grandchild has been adopted. Can I get visitation with my grandchild? *No.* Although your "grandparent's rights" were not legally terminated, the effect of the parental termination means you no longer have any rights to your grandchild. Laws prohibit you from petitioning the court for visitation once a new family has adopted your grandchild.

> **TIP:** Laws in some states allow grandparents to petition the court for visitation if a relative, as opposed to nonfamily member, adopts the child after parental rights were terminated.

My son and his wife refuse to let us see our grandchildren. If we sue for visitation, can we get an order from the court requiring our grandchildren to see us? *No.* Since the parents of your grandchildren are married, there is no reason for a court to interfere in the parents' decision to keep you from your grandchildren. Parents are the sole authority for what is in the "best interests" of their children where the family is intact and there are no abuse or neglect allegations.

My daughter is terminally ill. She and her children have been living with us. Can we be appointed our grandchildren's guardians? *Yes.* In situations where parents are chronically ill or dying, laws allow for "standby guardianships." The guardianship does not take effect immediately. Instead, when your daughter dies or feels unable to care for her children, you will become the grandchildren's guardians.

I am taking care of two small grandchildren and my financial situation will not allow me to keep them for much longer. What type of government assistance can I receive? There are several programs that may be able to assist you as the primary caretaker of your grandchildren. You should look into:

- Social Security dependent benefits–if you have worked, your Social Security benefits may be extended to grandchildren under 18 who are living with you.
- Supplemental Security Income (SSI)–SSI provides assistance to low-income children. You can apply on behalf of your grandchild.
- Medicaid–government medical care–is available for your grandchildren if they qualify for SSI or have substantial medical needs.
- Temporary Assistance to Needy Families (TANF)–this federal program allows you, your grandchild or both of you to receive benefits if you qualify. Information is available on the U.S. Department of Health & Human Services Web site at **www.acf.hhs.gov**.

> **TIP:** For questions concerning dependent benefits, SSI and Medicaid, go to the U.S. Social Security Administration Web site at **www.ssa.gov**.

CHILD SUPPORT

Both parents must provide for, or support, their children whether married or divorced. However, when a divorce occurs, the court determines the nature, amount and duration of the support so that one parent is not left with the entire burden. Child support has come to mean the payments one parent makes to the parent who has primary custody of the children.

AMOUNTS AND GUIDELINES

Courts and parents are guided in the amount of support payments required by state law child support guidelines. The amount is typically ordered in the form of a percentage of gross or net income. The guidelines also take into account the number of children being supported. However, the guidelines are just that–guidelines. Depending on the facts and evidence, the court may award more or less support. The guidelines differ among the states but the range is generally

a minimum of 20 percent of income to support one child up to 50 percent where there are six or more children.

> **TIP:** Parents sharing joint custody or joint managing conservatorship of children typically do not pay child support to each other where the child lives with them on an equal basis.

> When both parents have income, the calculation of a monthly support amount is based on the total income. However, the parent earning more money still pays support; it is just reduced by the percentage of her husband's income that contributed to calculating the monthly amount. For instance, if the monthly payment should be $1,000 based on both parent's income combined, but the mother is earning 75 percent of the combined income, she pays $750 in child support.

Can I make one lump sum payment instead of paying monthly child support? *Yes.* The court can order child support paid in almost any form, including lump sum payments, property held in trust, or the purchase of an annuity.

Will my ex-husband be ordered to pay child support if he is purposely unemployed? *Yes.* Parents who purposely limit their earnings will not obtain a decreased child support obligation. The court has the authority to order a payment amount commensurate with the income the parent has the capacity to earn or has earned in the past. Your husband's monthly obligation will not be decreased and if he fails to pay, his child support payments will quickly fall into arrears.

> A finding of "underemployment" requires evidence that the parent is purposely not earning more in order to avoid child support increases. A parent is under no duty to earn more money just because she can–she has the right to continue her employment in her current capacity.

My ex-wife's earnings are not large but she receives other forms of income. Do her other sources of income factor into the

child support calculation? *Yes.* The court uses income from all sources to calculate the net resources from which child support must be paid. For instance, royalty payments your wife receives are counted towards her net resources.

> **TIP:** Earnings or income from employment can include amounts other than what is reflected on a paycheck. The court considers commissions, overtime pay, tips, bonuses, dividends, interest income, trust income, annuities, unemployment and disability income and retirement income.

I added $500 to my last child support check because I received a Christmas bonus. Am I entitled to a credit on the next check? Under some laws, you may be allowed to decrease the next check by $500. You are not required to characterize the extra amount as a gift; it can be an advance payment on future monthly payments. Of course, you should notify your ex-spouse before you take the credit or at the time you make the advance payment.

We are deciding between which of three private schools our son will attend next year, so the exact amount of tuition is uncertain. Can the court order my ex-husband to pay 50 percent of the tuition as part of his child support obligation, rather than state a specific amount? *No.* The amount of child support cannot be speculative. The child support order must contain specific amounts. You should estimate the tuition and have the court require payment of half that figure.

Is child support automatically increased for inflation or other probable increases in expenses? *No.* If expenses change, the court must be presented with proof of the change, and the child support will be modified accordingly. The support cannot be based on an unpredictable future event, such as a statement that interest rates may go up and your mortgage is on an adjustable note.

Can I take a break from paying child support during the summer when the children are living with me? *No.* Typically, child support is calculated on an annual basis, and payments are spread throughout the year. Your obligation has already been determined by the court, and the court took into consideration that you would have the children during the summer. The fact the children are living with you does not extinguish your obligation.

My ex-husband is filing bankruptcy. Does he still have to pay child support? *Yes.* Your ex-husband's obligation to pay child support cannot be discharged. He cannot be released from this debt in the same way that a credit card debt is discharged.

> **TIP:** The ongoing bankruptcy may delay child support payments.

Does an ex-spouse who is in jail have to pay child support? Yes; however, since the ex-spouse is not earning any money, there are typically no funds available to pay child support.

> **TIP:** Some prison systems attempt to provide inmates with jobs so that some funds are available for child support payments. For information concerning families with a relative who is incarcerated, go to the Family and Corrections network at **www.fcnetwork.org**.

My ex-wife has put property in her parent's name to avoid paying off child support arrears. Is there anything I can do? *Yes.* Your ex-wife is making a fraudulent transfer or conveyance by placing property in someone else's name to avoid her legal obligation. You should contact your local or state child support agency to determine how to pursue an action to set aside the fraudulent transfers.

I have no idea where my ex-husband is living. He owes for many months of child support and is probably not working. Is there anything I can do to enforce the child support order? *Other than contacting the local or state agency responsible for enforcing child support orders and giving them whatever information you have on your ex-husband, the order cannot currently be enforced.* Since your ex-husband's whereabouts are unknown, the child support order is, unfortunately, difficult to enforce.

> **TIP:** Give the agency the names and addresses of all relatives with whom the person owing child support may be living, including current and past friends. It is difficult for a person to completely hide or disappear without the help of family or friends.

> **TIP:** A person's location can be tracked through Social Security information if that person is currently employed and not being paid in cash.

> **TIP:** Additional information is available on the Office of Child Enforcement Web site at **www.acf.dhhs.gov/programs/cse**.

> **The U.S. Passport office will deny passports to persons owing child support amounts exceeding $5,000. Any person in the Passport Denial Program can no longer use her passport.**

Increase or Decrease in Amount

Support is increased depending on the needs of the child, along with a parent's ability to pay more than called for in the guidelines. Children involved in many activities, attending camps, driving, taking music lessons, etc., may require more support if it is in their best interests to maintain that lifestyle. If the parent can afford it, the child's lifestyle should not be diminished because sufficient support is not ordered. Similarly, if the parent's income has increased significantly since the support order was entered, the court may increase the support payments owed by that parent. However, the parent can argue that the children do not require excessive support.

On the other hand, a parent may not be able to pay an amount that covers his support obligation under the guidelines. The father, for instance, may have other children to support, be disabled, unemployed, or have debts or judgments against him.

MEDICAL SUPPORT

The court can order either parent to provide and cover the costs of medical care and treatment for the child. Typically the noncustodial parent provides health insurance and medical care, along with a monthly support payment. Medical care is interpreted broadly, and can include tutoring, speech classes, or physical or occupational therapy. Dental and eye care are always part of the medical support provided to the child.

> **TIP:** The parent who is providing health insurance must provide the other parent with all information relating to the policy, including the policy number, insurance and prescription cards, and notification of benefit changes.

Qualified Medical Child Support Order ("QMCSO")

Along with the final divorce decree, a qualified medical child support order may be entered requiring a parent's employer-sponsored health plans to cover children of the marriage. The child is the alternate recipient of the health care benefits under the QMCSO. More information can be found in the U.S. Department of Labor's guide to QMCSOs at **www.dol.gov/ebsa/publications/qmcso.html**.

> **TIP:** Plans that do not provide dependent health care coverage do not have to comply with the QMCSO.

ENFORCEMENT OF CHILD SUPPORT ORDERS

Parents who routinely fail to pay child support have the amounts deducted from their wages under state and federal laws. All child support orders authorize a wage deduction from the paying parent's job income. Additionally, tax refunds can be seized if child support is owed. Commonly, the nonpaying parent is held in contempt of court and is fined or even jailed for failing to make child support payments. The parent who should be receiving child support payments (and is not) generally files a motion asking the court to enforce the child support payments.

> Holding the nonpaying spouse in contempt is a tricky remedy, because a person in jail obviously cannot earn income. Judges take this into consideration before placing a parent in jail.

> **TIP:** Interest accrues on unpaid child support.

Uniform Interstate Family Support Act (UIFSA)

The Uniform Interstate Family Support Act allows parents to more easily collect child support from parents who live in other states. The Act permits only one support order to be in effect for the child, which consequently allows for one controlling order (rather than several issued by the different states).

Significantly, the Act allows the state that issued the order to withhold income from the parent who is not paying, although he is employed in another state. "Direct income withholding" is accomplished by sending the child support order directly to the out-of-state employer who, under federal law, must comply with a "wage withholding order."

> **TIP:** Child support orders should be registered in the state where the paying parent lives.

Child Support Lien

Laws may allow the parent who is not receiving child support to obtain a lien on the nonpaying parent's property. A person with a lien can seize the property and sell it to satisfy an outstanding debt. Typically, personal property is seized by the sheriff and sold at auction. The proceeds go to pay off the child support arrears.

CHILDREN

Children have their own rights, and parents have duties toward them. These rights and duties arise in the context of pregnancy, abortion, birth, adoption and paternity.

RESPONSIBILITIES AND DUTIES OF PARENTS TO CHILD

Once a person becomes a parent, he or she has certain legal duties to the child. Parents must provide children with food, shelter, clothing, health care and education. Parents have a duty to protect their children from abuse and neglect. If parents do not provide a safe environment for their children, they may be held criminally liable and the child can be removed from the home.

Must parents continue to support children after they become adults? *No.* Once the child is no longer a minor, the parents' legal obligations to the child are terminated.

Parents' Rights Over Child

Just as they have certain duties, mothers and fathers also have certain rights regarding their children. Parents have the right to determine how the child will be raised, where and how the child will be educated, what religion will be followed and the type of medical treatment the child can obtain. Under some laws, parents have the right to any income earned by the child. Additionally, parents have the right to discipline their children within reason.

Service and Earnings

As long as a parent is supporting a minor child, the parent has the right to the child's earnings and labor. For example, the parents of a teen-aged boy living at home have the right to require him to work on the family farm. Once the child is an adult or the parent no longer supports him, the parent loses the right to his services and earnings.

Medical Treatment

When the life of the child is threatened because of a parent's decision, the state can intervene. Typically, these cases arise where the parents withhold medical treatment. Even if the parents have a religious belief that forbids certain treatment (e.g., a blood transfusion), a court has the authority to make the child a ward of the state and require the medical treatment.

Can a stepparent consent to a stepchild's medical treatment? *Yes.* However, the consent is authorized only in situations where an adult blood relative (such as a grandparent) cannot be reached and the parent is not available.

Can a parent authorize a hospital to take a child off of life-sustaining medical equipment? *Yes.* Laws generally allow parents to "let their child die" when the child is terminally ill. Under those circumstances, the parents do not have to consent to continued medical treatment, urgent or not. For example, a child with an inoperable brain tumor which will cause his death will not be legally forced to undergo invasive medical treatment if his parents do not wish him to have it.

> **Parents cannot withhold medical treatment from nonterminal children regardless of the severity of the disease, deformity or disability.**

Can a parent authorize a child to donate an organ to save the life of a sibling or parent? *No.* Parents are under a duty not to place their children in danger of injury. Since surgery has inherent risks, the child cannot be forced to donate an organ. However, other treatments may be authorized by the parents, such as donating blood or even bone marrow.

My 14-year-old daughter wants to donate a kidney to her brother. Can I authorize the surgery? *No.* However, the court can authorize the surgery under the "substituted judgment doctrine." If the court finds that your daughter, if she were an adult, would come to the decision to donate her kidney to her brother and that she would receive great personal benefit from her act, the judge may permit the surgery.

Can parents bar a child's access to contraceptives or birth control? *In some states, a physician can determine, without the parents' consent, whether to prescribe birth control medications.* Over-the-counter contraceptives can also be obtained by minors.

Can a minor seek confidential medical treatment? *Yes.* In certain circumstances, a physician may not be under a legal obligation to inform parents that she is treating their minor child.

> **Typically, laws allow minors to consent to their own treatment without the additional consent or notification of the parents, where:**
> - treatment is sought for an infectious, contagious or communicable disease of a type that must be reported to a local health board;
> - she is pregnant and seeking medical care (other than an abortion); or
> - treatment for an addiction is being sought.

> **TIP:** Minors on active military duty do not need parental consent for medical treatment.

> **TIP:** Minors who have left home and are supporting themselves can authorize their own medical care if they are at least 16 or 17 years old, depending on the laws of the state.

I am 17 years old. Can I consent to treatment for my baby? *Yes.* If you are the parent of a child, and have custody of that child, you can authorize medical care and treatment for your son or daughter even if you are a minor.

I am 14, and just found out that I am pregnant. Can the doctor tell my parents? *Yes.* Because you are a minor, the physician is not legally barred from advising your parents of the pregnancy. Although you can consent to your own treatment, the doctor does not have to keep the pregnancy and treatment a secret from your parents. Of course, your medical care is confidential as to any other person.

Can I donate blood if I am minor? Unless you qualify on a basis that allows you to consent to your own treatment, such as being pregnant, you must have your parents' permission to give blood.

Can I get an abortion without my parents' consent? *No.* Laws called parental notification acts typically require physicians to notify parents before an abortion is performed unless your life is in immediate danger.

> A court can issue an order giving a minor the authority to consent over her parents' objections.

LEGAL RIGHTS OF CHILDREN

Although not yet adults, minors have their own legal rights. Laws have been enacted to protect children from abuse and neglect, to give a child access to an education and to give them the right to receive certain federal and state benefits.

If my child inherits money from his grandparents, does it really belong to me? *No.* The money belongs to your child; however, you have some control over its use and management as long as it goes to the child's needs rather than your own. For instance, you are certainly entitled to prevent the child from giving it to his friends, but he is probably within his rights to use the inheritance to purchase a vehicle.

> Your child's earnings may belong to you under the law.

DETERMINING PARENTAGE

Because a parent and child are in a legal relationship, the issue of who is the parent is often litigated. As medical technology has advanced, the issue has become more complicated. The Uniform Parentage Act (UPA), enacted by several states, sets the guidelines for the presumption of parentage, recognizes the rights of unmarried parents and uses the term "child with no presumed father," rather than "illegitimate." Even states that have not enacted the entire UPA have generally enacted portions into law.

A child's legal mother is the woman who:

- gave birth to the child, or
- adopted the child, or
- has been adjudicated to be the child's mother when the child was born to a surrogate.

The issue of the identity of a child's father, or "paternity," is often litigated. The law presumes that a man is the father of a child born to his wife, or that he is the father to a child that he acknowledged as his child before the marriage. Fatherhood is also presumed when a man agrees to be the father and is named on the child's birth certificate.

> **TIP:** The mother of a child and a man claiming to be the father of the child conceived as the result of his sexual intercourse with the mother may sign an acknowledgment of paternity to establish the man's paternity.

EXAMPLE: A man who is living with the mother of a child during the child's first 2 years of life and who has represented to the public that he is the child's father, is the presumptive father. It is not necessary that the man married the mother.

Besides a paternity test, is there another way I can prove that the child my wife had is not mine? *Yes.* However, since you are presumed to be the father, you must be able to show that you did not have access to your wife at any time that the baby could have been conceived.

> **TIP:** Proof of a successful vasectomy or impotency rebuts the presumption of fatherhood.

My boyfriend alleges that he is not our son's father and has denied paternity. He refuses to submit to a DNA test. Can he still prove he is not the father? *No.* He was the alleged father because you say he is your son's father. However, by refusing to submit to a DNA test, he becomes the presumed father and can be made to pay child support.

Can my wife and her boyfriend sign an acknowledgment of paternity to establish that he is the father of our daughter, rather than me? *No.* If a child has a presumed father, the acknowledgment is not valid. Husbands are always presumed to be the father of their wife's children. Your wife's and her boyfriend's acknowledgment to the contrary does not affect this presumption.

How do I establish that a man is the father of my child? You file a suit to establish or adjudicate paternity in the state where you and the child are living.

> **TIP:** A suit to establish paternity cannot be filed once the child becomes an adult.

> **If the child already has a presumed father, a suit to adjudicate paternity, i.e., claiming a different man is the father, must be filed by the time a child is a certain age. For instance, the law in a state might require the suit to be filed by the child's fourth birthday. After that time, the presumed father's parental rights cannot be challenged by alleging that another man is the father.**

My child has not been born. Can I file a suit to adjudicate paternity? *Yes.* You may begin the proceeding before the birth of the child, but the matter will not be finalized, i.e. the identity of the father will not be determined, until after the child is born.

My wife and I have never lived together, and I know her daughter is not my child. Can I obtain a legal decree of some sort to establish that I am not the father? *Yes.* By virtue of your marriage, you are the presumed father. However, because you did not live with your wife when the child was conceived, you can bring a suit at any time to disprove paternity. Your paternity can be easily disproved with genetic testing.

Do I have to submit to genetic testing in a suit to establish paternity? *Yes.* If the court orders you to provide a DNA sample, you must provide one or risk being in contempt of court.

> **Genetic testing is not ordered over the man's objection until he has been notified of the proceeding, the court has held a hearing and listened to evidence, and the woman has established sufficient facts to allege the man is the father of the child.**

> **This testing is not considered to be a violation of a person's right to privacy or due process under the constitution. While blood and DNA tests may be considered invasive, the state has an interest in establishing a child's paternity in order to determine who has the duty to support the child.**

PREGNANCY AND BIRTH

Generally, a woman's decisions regarding her pregnancy and the birth of her child are solely within her control. She can decide to be under a physician's care, or not, during the pregnancy. She can give birth at home or in the hospital. In some instances, the woman can choose whether to have a vaginal birth or a caesarean section. In any case, her rights during pregnancy and birth are firmly established.

If I am not a minor, are there any legal requirements I must meet in order to have an abortion? *Yes.* A majority of states have laws that, at a minimum, require counseling, receipt of reading materials and viewing a video before a doctor can perform the abortion. Additionally, 26 states require a mandatory delay of 24 hours or more after meeting with the doctor (and receiving counseling services if mandated) before an abortion will be performed.

> **Many of these laws are being challenged as unconstitutional.**

Is the "abortion pill" available in the United States? *Yes.* A "medication abortion" is available to women. A medication abortion is a procedure in which certain prescription medications are administered that end a pregnancy without the necessity of any invasive procedures (other than an injection in some cases).

Are abortions in the second trimester illegal? *No.* However, laws have been enacted in many states banning second trimester abortions unless the health of the mother is in danger.

Is a parent's consent always required in order for a minor to obtain an abortion? *No.* However, nearly half the states have laws requiring parental consent. Nearly all of the remainder of the states require parental notification before the abortion can be performed.

> Currently, Connecticut, Hawaii, New York, Oregon, Vermont and Washington do not require parental consent or notice before a minor undergoes an abortion.

Can the biological father stop a woman from obtaining an abortion? *No.* A father
has no legal rights in the abortion decision. The father can neither stop a woman from having an abortion nor force her to have one, even if they are married.

Can I be arrested for taking illegal drugs during a pregnancy? *Yes.* Women who have
substance abuse problems while pregnant have been arrested and convicted under child abuse laws for harming their unborn child. Additionally, you can always be arrested, pregnant or not, for possession of illegal drugs.

> The charge typically arises after the child is born ill, disabled or drug addicted, i.e., "abused." The prenatal drug habit is evidence that the mother knowingly caused injury to the child.

> **TIP:** Some courts have overturned convictions because they interpreted child abuse laws to cover children and not a fetus. In other words, in these cases the court found that the term "child" as used in child abuse laws, does not mean an unborn child.

> In jurisdictions that have ruled "child" also means "unborn child," the mother may be prosecuted for ingesting drugs during the pregnancy even though the child is born without side effects. The theory is that the mother caused the child injury, harm and pain, which constitute child abuse.

Am I required by law to take certain measure to ensure the health and safety of my unborn child? *No.* There are no legal requirements
that mothers-to-be must follow to protect and guarantee the health of an unborn child.

> **TIP:** Even in states where mothers are prosecuted for abuse to unborn children, no requirements or duties are placed on the mother in caring for the unborn child's condition.

Can a hospital force me to undergo a caesarean section if the baby's life is in danger during labor? *No.* Since an adult can
refuse medical treatment, and the unborn child is still a part of the mother (not a separate person), only the mother's wishes should be considered. For instance, a Jehovah's Witness can refuse a blood transfusion, even if the chances are great that she and/or her unborn child could die.

> **TIP:** Because these cases usually arise in emergency circumstances and the court is called in to rule within hours on a life or death situation, the judge may side with the hospital and order the treatment. Caesarean sections have been ordered and performed over the objection of the mother.

Can a mother be prosecuted for leaving her baby at the hospital entrance? Yes; however,
some states have passed laws that allow the woman to overcome the charge if the baby is less than 3 to 30 days old, depending on the state, and was taken to a designated safe place.

TERMINATION OF PARENTAL RIGHTS

A parent's legal right to custody of a child can be terminated by a court. In an adoption, the natural mother voluntarily terminates her rights so that the child may be adopted. However, termination is often involuntary, and the grounds are typically the parent's neglect and abuse of the child. Grounds for involuntary termination of parental rights include:

- abandonment;
- knowingly placing the child in danger;
- failing to support the child;

- felony criminal conviction;
- sexual offenses;
- murder of one parent by the other parent; and
- causing the child to be born addicted to drugs or alcohol.

Parents who have children who are placed in foster care do not automatically lose their parental rights. Even a lengthy placement does not allow the court to terminate parental rights. However, parents who fail or refuse to participate in assistance programs that can improve their situation may have their rights terminated while their children are in foster care.

Father's Rights

A father who is not married to the mother of his child has parental rights, but he must exercise them. For instance, laws allow the father's rights to be terminated if he knew the woman was pregnant but remained completely uninvolved with woman and the pregnancy. He is considered to have abandoned the woman and his rights to the child as well. Generally, in these situations, the father is notified that his parental rights are being terminated and he does not contest the termination.

> **If the father's whereabouts are unknown, his parental rights can still be terminated. Laws do not require notification when the father cannot be located.**

However, a father has the right to oppose or contest the termination. If the termination is contested, evidence must be offered that grounds for terminating the father's parental rights actually exist.

Is a trial held to determine if a parent's rights should be terminated? *No.* There is a hearing before the judge where evidence is presented through testimony and documents that show the reasons for termination.

Who asks the court to terminate parental rights? The state agency involved in the care of the child asks the court to terminate parental rights.

> **Once the child has been removed from the home, she is in the custody of the state agency. The agency must attempt to move the child back home and out of foster care by helping the family create an adequate environment for a child. Agencies provide training and programs (such as drug rehabilitation programs) for parents who seek their child's return.**

When does an agency file to terminate a parent's rights? Under most laws, state agencies are required to begin termination proceedings once the child has been in foster care for over a year.

Can I oppose an agency's efforts to terminate my parental rights? *Yes.* You are permitted to explain your side of the story to the judge, present evidence and call witnesses to testify in your behalf.

> **Because a parent's rights are so important, the court must allow a parent, even one who is in jail, to present evidence opposing the termination.**

What do I have to prove to keep my parental rights? Assuming a legal justification exists for terminating your rights, you must show a compelling reason why the rights should not be terminated. There is not an exact set of circumstances that automatically provide a compelling reason, but some of the following reasons have allowed a parent to keep her child:

- that in 6 months or less, the parent will be able to care for the child again;
- that the child is old enough to state a preference that parental rights not be terminated;
- that the parent has maintained contact and the child would benefit from continuing the relationship;
- that the child is in a residential facility or home, adoption is unlikely and termination is not necessary to place the child; and
- that the length of time in foster care is due to circumstances beyond the parent's control, such as court delays or incarceration.

My children have told the judge they do not want my parental rights terminated. Can my rights be terminated over their wishes? *Yes.* The children's preference is only one of the factors a judge considers, especially where children are young and have a chance to be adopted by another family. If the judge finds that the children's emotional and physical well-being is threatened by returning them to you or that they have lived in foster care for many months and you have not shown improvements in your lifestyle, your parental rights will be terminated.

If I am unable to take care of my child and appoint my sister as his guardian, have I terminated my parental rights? *No.* You are still the legal parent of the child; however, all decision-making and custody of the child rests with your sister since she is the guardian.

> Appointing a guardian for a child is a court proceeding. The judge must approve of and order the guardianship.

Can I voluntarily give up my parental rights? *Yes.* In this case, you are relinquishing your rights to your child. Parental rights are routinely relinquished by birth parents that have decided to give a baby up for adoption.

Can the biological father's parental rights be terminated even where his paternity has not been proved? *Yes.* Any alleged biological fathers can have their rights terminated, along with the mother's and her husband (if she is married). If the mother names five different men that could possibly be the father of her child, then all five men will be part of one lawsuit to terminate parental rights. One of the men cannot go back and say that his rights were improperly terminated, because he did not believe he was the father at the time of the hearing.

Once my parental rights have been terminated, can they be restored in the future? *No.* If the child had not yet been adopted, you would have to adopt your child in order to regain your status as her parent. However, since your rights were terminated, it is highly unlikely a judge would find such an adoption to be in the best interests of the child.

EMANCIPATION OF MINORS

Minors can be adjudicated to be adults, or emancipated, if certain legal requirements are met and the court finds that it is in the best interests of the minor. Once emancipated, any legal limitations that are generally attached to minors are extinguished. For example, the emancipated minor can sign a lease contract.

Requirements

In order to be declared an adult, the minor must file a petition with the court. Generally, laws prohibit minors under 16 or 17 years of age from filing a petition under any circumstances. The minor may also be required to be living on her own and be self-supporting at the time she files the petition.

> The minor can file the petition in her own name.

> The court may be required to appoint an attorney (the attorney ad litem) to represent the minor.

If my 16-year-old daughter becomes emancipated, will I still be entitled to receive child support from my ex-husband? *No.* The obligation to pay child support usually terminates when the child becomes an adult. Once your daughter is emancipated, she is legally an adult, and your ex-husband no longer has to pay child support.

What is partial emancipation? Partial emancipation means that child is emancipated only:

- for a certain period of time, or
- for some special purpose (such as the right to earn and spend his/her own wages), or
- from a part of a parent's rights (such as the right to make decisions about a pregnancy).

> A minor that is partially emancipated is still entitled to support from her parents (although she is able to make her own legal decisions), and an ex-spouse would have to continue to pay child support until the child was 18 years old.

Can an emancipated minor vote before he turns 18 years old? *No.* Although considered an adult for some legal purposes, the law requires voters to be 18 years old.

Does the 21-year-old age limit for drinking apply to me if I am emancipated? *Yes.* You are still required to follow the law, and the law requires a person to be 21 years old before he or she can purchase or drink alcohol.

Am I automatically emancipated if I join the armed services? *No.* In fact, parental consent is required before a minor is allowed to join or enlist in the military.

> **TIP:** Under-age members of the military may consent to their own medical treatment.

Does getting married emancipate me? *Yes.* Laws in some states permit married minors to consent to medical treatment for themselves and their children, enter into contracts and make other legal decisions.

> Having a child does not confer emancipation upon a minor, although the minor parent can consent to medical treatment for the child.

I am 17 years old and signed an apartment lease. Is it valid? *Yes.* However, since you are underage, you can "void" or break the contract. Generally, minors cannot be held to the terms of a contract they enter into on their own. If you are emancipated, a court may require you to fulfill the lease obligation.

ADOPTION

Adoption is the legal process that allows a person to become the legal parent of someone not born to him or her. Although children are the persons who are typically adopted, adults can be adopted as well.

Adoptions follow a strict set of laws, and these laws vary from state to state. Whether the parents adopt through an agency or find a child to adopt on their own, the legal requirements of the state are the same. No child that already has a parent or parents may be adopted until those parental rights are terminated by order of the court. If the parental rights of the natural parents are not terminated, any later adoption is invalid.

CAUTION: States that have short waiting periods between the birth of a child and termination of parental rights are popular places to adopt. Typically, the adoptive parents take the baby home with them; however, they have no legal right to the child until the natural mother's rights are terminated. In states where termination takes up to a year, losing the child because the mother changes her mind is a wrenching experience.

Any eligible adult may petition the court to adopt a child. Marriage is no longer a requirement, although sexual preference may be a bar in some states. Foster parents may petition the court to legally adopt a child placed in their custody.

REQUIREMENTS

Laws require a myriad of filings, reports and studies before a child can be adopted. Generally, a social worker must interview the prospective parents and prepare a home study that is filed with the court. Additionally, health, social, educational and genetic history reports are prepared and filed. The adoption cannot be completed until the necessary reports are presented to the court.

> The adoptive parents' criminal records, if any, are searched and a criminal history report is prepared.

The court will grant the adoption at an adoption hearing if the court finds that the adoption is in the best interests of the child. Some laws permit the court to terminate the parental rights of the natural parents at the same time that the baby is adopted.

CONFIDENTIALITY

Laws generally require adoption records to be sealed if the adopting parents request that they be sealed. "Sealing" documents means that no one will have access to the information contained within them and that they will remain confidential.

How do I get my adoption records unsealed so I can locate my birth mother? *You can either file a petition to unseal adoption record or fill out a form with the probate or county court clerk requesting that the file be examined.* If your file contains a notice that your birth parent is looking for you, the records will be unsealed. Where a petition is required, you must show the court "good cause" to unseal the records, such as medical necessity.

> Laws have been enacted in some states that allow adoptees to request and obtain non-identifying information from the adoption records. Additionally, some states, such as Oregon and New Hampshire, have laws that allow adoptees access to their original birth certificate; Alaska and Kansas do not have sealed adoption records. Check your state laws for recent legislation allowing access to adoption records.

> Under the Indian Child Welfare Act, when requested, courts must unseal records for American Indian children in order to provide information to the adopted individual necessary to ascertain her tribal affiliation and membership.

BIRTH CERTIFICATES

When a child is adopted, a new birth certificate is issued. The clerk of the court typically sends the adoption order to the bureau or office that issues birth certificates. On receipt of the order, not only is a new birth certificate issued, any records relating to the children prior to the adoption are sealed.

GESTATIONAL AGREEMENTS

Parties can legally enter into agreements that require a surrogate mother to relinquish her parental rights when she gives birth on another couple's behalf. The use of these agreements protects couples who cannot have children on their own and who want to use a surrogate to carry their child through the use of an assisted reproductive procedure, such as in vitro fertilization.

The agreement prohibits the use of the gestational mother's eggs in the assisted reproduction procedure. Additionally, the intended parents must be married. The agreement is an enforceable contract.

> **TIP:** Laws authorizing the use of gestational agreements have not been enacted in all states.

What is an open adoption? *An open adoption generally includes ongoing communications between the birth mother (and father) and the adoptive parents.* Sometimes, the adoptive parents' duties to the birth mother are set out in a contract. The provisions might include sending a photograph once a year, regular telephone calls and e-mails, saving all letters and cards to the infant from the birth mother, and having the child meet the birth mother at a certain age. Typically, however, the birth parent and adoptive parents have an informal agreement.

What are "baby broker" laws? Baby broker laws prohibit unlicensed individuals from placing babies for adoption.

The laws require adoptions to go through licensed agencies; unlicensed persons are "baby brokers" and may be prosecuted for criminal offences.

If the adoption is never finalized, is a baby broker law still violated? *Yes.* The laws generally prohibit an unauthorized person from having any significant role in the placement activities. The actual finalization of an adoption is not required for the law to be violated.

Can the natural mother find adoptive parents without breaking baby broker laws? *Yes*. The natural mother, her parents or guardian, or other close relative may seek out adoptive parents.

Can an adopted child sue the placement agency if she was placed in an unfit home? *Yes*. It may be possible to file a lawsuit against an agency for negligent placement, if the agency did not fulfill its responsibilities to investigate the adoptive parents.

Once the adoption is finalized, the placement agency has no duty to continue to supervise, investigate or protect the child. Of course, the placement agency (typically the state's child protective service agency) has a duty to protect the welfare of a child in foster care prior to adoption.

Can an adoption agency charge a fee for placing a baby? *Yes*. A private placement agency may charge for its actual fees and expenses, and is allowed to establish a sliding scale based on the adoptive parents' gross income. For example, the agency may charge 15% of gross income up to $15,000. The formula varies according to state laws.

Laws prohibit charging fees unrelated to the adoption. Adoption-related fees are typically limited to the mother's medical and legal expenses, plus other expenses incurred as a result of her pregnancy (maternity clothes, for example). An adoption agency can also charge prospective parents for legal fees the agency incurs, an application fee, the cost of required home studies and reports, the cost of parental training, and the cost of counseling to all the parties involved.

There are laws that list allowable birth mother expenses. Payment of the following expenses is generally permitted:

- living expenses such as rent, food, utilities, and clothing (typically there is maximum such as $1,000 per month);
- medical expenses including prenatal care, delivery, and other pregnancy-related medical expenses (post pregnancy medical care for a number of weeks is usually allowable);
- transportation to access medical, legal, counseling and adoption services;
- legal services related to the termination of parental rights and adoption process;
- counseling to assure that the mother is aware of her rights and is not being coerced; and
- expenses relating to educational, vocational, recreational and religious services up to a certain amount.

What does a birth mother have to pay to give a baby up for adoption? *Nothing*. A birth mother is never charged a fee. The adopting parents pay for all her expenses.

Paying a birth mother's expenses is not the same as "purchasing" a baby, which is illegal. Paying the mother a lump sum after the child is born equates to buying the baby. Additionally, "cash up front" is typically considered an illegal payment.

My husband wants to adopt a child and I do not. Can he adopt the child on his own? *No*. Since you are his wife, you are required to participate in the adoption. When one of the parties is married, the petition to adopt must include both spouses.

Can a gay couple adopt a child? *Yes*. Laws in most states do not prohibit same sex couples from adopting a child. However, in some states the couple may not be permitted to jointly petition the court for an adoption.

> A gay individual can adopt because unmarried persons are permitted to adopt children in all states. Only Florida prohibits gay, lesbian and bisexual individuals from petitioning for an adoption.

> **TIP:** Adoptions by same-sex parents are also called "co-parent" adoptions or "second-parent" adoptions. Second parent adoptions occur when the partner of an adoptive parent wants to adopt the child as well.

Can a child be "unadopted?" *Since adoption is a legal process, and legal processes can be undone, laws may allow adoptive parents to revoke the adoption.* For example, California laws allow an adoption to be annulled if the child has a developmental disability or mental deficiency that existed but was unknown at the time of the adoption, and that is of such magnitude that the child is unsuitable for adoption.

WRONGFUL ADOPTION LAWSUITS

In recent times, adoptive parents have been successful in suing state and private agencies for placing children with known mental and physical disabilities, the existence of which was purposely withheld from the parents. All states have enacted laws requiring or allowing pertinent medical information concerning the adopted child to be released to the prospective parents.

CHILD ABUSE

Unfortunately, children may be neglected, abused or both. Such treatment is illegal. A neglected child is a child that has not been provided with proper care or support, is placed in a dangerous situation, or is abandoned. Abused children are victims of crime—they have been intentionally injured by another person. The injuries may be physical or mental.

REPORTING CHILD ABUSE OR NEGLECT

Laws require certain people (teachers, doctors, day care providers) with knowledge of child abuse to report the abuse to a local or state law enforcement agency. However, any person may report abuse or neglect. Proof is not necessary; all that is needed is a belief or suspicion that abuse or neglect has occurred or is occurring.

If I reported child abuse and was wrong, can I be sued by the person I reported? *No.* If you made the report in good faith, you are immune from liability. In fact, the failure to report suspected abuse is typically a misdemeanor offense.

How can I be sure I witnessed the treatment of a child that is at the level of abuse? Abuse is any:

- treatment of a child that causes physical or emotional injury;
- harmful sexual conduct towards a child;
- pornographic photographs, movies or other depictions of children; or
- exposure to drugs or alcohol.

What types of actions constitute neglect? You may need to report neglect if you are aware of a child:

- being left alone and exposed to harm;
- being placed in a harmful environment or where there is a risk of harm; or
- needing and not receiving food, shelter or medical care.

DOMESTIC VIOLENCE

Laws have been enacted that allow for better protection for victims of domestic violence.

Additionally, state agencies are charged with protecting children that are victims of child abuse. The agencies are legally permitted to remove the child from the home and take temporary custody of him or her. If the violence and neglect continues, parental rights will be terminated.

PROTECTIVE ORDERS

A protective order, or order of protection, is an order issued by a court prohibiting the abuser from communicating with family members and requiring him to stay away from the home, family members' places of employment, or the children's schools. Anyone who is a victim of family violence may apply for a protective order. If the abuser violates the protective order, he may be arrested immediately and taken to jail.

> **Protective orders are not available unless there is a relationship between the applicant and the person who is the subject of the order, such as ex-spouses, relatives, persons who live together or have a child together.**

> **TIP:** Although use of an an attorney is recommended, women's shelters and other programs that assist victims of domestic violence may have the forms necessary so that a person can obtain a protective order on her own.

Is the protective order permanent? If the facts warrant, the court will enter a permanent protective order. However, protective orders are usually issued on an emergency and temporary basis, with an expiration date.

I obtained a protective order for myself and my children against my ex-husband, but he has visitation with the children this weekend. Do they have to go? *No.* The protective order supersedes other court orders, such as custody orders. Under the terms of the protective order, your husband is not allowed near your home or family.

> **TIP:** Keep a copy of the protective order with you at all times in case it is violated and you need to show it to the police.

PARENTAL RESPONSIBILITY FOR CHILDREN'S ACTIONS

Laws hold parents responsible for the behavior of their children and liable for their misdeeds based on the theory that parents have a duty to control the child. Under the law, if the child is not controlled or reasonably disciplined, property damage caused by his behavior is the parent's fault.

LIABILITY

Laws automatically impose liability on parents of children who have maliciously caused property damage. These laws protect victims of property damage by requiring parents to pay some compensation, even if they were not negligent.

Parental liability laws typically make exceptions (and do not require compensation) for very young children under the theory that a very young child could not have formed the intent to behave maliciously.

NEGLIGENCE

When parents fail to supervise children in situations requiring it, the parents may be negligent. A negligent parent is responsible for any damage or injuries caused by the child's behavior in the unsupervised situation. The child's age and presence or absence of intent to do damage is not relevant. A parent who is not liable under parental liability laws because her child is very young (and incapable of malicious intent), could still be found negligent because she failed to properly supervise the child.

Am I always liable for injuries my child causes simply because I am the parent? *No.* Liability for your child's behavior is not based solely on the fact that a parent-child relationship exists—at a minimum, you must be negligent. In other words, you, as the parent, must have failed to do something you had a duty to do.

I told my 16-year-old son he had to mow the lawn with our riding lawn mower, as he does every Saturday, and he ran into the neighbor's car. Do I have to pay for the damage? *Yes.* Although you were not negligent, since your son knew how to operate the lawn mower and had used it many times before, in this instance he was mowing the lawn because you expressly directed him to. When a child is acting under your specific instructions and direction, you are liable for injuries and damage that occurs while he is performing the task.

My son and his friends were riding four-wheelers on our property when one of the children was injured while driving. Am I liable? *Yes.* Anytime you allow your child or any other minor to use a dangerous instrument, you may be liable. Four-wheelers and ATV's are generally considered to be dangerous instruments.

> Under some circumstances, liability may not be imposed when a child is allowed to use a dangerous instrument. For instance, you might not be negligent if your son's friend had ridden four-wheelers on your property before, you were supervising the activity, the children had to ride on a specified track, were given certain rules to follow, and had been trained in driving.

TIP: A dangerous instrument can be anything not commonly used by a child of a certain age, not suitable for that child's age or consistently used in a manner not suitable for the child's age.

CRIMINAL ACTS

Parents may be liable for their children's criminal acts to the extent they must compensate the victim for damages and injuries. For example, although the parents themselves cannot be convicted of arson where their child burns down a barn, the parents will be financially liable for the damage caused.

When am I liable for my child's criminal acts? In order to be liable, you must have some sort of control over your child. If your 17-year-old son that takes your car, drives drunk and fatally injures someone, he is not in your control. However, in that same situation, if you knew he was drunk and still gave him the car keys, you would be liable for his crime because you negligently entrusted him with driving your vehicle.

TIP: Before a parent can be liable for a child's criminal acts, the parent must have:

1. known or should have known that the child needed to be controlled because of previous similar bad behavior;

2. had the ability to control the behavior; and

3. had the opportunity to control the child.

Are the parents of children who take guns to school and shoot other students liable for their child's crime? *The parents are liable only if the child had behaved in a similar way in the past.* The parents must have been on notice that the child had a propensity for or likelihood of taking a gun to school and shooting other students.

Do parents who are liable for their child's crime go to jail for them? *No.* A parent is not convicted of the crime in place of the child nor is a parent required or permitted to serve time on behalf of the child.

> Parents may be separately charged and convicted with a crime they committed, such as buying an illegal firearm that the child then used in a separate crime.

> Parents of children who have committed crimes are typically sued in civil court. A jury decides if they are liable or responsible for the injuries to the victims because of their failure to control or supervise their child. If parents are found liable, they must financially compensate the victims for their injuries and other damages.

We know our son has a propensity for violence. What steps can we take to minimize our liability for his actions? *You should remove guns and other weapons from the house.* Additionally, you might:

- apprise school personnel of his behavior (and any changes);
- monitor his comings and goings;
- set curfews; and
- provide professional counseling.

TIP: Courts recognize that a parent's ability to control the child's behavior diminishes as the child matures and grows older.

If I take my son off his medication for Attention Deficit Disorder (ADD), will I be liable if he hurts someone at school? *Yes.* If the injury happened because he was taken off the medication and you failed to inform school authorities, you will be liable. However, if you inform the school authorities that he was taken off his medication, you cannot be accused of negligence and you will not be liable for the injuries.

> **TIP:** You do not have a duty to medicate your child in order to protect others from possible injuries that are caused by the disease, syndrome or disability for which he is being medicated.

My son, who has been in fights at school in the past, assaulted another student during the senior class trip. Am I liable for his actions? *No.* Although you knew your son was prone to get into fights, his age and the fact that he was miles from home means that you did not have the ability or opportunity to control his behavior.

JUVENILE LAWS AND PROCEDURES

Special laws have been enacted to address crimes committed by children. The disposition and sentencing of the crime is handled differently from an adult case since the minor's privacy must be protected. Any criminal issues concerning minors are addressed in juvenile courts. Minors do not appear in state courts to be punished for their crimes unless they are being tried as adults. Additionally, the minor starts with a "clean" record when he turns 18 years old. Juvenile crimes do not follow the child into adulthood—at least in public records.

DETENTION HEARINGS

Typically, minors are not sentenced if they commit a crime. Rather, they are detained and sent for rehabilitation in a juvenile facility for a period of time. Decisions concerning the minor's need to remain in the custody of the court and sent to a facility are determined during a detention hearing.

The hearing must be held within a very short period of time after law enforcement takes the minor into custody—usually no more than 24 hours. At the hearing, the juvenile court judge determines whether or not the minor engaged in the criminal conduct. If the child is not a repeat offender, he will be released; repeat offenders will

be detained. Additionally, a child will be detained if the court determines he is a danger to himself or to the public.

> **The commission of certain serious offenses converts the minor into an adult for the purposes of prosecution.**

> **TIP:** First offenders are not detained; they are usually released to the custody of a parent.

The child is detained in a special facility for several days. The facility can be a juvenile shelter, children's home or other authorized detention facility.

If my child is arrested, can he be held in jail? *Yes.* Minors can be taken into custody after an arrest just like an adult. However, children are held in a juvenile detention area rather than with the general jail population. Typically, your child must be allowed to make a phone call within an hour or two after his arrest and be released into your custody.

> **TIP:** Children in custody must be informed of their Miranda rights before they are questioned.

> **Federal laws prohibit detaining a child for longer than 6 hours in an adult jail setting. Additionally, during that time the child must be kept in an area that is out of sight and sound of adult inmates.**

If my child is charged with a crime, will she remain in custody until sentencing? *Yes.* At the detention hearing, the judge can decide that your child must remain in custody until sentencing. Juveniles are held in juvenile hall during this period of time.

> **TIP:** Juveniles are generally released into their parents' custody. However, a juvenile who is charged with a felony, is a fugitive from another jurisdiction, or is a physical threat to himself or others usually remains in juvenile hall.

My child is still in custody and waiting for a detention hearing. What do I do to get her released? *You should file an application for a writ of habeas corpus requiring law enforcement officials to show why she is being detained without a hearing.* Although laws require detention hearings to be held within 48 to 72 hours, sometimes officials do not follow the law and it is necessary to seek intervention from the court.

My child was arrested and a probation officer contacted me. Why is a probation officer involved? *In the juvenile system, probation officers are used prior to, rather than after a conviction.* When a minor is arrested, the juvenile probation department initially handles the case. In most situations, the probation officers assigned to your child's case will either reprimand the child or direct him into a community service program.

My child is going into a detention hearing. Do I have a right to speak at the hearing? *No.* Unless the court permits you to speak, the judge generally hears only from the arresting officer or probation officer. Typically, you and the probation officer will have come to an agreement prior to the hearing. For example, you may decide that your child's crime is so serious he needs to be sent to a facility and the officer will relay your wishes to the court.

What is a fitness hearing? *In a fitness hearing, the juvenile judge determines if the child is "fit" for prosecution in a juvenile court or should be tried as an adult.* Laws generally require children to be at least 14 years old before they can be tried as an adult.

TIP: A child is unfit for juvenile court if she is a repeat offender, shows criminal sophistication, demonstrates an inability to be rehabilitated before reaching adulthood, and has previously been unsuccessful in the juvenile system.

What is a dispositional hearing? *The dispositional hearing is the "sentencing" phase of the process.* At the hearing, the judge decides where to send a child for detention and the length of the stay.

My child's probation officer has recommended "diversion" rather than sending the case to the court. What is diversion? "Diversion" means your child is diverted into a community service or rehabilitation program rather than sent to a detention facility.

When a juvenile is arrested, the juvenile probation or prosecutor's department makes a decision to dismiss the case, divert the child into a community program, or request the judge to intervene by holding a disposition hearing.

What is a consent decree? *A consent decree is the court document outlining the conditions of dismissing or diverting the case against your child.* Typically, the decree sets out curfews, requires regular attendance at counseling sessions and school, and directs the child to make financial restitution to victims.

My son was sent to detention. Am I required to pay the costs of his stay in the detention facility? *Yes.* Typically, there is a daily charge for stays in a detention facility. The parent has the legal responsibility to pay the charges, plus any fines that might have been assessed.

Can I have my child admitted to a juvenile detention center? *No.* Only a juvenile judge determines if a child will be sent to a detention facility. You cannot "commit" your child to a facility.

How do I get my child's juvenile records erased or expunged? You must file a petition with the court. It is recommended that you hire an attorney to handle this matter.

Will my child attend school while she is in a detention facility? *Yes.* The law requires that children receive an education during their detention. However, the school is on the premises of the center and your child will attend classes there rather than at her regular school.

My son is being tried in juvenile court. Does he have the right to an attorney? *Yes.* Your son has the right to consult with an attorney during the proceedings.

My daughter was expelled from school. Why is she being referred to juvenile court? Laws may require schools to refer children that have been expelled to juvenile court. The expulsion creates a situation where the child becomes a delinquent in need of supervision.

Who has access to juvenile records? Access is limited to the child's attorney, court personnel, law enforcement and persons to whom the child has been referred for treatment.

> **TIP:** A child whom the court determines did not commit a crime has the right to have any juvenile court records destroyed.

> **TIP:** Children who do not have a parent willing to act in their best interests during juvenile court proceedings have the right to have a guardian ad litem appointed by the court.

7 LANDLORD & TENANT

Landlords and tenants are persons who enter into an agreement to rent property, such as a house or apartment. The owner of the property is the "landlord," or "lessor." The person who rents the property is the "tenant," or "lessee." The "tenancy" is the period of months or years the property is leased. This chapter covers issues relating to residential property leases, rather than commercial property leases (for example, office building space), although many of the same principles apply.

The landlord and tenant each have duties and responsibilities toward each other as well as duties to the property. Some of the duties are set out in the rental agreement. For example, the amount of rent the tenant must pay is a duty included in the agreement. Other duties can be found in federal and states laws—such as prohibiting discrimination in renting properties. State laws may require landlords to make specific repairs. A wide range of contract provisions and legal regulations cover your obligations as both a landlord and tenant.

FINDING A TENANT

Unless your rental property is occupied, you are losing money on your investment. Additionally, vacant properties tend to fall into disrepair, making them even harder to rent. Successful landlords must find tenants who will comply with the lease agreement. The landlord who is diligent in screening applicants will have fewer problems with his or her tenants during the lease period.

Your goal as a landlord is to find a tenant that can comply with the lease terms—which includes paying the rent on time and in full. You can advertise for new tenants, but you may get applicants you do not want. Some avenues for finding a quality tenant without advertising include:

- talking to existing tenants or neighbors—often they know someone who is looking for a house or apartment to rent;
- working with rental agencies—these specialist agencies charge a fee to search for a tenant; if you need a tenant quickly, they can often save you valuable time; and

- searching the Internet for useful Web sites that put landlords in touch with suitable tenants. (See, for example, the National Tenant Register at **www.thelpa.com/lpa/index.html**.)

Traditional methods of advertising for potential tenants are less selective. These methods include:

- putting a "For Rent" sign in one of the windows or in front of the rental property;
- posting a notice outside a local store and on church or community center bulletin boards; and
- posting a notice at college and university housing offices—this can be a very good resource, particularly if your property is near a college, and is reasonably priced.

ADVERTISING

A well written advertisement can save you time and money in the long run. Be specific in your description of the premises and provide the amount of monthly rent required so only those who can afford it respond to the ad. If a security deposit and first and last month's rent are required, include that in your ad as well. By making clear exactly what you are offering and requiring, you stand a better chance of getting a suitable tenant and avoiding possible problems in the future. For example, if you state in your ad that references from previous landlords are required, you automatically exclude applicants who are unable to supply such references.

Discrimination in Advertising

Your advertisement should not and can not in any way be considered discriminatory. Attempting to exclude applicants through advertising on the basis of race, ethnicity, national origin, gender, religion or disability violates the Fair Housing Act. Local ordinances and regulations usually re-emphasize these restrictions and may even broaden them. For example, the city of San Francisco prohibits discrimination in housing based on sexual orientation.

> **TIP**: Age discrimination laws prohibit discriminating against people over 40 years old in housing. Including terms like "students," "recent graduates," "college-aged," etc. that tend to exclude older individuals violates the law. Of course, by posting a rental notice at a college or university, you are most likely to get student applicants.

APPLICATION

Nearly all landlords require prospective tenants to complete a rental application.

The application requires information about the applicant's:

- income
- credit
- employment
- rental history
- Social Security number
- references

The application should also contain details about the property (for example, 2 bedroom, 2 bath apartment) as well as statements concerning:

- the amount of the application fee, if any;

- the amount of the security deposit;
- length of the tenancy ;
- what notice is required for terminating the rental agreement; and
- the applicant's consent to a background and credit check.

Although the application form is not a substitute for the actual lease agreement, including such basic information helps the tenant understand the fundamental terms of the lease he or she may be signing later.

The rental application should be:

- filled out completely, including Social Security number, driver's license number, current employment, and emergency contacts; and
- signed by the person applying to live in the rental property. By signing the application, potential tenants are consenting to credit and background checks (if a statement regarding a credit check has been included on the application), verification of the information provided (calling employers, banks, prior landlord, etc.) and allowing references to be confirmed.

An application fee may be required to cover the landlord's cost for credit and background checks. This fee should be less than $100; it will not be refunded if the application is rejected or the applicant decides not to rent the property (you should make the applicant aware of this provision by either telling them or including it on the application).

Application deposits are becoming more common. This fee is an advance security deposit and shows that the applicant is serious about renting the property. If the applicant ends up renting the property, it is applied toward the security deposit.

> **TIP**: Ask questions of prospective tenants from a prepared list. It is important to ask each of the applicants the same questions to avoid accusations of discrimination. Do not ask questions about age, ethnicity, sexual orientation, disabilities or religion.

Can I rent to a minor? *No. Minors cannot enter into real estate contracts.* If you do rent to a minor, the minor has the right to "disaffirm" the lease agreement, making it void and unenforceable. A minor can occupy the premises; however, an adult must sign the lease agreement. For example, college students typically have an arrangement where the parent signs the lease and the student lives in the apartment.

Can I ask about religious affiliation or martial status on the rental application? No, if it applies to your rental property, the Fair Housing Act prohibits questions concerning race, color, national origin, religion, sex, handicap and/or familial status.

I got a bad recommendation on an applicant from a previous landlord. Do I have to disclose this to the person who applied? *No. However, if you discriminate by refusing to rent to this person based on a previous landlord's information, you are acting illegally.* For example, if the previous landlord told you that prospective tenant had children and you decided against renting to him or her, you are discriminating based on familial status.

I completed an application and paid an application fee. If I have not heard from the landlord, have I been rejected? *Probably. If more than a week has passed, you can assume you have been rejected.* Some laws give the landlord seven days to notify an applicant that he or she has been accepted or rejected.

Some laws do not require you to enter into the lease agreement if the landlord has failed to notify you of your application's acceptance within seven days of submission. If these laws apply to your state you will have the right to rent elsewhere. Although you are not entitled to a refund of your application fee, all security deposits must be returned to you since the landlord was late in his or her acceptance.

My application was approved but I am moving to another complex. Can the landlord keep the application fee? *If you were approved and did not sign the lease, the application may allow the landlord to keep the entire deposit.* Typically, the fee is non-refundable under any circumstances.

Even without a written provision in the application, if the landlord turned away a potential renter before you told him or her you had changed your mind, the landlord may have a right to keep the application fee as compensation for their loss of a renter.

I paid an application fee at an apartment complex before my application was approved and decided that same day to rent somewhere else. The landlord wwill not return the fee. What can I do? *Review the application carefully.* Most applications contain a provision that the fee is non-refundable if you change your mind, the application was rejected or the application was approved.

If it turns out that the landlord is improperly retaining the fee, and you cannot convince him or her to return the fee over the phone, you need to write a demand letter. The demand letter should state that you are entitled to the return of your application fee and you are demanding it be returned by a certain date or you will sue. If you are still unable to get the fee back, you can sue for it. However, the amount of the application fee may not be worth the effort of going to court.

CREDIT CHECK

Landlords now run credit checks on all prospective tenants. Credit reports are accessed through one of the three major consumer-reporting agencies (CRAs) listed below. Any tenant who is unsure about the state of their credit can contact one of the agencies and request a copy of their credit report. (Beginning September 1, 2005, consumers may obtain one free copy of their report each year.)

Equifax Credit Information Services, Inc
P.O. Box 740241
Atlanta, GA 30374
To order report: 1.800.685.1111
Web site: www.equifax.com

Experian (formerly TRW)/National Consumer Assistance Center
P.O. Box 2002
Allen, TX 75013
To order report: 1.888.397.3742
Web site: **www.experian.com**

Transunion/Consumer Disclosure Center
P.O. Box 1000
Chester, PA 19022
To order report: 1.800.888.4213
Web site: **www.transunion.com**

The credit report notes all late payments on credit cards, mortgages, and loans. Any judgments—including foreclosures and evictions—or bankruptcies are also listed on the report. If a prospective tenant has a record of late payments or other negative history, the landlord may choose not to rent to that person.

> **TIP**: Typically, the rental application includes a statement that, by signing the application, the prospective tenant consents to a credit check. If you do not your credit report accessed, tell the landlord and then cross out the provision in the application—but do not be surprised if your application is rejected..

> **TIP**: Every time your credit is checked, it is reflected on the report. These checks are called "hard inquires" and they typically lower your score because the CRA assumes you are applying for loans or credit cards and that your debt will increase. You can learn more about consumer's rights concerning credit reports at the U.S. Federal Trade Commission's (FTC) "Web site on Credit" at: **www.ftc.gov/bcp/conline/edcams/credit/index.html.**

Fair Credit Reporting Act

The Fair Credit Reporting Act (FCRA) is designed to protect the privacy of consumer report information and to guarantee that the information supplied by CRAs is as accurate as possible. The FCRA requires landlords who deny a lease based on information in the applicant's consumer report to provide the applicant with

an "adverse action notice." If you receive such a notice, you are entitled to a free credit report (in addition to the one you are entitled to once a year) from the CRA listed in the notice.

Questions about the Fair Credit Reporting Act can be answered by calling 1.877.FTC.HELP. Information is also available online at **www.ftc.gov**.

> **TIP**: If your application is rejected on the basis of a report from a reference-checking agency, you are entitled to a copy of the report under the FCRA. However, a reference verified by the landlord or their employee is not covered by the FCRA if your application is rejected. You are not entitled to a copy of their notes or other documents regarding the references they obtained.

Banking History

Banks are unlikely to discuss specific details of a tenant's account; however they will generally confirm whether the applicant has an account and if it is in good standing.

> **TIP**: If the applicant has written you a check for the application fee, you may call the bank, ask for the accounting department, tell them the account number and amount of the check, and ask if the check will clear.

Employment and Income

Landlords want and need to know whether a prospective tenant can pay the rent. The applicant's employer may be contacted to verify employment and salary.

> **TIP**: If you have filled out a rental application, let the office manager or human resources department at your job know they may receive a call from a potential landlord.

I filled out a rental application and, although I never authorized it, the apartment manager went ahead and pulled my credit report. Is this legal? *Yes. Under the Fair Credit Reporting Act your credit report can be viewed* *"in connection with a business transaction that is initiated by the consumer."* In other words, by filling out a rental application you have begun a transaction—the process of renting an apartment—and the landlord has the right to use a consumer reporting agency to examine your credit.

The landlord who does not have a written authorization could be violating the FCRA if an apartment was not actually available to rent. In that situation, the applicant can successfully argue that there was no "business transaction" since there was no apartment to rent at the time the consumer report was pulled.

The property manager wants a co-signor on my lease because of some negative history reported in my credit report. Does this mean I can get a copy of the credit report? *Yes. Requiring a co-signor on the lease because of your credit history is considered an "adverse action" and federal law requires that the property manager give you an "Adverse Action Notice."* The agency that provided the report listed in the notice must provide you with a free copy of your credit report.

> **TIP:** Other actions that are considered adverse—even though you were able to rent the apartment—include:
>
> - increasing the security deposit;
>
> - requiring first or last month's rent when it is not normally required; and
>
> - raising the rent (to dissuade you from renting).

My apartment lease is up for renewal. Can my landlord check my credit history without my permission? *Yes. Laws do not require a landlord to get permission, written or otherwise, to check an existing tenant's credit history.* Since you are currently living in one of their apartments, the FCRA considers you to be in a business transaction.

A landlord can also pull a consumer report on a tenant that owes a debt, without the tenant's authorization. For example, the tenant who is routinely late with rent, has damaged the apartment in excess of the security deposit or moved out with time left on the lease, owes a debt, and his or her credit history can be examined without authorization.

I pulled the credit history for a rental applicant and checked with previous landlords. The applicant's history showed some late payments, but I primarily denied the application based on his or her rental history. Is he or she entitled to an Adverse Action Notice? Yes. Although your decision not to rent to the applicant was not based on their credit history, since it was part of what you looked at in deciding whether to approve the application, you must provide a notice.

If my property manager uses a consumer reporting agency to verify rental applications, am I, as the landlord, still responsible for notifying applicants of an adverse action? *Yes. Although you are using a reference-checking agency, any information you receive from them based on a consumer report that results in your decision not to rent, increase a security deposit, etc. triggers an Adverse Action Notice.* You must comply with the FCRA although you did not actually view the credit report.

If the property manager did not use a consumer reporting agency, you are not required to provide an Adverse Action Notice. Your obligation to notify an applicant is triggered only when you use a report from a consumer-reporting agency to make your decision.

> **TIP:** If you are a landlord and do not want to be subject to FCRA requirements, you or your employees should verify the application on your own. Although the consumer-reporting agency provides information you cannot obtain, you can still verify employment, income, check criminal history, and talk to previous landlords about the prospective tenant.

I am a landlord. Can an applicant I did not rent to and failed to give an Adverse Action Notice sue me? *Yes. If you used a consumer-reporting agency to make your decision not to* *rent and failed to give an Adverse Action Notice you can be sued.* The FCRA allows the applicant to sue you in federal court for compensatory damages, punitive damages (if the violations are deliberate), and attorney's fees. If you simply made an isolated mistake and you normally send out Adverse Action Notices, you are not liable to the applicant and the lawsuit will be dismissed.

My company will not give out salary information over the phone. What can I do to show the landlord I am employed? *Provide a copy of your most recent paycheck to the landlord and tell him or her it is against company policy to disclose employment information over the phone.* If your company will provide you with a letter stating your salary and length of employment, present a copy to the landlord or have one faxed to them from your place of employment.

BACKGROUND CHECK

You may be asked to provide the name(s) and telephone number(s) of previous landlord(s). Either the landlord you are applying to or a reference-checking agency may contact previous landlords or other parties you list on the application in order to check your rental payment history and compliance with lease provisions.

Your criminal history is also a factor in your ability to rent. It is becoming more common for landlords to conduct background checks to determine if you have been arrested or convicted of a crime. If you do have a criminal record, advise the landlord at the time you complete the rental application. The landlord may be more sympathetic to your side of the story if he or she hears it before completing the background check.

I am in the process of a rental application and the landlord is requiring a $35 background check fee. Is this legal? *Yes. Laws allow landlords to charge prospective tenants for the cost of a background check.* Landlords are not permitted to make a profit on the fee, however.

Can a landlord perform a background check without my authorization? *Yes. Landlords do not need authorization if the information is*

public and available. For instance, any person can check court records to determine if you have been convicted of a crime, or involved in a civil lawsuit, such as a divorce or a bankruptcy.

A greater amount of information is available publicly then you might realize. For example, records of real estate owned by an applicant are public, as well as some business filings. The military may disclose an applicant's name, rank, salary, duty assignments, awards and duty status without consent. Driving records are not confidential and if the landlord has a driver's license number, he or she can obtain information from the state Department of Motor vehicles. School and medical records, however, are not released without your express written authorization.

Police records and court records are two different documents. Court records are public records and accessible. Police departments, however, typically only release records to the individual involved in the report. For example, informal and unauthorized requests for police records using the applicant's name will be denied. On the other hand, requests for calls made to a police department concerning a certain address (an applicant's former apartment, for example) are often approved.

DECIDING ON A TENANT

A landlord may or may not have some basic requirements when he or she decides whether to accept or reject a prospective tenant's application. Typically, landlords set aside applicants with poor references or a credit report that shows a pattern of late bill payments or previous evictions. Landlords are also wary of tenants who do not have a bank account and offer to pay cash, since this could be an indication of illegal activity.

Discrimination and the Fair Housing Act

It is illegal to discriminate against prospective tenants. The U.S. Department of Housing and Urban Development (HUD) enforces federal laws and regulations prohibiting discrimination in buying, selling and renting housing properties. The Fair Housing Act prohibits any kind of discrimination in renting based on race, ethnicity, national origin, gender, religion or disability.

If you own more than three rental units or use a leasing agent, you must comply with federal laws prohibiting discrimination in housing. Additionally, many cities have passed their own anti-discrimination ordinances with which you will have to comply. For example, in some locations, discrimination is prohibited on the basis of sexual orientation, although there is no such prohibition in federal civil rights laws.

> **TIP:** The HUD Web site at **www.hud.gov** has information on compliance with federal anti-discrimination laws for landlords, tenants, and prospective tenants who believe they have been a victim of discrimination.

Landlords cannot reject an applicant because there will be children under 18 years of age in the household. The Fair Housing Act requires that children under the age of 18 living with parents or legal custodians, pregnant women, and people with custody of children under the age of 18 may not be denied housing.

However, properties that meet the definition of "senior housing" can deny housing to families with children. That is because senior housing is exempt from age discrimination prohibitions.

These properties can also deny housing to people over 40 years of age who would normally be protected under age discrimination laws where the property:

- is occupied solely by persons who are 62 or older;
- houses at least one person who is 55 or older in at least 80 percent of the occupied units; and
- is specifically designed for and occupied by elderly persons under a federal, state or local government program.

> **TIP:** If you are a landlord, whether you are regularly renting properties or not, keep organized files on each applicant. If a complaint is ever filed against you, the agency investigating the claim will ask about your basis for rejecting an applicant. You must be able to show that the applicant was rejected for a non-discriminatory reason, such as a poor credit rating. Always avoid making personal remarks about any of your applicants in your notes.

My mother's large home has been divided into four separate apartments. Does she have to rent to anyone who applies? *No. As long as your mother continues to live in the house, she can refuse to rent to whomever she chooses.* The Fair Housing Act does not apply to owner-occupied buildings with four or less units.

I own several duplexes and have instructed my rental agents to give people of my religion a rent reduction. Am I discriminating? *Yes.* The Fair Housing Act prohibits a landlord from offering different rental terms or deals to prospective tenants based on their race, color, national origin, religion, sex, handicap and/or familial status.

My brother just got out of a drug rehabilitation treatment center and apartment managers do not want to rent to him. Is this illegal discrimination? *No.* The Fair Housing Act does not prohibit a landlord from refusing to rent to a tenant who he or she believes would pose a threat to other tenants because of illegal drug abuse or severe mental illness.

Can a landlord refuse to rent to a gay couple? *Yes. Although the answer is "no" if the rental property is in certain states and cities that prohibit discrimination in housing on the basis of sexual orientation.* Federal law and the Fair Housing Act do not protect against discrimination based on a tenant's sexual orientation.

Can a landlord refuse to rent to unmarried couple? *Yes.* Although the answer is "no" if the state or city where the property is located prohibits discrimination on the basis of marital status.

My husband has AIDS and the manager of an apartment complex we want to live in is reluctant to rent to us. Can the manager refuse to rent an apartment to us? *No. The Fair Housing Act prohibits discrimination in housing based on disability, (meaning those individuals with mental or physical impairments that substantially limit one or more major life activities).* Since AIDS affects the major life activities of your husband, he is considered disabled under the Fair Housing Act. Remind the apartment manager that your husband has the same status as a blind or deaf person and he or she cannot refuse to rent to you on the basis of his illness.

Can a landlord require that I prove I am a U.S. citizen before he or she rents to me? *Yes. The FHA does not prohibit discrimination based solely on a person's citizenship status.* For example, the landlord has a right to know if your visa (allowing you to study in the United States) is going to expire soon, which could result in you leaving before the end of the lease.

> The landlord requesting citizenship information from prospective tenants must request the information from all applicants. The landlord cannot discriminate by only requesting documentation from certain applicants.

I am a single mother with two small children. A landlord recently told me that the only vacant apartment had been rented, when in fact it was available. Have I been discriminated against? *Yes. The landlord violated the Fair Housing Act by claiming that the apartment in question had already been rented when it had not.* Making a false statement that housing is unavailable for viewing, rental or sale based on familial status is prohibited.

We have signed a lease for an apartment by the pool, but now the landlord wants to put us in a part of the complex where most of the families with children are living. Is this legal? *No. The Fair Housing Act prohibits landlords from providing alternative or different housing facilities or services to specific groups or individuals based their race, color, national origin, religion, sex, handicap and/or familial status.* Your landlord is violating the law by attempting to force you to live in a certain section of the complex because you have children.

> **TIP:** The landlord is also prohibited from requiring an extra security deposit or other fee because you have children.

Because of a job transfer, I need to rent my home for a year and I do not want to rent to anyone with children. Am I breaking any laws? *No. The Fair Housing Act does not apply to single-family home rentals where a real estate broker is not involved.* As long as you handle the transaction yourself, you can refuse to rent to families with children (or anyone else) without violating the Fair Housing Act.

I believe that I was discriminated against when I tried to rent an apartment. What is the procedure for making a complaint? *You have one year to notify HUD (Office of Housing and Urban Development) of the discriminatory action.* You can call HUD's hotline at (800) 669-9777 or make a complaint at their Web site, www.hud.gov/fairhousing.

You can also make a complaint by writing a letter to HUD that that includes:

- your name and address;

- the name and address of the person your complaint concerns;
- the address of the house or apartment you were trying to rent or buy;
- the date when this incident occurred; and
- a short description of what happened.

The letter should be mailed to the HUD offices at:

> Office of Fair Housing and Equal Opportunity
> Department of Housing and Urban Development Rm. 5204
> 451 Seventh Street SW
> Washington, DC 20410-2000

How will HUD handle my complaint?
After HUD has received your complaint, an investigator will contact the person who allegedly discriminated against you and request a response. Typically, HUD attempts to mediate the matter. However, if the landlord continues to deny the discrimination and you stick to your story, the issue will be set for a hearing. Attorneys for HUD "prosecute" the matter on behalf of the United States Government. The attorneys are not representing you personally, although you have the right to be present and get your own lawyer if you choose.

What do I "win" if the landlord is found to have discriminated against me? *If the hearing officers make a finding that discrimination occurred, you have the right to move into the housing you were initially denied.* The landlord could be required to pay a fine of up to $50,000 in extreme cases of discrimination.

LEASE AGREEMENTS AND POLICIES

The lease agreement is the contract between the tenant and the landlord that sets out the duties and rights of each party. For example, the tenant has the duty to pay the rent on time and the landlord has the right to enter the premises for repair. Typically, tenants renting units in apartment complexes sign a standard lease form used by landlords in that state. A condominium complex owner or homeowner who is leasing will probably use a different form. A private landlord may use his or her own form or the standard form.

Some states have adopted the Uniform Residential Landlord and Tenant Act (URLTA), which covers many issues in lease agreements, as well as tenant rights and landlord remedies in lease disputes. A lease agreement may incorporate URLTA's provisions. For example, if the lease agreement states that return of security deposits is governed by URLTA, the landlord must follow those requirements.

Lease agreements that are less than a year in length do not have to be written. An oral agreement between the landlord and tenant is binding in these circumstances. In this situation, state law, rather than a written agreement, covers the duties and responsibilities of the landlord and tenant. Oral lease agreements are not recommended.

> **TIP:** Always get a copy of the lease agreement after it is completed and signed by all the parties.

Do I need a written lease agreement if I am renting from a good friend? *It depends. Without a written agreement, certain laws covering the rental and leasing of property apply, rather than the terms you and your friend agreed to.* Many states have laws that favor the tenant. For example, without an agreement, the law provides that you are in a month-to-month lease. The advantage is that you can move out with a month's notice. The disadvantage is your friend only has to give you a month's notice to end the lease.

NEGOTIATING THE LEASE

In large properties where there are many rental units, a standard lease form is used and it is not negotiable. The property manager may have some discretion in lowering or raising the amount of a security deposit or even the amount of rent, but written provisions concerning notice, termination, late charges, eviction, etc. are not negotiable. These items may be negotiable with a private landlord who is using his or her own form.

If the landlord does not want to change the lease agreement in writing, but will agree to the changes orally, do not expect him or her to follow through. The landlord's promise to you is not binding. The written lease agreement contains all the agreements between you and the landlord—conversations and promises cannot change its provisions.

> **TIP:** If you and the landlord negotiate a change, whether it is deleting a provision or adding one, you must both initial the change at its location in the lease agreement.

Unconscionable Lease Terms

Like any contract, a lease agreement can contain almost any terms to which the parties agree. Leases are typically written to favor the landlord and not the tenant. The tenant has the option to reject the lease and find another rental property if he or she does not like the terms of the lease. However, some leases can go so far beyond simply favoring the landlord as to make them patently unfair to the tenant. If this happens the entire lease is considered void because of its "unconscionable" lease terms. An elaborately lopsided lease provision favoring one party (usually the landlord) is unconscionable, or unreasonable.

In order to better protect tenants from unconscionable provisions, the Uniform Residential Landlord and Tenant Act (URLTA) prohibits provisions in a lease agreement that require the tenant to:

- agree to waive or forego rights or remedies under the URLTA;
- authorize a person other than the landlord to obtain a judgment against the tenant on a dispute arising out of the rental agreement;
- agree to pay the landlord's attorneys fees in a dispute; and
- agree to limit the landlord's liability for injuries or damages the tenant suffers through the fault of the landlord.

EXAMPLE: In New York State, courts have found the following provisions in lease agreements to be unconscionable.

- A clause prohibiting the tenant from asserting a defense in any proceeding the landlord brings against him or her.
- A clause raising the rent if the tenant brings a legal action against the landlord.
- A "singles only" clause that would allow the tenant to be evicted if he or she married or had a girlfriend/boyfriend move in.
- A clause prohibiting animals without the landlord's written consent and allowing the landlord to evict the tenant, when the landlord assured the tenants an animal would be allowed in order to induce the tenant to sign the lease.

Many states have not adopted URLTA. However, recently courts are ruling in the renter's favor in lease disputes based on unconscionable terms.

If a court determines that certain provisions are unconscionable, the entire lease may be unenforceable, since the landlord has a superior position to the tenant because:

- renters are not familiar with the carefully drafted legal terms in lengthy printed lease forms;
- the lease is usually carefully drafted and designed solely for the landlord's protection;
- the terms of the printed contract are usually non-negotiable;
- in most cases, the tenant is not represented by an attorney;
- the landlord not only possesses superior knowledge but also offers a scarce commodity; and
- the landlord is often assisted by expert legal counsel.

Waiver of Lease Terms

A landlord cannot enforce a lease provision if he or she has previously chosen not to enforce it. The landlord's previous non-action "waives" the provision. For example, if there is a rule against pets in the lease agreement and the landlord knows that the tenant has a pet when the tenant renews the lease, the landlord cannot later insist that the tenant comply with the rule.

EXAMPLE: If your monthly rent has increased, but your landlord continues to accept the original amount (say by cashing your check), he or she cannot terminate the lease for your failure to pay rent. The landlord's continued acceptance of the original amount means he or she has waived the right to terminate the lease on the basis on non-payment.

Utilities

Whether or not the landlord pays the cost of utilities for your apartment depends on the rental situation. Large apartment complexes typically handle water and gas bills and pay for trash service, while the tenants pay their own electric bills. Some properties are rented as "all bills paid," meaning that the landlords pays water, gas and electricity. Optional services such as cable television, Internet lines and phone service are the responsibility of the tenant.

POLICIES

The landlord has the right to restrict the tenant's use of the premises. The typical lease agreement requires that the landlord must approve any modification, addition, or change to the property. Additionally, the landlord may prohibit "visual clutter" such as flags, signs, outdoor decorations, plants, lights and additional items that can be seen by others.

Lease agreements also contain provisions concerning the behavior of tenants and their visitors, the landlord's treatment of the tenant's premises, and the tenant's use of facilities.

There are usually a variety of rules concerning parking, mail, trash disposal and the like, which may not be incorporated directly in the lease, but will be set forth in a separate document, often referred to as "house rules." The rules are still part of the lease (by reference), although they are not written into it. You should always ask for a copy of the house rules so you can avoid breaking them, and thereby inadvertently violating your lease.

Tenants' Use of Facilities

Tenants typically have the right to use swimming pools, tennis courts, exercise rooms, and party rooms under the terms of the lease agreement. However, the landlord has the right to control the time and manner of the tenant's use. For example, swimming pools are usually open during certain hours of the day only. The tenant's use of exercise equipment may be limited to an hour or two per day to give other tenants the chance to use the equipment. Tenants can reserve party rooms upon request, but may have to put up a deposit and sign a cleaning agreement.

> **TIP:** You should always read your lease and house rules, and ask about any policies that visitors using the facilities on the rental property must follow. For example, although you may be allowed to have guests at the pool, your guests could be prohibited from using the exercise room and equipment. It is always best to know the guest policy so you can avoid violating it unnecessarily.

Visitors

A tenant is allowed to have visitors and guests on the premises. However, if the visitors violate lease provisions or property rules regarding behavior, they can be required to leave. Most landlords reserve the right to exclude anyone who, in the landlord's judgment, disturbs other residents.

Can the landlord limit the number of my visitors? *Yes. As the tenant, you may be limited to a certain number of guests in your apartment at a given time.* Even if there is no specific number limit, if so many guests show up that they are disturbing other tenants, or creating an unsafe situation (such as too many people on a porch), some or all of them can be asked to leave. Restrictions may also be in place regarding who can use the swimming pool, tennis courts, exercise room or other amenities.

The landlord says I have to be at the pool when my sister and her children come to swim. Do I have to follow this rule? *Yes. Tenants are responsible for their visitors and any actions taken by their visitors.* If tenants are required to accompany guests when they use the swimming pool, you must follow the rule or the landlord could prohibit your guests from using the pool entirely. Additionally, landlords commonly limit the number of visitors who can use the pool or tennis courts in order to give all of the tenants the chance to enjoy the facilities without overcrowding.

Prohibited and Limited Behavior

A number of tenant activities and behaviors are prohibited, and will violate the lease agreement—resulting in possible eviction. Criminal activity is always a violation and will lead to termination of the lease. A tenant's disruptive behavior or even offensive conduct may also be cause for termination.

Standard lease forms commonly used by landlords prohibit a variety of conduct, including:

- behaving in a loud or obnoxious manner;
- disturbing or threatening the rights, comfort, health and safety of other residents and property employees;
- engaging in or threatening violence;
- disrupting business operations;
- possessing or displaying a weapon in a common area;
- tampering with electric and cable connections;
- storing gas appliances in closets;
- heating the unit with a portable cooking stove;
- using windows for entry and exit;
- drug possession and manufacture; and
- making libelous or slanderous allegations against the property owner and employees.

Not all bad behavior will automatically result in termination of the lease agreement. Some "limitations on conduct" set out in the lease may require the tenant to:

- dispose of trash every week in the dumpster;
- use passageways for exit and entry only;
- use non-glass containers at the pool;
- not cook on balconies or patios; and
- not operate a business on the premises, such as a daycare.

While violating rules which merely limit behavior may not result in immediate termination of the lease, repeating lesser offenses will eventually lead to eviction.

All limits on tenant behavior will also apply to the tenants' visitors and guests. Unruly conduct by a visitor or guest will result in possible termination of the tenant host's rental agreement.

How do I know if there is a policy regarding tenants' behavior? *Landlords are usually up front about their expectations.* Check the "Prohibited Conduct" provision in your lease for a list of behavior that violates the lease. It is in the landlord's interest to maintain a peaceful property, and you may have been given a list of behavior that is prohibited when you signed the lease. Also, the landlord may have had you sign a separate agreement concerning tenant conduct.

Signs are usually posted at pools, tennis courts, in laundry rooms, and on parking lots that spell out the behavior that is expected from (or prohibited by) a tenant. For example, signs posted at swimming pools set out the hours it is open, the minimum age for swimmers, as well as any glassware and toys that are prohibited.

Can I be evicted for my "bad" behavior? *Absolutely. The lease agreement prohibits most types of offensive behavior and allows the landlord to terminate the lease if your behavior violates policies.* However, landlords typically give you a warning and allow you to correct the behavior before terminating the lease. For example, one loud party will probably not result in eviction, if you quieted down after receiving a complaint.

Do visitors have to follow the behavior policies? *Yes. The landlord has the right to exclude guests and visitors who are violating rules and policies.* Further, the tenant can be penalized if his or her guests do not follow those policies. For example, if the tenant's friend insists on parking in another tenant's assigned parking spot every time he or she visits, the visitor friend can be "banned" from the premises. Or if the tenant's visitor leaves the apartment intoxicated and threatens another resident, the landlord will treat the incident as if the tenant had made the threat. Under the lease agreement, the tenant could be evicted. However, the most likely outcome will probably be that the visitor gets banned from visiting the property.

The lease agreement may give the landlord and his or her employees the right to ask visitors for photo identification and find out if the visitor is a resident or guest. If the visitor refuses, he or she may not be allowed into the complex.

Can the landlord make new policies that are not in the lease agreement? *Yes. Standard lease forms allow landlords to put new rules into effect immediately if they are distributed and are applicable to all rental units.* For example, a rule that all decorations must be removed from doorways and porches must be obeyed as soon as you are informed. A notice or warning that the new policy will begin in one week, for example, is not required.

New rules and policies cannot require tenants to pay a new fee or additional amount of money. The tenant's financial obligations are set out in the lease agreement and cannot be modified while the lease agreement is in effect.

Tenant's Privacy

Although the tenant has a right to privacy, the landlord typically has a right of entry to make repairs to the premises under the lease agreement. Some state laws allow landlords to enter to make health and safety inspections for dangers that present a hazard to the building and other tenants. However, in nearly all cases, the tenant must have notice that the landlord plans to enter or has entered the premises.

In California, for example, a landlord must give the tenant 24 hours notice, and even then may only enter the premises:

- to make necessary or agreed-upon repairs;
- to show the apartment to prospective tenants, buyers, mortgage holders, repair persons and contractors;
- when the tenant has moved prior to the expiration of the rental term;
- when the landlord has a court order authorizing entry; and
- in case of an emergency that threatens injury or property damage if not corrected immediately.

> **TIP:** Your landlord may not disclose information about you to other persons—with the exception of law enforcement agencies—without your express consent. Check your lease and make sure you "opt out" of the landlord's disclosure policy, if he or she has one. You do not want to receive junk mail and telephone solicitation calls as a result of renting a place to live.

Am I entitled to notice by the landlord before he or she enters my apartment? *Yes. Lease agreements generally require you to be notified at least 24 hours in advance if the landlord and their employees are coming onto the premises.* However, if you have requested certain repairs, you will not receive a separate notice.

In an emergency, a landlord is not required to give notice to the tenant that he or she is entering the apartment. For example, burst pipes that are flooding the apartment unit are considered an emergency situation, and the landlord may enter without notifying the tenant.

I received a message on my answering machine that the landlord was coming in to my apartment to do a general inspection. If I do not call back and agree, can my landlord still enter my apartment? *Yes.* Unless you call and tell the landlord "no" it is assumed that you have no objection to an inspection of your apartment.

You have the right to reschedule inspections, exterminations, etc. for your convenience. However, you cannot unreasonably deny the landlord access. For example, after rescheduling extermination twice, the landlord can give you notice and enter. The landlord has the right to maintain a schedule of exterminations and protect the health and safety of other tenants by making sure all of the units are free from insects and vermin.

Does my landlord always have legal access to my apartment? *No.* Your landlord can only enter the premises at your invitation, in conjunction with his or her duty to maintain the premises (with proper notice), if you have requested repairs or if there is an emergency.

Can the landlord show my apartment to potential tenants? *Only with notice and only if the lease agreement allows it.* Check your lease agreement for a provision allowing the landlord to enter and show potential tenants your apartment. If there is no such provision, your landlord is violating your right to privacy by going into your apartment. Even if the lease agreement gives your landlord the right to show the apartment, you are still entitled to notice.

Pets

Landlords typically have strict pet policies. Standard lease forms usually prohibit animals of all kinds, including mammals, reptiles, birds, fish, rodents and insects. A tenant must get the landlord's consent in order to have a pet on the premises. An animal or pet deposit is almost always required.

Landlords can create as many restrictions as they want when allowing pets on the property, including:

- limiting the number of pets allowed;
- requiring proof of rabies and distemper vaccinations;
- requiring proof of registration with the local municipality;
- creating leash and collar rules;
- restricting the presence of animals in common areas; and
- requiring spaying and neutering of pets, and declawing of cats.

Exotic animals are routinely prohibited on properties where other pets might be allowed. For example, large snakes are usually not allowed under the lease agreement. Also, many landlords will prohibit "vicious," poisonous or venomous pets, and certain dog breeds from the property.

However, "service animals" or "assistance animals" are excepted by a variety of local and federal laws, and cannot be barred from the property. They may still have to abide by certain rules, such as having appropriate vaccinations and being registered with the municipality, but they cannot be barred.

Can my mother bring her dog when she comes to visit? *Unless your lease provides differently, animals are not allowed in the premises, including those belonging to visitors and guests.* You can always ask the landlord or property manager and perhaps they will consent but, if you allow the dog in your apartment without consent, you have violated the lease agreement.

My landlord allows pets, but has prohibited me from getting any more. If my landlord has already allowed me to have two cats in the premisis, do I have a right to a third? *No. Limits on the number of animals, particularly cats and dogs are common.* Although the landlord has consented to pets and you may have paid a pet deposit, if you bring another cat to live with you, you will be violating the lease.

I have a friend who has a service animal. Can he and his dog visit me at my apartment? *Yes. Disabled individuals with service animals cannot be prohibited from bringing their* *pet onto the premises.* The best practice in this situation is to notify the landlord of the circumstances so he or she will not think you are violating the lease if the animal is spotted on the property.

My neighbor has complained to the landlord that my dog barks during the day and disturbs him. Do I have to get rid of my dog? *Very likely. Just as you are prohibited from disturbing your neighbors, so is your dog.* The lease agreement typically requires that the landlord give you notice so you can correct the problem (for instance, find a new home for the dog).

> If the dog must go and you decide to move before the lease ends, you are breaking your lease and the landlord can demand all the rent due on the months that are left on the lease.

Vehicles and Parking

Lease agreements commonly allow landlords to regulate the "time, manner and place of parking all cars, trucks, motorcycles, bicycles, boats, trailers and recreational vehicles." The number of vehicles a tenant is allowed is usually limited. For example, the lease agreement may permit two vehicles per unit or one per occupant.

Depending on the type of property that is being rented, the tenant may or may not be assigned a specific parking space. Visitors may be allowed to park in their host's assigned space with that tenant's permission. If not, they may not park in another tenant's assigned space and generally must park in a "visitor's parking" area if it is provided.

> **TIP:** Many apartment complexes require parking permits and will tow cars left overnight without one. If you have guests who will be staying with you for a few days, find out if you can obtain a temporary parking permit for their vehicles.

The term "vehicles" may include boats, trailers, ATVs, motorcycles or recreational vehicles. The landlord can prohibit those types of vehicles entirely from the premises if he or she chooses.

However, landlords generally permit boats and recreational vehicles to be parked in a less obvious location, such as the back of a parking lot. Keeping a recreational vehicle on the premises may require that the tenant pay an additional fee.

A motorcycle falls into the same class as cars and trucks if that is the tenant's primary mode of transportation. In that situation, the motorcycle can be parked in the tenant's assigned parking space or anywhere on the property a car would be allowed.

CAUTION: Inoperable vehicles typically violate the lease agreement and will be towed by the landlord if not removed.

I own a vehicle that is not operable and it is parked in one of my assigned spaces. Can the landlord make me move it? *Yes.* If your vehicle has become an eyesore, you may be asked to move it to a less visible part of the parking lot, or remove it altogether from the property.

Standard lease agreements do not allow unauthorized vehicles on the premises. A tenant may or may not be entitled to notice before the vehicle is towed. A vehicle is unauthorized and illegally parked if it:

- is inoperable (for instance, a flat tire);
- is on jacks, blocks or has wheels missing;
- takes up more than one parking space;
- belongs to a resident no longer living on the premises;
- is parked in a handicapped space without the proper tags, etc.;
- blocks other vehicles from entering or exiting the premises;
- is parked in a fire lane;
- is parked in another tenant's assigned space;
- is parked on the grass or sidewalks;
- blocks garbage truck access to dumpsters; and
- does not have a current license, registration or inspection sticker.

Alterations

Some alterations are acceptable and the landlord does not have to be notified if they are made. For example, pictures, photographs and other decorative wall hangings are usually allowed under the lease.

An issue that has become common is the tenant who wants to put up a satellite dish on his or her patio or balcony. Many lease agreements do not allow radio, television or other antenna to be erected or installed on or anywhere within the premises without the landlord's consent. However, the Federal Communications Commission (FCC) prohibits landlords from restricting a tenant from installing certain satellite dishes and other types of antennas, as long as the tenant meets FCC limitations.

Is hanging artwork on the walls an alteration? *Not usually. Lease agreements generally allow artwork, photographs and other decorative items to be hung on the walls or in the grooves of wood paneling.* You must use small nails and make small nail holes; large anchor bolts or expansion bolts may be considered an alteration.

Can I hang curtains in my apartment without "altering" the premises? *Yes. Window coverings are allowed and a tenant may hang them.* If you hang curtains and have to install the curtain rods, let the landlord know and assure the landlord you will repair any holes in the wall. Also, the landlord may not even mind the curtain rods at all if you plan to leave them when you move out.

CAUTION: If you want to install blinds, notify the landlord since you will be tampering with the woodwork around the window or the window frame. The landlord may consider this a major alteration.

If I make alterations without the landlord's consent, what will happen? *Making major alterations without the landlord's consent violates the lease agreement and you could possibly be evicted.* A major alteration is anything from repainting a wall to changing out a light fixture to structural modifications. After the lease ends, the landlord may deduct the cost of removing the alterations from your security deposit.

I want to paint my apartment at my own expense. Is this a problem? *Painting is considered a major alteration.* Additionally, paint can stain and damage the premises if it is not applied correctly. If you paint without the landlord's express consent, you are violating the lease agreement.

EXAMPLE: A standard lease provision prohibits "painting, wallpapering, carpeting and electrical changes."

Can I be prevented from hanging the American flag outside my rental unit? *Yes. If no flags of any kind are permitted, you cannot fly an American flag (or any other flag).* You can display the flag inside the privacy of your home, but not in the common areas of the rental property.

> **Typically, a person has the right to fly the American flag or any other symbol as protected free speech. However, since the tenant is on private property (the landlord's), he or she has no free speech rights in common or open areas.**

Can I place a satellite dish on my porch? *Under the Federal Communications Commission (FCC) rules, a tenant has a limited right to install a satellite dish or receiving antenna on their leased premises.* The landlord is allowed to impose reasonable restrictions regarding installation. The most significant of these rules:

- limit the size of a satellite dish to one meter (39.37 inches);
- restrict installation to areas exclusively within the tenant's use (meaning the dish or antenna, as well as installation hardware, cannot extend beyond the tenant's porch, patio or balcony); and
- allow reasonable restrictions by the landlord to prevent damage to the property (during installation and removal).

However, the lease agreement can be more liberal than the minimum requirements of the FCC. If satellite dishes are not mentioned in the lease, you are probably allowed greater latitude in the size of the dish and method of installation.

> **TIP:** More detailed information from the FCC on tenant and landlord rights regarding satellite dishes is available at: **http://ftp.fcc.gov/cgb/ consumerfacts/consumerdish.html**.

Can I hang Christmas lights outside my apartment balcony? *Unless Christmas or holiday lights are prohibited, you may hang Christmas lights as long as they are not a nuisance to a neighbor.* For example, if they are very bright and blink throughout the night, you may be required to turn them off at a certain time.

> The landlord, through the lease agreement, can prohibit you from publicly displaying religious symbols. Although you have the freedom to practice your religion, you are only protected from government interference, not a private individual's restrictions (such as the landlord) on private property.

Can I have a grill on my balcony? *Yes. You may have a grill on your balcony, although it is very likely you cannot use it on the balcony.* Grilling near the exterior of the premises is a fire hazard and is probably prohibited in the lease. Even if the lease does not mention grills, city codes typically prohibit open fire cooking within 10 to 15 feet of an exterior wall of a residence.

ADDITIONAL TENANTS/ SUBSIDIZED TENANTS

CO-TENANTS AND ROOMMATES

Two or more people are allowed to rent one property. In that situation, the occupants are known as "co-tenants." Landlords typically require all persons, not related, living on the premises, to sign their own individual lease covering the property. Although it is a common belief, co-tenants do not have half the obligations under the lease; they are each responsible for all the obligations. For example, if the rent is $500 per month and one of the tenants moves out or fails to pay, the other tenant is liable for the entire $500. Likewise, if one tenant damages the property and does not reimburse the landlord for the repairs, the landlord can demand all the costs from the other tenant.

> One co-tenant cannot keep the other tenant from living on the premises if they get into a disagreement. They both have a right to occupy the premises under each of their leases.

Can someone move in with me that is not on the lease? *Not without the landlord's consent.* Having another person move in usually violates the lease agreement. The landlord will give you notice that the person must move out and, if you fail to correct the situation, you can be evicted.

Standard lease forms usually state that no one else may occupy the apartment other than the tenant and the occupants listed on the lease when it is signed. Additionally, you can be limited to how many days in a month an individual can stay over as a guest at your apartment.

I am looking for a roommate. How can I make sure the person will pay the rent, clean the apartment, and be fairly quiet? *A good screening tool is a questionnaire you can have potential roommates fill out.* It should include questions concerning your personal preferences and pet peeves, such as whether you object to overnight guests. Other topics to ask about include:

- The hours they keep on the weekdays and weekends. (For example: Do you sleep late on the weekends? When do you leave for work or school? How late do you stay up? How much time do you spend in the bathroom?)

- Furniture and other items (For example: What furniture are you going to bring with you to the apartment? Do you have computer/stereo equipment and how much room do you need to set it up?)

- Visitors (For example: Do you have family and friends that will come over often? Will you have out of town guests? Do you expect to have overnight guests? Do you plan to entertain?)

- Working from home (For example: Do you work from home and what is your schedule?)

- Cooking (For example: Do you cook frequently? Do you expect your food to be kept separately from mine?)

- Alcohol consumption (For example: What types of alcoholic beverages do you drink? How often do you drink?)

- Smoking (For example: Do you smoke? Do you have friends and family who smoke that will visit?)

- Pets (For example: Do you have a pet? Do you object to pets? Do you expect any visitors to bring pets with them?)

- Cleanliness (For example: How important is cleanliness to you? What types of cleaning are will you do—bathrooms, kitchen, vacuuming, etc?)

- Sharing and borrowing (For example: Do you normally borrow items such as clothes or jewelry? Do you expect to share dishes, appliances, etc? Do you expect to borrow my car?)

- Leisure activities (For example: Do you watch a lot of television? Do you like to have music on while you are in the apartment? Do you object to television? What types of music do you object to?)

- Rent obligations (For example: How do you plan to pay the rent—by mail, in person, to me, etc? What will you do if you cannot pay the rent?)

- Repairs (For example: Can you pay for repairs if the problem is your fault? Can you be home if a repairman needs to come into the apartment? Do you have a problem talking to the landlord about repairs or other items that need to be fixed?)

- Rental history (For example: Have you had a roommate before? When and where? Did you move out early? Were you able to pay the rent every month?)

- Criminal history (For example: Have you been arrested or convicted of a crime? When and where? Have you ever had to call the police? Has anyone ever complained to the police about you?)

Do I need to have a written agreement with my roommate if we are renting an apartment together and have both signed the lease?

You do not have to have one, but it is highly recommended. If your roommate moves out, you are still obligated to pay the rent—including your roommate's half—for the remainder of the lease.

My roommate and I want to enter into an agreement with each other concerning our obligations while we are renting an apartment together. What needs to be included? *Your agreement is called a "Co-Tenant Agreement" or "Roommate Agreement."*

The following items should be covered in the agreement:

- Term of the lease (attach a copy of the lease to the agreement)

- List move-in and move-out dates for each tenant

- State which roomate gets what bedroom, bathroom, closet, etc.

- Each roommate must provide advance notice to the other of guests (For example: Each tenant will notify the other 24-hours in advance of an overnight guest.)

- List of expenses to be paid by each tenant and the amount (For example: Rent—$400; Utilities—50% of monthly bill; Telephone—50% of monthly bill; Internet service—$30; Cable—$40, etc.)

- Reimbursement (For example: The tenant that pays the telephone/utility/cable bill will reimburse the other tenant's portion within 24-hours of payment.)

- Repairs (For example: Each tenant will pay the entire amount charged for any repairs for which he or she is responsible.)

- Late fees (For example: The tenant who causes the rent/utilities/telephone payment, etc. to be late must pay the entire late fee.)

- Amount of security deposit owed to landlord (For example: Each tenant will pay a proportionate share of the initial security deposit.)

- Insurance (For example: Each tenant agrees to take out renter's insurance covering their items in the apartment.)

- Sublet by permission only (For example: Each tenant agrees that he or she will obtain permission from the other to sublet.)

- Eviction rights (For example: Each tenant has the right to evict the other if a tenant is charged with a crime.)

- Damage (For example: The tenant who causes damage to the apartment will reimburse the other tenant if the security deposit is withheld.)

The agreement should be dated and signed by each roommate. Although the landlord has no obligation under the Roommate Agreement, offer a copy to him or her for their files.

SUBLETTING

A "sublease" or "sublet" is a transfer of the tenant's right to occupy the rented premises to someone else. The sublease can cover all or a part of the rental property, such as the second story only of a town home. The tenant remains obligated under the lease agreement for rent if the sublessee fails to pay. Under a sublease, the tenant has the right to reoccupy the premises, taking it back from the person to whom he or she subleased. For example, the tenant with a six month lease who must leave the country for four months can sublease his or her apartment to a friend (now called the "sublessee") while he or she is gone. If the tenant returns before he expected, he can retake the premises and require his friend to move out.

An "assignment" is similar to a sublease. However, in the example above, if the tenant assigned his or her lease to a friend, the tenant cannot retake the premises. The lease assignment results in the friend stepping in the shoes of the original tenant. The friend is now the tenant under the terms of the original lease.

Subleases and assignments are commonly prohibited in a lease agreement. Standard lease forms usually allow subletting only when the landlord agrees in writing. However, a tenant does have a right to sublease or assign his or her lease, if there is nothing in the lease agreement or a law that prohibits it. Generally, laws require the prior consent of the landlord if the tenant wants to assign or sublet his or her lease.

> **TIP:** If you sublease, the security deposit you made may be credited to the sublessee, and you will not receive a refund until the original lease agreement ends. To protect yourself in case of damage to the apartment, collect a security deposit from the sublessee in the same amount as the one you paid to the landlord. When you get your security deposit back from the landlord, you can refund the one you took from the sublessee.

Can I sublet my apartment? *Unless your lease agreement prohibits subleasing, the law allows you to sublet your apartment.* However, you cannot lease to a person that you know will not comply with the terms of the lease.

What reasons do I need to sublet my apartment? *You do not need a reason to sublease.* Typically, a tenant subleases because of an extended vacation, job relocation, and marriage or family obligations.

If I sublet, do I have to notify the landlord? *Probably.* Since the landlord's consent is usually required (under the lease agreement and by law) before a tenant can sublease, you would likely be violating the lease by subletting without telling the landlord and getting his or her consent.

CAUTION: Check the rental laws in your state. Many states have laws prohibiting a sublease without the landlord's consent.

The act of subletting your apartment in violation of the lease agreement does not in and of itself terminate the agreement. Although subletting without notifying the landlord and getting his or her consent is probably a default under the terms of the lease, the landlord may or may not decide to terminate the lease and evict you (and the sublessee). For example, standard lease forms allow the landlord to "end the tenant's right to occupancy" on 24 hours notice for any default. After notice from the landlord, you would have 24 hours to remove the sublessee and be back in compliance with the lease.

Does the landlord have to consent to a sublease if I find a reputable person to move in and sublet my apartment? *Not really. If the lease agreement and the law prohibit subletting without the landlord's consent, he or she does not have to consent to the sublease.* And unless a clause in the lease states that the landlord may not withhold his or her consent unreasonably, you should probably assume that the landlord is not even required to be reasonable in making his or her decision. The landlord can refuse for any reason or no reason at all.

A few state laws may require the landlord to be reasonable in giving his or her consent to a residential sublease. New York law, for example, states that the landlord's "consent shall not be unreasonably withheld." In these states, the landlord must consent to a sublease to a reputable person of the tenant's same character.

Commercial leases are somewhat different, often requiring that the landlord be reasonable in granting consent to a sublease.

My landlord has consented to the subleasing of my apartment. Can I sublease my apartment for the rest of the lease term?
Yes. You can sublease if you have no intention of returning to the premises. However, you are ultimately responsible for complying with the lease agreement provisions regarding termination. You must notify the landlord, in writing, 30 days before it expires that you will not be renewing the lease. The sublessee and the landlord can make their own agreement to a new lease after your original lease terminates; you have no involvement in the new lease agreement.

Who pays the rent in a sublease?
The original tenant must continue to pay the rent. The tenant collects the money for rent from the sublessee and makes the rental payment.

In some cases, the landlord may agree to accept the rent from the sublessee directly. If the landlord is a party to the sublease, he or she can agree to accept rent from the sublessee, without letting the original tenant out of his or her responsibility to pay the rent under the original lease. However, the original tenant could then argue that the landlord's acceptance of rent from the sublessee means the original tenant is not responsible for the rent any longer. To avoid any confusion, contractual responsibilities of the parties should be clarified before the sublessee moves in.

TIP: If you sublease, plan on collecting the rent and paying the landlord yourself. You and the sublessee should have a written agreement as to when and where the sublessee will pay. Have the sublessee agree to pay you seven days before the rent is due. The extra time will give you the opportunity to resolve any rent issues that might arise between you and your sublessee.

If I sublet, will my furniture and other possessions stay in the apartment?
Quite often, yes. Part of the reason a sublease is attractive to a tenant is that he or she does not have to actually move any possessions while gone. Your sublet agreement should include a provision requiring the sublessee to care for and maintain your furnishings.

Is a written agreement required if I sublease my apartment?
There is no requirement for a written sublease agreement. However, without one you cannot enforce the sublease. For example, the person to whom you subleased can move out before the agreed upon date.

A written sublease protects both of the parties. You have a written agreement from the sublessee that he or she will pay the rent on time and comply with other provisions of the original lease, and the sublessee has proof of his or her right to occupy the premises for the length of the sublet agreement.

A sublet agreement should include:

1. the date;
2. the name each of the parties;
3. the address of the premises to be subleased;
4. the date the sublease begins;
5. the date the sublease ends;
6. the amount of the rent;
7. the date the rent must be paid by the sublessee to the tenant or to the landlord if he or she has agreed to accept payment;
8. the form of rent accepted (cash only, for example);
9. the amount of the security deposit the sublessee must pay and the conditions for its return (for example, you will return the security deposit when the landlord refunds the tenant's original security deposit);
10. a statement that sublessee must care for and maintain furnishings and other items left in the apartment;
11. a statement that sublessee is responsible for damage to tenant's furnishing, etc. that are left in the apartment;
12. the replacement cost or the amount sublessee owes for damage to tenant's furnishings, etc.;

13. the amount of tenant's original security deposit; sublessee will be responsible for any portion not returned to tenant;

14. the signature of both of the parties; and

15. the signature of the landlord, if his or her consent is required or he or she is a party to the sublease.

The agreement does not have to be lengthy. The items listed above can be covered in three or four paragraphs.

> **TIP:** Your landlord may have to approve the sublet agreement under the terms of the lease agreement. If this is the case, show the sublet agreement to him or her before you go to the trouble of having the sublessee sign it.

Do I still have any responsibilities once I sublet? *Yes. Not only are you obligated to make sure the rent is paid, you are ultimately responsible for any damage to the premises while they are being sublet. For example, if the person to whom you sublet y*our apartment breaks the glass in a patio door, you are liable for the landlord's repair costs.

I am leasing a house. If I take in a boarder or roomer, am I subletting? *No. You are not putting your boarder in possession of the entire rental premises.* He or she only has the right to occupy a room. The landlord may argue that the tenant has violated the lease agreement's prohibition against subletting by taking in a boarder. However, courts have held that an occupant is not a tenant and there is no violation of the lease agreement.

SUBSIDIZED HOUSING

The Department of Housing and Urban Development (HUD) subsidizes or pays a portion of the housing costs for low-income families and individuals. Federal subsidized housing, known as the Section 8 Program, was passed by Congress in 1974. The program allowed federal housing funds to be used for the construction of new low-income housing, rehabilitation of older low-income housing, or to subsidize rents in existing housing.

Under the Section 8 programs, either the housing complex is paid a "tenant based subsidy" for making units with lower rent available, or HUD provides a subsidy directly to a family that then selects their own rental unit from the private market.

Through HUD, the federal government pays up to 70% of the rent for households living in subsidized housing. The renter in a subsidized housing development typically pays rent equal to 30% of their income, after deductions.

No person or household is entitled to housing. Subsidized housing is limited and is occupied as it becomes available. To qualify for subsidized housing, a person must be below a set income limit, which varies by household size and location. Since only a limited number of subsidized units are available, after a qualified person applies he or she is put on a waiting list until there is a vacancy.

What is Section 8 housing? *Section 8 housing is low-income housing. However, there are two very different programs.* One Section 8 program distributes rental vouchers to households that cover a portion of their rent. The family gets to choose where it wants to live and use the voucher to pay for part of the rent.

The second Section 8 program concerns the housing development itself. The entire development is Section 8 housing and any person or family qualified to live there pays a reduced rent. They do not receive a voucher. Instead, federal funds are paid to the housing development to cover the portion of the rent the occupants do not pay.

Can a Section 8 housing development reject a qualified applicant? *Yes. Applicants with a history of drug use and drug-related criminal activity can be rejected.* Also, applicants with a poor credit rating do not have to be allowed to rent. A prospective tenant with no credit history cannot be rejected on that basis.

An applicant can never be rejected on the basis of race, color, religion, sex, familial status, national origin, disability and age. A single parent household or a family receiving welfare benefits cannot be rejected merely for their status.

Other than low-income families, is anyone else entitled to receive Section 8 rental vouchers? *Yes.* Elderly and disabled individuals can obtain vouchers so that they may rent decent housing.

How do you apply for a Section 8 housing voucher? *Applications are taken through the local housing authority.* However, funds are limited, there is a long waiting list, and it may be several years before an application is approved.

Does a private landlord have to rent to a tenant with a Section 8 voucher? *No.* Only landlords who participate in the program (including companies that own and operate apartment complexes) are required to take tenants with vouchers.

Can a landlord evict a Section 8 tenant? *Yes, for "good cause." Good cause includes failure to pay the rent, cr*iminal activity and repeated behavior that seriously affects the health and welfare of other tenants.

Section 8 tenants have certain rights if a landlord attempts to evict them. The tenant can contest the notice of eviction by requesting a hearing with the local housing authority.

> A landlord cannot prohibit a Section 8 tenant from keeping a pet. However, he or she can require a pet deposit and exclude "dangerous" animals from the property.

MOVING IN

INSPECTIONS

An inspection is a written record of the condition of the property and its contents (refrigerator, oven, furnishings) at the beginning of the tenancy or rental period. Most states have laws that require landlords to inspect the premises before renting it out—to insure that they are in good condition and habitable.

Landlord's Pre-Lease Inspection

Before the tenant moves in, a landlord should:

- check that all appliances and fixtures are in good working order;
- exterminate the premises to eliminate problems with rodents or insects;
- thoroughly clean the rooms, paying particular attention to the bathroom(s) and kitchen;
- repaint walls to clean and freshen the property;
- clean carpets; and
- re-key all the locks.

Tenant's Pre-Lease Inspection

Typically, at the time you sign a lease, the landlord or property manager will walk through the premises with you so you can see the condition of the property. If you discover any problems, tell the landlord right away and make sure it is noted on the lease. For example, the landlord may not have opened a closet door during his or her pre-lease inspection and failed to discover the door was off the hinges. If you try to open the closet door during your inspection and find out it is broken, you must inform the landlord immediately. If you do not, he or she might believe you are responsible for the damage and charge you for the repairs after you move in.

As you examine the premises with the landlord, he or she may be checking off items on a form. Typically, the landlord is noting which items are in the apartment and their condition. Again, if you believe something is not in good condition, immediately tell the landlord so it can be noted on the inspection form.

Check the inspection form for accuracy; it will be matched against another inspection form the landlord completes when you move out. The items usually covered in the form include:

- the decorative condition of the interior—carpets, curtains, fixtures and fittings, walls, and blinds;
- the condition of the furniture (if the premises are to be rented "furnished");
- the condition of floor, ceilings and doors;
- the condition of appliances; and
- the condition of any gardens or decks.

The property manager says the apartment I plan to rent is not available for inspection before I sign the lease and move in. I have looked at the model apartment—is this an adequate inspection? *No. The model apartment is not the apartment you are renting. In this situation, once you sign the lease, you will be obligated to pay rent on an apartment you have not seen or inspected.* Without an inspection, any problems that arise after you move in could be attributed to you rather than the previous residents. Tell the property manager you want to rent but will only sign the lease if the two of you can inspect the apartment first.

The property manager and I inspected my apartment, but then stated that he or she does not have time to let me walk through the entire complex and inspect the outside. Should I sign the lease anyway? *No. You should be able to walk through the entire property and inspect all areas to which residents have access.* For example, you want to make sure the weight room that is advertised is a working weight room in good condition. Other common areas to inspect include tennis courts, pools, party rooms, the mailbox area, parking areas and dumpsters. If the outside of the complex is not well maintained, it is a good bet that your apartment will also be kept in poor repair.

MOVE-IN DEPOSITS AND ADVANCES

It is the rare landlord that does not require a tenant provide some amount of money for a security deposit to insure the tenant does not damage the property. Additionally, a landlord may ask for "first and last month's rent." Both amounts are due at the time the tenant signs the lease agreement.

Advance Rent

Landlords usually require some amount of rent in advance for several reasons. For example, the tenant who pays advance rent will not suddenly change his or her mind about moving in and then leave the landlord with a vacant apartment. Additionally, advance rent keeps the tenant from living rent-free for a month if he or she decides to move out after 30 days—the landlord has a payment for the first month of occupation. Lastly, advance rentals are a large out-of-pocket expense to a tenant; the tenant who can afford to pay is probably going to be a tenant that does not break the lease and pays his or her rent on time.

The requirement for advance rent is part of the lease agreement. At the end of the lease, the advance payments are returned to the tenant or applied to the last month's rent. If the tenant breaks the lease, the agreement typically allows the landlord to keep the advance rent money.

The advance rent my landlord required was a very large amount of money. Can I require him or her to put it in an interest bearing account? *That depends on whether state or local law requires it.* Generally, a landlord must keep advance rentals and security deposits in a separate non-interest bearing account.

Is there a limit to how much advance rent a landlord can require? *Some laws limit the amount to a certain percentage of one month's* *rent.* For instance, a law may prohibit the landlord from collecting more than 150% of a month's rent as an advance rental payment.

Security Deposits

The difference between rent and a security deposit is that the landlord keeps rent and returns security deposits. The difference is important because laws require the landlord to handle security deposits in a certain manner.

Landlords typically require tenants to pay a security deposit to insure that the tenant will comply with certain provisions of the lease concerning damage to the premises and clean-up at the end of the lease. If the tenant complies, the deposit must be returned at the end of the lease.

A deposit that can be withheld for late rent or non-payment of rent is considered to not be just a security deposit. In such situations, the security deposit is also advance rent, and the landlord does not have to return the money if the lease is broken.

> **TIP:** When you sign the lease, ask the landlord what he or she considers to be "normal wear and tear." If the landlord cannot give you some examples, he or she may be the type of landlord who tries to withhold your security deposit even though the premises was not actually damaged. You might want to consider renting from a place where the landlord has a better understanding of the concept of "normal wear and tear."

Why do I have to pay a security deposit?

Landlords commonly require security deposits to insure that the tenant complies with certain terms in the lease agreement. For example, if, under the lease agreement, the tenant is required to clean out all appliances before moving out, and does not, the landlord can deduct the cost of hiring someone to clean from the security deposit.

> **TIP:** When you pay your security deposit, get a receipt or have the landlord note the amount paid on the original lease and on your copy. Standard lease forms have a blank for the landlord to fill in the amount of the security deposit.

Is there a maximum amount a landlord can demand for a security deposit?

Some states have laws setting a limit on the amount of security deposits, while others have no limit. As an example, California law requires security deposits to equal no more than 2 months rent on unfurnished rentals.

But remember, security deposits are different from advance rent. So although the California law has a limit on security deposits, it permits a landlord to demand six months rent in advance where a lease is six months or longer.

What happens to the money I paid as a security deposit?

Depending on the law in your state;

- there may be no requirements on the landlord;
- the landlord may be required to put security deposits in an escrow account; and/or
- the law can direct the landlord to place security deposits in an interest bearing account for the benefit of the tenant.

Can I be required to pay a non-refundable cleaning fee when I sign a lease?

Yes. In addition to a security deposit, the landlord may require a non-refundable cleaning fee. The amount is usually less than $100.

Even if you make a non-refundable cleaning fee, the landlord can still deduct expenses for "special" cleaning from your security deposit at the end of the lease. Special cleaning is beyond that needed for normal wear and tear. For example, if you were a heavy smoker in a furnished apartment, the upholstery and drapes may require special cleaning to remove the odor.

Pet Deposits and Fees

Most landlords are not fond of cats, dogs and other animals living in their rental properties. You may be required to pay quite a large deposit in order to have your pet on the premises. A $500 pet deposit, per pet, is not unusual. The deposit assures the landlord that he or she will be able to cover the cost of cleaning and repairing any damage the pet inflicts on the property. Typically, some portion of the deposit will be refunded to the tenant if the pet did not damage the premises. The lease agreement may set out an amount that will not be refunded, in order to cover the expense of shampooing rugs and ensuring any trace of fleas are removed from the property.

In addition to a "pet security deposit," the landlord may add an additional amount to the pet owner's monthly rent. This amount does not have to be applied toward cleaning costs or repairing any damage attributed to the pet. It is simply an added charge to the tenant, assessed for the pleasure of keeping a pet on the premises. Alternatively, a lump sum "pet fee" may be imposed in place of an increased rent amount.

Is there a limit to the amount a landlord can require for a pet deposit? *No. Generally, pet deposits (if pets are allowed) are at the discretion of the landlord.* Obviously, an exorbitant deposit will keep away pet-owners, and some landlords keep the deposit high for this very reason. You can attempt to negotiate a lower deposit. Also, it might help to provide references from a former landlord concerning your pet's behavior.

Laws in some states place a limit on the total amount of all advance fees and deposits that a landlord can collect for a pet deposit. For example, California law limits all fees and deposits, including pet deposits, to 2 month's rent in an unfurnished apartment.

> **A service animal must be allowed to reside with the disabled tenant; however, the pet deposit can remain the same for the disabled tenant as for a non-disabled tenant. However, if there is a "no pet" policy, then the pet deposit should be nominal since the law requires the landlord to accept the service animal.**

Is my pet deposit refundable? *Although the term "deposit" indicates that the amount paid may be refundable, some landlords retain the pet deposit at the end of the lease.* Before you sign your lease, ask the landlord if he or she treats the pet deposit as a security deposit (with amounts subtracted for damage) or a fee. If the landlord says all or part of the pet deposit is refundable at the end of the lease term, add that provision to the lease if it is not already included.

My landlord is charging me a pet deposit, but he or she also wants to add $25 to the monthly rent for "cleaning" since I have a cat. Is this legal? *Yes. The landlord can charge the amount of rent he or she believes is fair.* You always have the option of not signing the lease and renting somewhere else.

> **TIP:** If you do not keep the cat for the full length of the lease, you are still obligated to pay the extra $25 per month under the lease terms. Ask the landlord to include a provision that the extra amount will be waived if the cat is no longer living with you.

My roommate has a dog and paid the pet deposit that our landlord required. If the dog damages the apartment so that repair costs exceed the pet deposit, will part of my security deposit be kept? *Yes. Although the dog is your roommate's, you are jointly responsible for all damage to the apartment.* You need to come to an agreement with your roommate where he or she will reimburse you for any damage caused by his or her pet that is withheld from your security deposit. Alternatively, you can ask your roommate to pay you a pet deposit which you will return once you get your security deposit back.

RENT

The amount of money a tenant pays on a regular schedule to his landlord is the rent. The rent is the tenant's cost of living in the leased premises. Typically, rent is paid every month for a specified number of months according to the lease agreement. Unless both the landlord and tenant agree to a different amount, the rent does not change during the term of the lease agreement. At the end of the lease, the rent is again negotiable and the tenant can ask for a decrease. Of course, the landlord is under no obligation to decrease or change the rental amount and, in fact, he or she has the right to increase the rent when the lease ends.

TENANT'S DUTY TO PAY RENT

The lease agreement sets out the tenant's obligation to pay rent. Under the lease agreement, the tenant must pay the rent by a certain date. Typically, the lease requires that the landlord have the rent by the 1st or 15th of each month. If the payment of rent is late, there is usually a late fee charged. The late fee can be a set amount, such as $25, a daily fee or a percentage of the monthly rent.

When is the rent due? *On time.* Depending on your lease it could be any day of the month; however, if it is the first of the month, your landlord must have it in hand on or before that day. Check your lease carefully; the rent may be due by a certain time as well. If you have forgotten to pay the rent or get stuck at work and the rent was due by 6 p.m., it will be late if you pay it at 7 p.m.

What happens if I pay the rent late? *You will probably owe a late fee.* Leases commonly permit landlords to charge tenants a fee for failing to pay the rent on the day it is due. The fee is either a set amount or a percentage of the rent. Check your lease for a provision entitled "Late Charges" or "Late Fees" to find out what you will be charged for a late rental payment.

Late charges can be assessed on a daily basis, such as $25 for every day you are late—this can add up quickly. If the rent is due Friday, and you fail to pay on time, you may be stuck with 2 days worth of late fees if the management office is closed over the weekend.

> **TIP:** If you are constantly late paying your rent, even a day or two, your lease may not be renewed and you will suffer the inconvenience of having to move. Mark the date rent is due on every month of your calendar. You can also put the date into your e-mail system or electronic organizer. If you do not think you can keep up with the rent due dates, write out all the checks in advance and keep them in a prominent place so you can grab that month's rent and drop it by the management office on your way into or out of the property.

> **TIP:** If you have been a good tenant and have previously paid your rent on time, be apologetic if you are late and ask the property manager if he or she will waive the fee.

If I put my rent in the mail on the day it is due, has it been paid on time? *No.* Your lease almost certainly requires rent to be delivered to the landlord or property manager on or before the due date.

Do I have to take my rent payment to the landlord or management office? *You can typically mail your rent check or place it in a receptacle designated for rent in the management office.* However, if your lease agreement sets out a specific process for paying rent, you must follow it. For example, if you are renting from a private individual, he or she may require you to leave the check at a designated office and get a receipt from the receptionist. Taking your rent in person to the management office helps establish a relationship between you and the property manager that may be to your advantage in the long run.

When I hand over my rent to the landlord, am I paying last months or next month's rent? *You are paying next month's rent.* The tenant pays at the beginning of the rental period. This is why the landlord requires advance rent when you sign the lease agreement.

CAUTON: Your rent is "payable without demand." In other words, the landlord is not required to notify you that the rent is due—it is up to the tenant to pay promptly.

I have signed a lease but cannot move in for a month. Do I still owe rent for the first month even if I am not there? *Yes. If your delay is not the landlord's fault, you are required to pay the rent due under the lease.* This situation is no different from one where you left for a month on a vacation; you would have to pay rent for that month as well.

If you are unable to move in because the landlord is remodeling or the last tenant has not moved out, the rent is usually "abated" for every day of the delay. For example, if construction in your

$600 a month apartment has kept you from moving in for five days, you may deduct $100 from that month's rent ($20 per day x 5 days).

You may be able to terminate the lease entirely because of the landlord's delay. If you cannot wait until the apartment is ready, the lease typically allows you to terminate it and find another place to live. Read your lease carefully if you receive notification from the landlord that your move-in date is being delayed.

What forms of payment are accepted for rent?
Personal checks are the most common way that rent is paid, but you can also pay in cash, a cashier's check or money order. Some landlords also accept debit cards and credit cards.

A landlord can refuse to take personal checks. The landlord can and will charge a fee if the check is returned unpaid for non-sufficient funds (NSF fee). The NSF fee is usually noted in the lease agreement.

> **TIP:** Try to pay your rent in person and get a receipt for each month's payment. You will get an opportunity to know the property manager and develop a rapport; he or she may then be more approachable if you have a problem.

Can I be evicted for paying my rent a few days late every month?
Not if the landlord keeps accepting your rental payments. However, if you have always paid late but refuse to pay a late fee, the landlord can try to evict you for non-payment of those fees.

I was notified that the locks are being changed on my apartment. Can the landlord lock me out because I did not pay my rent on time?
Yes. Most states have enacted laws that allow landlords to lock-out tenants for late payment of rent after the tenant has been notified. If you do not want to be locked out, you must bring your current rent plus pay any late fees.

A lock-out does not mean that you cannot get back into your apartment. You must be given access to a key 24 hours a day.

Is there a limit on rent amounts?
Only in cases where rent is stabilized or controlled. Otherwise, landlords rent at the highest amount they are able to obtain. In locations without adequate housing and no rent controls, rents may be very high.

Can rent be increased while I am renting?
During the period of time that the lease agreement is in effect, the rent amount cannot change.

When I move out, can I apply my security deposit to the last month's rent?
No. You continue to owe rent until the lease is terminated. The landlord is holding your security deposit to insure you will comply with certain terms of the lease, such as giving notice and leaving the premises in good condition. If the deposit is used in place of the rent, then the landlord is left without a security deposit and has no way to cover the cost of repairing your damage, if any, to the property.

Can someone else pay my rent?
Yes. Someone else can pay as long as the landlord accepts the payment. For example, if your son is paying your rent, the landlord can accept his check for that month's rent payment.

When the landlord accepts a rental payment from someone else for the month, you do not owe for that month. However, you are still obligated to pay the rent on the remaining months of the lease. If your son, from the example above, pays the June rent, the landlord still looks to you for the July payment. The landlord does not have to wait for your son to make the payment; he or she can and will demand the July rent from you. Additionally, if the rent is late, you will be charged late fees—no matter who paid the rent late.

Withholding the Rent

Under some circumstances a tenant may withhold the rent. However, this option is not advised unless the tenant has talked to an attorney. Some laws allow "rent strikes," permitting the tenant to withhold rent as long as the landlord is not meeting the minimum standards under city housing codes. The landlord must be notified of the unsafe and unhealthy conditions-- and refuse to make the repairs before a tenant can withhold the rent or go on a rent strike.

In other states, laws prohibit the tenant from withholding rent to force repairs. Withholding rent will, at a minimum, cause the tenant to incur a late fee and may induce the landlord to begin eviction proceedings.

LANDLORD'S REMEDIES FOR NON-PAYMENT OF RENT

Although a landlord can evict a tenant for failing to pay the rent, eviction is an extreme option. The landlord has other remedies available that are less costly and contentious to convince the tenant to pay rent.

Late fees

The tenant is commonly charged for paying rent late. The late fee must be included in the lease agreement or the landlord cannot demand it. Generally, the late fee is a daily charge or a percentage of the rent amount.

> **TIP:** If the management office is not open, you will still be charged a fee for every day you are late, even if it is not your fault that you are unable to deliver the rent payment.

Demand in advance

Leases typically allow the landlord to accelerate the rent when the tenant is in default. Failure to pay rent is a default – a provision of the lease has been broken. The landlord now has the right to demand all the rent due for the remainder of the lease. If you have a $500 per month apartment and fail to pay the rent on time with 4 months left on the lease, the landlord can demand $2,000.

Lockout

Landlords may change the locks on the tenant's rental unit for non-payment of rent. Laws permit "lockouts" if the landlord follows certain procedures. Most often, the landlord must:

- notify the tenant in advance that the locks are going to be changed
- leave a notice telling the tenant where the new keys may be accessed

- make the new keys accessible 24 hours a day

The tenant can still occupy the premises; however, she does not have possession of a key. Obviously, the inconvenience to the tenant is the landlord's bargaining chip to get the tenant to pay the rent she owes.

My landlord has changed the locks to my apartment. Have I been evicted? *No. A lockout is not an eviction.* You are still allowed to enter your apartment and the landlord has to give you the new key as well. The landlord's motive is to get you to pay delinquent rent rather than evict you.

My landlord locked me out of my apartment and refused to give me a new key since the lease says I'm not entitled to one. Is this legal? *No. Laws pertaining to lockouts generally make any lease provisions that change the legal requirements of a lockout (such as requiring the tenant to be given a new key) void and unenforceable.* Although the lease might say that the landlord does not have to give you a key, the law requires him to do so.

What can I do if my landlord refuses to give me the new keys to my apartment after he changed the locks? *You can file a court action requesting a "writ of reentry."* The writ orders the landlord to give you a key immediately and allow you to reenter the apartment. You file the request in court, the judge issues the writ and the sheriff's office serves the landlord with it. Once the landlord has been served, he must comply with the writ or risk being in contempt of court.

> **TIP:** There is a filing fee as well as a fee to have the landlord served with the writ. If you cannot pay the fees, ask the court clerk for a "pauper's affidavit." The judge can order the writ to be served without a fee if he approves the affidavit.

Utility Interruption

Interrupting the tenant's utilities is illegal unless the rent covers all or a part of the utility payments. For example, if the rent payment also goes toward water service, the landlord may shut off the water since the rent (and the water service) has not been paid.

My electricity has been turned off because I'm late paying the rent. Is this legal? *Under no circumstances can a landlord interfere with the utilities that you are directly paying.* For instance, if you pay for your electrical service separately from the rent, and the landlord interrupts the service, he is committing a criminal act and you have the right to go to a small claims court to obtain an order requiring the landlord to restore the service. Additionally, you can ask the court for an order terminating the lease agreement and your attorney's fee.

However, if you are in an "all bills paid" lease agreement where your rent includes utility payments, the landlord may have the right to turn off your utilities for non-payment – this depends on local law. Even in this situation, the landlord may be prohibited from shutting off electricity and other utilities in extreme heat and cold. He may also be prohibited from shutting off electricity if you have verifiable health issues or needs. In either case, do not hesitate to call a health or building inspector if your health is endangered and explain the situation.

The landlord is not paying the electric bill in my "all bills paid" apartment complex. What are the tenants' options? *The tenants can pay the electric company and deduct the payment from rent; however the best option is to terminate the lease.* Laws generally allow tenants to terminate a lease within 30 days of receiving notice from the utility company of a future shut off, or notice of an actual shut off, whichever is sooner.

I live in a building divided into four apartments and the tenants split the utility payments. Can our landlord shut off the natural gas heating if one of us does not pay the rent? *No. If the tenants of the building are paying the utility bill separately from their rent payment, your landlord does not have the right to shut off the gas connection.* He can only shut off the connection for non-payment of the tenant's separate utility bill.

> Laws do not allow electricity to be turned off in any circumstances when it the temperature is below freezing or a heat advisory is in effect. Additionally, landlords cannot disconnect or shut off power to a unit rented by tenant who will become seriously ill as a result.

Landlord's Lien

The law allows a landlord to take possession of a tenant's property and sell it to cover rent in certain situation. The landlord has the ability to take the property because he has a landlord's lien. The lien is a provision in the lease that makes all of the tenant's property subject to sale if the rent is not paid. Since the landlord's lien is part of the lease agreement, a court order is not necessary.

> Laws require the landlord's lien to be printed in large bold-faced letters in the lease. If it is not, it may not be enforceable against the tenant.

Some property is "exempt" from the landlord's lien and cannot be taken and sold for rent. Depending on law of the state where the landlord is attempting to enforce his lien, he may not take:

1. clothing
2. tools, apparatus, and books of a trade or profession
3. schoolbooks
4. a family library
5. family portraits and pictures
6. furniture
7. beds and bedding
8. kitchen furniture and utensils
9. food
10. medicine and medical supplies
11. a motor vehicle
12. agricultural implements
13. children's toys not commonly used by adults
14. goods that the landlord knows are owned by a person other than the tenant or an occupant
15. goods that the landlord knows are subject to another creditor's lien

SEIZURE OF PROPERTY – The lien authorizes the landlord to take possession of the tenant's property only if he can do so peacefully. He may not break down the door, threaten the tenant or be disruptive when seizing the property. The landlord is prohibited from "breaching the peace" to enforce his lien.

NOTICE OF SEIZURE – The landlord must leave a notice with the tenant that the property has been taken for non-payment of rent along with an itemized list of the property.

The notice must state:

- the amount of past-due rent
- the name, address, and telephone number of the person the tenant may contact regarding the amount owed
- and that the property will be promptly returned when the past due rent is paid in full
- the fee for packing, removing, and/or storing the property (this fee must be part of the lease agreement or the landlord is not entitled to collect)

SALE OF TENANT'S PROPERTY – If the lease provides that the tenant's property may be sold for past-due rent, the landlord may go forward with a sale. However, the tenant must be notified of the date and time of the sale before it takes place. Laws typically require 30 days notice. The property is auctioned off to the highest bidder. After the past-due rent is paid, any remaining money must be sent to the tenant.

> When a tenant abandons the property, the landlord may remove all of the items in the unit. Under this situation, the landlord does not need a court order or a specific provision in the lease authorizing the removal and sale of the tenant's property.

My landlord is threatening to enforce his landlord's lien and seize my property for non-payment of rent. If there is nothing in the lease about this option, can he take my property? *No. The lease must specifically provide for the landlord to enforce a lien on your property for non-payment of rent.* Laws require that the provision allowing the landlord

to enter and seize your property be underlined or printed in conspicuous bold print in order to be enforceable.

Illegal Remedies

If the tenant fails to pay rent, the landlord must act lawfully in obtaining a remedy. For example, interrupting electrical service, entering the apartment without permission, removing appliances that the landlord furnished or threatening physical harm are illegal remedies. Landlords who put the tenant's belongings out on the street for non-payment of rent may be charged with trespassing, breaking and entering and any other criminal laws that apply.

CHANGES IN RENTAL AMOUNTS

Unless authorized by law, rent cannot change during the lease period. Of course, no tenant would oppose a rent decrease unless services were decreased as well. In rent-controlled apartment, laws may allow a rent increase if the landlord spends money on capital improvements, such as building a deck on the building's roof.

Rent Increases

The amount of rent that you pay under the lease agreement cannot be increased until the agreement terminates. The lease agreement is a contract and the landlord cannot change the most important provision – the amount of rent – on his own. If you have notified your landlord that you intend to renew your lease, the rent remains the same unless the landlord notifies you in advance. In a month-to-month tenancy, the landlord may increase the rent effective with the next month's rental payment as long as the tenant is given 30 days notice.

Rent Stabilization

Rent stabilization laws have taken the place of the old rent control system. In some areas of the country, notably New York City, tenants are "rent regulated" through rent stabilization laws. These laws prohibit or limit the landlord's ability to raise the rent on tenants occupying rental property under a current lease. Those tenants are known as "sitting tenants" and have the right to renew their lease and continue to rent the premises at the rate agreed to in the original lease, even if it was made years ago. "Sitting" tenants must be offered a renewal lease (at the stabilized rent rate) before the end of the current lease.

"Succession rights" allow a rent-regulated apartment to be passed on to an immediate family member who has been living there when the original tenant on the lease dies. The rights are only good for one generation. For example, the apartment may be passed from father to son, but not from the son to his children.

Landlords are allowed to impose substantial rent increases only when the rental unit is voluntarily vacated and a new tenant moves in. Raising rents to the current market rate after a vacancy is known as "vacancy decontrol." For example, if the previous tenant rented an apartment in Los Angeles (a rent control city) 5 years ago at $1,000 per month and the current rental rate for a similar unit is $1,500, the landlord can raise the rent to $1,500 when a new tenant rents the apartment.

> **TIP:** In addition to New York City, cities in California, Connecticut, Massachusetts, New Jersey and Hawaii have also enacted rent stabilization laws. Many housing departments from these cities have Web sites with more information.
>
> - Residential renters in New York City can find guidance at **http://tenant.net/main.html**.
> - The Los Angeles Housing Department has rent control information on its Web site at **www.lacity.org/lahd**.

LANDLORD'S DUTIES

FIT FOR HABITATION

A residential landlord is required to keep the premises in good repair and "fit for human habitation." This responsibility is mandated through several legal principles; and the lease itself most likely refers to certain standards of upkeep. If the premises are allowed to become unfit for people to live in, the tenant can terminate the lease agreement.

Implied Warranty of Habitability

Over the years, the law has evolved to create an implied duty for the landlord to keep the property in good condition. This duty is sometimes termed the "implied warranty of habitability," meaning that any person renting property guarantees, whether they say it or not, that it is fit for humans to live in by being safe and sanitary.

To be fit for habitation, rental property must be:

- structurally stable
- free from serious disrepair
- free from lead, mold, dangerous levels of air pollution (e.g., from gas or carbon monoxide), or other toxic and harmful pollutants that could damage the health of the tenant

The tenant must notify the landlord of the defects or conditions that are making the property unsafe or unhealthy. He cannot violate an implied warranty of habitability if he does not know that the premises are no longer fit to live in.

Some states have laws that specifically set out the tenant's rights when the property becomes uninhabitable, such as the right to withhold rent or terminate the lease. In states that do not have such laws, consumer protection fraud laws, which typically cover the seller and buyer of consumer goods, may apply to landlord tenant disputes.

Can I terminate my apartment lease if the landlord refuses to exterminate for mice and rats? *Yes. The landlord has breached the implied warranty of habitability by allowing vermin to infest your apartment.* However, if you have notified the landlord of the problem, he is allowed an opportunity to exterminate and put your apartment back into habitable condition.

> Not all unhealthy conditions make the landlord liable for a breach of the warranty of habitability. For example, some of the paint in older buildings may be lead-based. The landlord is not required to remove the lead paint. However, under the Lead-Based Paint Hazard Reduction Act of 1992, the landlord must disclose known lead hazards when residential premises built before 1978 are leased. Landlords must also provide a pamphlet on lead poisoning to the renter before the pre-1978 property is rented.

The water pressure in my apartment is so low I can barely take a shower. Does this make my apartment unfit to live in? *Probably not.* As long as the toilets flush, you can get drinking water, wash dishes, etc., the low water pressure is more of an annoyance than a health issue. If, however, the water becomes unavailable during some parts of the day, your apartment is unfit to live in, and if the landlord does not fix the problem, you can terminate your lease.

I want the landlord to replace the regular glass in my sliding door with safety glass. If he refuses, is he violating the warranty of habitability? *Not unless a state or city housing code specifically requires safety glass on doors in rental units.* Although the safety glass might be better security, leaving ordinary glass in the door does not necessarily put your safety at risk.

My wife is in a wheelchair and I want our landlord to lower the kitchen counters in our apartment. If he refuses, can we break the lease since the apartment is not habitable for my wife? *No. By renting you and your wife the apartment, the landlord has only guaranteed you a healthy, safe and clean place to live.* His duty is to keep the property in a condition that does not deprive you and your wife of essential functions, such as cooking. Although it would be more convenient for the counters to be lowered, the landlord's refusal does not completely deprive you of the ability to use the kitchen as it was intended.

If I rent a space in shopping center to open a bookstore, is there an implied warranty of habitability? *Yes, but it is different than the residential lease warranty. You have a commercial lease.* Generally, the warranty only applies to private residences. There are separate laws concerning the maintenance of commercial properties. Typically, in commercial lease situation the landlord warrants that the premises are suitable for the tenant's business purposes. The subject of commercial leases and their warranties are outside the scope of this chapter.

My landlord insists I pay an extra fee during the summer for the cost of air conditioning. Is this legal? *It depends on your lease agreement.* However, you should know that in some areas of the country, a landlord is required to provide cooling during high heat warnings so that it is "fit for habitation." You are not required to reimburse him for his expenses in complying with the law.

> **TIP:** Extra fees for heating are also illegal unless you are required to make the payments under the lease as additional rent or a separate utility.

My utilities are included as part of my rent. Can my landlord prevent me from running an air-conditioning window unit I've purchased? *Yes, if your lease sets a limit on the amount of energy or electricity you can use per month. If it does not, you are free to run the air conditioning unit and any other appliances.* If the lease does not allow you to use the air conditioner, the landlord is still required to provide adequate cooling to make your apartment livable in conditions of extreme heat.

> **TIP:** In regions where air-conditioning in not common, there may be a clause in your lease that says you need permission from your landlord in order to install an air conditioner. Unless your landlord agrees to it, do not run the air conditioning unit or you will be in violation of your lease.

My landlord gave me a deal on my apartment if I took it "as is." Is she free to ignore the problems I am having with the water supply in the unit? *No, your landlord must bring your apartment "up to code" or fit for habitation.* Your apartment must have a supply of running hot and cold water. The lack of water, heat, cooling, certain security and safety measures and other unsafe and unsanitary conditions mean the apartment is not fit to rent under the law. The landlord cannot get around the requirements by renting the apartment "as is;" i.e., he cannot have you waive your right to the implied warranty of habitability.

> **TIP:** If you rent an apartment "as is," you cannot later complain of dingy paint, stained carpet, and other cosmetic issues, as long as the basic requirements of safety and hygiene are in place.

The heat isn't working in our apartment and I've moved in with my mother. Am I still responsible for rent? *You must pay the rent until the lease is terminated.* If the heat is not working, laws typically require the tenant to notify the landlord and allow him time to make the repair. If after notice, the landlord does not make the repair, you can terminate the lease and move out.

At a minimum, your notice should be sent certified mail, return receipt requested and include:

- a description of the repairs needed;
- a statement that a threat to your health or safety exists;
- a request that the repairs be made in a reasonable amount of time (in an emergency as little as 24 hours is reasonable; otherwise, allow for 7 days).

> **TIP:** Notify the landlord immediately of the problem and that you have had to abandon the unit. He has a duty to make repairs to the heating unit in a reasonable period of time and notify you when the apartment is livable again. In very cold weather, requiring the heat to be repaired within 24 hours is reasonable.

I rented a condo in a non-smoking unit, but my neighbor's smoke is infiltrating my unit. What are my options? *You may be able to move without breaking your lease if you can show that the second-hand smoke is affecting your health to the extent that a major life function is impaired.* For example, if the second-hand smoke has caused severe asthma and you are now unable to breath without medication, your condo has become uninhabitable.

> **TIP:** Some city codes prohibit smoking in rental dwellings. Check with your local code enforcement office to determine if you can make a formal complaint.

Even if the condo has not become unfit for habitation, you may still be able to terminate the lease under the "nuisance clause." Many leases contain a clause that prohibits activities that "unreasonably interfere" with other residents' enjoyment of the premises. You can argue that the secondhand smoke has unreasonable interfered with your enjoyment of the premises because of discomfort or health problems.

State laws typically define a nuisance "anything which is injurious to health, indecent, offensive to the senses, or an obstruction to the free use of property so as to interfere with the comfortable enjoyment of life or property."

If the landlord refuses to correct the problem, he could be liable for the tenant's medical expenses as a result of health problems due to secondhand smoke as well as moving expenses.

> **TIP:** If you are a tenant smoking in a non-smoking unit, the lease may allow the landlord to evict you for breaking the no-smoking policy.

Does a leaking ceiling make my apartment unfit for habitation? *Yes, although minor leaks may not immediately impact your safety or health, roof leaks typically violate city housing codes making the apartment unfit to live in if the leaks are not repaired.* A constant leak can lead to mold, mildew, bacteria and other health hazards. For example, the upstairs neighbor who has a toilet that constantly leaks into your bathroom is an unsafe and unsanitary condition.

Housing Codes

In addition to the implied duties required of a landlord, municipalities typically enact housing codes requiring all landlords to maintain their properties in conditions that do not endanger the life, health and safety of the tenants. They must maintain the property so that the occupants will not be subject to conditions that are dangerous, hazardous or detrimental to life, health or safety.

Violations of the code are dealt with directly by the municipality, not the tenant. If a tenant complains that the landlord has failed to comply with the local housing code, city building inspectors will inspect the property and take action if the property is not being lawfully maintained. The landlord will be ordered to make any necessary repairs and may be fined. In extreme cases, such as where there is no running water, the rental premises are "condemned" and the tenants must vacate.

Under housing codes, residential rental properties must have, at a minimum:

- safe heating—a heating system that is in good working order and provides an adequate supply of heat to the property
- natural (or artificial) lighting that will allow normal indoor activities
- adequate ventilation
- satisfactory facilities for preparing and cooking food
- a sink with hot and cold running (and sanitary) water
- a flush toilet
- facilities for bathing
- a private entrance so that the tenant does not have to go through another property to get to the premises
- a means of escape from fire
- a working smoke alarm

Are there laws other than housing codes that my landlord is required to follow? *Yes. The term "housing codes" typically refers to a number of regulations concerning rental properties.* There are federal laws regarding the removal of lead paint and asbestos. Additionally, your landlord must follow certain city codes. Building codes cover the dwelling's electrical, plumbing and structural framework. Health codes concerning pests, rodents, garbage and other issues of cleanliness also apply to rental units. Finally, fire codes exist to ensure that smoke alarms, fire exits, extinguishers and alarms are present and working on the property.

> **TIP:** If you believe health or fire codes are being violated, contact the city health and fire departments as well as the code enforcement office. Excessive garbage and illegal trash dumping should be referred to your local environmental health or protection office.

What exactly constitutes a housing code violation? Violations vary from city to city, but typically one exists if your apartment has:

- dilapidated stairs, railings, balconies or decks
- no electricity or inoperable lights, outlets or switches
- a faulty or inoperable elevator
- sewer blockage
- no gas service
- no heat
- no hot water
- no smoke detector
- no exterior locks, or inoperable locks
- no water service
- required exits blocked
- roof leaks
- inoperable or broken windows

My apartment is very run down but the landlord says it is "up to code." How can I find out if the apartment complex is actually safe? *Contact the city code enforcement office and ask if the complex is properly registered and certified by the city as a safe rental unit.* You should also ask when the property was last inspected.

> **TIP:** Before signing the lease or moving in, contact the city code enforcement office for a formal code report history on the apartment unit or building.

If the landlord hasn't fixed the furnace in my apartment by winter, is the apartment unfit for habitation? *Yes.* City property and building codes require that rental units have adequate heating.

TIP: Cities have different requirements, but typically the temperature in a rental unit must be at least 60 degrees if the outside temperature is below freezing. For instance, Seattle requires a permanent heat source capable of maintaining an average room temperature of at least 65 degrees when outside temperatures are 24 degrees or above, and at least 58 degrees when the outside temperature is below 24 degrees.

We don't have heat in our apartment and I can't get my landlord to respond to my complaints. What can I do to get the heating unit repaired? *Since adequate heating is required under city building or landlord/tenant codes, you can notify the city building inspector or the code enforcement section of your local city government.* The building inspector will come to your apartment to verify your complaints. The inspector will then contact the landlord and require repairs to the heating unit. If the landlord doesn't comply, the city may begin imposing fines.

TIP: If it is very cold and there are children in the home, you should notify the building inspector immediately and emphasize that the lack of heating has become an emergency situation.

Because of a recent illness, I am now confined to a wheelchair. Is my landlord required to make any alterations or modifications to my apartment? *Yes. Because you are now disabled, your landlord should offer you an apartment that is handicapped accessible or modify your existing unit.* The modifications should include such things as bathroom and tub rails, lowered light switches and thermostats, and widening doors.

Can I rent out my condo as a 2-bedroom unit if the second bedroom does not have windows? *No. Building codes require windows in a bedroom in case of fire.* Your unit is not fit for habitation as a 2-bedroom unit.

The windows in my daughter's bedroom in our apartment are painted shut. Does the landlord need to make them operable? *Yes. Bedrooms must have escape routes in case of fire.* If the landlord will not repair the window, notify the city fire marshal. In the meantime, if you cannot unstick the window yourself, you should move your daughter out of the bedroom.

TIP: Generally, if an apartment unit is three stories or higher, an alternate fire exit (such as a fire escape) must be available.

My apartment is overrun with roaches although the landlord has brought in an exterminator. I threatened to report a housing code violation, but he says I'm responsible for the problem. Can I make a complaint? *You can complain, but the code enforcement inspector may decide the problem lies with you.* Although landlords must keep rental units in compliance with housing codes, tenants have responsibilities too. To help control roaches, rats and other vermin, you are required to keep:

- the apartment clean and sanitary
- the stove, oven, refrigerator, and other appliances clean
- put your trash and garbage in the garbage carts or dumpsters

Most leases permit you to be evicted for failing to maintain certain standards of cleanliness and safety in your apartment. For example, you cannot continually clog up plumbing fixtures, fail to remove trash and debris or tamper with smoke alarms and fire escapes.

The heat in my apartment isn't working and the landlord has provided me with several space heaters instead of making repairs. Is this legal? *No. Housing codes require a permanent heat source in rental dwellings, such as an oil, gas or electric furnace, or permanently installed baseboard or wall heaters.* Electric and kerosene space heaters are not legal as a primary heat source in rental housing. Your landlord is violating housing codes.

In this situation, contact the city housing code enforcement office immediately. Lack of utilities, such as heat, typically qualifies as an emergency and the repairs must usually be made within 24 hours. If the landlord still does not repair the heating, you can terminate the lease after notifying him of your intention to move out.

Can I withhold rent if the landlord is cited for housing code violations? *It depends on your location. Some cities and states have laws that allow the tenant to withhold rent once the dwelling is declared unfit for human habitation by the housing code inspector.* However, withholding rent does not mean you do not pay rent. Instead, your rent is typically deposited in a city escrow account until the landlord makes the required repairs.

If you have paid money into a rent withholding account and the landlord does not make repairs, your money will be returned after a period of time. For example, a landlord may have 6 months to make the repairs. During that time, you must continue to pay rent into the escrow account.

> Rather than withhold rent, notify the landlord you are terminating the lease because the premises are not habitable. Include a statement that your health and safety are in danger because of the violations.

I received a notice that my apartment complex has several housing code violations and that tenants will be relocated. Why do I have to move? *The city building inspectors have determined that your apartment is not fit for human habitation until the landlord makes certain repairs.* Tenants cannot, by law, occupy a dwelling that is unfit.

How do I find out more about tenant relocation because of housing code violations? *Contact the person on the notice you received or the city housing code office for assistance and ask for help.* In some instances, city personnel will work with tenants to find a new place to live, often making calls to apartment buildings on behalf of residents, as well as assisting with difficult problems such as deposits, move-in dates and pet issues.

> If you have been forced out of your apartment, you may have the right to sue the landlord for breach of contract (the lease) and breach of the warranty of habitability. Those types of lawsuits typically allow you to recover attorney's fee and court costs.

How do I file a complaint regarding housing code violations in my apartment unit? *You must contact your city building or housing code enforcement office.* You will likely be asked to complete a form, sometimes called a "request for service." Typically, an inspector will respond within 5 to 7 days, although a shorter time can be arranged in an emergency situation.

Some code enforcement offices require you to first contact the landlord by letter with your complaint and allow him a period of time to repair before the inspector will be sent out. An investigation of your complaint may be delayed until you comply with that requirement. Therefore, before contacting the code enforcement office, send a letter to the landlord listing all the problems and indicate a copy of the letter will be sent to the code enforcement office. Send one copy and keep another copy for your records.

What happens once I report a housing code violation? *Once you have made your complaint, a city building inspector is assigned to investigate.* The code enforcement office then writes the landlord a letter listing all the violations found during the inspection. The landlord is given a deadline to make repairs according to the severity of the problem. If the repairs are not made, the landlord is given a citation and must appear in court where he could be fined for his failure to repair.

> **TIP:** Mark your calendar to call the code enforcement office to check the status of your complaint within 7 days from the date you first complained. Get the name and numbers of the building inspector assigned to your complaint and call to check the status with her as well. Continue to mark your calendar to call the inspector every 7 days until the matter is settled to your satisfaction.

Can I be evicted if I report housing code violations? *No.* The landlord cannot evict you for reporting a violation as long as one exists, you have been paying your rent and there are no other issues that permit him to evict you.

> **Retaliatory or wrongful eviction is prohibited by law. You can sue in court and recover damages (moving expenses), attorney's fees and court costs.**

Can I report a housing code violation anonymously? *Most code enforcement offices require the name and address of the person complaining before sending out an inspector.* However, you can ask that your identity not be divulged to the landlord.

Constructive Eviction

When a tenant is forced to leave the property because the landlord has allowed it to become unfit for habitation, the tenant has been constructively evicted. The tenant should notify the landlord, in writing, that the lease is terminated because the premises are not habitable. A statement should be included in the notification that the tenant's health and safety are in danger because of the uninhabitable conditions.

The toilets in my apartment have never worked properly and I am forced to use a neighbor's bathroom. Can I move out? *Yes.* Assuming the landlord is aware of the ongoing problems with your toilets and has not made adequate repairs, notify him in writing that you have been constructively evicted because of the unsafe and unsanitary conditions, are unable to use and enjoy your apartment and are terminating the lease.

Despite numerous complaints to my landlord and calls to the police, my neighbors continue to "party" nearly every night and I am unable to sleep. Can I move out? *Yes. You are being deprived of the use and enjoyment of your apartment.* Since your landlord refuses to control or evict your neighbors, notify him that you are moving out because his failure to remedy the situation has resulted in constructive eviction from your apartment.

My neighbors have highly offensive posters in their apartment, with the windows open directly in my view; the landlord refuses to force them to put in window coverings. Can I move out before my lease ends? *No. You must be able to show that some portion of your apartment has become unusable due to the landlord's failure to remedy the situation with the neighbors.* Although their wall hangings may be offensive, in order to argue that you have been constructively evicted, you must be able to show that because of the wall hangings:

- your apartment has become unfit for human habitation
- conditions were created that were dangerous to your life, health or safety
- the essential functions of your apartment became unusable.

REPAIR OF PREMISES

Good Repair

I order to keep the premises fit for human habitation (and meet the implied warranty of habitability and the various local housing codes), landlords are responsible for making repairs to keep the property in good, safe and clean condition or "upkeep." State laws and housing codes require landlords to repair specific dangerous conditions and to keep the premises "up to code." Your lease may also set out items the landlord has a duty to repair, such as appliances.

Repairs to bring the premises back up to living standards are only required if the landlord knows about the defects or has been notified. Either a tenant, a community member or city employee can notify the landlord.

Structural Repairs

Landlords must make structural repairs in all cases since the tenants' safety depends on the integrity of the building. The structural repair can be minor, such as a broken step. However, minor problems may lead to serious injuries. For example, the broken step may cause an older visitor of the tenant's to lose his footing, fall and break a hip.

If the tenant is responsible for the breaking the step, she is also responsible for fixing it. The situation becomes complicated if the person who fell sues the landlord. Although he may not have had a duty to repair the step since the tenant was at fault, he does have a duty to keep the premises safe. If the step was in the front of the building and the landlord knew it was broken, he may be liable for the person's fall.

Heating and Cooling

Rental property must have working heat and cooling systems in order for the premises to be fit to live in. Any breakdown in the systems should be immediately repaired. The situation can turn into an emergency during very cold and very hot months. Children and the elderly are particularly susceptible to extreme weather. If you do not have working heat or air conditioning and you or your family's health and safety is at risk, call the city building inspector. City codes require adequate heating and cooling.

Is lack of heat a housing code violation?

Yes, in very cold weather the heat source in a rental dwelling must be capable of keeping the apartment at certain temperature. Depending on the outside temperature and local codes, an apartment must generally be between 65 to 70 degrees.

My landlord hasn't turned the heat on. Can I force him to?

Yes. Housing codes typically have strict guidelines, depending on the time of year and outside temperature, for heating and cooling of rental properties. Call your local housing authority and find out the requirements. If your landlord still refuses to turn the heat on although required to, you should file a complaint with the housing authority or city building inspector.

Mold

Mold in residences is big issue for homeowners, insurance companies, landlords and tenants. Some mold is harmful and can cause serious illness to the occupants of a home where mold is present. As a tenant, you can probably force your landlord to remove mold that is found on the premises since it is a health hazard. If it cannot be removed and your health is at issue, you may

have to option of terminating the lease early. As with all repairs, the landlord is not required to resolve the mold problem unless he is aware that it exists.

> **The bigger issue is whether the landlord is liable for the tenant's physical injuries and medical expenses. If he created the condition that caused the mold, the landlord may be liable. For example, if the pipes burst during an ice storm, the apartment was flooded and the landlord never had it properly dried out and replaced the carpet, he may have been negligent which in turn caused the tenant's mold induced injuries.**

I want my apartment inspected for mold but the landlord refuses to pay for the testing. What can I do?

Landlords are not required to pay for mold testing but they are required to provide tenants with a safe and healthy environment. Document the mold problem with photographs (if the mold is visible) or using a mold air test kit. Once you can show that mold is present in the apartment, make a written complaint to both the building code enforcement and health department in your city. The landlord may be forced to hire an inspector.

> **TIP:** Certified industrial hygienists can be hired to test environmental air quality. However, there are many self-proclaimed mold "experts" willing to test your home. Always check the person's credentials; those with Internet only training and certifications should be avoided.

What are some signs that my apartment may be infested with mold?

You should look for mold that is:

- blackish-green in color ("black mold")
- yellow, green and white colored mold ("trichoderma")

Other signs include:

- ceilings and walls with peeling paint
- condensation on walls, ceilings and floors

Physical symptoms include:

- stomach aches and diarrhea,
- extreme fatigue,
- eye and nose irritation,

- respiratory tract infections,
- skin rashes and hair loss.

Where do I look for mold? *If you believe there is mold in your apartment but have not been able to find it, pull out and look behind the washer, dryer and refrigerator.* Mold often grows under carpeting – pull up carpets and inspect the padding and floor underneath if you can.

My family has become ill because of mold in our apartment. Can we move out? *Yes; however, to avoid owing rent on the remainder of your lease term you need to notify the landlord in writing that the premises are unsafe, unsanitary and have become inhabitable.* Include a statement that because of the mold, you and your family have been constructively evicted. Copy the city health department and building code enforcement office with the letter.

Ordinary Repairs

The landlord is not required to make more than ordinary repairs. For example, if your refrigerator ice maker goes out and it would cost several hundred dollars to fix, the landlord is not required to have it repaired. The problem does not make the property unfit to live in, and the repair is not ordinary because of the cost. Further, the landlord is not required to make improvements or repair things that you, your family or visitors broke, such as a window that breaks when you son throws a ball through it.

My apartment needs new bathroom light fixtures, a hole in the wall repaired, new tile and caulking around the tub, and stove and kitchen sink repairs. Is all this more than ordinary repairs? *No. In combination, there are a lot of repairs to be done, but each one is an ordinary maintenance matter.* Your landlord is required to keep the basic functions of the premises in good working order.

It isn't a life or death situation, but our dishwasher has quit working and the landlord isn't responding to my requests for repair. Do I have to live without a dishwasher? *Although the landlord does not have to provide appliances, if he does, they must be maintained in working order.* He is violating the lease as well as the law by refusing the make the repair.

In situations where the repairs are small and the landlord is not responsive, the best option may be to "repair and deduct." You must give the landlord notice that you are exercising your option to repair and deduct and provide him with copies of your receipts at the time you pay the decreased rent.

My water heater is leaking but it still works. The landlord has tried to repair it several times and now I want I new one. Do I have a right to a new water heater? *Yes. A leaking water heater is an unsafe condition and your landlord must replace it since repairs are not working.* Remind him that the apartment could be flooded and he will be responsible for damage to your furniture and other possessions. Additionally, if the water heater is a gas heater, the leak could extinguish the pilot light creating the possibility of exposure to natural gas.

A leaky faucet or shower is typically not considered to be a health hazard and the landlord is not violating any law or breaching the lease by refusing to repair that kind of leak.

Severe hailstorms cracked the windows in the apartment units in my complex, as well as mine, more than a month ago. Isn't my landlord required to replace my windows now that I notified him in writing of the problem? *Not in this situation.* Where damage occurs as a result of an insured casualty loss the landlord can wait to make repairs until he receives the insurance proceeds.

If the loss is severe, such as a large fire, and the apartment is uninhabitable, the tenant can notify the landlord and terminate the lease before the repairs are made.

Limited Repairs

Sometimes a landlord agrees to make certain limited repairs, for example, replacing boards in a backyard deck that have rotted. By replacing the boards, the landlord is not agreeing to replace the entire deck.

Tenant's Duty to Repair

A tenant must repair or pay for the costs of repair for damages to the rental property that she caused. For example, if the tenant runs her car through the garage wall, she is responsible for the costs of those repairs. If she does not pay them, the landlord can sue her to recover his repair expenses. He cannot recover the amount that the value of property decreased because of the damage to the garage wall. If the repairs cost $500 but the value of the house, since its garage was unusable, decreased $5,000, the landlord only recovers $500.

My ex-boyfriend punched a hole in the wall of my apartment. Am I responsible for the repairs? *Yes. The actions of anyone you invite into your apartment are your responsibility.* If your ex-boyfriend illegally broke into the apartment, you can argue the landlord should repair the wall since security is obviously lax. On the other hand, if your ex-boyfriend gained entrance into the apartment because you let him in, or he still had a key, he is an "invited" guest and you are responsible for the damages.

Do I have to pay for a friend's damage to the complex's fence when she drove away from my apartment? *Probably not. Although she was visiting you, once she left your apartment, you no longer had any control over her.* Unless you knew or believed she would get into an accident with the fence, you are not liable. However, if she left your apartment intoxicated, the landlord can argue you should have known your friend might drive into the fence and you had a duty to prevent her from driving. Since you let her drive, under the landlord's theory, you would be liable for the damage.

LANDLORD'S FAILURE TO REPAIR

If problems exist that put the health and safety of the tenants in danger, the landlord is required to make repairs when he is notified, by either the tenant or the municipality.

Tenant's Options

If the landlord fails to make repairs that affect the health or safety of the tenant, the tenant has the right to break the lease and move out.

Alternatively, (and only in extreme cases), the tenant can stay on the premises and withhold all or a part of the rent until the repairs are made. The tenant can also file a lawsuit against the landlord for breaching the implied warranty of habitability. The tenant's options are:

Repair and Deduct

If you wish to deduct an amount from your rent because your landlord is not making repairs and you had to correct the problem, you must:

1. notify him in writing, with the date at the top of the letter, of the problems you are facing and request repairs within a reasonable time (for example, 7 business days)

2. keep a copy of your written notice to the landlord

3. contact at least two contractors for repair estimates

4. if the landlord does not make the repairs by the deadline, hire the person with the lowest bid to do the job.

5. keep the costs reasonable and save all your receipts.

6. when the next rent payment is due, deduct the cost of the repairs from your usual rent payment and attach copies of the repair receipts.

> **TIP:** It is a good idea to take a picture of the problem and enclose the photo with your notice. This lets the landlord know you are serious about getting the repair made.

The "repair and deduct" remedy is for minor repairs only. It should never be used with major repairs, like new carpeting or appliances. Your rent payment will be so greatly reduced after you deduct those costs, it is likely your landlord will attempt to evict you for non-payment of rent.

> **TIP:** If you do the repairs yourself, your only receipts are the ones for materials. You cannot put a price on your time and labor and deduct from the rent.

Withhold Rent

Some states have rent escrow funds where a tenant can deposit rent that she is withholding while the landlord refuses to make repairs. Typically, the tenant deposits the rent payment with the court when she files a "rent escrow action." There may be a filing fee. To file a rent escrow action, you must:

1. notify the landlord in writing, preferably by certified mail.

2. wait a required amount of time, such as 7 days, for the landlord to respond.

3. complete the forms for a rent escrow action, deposit the rent with the court's clerk or administrator, along with a copy of your notice to the landlord.

The rent escrow action is set for a hearing, and if the tenant proves the landlord refused to make necessary repairs, the judge can order:

- the landlord to fix the problem,
- fine the landlord,
- require the tenant to "repair and deduct,"
- order future rents paid to the court until the repairs are made, and
- return all, none or part of the rent to the tenant.

Terminate Lease

If the landlord refuses to make repairs, the tenant may terminate the lease after giving the landlord a notice of the problem and demanding repairs. However, termination is only permitted when the conditions are unfit for habitability and the landlord has been given a reasonable opportunity to repair. For example, a leaking ceiling that is about to cave in and has caused water damage to the tenant's furniture makes the premises uninhabitable and the tenant can terminate the lease. Mere inconvenience, such as dripping faucet, due to the landlord's failure to repair is not a valid reason for terminating the lease.

File Suit

The tenant always has to option to file a lawsuit against the landlord for breach the implied warranty of habitability if the failure to repair is a threat to the tenant's health and safety. The tenant must first send a demand letter to the landlord, demanding repairs. Once the lawsuit is filed, the tenant may recover damages – i.e., damage to property as a result of repairs not being done, costs of moving, plus attorney's fees.

SAFETY AND SECURITY

The landlord has a duty to the tenant to maintain the tenant's safety and security. In locations where there is a probability of crimes being committed against his tenants, the landlord should install sufficient security devices. For example, if there have been several purse-snatching incidents as female tenants get out of their cars, the landlord could install high fencing and locked gates around the parking lot to help prevent the crimes and limit his liability.

Laws commonly require all rental units, including apartments, houses, condominiums, duplexes, etc., to have the following security devices installed at the landlord's expense:

- a viewer or peephole on each exterior door
- window latches on exterior windows
- pin locks on sliding doors
- security bar or door handle latch on sliding doors
- keyless deadbolt locking device on each exterior door
- either a keyed deadbolt or doorknob lock on each exterior door (locks must be re-keyed after prior tenant moves out

If the required security devices are not installed, such as a keyless deadbolt lock on the front door, the tenant has the right to install it herself and deduct the cost from her next rent payment. Some laws also permit the tenant to terminate the lease if the she requested that the keyless deadbolt lock, for example, be installed and the landlord fails to do so.

> **TIP:** Always make your request to the landlord for installation of a security device in writing. Laws generally require the landlord to comply with your request within 7 days or less. If there have been any intruders in your apartment, many state laws require that the landlord comply with your request within 72 hours.

The lights in the stairwell and outside my door no longer automatically come on at night. Is the landlord required to repair

the problem? *Yes. The lighting you describe affects your safety and security.* The landlord must make the repairs promptly. Additionally, the landlord must replace bulbs in lighting in common areas in order to maintain the safety and security of his tenants.

Is my apartment required to have a smoke detector? *Yes. State laws and city housing codes require landlords to install smoke detectors in rental units.* The location and number of smoke detectors required varies from state to state, but laws requiring a smoke detector outside each bedroom are typical.

The units in my apartment complex have fireplaces and I want my landlord to install a carbon monoxide detector. Is he required to pay for the installation? *Yes. Laws generally require carbon monoxide detectors in rental dwellings to ensure the tenants' safety.* Your landlord must pay for the immediate installation of the carbon monoxide detector or he is likely violating building codes in your area.

> **TIP:** The tenant is responsible for replacing the batteries in smoke and carbon dioxide detectors.

The electrical outlets in my bathroom are not grounded and I want them replaced with ground-fault circuit interrupters. Does my landlord have to make the replacement? *Probably. Most building codes require updated electrical outlets in all rental dwellings.* An ungrounded outlet, especially in an area where water is present, is a serious safety hazard.

However, if you are renting an older home from the homeowner, the building codes may not require updated outlets. You should not attempt to replace the outlets yourself since electrical work must be permitted and performed by a licensed electrician.

Locks

Laws require landlords of residential property to install particular locks and security devices. At a minimum, locks are required on all exterior doors and windows. Additionally, the landlord may be required to install key and keyless deadbolt locks on the exterior doors. Sliding doors and French doors may require special security devices as well.

What locks are required to be installed in my apartment? At a minimum, all the exterior windows must have a window latch; exterior doors must have keyed doorknobs and a keyless bolt, and sliding glass doors must have both a pin lock and a handle latch or security bar.

Is the landlord required to change the locks after the former tenant leaves and I move in? *Yes.* Laws require landlords to "re-key" locks so that only the new resident has access to the rental unit.

I moved into my apartment today and the landlord can't change the locks for 2 days. Can I change the locks myself? *Yes.* You can either install the locks or re-key them without any notice to the landlord and deduct the cost from your rent.

I want to change the locks on my apartment so my boyfriend can't get in. Do I have to pay for the new locks? *Yes.* Generally landlords are only required to change locks at their expense when a new tenant moves in or a break-in has been attempted (or occurred).

Your landlord cannot refuse the right to change the locks. Laws give tenants the right to have new locks installed or re-keyed at the tenant's expense at any time. However, the lease will require you to provide the landlord with a key to any new lock.

My landlord hasn't changed the locks in my apartment since the previous tenant moved out. Can I terminate the lease? Yes, after written notice to the landlord requesting the lock change and allowing him a reasonable amount of time to make the change, laws in some states allow you to move out and terminate the lease.

LANDLORD'S LIABILITY

Liability for Injuries

Depending on whether an injured person is a tenant, visitor or trespasser, the landlord may be at fault for injuries on the premises. However, he is only at fault if he failed to maintain the premises in a safe condition. A landlord is required to correct any open and obvious defects, as well keep his rental property safe and clean. An open and obvious defect is a hazard that can be readily observed, such as a broken gate around the pool area.

Liability for Children

Parents or legal guardians are responsible for supervision of minors at all times. However, the landlord will be liable for a child's injuries if the property is not in good repair or obvious hazards have not been corrected. The landlord is not liable for injuries that occur within the rental unit itself. For example, the landlord is not liable for a child's burns because the stovetop gets hot very quickly. He is liable if he is supervising the repaving of his parking lot, then leaves the area unattended and the child burns himself on hot asphalt.

Liability for Criminal Activity

The landlord guarantees safe and secure premises as part of his warranty of habitability. Security is a concern for every landlord, since he may be liable for any injuries that tenants or visitors receive due to poor security.

Tenants, guests and visitors who have been the victims of criminal acts have been successful in suing landlords for failing to provide proper security. Typically, a landlord is not responsible for the acts of third parties, such as criminals or trespassers. However, if the landlord could have foreseen criminal behavior that would result in injuries to his tenants and their visitors, he may be at fault. The outcome of court cases on this issue depend on whether the specific crime that occurred was foreseeable. If the victim was assaulted, for example, some factors that made the assault predictable include:

- past criminal assaults on the premises
- reports of assault in the area bordering the premises
- poor lighting
- absence of secure fencing and gates
- absence of a security guard

If those factors are present, juries may find that the landlord could have foreseen the assault. Since the assault was predictable, the landlord had a duty to try and prevent the attack. Accordingly, he is liable for the victim's injuries, and she will be able to recover damages from him.

Whether a crime is predictable or foreseeable varies. A victim who was assaulted and suffered emotional damage might not win her lawsuit, if only minor pilfering of newspapers and mailboxes could have been predicted – not assault incidents. However, if the landlord should have foreseen assault situations (since assaults had occurred nearby), then he would be liable for the victim's injuries.

> Where "front line defenses" against crime are in poor repair, the landlord may be liable for the victim's injuries regardless of the crime. Front line defenses include a strong front door with a deadbolt, secure locks on other doors and windows, or lobby doors that are passkey protected.

LEASE TERMINATION AND RENEWAL

The lease agreement sets out the number of weeks, months or years that the property will be rented to the tenant. The length of time the premises are rented is solely within the discretion of the landlord and the tenant and is called the "tenancy." Typically, an apartment lease is for a 12-month term or period of time. Also, renting a single-family home usually requires a year-long lease. At the end of the term the lease terminates.

END OF LEASE TERM

Leases are not forever, and eventually the lease period ends. Leases lasting over a year are not common. Many apartment leases are for 12 months with an option for the tenant to renew at the end of the 12-month period. The tenant usually must notify her landlord in writing 30 days before the end of the lease that she plans on renewing. Likewise, if the landlord is not renewing the lease, he must notify the tenant at least 30 days in advance.

Notice

The lack of notice is one of the biggest reasons for lease disputes. As a tenant, your lease agreement probably requires that you give the landlord written notice that you are not renewing the lease. If not, oral notice may suffice.

> **TIP:** Mark your calendar for 45 days before your lease ends so you can begin thinking about whether you want to renew or not. You will also have time to look at other properties if you are not happy with your current rental. Also, mark your calendar for 30 days before the expiration of the lease, as that is the deadline for notifying the landlord of your plans.

My landlord notified me that he is not renewing my lease. Is there anything I can do to make him renew it? *No. The landlord has the right not to renew at the end of the lease as long as you have been give proper notice (usually 30 days before the lease ends).* However, if you believe your lease is not being renewed for a discriminatory reason (your race, religion, sex, age, or ethnicity), you can contact the local housing authority and claim discrimination in housing.

Agreement

If both the landlord and tenant agree, the lease agreement can be terminated at any time during the lease. Some landlords are more understanding than others, and may be willing to end the lease early (for example, if the tenant takes a job in another city).

If you can get the landlord to agree to early termination, take a copy of your lease and ask him to write in and initial the new termination date for your records. The initialed copy will also be evidence that your landlord agreed to the early termination if you are sued for unpaid rent under the original lease.

RENEWAL

Automatic Renewal

A lease agreement may provide for automatic renewal if the parties do not give notice to each other ending the tenancy. In that situation, the tenant who forgets to give notice must continue to live in the apartment another 12 months and give notice in the eleventh month that she is leaving. A tenant who leaves after the initial lease terminates, although it has been automatically renewed, will forfeit her security deposit. Laws in some states may prohibit automatic renewal clauses in lease agreements, but they generally are not considered unconscionable.

Holdover

A tenant who continues to live on the premises after the lease period is up or after receiving a notice to vacate is "holding over." Laws refer to the extra time the tenant is living in the rental property as the "holdover tenancy."

If the holdover is with the consent of the landlord, a "periodic" or "month-to-month" tenancy is created. However, if the holdover is without the landlord's consent, the landlord can bring eviction proceedings against the holdover tenant, and may be able to increase the rent up to 200% during the holdover period.

Once he accepts a rental payment, the landlord cannot attempt to evict the tenant for holding over, since he has consented to a periodic tenancy. But the landlord can give notice that he is terminating the tenancy in 30 days, and that the tenant must leave within that period.

> **If you have sublet your apartment and the sublessee does not vacate, you are the holdover because you are the original tenant under the lease agreement.**

Month-to-Month Tenancy

If the lease ends with no provision for automatic renewal, and the tenant continues to live on the property, she does so as a "periodic" or "month-to-month" tenant. Since there is no lease in effect, the tenant and landlord's duties and responsibilities to the premises and each other are covered by the laws of the state. The tenant's payment of rent every month, and the landlord's acceptance of that rent, create an agreement that the tenant has the right to occupy the premises for another month. The tenant must give the landlord 30 days notice of termination in a month-to-month lease, since that is new term of the lease. (In some jurisdictions, a commercial lease may be extended for another year.)

If you are in a month-to-month tenancy, the landlord has the right to advise you that she is not "renewing" your tenancy. You are required to be given 30 days notice, but you will still have to move out. Therefore, although a month-to-month tenancy gives you more flexibility, you also run the risk of being asked to move in 30 days whether you want to or not.

BREAKING THE LEASE

A tenant can violate or break a lease intentionally or unintentionally. Lease agreements typically include "default provisions" which list actions by the tenant that violate the lease and allow the landlord to terminate the lease before it ends. Of course, by paying the rent late or failing to pay it entirely, the tenant is in default and has violated the lease agreement. However, the tenant also defaults if she:

- violates criminal laws, whether any arrest or conviction occurs
- gives false information on the rental application
- possesses, manufactures or delivers a controlled substance, marijuana, drugs or drug paraphernalia
- makes a false complaint concerning the habitability of the premises to a government agency

Purchasing a home does not permit a tenant to break a lease, unless the lease specifically permits it. Additionally, other common reasons that do not allow a tenant to break the lease, including:

- marriage
- separation
- divorce
- reconciliation
- leaving or withdrawing from school voluntarily or involuntarily
- voluntary or involuntary job transfer.
- loss of roommate or co-tenant
- loss of employment
- bad health
- criminal activity in and around the area

TIP: If you are in the military, or enlist while you are leasing and ordered to active duty or to relocate, you may lawfully terminate your lease before it ends. You must give the landlord notice, preferably 30 days in advance, if you are able. You will not be responsible for the rent due on the months left on the lease after you move out.

Do I have pay to for the months left on the lease if I break it? *Yes. You are responsible for paying the rent for every month left on the lease.* Additionally, your lease agreement may allow the landlord to "accelerate the rental payments" or call them all due at once. For example, if you break the lease and leave with 3 months left on a $500 month apartment, the landlord can demand $1,500 ($500 x 3 months).

TIP: Most laws require landlords to "mitigate" damages or attempt to rent out the apartment that was vacated early. In the example above, if someone moved in 30 days after the tenant left, the tenant must pay for that month only or $500.

Do I lose my security deposit if I move out early? *Probably. Not only do security deposits insure that the tenant will keep the premises maintained, they also act as a deterrent to breaking a lease.* Even if the landlord does not go to the trouble to sue you for the remaining rent owed under the lease, he is still somewhat compensated by keeping your security deposit.

TIP: You still owe rent for the months left on the lease, even if you forfeited you security deposit. Since the lease is a contract, most laws give the landlord 2 years to sue for the remaining rent.

I had to break my lease, but I found a replacement tenant to move in the day after I moved out. Can the landlord still keep my security deposit? *No, assuming that the premises were left in good condition.* If the lease allows the landlord to keep the security deposit as a penalty for breaking the lease, but you find a replacement, he must return the security deposit. However, the landlord has to approve the replacement tenant, and if he does not, he keeps the security deposit.

I broke my lease because I had to move. The landlord is keeping $500 of my $1,000 security deposit for the cost of finding a replacement tenant, although the apartment was left in perfect condition. Can he keep half my security deposit? *Yes. The landlord is entitled to deduct the cost of his actual expenses in finding a tenant to take your place and occupy the vacant apartment.* If the rental agency he used charged $500 to find a new tenant, then he has a right to deduct that amount (or whatever the amount is) from your security deposit when it is refunded to you.

The cost to the landlord for having to find another tenant is sometimes called a "reletting fee" in the lease agreement.

RETURN OF SECURITY DEPOSITS

Because of the frequency of security deposit disputes between landlords and tenants when the lease ends, laws place specific duties on the landlord when he keeps a tenant's security deposit. Typically, the landlord is allowed to deduct the cost of damages to the premises from the tenant's security deposit. However, the landlord may not keep all or a portion of the security deposit for normal wear and tear. The landlord may also be required to give the tenant an itemized list of the damages deducted from the security deposit.

If you don't receive an itemized list, check to see if one is required under your state laws by calling the local housing authority. If it is required, ask the landlord for one. By not providing you with an itemized list, the landlord may have to return your entire security deposit and will have waived his right to sue you for the damages.

TIP: Your security deposit is normally returned if you leave the premises in good condition. Failing to clean the oven and leaving the refrigerator dirty is not good condition. To avoid deductions from your security deposit make sure to:

- sweep and mop floors
- vacuum carpets
- clean sinks, tubs and showers
- wipe down walls with fingerprints or other stains
- clean out the oven, refrigerator and microwave
- sweep and clean off the patio and balcony
- remove all tacks and nails from the wall
- clean out the fireplace if you used it
- clean glass in patio doors
- remove shelf and drawer paper

Is there a deadline for returning my security deposit? If the lease sets out the time for returning a tenant's security deposit (for example, 10 days after tenant surrenders possession), then your security deposit must be returned to you by that deadline, minus any deductions for damages.

If the lease does not set out a date, state or local laws may require the security deposit to be returned (minus deductions for damages) within a certain time frame. A typical deadline prescribed by law is 30 days after the tenant surrenders possession.

Do I have to make a written request to get back my security deposit? *It depends on the lease agreement.* Check to see if you must request the return of the security deposit in writing under the terms of the lease. If a written request is required, present it to your landlord when you turn in your keys so that you are in full compliance with the lease agreement.

What types of lease violations permit the landlord to keep my security deposit when the lease ends? *Some of the provisions a tenant must follow in a standard rental agreement in order to have her security deposit refunded include:*

- remaining a tenant for the entire length of the lease – moving out in the tenth month of a 12-month lease is "breaking the lease," and you will forfeit your security deposit
- providing written notice – you should inform the landlord that you will not be renewing the lease at least 30 days before it ends
- being up-to-date on the rent – if the lease allows the landlord to keep the security deposit when you move out and are behind on the rent, you will not get it back

My landlord says he can't refund my security deposit because he owes the electric company several thousand dollars. Do I have to wait until the electric company is paid before I get my deposit back? *No.* The landlord's debts and bills do not take precedence over the return your security deposit.

If my landlord won't give me back my security deposit, is there anything I can do? *Yes, you can file a lawsuit against your landlord for failing to return your security deposit.* Generally, laws require the landlord to return your deposit if he kept it without a permissible reason. Additionally, the landlord may have to pay "penalty" damages (twice the amount of the deposit, for example), plus your attorney's fees.

EVICTION

When a tenant does not comply with the terms of the lease agreement, the landlord has the right to evict or remove him from the premises. Generally, the only legal basis for an eviction is the tenant's:

- failure to pay the rent
- defaulting or breaking a lease provision
- refusing to move out when the lease ends

An evicted tenant is a tenant who has been physically removed from the property. The tenant's property is also removed along with any other occupants (and their property) living on the premises. Once he has been evicted, the tenant is under no obligation to continue to pay rent.

PROCESS FOR EVICTION

In order to evict a tenant who has violated the terms of the lease, such as continuing to live on the premises without paying rent, the landlord is required to follow a precise legal procedure. The specifics vary from state to state, but generally all laws require:

- a legal purpose for eviction,
- notice to the tenant,
- a trial before a judge,
- an order of eviction and
- removal of the tenant.

Notice to Vacate

Typically, laws require between a 3 and 10-day written notice to the tenant that the landlord is seeking to evict him. The notice may be called the "notice to vacate," the "notice to quit," or some other term. Some laws allow the landlord to notify the tenant himself. Others require that law enforcement personnel, usually a sheriff's deputy, "serve" the tenant with notice.

If a deputy must serve the notice to vacate, the court clerk typically prepares the notice for a fee. The clerk then sends the notice to the sheriff's office for service. The sheriff can either give the notice to the tenant personally or post it on the door of the rental unit.

Once the notice is served, the tenant has a short time period to pay the past due rent, (if that is the issue), or to vacate the premises. For example, if a tenant is served with a 5 day notice to vacate on a Monday morning, he must pay the rent that is due or vacate by Saturday morning.

Holidays and weekends are included in the tenant's time to pay or vacate before the deadline. In the example above, the tenant must vacate on a Saturday. Although Saturday is part of the weekend, it still counts as a day in the notice period. The tenant does not get to skip Saturday and Sunday and wait until Monday to pay or vacate.

The sheriff's office does not serve notices and other legal papers on the weekends or holidays. If you are a landlord, keep in mind that there may be a delay before your tenant gets the notice to vacate during holiday periods.

My landlord gave me a 24-hour notice to vacate and I immediately paid the past due rent. Can I still be evicted from my apartment? *No. You did exactly what the landlord wanted to accomplish by giving you the notice – you paid the rent.* The landlord has no basis for an eviction. As long as you continue to pay the rent and comply with other provision of the lease agreement, you can stay in your apartment until the lease ends.

The landlord gave my teen-aged daughter a notice to vacate. Is this valid? *Yes, in some cases.* Laws allow the notice to vacate to be given to other residents of the apartment if they are a certain age. You need to check the law in your state concerning eviction notices. In Texas, for example, if your daughter was under 16 years old, the landlord's notice to vacate has not been properly given to you.

The law in my state gives tenants 3 days to vacate but my landlord has given me a 24 hour notice to vacate. Is this legal? *In some jurisdictions, if your lease specifically provides for only a 24-hour notice, then state law does not apply.* Under the lease, the landlord is acting legally and you have 24 hours to vacate the premises or to remedy the issue that prompted the notice.

I gave my tenant a notice to vacate but she hasn't left the apartment. Can I change the locks and move her furniture and other belongings out? *No.* You must file an eviction lawsuit and obtain a court order requiring the tenant to leave.

> **TIP:** If your lease gives you a landlord's lien, you do not need to go to court to move out the tenant's belongings.

I received a notice to vacate. Do I have to move by the deadline? *No. Your landlord must obtain an order from the court.* Until he has the order, he cannot forcibly remove you or your belongings (unless he has a landlord's lien) from the apartment.

Filing Suit

Once the landlord has given the tenant a notice to vacate, or the notice has been served, and the deadline passes without the tenant paying the past due rent or vacating, the landlord will file a lawsuit to evict the tenant. The lawsuit may be termed an "eviction suit," a "forcible entry and detainer suit (FED)," or a "dispossession suit." In such lawsuits, the landlord is requesting a judicial order allowing him to remove the tenant, the occupants and any property belonging to them that is on the premises

Once the lawsuit is filed, the tenant must be notified of the filing. This is accomplished by serving him with a copy. The tenant has the right to respond or "answer" the landlord's suit. The deadline for a response (called the "answer date") begins to run once the tenant is served. Typically, the response time is short – about 10 days.

Tenant's Deadline to Respond

The tenant's answer must be in writing and filed by the deadline or he automatically loses the case. Once the tenant files his answer, the court sets a trial date for the eviction case. The tenant must be notified of the time and date of the trial by the court. He has the right to appear before the court at trial and show cause as to why he should not be evicted.

> **TIP:** Call the court clerk and ask if there are forms available for answering an eviction lawsuit..

> **TIP:** The tenant's answer date (the deadline to respond to the lawsuit) may also be the date the judge plans to hold the "trial." If you have been served with an eviction or forcible entry and detainer suit, call the court clerk and ask if the judge will hear the case on the answer date. If the answer is "no," you only need to be concerned with getting a written response to the court by the answer date. If the judge is going to hear the case, you must be prepared to defend yourself against the landlord's contention that he is entitled to evict you.

The answer should include a statement that the tenant "denies all the claims set out in the lawsuit." Additionally, a "counterclaim" against the landlord can be included. A counterclaim is an allegation that the landlord owes the tenant an amount of money. Typically, the tenant's counterclaim is for repair expenses that the landlord has refused to cover. For example, if the toilet did not flush and the tenant was forced to call a plumber, the tenant can counterclaim for the cost of the plumber.

> **TIP:** You will only win on your counterclaims for repair costs if the landlord knew he needed to make the repairs and refused. At a trial, you must have proof of notice to the landlord in the form of a written demand, or a witness that can testify that the landlord knew about the problem.

I've been served with a lawsuit for eviction. Is it too late to settle with the landlord? *No.* You can settle any time before the judge makes her final ruling, even during the trial itself.

If you and the landlord came to an agreement before the answer was due, you can go ahead and file an answer denying the claims in the lawsuit. After denying the claims, include a description of the settlement. For example, "the landlord and I have agreed to settle this case and a trial is not necessary." Then ask the court to dismiss the case.

If my landlord and I have settled the eviction lawsuit, do I need a written settlement agreement? *Yes, otherwise you have no proof of your agreement with the landlord.* Additionally, if the court has not dismissed the lawsuit, the landlord can request a trial date at anytime.

What happens if I don't respond to or answer the eviction lawsuit? You automatically lose the lawsuit and your landlord may be entitled to possession of the premises within 48 hours or less.

Trial

The eviction lawsuit is set for trial whether or not the tenant responds. If the tenant has disputed the landlord's allegations, the judge will hear from both parties during the trial and decide if an eviction is warranted. The judge's decision is the "judgment."

The landlord must show cause as to why then tenant should be evicted. The tenant is allowed to defend the eviction suit. His defenses are the reasons he should not be evicted. For example, one of the tenant's defenses may be that he did, in fact, pay the rent to the landlord if non-payment is the basis for the eviction.

> **TIP:** The tenant may represent herself at trial. The landlord can only represent himself if he is a private owner of the property. Corporations that own property and seek to evict tenants must be represented by a lawyer at trial.

> **TIP:** The tenant has the right to a jury trial. If your landlord has brought an eviction suit against you, a jury may be sympathetic to your situation. Additionally, the time and expense of a jury trial may force the landlord to settle the case, and you can avoid a trial entirely. On the other hand, a deadbeat tenant who is refusing to pay the rent will probably fare badly in front of a jury.

At trial, can I raise the issue of money owed to me by my landlord for a personal loan?
No. The court only hears evidence relating to who is entitled to possession of the premises. Other matters, including ownership and title to the property, may not be tried at a forcible entry and detainer trial.

Evidence

"Evidence" is the proof each of the parties presents to the court to show the judge why she should rule in the landlord or tenant's favor. Evidence can be testimony from the parties or their witnesses, or written agreements, including the lease agreement, cancelled checks, receipts, correspondence between the parties, including repair demands, and photographs.

The landlord presents his evidence first. He will show the court the lease agreement and testify that he has not received a rental payment for however many months the tenant is overdue.

The tenant may present evidence as well. If the tenant has paid the rent, she can show the court a copy of cancelled check. If the tenant has a counterclaim, she presents proof of that to the court as well. For example, if the landlord owes her for repair costs, the tenant can show the court her repair receipts. Photographs of the repairs can also be used as evidence.

> **If the tenant does not answer by the deadline, or fails to appear for trial, the landlord gets a "default judgment." A default judgment means the tenant has automatically lost the case. When the landlord appears in court, the judge accepts his evidence (since the tenant did not dispute it in writing by the deadline or appearing at trial) and will issue an order directing the sheriff to evict the tenant.**

Tenant's Appeal of Eviction

The tenant who loses an eviction case always has the right to appeal the court's decision. Some state laws require an appeal to be filed within 5 days of the court's ruling in the landlord's favor. If the deadline is missed, the case cannot be appealed.

> **TIP:** Although judges cannot give legal advice, ask the judge at the time that she rules in the landlord's favor, how much time you have to appeal. She will probably tell you since you are representing yourself.

Appeals are complicated and there is no room for error. Additionally, a higher court considers appeals, and the judge will not be as patient with the tenant who represents herself. If you are considering an appeal, talk to an attorney as soon as possible. The deadline for filing an appeal will be fast approaching and you need immediate legal advice.

What is an appeal bond? *An appeal bond is the amount of money you are required to pay in order to appeal the eviction order against you to a higher court.* If you cannot afford the appeal bond, you can file a "pauper's affidavit" stating you do not have the resources to pay the bond and the judge may waive it.

I'm appealing the eviction. Do I have to continue to pay rent? *Yes.* However, during the appeal, the rent is paid into the registry of the court rather than to your landlord.

> If non-payment of rent was not the reason for eviction, you must continue to pay rent directly to your landlord.

Obtaining and Serving the Eviction Order

After she hears the evidence, the judge decides whether or not to grant the landlord's request for an order evicting the tenant. If the court issues the order and the tenant is present, the judge informs the tenant in person that he has a set period of time to vacate the premises. Some state laws require only a 24-hour notice. Other laws require a longer time to allow the tenant to vacate.

The landlord won his eviction suit and I have 6 days to vacate. Do I have to notify that court if we've come to an agreement on the amount of past due rent and the landlord has agreed to let me stay in the apartment? *Yes. Your agreement does not change the court judgment evicting you.* Unless you notify the court, the landlord can have you evicted at any time in the future without further court proceedings. The landlord must sign a statement that he will not enforce the court's judgment and file it with the court. If he does not file the statement, then you must file it.

CAUTION: If the landlord will not sign an agreement promising to not enforce the judgment, you are in the risky position of being evicted in the future, even if you are paying rent. In this situation, you should vacate the premises although you have an oral agreement with the landlord.

The eviction order is sometimes termed a "writ of possession" or "writ of ejectment," which gives the landlord the right to have the tenant physically removed and retake possession of the rental property.

The landlord does not personally carry out the writ of possession. Typically, a sheriff's deputy arrives at the premises with the writ and orders the tenant to immediately vacate and takes his possessions, under threat of arrest. The deputy stays until the tenant is completely moved out of the property. The landlord is not involved with this part of the process, since court orders are enforced by law enforcement personnel. He may watch and observe only.

My tenant finally vacated after I won an eviction suit; however, he left behind all his property. What do I do? *Most laws require the landlord to keep the property for a period time.* You can leave it in the apartment or store it. Once the required amount of time has passed, you may sell or dispose of the property. For example, if you are required by law to keep the property for 14 days, you cannot dispose of it until 14 days from the time the tenant vacated the apartment has passed. You must store the property or leave it in the apartment.

The judge ruled in my favor and I can evict my tenant. Do I have to let her in to retrieve her property after the trial? *Yes.* The tenant has a right to take her belongings with her when she is evicted or before the order is served on her.

> **TIP:** The tenant still has the right to enter the apartment after she has lost at trial and before she is served with the writ of possession.

I know the sheriff is trying to serve me with an eviction order. Can I stay in the apartment if I continue to avoid him? *No. Laws permit the law enforcement officer that is attempting to serve an individual to post the eviction order in a conspicuous place or mail it if she cannot serve you personally.* After the order has been posted or mailed, you must vacate or risk being removed bodily by the sheriff.

The sheriff served me with an eviction order and I attempted to pay my landlord the past rent I owe. Can she refuse to accept the rent? *Yes. Your chance to pay the past-due rent ended once the landlord obtained an eviction order.* She is under no obligation to accept the rent and the eviction order continues in full force.

I paid my past due rent to my landlord after I was served with an eviction order. How do I know I still won't be evicted? *You can be* *still be evicted as long as the eviction order is in effect.* Your payment to the landlord does not extinguish the judge's order.

> **TIP:** To make certain you will not be evicted, you must get a written agreement from the landlord stating she will not evict you based on the current order, and file the agreement with the court.

I've been served with an eviction order, but it's snowing outside. I can't be evicted in bad weather, can I? Unfortunately, you can. Despite rain, snow or cold weather, you have to move out by the date specified in the eviction order.

Self help

The landlord who decides to "evict" a tenant without the proper court orders, is committing an illegal self-help action. The landlord must go to court to evict a tenant. Changing the locks, turning off utilities, entering the unit and removing the tenant's property or threatening the tenant or other occupants violates the law. The tenant has the right to sue the landlord for damages as a result of any of these actions. The fact that the tenant has not paid rent in months, for example, does not extinguish his right to sue.

8 THE LEGAL SYSTEM

The American legal system is rooted in English common law, which is reflected in the federal and state laws that currently govern the United States. Federal, state, and local courts and administrative agencies interpret and enforce laws, litigate disputes and render decisions based on those laws every day.

COMMON LAW

Before statutes, regulations and the Constitution existed, people were governed by "common law"—legal customs that regulated behavior and business activities. Common law is the end result of a multitude of customs and general principles that began centuries ago in England and continues to develop today in judicial case law.

For example, a person who engages in reckless behavior and injures another person may be liable for damages under common law. Of course, there are statutes addressing reckless behavior while driving or setting out standards for safety on construction sites, but not all situations concerning liability for reckless behavior are covered in statutes. Thus, the common law principle that a person's reckless behavior may result in liability can be applied to a scenario the statutes do not address.

THE UNITED STATES CONSTITUTION

Although the U.S. Constitution importantly sets out the basic rights guaranteed to all citizens, its greatest impact on the American legal system is the division of power among the three branches of government, which creates the boundaries between federal and state law. The legislative, executive and judicial branches of our government each make distinctive contributions to the legal system.

The Constitution directs Congress in the types of laws it can enact. Once those laws are passed, the executive branch (the President) can veto or sign them. The courts then interpret and enforce the laws.

STATUTES

Statutes (laws that have been passed by Congress or state legislatures) are the most obvious source of the many kinds of laws that regulate conduct. Criminal laws describe and define illegal conduct. Civil laws provide a framework for actions that affect other individuals.

For example, laws concerning the family relationship are the civil laws that control the marriage, divorce and adoption processes. Likewise, there are statutes directed at certain businesses and occupations, real estate matters and contracts between individuals. Although there are a great many statutes, both federal and state, not every potential legal issue can possibly be addressed by a statute. In those situations, common law applies.

Federal laws are enacted in the U.S. Congress and apply to all persons living in the United States, regardless of their state of residence. State laws are enacted in state legislatures and apply to citizens of those states or any dispute that occurs there.

JUDICIAL PRECEDENT

When the verdict in a trial is appealed, a specific point of law may be examined and interpreted by the appeals court. The appellate courts' decisions are often published and become "judicial precedent." Lower courts and other appellate courts then apply the appeals courts' interpretation so that a precedent is eventually created. By following another court's interpretations of a law, consistency and predictability is ensured.

EXAMPLE: A statute might require a builder to use "reasonable safety standards" on the building site. If a lawsuit is filed claiming that reasonable safety standards were not used, the judge will review other cases that involved that statute to determine exactly what the "reasonable" standards are in the situation. A previous case may have held that requiring a builder to have his workers undergo medical examinations before employment was reasonable. If the builder in the present case did not provide medical exams, the judge can rule that the statute was violated because judicial precedent holds that the builder did not follow reasonable safety standards.

TIP: Parties involved in cases where judicial precedent is unfavorable to their claims try to distinguish their facts from the facts in the cases that produced the earlier decisions. For instance, in the builder example, the builder might claim that the workers gave him false medical documentation so it was reasonable for him to believe another exam was not necessary.

REGULATIONS

Regulations are typically enacted by federal and state agencies to provide specific direction for broader laws. Administrative agencies are authorized by Congress to adopt such rules.

EXAMPLE: Federal law provides that disabled children receive the same education as nondisabled children. Because this is a broad mandate, regulations created by the U.S. Department of Education guide educators in this process. For example, a regulation may provide that children with disabilities must be tested within a certain amount of time after enrollment in a school. The statute itself does not go into such detail.

ORDINANCES

Cities and municipalities do not pass statutes; they enact ordinances. Ordinances are municipal laws that have force and effect only within the boundaries of the city where they were enacted.

EXAMPLE: Cities commonly enact zoning ordinances. An ordinance may prohibit retail businesses in a certain neighborhood in the city. However, because the ordinance applies only within the city, a business across the street from the neighborhood is perfectly legal if it is outside the city limits.

The primary function of city ordinances is to prohibit certain actions that put the public's health, safety and welfare at risk. When an ordinance is violated, a city attorney handles the prosecution in municipal court. Some offenses addressed by city ordinances include:

- unlawful possession of alcohol by minors
- possession or purchase of tobacco products by minors
- prohibition of smoking in specified public areas and places
- possession of drugs and drug paraphernalia
- retail theft or shoplifting
- criminal trespass to land
- curfews for minors
- disorderly conduct
- cruelty to animals
- truancy
- noise

Additionally, cities enact ordinances concerning building safety. These ordinances are part of city building codes, fire codes, plumbing and electrical codes.

If I violate a city ordinance, have I committed a crime? *No.* Only violations of state criminal statutes are "crimes." Violating a criminal ordinance is considered a "quasi-criminal" violation, or a civil infraction.

> **The distinction is important because persons accused of a crime are typically afforded more rights than someone who violated an ordinance. For example, to prove you violated the disorderly conduct ordinance, the city attorney's burden of proof is a preponderance of the evidence (more likely than not you were disorderly) versus the much higher "beyond a reasonable doubt" standard that is required in criminal trials.**

Can I go to jail for violating a city ordinance? *Yes.* Violations of some ordinances could result in jail time, a monetary fine or both.

Can an attorney represent me in municipal court? *Yes.* An attorney may represent anyone charged with violating an ordinance.

> **TIP:** If there is a possibility of jail time and you cannot afford a lawyer, cities may appoint a public defender to represent you in court.

State law does not prohibit me from renting an apartment to a gay couple. How can my refusal to rent violate an ordinance? *Ordinances are usually much stricter than state laws.* Many cities have passed antidiscrimination statutes, which prohibit housing discrimination because of sexual preference.

THE COURT SYSTEM

The court system in the United States operates on a national, state and local level. Lawsuits are filed in certain courts at different levels depending on the type of case and the amount of money involved. For example, a case involving injuries

to a person by police officers could be filed in federal court because civil rights under the U.S. Constitution are an issue.

LOCAL COURTS

There are many different types of local courts:

- A municipal court handles violations of city ordinances—everything from traffic tickets to disorderly conduct cases.
- Small claims courts are civil courts created to resolve disputes between individuals without the necessity of a lawyer. These courts cannot hear cases that involve more than $2,000 to $5,000 in money or property.
- Juvenile courts hear cases where minors have committed offenses.
- Justice of the peace courts exist to adjudicate certain matters, such as evictions.

Verdicts in local courts are generally appealable to the state trial court.

STATE TRIAL COURTS

A case involving a state's civil and criminal laws is tried in state courts. Many states have specialized courts that handle only criminal, civil or family law matters. However, in another state, the court may have the jurisdiction to handle any type of matter.

There are many different terms for state courts. For example, the court may be called a Municipal, County, District, Circuit or Superior Court.

STATE APPELLATE COURTS

Litigants have the right to appeal state trial court verdicts and ask an appeals court to examine the mistakes made during the trial. These courts have the power to reverse the trial court's verdict, remand the case (send it back to the trial court for a new trial) or render another verdict. Appellate courts are a step between a state's trial court and a state's supreme, or highest, court.

There are many names used for appellate courts, including Court of Appeals, District Court of Appeal, Court of Appeal, Intermediate Court of Appeals and Appellate Court.

STATE SUPREME COURTS

If a litigant loses at the appellate court level, she may appeal to the state's highest, or supreme, court. This is the last opportunity she has to change the outcome of the trial. State supreme courts are the final court of appeal in that state.

There are many names used for state supreme courts, including Supreme Court, Court of Appeals and Supreme Judicial Court.

> In cases where a constitutional issue is involved, an appeal to the federal court of appeals may be permitted.

U.S. DISTRICT COURTS

A federal trial court is known as a U.S. District Court and there are several assigned to each of the states. Larger states are divided into districts, such as the Northern or Southern Districts of Texas. Each district may have several district courts.

U.S. District Courts handle civil and criminal cases that involve federal laws (such as kidnapping offenses), the U.S. Constitution (such as discrimination in employment because of race) and civil cases where the parties are residents of different states.

U.S. APPELLATE COURTS

All U.S. District Courts belong to a specific "circuit." For instance, federal cases from the U.S. District Courts in the southern part of the United States are appealed to the Court of Appeals in the Fifth Circuit. These federal appeals courts review verdicts from U.S. District Courts.

U.S. SUPREME COURT

Once a case reaches the U.S. Supreme Court, there is no further appeal. The U.S. Supreme Court is free to accept or reject most cases that are appealed to it. Only cases with important constitutional questions or where there is a conflict between states are generally accepted.

Cases may be appealed to the U.S. Supreme Court from the U.S. Appellate Courts or from the highest court in the individual states.

OTHER FEDERAL COURTS

There are several other federal courts that were created to hear specific issues only. Some of these include U.S. Tax Court, bankruptcy courts, maritime courts, the U.S. Court of Federal Claims and courts of veterans' appeals.

> **TIP:** For an overview of the federal court system, go to the U.S. Courts Web site at **www.uscourts.gov**.

ADMINISTRATIVE COURTS AND HEARINGS

Federal, state and local agencies have oversight over different areas of public interest and create regulations that must be followed. For example, the state education agency oversees public schools, administrators, teachers and licensing. It creates regulations to guide persons involved in the educational system.

Administrative agencies make decisions affecting people based on the regulations. For instance, the Social Security Agency may decide that an individual does not qualify for disability payments. That individual has the right to appeal the administrative decision. A hearing officer or administrative law judge (ALJ) hears the appeal at an administrative hearing.

Can I bring a lawyer with me to an administrative hearing? *Yes. Additionally, in some cases, you may have a nonlawyer representative.* For example, a special education advocate is allowed to appear in hearings concerning a disabled student.

What happens at an administrative hearing? The ALJ or hearing officer explains the issues, questions you and your witnesses and looks at any evidence you have submitted.

> **TIP:** Hearings are tape-recorded and you are typically entitled to a copy of the tape.

I am unable to travel to the hearing location. What can I do? *You may request a telephone hearing.* Telephone hearings are not uncommon in administrative procedures as it is often difficult for people to travel to the state or federal agency's location.

> **TIP:** Some state agencies hold all hearings over the telephone or by video call.

Will a decision be made on my case at the close of the hearing? *No.* You will receive the decision in writing.

What happens if I fail to show up for my hearing? *The officer or ALJ may rule against you.* You should always contact the person handling the hearing and explain the situation.

Can I appeal a hearing decision? *Yes. In some situations you can appeal the hearing officer's decision to a court.* In other cases, such as educational hearings, the officer's or ALJ's decision may be final.

SELECTING A LAWYER

Choosing a competent attorney to represent you on a legal matter is one of the most important decisions you may make. Because most people are rarely involved in lawsuits, being involved in one is typically stressful and traumatic. A good lawyer will give you confidence and make litigation more bearable.

Laws allow attorneys to advertise on the radio and television, in newspapers and phone books, and on billboards. It is not recommended that you choose a lawyer based on his advertisement. However, the advertisement may be a helpful starting place. For instance, you can find out if the lawyer has a certified specialty, get access to the firm's Web site and perhaps get information on fees from an advertisement.

> **TIP:** Phone books typically list attorneys by their specialty or board certification. This is important information because attorneys board certified in a certain field are perceived as being more qualified. Additionally, complex cases (mineral law, patents, appeals) are generally better served by a board-certified lawyer in that specialty.

It never hurts to use an Internet search engine to compile a list of possible attorneys in your area. You can then search a single attorney's name to find papers or legal articles she has written as well as cases she has handled.

> **TIP:** There are a tremendous number of Web sites that promise attorney referrals or list lawyers supposedly competent in their field. Do not use these Web sites to find an attorney. Remember the attorneys utilizing the Web sites are simply paid advertisers. Do not expect to find an attorney by filling out a form and checking off your "issue." Selecting an attorney is not like shopping for a car online. No form can unearth the right "make and model" lawyer for your situation.

Talking to family, friends and colleagues is an excellent way to find an attorney. These people have had dealings with specific attorneys and can tell you what their experiences were with that lawyer.

All states maintain an official Web site listing attorneys licensed to practice law in that state. The Web site should have information on the attorney's years in practice, specializations, the law school she attended and whether any disciplinary actions have ever been initiated against her.

> **TIP:** State bars generally have sections or committees of lawyers who practice in one area. If your case involves a business contract, you can contact the president of the business law or litigation section for some direction in selecting an attorney.

Lawyers practicing in a city or area are usually members of the local bar association. The local bar association has an office that you can contact for a lawyer referral. The referrals simply come from a list. The name you are given is not necessarily an individual personally recommended by the local bar association. He is simply a member who is available for referrals.

How do I know if my situation warrants hiring an attorney? *You should consult with an attorney if you or your property has suffered* *a serious injury.* Personal injuries with pain and suffering and out-of-pocket expenses definitely warrant a consultation (usually free) with an attorney.

> **TIP:** If your business or property is injured or injury is threatened, and your livelihood is likely to be affected, it is important to talk to an attorney as soon as possible.

> **TIP:** If you have been a victim of discrimination or a civil rights violation, you should first contact the Equal Employment Opportunity Commission (EEOC) or the U.S. Office of Civil Rights (OCR). Those Web sites are **www.eeoc.gov** (EEOC) and **www.hhs.gov/ocr/index.html** (OCR).

I am meeting with an attorney today to discuss my case. What questions should I ask him? *You should ask:*

- How long have you been practicing law?
- How long have you been practicing in this area (city, county)?
- How long have you been with this firm?
- Are you board certified in a specialty and, if so, when were you certified?
- How many cases have you handled similar to mine?
- How many cases have you tried in front of jury?
- Do you usually represent plaintiffs or defendants?
- Will you primarily handle the case or will it be assigned to another attorney? (then ask the same questions of the attorney who will get the case)
- Will you take the case on a contingency basis?
- If not, explain your fees. How is your hourly time segmented?
- What do you anticipate the expenses (not fees) will be to handle this case? Will I have to front the expenses?
- Will your paralegal or legal assistant be working closely on the case? Will I be talking to him on a regular basis?

After you have established answers to basic questions, you should question the attorney about the specifics of your case:

- What do you see as the legal issues?
- How strong is my case, in your opinion?
- Do you have a sense that the case can be settled?
- How much preparation, research, investigation and discovery will be necessary to handle the cases?
- If I do not want to settle, are you willing to take the case to trial?

ATTORNEY'S CONSIDERATIONS

Although it may be a simple matter to hire an attorney, especially in cases of divorce, bankruptcy and even criminal law, there are many times lawyers may be reluctant to take on your case. Lawyers accept cases and clients based on several considerations.

▸ **SPECIALTY INVOLVED.** Some legal matters are extremely specialized. Patent law, for example, should never be handled by any attorney that is not highly experienced in the process. If you live in a city where there are no patent attorneys, it will be very difficult to hire a general practice attorney to handle this situation. Additionally, although most lawyers are capable of drafting wills, probate litigation can be complex. Thus, the same attorney who drafted your father's will may not want to continue on as the family lawyer if the will is contested.

▸ **CLAIM OR ISSUE.** Some problems that a client brings to an attorney do not rise to a legal claim. Your neighbor's purple fence may bother you, but the law may not give you any particular legal options.

▸ **CLIENT'S ATTITUDE.** Lawyers do not want to represent clients who are unreasonable, unwilling to negotiate or consider settlement offers. Of course, the client can turn down a settlement offer, but attorneys want to represent individuals who will consider all of their options. Lawyers also want likeable clients, especially in a civil matter that is going to trial. A client with an unsavory past, spotty employment or a criminal record may have a difficult time finding representation in noncriminal matters.

▸ **THE ADVERSARY.** Taking on a neighbor is different than pursuing a claim against the local rabbi. Believable adversaries with good reputations in the community usually make a case more difficult because a jury is ultimately affected by the adversary's well-known character. Attorneys always consider the individual or company that will be on the other side before taking a case. Some adversaries, particularly corporations who can afford substantial legal fees, will drown the lawyer in paperwork, motions and depositions making it unattractive for the attorney to go up against such an adversary. Clients that have claims against such companies will have to find a lawyer with the resources, office staff and experience to take on adversaries that wear down the lawyer and the client.

▸ **COST OF CASE.** Although most people think of lawyers' fees as the primary cost of representation (and they are), other expenses can be quite steep. For instance, ordering and copying records (personnel, medical); travel expenses; and court reporter and videographer fees (for depositions) quickly add up. The attorney typically fronts the payment for these services and if expenses will run into thousands of dollars just to explore the client's claims, a lawyer may be unwilling to take on the case.

> In contingency cases, the lawyer pays the expenses, then deducts those costs from the settlement or jury award.

▸ **POTENTIAL AMOUNT OF RECOVERY.** A client may have a good claim; however, the damages she can obtain under the law may not be worth the cost of representation. This is especially true in personal injury cases where attorneys typically take the case on a contingency basis. The 30- to 40-percent contingency fee may not make up for the attorney's time in pursuing a case where only a small amount of damages are recoverable.

▸ **LIKELIHOOD OF RECOVERY.** In all cases, lawyers consider the probability of success. Your attorney should be frank with you and never make guarantees. If the chances are slim that the client will prevail, a lawyer is usually unwilling to take on the matter since the client is ultimately disappointed and dissatisfied.

> A criminal case is unique because a person's freedom is at stake and the defendant does not have to prove her innocence. The client may look guilty but the defense lawyer still advocates for her client—a plea bargain or hung jury is always a possibility.

▸ **COURTS AND JUDGES.** Depending on the nature of the claim, a lawsuit must be filed in a specific type of court. Bankruptcies are filed in federal bankruptcy courts; will contests are handled in probate court; and constitutional claims must be filed in federal court. Lawsuits in federal courts usually mean higher fees for the client. Federal courts have complex rules, short time schedules and the judges are typically extremely strict with attorneys and their clients. For instance, postponing a hearing in state court may be easy to obtain but not permitted by a federal judge.

> **TIP:** Some federal judges have such fierce reputations that lawyers have fee agreements specifically increasing their fees if the case should land in that judge's court.

ATTORNEY FEES AND EXPENSES

Attorneys' fees are one of the biggest factors in any client's decision to hire an attorney. Some lawsuits are handled on a contingency basis where attorney's fees are contingent on the lawyer recovering some sum of money for her client. Other lawsuits, such as bankruptcies, divorces and DUIs are often handled for a flat rate fee. The traditional method of billing by an attorney based on his hourly rate is generally the most costly method.

Fee-Based Billing

Lawyers set an hourly price on the legal services they provide based on their experience, education, location and specialty. For example, a partner in a law firm that specializes exclusively in oil and gas law may charge a minimum of $300 per hour. A young attorney just out of law school (known as an "associate") may have a rate of $100 per hour.

My lawyer charges $200 an hour. If we meet for 30 minutes, how much am I charged? *Lawyers break down their hourly rate in segments within the hour.* A 30-minute meeting will cost you $100.

Why have I been charged 15 minutes worth of fees when I only spoke to my lawyer on the phone for 5 minutes? *Your attorney has broken his hourly rate into 15-minute time segments.* The phone call was rounded up to 15 minutes for billing purposes.

Flat-Rate Case

The most common legal problems people encounter in their lives are often handled for a flat fee. These attorneys commonly handle one type of case over and over, and their offices are set up to efficiently represent the clients.

The attorney sets a rate based on the type of case, and the client is charged that amount only. However, the flat rate remains effective only if the case proceeds as expected by the attorney. For example, an attorney that agrees to handle an uncontested divorce for $2,000 will no longer apply the flat rate if the other spouse decides to fight or contest the case.

Why does my bill contain charges for "memo to the file" after every phone conversation I have with my attorney, no matter how brief? *Lawyers keep written documentation of all phone calls with their clients.* These memos are an important part of the file and help refresh the attorney's memory when he next talks to you. Remember, your attorney could be handling 50 different files at one time.

My bankruptcy is being handled for a flat fee of $1,000. I signed a contract with my attorney stating that if the matter is litigated, I will be billed on an hourly basis. What does this mean? *You have agreed to pay your attorney her hourly fee if one of your creditors objects to the bankruptcy.* Your attorney set her flat fee based on the assumption that there would be no objections to your bankruptcy and the bankruptcy trustee would approve it.

Are attorneys' fees negotiable? *Yes. Some attorneys may cut their hourly rate depending on the situation.* You can also ask if the associate rate could be reduced.

My husband is fighting our divorce and I cannot afford to pay my attorney now that his hourly fee that has gone into effect. What happens now? Unless you can work out something with your lawyer, she will probably ask the court to permit her to withdraw as your attorney because you cannot pay.

Lawyers are routinely allowed to withdraw from representing a client when the client has not paid. The lawyer must file a "Motion to Withdraw," which the judge typically grants. Only if the lawyer is in the middle of a trial will she be forced to continue to represent the nonpaying client.

My bill includes 3 hours for "research." What does this mean? Research is the time the lawyer puts in studying case law, statutes, regulations and investigating the legal status of your claim.

Contingency Fee Cases

Being represented on a contingency fee basis is the most advantageous way to pursue litigation. The client pays nothing unless the lawyer recovers money on his behalf. However, because the lawyer is essentially working for "free" until the case ends and money is recovered, attorneys are extremely picky about the contingency cases they take.

Attorneys take cases on contingency only when there is a good chance of recovery, the client would be believable and likable in front of a jury and the amount of money at stake is not insubstantial. For example, an attorney is likely to take a medical malpractice case on a contingency basis that involves a child's death where the health care personnel made obvious mistakes.

The typical contingency contract provides that the attorney will get 40 percent of any recovery, before expenses have been deducted. If the lawyer settles a client's case for $10,000, she is due $4,000. The client gets $6,000 minus any expenses paid by the attorney, such as filing fees, expert fees and the like. Fifty percent contingency fee contracts are becoming more common.

I know I do not have to pay attorneys' fees because my case is being handled on a contingency, but what about expenses?
Lawyers' attitudes toward expenses vary. Most attorneys pay expenses on behalf of the client as the case proceeds then deduct the expenses from the client's portion when money is recovered. However, you may be asked to cover some or all of the expenses.

> **TIP:** If you are paying expenses, make sure you have a written agreement limiting certain types of expenses. For instance, you do not want to be charged $.10 for every copy when copying can be done at $.03 a page.

If my case is being handled as a contingency, do I have to accept a settlement offer? *No.*
You do not have to accept a settlement offer even if your lawyer advises you to take the money. Just because yours is a contingency case does not mean you must immediately settle so that your attorney will get paid.

> **Clients who repeatedly turn down reasonable settlement offers against the advice of their attorney may lose their lawyer. The attorney can ask the court to let him withdraw on the basis that the client is being unreasonable.**

If the person who sued me loses the case, will they have to pay my attorney's fees?
Generally, your attorney's fees will not be reimbursed for defending a civil lawsuit.

> **Lawsuits brought in bad faith or for harassment could possibly be dismissed by the judge, along with an order that the defendant's attorney's fees be paid.**

LEGAL MALPRACTICE

A lawyer who fails to competently represent his client may have committed "legal malpractice." For instance, a client who suffers damages (loses her case at trial) may have a claim against her attorney for malpractice. Typically, malpractice claims are based on the lawyer's:

- negligence,
- breach of fiduciary duty, and
- breach of contract.

Proof of Legal Malpractice

To win a legal malpractice cases against your attorney, you must show that all the following facts exist:

1. An attorney-client relationship existed between you and your lawyer.

2. Your lawyer acted negligently (the most common claim) by not performing up to the standards practiced by other attorneys in the area.

3. The lawyer's behavior (typically failure to attend to the matter) caused damage to you, the client.

4. The legal result or outcome would have been different if the lawyer had not acted negligently.

5. You suffered a financial loss as a result of the lawyer's malpractice.

The fourth element is the most important. Unless the client can show that the underlying case (the case the lawyer neglected) had merit and she likely would have won that case, she does not a claim for legal malpractice. Because of this element, legal malpractice claims are really a "case within case." The client has to prove the lawyer's negligence as well as show the underlying case could have been won.

> **TIP:** Even if a million dollar verdict would have been awarded, unless the judgment could be collected, the malpractice claim may fail. For example, the absolutely winnable case against a hospital for medical malpractice (which the lawyer neglected to such an extent the case was lost) does not establish a cause of action for legal malpractice if the hospital is bankrupt and the judgment could never have been collected.

Grievance or Complaint

Clients always have the option of complaining about their lawyer's acts to the state bar, the office that oversees attorneys practicing in that state. If the misconduct rises to the level of a grievance, the lawyer will be reprimanded. However, the misconduct may not be malpractice.

Grievances arise out of an attorney's unethical conduct. All attorneys are bound by certain rules of ethics. Lawyer who do not comply are subject to disciplinary action by the state bar. The discipline can be a private or public reprimand, suspension of the lawyer's license and, in the most egregious of cases, the lawyer must permanently give up his law license.

How do I file a grievance against my attorney? Contact the local bar association in your city. They should have information on how to file a grievance. There may be a form to fill out or you may just write a letter to the state bar requesting an investigation.

What do I say in my letter requesting an investigation? Your letter should give:

- your name, address and telephone number,
- the name, address and telephone number of the attorney you want investigated (include the lawyer's full name and law firm name),
- the name of your court case (if one has been filed) including the case number,
- a description of what your attorney did or did not do that may have been incompetent, improper or unethical, and
- copies of any documents that you have, such as letters, agreements or correspondence that help support your complaint.

Can I find out if my attorney has had previous grievances filed against her or if the state bar has disciplined her? *Yes. Most states have an Attorney Registration and Disciplinary Commission (ARDC).* These agencies maintain discipline information for lawyers licensed in your state.

What do I get if I win my case against my attorney for malpractice? *You recover the money you would have potentially received if you had prevailed on the underlying case.* For example, if it were clear you would have been awarded $10,000 for your personal injuries, you would recover that amount.

> **TIP:** The attorney's malpractice insurance pays the claim, plus the cost of defending the attorney.

> **Attorney malpractice claims have a statute of limitations just like any other claim. If the client fails to sue within the time frame set out by state law (2 to 4 years), she has lost her right to file a lawsuit.**

Is it malpractice if my lawyer will not return my phone calls? *No.* However, if your lawyer is not regularly returning phone calls in a timely manner (at least by the next day), you may want to consider hiring another attorney.

> **TIP:** If leaving messages for the attorney does not work, ask for the name of his legal assistant and leave messages for that person. Typically, the legal assistant will return calls. Of course, she should have returned your calls to the attorney if he was unable to get back to you.

> **TIP:** If communicating with you attorney's office has become impossible, fax the office detailing the dates you called and the fact that the calls were not returned. Ask him to call you with 24 hours. If you still do not hear from your lawyer, contact the local bar and make a complaint.

I hired my current attorney because she said I had a great case and could probably settle it for at least $100,000. Now she is pressuring me to settle for $10,000. Is this malpractice? *No. Lawyers should never guarantee a result, and it appears she overestimated the value of your case.* However, you need to get your file, take it to another attorney and get a second opinion about the value of your claims.

I think my lawyer purposely overcharged me. What do I do? *You have several alternatives, but initially you should speak with your attorney about your concerns and ask that certain portions of the bill be cut.* Most attorneys are willing to work with clients on bills. However, if you cannot get your attorney to reduce a portion of the bill, try one of the following options:

- Pay the portion you believe is reasonable, accompanied by a letter explaining your position.
- Pay the entire bill then sue in small claims court (if the amount is just a few thousand dollars) and ask for a partial refund.
- Pay the bill and file a complaint with the local bar and state agency that regulates lawyers complaining of inflated billing.
- Request fee arbitration.

> **Fee arbitration is a process available in most states where the client and attorney present their sides of the issue to a panel of neutral arbitrators. You should never agree to binding arbitration because you will waive your right to sue for a refund.**

My divorce is final and the case has been completed, but my lawyer refuses to give back my retainer. What do I do? *Lawyers are required to return a client's retainer when the case is finished and there are no bills left outstanding.* Complain immediately to the state bar that regulates attorneys. If your lawyer has "stolen" your money or mishandled it in such a way that it is gone, most state bars have a fund that will reimburse you.

My attorney has been disciplined by the state bar because of my complaint. Is this proof that he committed malpractice? *No.*

A malpractice claim requires that you suffered some sort of financial loss, which you would not have suffered, but for the lawyer's unethical and incompetent behavior.

EXAMPLE: If you hired the attorney to file a lawsuit for personal injuries you received in a car wreck and he did not file before the legal deadline (the statute of limitations) and you can prove you would have recovered some amount of money (either through settlement or a jury award), you may have a malpractice claim. On the other hand, if the lawsuit was filed in a timely manner but handled incompetently (the lawyer missed hearings, did not answer discovery), there is no malpractice.

> **A claim for malpractice cannot be solely based on the lawyer's violation of a rule of ethics or rule of conduct.**

I do not think my lawyer is really working up my case. What should I do? Talk to your attorney immediately and ask that you be kept informed of what is going on in your case by either her or her legal assistant.

> **TIP:** Follow up with a letter setting out your expectations. If the lawyer made verbal or written promises (such as "I'll get interrogatories out by next week"), include those statements in the letter as well. The letter creates a paper trail of communication with your attorney. If the attorney still continues to neglect your case, you have proof to back up any complaint you make.

LEGAL SERVICE PLANS

Because the costs of hiring an attorney are often prohibitive, legal service plans have become an option for some people. The plans require payment of an annual membership fee or retainer in return for access to legal services. Like insurance policies, legal plan coverage is greatly varied; however, the plans generally provide adequate legal services for the most basic issues (e.g., wills, uncontested divorces, property transfers, adoptions and landlord-tenant disputes). Some plans offer unlimited phone access to an attorney as part of the plan, but office visits may be limited.

> **TIP:** It is becoming more common for employers, unions, school districts and other organizations to offer legal plans to their employees and members at a reduced cost.

The cost of prepaid legal service plans varies from $100 to $400 per year. Business plans may cost more. Some plans add services and access to attorneys with every year's renewal.

> **TIP:** The American Bar Association Web site has information on prepaid legal service plans at **www.abanet.org/legalservices/prepaid/home.html**

Legal service plan companies typically offer two types of plans:

Access Legal Service Plans

The least costly legal service plan is one that allows the member to quickly access an attorney for uncomplicated advice and simple legal services. For instance, an access plan may include the preparation of a simple will for you and your spouse but exclude the preparation of other legal documents.

Comprehensive Legal Service Plans

Comprehensive prepaid legal plans allow the member to access a broader range of legal services. Generally, matters that require extensive time and effort on the part of an attorney are only covered in a comprehensive plan. For instance, setting up trusts and drawing up papers for the sale of business would not be covered under the basic access plan but may be available in the comprehensive plan.

Some comprehensive plans may provide legal representation in some types of court cases, such as child custody lawsuits. Additionally, representation in criminal matters may be provided. Individuals who own several real estate properties, have family trusts and partnerships,

issues with complicated heirships or who need regular business advice should look at comprehensive prepaid legal plans.

How do I determine if a legal service plan will benefit me? *The plan will be beneficial to you if you own a small business and have frequent, but basic, legal questions.* Additionally, if you believe you may encounter legal problems in the future, you should consider a plan.

What do I look for in a legal service plan? Some items to look at include:

- the specific types of matters that are not covered by the plan
- the limit, if any, on matters that the plan will handle during the plan period
- the time frame for addressing a matter (length of time before a demand letter goes out, for example)
- extra expenses for which you may be responsible
- whether you can pick the attorney you want to use
- whether you can change attorneys
- the cancellation policy if you want to leave the plan
- geographical limitations of the plan (does the plan work in Florida and California if your family moves?)
- whether you can be terminated (kicked out) from the plan
- how are complaints about the plan are resolved
- how coverage appeals are handled

What is the difference between a prepaid legal plan and legal insurance? *Legal insurance works like homeowners' insurance.* Its purpose is to protect the policyholder against all legal costs (as opposed to provided specific services only as in prepaid plans).

> **Legal insurance policies reimburse the policyholder for any fees, costs and expenses incurred for legal services including money judgments, up to the policy's limits.**

Will a prepaid service plan defend me in a DUI charge? *Yes, but with exclusions. For instance, if you have a prior record of motor vehicle-related arrests or accidents, the policy* *will not cover you.* Also, you may be limited to 2 to 3 hours of the lawyer's time. Your policy will probably not cover any court appearances by the attorney, although you may be eligible for a discounted lawyer's fee.

Are tax matters covered in prepaid plans?
Yes. Some plans provide legal advice and services for personal income tax matters, including audits, negotiating a settlement with the IRS and even litigation in tax court. The total amount of hours on the entire matter is typically limited to 50 hours of lawyer time. On the other hand, some plans exclude any and all tax matters from plan coverage.

> **TIP:** Business tax matters are highly specialized and universally excluded from nearly all the plans.

I want to sue my builder for building me a defective house. Will a prepaid plan cover this situation?
No. Plans typically provide preventive legal services (wills, for example) and represent members who must defend an action. The plan may provide an attorney to negotiate with the builder or write a demand letter, but the plan will not pay the costs when you are pursuing the lawsuit.

> The typical plan provision excludes "any legal proceeding in which the Participant is the plaintiff, petitioner or movant, with the exception of the Bankruptcy; Divorce, Annulment or Separation; Adoption; Consumer Protection and the Name Change coverages."

PRO SE REPRESENTATION

You do not need to be a lawyer to appear in court, even the U.S. Supreme Court. Any person has the right to represent herself. Persons who represent themselves in litigation are known as "pro se plaintiffs" and "pro se defendants." A pro se party is subject to the same rules of court that apply to attorneys. The pro se litigant that fails to follow court rules and orders is subject to the same sanctions as an attorney.

> **TIP:** For information and help with pro se representation, go to **www.selfhelpsupport.org**.

What types of cases can I represent myself "pro se?"
You may represent yourself in any type of case. Though acting as your own attorney in a murder trial is highly questionable, some types of cases can be handled pro se with success. For example, it is not uncommon for a spouse to file a pro se divorce petition because the pleadings are typically forms that can be changed to suit the situation.

ALTERNATIVES TO TRIAL

DEMAND LETTERS

Attorneys almost always send out a "demand letter" on behalf of their clients before an actual legal proceeding (a lawsuit, for example) is commenced. Depending on the client's situation, the demand letter can be as simple as a demand for payment owed to the client, or cover several issues related to complex real estate litigation.

Demand letters should be simple and concise. The most effective demand letters set out a deadline for the recipient to act (pay the money, for instance) and clearly set out the consequences of failing to meet the demand.

My neighbor owes me for repairing his plumbing. My lawyer is sending out a demand letter but is not sure if she wants to file a lawsuit if the letter does not get a result. Is this a good strategy?
No. Unless your attorney is willing to follow up her demand with legal action, the letter has no effect. As the deadline passes and your neighbor realizes the lawyer has not acted, the letter loses its impact. Additionally, your concerns may begin to be seen as frivolous if legal proceedings do not commence.

I cannot afford a lawsuit, but I want to hire an attorney to write a demand letter for me. Is this an appropriate service?
Yes. However, most attorneys are reluctant to send out demand letters with the idea that the letter is a "scare

tactic" only. Letters that are sent out and not followed up on can diminish the effectiveness of your threat.

> **TIP:** It is conceivable that the recipient may hire her own attorney who will then contact your lawyer. If your lawyer was hired only to write a letter, then you end up dealing with the attorney.

NEGOTIATION

Negotiation is an informal process conducted between the attorneys for both sides. The clients are typically not involved initially, and the lawyers discuss the matter. In most cities, attorneys are at least acquainted and able to discuss the pros and cons of their respective cases in a friendly manner. It is possible that an agreement can be worked out over the telephone in the initial stages of the lawsuit.

An attorney never agrees to any type of settlement terms without first discussing the offer with her client and obtaining the client's authorization to accept the settlement. Agreeing to settle without the client's authorization violates rules of conduct and ethics.

MEDIATION

Mediation is a negotiation, but it is a fee-based process, often ordered by the court. The mediator does not decide the case and does not give legal advice. Mediation allows both sides to talk about the dispute and voluntarily reach a mutual agreement in an informal setting.

How much does mediation cost? *The cost depends on how many hours you use the mediator. If a mediator charges $100 per hour then an all-day session could cost as much as $800.* Additionally, if your attorney is with you, she will be billing for her time as well.

Who pays for mediation? The party requesting the mediation generally pays. In court-ordered mediation, the parties may have to split the fee.

How long is mediation? Mediations generally take a minimum of 2 hours but can take an entire day.

Does my attorney come with me to the mediation? *Yes.* Your attorney is there to advise you and help you come to a decision to settle. If there is an agreement, the attorney makes sure it reflects what was discussed and agreed to during the mediation.

ARBITRATION

Arbitration is the resolution of a dispute by a neutral third person (the arbitrator) that listens to the arguments of each party, reviews the evidence, and issues an arbitration award. The arbitrator simply "hears" the case. Unlike the mediator, she does not work to persuade the parties to come to any kind of an agreement. Additionally, the arbitration award is a legally binding decision on both the parties. Generally, parties who submit their differences to arbitration are bound by the decision of the arbitrator and cannot go to court on the issue once a final decision has been made.

Mandatory arbitration is becoming common. For instance, most credit card company agreements require that customer disputes go to arbitration and do not permit the customer to file an action in a court. Consumers are generally unaware that they have signed an agreement containing a mandatory arbitration clause. These clauses are found in car lease contracts, cell phone contracts, insurance policies and HMO enrollment forms, to name a few.

> **Mandatory arbitration clauses typically require the consumer to arbitrate through a preselected arbitration service. The service may require hundreds of dollars in filing fees and an advancement for the arbitrator's time. Consumers frequently spend several thousand dollars arbitrating their dispute.**

> **TIP:** The Federal Trade Commission maintains information on arbitration on its Web site at **www.ftc.gov/bcp/conline/pubs/general/dispute.htm**.

State and federal courts enforce arbitration awards. Parties who do not comply with the arbitrator's decision may be forced to defend an enforcement action.

Who chooses the arbitrator? *Ideally, the parties agree on an arbitrator.* In some cases, there is a panel of arbitrators (one chosen by each side plus a neutral arbitrator). Companies may require customers or employees to choose or agree to an arbitrator from a preselected list.

> Choosing an arbitrator often involves each side eliminating names from a list until one is left.

Who pays for the arbitrator? *In voluntary arbitration, the parties can split the cost or one party may offer to pay.* In mandatory arbitration, the person bringing the dispute is responsible for the arbitrator's fees.

> **TIP:** Local Better Business Bureaus (BBBs) have arbitration programs for individuals who agree to arbitrate their disputes. The BBB typically bears the cost of the arbitration. The arbitrator is usually a community volunteer and does not charge a fee.

Where does arbitration take place? *The arbitration often takes place at the arbitration services offices.* If a mandatory arbitration clause is in effect, the location could be anywhere in the nation.

Can I appeal the arbitrator's decision? *No.* Arbitration awards are final and binding.

Do I need an attorney to represent me at arbitration? *No. However, if you are dealing with a large company and complex issues, an attorney will be invaluable.* Additionally, it is not uncommon for an arbitrator to require written memoranda of the legal issues in the case with cites to relevant statutory or case law.

Can a judge order my case to binding arbitration? *Yes.* Laws in some states permit courts to send cases to arbitration where the amount at stake is below a certain sum, such as $25,000.

> To remove a case from binding arbitration ordered by a judge, a party must file a motion for removal.

COLLABORATION

Another form of negotiation is the use of the collaborative law process—an alternative to court. The process of collaboration means the parties are agreeing to participate in nearly any forum that is likely to bring about a settlement and avoid litigation. Collaboration encompasses mediations, settlement conferences, discussions with experts and other nonadversarial alternatives to a trial.

Like mediation, the parties and their attorneys participate in an informal discussion to reach a settlement. However, the discussions are ongoing until an agreement is worked out. The clients and attorneys enter into a participation agreement, which sets out the ground rules for collaboration.

Unlike mediation, there is no neutral third party helping to obtain a settlement. Instead, the clients and their attorneys are working through their differences over a period of time with the goal of avoiding court intervention.

What disputes are best handled by collaboration? *Family law disputes, such as divorces and child custody cases, benefit greatly from the collaborative process.* Spouses and their attorneys, children who are old enough to participate and other professionals working with the family, agree to resolve all their issues without initiating contentious court proceedings. The participants work together to create an agreement that works for the entire family.

SMALL CLAIMS COURTS

Every city, county or municipality has one or more small claims courts. These courts were created to allow individuals to litigate in an inexpensive and efficient forum without the necessity of an attorney.

Maximum Amount of Claim

Small claims court is just that—a court for litigating over smaller amounts or claims of money. The court's jurisdiction (its power to adjudicate only certain types of cases) is based on the amount of money requested in the lawsuit. Typically, the amount cannot be over $5,000. Laws in some states may permit the court to hear claims involving higher amounts or set the limit much lower. The court does not have the jurisdiction to hear matters that involve amounts beyond the set limit.

Type of Claim

Small claims courts hear only civil cases where an individual is seeking a cash judgment or recovery of personal property. If the court's jurisdiction is capped at $5,000, the value of the personal property cannot exceed that amount.

Notifying the Defendant

Although litigation in small claims court is an informal process, notifying a person that he has been sued is the same as in any court. The defendant must be properly served with the lawsuit. Without service of the defendant by a law enforcement official or a private process server, the court cannot enter a judgment.

Who can file a lawsuit in small claims court? *Any adult (over 18 years of age) can file a claim.* Anyone under 18 years old must have a guardian ad litem appointed by the court to protect his interests.

Is there a limit to the number of claims I can file in one year? *Yes.* Some courts limit filings to 12 per year, for example.

Can a lawyer represent me in small claims court? *No.* You can discuss your case with an attorney but she cannot appear before the judge on your behalf.

How much does it cost to file a case in small claims court? *Costs vary, but typically the fee is less that $50.* By contrast, the fees for filing a petition in a state court are often at least $200.

How long do I have to wait before the judge hears my case? Judges usually set cases within 30 days or so in small claims court.

Do I need to bring evidence with me to court? *Yes.* Evidence, such as receipts, helps prove your case to the judge. For example, you can bring:

- photographs
- bills

- receipts
- correspondence
- contracts

Am I allowed to have a witness testify on my behalf in small claims court? *Yes.* If you have a witness, you should definitely ask her to appear and testify for you. A witness's testimony will help convince the judge of your case.

> **TIP:** To ensure the witness's appearance at trial, he must be formally subpoenaed. The court clerk prepares the subpoena and forwards it to the sheriff for service. If the witness fails to appear, you have the right to ask for a postponement until the witness can be found.

> **TIP:** There is a fee for serving a witness subpoena and you may also be required to attach a witness fee to the subpoena.

Is discovery allowed in small claims court? *No.* The usual discovery (depositions, interrogatories and requests for production) is not permitted in small claims court.

When does the judge make her decision? *Usually, judges rule immediately on the matter.* For example, if you claimed you were owed money, and the judge agrees, she will rule in your favor and enter a judgment for you for that amount.

> **TIP:** Some judges do not make a decision immediately. The judge's verdict is mailed to the parties at a later date.

If I do not like the judge's decision, can I appeal it? *Yes. However, the deadline for filing an appeal is short.* In some cases, you may have as little as 10 days to file the appeal. If you miss the deadline, the verdict is final and no longer appealable.

I sued someone in small claims court but am unable to make the court date. Can my wife go in my place? *No. If you fail to appear, your case will be dismissed.* You are the only person who may appear in court to litigate your claim.

> It is possible that the plaintiff or defendant in small claims court may be represented by another person if, in the judge's opinion, he is unable to understand or participate at the trial. The person acting as the representative cannot be an attorney and must be familiar with the facts of the case. For example, a person with a physical disability that makes it difficult for her to speak and be understood could have her sister act on her behalf.

> **TIP:** Ask for a continuance if a conflict arises with your court date. Call the court clerk and explain the circumstances. If your reason is valid, you can probably get a new court date.

CIVIL CASES

When negotiations or mediation fails, often the only remaining option is to file a lawsuit. A civil lawsuit alleges that an individual or company (the defendant) violated a law or failed to perform in a certain manner (finishing the painting job specified in a contract, for example).

All states have enacted laws that protect its citizens. Criminal statutes are, of course, the most visible. However, there are other state laws that make certain noncriminal actions illegal. For example, an automobile dealer cannot represent he is selling a new car when it is really used. These types of laws are known as consumer protection statutes.

Although most laws are set out in written form, the laws themselves evolved from certain duties required of individuals. For example, we all have the duty to not recklessly injure another person. Because laws cannot be written to cover every conceivable situation where an injury might occur, the common law of torts applies.

TORTS

A tort is a legal "wrong." Because it is impossible to make laws for every conceivable wrong that might occur, the law of torts allows injured parties to recover when another party has been negligent. For instance, the driver who rear-ends you is probably negligent. Your resulting lawsuit is based on that tort.

> Lawsuits based in tort also include situations involving medical malpractice, defective products and unsafe premises.

Torts do not apply to criminal acts. The law of torts allows a person who has suffered an injury to pursue a remedy. Though the party who caused the injury may have committed a criminal act, his penalty is provided under criminal laws.

> **TIP:** A crime victim can always sue the criminal in a civil lawsuit for the injuries she suffered. The civil suit is completely separate from the criminal prosecution.

> Civil "punishment" does exist in the form of punitive damages—an amount of money awarded to the plaintiff to deter the defendant from further reckless acts. See DAMAGES, below.

Duty

Every lawsuit based on a tort hinges on whether a duty exists to act in a certain way. Because drivers have a duty to drive safely and cautiously, the person who rear-ends another vehicle has generally breached the duty.

Without a duty, there cannot be an action based on tort. For example, a trespasser who injures himself on your deck does not have a cause of action against you because you have no duty to make your deck safe for trespassers. On the other hand, an invited guest would have a cause of action if you knew the deck was unsafe.

Foreseeability

Whether a tort was committed depends not only on the existence of a duty but also on the foreseeability or likelihood of the injury. Without proof of foreseeability, the tort case fails because a required element is missing. The most common cases involving questions of foreseeability are "slip and fall" cases.

EXAMPLE: The situation where vegetable oil, for instance, has spilled all over a grocery store aisle which employees knew about but failed to clean up (or warn customers) is the type of scenario where it was foreseeable a customer would slip and fall. On the other hand, the customer who slips and falls on a grape in the produce section would have to prove that the store employees knew about the grape and did not pick it up. Foreseeability for an injury because of the grape does not exist because its presence was unknown to store employees.

LIABILITY FOR OTHER INDIVIDUALS

Sometimes a situation occurs where a person is liable for another person's injuries although he did not actually cause them. For example, the owner of a vehicle who knowingly loans his car to a drunken friend who then has a car wreck may be liable for injuries caused to another person involved in the wreck. The drunken friend's liability is imputed to the car owner. This type of liability is known as vicarious liability.

Third-party liability often occurs in commercial settings. For example, an apartment complex that failed to provide proper lighting at night might be liable to a tenant who was mugged in the dark parking lot. A software company might be sued under this theory if a computer game it manufactured resulted in a player violently attacking another person.

DEFENSES TO LAWSUITS

Once an individual is sued, he becomes a defendant and must defend himself against the plaintiff's allegations. Some defenses are simple. For example, if a homeowner is sued by a plumber for not paying the bill, his defense is "payment" and his proof is his cancelled check. In a slander or libel suit, truth is always a defense.

REMEDIES

A remedy is the amount of money or specific action that the person filing the lawsuit requests the court to order. A remedy can be as simple as recovering payment for painting your neighbor's home or as complex as halting construction of a road. In contract cases, the remedy requested is often the specific performance of some action by the person sued.

EXAMPLE: An employee may agree in writing not to compete with her employer in the same clothing business if she quits. If she then starts her up her own competing clothing store, the employer's requested remedy is to make her perform under the agreement, i.e., stop operating the competing store.

Legal Remedies

The plaintiff who is requesting monetary damages is asking for a legal remedy. The money she recovers will compensate her for her injury. However, there are cases where an award of money does not provide a complete remedy (or any remedy at all). In those situations, the court may order equitable relief.

Equitable Remedies

An equitable remedy requires a specific act instead of a tangible award of money or property. Injunctions and restraining orders are common examples of equitable remedies.

EXAMPLE: The court that orders a farmer to cease operation of a pig farm (which creates a terrible odor) at the request of a neighbor has entered an injunction. Because an award of money will not remedy the neighbor's problem with the odor, the judge decided equitable relief was appropriate.

DAMAGES

The right to a remedy depends on whether there have been damages. "Damage" is a loss or injury to a person, their property or reputation. In a lawsuit, damages typically refer to monetary compensation. The party at fault (if fault is proved) compensates the injured party if a verdict is rendered in the injured party's favor.

Compensatory Damages

Compensatory damages are calculated on the basis of the cost of making the person "whole." For example, a man who was fired because of his advanced age recovers all the salary he would have earned if he had not been terminated. The family whose fence was destroyed by a reckless driver recovers the cost of replacing the fence.

Punitive Damages

Generally awarded where a lawsuit involves a corporate defendant, punitive damages are recoverable in order to punish the company and deter future bad acts. An attorney arguing for punitive damages typically asks for a percentage of the corporation's net worth. For example, the trucking line that has consistently employed unsafe drivers, one of whom finally caused a death, may be required to pay 1 percent of its net worth in punitive damages. If the company is worth $100 million, punitive damages are $1 million.

What are my damages if I was injured in a car wreck? *The most easily calculated damages are the cost of your medical care and the repairs or replacement of your vehicle.* However, you are also entitled to damages for your pain and suffering.

FILING A LAWSUIT

Lawsuits proceed based on certain rules concerning deadlines, the form of pleadings, service of process, discovery, pretrial motions and more. Although laws vary from state to state, the basic requirements are the same.

STATUTE OF LIMITATIONS

With the exception of certain criminal laws, such as murder statutes, all lawsuits must be filed within a certain amount of time or the claimant forever waives her ability to sue. For instance, if the painter did not finish the job he was hired to do under a contract yet kept your entire payment, depending on the state, you must sue to recover the money within 2 to 6 years. After that time, the deadline has passed, and any lawsuit filed will be dismissed for exceeding the statute of limitations.

We had a pool installed several years ago. Now it is cracked and leaking. Is it too late to sue the pool contractor? *No. Typically, the statute of limitations begins to run when the injury (the pool defect) is discovered.* In your case, a consumer protection law probably applies and you will have 2 to 4 years to sue the contractor from the date you discovered the problem.

> The discovery rule is an important factor in lawsuit filing deadlines. Typically, the statute of limitations begins to run from the time the act was performed (the date the pool was installed). However, when a defective situation is unknown and only discovered after the statute of limitations has run, the deadline for filing is changed to begin running from the date of discovery.

PLEADINGS

A pleading is the initial narrative of the claim that is filed with the court. The person filing the pleading is the plaintiff and the pleading is the plaintiff's original petition. The person being sued is the defendant.

There is no universal form for pleadings, but all pleadings must include:

- the name of the plaintiff and where he resides;
- the name of the defendant and where she resides;
- a statement setting out the law or laws upon which the claim is based;
- a statement of facts explaining how the claim arose; and
- a request for relief in the form of money, performance or both.

> **TIP:** Federal courts have strict rules concerning the form of pleadings and many states courts have created local rules setting out the form preferred. Do not file a pleading without knowing these rules.

> Pleadings based on money owed on account, such as past due payments to an appliance store, must be verified. The person claiming that money is owed must swear to the truth and sign before a notary public that the amount specified in the pleading is accurate.

ANSWERS

The defendant's response to the plaintiff's petition is called the "defendant's original answer." The defendant's answer must be filed by a certain date. The summons or citation gives the deadline for answering. For example, the deadline to answer may be "the first Monday after the expiration of 10 days after the date the citation is served."

Initially, the answer is a simple denial of all the plaintiff's allegations. Later, it is common for defendant's to amend their answer to include specific defenses.

> **TIP:** Failure to answer in time means a default judgment can be taken against you.

> The "default judgment" grants the relief requested by the plaintiff in her petition. There is no limit to the amount of money that can be granted in a default judgment.

COUNTERCLAIMS

Sometimes the defendant has a claim against the plaintiff. In that situation, the defendant can file a counterclaim against the plaintiff in the same lawsuit. By filing the counterclaim, all the disputed issues between the plaintiff and defendant are before the court at the same time.

> A mandatory counterclaim is a counterclaim the defendant is required to file in the plaintiff's lawsuit because it concerns the same facts and legal issues as the underlying lawsuit. For example, if a tenant is sued by her landlord for damages to an apartment and has a claim for wrongful retention of her security deposit, she must file a counterclaim or waive her right to sue on that issue. In other words, she cannot file a separate lawsuit in the future asking for return of her security deposit.

I filed a lawsuit against my neighbor but did not include her husband in the pleadings. Do I have to file a new lawsuit? *No. You do not file a new lawsuit; you file a new pleading* *with the husband added.* Anytime you want to add or remove from your initial pleading, you are amending the previous pleading.

> **TIP:** Amended pleadings should always be titled "First Amended Petition," "Second Amending Petition" and so on. The amended pleading takes the place of all previous pleadings.

SERVICE OF PROCESS

In the United States, any person who is sued is required to be notified. If the plaintiff fails to notify the defendant, the lawsuit cannot proceed and a judgment cannot be entered.

A defendant to a lawsuit is notified by "service of process"—the individual is given a copy of the lawsuit by an official, usually by a sheriff's deputy, along with a summons or citation to appear in court by a certain date. Once the individual takes the lawsuit, he has been "served," and the deputy verifies that service was made on a written form that is filed with the court.

> **The defendant does not physically "appear" in court; he appears by filing a written answer to the plaintiff's petition.**

Although it is generally believed that service of process requires a face-to-face meeting between the process server and the defendant, in fact, service is accomplished in many different ways.

Service by Publication

In certain situations, where the defendant's whereabouts are unknown, notification of the lawsuit is published in the newspaper. For example, in adoption cases where parental rights must be terminated, the father might be notified by publication.

Service by Certified Mail

Corporations are often "served" by mail directed to the corporate president or secretary. The mailing typically issues out of the state secretary of state's office.

> **TIP:** Some companies have a designated "agent for service."

Service Left at Residence

Service can be accomplished by leaving the paperwork at the defendant's "usual place of abode." Typically, laws require that a member of the defendant's family that is at least 16 years old be present to accept service.

Posting Service

When the defendant cannot be located and no one in the family is available for service (or actively avoiding service), the sheriff or private process server may "post" or attach the summons or citation to the front door of the defendant's usual place of abode.

DISCOVERY AND DISCOVERY METHODS

All lawsuits include some sort of fact-gathering process, known as "discovery," that helps attorneys and clients better evaluate their case. The purpose of discovery is to uncover and gather any evidence and information relevant to the lawsuit. Each party has the right to discovery from the other side as well as any other persons connected to the case (witnesses, for example.)

> **Although, the scope of discovery is broad, it operates under specific rules of court. For example, the rules may limit a party to 30 questions or "interrogatories" that can be asked of the other side.**

What exactly is my lawyer attempting to "discover"? *Discovery includes obtaining basic facts such as the names and address of anybody with knowledge of the case.* From those basic facts, discovery becomes more specified. For instance, information on a witness's medical and employment history may be discovered once her name is revealed. The medical records may not be admissible in court but are allowed to be "discovered" because admissible evidence (the name of witness) may be found as a result.

Depositions

Most lawsuits include at least one deposition, or formal interview, of one or both of the parties to the lawsuit. The person being deposed is called the "deponent." Anyone can be deposed; you do not have to be a party to the lawsuit to be deposed. For example, witnesses in car wreck cases are routinely deposed. All depositions require formal notification known as the Notice of Deposition.

Anything said in a deposition is sworn testimony, made under oath, just as if the person was in the courtroom before a judge and in the witness chair. Lawyers for both sides are present. The lawyer for the party who requested the deposition questions or "examines" the deponent first. When the initial examination is over, the lawyer for the opposing side questions the deponent (usually his client), hoping to correct mistakes or provide additional explanation.

Do I have to travel out of state to give a deposition? *No. Typically, the deponent is not required to travel beyond the court's jurisdiction, or a certain distance.* The person who wants to depose you usually must come to you.

Who pays my expenses? The party requesting the deposition generally pays your expenses.

Can I get a copy of my deposition? Yes. If you are a party to the lawsuit, your lawyer will provide you with one. However, if you are not a party, you may have to request one directly from the court reporter.

Can I refuse to be videotaped? *No.* Unless your attorney files a motion with the court and the court orders no videotaping, you will probably be videotaped.

Can I talk to my lawyer during the deposition? *Yes.* However, excessive conversations may be limited by a court order if you are perceived to be purposely disrupting the flow of the deposition.

I am too upset to continue my deposition. Can I stop? *Yes.* Generally, lawyers will not require a deponent to continue to testify when she is too emotional to answer accurately.

> **The lawyer taking the deposition is not required to stop the deposition in consideration of the deponent's feelings. However, if she insists, the deponent's lawyer may object, end the deposition and let the judge decide later if stopping the deposition was proper.**

Can I refer to my notes during the deposition? *Yes. You can refer to almost anything during your deposition, and the lawyer deposing you has the right to examine them if you do.* Thus, it is highly inadvisable to take in personal notes because, once you use them, the notes are considered "discoverable."

Can I refuse to answer a question? *Yes.* However, you may be later sanctioned by the judge for your refusal to cooperate.

> Generally, the deponent's lawyer objects to a question for a specific reason and refuses to let the client answer. The judge rules later whether the objection was appropriate. If the objection is overruled, the question must be answered.

Can my sister sit in on the deposition with me for support? *No.* Only named parties to a lawsuit and their attorneys are allowed to present during a deposition.

> **TIP:** Minors are allowed to have a parent, guardian or court advocate present.

If it is difficult for me to understand English, can I have an interpreter present? *Yes.* In fact, your entire testimony may be inadmissible if it is later shown that you did not understand the questions because you were not provided with an interpreter.

> **TIP:** The party requesting the deposition pays for the interpreter. During the actual trial, the court provides the interpreter.

Now that my deposition is over, what is my lawyer going to do with it? *Your lawyer uses your deposition testimony to get you ready for trial.* What was said in the deposition must agree with your trial testimony or the inconsistencies will be pointed out by the opposing side to discredit you.

Interrogatories

Prior to trial, each party has the right to send written questions to the other side. The written questions are called interrogatories and are governed by specific rules relating to their form, the deadline for answering, the number of questions that can be asked and what types of questions can be asked.

> Many courts have created standard interrogatories, which lawyers are encouraged to use in order to avoid disputes. For example, courts may have matrimonial interrogatories for divorce lawyers to use. Because the interrogatories are of the court's own design, the answering party cannot argue that the questions are improper and refuse to answer.

Request for Production

A request for production is a formal document listing tangible items that the other side must produce. Like written interrogatories, requests for production are governed by specific rules relating to their form, the deadline for producing the item, the limit on items to be produced and the types of items that must be produced.

Typically, a party is asked to produce any documents, reports, medical records, contracts, deeds and correspondence relating to the lawsuit. At times, an item must be produced, such as the vehicle involved in a car wreck case.

> **TIP:** "Producing" records does not necessarily mean copying and delivering boxes of documents to the other side. It is permissible to make the documents available. For example, if the other party wants to go through years of warehouse invoices, the company can make the warehouse open and the documents available on-site.

> **TIP:** The party making the request pays the copying expenses.

> Many documents are "privileged," such as correspondence between the lawyer and the client even though it relates to the case. Privileged documents do not have to be produced.

Request for Admission

Parties are permitted to require the other side to admit certain facts under oath. Requests for admissions are particularly useful to prove obvious facts (admit that it is your signature on the contract, for example) and prove that documents are authentic (admit the attached document is your father's last will and testament, for example). When trial commences, it will not be necessary to introduce evidence concerning the admitted facts, and the attorneys can move on to litigating disputed facts, saving time and legal fees.

Physical and/or Mental Examination

If relevant to the case, one party can request that the other party submit to a physical or mental examination by a doctor chosen by the requesting party.

Inspection of Real Property

A party is permitted to request and obtain an order from the court allowing him and his attorney) to go onto and inspect real property owned by another party.

Records Subpoena

Records can often be obtained directly from the source rather than by requesting their production from the other attorney. For example, in cases where there is a personal injury, the injured party typically signs a medical release that allows the opposing attorney to subpoena medical records directly from the hospital or doctor.

Motion to Quash

Nearly all pretrial discovery includes at least one dispute where one party refuses to answer an interrogatory or produce a document. In those instances, the refusing party files a Motion to Quash with the court requesting that the interrogatory, for example, be quashed or ruled improper. If the judge agrees and grants the motion, the party does not have to respond to the objected discovery.

Sanctions

Parties who refuse to cooperate with the discovery process (and their attorneys) are subject to sanctions. Discovery rules permit the court to fine parties and their attorneys, refuse to allow certain evidence at trial and even dismiss the entire lawsuit if a party is uncooperative.

PRETRIAL MOTIONS

To speed a trial along, judges make rulings on certain issues prior to the beginning of the trial by hearing pretrial motions. The defending party typically files a motion to dismiss, arguing that the plaintiff has no legal cause of action. The court sets a hearing and decides whether the grant the motion. If the motion to dismiss is granted, the case is dismissed and the time and expense of a trial is avoided.

In other instances, where neither party can dispute the facts, one party may file a motion for summary judgment. Because the facts are not at issue, the judge can apply the law without the necessity of a trial and enter a judgment.

SETTLEMENTS

A settlement ends the lawsuit, and nearly all cases are settled before trial. Settlement discussions are typically ongoing during the entire case, but as a trial date nears, one party (typically the defendant) makes a settlement offer to the plaintiff.

> **TIP:** Almost all courts require settlement discussions by ordering the parties to attend at least one court-ordered mediation.

Settlements are written agreements between the parties. The settlement agreement is generally not filed with the court, and its provisions are confidential. Some of the points covered in a settlement agreement include:

- the exact amount of money to be paid
- the identity of the party paying the money
- the identity of the party who receives the money
- the form of payment
- the due date of payment (settlement checks are sent to the attorney)
- a provision regarding how the attorney's fees will be paid (one party pays the other party's fee, each party is responsible for their own attorney's fees)
- who is paying court costs
- an agreement to dismiss the lawsuit with prejudice—that is, forever waiving the right to file another lawsuit based on the same facts

I think a have a good case. How do I decide whether to accept a settlement? *Settling your case is a big decision.* Here are some things to think about:

- Your chances of winning at trial. If there are problems with your evidence, settling the case may be the best option.
- The defendant's "deep pockets." It is common for insurance companies to handle the defense of their policyholders. The company typically has a large amount of money at its disposal to settle your claim and wants to avoid a trial at all costs. If this is your situation, push the case as close to trial as you can, then take the settlement if it is reasonable.
- The emotional and physical impact of a trial. Foregoing a trial and accepting a settlement check will relieve you and your family of a lot of stress.
- Your attorney's fees arrangement. If you are paying your attorney, her fees will climb astronomically during the trial. You should consider settling if the money will cover your attorney's fees to date yet still leave you with something. You do not want to lose at trial and owe your attorney thousands of dollars when the case could have been settled.

If we start the trial, is all chance of settlement gone? *No. Cases are regularly settled during the trial.* Up until a verdict is rendered, the parties can agree to settle and dismiss the case.

TRIALS

There are two types of trial available to litigants. Every party is entitled to a jury trial; however, sometimes it is advantageous to waive the jury and let the judge decide the case. A bench trial is a trial without a jury. The case is tried before the judge only and she decides the outcome rather than a jury. Bench trials have the advantage of being much more efficient and quick, thus potentially saving the client the expense of a lengthy jury trial.

I do not want to have a jury trial, but the person I am suing insists on a jury. Can I force a bench trial? *No.* Except in minor misdemeanor cases and other special situations, everyone is entitled to present their side of the case to a jury. You cannot force a bench trial.

Am I entitled to a jury in a civil trial? *Yes.* The U.S. Constitution guarantees each U.S. citizen the right to trial by jury in both criminal and civil matters.

JURY SELECTION AND VOIR DIRE

Jury selection is the process of selecting a group of people to hear the evidence in a case and decide the outcome of a trial. Depending on the complexity of the case, jury selection can last half a day or an entire week. Selecting a jury is governed by certain rules.

Voir Dire

Voir dire is the part of jury selection where attorneys for both sides (and the judge) ask questions of the individual jurors or the group as a whole. Translated from the French, the term means "to speak the truth." Voir dire is the opportunity to preliminarily question a prospective juror to decide whether that person is qualified to serve on a jury.

For instance, in a lawsuit between a homeowner and the builder, the panel may be asked if any of them have ever hired a builder. Those who indicate that they have had dealings with a builder may be questioned about their attitudes toward homebuilders and how their specific situation turned out. The lawyers are trying to determine who will be most sympathetic to their side of the case.

Challenges

As voir dire proceeds, the lawyers or the judge may excuse potential jurors for various reasons. If an attorney believes a juror should not serve on the jury, she must use a "challenge" to excuse that juror. There are two types of challenges, or reasons, to dismiss a juror:

1. **FOR CAUSE.** Laws set out various reasons why jurors may be excused "for cause." For instance, a juror who is related to one of the parties (or the judge or attorneys) in the case may be excused for cause. An attorney may challenge jurors for cause as many times as necessary; however, the other lawyer can object and it is possible the judge will rule that the juror may stay.

2. PEREMPTORY. Before voir dire begins, each side in a case has a certain number of peremptory challenges or "strikes" that can be used to excuse a juror without giving a reason. Each side is entitled to request that the judge excuse a particular juror as long as they have peremptory challenges left. The number of peremptory challenges lawyers have in a trial varies according to the laws of the state.

Who is eligible to be a juror? *Any U.S. citizen over 18 years of age and residing in the county where the trial is to take place is eligible to serve.* It is unconstitutional to disqualify anyone because of race, creed or color.

> **Additionally, jurors must:**
>
> - be able to understand English;
> - have the mental and physical capacity to carry out the duties of a juror; and
> - not have served on a jury in previous months (typically 12 months).

I was convicted of a felony years ago. Will I ever be able to serve on a jury? *Yes. Your rights to serve on a jury, vote and hold certain licenses can be restored.* In some states, the right will be automatically restored once you have served your time and completed probation. Laws in other states require you to petition the court to have these rights restored.

Why do I have to fill out a personal history questionnaire? *The answers to the questions assist the attorneys and the judge in selecting (and disqualifying) potential jurors.* For instance, a person whose husband works for the company being sued is automatically disqualified because of potential bias.

> **TIP:** The questions asked are mostly related to the socioeconomic status of potential jurors. For instance, occupation, marital status and the juror's (or his family's) prior experience with the court system are typical of the type of questions asked on the personal history questionnaire.

Who will see my answers to the questions on the form? The attorney, their clients and the judge are usually the only people with access to the questionnaires.

If I am Hispanic, am I entitled to at least one Hispanic juror? *No. You are only entitled to a jury that is representative of your community.* If there are a variety of ethnicities living in your community, it is possible that a Hispanic will not be picked.

> **The jury pool, however, cannot exclude Hispanics. The pool is the large group of citizens (sometimes 100 or more) picked for jury duty and from which specific trial juries are chosen.**

Is anyone automatically allowed to be exempt from jury duty? *Yes. Most states have laws permitting exemptions on the basis of age. For example, a person over 70 is not required to serve, although she may if she wishes.* Eighteen year-olds still in high school during the school year are also automatically exempted.

I am not exempt from jury service, but can I get excused? *Yes. There are many valid excuses. However, this generally only postpones eventual jury duty.* Some excuses that courts are willing to accept include:

- caring for young children or a disabled individual
- health problems or a disability that makes jury service difficult
- a scheduled vacation already booked and paid for
- personal commitments (a marriage, for example) that cannot be rescheduled

My employer says I will be fired if I get picked to be on a jury. Can he do this? *No. The law requires that employees be allowed time off to serve on a jury.* It is illegal for your employer to harass or fire you because you are a juror. Contact the court if this happens.

How much will I get paid to be on a jury? *Payment varies from state to state. You may get as little as $10 per day or as much as $75.* You are also entitled to reimbursement for parking and travel to and from the courthouse at a per-mile rate, such as $.10 per mile.

What will happen if I do not show up for jury duty? Failure to appear as summoned could result in a large monetary fine, a jail sentence and other legal consequences.

BEING A JUROR

Jury service is considered a duty and must be taken seriously. Jurors are typically ordered to be present at a certain time each morning, to talk to no one about the case and to refrain from reading outside material or doing their own research on the issues. Jurors who disobey the judge's orders will be dismissed from the jury.

Deliberations

Deliberations are the discussions that take place between the jurors in the jury room about the case. If the jurors have obeyed the court's instructions, deliberations are the first time the jurors have talked about the case among themselves. During deliberations, the jurors discuss the evidence and testimony and attempt to reach a verdict. Jury deliberations are secret and never include any persons except the jurors.

Foreperson

At the beginning of deliberations, the jury votes to select one member to be the foreperson. The foreperson has a duty to see that deliberations proceed in an orderly manner and that the case and issues are fully and freely discussed. The foreperson makes sure that every juror is given a chance to participate in deliberations. If there are problems or issues during deliberations, the foreperson notifies the court through a handwritten note. When a verdict is reached, the foreperson completes and signs the verdict form.

I am happy to serve as a juror, but in 2 days I have an important medical appointment. Do I have to cancel my appointment? *No. The judge is typically willing to work around situations involving important personal matters.* The trial may be delayed a few hours until your appointment is over or end early that day, depending on the time of your appointment.

> **TIP:** Personal requests must be relayed through the bailiff who will then advise the judge of the issue. You will be called into the judge's chambers and asked to explain the conflict. The lawyers will be present. Generally, the judge and the attorneys are happy to accommodate your request.

What do I do if I know one of my fellow jurors has had a conversation with one of the parties in the trial? *You must immediately report what you saw to the bailiff.* Any misconduct or suspicious behavior should be reported because that juror can "taint" deliberations with her bad behavior.

Are juries always sequestered? *No. "Sequestering" a jury means that the jury is taken to a location, away from their homes, during the duration of the trial.* Sequestration is rare and expensive for the county that bears the cost of lodging, transportation and meals.

Can I talk to a fellow juror about the trial? *No. The trial may only be discussed when it ends and the jury goes into formal deliberations.* The judge should have made this clear when you were first instructed on your duties as a juror.

OPENING STATEMENTS

Once a jury is chosen, the trial begins with opening statements. The opening statement sets out the framework of the case that is about to be tried in front of the jury. The attorney for each party gives the jury an overview of their case (or statement of facts), tells about the testimony jurors may hear, describes evidence that may be introduced and discloses any "problems" with her client or the evidence.

An opening statement typically includes some discussion about the other side's view of the case (and how wrong it is) and brings into question the credibility of the opponent's witnesses and evidence. Importantly, during the opening statement, the attorney explains the law to be applied. For instance, in a negligence case, the lawyer may emphasize that if the jury finds that the other party acted unreasonably, then that party must be found negligent.

Are objections permitted during an opening statement? *Yes. Although the attorney is given a lot of leeway during the opening, a comment referring to evidence that is patently irrelevant is subject to objection and could result in a mistrial.* For example, in a case that concerns a contract dispute, the lawyer cannot tell the jury the other party has several DUI arrests.

EVIDENCE

Evidence is the facts that support each party's versions of the events that are the basis of the trial. Evidence can include:

- testimony
- documents
- photographs
- official records
- personal notes, diaries, correspondence
- computer generated invoices, billings and statements

In fact, nearly anything can be evidence; however, it must be admissible. Admissible evidence is evidence that is both relevant and truthful or authentic. For instance, evidence concerning the sexual predilections of the homebuilder in a case against him for faulty building is probably not relevant. On the other hand, even if the information is relevant it cannot be admitted (or brought before the jury) unless there is a witness (such as an eyewitness) or documents that proves he engaged in the behavior firsthand. A person's secondhand version of events is hearsay and not admissible.

BEING A WITNESS

A witness is a person who can give a firsthand account of something he has seen, heard or experienced. Anyone can be called as a witness. Witnesses testify in open court, under oath. The attorney for each party has the opportunity to question or examine the witness. Judges can also ask witnesses questions, although it is rarely done in state courts. Jurors may not question witnesses.

> Even a child may testify if she can prove to the court she understands the difference between the truth and lie.

> **TIP:** Witnesses do not attend the trial until after they have testified.

My friend is in the middle of a trial and wants me to testify on her behalf. Do I have to go? *No.* You can only be compelled to testify at trial if you have served with a subpoena ordering your presence.

> **TIP:** A subpoena is an official order to attend court at a stated time. The subpoena is a legal document typically given to you by a sheriff's deputy with a witness fee attached.

CLOSING ARGUMENTS

Closing arguments are the final opportunity attorneys have to persuade jurors.

Attorneys carefully go through the evidence that was presented at the trial during the closing and show jurors how it supports a verdict in favor of their client. Importantly, closing arguments are the forum for an attorney to highlight the weaknesses in the opposing party's case. The lawyer reminds the jury of evidence that damages the other side's position and points out any inconsistencies.

I am representing myself in small claims court where there is not a jury. Do I still get to make a closing argument? *Yes. The judge should allow you to briefly summarize the strengths of your case and the weaknesses of your opponent's position.* However, because you are arguing before the judge, who has heard all the evidence and understands the law, you should avoid getting emotional or righteous. Those tactics are for juries, not judges.

COLLECTING JUDGMENTS

The court's judgment only entitles the prevailing party (the judgment creditor) to recover money from the other party (the judgment debtor). For example, the judgment does not direct that money be handed over at a certain date or time. It is up to the judgment creditor to collect the judgment.

The judgment is collected by obtaining payment from the judgment debtor; however, there may be no cash available to pay the judgment. In that case, the judgment creditor may seize and sell certain assets owned by the judgment debtor.

> Laws in every state exempt certain assets from seizure. For example, a person's home cannot be seized and sold to pay off a judgment.

Before the assets can be seized, the judgment creditor may be required to obtain an Abstract of Judgment to file in the county deed records. Once the judgment is recorded, the judgment creditor has a lien on any real estate the judgment debtor owns. The lien means that before the judgment debtor can sell her house, she must pay the judgment.

A judgment creditor can garnish the judgment debtor's bank account if he has the proper information. A writ of garnishment is prepared and served on the bank (not the judgment debtor) by the sheriff. The writ orders the bank to turn over any funds available up to the amount of the judgment.

CAUSES OF ACTION

There are many different causes of action, or legal reasons, for filing a lawsuit. The following are some common causes of action.

ASSAULT/BATTERY

Assault is the intentional act of causing injury to another person, the attempt or threat to physically injure another person, or intentionally physically contacting a person knowing they will be provoked. Battery is the unlawful beating of another person, or other physical violence directed by the accused to the victim or victims.

Not only is it a criminal act for which the perpetrator can be prosecuted, assault and battery is the basis of civil suit for damages the victim can bring against her batterer.

LANDOWNER LIABILITY

A landowner may or may not be liable for an individual injured on his property. For example, a homeowner is not liable for a guest who is injured when she trips on the front porch steps. The homeowner's only duty to guests is to warn them of, or to repair, dangerous conditions. Unless the porch step was old and rotted, it is not a dangerous condition.

> Trespassers are owed no duties. A landowner is not required to post warnings that dangerous conditions exist as a precaution for potential trespasser, for example. However, the landowner may not intentionally injure the trespasser (set a trap, for instance) although he does have the right to use force to protect himself or his property.

> A landowner that is sued is typically defended and protected under her homeowner's insurance policy. Under the policy, the insurance company has the duty to pay for the costs of defending the lawsuit (the "duty to defend"). If the landowner loses the suit and damages are awarded, the company pays the plaintiff (the "duty to indemnify") up to the limits of the policy.

Additionally, states have enacted laws that provide that landowners do not owe a duty of care to recreational users of their property. These laws are generally knows as "recreational use statutes." The statutes relieve the landowner from liability because they provide that he does not have a duty to keep the property safe for entry or use, or to warn of a dangerous condition on the property to recreational users. For example, these laws protect a landowner who gives permission for horse owners in the area to ride across his property.

> **TIP:** Recreational uses include hunting, fishing, trapping, camping, hiking, sightseeing, operating snow-traveling and all-terrain vehicles, skiing, hang-gliding, dog sledding, equine activities, boating, sailing, canoeing, rafting, biking, picnicking, swimming and other outdoor activities.

> **TIP:** A landowner that charges for the use of his land (a dirt bike trail, for instance) typically loses any protection under the recreational use statute in his state.

A landowner, for purposes of the recreational use statutes, includes the legal owner of the land, a tenant, lessee, occupant or person in control of the premises.

The attractive use doctrine is a special category of landowner liability. Where normally the landowner would not be liable to trespassers, in cases where some dangerous feature on his property attracts children, he has higher duty of care. Swimming pools, for instance, are considered an attractive nuisance. The landowner who fails to fence her pool in a neighborhood full of children may be liable for a child's injuries even if he is a trespasser.

MEDICAL MALPRACTICE

Medical malpractice is any act or failure to act by a health care provider (medical doctor, dentist or nurse) that results in injury to a patient while under the care of health care provider.

NEGLIGENCE

Negligence is the failure of a person (e.g., a corporation, city, county or school district) to use reasonable care, which causes an injury to a person or property. Reasonable care is doing or not doing something, which a reasonably prudent person would or would not do in similar circumstances. For instance, a reasonable person does not tailgate another car because a rear-end collision is likely.

Gross negligence is more than ordinary negligence. The negligence is a reckless disregard for the safety of persons and property. It is more than an oversight; gross negligence appears to be a conscious violation of another's rights to safety.

NUISANCE

A person has a right to sue for unreasonable interference with the use and enjoyment of his property. For example, a company that builds a cell phone tower directly behind a residence with high-powered lights shining on the house during the night is committing a nuisance.

PRODUCT LIABILITY

Product liability is liability imposed on a manufacturer, distributor and seller that has put a defective product into the stream of commerce, which caused injury to persons or property.

SLANDER

Slander is a civil tort where a person makes an untrue verbal statement about another person, which damages that individual's reputation.

TRESPASS

Trespass is the unauthorized entry on another person's property. If the trespass results in damage, the landowner has a civil action for trespass and may recover damages.

9 PURCHASING & SELLING REAL ESTATE

Purchasing and selling real estate are heady but often complex and confusing transactions. There are pitfalls to watch out for, decisions to be made, and documents to wade through. Do not commit yourself to what could be the biggest purchase or sale of your life without considering all aspects of a real property transaction.

BUYING A HOME

Buying a home is time-consuming, expensive and, to varying degrees, stressful. Before you start shopping, take some time to reflect on whether buying a home is right for you.

WHAT YOU SHOULD CONSIDER BEFORE BUYING A HOME

Do my personal circumstances warrant moving? The following factors are strong motivators for making a move:

- I need extra space because there is a baby on the way or for another reason.
- My job is changing and my commute would be too far if I stayed here.
- I make more money now and can afford to buy and maintain a house.
- I have the funds also to pay for moving expenses, repairs to a new home if they are needed right away and decorating.
- I am tired of paying rent and getting nothing for it.

Do I have the ability to make the commitment and take responsibility for a home? If the following statements honestly reflect your situation and abilities, you can financially afford to buy a home:

- I have a good job I intend to keep that is a reliable source of income.

- I pay my bills on time every month.
- My other long-term payments that I have considered are a car payment, or child support or other debt.
- My credit history is good.
- I have the money saved to make a down payment.
- I can also pay the closing costs of at least 5 percent of the home's price.
- I will make my mortgage payments and not incur late payment penalties.
- I know my mortgage payment will be more than the rent I pay now.
- I will pay property taxes, insurance and utilities.
- I will pay to maintain the house; if it needs a new roof, I will save for it.

> **TIP:** Sometimes you may be better off not moving from your existing home. It is costly, stressful and time-consuming. If you move, you may encounter serious problems such as expensive repairs or other concerns. An alternative to moving is remodeling your current residence.

What are the advantages of buying over renting? *Buying a home may be better for you because mortgage payments usually stay about the same and you own the property, a benefit especially when your property value increases.*

The investment in your home generally pays off when you sell the home. When you rent, you do not have an ownership interest in the property and the rent continually goes up. When you are ready to move, you have nothing to show for all those rental payments.

A significant consideration to owning a home is the tax advantage. The IRS allows homeowners to deduct mortgage interest, which reduces the total amount of tax you pay to the government every year. During the early years of a mortgage, most of the payments go to pay off interest, and these payments can be deducted from your total tax bill. In addition to this significant tax advantage, you can deduct property taxes from your income. In the year you buy your home, you may be able to deduct closing costs and moving expenses. If you have a home office, you can deduct a percentage of the expenses to run it.

Also, when you own a home you may be able to get a home equity loan to remodel the house, pay for your child's college education or provide cash after you retire.

Most renters like renting because they do not have to do any residence maintenance or yard work. But they also do not have equity in their home, may not be able to decorate like they want to, and do not receive the tax benefits that homeowners do.

SHOPPING FOR A HOME

Okay, I have decided that I want to move. How do I begin to look for a home? W*hen you are ready to make a move, start by looking at the "Homes for Sale" section of the newspaper, talk to your family and friends, drive through neighborhoods, and check the real estate sales brochures that many grocery or drug stores have out front.* See what homes are out there on the market now. This will give you an idea of current housing prices and the variety of homes on the market.

How much time will buying a new home take? *Allow 6 months to get to know the real estate market in the area you want to buy in, house hunt, make an offer on a home, secure a mortgage and close on the sale.* It may take longer if your financial documentation is not in

order. On average, home buyers view 15 houses before making an offer on one. Be patient, as it will take time to make what may be your largest lifetime purchase.

The key to timing when buying a home is continuing your present residence until you close and move into your new home. If you currently live in an apartment, you may be able to arrange for a month-to-month lease. If you must sell your current home before you can close on a new home, you may need to consider temporary living arrangements, storing your furniture and moving within a tight time period. It can be a juggling act and can take considerable time.

When is the best time of year to buy?

Real estate sales are highly influenced by the economy. Generally, home sales increase when the economy is good, with a good percentage of people employed. Within this general framework, the real estate market has certain cycles. In the spring, because school is about to end for the year and job changes often occur, many families do their house hunting. Many buyers start looking, and many sellers put their homes on the market.

In the fall and winter, home prices tend to be lower in most parts of the country because of uncertain weather and travel conditions, the pessimism people feel during colder and darker weather, and the time taken away from house hunting by the holidays. In particular, viewing a cold or vacant home can be a turnoff. In warm-weather areas, the market generally is more active during the fall and winter when it is cooler to house shop; it is not as active in the spring and summer when everyone is at the beach or busy with activities.

WHAT THIS MEANS FOR YOU: As a buyer, you may want to do your house hunting in the off-season. You might find that perfect home and at a lower price than if you bought it in the spring when everyone else is moving. There will be fewer other shoppers in the market to compete against. However, fewer sellers put their homes on the market during the fall and winter.

How do buyers' and sellers' markets affect when I decide to buy? *When there is a relative balance of buyers and sellers in the*

market, home prices will be driven by economic factors. When there are few homes on the market to sell and many buyers who want to buy, it is a seller's market: the seller can set a high price and the buyer may have to act quickly to get the home the buyer wants. When there are many homes on the market and only a few buyers who can afford to buy, it is a buyer's market: the buyer has a large selection of homes to view and sellers may be forced to lower their prices to get a sale.

WHAT THIS MEANS FOR YOU: The place in the real estate cycle when you decide to buy your home is important to how much you will pay for your home. If you can wait and house hunt during a buyer's market, you may get the home of your dreams at a good price. If you must buy during a seller's market, it likely will take more time to find an affordable home that is one you like.

What other issues affect when I should buy a home? *Another timing issue to consider is whether you will have more funds to buy a home during a certain time of the year. In the spring you may receive a large refund from your income taxes that can be used for a down payment.* During the holidays you may incur substantial bills and have less in savings to spend. Also, you may want to buy as early in the year as possible to get a full 12 months of interest payment deductions to offset your taxable income.

How much home can I afford? *The Federal Housing Administration (FHA) has established certain criteria to let first-time home buyers determine what should be their "debt-to-income" ratio, how much income they have and how much can be spent on a home mortgage, housing expenses, and other debt.* For FHA loans, 29 percent of income should be used for housing costs (mortgage principal and interest, taxes, and insurance) and 41 percent of income should be used for costs and debt (utilities, maintenance, credit card payments), including long-term debt (like car or student loan payments, child support and alimony). For conventional loans, the ratio for qualifying for a mortgage is 28 percent toward housing costs and 36 percent toward costs and debts.

TO PUT THIS IN REAL TERMS: If your income is $75,00 per year, as a first-time home buyer getting an FHA loan you can spend $21,75of this year's income on mortgage payments (about $1,813 per month) and $30,75 (about $2,563 per month) on costs and other long-term debt. The remainder of your income goes to other spending and savings.

TIP: A quick but oversimplified way to determine how much home you can afford is to take twice your annual household income to determine how much mortgage you qualify for.

For example, if you and your spouse earn $75,00 a year combined, you qualify for a $150,00 mortgage. If you have about $20,00 for a down payment, you can afford a home with a sales price of around $170,000, more or less.

You will be required by mortgage lenders to make a down payment of between 5 percent and 2 percent of the home's selling price. One aspect you need to consider is the amount of mortgage loan you can get,or how much you can borrow compared with the price or appraised value of the home you want to purchase. This is called the "loan-to-value" ratio (LTV). Every loan has its own LTV limit.

TO PUT THIS IN REAL TERMS: With a 95 percent LTV loan on a home priced at $75,000, you can borrow up to $71,25 (95 percent of $75,000) but must pay $3,75 as a down payment.

However, lenders would prefer that you make a larger down payment and that they loan you money at a lower LTV. To help protect the lender against risk from a loan default when a larger down payment cannot be made, they will require a mortgage insurance policy (PMI). You may be allowed to cancel the PMI (and save the cost) when the equity in your home reaches 2 percent of the value of the home. However, canceling PMI is often time-consuming and requires significant effort on your part, as lenders are reluctant to cancel it, even when you have every right to have it cancelled.

Chart out these factors to get a clear picture of how much home you can afford:

What are all of my sources of income?'

- Hourly wage/seasonal pay/salary
- Unemployment compensation
- Veteran's benefits
- Military pay
- Social Security
- Interest from banking accounts
- Child support
- Retirement pension payments
- Alimony

What debt do I have?

- Car payment
- Child support
- Credit card debt
- School loans
- Doctor bills
- Debt that has gone to collections

What expenses do I pay regularly?

- Personal and real property taxes
- Child care costs
- Health care costs not covered by insurance, including copayments, doctor fees, prescriptions, eyewear and dental care
- School activity and other fees
- Utilities
- Groceries
- Lunch while at work and occasional restaurants
- Car maintenance and annual inspection fees

How much savings is accessible to me?

- Money market fund
- Savings account
- Checking account
- Stocks, bonds, trusts

WHAT THIS TELLS YOU ABOUT YOUR ABILITY TO BUY A HOME: Once you know your income, debt, regular expenses and savings, you can determine how much home you can afford. This is the target price that should be considered before house hunting to avoid unrealistic expectations and disappointment.

What kind of home is right for me: single family, multifamily, condo or co-op? *The home you will want to buy is one that fits the way you live and meets your needs.* Just because a home looks good does not mean it fits your entire family. It should have spaces and features that work for all family members.

First, make a list of your priorities: location, number of bedrooms and bathrooms, features like an eat-in kitchen, nearness to schools or work or public transportation and the size of the yard, for example. Then, make a wish list of things that you would like but are not essential. Now you have a good idea of the features you want and how important they are to you. Next, decide what type of home you are looking for.

Consider the following factors to determine the home best suited for you and your family:

Do I want a single-family home?

- I like the homes I have seen in a certain neighborhood that I can afford.
- This type of home offers more privacy than other types.
- My family is growing and a smaller living space is not big enough.
- Have I considered all of the yard work and house maintenance?

Would I prefer a multifamily home?

- If I bought a duplex and rented out the other half, I could defray my mortgage cost.
- I would have lots more maintenance to do.
- Have I considered the problems of dealing with renters?

- If the other unit is vacant, can I still make the mortgage?

Is a condo or cooperative right for me?

- I am single and a smaller place would be best.
- I do not want yard work or exterior maintenance to do.
- I feel safer when others live around me.
- A condo may have other amenities, like a pool or tennis court, that a single-family home does not have.
- I may have to pay monthly fees for use of the amenities, for security, or for common area maintenance.
- I will have to adhere to the rules and regulations of the building.
- The noise level can sometimes be bothersome between units.
- Have I considered that it can be difficult to sell a condo or co-op later?

Is a newer or older home where I want to live?

- I dislike always having something needing repair; an older home may not be what I want because frequently repairs need to be made.
- I love the charm of an older home and am interested in maintaining its features.
- Older homes usually are located in established neighborhoods.
- The tax rate on an older home may be lower than a comparable newer home.
- Newer homes often have less problems and I have a busy work schedule so a newer home may be better for me.
- I like the newer appliances and energy efficiency of newer homes.

As you answer these issues, and think of others for your own special circumstances, you will see which type of home suits you best.

Which community is right for me? Consider the following to decide on where to begin looking for a home:

- The neighborhood I live in now is where I want to be.
- A neighborhood with better schools is important—I would move for that.
- An area closer to work would be better.
- My friends all live in another part of town.

- I think a newer development is where I want to live long-term.
- I want to be in an urban or rural environment.
- I would move to live in a safe, low-crime neighborhood.
- An area where the home values are appreciating is important to me.
- I want to be closer to shopping than I am now.

How can I find out more information about a new community?

▶ **SCHOOL INFORMATION.** Home buyers often make a decision based on the schools in an area. Often, your real estate agent is knowledgeable about certain schools, including testing history and other significant information. In addition, the local school board or individual schools can provide information on admission procedures, activities and the students.

▶ **COMMUNITY INFORMATION.** When you find an area you like, contact the local chamber of commerce. They can provide a wealth of information on the communities they represent. A local library is a great source for events, service providers, and special services, and the librarians are available to answer or locate the answer to most questions you may have.

> **TIP:** Rural locations may offer less in the way of services and amenities (i.e., sewer, utility, cable, snow plowing, road maintenance, fire and police protection and zoning regulations). This may be a detriment to you or this may be why living in a rural setting, especially the privacy it provides, is appealing. In any case, keep in mind that you may not have all of the services you are used to if you buy in a rural area.

What if I have been discriminated against when selecting a new residence? *If you feel actions have been taken to exclude you from a neighborhood, contact the U.S. Department of Housing and Urban Development (HUD) or your state fair housing agency.* A violation of the Fair Housing Act (Title VIII of the Civil Rights Act of 1968) may have occurred. The HUD hotline for reporting discriminatory actions is 800.669.9777 or 800.927.9275 for the hearing impaired. To document the discrimination, make a record of every meeting and phone call and what occurred. Keep all written papers, business cards or applications that may be relevant to the discrimination.

How can I get the best deal on a house?

Everyone wants to buy a home at a bargain price, or one that will appreciate and reap significant profit when it is sold. There are a few important aspects to consider to obtain the best deal you can:

- Buy a structurally sound home that does not have major defects.
- Buy a home that is located in a good, or up-and-coming, area.
- Find a highly motivated seller (one who must move quickly).
- For a home that is not in excellent condition, the home will need repairs; offer below-market value to compensate for the needed repairs.
- Shop for your financing as this will save significant interest in the long run.
- The difference in the homeowner's past purchase price and the current listing price should provide negotiating room.

> **TIP:** If the homeowner bought the home many years ago, the owner may have paid significantly less than the home's current listing price. The owner may negotiate on the price because of this. If the home has been owned only a short time, there may be little or no negotiating room on the price.

CAUTION: Do not buy a home needing significant work, such as one needing an "extreme makeover." Even the best estimates of what it will cost to make repairs or renovate will likely not be accurate and may result in a "money pit."

What significance do homeowners' associations and restrictive covenants have on my home shopping?

Homeowners' associations are legal entities created to maintain common areas, such as swimming pools and green belts, to enforce private deed restrictions, and provide services, such as recreational activities and security. Some single-family subdivisions and most condominium and townhome developments have homeowners' associations, which are usually created when the

development is built. Homeowners' associations generally are governed by a volunteer board of directors consisting of other homeowners in the development. Larger homeowners' associations may have paid staff that provides operational, accounting and recreational services. These associations are funded by annual assessments charged to the homeowners in the association.

One of the primary purposes of a homeowners' association is administration of covenants. All homeowners governed by the association agree at the time of purchasing their home to be governed by the association covenants. The covenants usually restrict changes to the exterior of the home (e.g., you can paint your home a color only from a select color palette) and provide for maintenance criteria (e.g., you must maintain the exterior of your home and replace deteriorated siding).

> **TIP:** A distinct advantage to a homeowners' association is the consistent and quality appearance of the homes because of the restrictions governing the property. A disadvantage is the association assessment is an annual fee in addition to real property taxes. If the assessment is not paid, a lien may be placed against the home.

As a buyer looking at a home located in a homeowners' association area, you must:

- Read all of the association's governing documents, including the covenant restrictions, carefully and thoroughly. If these documents are not provided to you before you make an offer on a home in the association, insist that these documents be given to you for review. The documents will state the rules that all homeowners must abide by and all restrictions the association places on the use of your property.
- Request information about the financial and legal status of the association. You should determine if the association is financially sound and if any lawsuits are pending against it. The association should have sufficient funds to pay for common area repair, pay its staff and have reserves. There should be no lawsuits that may result in the potential for a large assessment against the homeowners.
- You may want to talk to neighbors in the area and inquire whether the association provides

quality services and is respected by the homeowners.

- If you have any questions about the association and how it impacts the purchase of your home, consult with an attorney.

What issues affect buying an older home?

Every home comes with small or large problems, but these may be magnified to a greater extent in an older home as there is always something to repair. Besides repairs, older homes often need to be updated and improved. This may involve the remodeling of kitchens and bathrooms, the most expensive rooms in a home to upgrade. Consider this hidden cost if you find that your dream home is an older home.

> **TIP:** Property taxes on an older home are often lower for a comparably sized newer home.

I am fairly handy and found a "fixer-upper." My friend said not to bother. Who is right?

Certain homes may be labeled "handyman's special" or "fixer-upper." These homes likely will be sold "as is," meaning repair of all defects will be at the expense of the buyer, with no recourse against the seller for later discovered problems. Unless you are experienced or have the skills to do extensive home repair, be cautious about the fixer-upper. If this type of home is of interest to you, have an inspector carefully go through the home and list all problems. You may also want to hire an appraiser to estimate the home's current market value and its value after you have expended funds and made improvements to determine if buying this home is a worthwhile investment.

I have found a home in a charming neighborhood with landmark status. What are the pros and cons of buying landmark property?

An important consideration when thinking about buying an older home is whether the home has historical status or a landmark designation; these have there own unique concerns, including restrictions on what can be remodeled or changed.

Many cities and states have laws governing these structures, what can be changed or remodeled, what colors can be used on the exterior, even what can be removed and what must be preserved. In addition, a city or county may have a historical commission governing the use of landmark properties, or that may designate certain areas as landmark districts or neighborhood conservation areas.

Generally, a landmark is an individual place, structure, feature or object that is historically or architecturally significant by itself or because it is associated with events, persons or trends significant in the history of the city. Some properties are protected by preservation easements. If a property is located in a historic district or is a protected landmark, the property owner may be required to obtain approval from the local historical commission before a building permit is issued and any work can be conducted.

> **TIP:** One benefit of owning a historical home is that some areas provide a real property tax incentive. This may take the form of abating a portion of the taxes in the year renovations are made.

CHOOSING A REAL ESTATE AGENT (OR NOT)

How do I go about selecting an agent? *There are many ways to go about choosing an agent. Start by asking family and friends if they can recommend an agent, or talk to an agent you may have met at a Sunday open house.* Many agents specialize in certain geographic areas or types of homes. Before settling on one agent, compile a potential agents list and then talk to each of them and check their references. Select an agent who:

- Listens well and shows an interest in finding the type of home that would be best for you. The best agent is very familiar with the area you are looking in and can give you a broad range of housing prices in that area.

- Has a series of resources available and can provide the services you want and who will help find a home that fits your needs.

- Answers your questions completely and clearly. If you do not understand something an agent tells you, ask again and have the agent clarify what he or she is saying. In particular, if an agent uses a term you are not familiar with, such as "points" or "debt-to-income" ratio, have the agent explain as this is a major purchase and you are entitled to understand all of its aspects.

What is the difference between a real estate agent and a broker?
Real estate agents generally are licensed by the state they work in, and may be members of the National Association of Realtors. They are usually independent salespeople who provide their services to a real estate broker. The broker pays the agent part of the commission earned from the agent's sale of the property.

Real estate brokers are independent businesspeople who manage their own office for the purpose of selling real estate. Whereas brokers and agents may have many of the same job duties, a broker will essentially supervise an agent working for her office. Brokers may also help find financing for a buyer, arrange title searches, rent or manage properties for a fee and perhaps sell insurance out of their real estate business.

Depending on the custom in your area, agents usually receive a 6 percent to 7 percent commission on the sale of the home. If both the buyer's and the seller's agent assist with the sale of the home, they generally split the commission. If a broker listed the home for sale, the broker will receive a portion of the commission also.

What is a Multiple Listing Service (MLS)?
Multiple Listing Services are large computer databases of homes currently for sale. Your agent should have access to a Multiple Listing Service and should be able to provide printouts of homes you may be interested in. Ask for comparable listings that show housing prices.

What information can a real estate agent provide me with?
In addition to providing access to the Multiple Listing Service in your area, an agent should furnish specific information about the home and community. Before you buy a home, talk to the real estate agent about all concerns you have, as they are earning their commission by assisting you. Ask about the zoning in the area as this may affect any remodeling you want to do. Ask about whether the house meets local building codes. Ask if the area is prone to flooding or other natural disasters. Ask what the monthly utility bills are. The agent should have this information from the listing or can obtain it from the seller. Ask if there are any area fees, such as for use of a community swimming pool or tennis court. The agent should also be able to provide you with information about property taxes in the area and on a specific home.

What is the difference between a listing agent, a buyer's agent and a seller's agent?
The listing agent handles the listing of real property for sale. This person may or may not be involved in the actual selling of a home. The selling agent represents the seller, not the buyer, and conducts business on behalf of the seller seeking the best, and highest, price for the seller in the shortest period of time. This agent's responsibilities include doing what needs to be done to close the sale.

Some agents present themselves as buyers' agents, providing services for the benefit of the buyer and representing only the buyer. A buyer's agent may contract with a buyer for an additional commission, above the regular commission rate.

When you are speaking to agents, ask them who they will represent in the transaction and decide which type of agent works best for you.

What questions should I ask a potential agent?
- How long have you been a real estate agent?
- How long have you been with your current firm?
- How many homes in which you represented a client have closed in the last 6 to 12 months?
- Look for an agent who is a career real estate agent and not in real estate as a temporary or part-time position. You may receive better service from a professional agent or broker.
- What references can you give me?
- Ask for references of past and current clients and phone them to determine the quality of the agent's services. You may ask whether they were satisfied with the price they paid, if the agent was helpful and if they would use this agent again.
- What services do you and your agency provide?
- Do you or your agency receive fees for the referral of additional services?
- The real estate agency may work with a limited number of mortgage lenders, home inspectors, title companies, contractors doing repair work or insurance companies. You will want to consider if the agency gets a fee for

a referral when you are shopping for these providers.

- Generally, how do you go about finding a home to buy for your clients?
- For example, does the agent do a drive-around with clients to view locations, evaluate the homes for sale in their price range in a multiple listing service and schedule appointments to see homes?

Decide which agent works best with and for you. Once you have chosen the agent, tell that person specifically the features you want in a home and communicate clearly other aspects that you have considered, such as schools and neighborhoods. Time will be saved if you can communicate specifically what you are looking for.

What if I look for a home without using a real estate agent? *Buying a home without hiring an agent is possible but will take significant effort and time on your part. You must take the time to review the market, carefully determine what is available and understand all aspects of home-sale documentation.* In addition, you may need to find and hire certain professionals, such as home inspectors, a title company, an insurance company and perhaps an attorney to review the final contract, among others.

What home buying resources are on the Internet? *There are many sources on the Internet that can provide information about the real estate agents working in your area, houses for sale where you want to live, mortgages and county real property taxes, for example.* Additionally, there are a number of Web sites where owners are selling their homes directly to buyers and bypassing real estate agents. The following sources may assist you in finding information concerning the home you want to buy:

First-Time Home Buyers

www.homebuyingguide.com – The Federal National Mortgage Association, Fannie Mae Foundation, "Want to Buy a Home? Let Us Point You in the Right Direction"

www.freddiemac.com/homebuyers – Freddie Mac, "Your Route to Home Ownership"

www.hud.gov/buying/index.cfm – HUD, "Buying a Home"

www.abanet.org/publiced/practical/buyinghome.html American Bar Association, "Buying or Selling a Home"

www.consumer.gov/yourhome.htm – "First Gov for Consumers," "Real Estate/Mortgages" and "Moving Tips"

Homes for Sale

There are many Web sites listing homes for sale including sites specific to each state.

www.realtor.org – National Association of REALTORS

www.realtor.com – National Association of REALTORS "Find a Home"

www.forsalebyowner.com – For Sale by Owner

Mortgages

www.ftc.gov/bcp/conline/pubs/homes/bestmorg.htm – Federal Trade Commission, Consumer Publications, "Looking for the Best Mortgage"

www.mbaa.org – Mortgage Bankers Association

Home Inspections

www.nahi.org/consumer_info – National Association of Home Inspectors, Consumer Information, "Locate an Inspector"

DECIDING ON A HOME

What should I look for when walking through a home? Pay attention to the following when you walk through a home for the first time:

- Are there enough bedrooms and bathrooms?
- Is the kitchen functional for the way I cook and use the kitchen?
- Is there place to eat in the kitchen or is the dining area easily accessible?
- Does the house have the features I need and a few from my wish list?
- Is there enough room for what I need presently and some extra for the future?
- Do I like the floor plan and the way the rooms flow?
- Does the house seem structurally sound?

- Do the mechanical systems and appliances seem to be in working order?
- When was the roof, furnace, plumbing and electrical last replaced or repaired?
- Is the yard the right size?
- Will my furniture fit into the house?
- Is there enough storage for all my extra things?
- What do I see that needs to be repaired or replaced right away (e.g., appliances, carpeting?)

> **TIP:** Ask your real estate agent what he or she sees as the features and detriments to each home you see. Your agent may point out things that you do not see.

How do I keep track of all the homes I have looked at? *Take notes on the sales sheet or in a notebook for each home you see. After viewing several homes in one day, these notes will help you recall a specific home when all of their features tend to blur together.* Also, these notes will help you to compare homes when you are about to make an offer. If possible, take photos of the homes you like the most, including the outside, the major rooms, problem areas and special features.

> **TIP:** Bring a tape measure with you when you go out looking at houses. They often come in handy for determining if your furniture will fit in the house, if the bedrooms are big enough, if the height of the counters or showerhead fits you well, or to answer many other unanticipated questions.

What should I know about open houses? *If you are visiting an open house without being represented by an agent, be aware that most open houses are held by sellers' agents.* This agent likely will ask that you add your name to a list showing that you visited the home. It is important, to avoid possible future commission misunderstandings, that you make clear that you either represent yourself or you are represented by an agent already.

MAKING AN OFFER

Always return for a second look before making an offer on a home. Even if you saw the home at 8:00 in the evening, go first thing the next morning. Seeing a home in different light, seeing it a second time, or seeing it with a spouse may make the difference between a good or poor decision.

How do I determine what price to offer? *This is a very important part of the home-buying process, and making an offer should not be done impulsively or lightly.* If your agent is a buyer's agent, discuss the offer price with her; she can point out features that make the sale more or less attractive to you and help you to adjust your price. If your agent is not a buyer's agent, the agent works for the seller, not you. Request that the agent keep any discussions you have about the offer confidential. However, rely on your determination of what a fair offer should be. The things to consider are:

- The prices of homes that have recently sold in the area
- The highlights and problems with the home, such as major items that need replacing within the next year or two
- How long the home has been on the market
- Whether it is a seller's or buyer's market—that is, whether homes are selling fast or slow
- The financing of the home purchase
- The seller's situation, such as a job transfer in which the seller has already moved to a new city, a divorce, or financial difficulties
- Whether the time of year is a factor (e.g., sales generally take longer in winter)

Consider whether you want to include any household items in the offer. *Did the furnishings in one of the rooms go particularly well with the décor? Was there portable shelving in the garage that would be difficult to replace?* Did the kid's play area have equipment that you would like? You may want to approach the seller and ask if you can include some of these items in your purchase of the home for an additional payment. The seller may not want to move the play equipment or has plans to buy new furniture and would welcome the extra cash. Consider these special items before you make the offer.

What are some bargaining tactics to consider?

- The asking price for a home is usually 5 to 1• percent above what the seller really expects to receive. Take this into consideration, but also consider that making an offer of less than 9• percent of the asking price may be considered insulting or cause the seller to be reluctant to negotiate with you.

- If your agent informs you that the price is firm, or that the price has already been reduced and will not go lower, you may still try to bargain for help with closing costs, paying for repairs, or for new appliances.

- If a property has been on the market a long time, it may be that there are problems, it is overpriced, or the seller is unrealistic. Consider this factor when you are negotiating.

- If the seller is relocating and wants to move, he may be flexible as to when you move in or even consider lowering the price. Find out the seller's motivation for the sale.

- The seller may have another buyer or simply state that there is another buyer ready to make a full offer. Depending on your situation, you may want to counter the bluff, saying there is a similar home in the area at a lower price, or you can wait until a better-priced home comes along.

What goes into the offer? *When you are ready to make an offer, your agent will assist you with the paperwork.* Here is where all of your prior preparation and gathering of documentation will help, as the offer will require the following information:

- A legal description of the property
- The price you are offering
- The amount of earnest money
- Your down payment and financing details
- The proposed closing and moving-in dates
- The length of time the offer is open
- Other details or contingencies of the sale, such as the requirement of an inspection and repair by the seller, or other unique concerns

Other details the offer will contain include:

- The names of the real estate agents and the commission to be paid
- A provision that the sale is contingent on a satisfactory appraisal and clear title

- A statement of the total purchase price and the amount due upon signing the real estate sales contract
- A provision for the time period in which the buyer must:
  - obtain a mortgage;
  - conduct the home inspection; and
  - close on the home.

Enticements for the seller to accept your offer:

- Offer more than the listing price
- Offer to pay some of the seller's expenses such as the title or appraisal fees
- Be flexible about the closing date
- Offer more earnest money
- Show documented proof of mortgage preapproval
- Limit contingencies

> **TIP:** Use these enticements only when it is a seller's market, there appears to be tight competition for the home, or there are other reasons for enticements.

What is earnest money and how does it affect my offer? *Earnest money is a deposit you pay to show good faith and hold the home seller to the sale. It demonstrates your seriousness and is usually 1 to 5 percent of the purchase price.* If your offer is accepted, the earnest money is made part of the down payment or closing costs. If your offer is rejected, your earnest money is returned. If you back out of the sale, such as if you were to find another home you like better, the earnest money will be forfeited. Therefore, make sure that this is the home you really want to make an offer on before you write an earnest money check.

I have made my offer. Now what happens? *Once you make an offer, the seller has a stated period of time to accept or reject the offer, usually 24 hours.* This can be a stressful time. Be prepared to continue house hunting or make a second offer if your offer is rejected, or celebrate if your offer is accepted.

When your offer is accepted, you still must negotiate a satisfactory real estate sales contract covering all of the details of the sale. It will be based on the offer. An accepted offer takes the property off the market.

> **TIP:** Be prepared to negotiate the offer. It is common for the seller to come back with a higher price or certain conditions in a counteroffer. There may be some back and forth before the price and conditions can be finalized.

What happens if I have made an offer on a home and then find another I like better?

You should immediately give written notice to the seller's agent that you are withdrawing your offer. Generally, if the seller has not accepted your offer by signing the purchase contract, you can withdraw. If the seller has signed but your agent has not received the contract in hand, you may be able to withdraw. However, if the seller has signed and your agent has received the contract, you are obligated to purchase the home or face legal consequences, including losing all or part of your earnest money.

What goes into the real estate sales contract?
A real estate sales contract should contain all of the provisions necessary to protect your rights and cover all aspects of the sale.

Your real estate sales contract should include the following items:

- The address of the property
- A legal description of the property
- The purchase price
- The earnest money amount
- The amount of down payment
- Mortgage information, including the interest rate
- A listing of all that is included in the purchase price, such as any appliances or furniture that stays with the house, certain fixtures such as a unique dining room chandelier, the riding lawnmower, or any draperies or window coverings
- A statement that any unwanted items the seller leaves behind will be disposed of by a certain date

- A listing of all systems and appliances that should be in working order
- A listing of all closing costs and fees
- The agent's sales commission
- A statement that all utility and insurance bills are prorated to the time of settlement
- The closing date
- The date the contract expires (usually between 3 and 9 days)

Contingencies that your contract may include:

- The contract is subject to inspections satisfactory to the buyer
- The contract is subject to an appraisal satisfactory to the buyer
- The contract is subject to the approval of your attorney, a relative, or another person who may withhold approval if a significant problem is discovered

> **TIP:** Include specifics about which companies will conduct the inspections and appraisal, who will pay for these services, and what will happen if the home does not pass the inspections or if the appraisal is lower than anticipated.

What if the contingencies in my contract are not met by the seller? *You may want to withdraw from the contract or have the price reduced.* You can negotiate with the seller's agent to find the best resolution.

UNDERSTANDING AND OBTAINING A HOME MORTGAGE

There are many lenders willing to provide a mortgage for your new home. Take the time to evaluate the different types and terms of the available mortgages and to locate a lender. Diligent comparison shopping may result in trimming your monthly mortgage payment and saving thousands of dollars in interest over the life of your mortgage.

To begin your search, mortgage information can be obtained from your real estate agent, from the Federal Trade Commission's (FTC) Web site (**www.ftc.gov/bcp/conline/pubs/homes/**

bestmorg.htm), from the newspapers in the Real Estate section, from a mortgage lending institution, from a credit union, or from a bank.

What kinds of mortgages should I consider?

Each mortgage is different and you must find one that you qualify for and meets your needs. They vary in qualifying conditions; interest rates and whether the rate is fixed or variable; points to pay; down payments required; and monthly payment amounts. The types of mortgages usually obtained are:

- **CONVENTIONAL MORTGAGE.** The features of a conventional mortgage are its fixed interest rate and fixed monthly payment, typically over a 30-year period. A conventional mortgage option is to decrease the payment period to 15 or 2 years, thereby decreasing the total amount of interest paid significantly. However, your monthly payment will increase under this option.

- **ADJUSTABLE RATE MORTGAGE (ARM).** The primary feature of an adjustable rate mortgage is that you can obtain and begin paying this mortgage at a lower than conventional mortgage interest rate. However, because the rate is usually tied to a market index, the interest rate changes annually, or even monthly, sometimes in your favor but often at a higher rate. This makes this type of mortgage unpredictable.

> **TIP:** If you decide this is the best mortgage for you, find an ARM that contains an interest rate cap that limits rate increases to two percentage points per year and five to six percentage points over the life of the mortgage. You may want to bargain for an option to lock in a fixed rate or refinance at a certain time.

- **GOVERNMENT PROGRAMS.** A mortgage may be obtained through a state or federal program. For example, the Federal National Mortgage Association (Fannie Mae) provides guaranteed mortgage loans to families with lower incomes which require a smaller down payment.

Other, less common, mortgage types include:

- **BALLOON MORTGAGES.** This mortgage is structured like a fixed-rate mortgage for a set time period, usually 5 to 7 years, after which the entire balance of the mortgage is due—the "balloon" payment. Because most homeowners

cannot pay off their mortgage balance at that time, they will refinance this type of loan. These mortgages offer lower interest rates than fixed-rate loans.

- **GRADUATED PAYMENT MORTGAGES (GPM).** The feature of this type of mortgage is the initial low monthly payments that increase over the life of the mortgage. If you anticipate that you will have a lot more income in the future, this type of mortgage may allow you to buy a more expensive home than you could obtain under a conventional mortgage. However, the danger with this type of mortgage is that if your income does not increase and you cannot make the higher monthly payments, you will not have significant equity in your home even after making regular monthly payments for years. A forced sale will result in little or no investment return.

- **SHARED APPRECIATION MORTGAGE (SAM).** The lender under this type of mortgage obtains an ownership interest in the property according to the conditions of the mortgage and on a specific date. The lender receives a portion of the future increase in the value of the mortgaged property when it is sold in return for a lower rate of interest.

Explain the types of mortgage lenders that are out there. Depending on your circumstances, one of these five types of mortgage lenders will be right for you:

- **LARGE BANKS.** The traditional mortgage provider is a large bank. It has the strictest requirements and qualifying formulas but often the lowest interest rates.

- **CREDIT UNIONS OR LOCAL BANKS.** There may be more flexibility with a credit union or local bank as they often take into consideration your current financial situation, your present ability to pay and your financial stability in addition to your other financial documentation, such as your credit history.

- **MORTGAGE COMPANIES.** Mortgage companies are in the business to make home loans. They often advertise in the newspapers the interest rates and points required of their mortgages to obtain your business.

- **MORTGAGE BROKERS.** Mortgage brokers represent banks, organizations and private individuals with money to lend. A mortgage broker has access to the largest number of loan options for most borrowers, and can often secure lower interest rates than local banks offer. Mortgage broker fees are commonly paid by the lending institution providing the loan, as a percentage of the loan amount.

▸ **GOVERNMENT AGENCIES.** The Federal Housing Authority (FHA) and the Veteran's Administration (VA) insure a significant amount of the mortgage lending in the United States. These agencies guarantee a mortgage loan if the applicant qualifies. An FHA guaranteed loan may require only a 5 percent down payment. A loan guaranteed by the VA requires you to be a qualified veteran. Contact the FHA, VA, a bank, your credit union or your real estate agent to determine if you qualify for an FHA or VA guaranteed loan.

TIP: Before shopping for a mortgage, gather all financial statements and documentation required by your lender. Set aside the last two paycheck stubs for each wage earner in the family, outstanding loan payment books or account numbers and balances, bank account numbers, credit and debit account numbers, and your two latest tax returns with accompanying W-2 and 1099 forms. Check the three major credit reporting agencies for any errors in your report before applying.

What should I ask when shopping for a mortgage? *Knowing the monthly payment calculated on the price of the home you are considering is not enough. Ask for the interest rate and points on the type of mortgage you want for the term you want.* Ask what percentage of the purchase price will be needed for the down payment and if private mortgage insurance (PMI) is required. Make sure that there are no prepayment penalties (so you can pay off your mortgage earlier than the loan term), what the late payment terms are and what refinancing options are provided for in the mortgage. You will also want to know if the lender charges origination and other fees. The lender must give you a breakdown and estimate of all anticipated fees. Once you have all of this information, you can compare mortgage loans.

TIP: See **www.ftc.gov/bcp/conline/pubs/ homes/bestmorg.htm** for a "Mortgage Shopping Worksheet." The worksheet was developed by the Federal Trade Commission in conjunction with other federal agencies providing home mortgage services.

My agent keeps using the terms "prequalify'" and "preapproval" regarding my mortgage. What do these mean? *You can go to any real estate agent or lender and find out the amount of mortgage loan you can qualify for.* This is called prequalification and is an unofficial initial estimate of the mortgage you can afford. You will be asked to supply your income and debt information, which will be used to prequalify you.

Preapproval is a more extensive process conducted by the mortgage lender and serves as a guarantee of a specific loan amount. It certifies the lender has reviewed all of your paperwork, including tax returns, check stubs, credit reports, net worth statements, budgets and other documentation. It verifies that you are financially ready to buy a home and speeds up the loan process once you make an offer on a home.

What are points and how do they affect my mortgage? *Many lenders charge fees—known as "points"—to borrow mortgage money. A point equals 1 percentage point of the amount of the mortgage loan.* In general, the more points you pay to the lender, the lower your interest rate will be. Look in the real estate section of your newspaper to compare rates and fees. Shop carefully for a mortgage lender, comparing rates, fees and service.

TIP: Do not hesitate to negotiate with your mortgage lender. Often, they can reduce their fees or work with you to minimize your costs to obtain the mortgage.

I heard a lender talking about "net worth." What does this mean for my loan borrowing power? *In addition to these considerations, a mortgage lender will consider an applicant's net worth, i.e., your total assets minus your total liabilities.* A low net worth may subject the applicant to higher interest rates and may require a larger down payment or a smaller mortgage loan.

What other options are available instead of a traditional mortgage?
If your circumstances do not fit with any of the other mortgage types, you might consider these options:

- **COSIGNED MORTGAGE.** A family member or relative may be willing to cosign or guarantee your mortgage loan. Banks often find this acceptable. This may entail the cosigner having a part of the title ownership in the home. Cosigners are often reluctant to participate because if you default on your mortgage, the cosigner becomes responsible for the mortgage payments. If you do default, the cosigner may bring a lawsuit and become sole title owner to the home.

- **LEASE WITH OPTION TO PURCHASE.** If you do not have enough for a sufficient down payment, one option is to enter into an agreement with a home seller to lease the home until a time when you can purchase it, usually 6 months to 2 years. The contract should be written so that all lease payments are credited to the purchase price. The seller may require a down payment.

CAUTION: If the contract does not contain a provision crediting all rent to the purchase price at the end of the option term, the seller may be able to evict you and keep the down payment if you do not qualify for a mortgage.

- **EQUITY SHARING.** In this arrangement, you and an investor buy the home together; the investor may make the down payment while you agree to make all of the mortgage payments. This arrangement provides that when the home is sold, both you and the investor share in the proceeds of the sale. An attorney should be consulted as this arrangement is complex.

- **OTHER SOURCES FOR HOME LOANS.** Examine your pension plan, profit-sharing plan, union membership and life insurance. These may be sources you can obtain a loan from to buy a home.

Because these are less conventional types of loans for home buying, higher fees may be charged. Determine and compare the fees charged.

Would seller financing work for me instead of a traditional mortgage?
If your circumstances prevent you from obtaining a traditional mortgage, seller financing is an option to consider. This is also known as a "purchase money mortgage" or "owner financing." This option may be desirable if you are a first-time home buyer, are self-employed, or have a poor credit history. The buyer borrows funds from the seller, instead of, or in addition to, a bank. The seller allows the buyer to use the equity in the home to finance the purchase. However, there are risks with this type of mortgage financing.

The seller holds title to the home, not the buyer. The buyer makes payments to the seller, not a bank or mortgage company. If you cannot make your payments, the seller can foreclose on the home, even if you have made consistent payments for a considerable period of time.

What is "locking in" an interest rate?
Once you have found the mortgage you want, ask for a written "lock-in." This will state the agreed-upon interest rate, the period the lock-in lasts, and the number of points to be paid. A fee may be charged for locking in the loan rate. However, a lock-in protects you from interest rate fluctuation, particularly a costly increase in the interest rate while your loan is processed.

What protection do I have if a mortgage lender discriminates against me?
The Equal Credit Opportunity Act prohibits lenders from discriminating against credit applicants in any aspect of a credit transaction on the basis of race, color, religion, national origin, sex, marital status, age, whether all or part of the applicant's income comes from a public assistance program, or whether the applicant has in good faith exercised a right under the Consumer Credit Protection Act. You cannot be refused a loan and cannot be charged more for a loan or offered less favorable terms based on these characteristics. Contact an attorney if you feel you may have been discriminated against.

What other costs and fees will I have to pay to buy a home? *Some lenders charge an origination fee of about 1 percent of the loan to pay for the loan application process.* This fee is often negotiable.

Some lenders also require an escrow account holding of up to 14 months of prepaid taxes and insurance. The escrow account may be waived by the lender if you are making a 2 percent down payment on your home. Some states require interest to be paid on escrow account funds, but many do not.

You will need cash to cover the closing costs. These are typically are 2 to 4 percent of the loan, excluding points. These costs include the survey, appraisal, escrow account set-up, closing attorney fee and broker commission. They may also include research, copying and other miscellaneous or "junk" fees. Review all fees charged by your lender to avoid paying unnecessary fees.

What is a mortgage servicing company? *Most lenders who make mortgage loans do not hold and service the mortgage over its life.* More often, a mortgage servicing company will "buy" the mortgage at some point, and you will receive notice in the mail, one from the lender and one from the service organization, usually 15 days before the effective date of the transfer. Your mortgage payments are then made to this company, as it is responsible for collecting your monthly loan payments and crediting your account.

> **TIP:** Keep all of your records regarding a change in the company servicing your mortgage. If you have a question, you then can easily determine who is currently handling your mortgage and how to contact them.

When should I submit my mortgage loan application? *Right after you and the seller sign the real estate sales contract is the time to go to your mortgage lender and submit your loan application.* Bring any information necessary to process your application, such as identification, copies of your last 2 years' income tax returns, pay stubs, bank statements, titles to your car, and any other proof of income and assets and debts.

What will happen at the lender's office? *Together with the mortgage lender, you will complete the loan application. You will also pay several fees, including the loan processing fee, the property appraisal fee and credit reporting fee.* If the mortgage you are applying for includes points, you will pay these, too. If you are assuming a seller's mortgage, you will pay a loan assumption fee.

> **TIP:** Be sure to have funds in your checking account for these fees and bring your checkbook with you when you apply for the loan.

The mortgage lender should inform you of the following:

- The interest rate for the loan and whether it can be locked in
- The amount of the loan origination fee (usually 1 percent of the loan) and when it should be paid
- Whether the lender is requiring private mortgage insurance (PMI)
- If there are other considerations regarding your ability to be approved
- The amount of the closing costs

> **TIP:** As required by law, you should receive a good faith estimate of the closing costs within 3 business days of submitting your loan application. If you do not, phone your lender and have the lender fax this statement to you.

What happens after I have applied for the loan? *Once you have applied for the mortgage loan, it usually takes time to be approved. Some lenders are faster than others.* If you have not heard from your lender within a reasonable period of time, 2 weeks or more, phone and inquire about the status of your loan approval.

The lender will review your documentation and initiate certain services. An appraisal will be conducted to determine and confirm the market value of the home. A title search will be conducted in the public records checking for unpaid taxes, judgments, mortgage payments or outstanding liens. A survey may be conducted to verify the location of the property.

When you are approved, the lender will provide a letter of commitment, which states the terms and conditions of the mortgage.

> **TIP:** Read the letter of commitment carefully, checking for misstatements or errors. If this occurs, phone the lender immediately to have the problem remedied or clarified.

Once you are satisfied with the letter of commitment, sign and date it, make copies for your file and return the original to the lender.

I have been approved for my mortgage! Are there any more steps to secure my loan?

At closing, you will be required to sign the mortgage note that secures the loan. By signing the note, you will be giving the lender a lien on your property, which allows the lender to bring a lawsuit if you default in making payments. Alternatively, you may be required to sign a deed of trust, which gives the lender the right to have the property sold if the event of a default.

PREPARING FOR THE CLOSING

Do I need a lawyer when buying a home?

Most states do not require a lawyer when buying a home, but do require the involvement of a qualified real estate professional, such as an escrow agent or title company. However, some states require a lawyer to assist with some aspects of the sale, such as closing. A lawyer can represent you in negotiating the contract or clarifying aspects of the deal. Hiring a lawyer to review the real estate sales contract, particularly if anything is even slightly out of the norm with the sale, may be a wise decision. In addition, the lawyer will be familiar with the situation in the event there is a dispute or delay.

How do I locate a real estate lawyer? *Real estate agents often can recommend a lawyer they have worked with in the past. Family and friends may be able to recommend a lawyer. You can phone the local bar association as they often have referral services.* Make sure to discuss the lawyer's experience representing homebuyers, the fee, the services covered by the fee and any costs associated with the representation, such as photocopying and filing fees.

> **TIP:** See www.abanet.org/legalservices/lris/directory.html for the American Bar Association Lawyer Referral Services locator.

Should I bother to get a home inspection?

A home inspector examines a house's structure, construction and mechanical systems and lets you know the repairs that are needed or problems that are found. Getting a home inspection is very important and should not be bypassed to save money or time. You do not want to find out about these concerns after you buy the home, so take the time to get an inspection. An inspector will not tell you if you are getting a good price for the house, but will tell you if the home is sound.

Specifically, the inspector will look at the home's foundation, the electrical system, the plumbing and waste disposal, the water heater, insulation and ventilation, the air conditioner, water systems, the potential presence of pests such as termites, all doors and windows, ceilings, floors and the roof.

There should be a clause in your offer covering the inspection. The clause should state an inspection is required and if serious problems are found, the offer can be rescinded. This will give you an out so that you do not have to buy a defective house. Or, if minor but costly problems are found, this clause may give you some leverage to renegotiate the price. The clause also may specify that the seller must fix any discovered problems before you purchase the home.

> **TIP:** You are not required to be there at the time the inspection is conducted. However, it is a good idea to be present so that the inspector can answer questions you might have as the inspection proceeds.

What are specialized inspections?

Specialized inspections are required to check for radon gas, asbestos, water or air-related issues, mold or lead-based paint. In some geographic areas, radon is a significant concern, or termites are prevalent. These problems may be costly to remediate.

You may want to check a fireplace chimney and have it cleaned before you move in. Also consider having septic tanks and water wells inspected. For new septic systems, a "perk test" should be conducted to test the soil for compatibility with septic. This is very important and should not be overlooked.

What does the seller need to disclose about the house I am buying? *Sellers in most states are required to disclose "material defects" that cannot reasonably be discovered by a buyer. However, when a defect is open and obvious, the seller is not under this disclosure obligation.* Material defects may include asbestos, urea formaldehyde insulation, remodeling or alterations that do not comply with building codes, crimes that occurred in the home, or other defects that materially affect the market value of the home.

In most states, the seller is not obligated to make any guarantees about the future condition of the roof, heating and cooling, and other systems.

If a defect is encountered, you must consider your options. First, any problems or undisclosed material defects should immediately be pointed out to the seller. The seller may then correct these problems. If the seller does not, your payment on settlement day may be reduced to reflect the discovered problems. If an egregious or undisclosed problem is discovered, you may want to consult your attorney regarding continuing with the purchase and the costs of ending the sale.

> **TIP:** Consult your attorney if a material defect is discovered after you have closed on the sale of your home. You may want to consider a fraudulent misrepresentation lawsuit.

Should I buy a home warranty? *Home warranties offer a new home buyer some protection for a period of time. They warrant against potentially costly problems, such as furnace failure, that are not covered by homeowner's insurance.* Consider the age of the home and its major systems and whether there is significant potential for problems. During the first year after the purchase of a new home, homeowners are often cash-poor. The purchase of a home warranty may be a wise investment.

Will I need homeowner's insurance? *A homeowner's insurance policy is required to close on your home. Speak to several insurance agents to learn about coverage and to get premium quotes. Homes constructed of newer materials and those located near a fire station may reflect a lower-cost premium.* Premiums will increase, or coverage may be excluded, in certain areas such as those prone to flooding or that encounter repeated natural disasters, such as hurricanes or earthquakes.

What is title insurance and why do I need it? *Title insurance is issued by a title company and protects the buyer against loss from a defective title. The title company searches and examines public records at the county recorder's office or registry of deeds, looking for unpaid taxes, judgments, mortgage payments or outstanding liens.* The examiner also looks for third-party claims such as for monies owed to a former spouse or business partner or to a homeowner's association.

If there are unpaid monies owed or third-party claims, the title will be designated as "not clear" or "marked-up" or "with encumbrances." These are problems that must be fixed before a lender will approve a mortgage loan.

CAUTION: Do not accept a title that is not clear as it will result in problems to the buyer in the future. Either demand that title be made clear before you purchase the home or cancel the purchase if the problems appear significant. Also, consult your attorney to fully understand the condition of the title.

Title insurance should be purchased to protect you from any problems with the title that the searcher does not locate and that are discovered after the purchase.

What are the types of ownership interest, and which should I choose for my title to the property? *If you are a single person, and no one else will own or have an interest in the home with you, you will hold title to the home in "fee simple," without limitation to any other*

person. It is the most common form of property ownership and reflects the type of estate you have in the property.

If you and your spouse are purchasing the home, depending on the state you live in, you will hold it as "joint tenants with right of survivorship," as "tenants in common" or in "tenancy by the entirety."

- ▶ **JOINT TENANCY WITH RIGHT OF SURVIVORSHIP.** Two or more persons own and have equal interests in the same property, and if one person predeceases the other, the other is sole title owner
- ▶ **TENANCY IN COMMON.** Two or more persons own and have equal interests in the same property.
- ▶ **TENANCY BY THE ENTIRETY.** Spouses own the property as one party with survivorship, but neither spouse can sell his or her interest.

CAUTION: This form of home ownership is not legal in some states.

Why should I bother with a final walk-through? I have seen the home several times already. *The final, or presettlement, walk-through may be your first opportunity to see the home empty, without furniture and other decorating. Examine the house carefully. Look at the walls and ceilings, checking for cracks or water damage or other signs of structural problems.* Check to make sure all work the seller agreed to do was completed. If any of these problems were not fixed, this should be brought up and handled prior to closing. Check to see if everything that is supposed to be included with the home is there, such as draperies, the washer and dryer or other appliances. Try the various systems to make sure everything is in working order.

> **TIP:** Conduct the final walk-through in the middle of the day when the best light is available. This also will give you the opportunity to walk around the outside of the home.

What happens at closing and settlement?
Closing often occurs at a title insurance company or an attorney's office. The buyer and seller usually attend and closing documents are reviewed and signed. If you have not already provided a paid homeowner's insurance policy or a binder and receipt showing the premium has been paid, this is the time to do so. The closing agent will present forms listing all of the money you owe the seller, such as the remainder of the down payment, and any money the seller owes you, such as any prior agreed rent for staying for a longer period. The seller provides proof of any agreed warranty or repairs made. The mortgage will be reviewed and signed by you in addition to the mortgage promissory note. You will then receive a deed to the property.

The deed and mortgage are recorded with the local authority, such as the county recorder or registry of deeds office. This should be completed by the closing agent within a reasonable period of time.

The buyer must bring to the closing:

- The down payment (usually a certified check)
- A deposit for prepaid taxes and insurance to the escrow agent
- The real estate agent's commission
- Various fee payments for the attorney and lender

The seller must bring to the closing:

- The deed, title and keys to the home
- Inspection reports not previously submitted
- Any documents that will be transferred, such as for property taxes or insurance policies
- A bill of sale for any furniture or other personal property included in the sale

The documents and items you will receive include:

- Settlement statement or HUD-1 Settlement Statement Form
- Truth-in-lending statement
- Mortgage note
- Real estate sales contract
- The deed to the property
- Keys to the house

CAUTION: Make sure to check the deed, that you and your spouse's names are spelled correctly and that your title designation is correct (i.e., you and your spouse are listed as joint tenants with right of survivorship or as tenants in common or tenancy by the entirety).

What costs will I pay at closing? *At closing, the lender's agent receives payment from you for all of the closing costs and gives you a settlement statement.* Closing costs vary, but generally cover the following:

- Attorney or escrow fees
- Property taxes for the remainder of taxes due during the tax period to date
- Interest paid from the closing date to 3• days before the first monthly payment
- Any loan origination fees required
- Deed recording fees
- A survey fee
- The first premium covering the mortgage insurance
- Title insurance fee
- Loan discount points
- The first payment to the escrow account for future real estate taxes and insurance
- Homeowner's insurance policy, other insurance policy (such as flood or fire insurance policy) receipts
- Miscellaneous fees, such as for documentation preparation

> **TIP:** Some closing costs may be waived by the closing agent prior to the actual closing. Shop for closing agents to determine who will provide the requested services at the lowest fee. Have the agent fax or mail a listing of the fees they will charge. Some fees, however, cannot be waived, such as the fee for recording the deed.

There is so much to do! How can I organize my upcoming move? The following checklist will help alleviate the stress of moving:

- Put in a change-of-address form at the post office.
- Notify important personal contacts, such as your employer and emergency contact listings, of the new address and phone number.
- Make an inventory of your possessions to ensure that they do not get misplaced during the move.

- If you intend to use a moving company, get three estimates and check their references for reliability and careful handling.
- Phone all utility companies so that you will have water, electricity, telephone and gas the day you move in.
- Determine the location of the water heater, fuse box, and gas and water shut-offs.
- If appliance manuals, warranties, and service records were not left in the home, contact your real estate agent to request these from the seller.
- Consider changing the locks on the exterior doors.
- Plan and test emergency procedures if you have children.
- Familiarize your pet with the new home and yard.

SELLING YOUR HOME

Why sell your home? There are many reasons, some of which are to upgrade to a nicer or newer home, to have more room for a growing family, to downsize after divorce or retirement, to relocate for a new job, to repay debt, to take out the profit from a sale because of unemployment or a death, or to get rid of depreciating property.

Be clear as to why you are selling your home as this will impact the selling price. If you must move quickly, you may have to accept a lower sales price. If you can take your time and wait out a poor market for selling homes, this may garner a higher profit for you.

> **TIP:** The federal government has many pamphlets that assist consumers who are thinking about selling their home. See the Consumer Information Catalog, Pueblo, CO 81009, 888.8.PUEBLO, or find the catalog on the Internet at **www.pueblo.gsa.gov**.

PREPARING YOUR HOME FOR SALE

What is the first step in selling a home? *Selling your home is more than just setting a price, finding a sales agent and keeping the place clean. It involves careful planning and consideration of the current market.* You should look at your home as you have not before and decide whether its condition warrants repairs, painting, renovation or replacement of worn decorating is necessary. If you do not do these repairs before you put the house on the market because you have lived with the problems for years, do not be surprised when a buyer demands that you make the repairs before the sale can be closed. These things take time and cost money but will enhance the value you receive from a sale.

> **TIP:** Consider hiring a home inspector yourself before any potential buyers ever see the house. From the results of the inspection, you can decide which projects are the most important to do and which may be foregone. A real estate agent can also make suggestions that will make your home more saleable.

My real estate agent told me to remove everything from my house that I do not need for the next month. Why does she want me to remove the clutter? *Nothing discourages a potential home buyer quicker than clutter.* You want the buyer to see your house and its possibilities, not your possessions. The less that remains in your house, the better the buyer can do this.

If there are too many family pictures on the mantel, box them up. If there are not only books on the bookshelves but figurines, mementos, CDs, and videotapes, box the extras up and put them away. If your child has an excessive amount of stuffed animals in their room, store some away. Make all kitchen and bath counters shiny and clutter-free. Also, remove any items that might make a statement that would be offensive to others who may not share your same views, beliefs or sense of humor. After you have boxed up what you do not need, consider storing it all in a rental locker so that the clutter problem does not just move to your garage, attic or basement.

What are some easy things I can do to my home's interior to make it more appealing to a buyer?

- Clean as much as possible until your home sparkles, particularly the windows, floors, kitchen and bathrooms
- Change or clean heating and air conditioning filters

- Repair dripping faucets and oil squeaky doors
- Pick things up off the floors that do not belong there
- Clean your oven
- Paint any areas that do not look fresh, use a neutral color
- If your furniture makes a room look crowded, remove the excess furniture and pout it in storage
- Put fresh flowers in the dining and living rooms
- Put a new comforter on the master bed
- Put new guest towels in the bathrooms
- For showings and open houses, make coffee and put cookies on the counter and possibly use an air freshener

Your goal is to leave a potential buyer with a good impression, that your home has been well maintained and is a place they will want to live.

> **TIP:** Cigarette smoke and pet odors can kill a sale. Have the home professionally cleaned, including all carpets and window treatments to remove as much odor as possible. If you smoke, smoke outside, and consider having your pet stay with a relative during the time you are trying to sell your home as air fresheners do not mask these smells adequately.

What can I do to improve my home's curb appeal? *A home that is visually appealing and in good condition will attract potential buyers.* Use this checklist to view your property through an outsider's eyes:

- Are the lawn and shrubs well maintained?
- Are there cracks in the foundation or walkways?
- Does the driveway need resurfacing?
- Are the gutters, chimney and walls in good condition?
- Do the window casings, shutters, siding or doors need painting?
- Are any bicycles or other items in the yard removed and debris stored out of sight?
- Are lawnmowers and hoses properly stored?
- Is the garage door closed?

- Are there attractive yard lights that can be put on?
- Is there a pot of flowers on the porch?

How much time will selling my home take?

This is not an easy question to answer and is different for every sale. Consideration of whether you are attempting to sell your home during a buyer's market or a seller's market affects whether the sale will take a long or short time. If it is a seller's market, when there are few homes on the market to sell and many buyers who want to buy, you may be able to set a high price and the buyer may have to act quickly before the home is sold. When there are many homes on the market and only a few buyers who can afford to buy, it is a buyer's market—the buyer has a large selection of homes to view and a seller may be forced to lower his price to get a sale. In addition, during a buyer's market, a home for sale may remain on the market for a considerable time.

CHOOSING A REAL ESTATE AGENT OR "SALE BY OWNER"

Should I avoid a real estate agent and sell my home through a "sale by owner" organization? *You can sell your home without using an agent—there are a number of "sale by owner" organizations on the Internet.* However, there are several disadvantages to this method, including creating and following up on the local marketing of your home and taking a significant amount of time to properly understand and handle the documents involved. Keep in mind that handling your own sale means you will be responsible for placing ads, answering phone inquiries and showing your home to strangers.

If a buyer knows you are selling your home without an agent, presumably to save on the agent's commission, the buyer may offer less for your home. Also, if you intend to sell your home by owner, it would be best to consult an attorney before accepting a buyer's offer and signing the real estate contract. Keep in mind you must comply with the disclosure statutes of your state as well as the state and federal fair housing laws.

What are the pros and cons of using a real estate agent to sell my house? Advantages of selling your home with an agent:

- The agent handles all marketing and advertising costs.
- The agent can make suggestions about ways to make your home more attractive.
- Your home likely will be listed on a Multiple Listing Service, giving it wider exposure to potential buyers (though some "sale by owner" organizations also offer this option).
- The agent will help establish a fair asking price for the home.
- Open houses and showing of the home are coordinated by the agent.
- The agent will weed out buyers who do not qualify for a mortgage.
- The agent prepares the forms and agreements needed to sell the home.
- The sales negotiations are handled by the agent.
- The agent can assist you and the buyer to locate financing, inspectors, insurance, and legal counsel.

Disadvantages of selling your home with an agent:

- You will pay a commission of 5 percent to 7 percent of the selling price, on average.
- You must forego some degree of control over the sale of your home and you may experience some disagreement with the agent over marketing of the home.

> **TIP:** If you determine it is a "hot" seller's market, you may want to try to sell your home on your own first to save the commission.

How do I go about selecting an agent to sell my house? *Find and phone several agents to determine who you can work with. Do not hire the first agent you speak to.* Ask how they will market the house, what publications they will list your house in, whether they use yard signs and hold open houses, and if they will put your house information on the Internet.

Features that you should look for when considering an agent include:

- You are comfortable and confident with the agent.

- You do not feel pressured by the agent.
- The agent specializes in the area you live.
- The agent returns calls promptly and answers questions fully.
- The agent keeps you informed about the sale's progress, telling you other agents' comments about the home and potential buyers' level of interest.
- The agent suggests new strategies during the listing period.
- The agent has a track record of good sales and satisfied sellers.
- The agent is a good negotiator.

What is an agent's listing agreement? *When you have found an agent to represent you in selling your home, the agent will have you sign a listing agreement. This contract will bind you to that agent's services for a specific period of time.* The usual time is 6 to 9 days. It is not wise to bind yourself to a listing of a longer duration as you do not know how well you can work with this agent or if the agent will market the house vigorously. If you find you want to change agents, review the listing agreement and follow the steps required to terminate the agreement. Or, you can wait until the listing expires; however, the sale of your home may take longer.

Should I agree to hold an open house?
Holding open houses to market your home to potential buyers sounds productive, but it actually produces little sales results. Instead, it produces a number of new clients for the agent holding the open house. However, an open house to other real estate agents does generate interest, and often results in agents bringing their buyers to tour the home.

I am a little nervous about all thee people marching through my house. What should I be aware of when opening my doors to strangers? *Make your home accident proof when it is on the market and many people will be coming through. They will not be aware of the hazards that you overlook daily.* Remove obstacles that could injure someone. Post "watch your step" signs where needed. Check for uneven steps, loose railings, objects like plants or vases that could easily fall, or objects like toys that a stranger could easily trip over. Roll up and store rugs that slip. Clean up any wet areas in the kitchen or bathrooms.

> **TIP:** Remove small valuables such as jewelry, loose money and important documents. You may want to put these in your safe deposit box while your home is on the market.

How should my home be marketed? *Your home should be listed in a Multiple Listing Service (MLS) to gain exposure to the widest range of home buyers.* This service can be provided through your real estate agent or through a "buy owner" Web site. You or your agent may print brochures that can be placed in a box at the curb for drive by house hunters. You may want your agent to put pictures and information about your home on the Internet on the agency's Web site. All of these are good marketing methods that may result in a sale.

You or your agent should also run advertising in the local newspapers. Classified ads use abbreviations, and understanding these takes some learning. For example, "Condo, 2B, 2BA, frpl, HOA/Condo fee" means a two-bedroom, two-bath condo with a fireplace and a homeowners' association annual fee. The ads also may use code words such as "fixer-upper," meaning significant work needs to be done on the home, or "low upkeep" meaning there is no or little yard. Study other newspaper sales ads to get up to speed on what the ads are really telling the buyer; then make sure your ad reflects your home in its best light.

What is a market analysis and how can I get one? *An agent who is interested in selling your home can provide a market analysis for your review.* The market analysis will contain:

- descriptions of comparable homes
- the price that the comparable homes have sold for or are currently selling for in your area
- the amount of time they were or have been on the market
- the dates of each sale

BUYERS AND FINANCING

How should I go about pricing my home? *A real estate agent can give you the price of several comparable homes that have sold in your area. Or you may be able to find prices and statistics for recently sold (comparable) homes in the area using the Internet.* These are made available through the county recorder, or are sponsored by the real estate section of your local newspaper. Use these prices as the basis to set the selling price. Avoid overpricing in an effort to provide yourself negotiating room; you may never see a group of potential buyers if the price is higher than they can afford.

Factors to consider when establishing a fair price include:

- The present economic situation
- The supply and demand in the local housing market
- Seasonal influences and holidays
- Local schools
- Average home prices in the neighborhood
- The condition of your home
- Your home's features or extras, such as a pool, fireplace, children's play area, new roof, updating of the heating/cooling systems, fenced yard or special landscaping

How do I or a real estate agent find a qualified buyer? *Either you or your agent will want to quickly weed out potential buyers who cannot afford to purchase your home.* The following factors will help determine whether you are wasting your time negotiating a sale:

- The buyer's debt and credit history
- The buyer's current income and employment
- The buyer's cash position and availability of a down payment
- The length of time the buyer needs before closing on your home
- How interested the buyer appears to be in your home versus others

A real estate agent will determine if a prospective buyer is able to afford your home by asking if they are prequalified for a mortgage loan and for what amount, or by having the buyer complete basic income and debt information forms.

What is seller financing and how does it work? *If a buyer's circumstances prevent her from obtaining a traditional mortgage, the seller may choose to finance the mortgage loan. This is also known as a "purchase money mortgage" or "owner financing."* A seller should consider this option only if the buyer appears to be financially stable, but for some reason did not qualify for a traditional mortgage loan or for the full amount of the loan needed. Such reasons may be if the buyer is a first-time home buyer, is self-employed but does not have several years of documented income, or has a poor credit history but seems to have turned this around.

In essence, the buyer "borrows" funds from the seller, instead of, or in addition to, a bank. The seller allows the buyer to use the equity in the home to finance the purchase. The seller may carry back a promissory note at the current interest rate and enter into a deed of trust, mortgage, or contract with the buyer for the home sale.

There are risks with this type of financing for both the buyer and seller. The seller likely will hold title to the home, not the buyer. The buyer makes payments to the seller, not a bank or mortgage company. If the buyer does not make the payments, the seller can foreclose on the home.

CAUTION: Think carefully before you provide seller financing, weighing the risks of nonpayment with the benefit of a buyer for the home. Make sure this is the financial decision you want to make with your money.

What is a bridge loan? *If you intend to sell your home and buy a new one, place your home on the market as far in advance as possible of purchasing the new one.* If you find a new home first and are unable to quickly sell your present home, you may wind up with two mortgages. If this happens, ask your real estate agent or banker about a bridge loan to help you make the double payments. Lenders use the same criteria for offering bridge loans as they use for mortgages. Be aware that bridge loans can be expensive.

OFFERS AND SELLERS' COUNTEROFFERS

What do I need to know when reviewing an offer on my home? *There may be a considerable period of time after you have put your home on the market before an offer comes in. Do not let this lag of time lull you.* Once you receive an offer, you must act quickly. Often, an offer is open for 24 to 48 hours only, or must be accepted by a certain date, or accepted "upon presentation of the offer."

Review not only the purchase price being offered, but the terms and conditions of the sale. Consider the following issues:

- What are the contingencies this buyer has placed on the sale? An inspection? The sale of a current home? Approval by a third party? Approval of financing?
- What repairs are demanded by the buyer; do you want to and can you afford to make them?
- What inspections is the buyer requiring and who pays for these? Termites? Radon? Lead paint? How much will they cost?
- What fixtures or other items does the buyer expect will be conveyed with the home? All draperies? The garage work table?
- Are there any items the buyer wants to purchase? The riding mower? The kitchen chairs? Play area equipment?
- How long do you have to accept or reject the offer?

CAUTION: Read the offer carefully so that there are no misunderstandings later. It is advisable to have your attorney also review the offer. Get your real estate agent's opinion of the offer.

I can agree to most of the buyer's offer, but I would like to negotiate a few terms. What are my options? Once you have reviewed the offer, you have several options; negotiating the sale of a home is an accepted practice. Your options are:

1. accept the offer as it is;
2. reject it stating clearly why the offer was unacceptable. Making your reasons known may result in the buyer coming in with another offer that might be acceptable to you; or
3. make a counteroffer, accepting parts of the offer and amending other parts. The counteroffer should contain a time limit for

acceptance from the buyer. Often, specific provisions are discussed by phone with the real estate agents acting as liaisons to come to a conclusion.

Do not let a potential buyer get away without first attempting to work through any problems to the sale. A ready and willing buyer may not come along again for a long time, and most reasonable offers should be carefully considered.

I made a counteroffer, then the buyer withdrew. Can she do that? *If you make a counteroffer, the buyer can withdraw from the sale at any time, up until she accepts your counteroffer.* Once the buyer accepts the counteroffer, you have a sale.

What happens if someone else comes in with a higher offer after I accepted the first one? *Once you accept an offer, you have sold your home.* If you accept another, higher offer, you have broken the contract with the first buyer.

CLOSING THE SALE

What documentation do I need to sell my home? *The sale of your home requires significant documentation to comply with real estate law.* Make sure you have these documents on hand before you put your home on the market.

- Your deed, a deed of trust, or your mortgage agreement
- Your most recent real property tax bill
- A plat or survey of your property (additionally, a survey may be made later in the process)
- If your home is a condominium or cooperative or part of a homeowner's association, the governing documents and any assessment documents (these may be obtained later in the process)
- Any documentation that adversely affects your property, such as a lien or lawsuit

What are the tax consequences of selling my home? *Selling your home will impact your federal and state tax payments and must be reported on your tax returns.* Seek the advice of a tax consultant on how the sale of your home may affect your tax liability.

You and your tax advisor will consider:

- Whether you purchased the home or acquired it by gift or inheritance
- Whether you used your home partly for business or as a rental
- The costs associated with selling your home and whether they may be deductible
- Home improvements or additions, which may help to offset capital gains
- The gain or loss from the sale of your home
- Any applicable exclusions, such as for certain married couples or for specific amounts of capital gain

What can I take with me and what do I have to leave with my home when I move? *"Fixtures" are the items that you can think of as being affixed to the home.* They convey with the sale of the property and include wall-to-wall carpeting, major appliances, plumbing fixtures, built-ins such as bookcases or eating benches, track lighting and garage shelving, if attached. Some items, such as draperies, are not fixtures but often stay with the home.

> **TIP:** To avoid any misunderstandings, make sure the real estate sales contract spells out only those items that are actually staying with the property.

BUYING REAL ESTATE FOR YOUR SMALL BUSINESS

WHAT YOU SHOULD CONSIDER BEFORE BUYING REAL ESTATE FOR YOUR SMALL BUSINESS

During the life of a small business there comes a time when determining whether to continue leasing space or buying property becomes a critical question. Purchasing real property may be the single largest purchase for a small business. The small business owner needs to make a series of decisions before purchasing property for her business.

Is purchasing property the best option for my business? *Whether to remain in a current space or purchase real property?* The small business owner needs to look at the short- and long-term benefits and disadvantages of each alternative when resolving this dilemma.

Financial impact

- What is the financial impact of remaining in leased space (e.g., no equity in property versus no real property taxes to pay)?
- What is the financial impact of buying property (e.g., financial drain from a purchase versus equity that can be borrowed against and sold at higher value later)?

Product and services

- What is the impact on product or services and employees of remaining in the current space?
- What is the impact of moving to larger or better configured space?

Mechanics of moving

- How will moving to another location and another facility affect the business?
- What will moving cost?
- How much time is needed to move?
- Are there any special requirements for a move, such as moving a computer or manufacturing system?

Furnishings/renovations

- What facility changes or renovations will be needed?
- Are new furnishings, such as lobby furniture or new cubicles, needed?
- How much will this cost?
- How much time will this take?

Lease/purchase

- Is an outright purchase best?
- Is a long-term lease the best way to go?
- Is a lease-purchase option a consideration?

How can I narrow down properties to look at? Before beginning a search for business property, consider exactly what it is you are looking for.

- Are you looking for office, retail, or industrial space?
- Do you need more space for customers, employees or manufacturing?
- How much square footage do you estimate you need?
- Which weaknesses do you want to avoid that are present in your existing space (e.g., space

is not configured properly, does not have capability for newer technologies or has older public areas)?

- Do you need property better located to downtown, to where you live, near suppliers, or closer to customers?

CAUTION: Write down exactly what you are looking for before going property shopping. If you do not, you may find space that at first glance appears to be right for your business but when put to use is not really what you needed.

How does buying commercial real estate differ from buying residential property?
Unlike the purchase of a home, there are many additional considerations when buying commercial real estate. Consider these before you invest in the purchase of business property.

Environmental concerns: toxic chemicals, ground water contamination, asbestos, lead and other issues. A significant concern when considering the purchase of commercial property is whether the purchaser will be liable for clean up costs from prior contamination, even when the new owner did not contribute to or know of the contamination. Environmental contamination may impair a purchaser's ability to finance the property acquisition. The future marketability of the property also may be impacted by the contamination.

EXAMPLE: For example, dry cleaning establishments provide services that may be accompanied by a release of chemicals that can contaminate ground or surface water, and may result in hazardous waste or polluting air emissions. The state of Ohio, which has almost 4 percent of the nation's dry cleaners, has developed environmental regulations governing this business, including establishing proper handling and disposal procedures and reporting requirements. (See **www.epa.state.oh.us/dhwm/ drymain.htm**.)

Current zoning and how it affects the property. The use of land is controlled by zoning regulations whose purpose is to regulate the development and growth of a community in a way that is best for the general public. Zoning divides the community into areas (zones) that can be used only for certain purposes, such as residential, commercial, industrial and

agricultural. These zones may be further divided, such as a residential zone may be zoned either single or multifamily, and an industrial zone may be zoned either light or heavy industrial.

The use of the business property you purchase is regulated by the zoning of the area where the property is located. It is important to determine exactly how the property is zoned as this affects how the property can be used now and in the future. Zoning can be changed or a variance or conditional use permit applied for, but only after a costly and time-consuming process. Zoning changes often involve public hearings.

CAUTION: Fully understand the risks of purchasing real estate for a business that is not currently zoned for that type of business. There is no guarantee the zoning can be changed or a variance granted.

In addition to zoning, what other municipal restrictions apply to building or renovating my business property?
Municipalities restrict the building on and renovation of property through building codes. The codes regulate how a building is constructed, what size it can be and where it may be placed on the property. Building codes are enacted to protect the public health and safety. To ensure compliance with building codes, many municipalities require that property owners get building permits before they begin any type of construction or development. Another way communities enforce codes is by issuing a certificate of occupancy (without which a building cannot legally be occupied) to buildings that pass code requirements.

CAUTION: If you plan to renovate the property you purchase, consult the building codes in your city or town to determine if the improvements you want to make are allowed and what the permit requirements and costs will be.

What do I need to know about restrictive covenants in a business park or association?
Similar to residential homeowners associations, business associations are legal entities created to maintain common areas, enforce covenant restrictions and provide services, such as security. Business associations are often set up in business parks or large office buildings with

many, varied tenants. They provide the members with a voice in how the property is improved and used.

A business association will set up a series of restrictions to protect the investment of the owners by ensuring that only appropriate and attractive facilities are located in the development. The restrictions may cover the building's exterior materials and signage, landscaping, compatibility with current businesses, availability of parking and the establishment of loading zones. These restrictions will be made part of the deeds of all of the properties in the business development, known as restrictive covenants.

The benefit of such covenants is that the maintenance of common areas and the provision of services, such as security, enhance property values. In addition, enforcement of the restrictions provides a uniform, aesthetic look and well-maintained property. The drawback is that a new owner may not be able to do all that she wants to with the property.

> **TIP:** If you are interested in purchasing business property in a business park, request all documentation regarding any deed restrictions affiliated with the business park or association. Carefully consider the restrictions contained in the documents and how they will impact your business before you buy the property.

SELLING YOUR SMALL BUSINESS PROPERTY

When you own the property where you conduct your business, there are many issues to consider before selling the property. If you are selling your business in addition to the real property, this sale likely will represent the culmination of years of hard work.

DECIDING TO SELL YOUR SMALL BUSINESS PROPERTY

How do I know if I am ready to sell my business property? Consider the reasons why you might want to sell:

- You want to sell to buy larger/better property or facilities.
- You are retiring.
- You want out of the business.
- You and your partner are dissolving the business.
- You have been offered a position with another company.

Any one of these reasons may impacts whether you decide to sell. It may be that you can hold onto this property as an investment. It may be that you need the funds you can take out of this property to buy larger or better real estate. You may want to or have to sell quickly. Understand your motivation for making a sale before you put the property on the market. The price you accept may be higher or lower depending on that motivation.

What factors determine if selling now makes economic sense? Consider the climate you want to sell in:

- Is there significant office space available for rent in your area?
  - If so, you would be selling in a down market and may not get the best price.
- Is your property in good condition?
  - If not, you may need to complete repairs before you can sell.
- Is your property suited to a specific need?
  - This may be a selling point. For example, the only veterinarian office in a high-traffic area is likely more desirable than one close to another vet office.
- Would it take a lot for a buyer to reconfigure your property?
  - This may be a determent to a sale if it is costly to renovate. You may consider paying for a portion or all of the renovations to make a sale.

Consider your finances:

- Must you sell?

- Can you afford to move to another property?
- Are you selling to get funds?
- If you bought another property, do you have funds to renovate or repair it?
- Can you use this property as an investment and hold on to it?

Consider the type of buyer who may want your business property:

- Can only a certain type of buyer purchase the property, thereby limiting the pool of potential buyers (e.g., is another veterinarian your only market)?
- Your company is being bought out and you have agreed to sell as soon as possible to any buyer who will take the property; you may have to take a loss on the property.
- Will the buyer be the type of business person who will want to negotiate and dicker about the details, making the sale time-consuming? If time is of the essence for you, be wary of this type of buyer.
- Will the buyer want a quick sale and pressure you to accept unreasonable terms?

These factors will all play a part in your determination of whether selling your business property makes economic sense for you. Before you put your business on the market, consider these factors and any others unique to your business.

What options are there to selling my business property? There are several options to consider before you commit to selling your property:

- ▸ **HOLD IT AS AN INVESTMENT.** Often, holding the property for a period of time may result in a higher return on the investment in your property. If possible, consider this option if the market looks strong and a market value increase is likely.

- ▸ **LEASE IT TO ANOTHER BUSINESS.** You can lease the property to another business. However, this gives you the added responsibilities of a landlord. This may be mitigated by hiring a management firm that provides certain management services, such as contracting to make repairs, collecting lease payments, and handling all contact with the lessee.

- ▸ **EXCHANGE OR TRADE IT.** You may enter into an exchange, trading your property for property with a similar market value. The transfer of the property to satisfy a debt can occur. These transactions can be complex and require the assistance of an attorney. Some exchanges are virtually tax-free.

- ▸ **EQUITY LOAN.** If your reason for selling the property is a need for funds, you might consider getting a business equity loan, a real estate investment partner, or finding another funding source. There are many sources of small business loans on the Internet.

CHOOSING A BUSINESS BROKER

Selling commercial real estate has many aspects similar to selling your home. However, there are special considerations to selling business property.

What is a business broker? *There are numerous business brokers who can assist the sale of your business property. A business broker is an agent for the owner who wants to sell a business.* Some real estate agents also broker businesses. Most business brokers are small local businesses representing particular industry businesses and small businesses.

How do I locate a business broker and what should I negotiate with him? *Finding a business broker. You can find a broker by asking business associates or looking in the Yellow Pages or on the Internet.* For example, see **www.globalbx.com**, which lists itself as a free business-for-sale listing exchange that provides a confidential forum to facilitate the buying and selling of businesses and helps find business brokers.

BROKER COMPENSATION. Take the time to understand all aspects of the compensation agreement, particularly the term for the broker's services, how the compensation is calculated and on what basis the compensation is determined. For example, if your business property does not sell in 6 months, can you get out of the compensation agreement? If the property is sold by a third-party broker, what compensation do you owe your broker?

MARKETING YOUR PROPERTY. Discuss with the business broker exactly how the broker will market your property. Will it be listed only in the local newspaper? Will it be placed in professional journals? Does the broker represent buyers also? Will print brochures or other advertisements be used?

OBSTACLES TO SELLING YOUR BUSINESS PROPERTY

What do restrictive covenants mean to the sale of my business property? *If you are attempting to sell your business property, these same restrictive covenants that may have favored your business may be a hindrance to the sale of that property.* For example, a buyer who would like to install a specific and widely recognized sign to attract business may not be able to do so because the covenants restrict certain signage. A buyer who would like to open a food store or pet store in the building may not be able to do so because of the restrictions.

If the restrictions are problematic to the sale of your business property, you may have to lower the sales price to offset the concern of the buyer and compensate him for not being able to use the property in the way they want.

CAUTION: Membership in a business association and the covenant restrictions must be disclosed to the buyer before a sale.

10 SMALL BUSINESS

People follow many paths to the point where they start their own business. For some, it is the American dream, a desire they hold all their lives. Others realize that they do not like working for other people—they just want to be their own boss.

Still others see themselves as pushed into going into business for themselves, perhaps because they have lost a corporate job they had always believed was secure. Some business owners start because they want a particular lifestyle, as might a mother who wants to work from home to be near her children. And then there are those who have the vision and drive to create a unique new product or service.

Whatever the reason for starting a business, many experts say that small businesses—which make up 99.7 percent of all employers in the United States—are a prime fuel of the American economy. And each of these business owners confronts a maze of decisions as they establish and move forward with their enterprises.

While there are virtually infinite ways to manage a business and an array of support services available, laws and regulations put boundaries on the choices that a business owner will make. If the business owner has a basic knowledge of the options, he or she can make smarter choices and avoid time-consuming and expensive problems.

One of the earliest decisions a potential business owner makes is how exactly to begin. Selecting a business that fits the owner's personality, knowledge and resources is a step that usually takes both research and thought. Many people just assume that they will start a business from scratch. But others do not want to do so, and they decide to buy an existing business or a franchise.

BUYING AN EXISTING BUSINESS

Why would you want to buy an existing business rather than start your own? For some, an ongoing cash flow is an attractive reason to buy. Another reason is a chance to grow an existing business more quickly.

Many people who buy businesses say that it is easier than a startup, although they may spend months scouting and researching a potential purchase. One thing is clear—researching the industry, the market and ultimately the company is key to future success.

JUST A FEW QUICK FACTS

You and your fellow small-business owners play a huge role in keeping the U.S. economy strong. The government says that small businesses:

- employ half of all private sector employees;
- pay 44.3 percent of total U.S. private payroll;
- have generated 60 to 80 percent of net new jobs annually over the last decade; and
- are 53 percent home-based and 3 percent franchises.

DUE DILIGENCE

Once you get to the point of seriously considering the purchase of an ongoing business and have signed a letter of intent with the current owner, you need to thoroughly investigate all aspects of the business so there are no surprises once the transaction is complete.

What does "due diligence" actually mean? *Due diligence is the process of investigating a business to make sure that you have up-to-date, accurate and complete information that will later affect your operation of the business.* This means verifying the seller's statements and the business's documents and records.

What is a letter of intent? *A letter of intent is signed by both the buyer and seller after most of the terms of the purchase are generally agreed upon.* It shows that each is serious about completing the transaction and opens the way for the buyer to look more closely at the business records of the seller.

What if I am not familiar with all the regulations or if I do not feel very comfortable with all the bookkeeping and financial statements? Even if you are on a tight budget, the time to bring in your lawyer and accountant is before you have written a check to the seller.

What should I look for when completing due diligence? Here are some items you want to be sure to investigate when you are buying a business.

PAPERWORK: A good part of your due diligence time will be spent reviewing the company's documents. This includes reviewing all financial records, such as income statements, balance sheets, cash flow statements, payroll, tax audits and a list of all physical assets owned by the company.

Other records, reports and contracts to study would include lease and loan agreements, any lawsuits past or present and insurance policies. Records of dealings with customers can give you valuable information, as will a thorough look at the company's marketing materials—catalogs, brochures, Web site and sales letters, for example.

COMPLIANCE: If you were starting a company from scratch, you would need to research the registrations, licenses and permits required for the business. Ensuring compliance with local and national laws and regulations is just as important if you are buying a business.

OPERATIONS: You might want to roll up your sleeves and spend some time on the factory floor if you are considering a manufacturing facility. This is the time to talk with employees to get a better feel for the business.

You can check the company's facilities with an eye toward safety and efficiency. Look at physical inventory and compare with corporate reports. Some potential buyers have been known to actually work at a company for several weeks before finalizing the deal.

SALES—CURRENT AND POTENTIAL: You have most likely studied and researched a potential purchase's market and industry before you sign a letter of intent. Now that you have the opportunity to dig deeper, you can talk with suppliers and customers. You may be able to get a better sense of the competition.

I am selling my business. What due diligence should I complete? *As the buyer is studying the prospective acquisition, you should be studying the buyer.* Of course you want to know if he or she can make the one or more payments called for in the contract. Even if the buyer is paying cash and you are retiring, you have an interest in maintaining a positive reputation for the business within the community.

BUYING A FRANCHISE

For many people, buying a franchise is just the right blend of entrepreneurship and predictability. They have the opportunity to run their own operation, yet have the guidance and knowledge of an ongoing business organization.

Nearly one-third of the United States' retail trade is conducted through franchising. Industries from fast food restaurants to health clubs to carpet cleaning are involved in franchising. If you are considering purchasing a franchise, talk with an attorney who specializes in the field. The franchise agreement is drafted in favor of the franchisor. It is not uncommon for a franchisee to find himself or herself with little or no recourse if the franchise does not work out.

How do I distinguish between an actual franchise and a simple business opportunity? A franchise requires:

- the use of the seller's trade name or trademark;
- payment for the use of that trade name or trademark; and
- an agreement giving the seller certain controls (for example, you must use packaging they provide rather than less expensive packaging that you find on your own).

Why should I consider getting into business with a franchise? *For one thing, you may already have had a personal experience with the franchise.* If you buy a hamburger at McDonald's® or a muffler from Meineke, you may be patronizing a franchise. In other words, a franchise can be more of a known quantity than a startup or an ongoing, but nonfranchised, business.

What should I expect from the franchisor? You should get a complete business package from the franchisor—a product, a business plan, advertising and marketing support, processes and site selection.

What are the advantages? Strong franchises have a high success rate, and it is in the franchisor's interest for you to succeed at the business.

> **TIP:** According to the U.S. Small Business Administration, approximately 35 percent of new business startups fail in their first year. However, after 5 years, approximately 90 percent of all franchises are still in business.

Besides the advantages that come with the complete business package, financing may be easier. The franchisor may provide financing. Or if you go to a bank or other lender, they may be more willing to provide financing, since they are familiar with the franchisor.

What if I do not have much experience in the business? *That is one of the best advantages of franchising.* You will most likely have a chance for a thorough training program.

How do I know I am signing up with a reputable franchise? You should be cautious if the company is using high-pressure sales tactics, promises huge and immediate returns on your investment and does not have a structure in place for assistance and training.

> **TIP:** Avoid franchise "seminars" where you are encouraged to "sign up before the opportunity is lost" at a so-called special price. These opportunities typically require the buyer to sign up very quickly before the "discounted" price of the opportunity expires. A reputable franchise will not rush the buyer.

Where can I get information about buying a franchise? The SBA's Web site, www.sba.gov/starting_business/startup/franchise.html, provides answers to many basic questions concerning a franchise purchase.

How are franchisors regulated? *The Federal Trade Commission oversees franchising at the national level. When you first begin talking with a prospective franchisor, you should be provided with offering documents that*

outline information about the franchise. These have now been standardized into the Uniform Franchise Offering Circular (UFOC).

What is included in the Uniform Franchise Offering Circular? The UFOC includes a company history, financial statements, fees that will be required, description of quality controls and information about ending or renewing the contract.

So are all franchise contracts the same? *Each franchise agreement will be different. As mentioned, you will be expected to pay an initial franchise fee and a royalty fee and most likely make a contribution to a pooled advertising-marketing program.* You may be required to buy your supplies from the franchisor. And you will need to follow many operating requirements set down by the franchisor.

What kind of fees can I expect? *There are several types of fees that your franchisor will expect.* The first one due is called the franchise fee, which essentially buys your license or right to the products and bundle of services that you are buying.

On an ongoing basis, you will likely be expected to pay two other fees. The first, usually figured as a percent of sales, is a royalty fee. Second, you will be asked to contribute to a cooperative advertising and marketing program. The franchisor will probably make the decisions regarding the publicity program, and your business will have access to major media that a stand-alone small business could never hope to have.

Do I need a franchise attorney? *All franchises must comply with complicated state and federal regulations.* An attorney that specializes in franchise law will protect your interests and make sure you do not violate any laws.

DUE DILIGENCE

Just as you would thoroughly investigate an independent business before you make the purchase, you will want to check out the franchisor. Look for overall reputation, financial strength and desirable products and services. Find out what the rate of growth is overall and whether they are growing at a rate that is reasonable.

Be sure to check with other franchisees for their views on the business. You can request a list of references from the franchisor.

What are some disadvantages of buying a franchise? *For starters, franchises are not cheap. You will spend a lot of money for the initial purchase of the business. In addition to the initial outlay of money, you will be paying the franchisor on an ongoing basis for royalties, advertising costs and more. You will not have much wiggle room with the franchise agreement.* If you are an entrepreneur who likes to do things your way, you may find answering to the franchisor's demands too restrictive. You may also find it difficult to sell your franchise if things do not work out. In some cases, the franchisor has the right to approve or disapprove of a potential buyer.

SELECTING A LEGAL STRUCTURE FOR YOUR BUSINESS

One of your first decisions in setting up a business is the legal structure. The options range from a sole proprietorship, which is usually operated by a single person, to a full-fledged corporation that is flexible enough to employ hundreds of thousands of people and generate billions of dollars in revenue.

Each of these types of business entity differs as to where liability resides, the type and rate of taxation and the amount of formal reporting to state and federal governments, among other things.

Your choice will depend on the kind of business you are or will be starting and your vision for the business's future. If, for example, you are a freelance graphic designer who works alone from home with no plans to expand, the simplicity of a sole proprietorship might be just what you are looking for. As a business becomes more complex—with many employees, a more specialized management team, perhaps with facilities such as a manufacturing plant or warehouse—a more formal corporate structure would be necessary.

This section discusses the major types of business structure:

- sole proprietorship
- partnership
- C corporation
- S corporation
- limited liability company (LLC)

> **TIP:** The U.S. Small Business Administration has a wizard to help you in "Choosing a Business Structure." A series of short questions will help narrow your options. See **http://app1.sba.gov/exsysweb/client/bizform/bizformmenu.html**.

SOLE PROPRIETORSHIP

The simplest and most common form of business entity is the sole proprietorship. It is the easiest to set up, as there are no outside owners or investors. Unlike a corporate structure, there is no requirement for corporate officers or a board of directors, and there is less paperwork.

The business is run by an individual, although it may use a trade name. A sole proprietor can hire employees. In fact, one of the employees could be the proprietor's husband or wife.

There are no outside owners or investors. There is no potential to expand through bringing in additional owners or their capital.

A drawback to a sole proprietorship is that the owner is personally liable for every activity and all debt incurred by the business.

Another possible concern is that if the owner is ill, disabled or dies, the business is not structured for a backup manager to keep the business running. A sole proprietorship ends when the owner dies, so there may be complications with estate planning.

Tax Aspects of a Sole Proprietorship

A sole proprietorship structure avoids the potential for double taxation that may occur with a corporation.

Taxes are paid on an individual's 1040, Schedule C (Profit or Loss from a Business, Sole Proprietorship) and Schedule F if farming is involved. As a sole proprietor, the IRS does not consider you an employee, and you must pay the full amount of Social Security and Medicare taxes, currently 15.3 percent, which is calculated on Schedule SE.

An important difference between a corporation and a nonincorporated business is the tax treatment of medical expenses for the owner and his or her family. A sole proprietor can deduct 40 percent of health insurance premiums on Form 1040. The remaining 60 percent of the premiums and other uncovered medical expenses are deductible only if they are more than 7.5 percent of adjusted gross income. A corporation can pay for all insurance premiums and uncovered medical expenses and deduct the costs as a business deduction.

What can I do about retirement plans? *A nonincorporated business can take advantage of several tax-sheltered retirement programs.*

A Keogh plan permits a sole proprietor to put aside 25 percent of after-tax income, up to $30,000 per year. Under a Keogh plan, employees must be covered at the same percentage rate, and the employer makes the contribution. Deferred vesting is allowed, so employees can be required to work up to 3 years before they are covered.

What other retirement possibilities are there for a non-incorporated business? A*nother option is a Savings Incentive Match Plan for Employees (SIMPLE plan).* As an individual, the sole proprietor can also participate in a traditional Individual Retirement Account or a Roth IRA.

PARTNERSHIPS

When two or more people agree to maintain a business for profit, it is considered to be a partnership. A partner may contribute money, expertise, time or energy to help the business grow and expects to receive a share of the profits in return. The potential for business success may be increased if each partner brings a unique set of capabilities that are complementary.

A partnership is similar to a sole proprietorship, but it allows more than one person to share in the ownership of the business. There is no legal separation between the business and the owners, and as with a sole proprietorship, there is less paperwork than there would be with a corporation.

Since a partnership does not file papers with the state as with a corporation, does that mean there is no paperwork? *You still need to get all required permits and licenses from the federal, state and local governments.* You might need to register the business's name with your state. (It may be called an Assumed Name Certificate.) If you are hiring employees, you will need an employer identification number (EIN) from the Internal Revenue Service, and you may need to register as an employer with your state.

Do we really need a partnership agreement? *Although a partnership is simple to form, many business advisors believe it is one of the most difficult to keep going.* There is no legal requirement, but experts recommend that a formal partnership agreement or contract be completed. The contract should define the duties and responsibilities of each partner, how much time each partner will devote to the business and how profits will be divided. The amount and kind of capital contributed by each participant should be recorded.

A partnership agreement should also deal with how the partnership may be split up—the process for one partner being bought out by the remaining partner or partners or division of assets if the business is later dissolved for any reason. An enterprise should not be started unless everyone is optimistic that it will succeed, but it is to each partner's advantage to anticipate a change in ownership or time devoted to the business.

What else should be in a partnership agreement? *You might want to include how to handle profit-sharing; it would be assumed to be an equal split unless otherwise specified.* You can also agree to the process for removing or adding a partner so that the partnership does not get dissolved. A method for appraising the assets of the partnership should be specified in the agreement.

Why should I consider the partnership form of business? *One of the primary reasons people choose to start their business as a partnership is that there is no initial governmental paperwork, so it is simple and straightforward.* (Remember, however, partners need to have a clear understanding of what each will contribute to the business, and that understanding should be in the form of a written agreement.)

As partners need to raise capital for their business, they may be able to present a stronger case for loans or simply have a wider network to draw on for funding resources. Also, in order to attract high-quality employees, the firm can offer the opportunity to become a partner.

What are the problems with a partnership form? The partnership form shares some of the drawbacks of the sole proprietorship as well as some additional shortcomings.

Liability is a significant issue. Each partner is liable for the actions of the other. For example, business debts incurred by one person become the responsibility of all partners. Decisions such as how to share profits, as well as differences on how to manage the business, can trigger disagreements.

A partnership does not have a perpetual life. It can end when a partner leaves, either voluntarily or through death or disability.

How do taxes work for a partnership? *Generally, tax treatment for a partnership is similar to a sole proprietorship.* Profits from the business are taxed at the partners' personal tax rates, rather than the typically higher corporate tax rate.

Benefits such as health insurance cannot be deducted by the partnership, and they become part of the personal tax schedule of the partner.

What are the different types of partnerships? Besides the general partnership that has just been described, there are two other types of partnerships.

▸ **LIMITED PARTNERSHIP.** Like a general partnership, a limited partnership is made up of two or more people who agree to own and operate a business. The difference is that one or more of the partners does not manage the business and has limited liability. There must also be at least one general partner.

In addition to meeting the requirements of a general partnership, a written agreement is required and the words "Limited Partnership" must be included in the name. Your state will most likely require that you file a Certificate of Limited Partnership and keep certain records.

The partnership files an information return annually, but income or loss flows directly to the partners. Partners report their share of the profit or loss on their individual income tax returns.

▸ **JOINT VENTURE.** A third type of partnership, the joint venture, is set up for a special purpose and has a limited time frame. A corporation can be the "person" in the partnership, and joint ventures can be combinations of large corporations as well as small businesses.

C CORPORATION

A C corporation is a form of business that is completely separate from the owners and managers. It has a "life of its own." A major advantage to a corporation is that, in most instances, individual owners (shareholders), directors and employees do not assume personal liability for its actions.

Some important features of a corporation include the following:

- A corporation is state-chartered based on where its headquarters are located.
- A corporation has a perpetual life and ceases to exist only when it is formally dissolved.
- The corporation is owned by the shareholders, who elect the board of directors.
- The board directs corporate strategies and policies. The board also elects the corporate officers (president, vice president, secretary and treasurer).

What does a "controlling interest" mean?
The percent of stock owned by a shareholder governs the amount of voting power he or she has. The vote of a shareholder who owns more than half the stock (51 percent) will be able to control the outcome of any ballot, so that shareholder is considered to have a controlling interest.

How many shareholders are needed to form a corporation? Only one shareholder is required, and one person can comprise the board of directors and all corporate officers.

Forming a C Corporation

Forming a C corporation calls for meeting requirements set forth by your state. An Internet search under "[your state name] Secretary of State" should lead you to the forms you will need.

Steps that you will take to incorporate include:

1. File the forms for your state's articles of incorporation and pay the incorporation fee.
2. Establish corporate bylaws and maintain a minute book to record board of directors' meetings and the corporation's annual meeting.
3. Distribute stock certificates to shareholders.

Once you have incorporated, you will be required to hold an annual shareholder meeting, file an annual report with your secretary of state and pay any required annual fees.

What information will I need to file articles of incorporation? The forms will ask you to list the business's official corporate name and the purpose of the business, the name and address of the registered agent and details of share ownership.

How do I decide on a corporate name? *This is an important decision. To avoid potential legal problems, you must avoid choosing a name that duplicates or can be considered too close to a name used by an existing business.* Your state will make sure that you do not duplicate a name that is registered with the state, but you may want to do a national search for an identical or nearly identical name, especially if you intend to do business outside of your state.

You will also want to make sure that the business name includes the words "corporation," "company," "incorporated," "limited" or an abbreviation of those words.

What is a "registered agent"? A registered agent is a person or entity who will receive tax and legal documents for the corporation. This can be a manager or shareholder of

the company, or there are services that will handle the function for a fee. The registered agent must have a legal address within the state or jurisdiction that the registration covers. The corporation may be invalidated if the registered agent is not maintained.

What about raising capital for a corporation?

Like a proprietorship or partnership, a corporation can borrow money from a bank or other lender. But it can also raise funds by selling stock to shareholders. This money becomes a permanent part of the company's resources and does not have to be repaid as a loan does.

Ongoing Legal Requirements for a Corporation

One of the continuing duties of a corporation is to maintain business and accounting records. It will need to keep the following at its home office:

- articles of incorporation and bylaws and any amendments that are up-to-date;
- any resolutions adopted by the board;
- copies of written messages to shareholders, including financial statements that are required for shareholders;
- names and addresses of directors and officers; and
- the annual report most recently filed with the secretary of state.

Tax Aspects of a C Corporation

One of the drawbacks to the owners of a C corporation is the potential for income to be taxed twice—first as a corporation and second as a shareholder.

This can happen because the C corporation files its own tax returns as a stand-alone entity and pays any taxes that are due. The corporation then pays after-tax profits to shareholders in the form of dividends, and the shareholders will most likely have to pay personal income tax on the dividend money.

Is there any way to avoid double taxation?

If the shareholder is also an employee, the company can pay the shareholder-employee a salary, as long as it is considered a reasonable amount. The corporation can deduct the salary as a business expense so that it is taxed only once (as income by the employee).

Another option is to elect Subchapter S status if the business qualifies.

Shareholder Liability

As a shareholder, you are not liable for the debts and liabilities of a corporation. Generally, you are not risking your personal assets. You may, however, lose the amount of your investment if the corporation is not profitable or ceases to stay in business.

You may also be at risk if you personally guarantee a debt of the business. Also, if the corporation does not follow legal requirements or if corporate and personal funds are commingled, you might be liable.

Can directors be held liable for issues that relate to their service to the corporation?

Yes, directors, as well as corporate officers or employees, can be considered liable. This can be a problem in attracting directors or employees with the needed expertise. Companies can purchase insurance that will provide compensation for losses sustained due to actions of the directors and employees while they are performing their responsibilities to the corporation.

In addition, depending on the nature of the business, the corporation's leaders must be sure that insurance is sufficient to protect the corporation from losses due to property damage or personal injury.

What if I want to close my corporation? *You need to gain shareholder approval and file a notice with the secretary of state.* After taxes and other debts are paid, any remaining assets are distributed to shareholders.

SUBCHAPTER S CORPORATION

An S corporation has the same formal organization as a C corporation, but the income flows directly to the owners, who are taxed at their personal rate. Thus, the owners avoid the potential double taxation of a C corporation, yet they retain the advantage of limited liability.

Incorporating an S corporation includes the same procedures and filings as a C corporation. The owners must elect Subchapter S status with the IRS by filing Form 2553, Election by a Small Business Corporation, and they must meet certain criteria.

All of these criteria must be met in order to qualify as an S corporation:

▶ **DOMESTIC CORPORATION:** organized under the laws of the United States, a state or a territory;

▶ **SHAREHOLDERS:** cannot be a nonresident alien; cannot be a partnership or a corporation and must meet additional similar measures;

▶ **NUMBER OF SHAREHOLDERS:** cannot be more than 75;

▶ **STOCK:** can only be one class of common stock with no preferred stock; and

▶ **CERTAIN TYPES OF CORPORATIONS:** are not allowed, such as an insurance company or a domestic international sales corporation.

Can I convert a C corporation to an S corporation? Yes, if certain of rules are followed:

- All shareholders must agree to the election.
- No more than 25 percent of the company's gross receipts during the 3 prior years may be considered passive income (such as rent from a real estate investment).

Can I convert to a Subchapter S corporation whenever I choose? *Timing is important in becoming a Subchapter S corporation.* If you want to convert from a C to an S corporation immediately after starting the business, you must file with the IRS within the first 2_ months of the company's first taxable year. If you do not meet the deadline, your business will be taxed as a C corporation.

If your business has been ongoing for some time as a C corporation, you can still elect Subchapter S status if you file with the IRS during the 12 months before the tax year that you want the company's status to change.

Tax Aspects of an S Corporation

Since an S corporation is treated like a partnership for tax purposes, each shareholder's portion of the profit or loss is included on his or her federal and state tax returns. This means that profits from the S corporation are only taxed once at the individual's personal tax rate. Shareholders are personally responsible for any related taxes and for estimated income taxes.

So profit and loss are allocated among shareholders just the way it is done for a partnership? *For an S corporation, profits and losses are allotted in the same proportion as the stock ownership.* If someone owns 10 percent of the stock, their share of the profit or loss is 10 percent. This might differ from the allocation of a partnership, as a partnership agreement can specify a distribution of the profit or loss that might be different that the proportion of stock ownership.

Shareholder Liability

Other than its distinctive tax treatment, an S corporation has the same features as a C corporation. That is, beyond his or her investment in the business, a shareholder is not personally at risk for debts or other liabilities of the business.

Can I convert an S corporation back to a C corporation? Yes, if the conditions for an S corporation are no longer being met.

Can an S corporation have ownership of a C corporation? *An S corporation can own 80 percent or more of a C corporation.* It can also hold subsidiaries if it meets certain qualifications.

LIMITED LIABILITY COMPANY

The Limited Liability Company is another hybrid form of organization, blending features of a corporation and a partnership. It has the limited liability advantage of a corporation and the tax advantage of a partnership. Although LLCs are a fairly recent form of business, they are now recognized by all states and the District of Columbia.

Owners of the LLC are called "members." If there is no written operating agreement, each member is considered to be a "manager." An operating agreement can identify specific members to be managers.

Forming a Limited Liability Company

As with a corporation, there are a series of steps to form an LLC:

1. Apply to your Secretary of State for your company name. The name identifies the form of business by using the words "Limited Liability Company" or "LLC."
2. Plan and agree to an operating agreement.
3. File articles of incorporation with your secretary of state, including the required filing fees.
4. As with other incorporations, you will need a designated registered agent and office to be filed with your secretary of state.
5. Be sure to obtain licenses and permits at the local, state and federal level and pay the necessary fees.

What other forms do I need to operate an LLC? Each year, you will need to file an annual report with your secretary of state.

Tax Aspects of a Limited Liability Corporation

If an LLC is structured properly, it is taxed in the same way as a partnership or S corporation. That is, each member/owner is allocated a share of the profit or loss, which is included on his or her state and federal tax returns. For tax purposes, LLC members are generally considered to be self-employed. That means they are responsible for their own estimated income taxes and related taxes.

It is important to make sure that an LLC is structured properly, or it can be taxed like a C corporation.

Liability for LLC Members

Beyond a member's investment in the business, he or she is not personally at risk for debts or other liabilities of the business. A member's personal assets are not considered to be liable for the actions of the business, unless the member guarantees a debt of the business or acts in a way that opens opportunity for liability.

Dissolving or Closing an LLC

The LLC is considered to be perpetual unless certain events take place. The LLC would be dissolved if a time is specified or a triggering event takes place as specified in the articles of organization. Other events that would trigger dissolution are:

- A member withdraws from the organization, and remaining members do not agree to continue the business. (This possibility can be anticipated and become part of the operating agreement.)
- All members agree and give their written consent to dissolve.
- A court order requires dissolution.

SMALL BUSINESS: FORMS OF BUSINESS CHART

Form of business	Legal filings	Taxation	Structure	Advantages	Disadvantages
Sole proprietorship	Required licenses and registrations	Personal rates, filed using Schedule C on Form 1040	Business ceases when proprietor leaves the business	Easy to set up	Does not protect against personal liability
Partnership	Assumed name filing, required licenses and registrations	Profit shared by partners at personal tax rates	Dissolves when a partner leaves	Fairly easy to set up; partnership agreement recommended	• Does not protect against personal liability • Only partial deduction for health expenses
C corporation	• Annual reports • Board of directors meetings	• Separate tax return, taxed as separate entity • Corporate tax rates • Dividends taxed to shareholders	• Perpetual existence • More than one class of ownership are possible (e.g., common and preferred	Can protect against personal liability of individual shareholders regarding claims against the business	• Corporate tax rate is higher than individual • Double taxation of dividends • Additional administrative costs
S corporation	Similar to C corporation	• Taxed at individual rate, Form 1040, Schedule C, E, and SE • Form 1120S, Income Tax Return for S Corporation and Form 1120S K-1 • Must close books at end of year	Similar to a C corporation except must meet certain requirements to be treated as an S corporation	• Eliminates double taxation of dividends	• Cannot deduct benefits such as health insurance for shareholders owning 2% or more of the company • Cannot own subsidiaries • Cannot retain earnings • Typically fiscal year must be a calendar • No more than 35 shareholders
LLCs	• Exempt from corporate filings in most states • Operating agreement required	• Taxed at individual rate, Form 1040, Schedule C (need approval of IRS) • Usually more accounting flexibility than C or S corporations	Somewhat of a hybrid between an S corporation and a C corporation	• Taxed at personal rate • Limited liability as a corporation	

NAMING YOUR BUSINESS AND PRODUCTS

One of the first and most important decisions you will make is the naming of your business. You may also identify specific names for products that you offer, either when you start the business or as they are developed along the way.

The name you choose must meet legal requirements, and it is also linked with the success of the business. The basic principle is that the name be distinct and does not infringe on a name chosen by another business, especially a competitor. Besides meeting federal, state and local regulations, a unique name that enhances your marketing initiatives will give you an advantage in generating sales.

Brainstorming and creativity—along with solid research—will give you the name you need to protect your business's identity and avoid a potentially expensive conflict with another business.

DIFFERENT TYPES OF BUSINESS NAMES

The law distinguishes among different types of names that are used by businesses, and it is important to understand these differences:

1. Legal Name

When a business registers with the state, part of the process is to declare its legal name. This name will be used on all official filings and registrations.

Other terms for a business's legal name might be "corporate name" or "registered name." Depending on the form of business, states will require certain attributes and restrictions to the legal name.

2. Assumed Name

Have you ever seen the letters "dba" and wondered what they meant? The answer is "doing business as," which shows that the business name being used is not the official, legal name of the business. Other terms for a "dba," or assumed name, are "fictitious business name" or "trade name."

EXAMPLE: The legal name of a business might simply use the name of the owner, "Robert Smith Corporation." But Robert Smith might want to use a more descriptive business name for advertising and marketing reasons. He might select an assumed name, something like "Taco Treats" or "Tortilla to Go," to get instant customer recognition.

The business owner will need to register his or her assumed name with the state and possibly with the county. Just as states require the use of "Inc." or "Company" in an official corporate name, they usually do not allow those official designators in an assumed name.

3. Trade Name

A trademark, or service mark, registered with the United States Patent and Trademark Office can protect the name of the business or its product from use by others. There is no legal obligation to register the mark with the USPTO, but doing so has potential to avoid expensive and distracting efforts to protect valuable intellectual assets in the future.

How can I go about selecting just the right name for my business? *Picking your business name balances legal requirements with creativity and marketing.* The first name you pick may have already been spoken for by another business. If you begin by brainstorming many different ideas, you have the best chance of identifying the perfect name.

One way to begin is by writing down all words that have something to do with your product. If you are starting a candy store, perhaps your list will include words like "sugar, sweet, honey." You might have words like "happy" or "pleasant" or "smile"—the ways that your candy will make the customers feel.

What should I consider in picking a name for my business? *The name of your business might help people understand what your product or service is—something like "Candy Cottage."* Ideally it will be easy to remember, easy to spell and encourage customers to try what you have to offer.

Many corporations pay big dollars for consultants to come up with made-up names. The oil company, Exxon, is an example of that. Microsoft is a combination of two computer-related terms. You can try ideas like that when you are developing your ideas.

Some advisors suggest not using a person's name or a location, but many successful companies use the founder's name or the name of a city or region.

What do I need to do in choosing a legal name for my business? *When the new business is first registered with the state, it is automatically registered under its legal, or "registered," name.* At least part of the legal name will be regulated by the state and will depend on the form of business.

Do I need to choose a legal name for my business if it is set up as a sole proprietorship or partnership? *Since a sole proprietorship is legally an extension of the owner, it is presumed to operate under the owner's name.* If you want to operate the business using another name, file for an assumed name with the state and/or the county.

For a partnership, the business name will be made up of the last names of the partners. If the partners decide to use an assumed name for the business, they can do so by including the name in a written partnership agreement and making the proper assumed name filings.

What are the requirements for a legal name for a corporation or subchapter S corporation? *Most states require that the name of the business include an indication of the corporate status. "Incorporated," "company" or "corporation"—or an abbreviation of one of these—are typical of those requirements.

Similar to a corporate name, states will require a business name that indicates the limited liability status. "Limited Liability Company" or "LLC" are common phrases.

RESEARCHING BUSINESS NAMES AND TRADEMARKS

The good news about researching a unique name for your business is that most of the search can be handled with a few clicks of your computer keyboard. The bad news is that there is no single spot to search; you will have to take several different paths to make sure your exploration is complete.

If you find a name that is so close to the one you have chosen that you sense you might need to defend your choice, start thinking of another one.

How do I research my business name? *Your state's corporate registrar, usually the secretary of state's office, is a good place to begin your search, since both legal names and assumed names will be registered with that office.* Most likely, there will be a database available that you can search via the Internet.

To look at the national level on an informal basis, you can use search engines such as Yahoo!® or Google to try variations of business names you are considering.

Along those lines, test Web site names (URLs) that you would like to consider for your business. The results will tell you whether the name you are considering has been taken by another business, and they will tell you whether you can secure a domain name that aligns well with your business or product's name. With the dominance of the Web in selling products and marketing, it only makes sense to make sure that the business name (1) is legally available, (2) will not infringe on other similar names and (3) can be used freely as the name for your Web site.

You can check domain name availability by using any of the many services who will sell the name to you along with hosting your Web site. A central source of information—including who owns domain names that have already been purchased—is **www.whois.net**.

How can I research trademarks? *You may decide to trademark the name of your business or products that you have developed.* Before moving ahead, you will need to make sure the trademark is not already in use. This includes checking for trademarks which are registered—usually with a

county or the USPTO—or unregistered, a mark which has not been formally registered but has validity due to continuous use.

Since states and many counties require trademark registration, you can search their databases to make sure your name, or one that is very similar, does not infringe on a name that has already been recorded.

> **TIP:** Be sure to take advantage of the search function at the USPTO Web site: **www.uspto.gov**. You can also check a database of trademarks registered in all 50 states at **www.trademark.com**.

A search engine or the Thomas Register (online or in the library) may help turn up trademarks which are not formally registered.

Can I trademark my Internet domain name?
Some domain names can be trademarked, and others cannot. If a name is distinctive—such as eBay® or Google—it will probably qualify for trademark protection. A Web name that is primarily the name of a generic service— "housekeeper.com," for instance—may not qualify.

It is possible to have a registered trademark and not be able to obtain a trademark for the domain name. For example, a business might have the name "housekeeper" in its trademarked name, along with many others, but it is possible that another business has already acquired the "housekeeper.com" domain name.

What if some business is offering to sell me the domain name I want, but it seems like the price is too high? *In some cases, you might benefit from a law called the ACPA.* The Anticybersquatting Consumer Protection Act prohibits cybersquatting—registering a domain name with the sole purpose of profiting by the good reputation of a trademark already owned by another business.

You can also go to ICANN, the Internet Corporation of Assigned Names and Numbers. This organization sponsors an international arbitration system to deal with trademark infringements by cybersquatters.

REGISTRATIONS, LICENSES AND PERMITS

One of the first items on your business startup agenda is to learn what regulations you will need to follow at the local, regional, state and national level. It could be a setback of major proportions to discover that you should have a special type of permit for your business and that the government can require you to stop doing business until you have corrected the problem.

EXAMPLE: If you are in the restaurant or other food-related business, you will need to comply with health-related requirements. This might mean dealing with your local health department for permits to store and handle food; the zoning commission will be interested in a preliminary site analysis. Further, you will also need to be aware of license and permit requirements for serving alcohol or to have a sidewalk café, and you will need to have a plan for litter removal.

Making sure that your business is complying with regulations and has the necessary licenses and permits is a challenge. As you begin learning the steps you will need to take for your particular business, it might be helpful to think of each of the governmental entities that may be regulating your business—at the federal, state and local level. (In some cases, regional authorities may also have requirements.)

This is confusing! Where should I start looking to make sure my business is complying with all the rules? *For starters, your business is likely part of a national trade organization. For instance, if you are in the retail business, the National Retail Federation has members from all kinds of retail businesses.* Their Web site provides links to state retail federations. A more specific trade group is Shop.org which is comprised of Internet-based merchants.

Where else can I look? Many public libraries have business resource sections that can be helpful. For instance, the New York Public Library has a section on its Web site that gives an overview of regulations in New York City and New York State and provides links to many resources that can help a you track down what is necessary for your specific business.

LOCAL REGULATIONS: CITY AND COUNTY

Although you may need to obtain permits and licenses that are unique to the kind of business you are in, there are several types of regulations that apply to many kinds of enterprises. Be sure to review these categories in light of your own organization.

Business License or Tax Registration Certificate

Many towns and cities require a business license or tax registration certificate for virtually all types of businesses. The purpose of these licenses is to give the local government a means of tracking business activity in its jurisdiction—information that can be used to develop economic data and track economic trends within its boundary. The fees, of course, support a safe, attractive shopping and working environment within the municipal area.

Does every business need a business license? *As an example, one large suburb near Chicago requires that all for-profit businesses that are not required to be licensed by a state or federal regulation must be licensed by the city.* An exception is home-based businesses, which are not required to have a license.

If I am a landscaper and I just go into another city to take care of lawns during the day, I will not need a license, will I? *Actually, you might. The same city mentioned above requires that certain businesses which are based outside the city obtain a license if they want to carry out business within its boundaries.* These are businesses like landscaping services or those that operate pickup and delivery within the town, such as garbage collection.

Zoning and Building Codes

No matter where your place of business is—from home-based to a sophisticated manufacturing facility—you will need to adhere to local zoning and building codes.

Starting with a simple form, most home-based businesses are regulated primarily with the idea of minimizing disruption in the neighborhood. That means, if your work generates activity from large numbers of people and vehicles, you may encounter restrictions that prevent you from pursuing your business from home. It is possible that you will be required to have a home business permit.

More complex and sophisticated businesses will require close attention to zoning and building ordinances. Zoning and building codes will most likely be enforced by different municipal offices.

What does zoning actually mean? *Zoning rules and regulations direct the use of land, so that is the first area to check when thinking about locating a business. Zoning ordinances break out sections of the city based on commercial, residential, industrial or agricultural uses.* Characteristics like building height, noise, parking and open space are regulated through zoning. Your town may require you to obtain a zoning permit before the business can open.

What if I find a great location for my business then find out that zoning rules will not allow me to locate there? Is there any other option besides looking for a new location? *Yes, you can apply for a "variance." A variance allows you to deviate from the zoning rules on the books in your municipality. If you think your business is suitable for the area where you want to locate, you should ask for a variance.* This usually entails presenting your case before the local zoning commission.

Typically, neighbors must be notified that you are seeking a variance, so they have a chance to state their concerns before the zoning board. This is an important part of the process, and you might want to informally communicate with the neighbors beforehand.

What about the actual building that I want to use for my business? *Building ordinances regulate the space that you will actually be using for your office and other facilities. Usually a separate municipal department enforces the building codes.* Beginning with a review of your construction plans, they will issue building permits, then conduct periodic inspections during the construction and provide a final sign-off that the space can be used for the purpose you intend.

You will find that building ordinances cover a wide spectrum—things like construction methods and materials, size and setback requirements, even the days and times when construction is allowed to take place. You may need to make sure that your business has access and facilities for the disabled.

Building codes are designed to maintain public health and safety, and they are updated frequently as new products and methods become available.

What does "grandfathering" mean? *When building codes are updated, they often apply only to new construction or changes in tenancy or ownership.* That means if you take on a space that someone else has been using, you may be required to make updates to meet the code. It could be a costly mistake to assume that you can continue what the prior owner or tenant has been doing without checking on local ordinances.

> **TIP:** The best ways to find out what local permits and licenses you will need:
>
> • Some larger towns have an organization that deals with helping business startups.
>
> • If you are in a smaller town, you might check with local trade associations or people who operate businesses similar to yours. The Chamber of Commerce could point you in the right direction.
>
> • You can check with the police and fire departments, the health department and your city or town's tax office. To make sure your place of business will meet local requirements, check with the planning and zoning department as well as the building inspector.

STATE REGULATIONS

Depending on the kind of business you are in, your state may require you to be licensed based on your occupation or on the products that you provide or handle. There are also taxes that many states impose—most commonly sales tax, which you may be responsible for collecting, and a business income tax.

Licenses for Some Occupations

States typically require people in certain professions to be licensed. These include many of the health care careers—doctors, dentists, nurses, pharmacists and psychologists. Other professions that are typically licensed by a state include lawyers, accountants, architects and engineers.

There are more. If you are a barber, auto mechanic, private investigator, cosmetologist, real estate agent or tax preparer, you may need to obtain a license from your state.

Do I have to pass a test to get a license? *It is possible that you will need to take and pass a state-sponsored test for a license. For example, this is generally true if you want to be licensed as a real estate or insurance agent.* You may also need to show that you have the appropriate education to be licensed.

Is the occupational license for myself as an individual or obtained through my company? *Again, this depends on the type of business.* Some licenses are obtained through a partnership or corporation; others must be obtained by the individual.

Licensing for Certain Products

States require licenses for certain products. Cigarette manufacturing or distributing, motor fuel and liquor distribution, sale of firearms and gaming devices are some examples.

Sales Tax Licenses

If you are selling or reselling items, you will most likely need to become licensed at the state level. This might be called a sales tax license or a seller's permit.

You will be collecting sales taxes on your products, which you then pay to the state. Even if your customers are nonprofits, and thus are exempt from paying a sales tax, you will still need to obtain the sales tax license.

Business Income Tax

Your state may impose a business income tax, and you will need to file a return. You may also need to file quarterly reports.

FEDERAL REGULATIONS

Tax Registration

You will need an EIN, which can be obtained through the IRS by filling out Form SS-4. Experts recommend that you secure an EIN even if you are a sole proprietor who does not intend to hire employees. Using an EIN will help protect the privacy of your Social Security number as well as help separate your business life from your personal life.

Also, if you choose to elect status as a Subchapter S Corporation, you will use IRS Form 2553.

Licenses and Permits

It might surprise you to find out that the U.S. government does not license many types of businesses. However, if your business is overseen by a specific federal agency, there is a good chance that you will need a federal license or permit.

FINANCING YOUR BUSINESS

Fortunately, there are many ways to secure financing for your business. A wise business owner will not just grab the first dollar he or she can get, but will consider the pluses and minuses of the funding options available.

Ideally, you will find a lender or investor whose interests are aligned with your success, who understands the vagaries of your particular business and who may even be able to offer fresh ideas or guidance that will help the business grow.

BUSINESS PLANS

What is a "business plan"? *Every business needs a well-defined description. Whether you are seeking financing or not, you should document your company's business plan in order to have a clear statement of purpose, goals and strategy.* Business plans also detail the company's financial situation.

Business plans are useful to owners and employees because they help everyone participating in the business to understand the company's mission. Putting a business plan together is an opportunity to analyze the marketplace, including customers, suppliers and competitors, devise a marketing strategy, and project future costs, sales and profits.

Business plans are essential to obtaining financing, either from lenders or investors.

What are the different types of business plans? *The type of business plan you choose depends on the type of company you have.* They can vary considerably in presentation in order to emphasize what is important about your business.

Entrepreneurs may create a very short business plan of 10 pages or less, briefly covering all the important topics, as a kind of first draft before attempting a more comprehensive plan. Expanding it into a working plan is a more involved and lengthy next step, but it will still lack depth and polish. If you simply need a business plan for internal purposes, this may be sufficient.

But if you are going to show your business plan to anyone outside the company, you will want to take it to the next level and turn it into a presentation-worthy business plan. Use plain, jargon-free language understandable to everyone. All facts must be accurate and consistent. The plan should be printed and bound using high-quality materials.

You may also want to create an electronic version of your business plan for ease of transmission or use on an overhead projector. Some investors may prefer an electronic version over a printed one.

Do I have to create a business plan to get financing? *Yes.* You will definitely need a comprehensive formal business plan to present to lenders in your loan proposal.

What should my business plan include? First, a business plan should have a cover, title page and table of contents.

If you intend to use your business plan to borrow money or attract investors, your business plan should include a description of the business, including its purpose, how it operates and your marketing strategy; an analysis of the marketplace and your competitors; a discussion of your professional experience and accomplishments; and a detailed financial summary with projections.

The business plan can be broken into three major areas that cover the business idea, the marketplace and financial information. Within that overall structure, you should include the following sections:

Executive summary

First, clearly state what you want. If you are seeking a certain amount in business loans or equity funding, say so right up front. The reader is most likely someone who can provide you with the capital, and they do not want to have to search the document for that information. Let them know from the start what their participation in this venture might be—that is, how much money they would need to give you to meet your needs.

Second, describe the basic concept of your business—what product or service you provide, what market you serve and what competitive advantage you have.

Third, briefly summarize important financial information, including sales, profits and cash flow.

Fourth, explain how much total capital you need—from the reader and other sources—to meet your goals and how the money would be used.

Finally, discuss the background of the company, including its legal structure, the owners and management, and what milestones have been achieved so far.

The executive summary should be short—usually less than one page. So be concise in your wording.

Business description

Begin the business description with a brief discussion of the industry, including current trends, the future growth outlook and how potential developments could affect your business. Make sure any data you cite is accurate, and reference the sources you use.

Describe the type of company you have—for example, whether it is a retail business or a manufacturing operation—and what type of legal structure it is, such as a partnership or corporation. Explain why you chose that structure and what the partners or owners bring to the business in the way of experience, contacts and equity.

Inform the reader about your products and services, how they are distributed and what sort of promotional and customer support they have. Make sure you emphasize any competitive advantages.

Finally, give all the reasons why your company will be profitable—and why additional funding will boost that profitability.

Market strategies

Before you complete this section, you need to do a thorough market analysis, which is an important exercise for you as the business owner. This type of evaluation can help you better understand the industry you operate in, narrow your target market more accurately and position the company accordingly.

Through market analysis, the company can decide on the best pricing and promotional strategies to profitably compete and what type of distribution works best in this market. The company can then develop an estimate of its own growth potential in the market.

In this section, outline the findings of your market analysis—including the size of the market, total sales, competitive environment and growth outlook. Detail what segment of the market you plan to target as well as your potential market share in light of your positioning, pricing, promotions and distribution channels.

Competitive analysis

While market analysis takes a look at the big industry picture, a competitive analysis focuses on the specific players in that industry. Through this type of analysis, you identify your competitors, evaluate their strategies, pinpoint their strengths and weaknesses and compare them to yours.

In this section, readers will want to learn what competitive challenges you face, what advantages you have and how those advantages are exploited in your company's strategies.

Design and development plan

In this section, you should describe the design of your products in depth in terms of both production and marketing. You should also outline your product development goals, strategies for achieving them, development funding needs and product revenue potential.

Readers will want to see what procedures you have put in place for product development as well as for the market and organizational development needed to support those products. Determine a schedule for each stage of product development and a budget that takes into account all expenses that go into the process, including materials, labor, overhead, equipment, personnel, and marketing and sales.

You should include some discussion of personnel expertise in product development. Detail your goals in recruiting and training personnel and how much skill is required of them. Each position should have a specific job description and occupy a specific place on an organizational chart.

Finally, lenders and investors will want you to identify and address all risks in the product development process.

Operations and management plan

This section lays out the ongoing operations and management functions of the company, including the organizational structure of the company and the expense and capital requirements associated with its operation.

The organizational structure usually consists of marketing and sales, production, research and development, and administration. Identify which tasks each division performs as well as what responsibilities the managers of each division have.

You also need to detail the capital and expense requirements of operating the business. Decide on the number of personnel needed and total labor expense for each department. Calculate overhead expenses, or all nonlabor expenses, including loan payments, rent, equipment leases, utilities, maintenance, supplies and insurance, noting which are fixed and which are variable.

Here, you will build the foundation for the financial statements later on by tabulating operating expenses, capital requirements and cost of goods.

Financial information

Financial data always comes last in the business plan, but this information is of crucial importance to lenders and investors. They will consider this section very carefully because it quantifies a company's current value and future prospects. However persuasive you are in describing your business idea and strategy for executing it, the financials will provide hard evidence of that fact.

You should include an income statement, a cash flow statement and a balance sheet. These three documents are interrelated and equally important.

During the first year of business, companies should generate an income statement and cash flow statement monthly. During the second year, they should generate these reports quarterly. After that, they can be generated annually. The balance sheet only needs to be generated once per year.

Essentially, the income statement shows the company's profitability. The income statement includes:

- income
- cost of goods
- gross profit margin
- operating expenses
- total expenses
- net profit
- depreciation
- net profit before interest
- interest
- net profit before taxes
- taxes
- profit after taxes

The cash flow statement indicates how much cash the company needs to spend and where it comes from. The cash flow statement includes:

- cash sales
- receivables
- other income
- total income
- material and merchandise
- production labor
- overhead
- marketing and sales
- research and development
- administrative labor expenses
- taxes
- capital
- loan payments
- total expenses
- cash flow
- cumulative cash flow

The balance sheet summarizes all the preceding financial information. It organizes that information into three categories:

- assets
- liabilities
- equity

Assets include current assets and long-term or fixed assets. Current assets will be converted to cash or used by the company in 1 year or less. Long-term assets last more than 1 year.

Current assets include:

- cash
- accounts receivable
- inventory
- total current assets

Long-term assets include:

- capital
- investment
- miscellaneous assets
- total long-term assets
- total assets

Liabilities are also classified as current or long-term, depending on if they are due in less than 1 year or more than 1 year.

Current liabilities include:

- accounts payable
- accrued liabilities
- taxes
- total current liabilities

Long-term liabilities include:

- bonds payable
- mortgage payable
- notes payable
- total long-term liabilities
- total liabilities

On the balance sheet, the difference between the total assets and the total liabilities equals the owner's equity. The amount of equity in the business is an important factor to lenders and investors in determining how much capital to lend or invest.

Some business owners provide brief analysis and explanation following each report.

What financial projections should I include in my business plan? *Forecasting your company's finances is a matter of making informed estimates about how much the business will make and how much it will spend in the future.* Financial projections give lenders and investors an idea of how profitable your company will be.

Your financial projections should include:

- a startup cost estimate: the total expenses needed to launch the business;
- a break-even analysis: income and expense estimates indicate whether your company can generate enough money to meet costs;
- a profit-and-loss forecast: take the income and expense estimates from the break-even analysis and create month-to-month profit projection for the first year of operation; and
- a cash flow projection: money coming in minus expenses going out equals net cash flow; estimate how much cash flow your company will generate each month.

How long should my business plan be?
Business plans are typically 15 to 20 pages in length, but they can run more than 100 pages in some cases. The length largely depends on the type of company and the complexity of the business idea and financials.

When should I update my business plan?
Companies update their business plans monthly, quarterly or annually. You will want to do an update before you seek any financing because lenders want to see the latest numbers. Management changes, new products or services or shifts in market trends also necessitate an update.

How do I put together a loan proposal? *In addition to standard loan documents, you should put together a written loan proposal once you have finished writing your business plan.* The business plan is the centerpiece of the loan proposal, but the proposal should also separately communicate how much you need and how you plan to pay it back.

The loan proposal should include:

- the business plan;
- a cover letter stating the amount that you are requesting and how you will use the loan;

- a proposal of terms for repayment; understand that you will negotiate this point with the lender;
- personal financial statements; these statements should list your assets and your liabilities; provide copies of your personal tax returns and a list of credit references;
- supporting documents, such as letters of reference, contracts, leases and certificates of incorporation or partnership agreements; and
- collateral; list business and personal assets that could be used to secure the loan.

After you present your loan proposal, lenders will take some time after the initial meeting to review your business plan. If your loan is approved, make sure you review all documents and understand everything before signing.

TYPES OF FINANCING: LOANS OR EQUITY

Before you begin searching for specific sources of funds, consider whether you will be better off with a loan or by offering a part ownership (equity) in your business. Each of these types of financing has advantages, and each has a few strings attached.

A loan, or debt financing, means that you will be paying interest until the money is repaid. This is a commitment that you want to be sure to be able to meet, as there will be penalties if you fail to meet the terms of the loan agreement. The good news is that you retain complete ownership and control of the business. Another positive side to borrowing is that any interest you pay is tax-deductible.

Debt financing can be either short-term (full repayment due in less than 1 year) or long-term (repayment due over more than 1 year).

Equity financing means that the person or business that provides financing will become a partial owner of the company. Unlike a bank, they do not expect to be paid interest nor do they expect to be paid back. On the other hand, they may want to become a decision-maker in the business, often by becoming a member of the board of directors.

What is the tradeoff with equity financing? *If you give a share of ownership in your business in return for funding, your ownership becomes diluted. You may be expected to share in the*

profits of the business by paying a dividend to all owners, and when the business is sold, the other owner or owners will expect a proportion of the sales proceeds. And you can expect to lose some control to an expanded board of directors.

What about a combination of debt and equity?

Businesses can use both debt and equity financing. In fact, many professionals believe that a proper balance of debt and equity is an ideal combination.

About Debt Financing

The first source for a loan that most people think of is a bank (savings bank or commercial bank). Commercial banks may have tight requirements and traditionally are not willing to take on much risk. They are strictly lenders, so they do not expect to exert the influence and control that a venture capitalist would. If you are not looking for a large amount of money, you may be able to get a loan guaranteed by your personal credit.

A bank loan can be short-term or long-term; the term usually matches the life of the item that is being financed. Like a long-term mortgage on a house, a long-term loan would be given to purchase a building or machinery that will be used for more than 10 years. A short-term loan would finance a seasonal cash flow situation.

You might also need to put up collateral—a specific asset—to guarantee repayment of the loan. This is considered to be secured financing and is most often required for a small business. An unsecured loan is simply a promise to repay under the terms of an agreement. Lenders know that an unsecured loan puts them at the end of the line if a borrower defaults on a loan, and they would require strong credit history to issue such a loan.

When should I consider leasing equipment for my business?

Equipment leasing helps manage cash flow. Many types of equipment are routinely financed with leases—copy machines, computers and vehicles, for example.

What other types of loans are there?

In effect, trade credit is a loan from your suppliers or customers. When a buyer and seller agree that the buyer will pay for the goods at a later- than-normal time, the buyer is financing using trade credit. This is a common form of financing for businesses, in which the supplier knowingly participates. In fact, the supplier may extend additional trade credit as the buyer proves creditworthy.

What about my insurance policies as a source of financing?

Most insurance policies permit borrowing against the cash surrender value. This essentially means taking a personal loan, which you can use to fund the business.

What are some other types of business loans?

In addition to the loans discussed above, business financing can come from one or more of the following sources:

- ▶ **LINES OF CREDIT** are a type of revolving credit that allow you to borrow money up to your credit limit, usually up to $200,000, pay it back with the revenue generated by that money and borrow from it again and again without having to reapply for the amount each time. Lines of credit usually require no collateral, but are extended on creditworthiness instead.

- ▶ **BRIDGE LOANS** are short-term loans that tide a company over with capital until a specific event occurs that enables the company to pay it back, such as the sale of an asset or another form of financing becoming available.

- ▶ **MORTGAGE LOANS**: When purchasing property, business owners can take out a loan similar to a home mortgage. The term of a business mortgage loan is usually 20 years. The property being purchased with the loan can be used as collateral.

- ▶ **FRANCHISE LOANS:** These loans are specially tailored for borrowers who are starting a franchise of a national company.

- ▶ **PROFESSIONAL LOANS.** Lenders may offer loans that specifically meet the needs of professional small-business owners, such as physicians and attorneys.

How do I figure out how much to borrow?

The first step to getting a loan is determining how much you need—an important calculation, not to be taken lightly. You want to borrow enough to meet your capital needs, grow the business and increase your profits. But you do not want to borrow so much that you struggle to generate enough profit to pay it back. You also want to expand your business at an appropriate rate. Make sure your ideas work before you bet the farm on them. Building a successful track record with as few missteps as possible will keep your company's finances in top shape and help you get greater amounts of financing later on.

You should estimate all business costs for several months out, which will vary considerably depending on the type of company you have. Identify which costs will be one-time and which will be recurring, which must be paid immediately and which can wait, which are fixed expenses and which will vary over time.

> **TIP:** You can use the startup costs estimate calculator at **www.bplans.com/contentkit/ index.cfm?s=tools&affiliate=sba**

I do not have the best personal credit history. Will that be a factor in getting a loan? *Yes, lenders will consider your personal credit history in their decisions to give you a loan.* Because new businesses often have no credit history yet, the lender will use your personal credit history instead.

Get a copy of your credit report from at least one of the three major credit bureaus—TransUnion, Equifax or Experian. Keep in mind that each credit bureau presents your credit information in a different way on the report. Your credit report lists all the credit you have used in the past, including mortgages, car loans, student loans and credit cards. The report also states your payment history—whether you paid on time and as agreed or you were late in making payments. The report will also reveal if you filed for bankruptcy in the last 10 years.

If your credit history was damaged by a divorce or personal crisis, you should provide a written explanation to the lender and establish that you managed your credit responsibly before and afterward and that you have tried to pay back your debts.

If there are any errors on your report, have them corrected before you apply for a loan. It can take 3 to 4 weeks to get an error fixed.

> **TIP:** You can visit the three major credit bureaus online at:
>
> Equifax: **www.equifax.com**
>
> TransUnion: **www.transunion.com**
>
> Experian: **www.experian.com/consumer/ index.html**

You also want to get your household finances in order. Your small business might not turn a profit right away, but you still need to pay your living expenses. Create a conservative monthly budget and make sure you have enough money saved to live according to that budget for many months or until you expect to receive an income from your business. Putting away an additional emergency fund is a good idea in case your projections are wrong.

What other factors will lenders consider?
Lenders are very discriminating about whom they lend money to, and they will evaluate many different factors that indicate whether or not you are a good business risk that they could potentially profit from.

First, you must demonstrate your ability to repay the loan. Lenders may look for two sources of repayment, such as cash flow and collateral. Cash flow projections are derived from past financial statements. The longer your company has been operating the more of a financial history it has and the more trustworthy the projections that are based on it. Borrowers must put up some collateral, either personal or business assets, as a backup repayment source.

Second, lenders consider how much equity the business has. Equity usually comes from owners who have put their own money into the company, investors who have provided capital in exchange for interests and retained earnings. Debt should not usually exceed more than four times the amount of equity.

Third, borrowers must show that they have experience in the business and a track record of success in managing a similar company.

How do I determine how much my collateral is worth? *The value of assets put up as collateral is not equal to their market value,*

but discounted because some value would be lost if the assets were liquidated. For example, according to most lenders, the collateral value of your house is 75 to 80 percent of the market value minus the mortgage balance. The collateral value of heavy equipment is usually 50 percent of the depreciated value. The collateral value of stocks and bonds is 50 to 90 percent of their market value.

If I do not have any collateral, can someone who does have collateral co-sign my loan?
Yes. If you have no collateral, getting someone who has collateral to co-sign the loan may be the only way you can get financing. When someone co-signs your loan, they are risking their assets if you cannot repay the lender.

What is a personal guarantee? *Normally, lenders have no claim to personal assets that you have not put up as collateral in the event that you cannot repay the loan.* Your liability is usually limited to the company's assets. But since small businesses are risky ventures, lenders want you take a personal stake in paying back the loan as well as provide them with the added protection of claim to your personal assets if the business fails.

Therefore, many lenders ask you to give them a personal guarantee. Even if your business has been formed with limited liability protection under the law, you are pledging your personal assets to guarantee repayment of the loan.

If you make a personal guarantee and default on the loan, the lender could claim all of your property and half of any property you jointly own. If you are married, the lender may require that your spouse co-sign the loan, in which case, the lender could claim all of your jointly owned property as well as anything your spouse owns separately.

What are the different types of repayment schedules?

▸ **AMORTIZED PAYMENTS:** This is the type of repayment schedule most people are familiar with, as car loans and home mortgages are usually repaid this way. With amortized payments, you make equal monthly payments over a certain period of time, with a portion of each payment paying off

principal and a portion paying off interest. The principal and interest are fully paid with the last monthly payment.

▸ **EQUAL MONTHLY PAYMENTS AND A FINAL BALLOON PAYMENT:** This type of schedule also involves making equal monthly payments that go toward both principal and interest, but the payments are relatively lower and for a shorter period of time. However, at the end of that time period, you must pay off the remaining principal and interest in one large balloon payment. Many business owners choose this repayment schedule because the lower monthly payment frees up funds for other uses, but you must have a plan for making the final balloon payment. Some borrowers plan to take out another loan to pay it if they expect interest rates will be the same or lower at that time, while other borrowers plan to sell an asset to pay it—both of which carry risks.

▸ **INTEREST-ONLY PAYMENTS AND A FINAL BALLOON PAYMENT:** This type of schedule involves making equal monthly payments that pay off only the interest over a certain time period. At the end of that period, one large balloon payment of the principal and remaining interest is due. This method of repayment also involves relatively lower monthly payments, but you will pay more interest than with the other two methods because you are borrowing the full amount of principal for a longer period of time.

▸ **SINGLE PAYMENT OF PRINCIPAL AND INTEREST:** When you borrow money from friends or family members, they often do not require that you make regular payments, but rather, ask that you pay them back all at once by a certain date.

Regardless of the type of repayment schedule you choose, make sure you have the right to prepay the loan at any time without penalty.

What kind of interest rate can I expect to pay?
Interest rates for small business loans tend to be relatively high because of the higher risk to the lender to finance a small business venture. However, state laws prohibit lenders from charging unreasonably high interest rates on small business loans. In general, a lender can legally charge interest of up to 10 percent per year, but most charge less than that.

If the business is borrowing money from a shareholder in the company, the interest rate cannot be unreasonably low or the IRS will regard the loan as a capital investment and the loan repayments as dividend payments for tax purposes.

Types of Equity Financing

The equity investor does not expect an immediate payback, but invests with the idea that his or her ownership in the business will grow in value and perhaps pay some cash dividends along the way.

An ownership interest also gives investors the right to participate in certain business decisions, including determining your salary. It is important to remember that the more shares you sell in the company, the more diluted your ownership stake becomes. Equity financing can also take much longer to obtain—months instead of days. But for many companies, especially those with little or no track record, equity financing may be the only option.

Investors assume more risk than lenders. If the business fails, investors have no claim to corporate or personal assets to recoup their investment. When assets are liquidated, all creditors must be paid in full first. Only what is left over is distributed to owners. Essentially, they can lose their entire investment. Investors expect a much higher return than lenders in exchange for taking on so much risk. In order to get equity financing, you must demonstrate that your business has the high-growth potential to generate the kind of returns investors are looking for.

It can take years for a company to mature to a point where equity investors realize gains. They usually only profit once their shares become publicly traded through an initial public offering (IPO), the business is acquired by another company or through some other exit strategy.

Who provides equity financing?

- Family and friends are a first option for many business owners. As these are people you usually deal with in an informal way, it is wise to be clear and make a formal agreement regarding their rights in regard to ownership of the business.

- You might find an "angel investor" for an early-stage funding, even before a venture capital person. An angel investor is a private investor, usually close to home, offering advice as well as funding. These investors may be highly involved in the business, bringing their own expertise as well as connections to ensure your business succeeds. An angel investor might be willing to take on more risk than a bank and have a fairly long horizon before expecting a return. Some cities have informal groups of angel investors.

- Venture capitalists often specialize by industry. Traditionally they have held a long time horizon for a return, but in recent years the time frame has shortened to 3 to 5 years. Venture capitalists typically expect an equity stake in the firm, may want board representation and will take an active role in company strategy.

- The government has a venture capital business, its "Small Business Investment Corporations." SBICs are located around the country and combine private and public funds to provide equity capital or long-term loans for businesses. They also offer assistance to business owners.

- Another form of equity financing is the Employee Stock Option Plan (ESOP). In this arrangement, employees own shares of the company. This serves a dual purpose: providing the company with capital and giving employees an incentive to perform in a way that benefits the business.

If I want to attract investors, how should I structure my company? *Investors will be most interested in corporate structures that limit their risk.* They may be willing to lose their investment, but they probably will not be willing to risk their personal assets.

- **GENERAL PARTNERSHIP:** If anyone invests in your sole proprietorship, your business becomes a general partnership, and your investors become general partners who are personally liable for business debts, even if they do not participate in running the business. Investors may not want to assume personal liability and may not be interested in joining a general partnership.

- **CORPORATION:** Corporations offer investors limited liability—that is, they are not personally liable for business debts if they do not participate in running the business.

Setting up and maintaining this corporate structure involves paperwork and costs.

- ▸ **LIMITED PARTNERSHIP:** If your company is structured as a limited partnership, your investors become limited partners who have limited personal liability for business debts as long as they do not participate in running the business, just like a corporate shareholder. But in a limited partnership, there must be a general partner who is personally liable for business debts, and that role would probably fall to you, the owner.

- ▸ **LIMITED LIABILITY COMPANY:** A limited liability company sells membership interests in the LLC to investors. LLCs offer the same limited personal liability of a corporation and a limited partnership.

What if I have a group of investors lined up?

If you are looking at gathering funds from a number of investors, you should be aware of regulations supervised by the Securities and Exchange Commission. There are rules limiting the number of investors and amount of money raised before a business must comply with regulations that apply to a public company.

Are the interests I am selling in my company considered securities?

Shares of a corporation and interests in a limited partnership and limited liability company are, by law, considered to be securities. Therefore, as a business owner, you need to comply with federal and state securities laws if you sell equity in your company in exchange for capital investments. Most small businesses can sell ownership interests in the company to a limited number of investors with minimal paperwork required to comply with securities laws. As a rule of thumb, you should be completely forthcoming with any details that are pertinent to investors making a fully informed decision about the company. If your company grows considerably larger, you may have to meet more complex disclosure requirements and eventually register the securities with the SEC.

How do I go about asking investors for money?

Companies seeking equity funding usually make a presentation to a group of potential investors. Entrepreneurs should put a great deal of time and effort into preparing these presentations, as they could be the most important sales pitch in the life of your company. Explain in detail the idea for your business, your plan for executing it and how the company will profit from it. Put technical or insider jargon in plain language investors can understand. Also, sell yourself as a proven, experienced manager who has the skills to make your company succeed. Honestly address the challenges the company faces and how you plan to overcome them. Investors are more focused on the downside of risk than the upside of a great idea.

What are private placements?

A private placement, or private stock offering, is the sale of securities to a limited number of qualified private investors. While a public stock offering is the sale of shares to the general public, a private placement is the offering of shares to only institutional investors and accredited high-net-worth individuals.

When does a private placement make sense?

Companies usually make private stock offerings after they have already received several rounds of private equity funding and now need greater amounts of capital, but they are not ready to go public.

Private placements enable companies to raise capital more quickly and less expensively than a public offering. Companies also have more control over private placements than they do over public offerings. Owners can decide how much to sell, at what price and to whom. Private placements do not need to be registered with the SEC, but they do have to comply with state and federal securities laws. While companies do not have to make public disclosures of financials, they do have to disclose all relevant information to potential investors in the private placement.

As with all private equity investments, companies must demonstrate that they have a strong future growth rate and a potential exit strategy for investors.

How do private placements work?

A company making a private stock offering issues a Private Placement Memorandum, or PPM. The PPM includes the company's financials and business plan as well as any other relevant information. Preparing a PPM involves hiring attorneys who specialize in private placements to oversee the paperwork and make sure the process complies with SEC and state laws. The issuing company and potential investors usually work with an investment bank as a go-between. Investors who decide to invest complete a subscription agreement.

How are profits distributed to investors?

- **EARNINGS DISTRIBUTION:** A portion of the company's earnings can be distributed to shareholders, usually in the form of dividends. Most investors prefer that companies reinvest earnings in the business instead of distributing them to shareholders. If the company grows and performs well, the value of their shares grows, eventually resulting in a capital gain from the sale of the business or the sale of their shares.

- **SALE OF THE BUSINESS:** If the company is sold, equity investors get a cut of the proceeds, depending on the number of shares they own. If the investor makes more money than they originally invested, the excess amount is called a capital gain.

- **SALE OF EQUITY INTEREST:** Investors can sell their interest in the company and realize a capital gain if the value of their shares has become greater than what they originally paid.

What is a public stock offering? *A public stock offering is the sale of equity in a company, in the form of shares of common stock, through an investment-banking firm to the general public.* A private company "goes public" by selling its stock on the open market for the first time through an IPO.

Why do companies go public? *Companies become publicly traded in order to raise greater amounts of capital to expand the business, fund research and development, make acquisitions and pay down debt.* Once public, a company can raise more capital by issuing additional stock in a secondary offering. Public companies can also more easily raise private funds and get better rates when issuing debt.

Investors who purchase equity interests in a private company need an exit strategy to unlock the value of their shares. Going public provides them with an opportunity to sell their holdings for potentially much more than they paid for them, or at least see them increase in value. And, as a founding owner and large shareholder, you personally would also stand to make a great deal of money.

What does the IPO process involve? *In order to go public, companies should be able to demonstrate they have the potential to generate minimum annual earnings growth of 20 percent.* They must also have the ability to achieve a valuation—that is, shares outstanding times stock price—of around $100 million.

The IPO process is a long and involved one. Before going public, the company hires an investment bank to handle the offering, registers with the SEC, issues a preliminary prospectus and markets the IPO to institutional investors in a "road show." After the SEC approves the offering, an "effective date" is set—that is, the day the stock will be offered. The investment bank and the company then decide on the opening stock price, which is largely determined by market conditions and institutional investor interest. Most of the IPO shares are allocated to large institutions, but individual investors can sometimes get shares.

On the day of the initial public offering, the company's stock trades on the open market for the first time. From that moment forward, market demand dictates the stock price. Stock prices frequently spike on the first day of trading and settle back down in the days following. After 180 days, people who held shares before the IPO are allowed to sell them.

What are the drawbacks to going public? *Going public is expensive—more expensive than other means of business financing. A company must give up at least 25 percent of its equity in the offering, perhaps much more.* Taking a company public is complex and requires the hiring of many experts to help with the process. Tackling the mountain of paperwork involved costs a great deal of money. Fees and expenses can add up to as much as 20 percent of the deal. Once public, companies are required to follow strict rules and disclose financial information regularly, which are costly a consuming endeavors.

When going public, the original owners relinquish some of their ability to make independent decisions. The company is now largely owned by public shareholders. Even though they might not have a majority stake in the company, their holdings are significant enough that companies must hold shareholder meetings, notify shareholders of company developments and allow them to vote on certain business decisions. Finally, if shareholders do not like how you are running the company, they can vote with their feet and sell their shares, hurting both the company and your personal fortune.

SBA Programs

The Small Business Administration is a valuable resource for more than just financing. It offers a range of programs—several large ones and others for special circumstances—that may be just what you need to start a business or grow to the next level. (Your state and local community are also potential resources.)

Although sponsored and funded by the SBA, these programs are administered by banks.

- Section 7(a) guaranteed loans include the "LowDoc" program. It is designed to minimize the amount of paperwork required, and, in fact, the application is a one-page form with the application on one side and a bank or other lender's request for guarantee on the other side. These loans are available to a maximum of $150,000.
- Section 504 Community Development Corporation program provides financing for fixed assets like real estate and machinery. It is geared toward existing businesses that want to expand and set up to encourage job development within a community.
- SBA microloan program provides small amounts of financing (up to $35,000) for both startups and ongoing businesses. It is managed by nonprofit organizations.

> **TIP:** To find an SBA microloan intermediary in your area, visit: **www.sba.gov/financing/microparticipants.html**

The SBA also provides special areas of funding for Small Business Development, Women's Business Centers, veterans and Native Americans programs. It also provides assistance after some disasters. Further, the SBA has resources for businesses that want to export goods to other countries.

My business generates plenty of money to repay a loan, but I have very few personal or corporate assets to put up as collateral. What can I do to get financing? *The SBA, an independent federal agency, offers programs to help small-business owners get financing.* The SBA has federal funds to provide guarantees on loans to small-business owners that are structured according to the SBA's requirements.

Most banks and many commercial finance companies offer SBA-guaranteed loans. About 850 lenders qualify as SBA-Certified Lenders, which means they meet certain SBA criteria and have experience in making SBA-guaranteed loans. The agency can process a loan with one of these lenders in about 3 business days. About 500 lenders qualify as SBA Preferred Lenders and handle about 30 percent of all SBA-guaranteed loans. They have full authority to process SBA loans and can complete applications in 1 business day.

> **TIP:** To find SBA lenders, go to **www.sba.gov/financing/basics/lenders.html**.

While the SBA sets the guidelines for the loans, the lenders provide the actual funds to the borrowers. The SBA guarantees as much as 80 percent of the principal of the loan with the full faith and credit banking of the federal government, significantly reducing the risk to the lenders.

Many small businesses are fully capable of repaying a loan, but do not have enough collateral to get one. SBA programs make it possible for those types of companies to get financing. It is also hard for small-business owners to get long-term loans because they involve increased risk to the lender, but long-term loans mean lower, more manageable payments. SBA-guaranteed loans mitigate the risk and encourage lenders to make loans with terms of up to 10 years.

SBA loans are also relatively inexpensive. The maximum allowed interest rates range from the prime rate plus 2.75 percent to the prime rate plus 4.75 percent. Lenders of SBA loans also cannot charge repayment fees. Applying for an SBA loan may be a more involved and lengthy process than applying for a traditional loan.

LEASING OR BUYING YOUR BUSINESS LOCATION

Many factors will go into the decision on locating your business. For example, if you are planning a retail business, you most likely want easy access for customers. Or, if you are in distribution or manufacturing, you will want a workable setup for equipment and product delivery and shipping.

Most new businesses rent, or lease, their facilities, so the discussion here will focus on the legal aspects of leasing. There are, however, some solid reasons for buying a space.

Why purchase a business facility? *Leasing has many advantages in terms of maximizing cash flow and the ability to change locations, but buying offers opportunities to consider.* Some reasons to buy are:

- You are confident that the business will be in the same place for years to come, and you expect to make alterations to the property as the business grows and changes.
- You believe the value of the property will grow over time, and, measured against cash flow and actual lease cost considerations, the business should benefit from appreciation of the property.
- Tax considerations may encourage a purchase. Rent is deductible for tax purposes, and it is a cash outlay. Depreciation is not a cash outlay, but it is deductible for tax purposes. Interest payments from financing a purchase are also tax deductible.
- More control and flexibility in making decisions about the property will be available without the need to accommodate the lessor or landlord.

What are the advantages of leasing?
Especially when starting out, business owners see the advantages of leasing versus buying a business facility. Some key considerations in making that decision include:

- There is less up-front cash required with a lease. Cash is preserved for other needs of the business—sales and marketing efforts, hiring employees, buying equipment. Rent is deductible for tax purposes.
- Unlike a typical residential lease, terms of a commercial lease are open to negotiation. You can decide what is important to you and work with the landlord to accommodate the needs of your business.
- Maintenance can be shifted to the landlord. This includes routine concerns such as landscaping or snow removal. It could also apply to building repair and upkeep.

A lease means there are periodic opportunities to reconsider and move on to another space.

What should I look for in a commercial lease? *The amount of rent is usually calculated per square foot.* Commercial real estate brokers can help by giving you the average price per square foot for similar properties, and rents for larger properties are often published.

The length of the lease is a factor. Can you sublease? What is required to terminate the lease early? *Another area to check is the description of the area you are renting.* Does it fit with your verbal understanding with the lessor?

How can I make sure a leased property will really suit my business? *Be sure to read the lease carefully and think through the details as they apply to your business.* What will the landlord do in the way of maintenance? What restrictions on signage might discourage customers or make freight deliveries difficult?

What are some features of commercial leases? *A commercial lease is a legal document, enforceable in a court of law.* Because commercial leases are tailored to specifics of the business and the facility, they are not standard documents. Terms are negotiable.

The fact that commercial leases are not standardized gives the business owner opportunity to structure terms that support the business. A "build out" that tailors the property to the lessee's specifications may be included as part of the lease.

Commercial leases tend to be long term—10 or 15 years—and it is difficult to break them. Over time, the amount of money involved can be significant.

There are no tenant advocates as you might find in a consumer lease situation. For these reasons, it is important to make sure an experienced third party, most likely a lawyer, reviews the document.

Do I need to worry about zoning if I am moving into a space that has been occupied by a similar business? *Yes, you need to check the zoning, and you should not count on the existing business or landlord to advise you on this.* If the zoning rules have changed, the current business might be "grandfathered" in—that is allowed to continue their business as long as they stay, but the new occupant must adhere to the new zoning rules.

It is unlikely that you will avoid the scrutiny of your local government when you move into a new location as you will be applying for business permits and licenses that will trigger a zoning review.

Should I just hire a commercial broker to find a facility for my business? *A commercial broker knows the territory and current pricing and can be a great asset in your search for a location.* You might also want to check for economic development zones, small business incubators and other government-sponsored programs that help businesses find appropriate locations.

Will the landlord take care of the "Certificate of Occupancy"? *Many cities require a Certificate of Occupancy or a similar document that shows a building confirms to city requirements.* For example, in Chicago, there are three types: covering a full building, part of a building or a temporary certificate for a special event.

Checking the Certificate of Occupancy will tell you that the building meets local building codes as well as the kinds of uses permitted for the building.

BUSINESS INSURANCE

As you decide on your business's insurance needs, think about two broad categories—property and liability. While these two types of insurance are not required in a legal sense, you will have many good reasons to make sure that you have adequate coverage. Besides protecting your personal and financial investment, insurance may be required as part of a lease or loan agreement.

What is liability insurance? *Liability coverage protects against situations like accidents that cause an injury to someone who is on your property.* Another type of liability insurance protects against lawsuits from people who have used products that you produced and claim to be injured by them.

You can also obtain auto liability insurance, which covers damage in a business-related accident. It is legally required in almost all states and is not included in general liability policies. Even personal cars that are used for business purposes should be covered by auto liability insurance.

Comprehensive general liability insurance covers any liability for property damage or personal injuries, unless they are designated as excluded. The general liability policy covers an "occurrence"—meaning personal injuries or property damage to another party. It is important to keep the policy in force. Once it has lapsed, the insured is no longer covered.

Can the insurer make exclusions from its general liability coverage? *Yes. If an insurance company can prove that the insured "expected or intended" certain damage, it can be excluded from coverage.* This is difficult to prove since the insurance company has to show what the company was actually thinking at the time.

Will my liability insurance cover my intellectual property? *Insurance companies are beginning to exclude coverage for personal injury to others that result from events such as* *slander, copyright infringement, trademark infringement or invasion of privacy.* As a small-business owner, you can request an endorsement to include this coverage. Cyberspace insurance policies are now available for companies that do a lot of business on the Internet.

Beyond intellectual property, an insurance policy may specify that coverage for damages is limited to "tangible" property or physical damage that has occurred. This creates an opening for computerized data to be questioned on a claim.

If your company provides computer hardware, software or programming services, find out whether the standard policy includes this coverage. If not, seek an endorsement from your insurer.

Can I get specialized forms of liability insurance? *Specialized liability insurance is focused on covering endorsements that might be excluded in the general liability policy.* This might be in the form of an endorsement to the general liability that covers an item that would otherwise be excluded.

Or, if a liability is related to a risk unique to a profession, it will call for a specialized policy such as errors and omissions (E & O).

Can I get insurance against liability for cleanup to a polluted site? Yes, you can ask for an endorsement that covers liability for environmental hazards. It is possible that cleanup costs will be charged to a new owner or party that did not actually cause the damage.

It is likely that the insurer will require an environmental inspection to be conducted. One difference between an environmental inspection and a standard inspection is that the environmental inspection is concerned with pollution that could harm property or people outside the boundaries of the insured property.

Do I also need property insurance for my business? *Property insurance is exactly what it sounds like. It covers physical property against loss or damage.* Typically, you can expect property insurance to cover furniture and fixtures, machinery, office equipment, computers and inventory.

You can choose between several types of property insurance—basic, broad or special coverage. A basic policy covers damage from fire, storms, smoke, riots and vandalism. The broad form might add broken window damage and water damage to coverage.

Is theft covered in my business property insurance policy? *Many business owners are surprised to find that theft is not covered under their basic or broad property insurance policies.* To get theft coverage, a special form policy is needed, or an endorsement to a general policy.

What does "special form" property insurance cover? *This is the strongest form of property insurance protection.* It normally covers all risks unless they are specifically excluded.

What else should I look for in property insurance? *Check the limits on the coverage you have. Be sure you know what your deductibles are.* Guaranteed replacement cost can be an important component of your insurance plan. With replacement cost, you will be reimbursed at the current price of items that have been damaged or totally destroyed.

How do I find and buy business insurance? *If possible, try to find an insurance broker who is knowledgeable about your particular business.* He or she might show you policies that are specifically designed for your type of business. The most important point is to understand exactly what your policies do and do not cover.

ADVERTISING AND MARKETING

Millions, perhaps billions, of dollars are spent on advertising every day, and it is a rare advertiser who is called to account for deceptive or misleading advertising. It is, however, important to know the boundaries so you do not stray outside the law.

Advertising is regulated by both federal and state law. Under the law, your ad is unlawful if it tends to mislead or deceive. It is possible to run an ad that is unlawful, even if you did not intend to mislead. Ignorance or your intentions are not a defense in this case.

What agencies regulate advertising? *At the federal level, the Federal Trade Commission is primarily responsible for supervising advertising. Often an investigation is triggered by a consumer complaint or a report from a competitor.* Initially, the FTC may try to encourage compliance through voluntary action. If that does not work, they can take a business to court. They can also compel the advertiser to run ads that acknowledge deception and state the truth.

State and local governments also have laws that regulate advertising. The state's attorney general is usually charged with monitoring and prosecuting violations.

If customers feel that they have been misled by an advertiser, do they have the right to sue? *Yes, states have enacted consumer protection laws that give individuals the right to sue.* Competitors can also sue if they believe an ad is misleading. Plaintiffs can also seek punitive damages that far exceed the value of the advertised item in question.

What are some advertising guidelines that I should keep in mind? Here are some tips for keeping your ads within legal limits.

BE TRUTHFUL. Neither words nor pictures should mislead consumers. Promises made in the ad should be kept, and language should be accurate. Fire-resistant is not the same as fireproof. Illustrations, whether they are photos or drawings, should be accurate.

BE FAIR WITH COMPETITION. Comparing your service or product with a competitor's can open up potential problems. Make very sure you have all the facts before running the ad.

PRICING CLAIMS MUST BE ACCURATE. If you are promoting a sale or savings, be careful when you compare with a base or standard price. You can get in trouble by artificially raising a price in order to lower it for a "sale."

BE CAUTIOUS WITH THE WORD "FREE." If the offer has a qualification—for example, you must buy one item for the other to be "free"—then you must clearly state the condition.

GET PERMISSION FOR QUOTES AND ILLUSTRATIONS. If your ad includes language that you have "borrowed" from someone, be sure that you are not violating copyright laws. A short, limited quotation is usually considered fair use under today's copyright laws, but you would be wise to get permission in advance if there is any doubt. Likewise, permission should be obtained to use a photo or other image.

DELIVER THE GOODS. If you have ever made a special trip to the store for an advertised item and found that it is out of stock, you know the reason behind this rule. The advertiser should be sure to stock enough product to meet anticipated demand. If you have any doubts about whether you will have enough, the ad should state that "limited quantities" are available.

DO NOT MISLEAD ON OFFERS TO EXTEND CREDIT. In the spirit of honest advertising, offers to extend credit should not be misleading. An example: Your ad claims that you will extend credit to anyone and then you fail to extend credit to buyers with bad credit ratings (or you charge a higher interest rate). Buried details in the credit terms and overly aggressive collection efforts can also lead to false advertising charges.

INTERNET AND E-MAIL MARKETING

The Internet has opened up new methods of advertising and marketing—some of which, as in the case of spam, has not been welcomed by most people. The Controlling the Assault of Non-Solicited Pornography and Marketing Act (CAN-SPAM) took effect in 2004 and set out rules for unsolicited e-mails. More legislation is pending.

Current concerns in Internet marketing include copyrights and trademarks, privacy and order fulfillment. In many ways, these issues parallel the rules that have been in place for ads via print and the airwaves.

▸ **COPYRIGHT AND TRADEMARKS:** Usually a short quote is okay; more than that calls for permission. Writers have found entire articles picked up and used without their permission. Likewise, trademarks used on the Web should be in line with trademark law.

▸ **PRIVACY:** If you want to use customer or client testimonials, you should not post names or pictures without the consent of the client. You need approval in writing.

- **ORDER FULFILLMENT:** If you promise delivery within a specified time, you can get in trouble with the law and possibly have to pay some expensive fines. By default, the law says you must deliver within 30 days (if you do not note another time frame).

> **TIP:** How do you use e-mail to market products on the Internet without people thinking that it is spam? Experts suggest the following:
>
> - Ask people to sign up for an e-mail newsletter that you distribute.
>
> - Use the speed of the Web to keep your subscribers up-to-date on the topic of interest to them.

What does CAN-SPAM say I can and cannot do in an e-mail? *CAN-SPAM requires that any unsolicited commercial e-mails must be labeled as such (although the law does not specify how the labeling is done). It prohibits the use of misleading headers and subject lines.* It also requires that the e-mail include a way for the recipient to opt-out of any future mailings, and it should have the sender's physical address.

BOOKKEEPING AND ACCOUNTING

As a business owner, you will be required to produce financial statements for outsiders, such as banks, and to report financial information for tax purposes to federal and state governments. But equally important, the biggest beneficiary of good record keeping and reporting is you, the business owner.

Effective bookkeeping and accounting practices greatly increase your ability to control your understanding of your business finances.

Your system for keeping track of receipts and expenditures is bookkeeping. While there are many good systems that you could use or adapt for your own use, there are no rules as to which process you must follow. If by some chance you are audited for tax purposes, you will be asked to produce the detailed records kept with your bookkeeping system.

Depending on the size and complexity of your business, you will want to produce reports that help manage the business and meet tax and other regulations. For this, you may want to get the help of an accountant.

How do I set up a bookkeeping system?
Setting up a bookkeeping system has several stages.

- Keep track of your receipts and associated payors, dates and products or services purchased.

  Your system might be as simple as logging checks received against copies of invoices you have sent out. Or it could be a system in which your cash registers are connected with a sophisticated computer system. The number of receipts you receive will help determine the way you keep track of them.

- Record your transactions in a ledger.

  A ledger summarizes revenues and expenses and the pertinent data that you will need later. Whenever you feel it will be useful, you can use the ledger to create reports that will help you analyze the flow of your business. You can create reports for special purposes; for instance, you might want to know how many boxes of stationery have been sold over the past month, and your bookkeeping system can help answer the question.

  When you transfer the information about your receipts and purchases into the ledger, it is called posting. There are many software programs available that automatically post to ledgers and later reports that you can use as managing tools. An alternative or supplement to a computer program is an outside bookkeeping service.

- Use your financial information to create financial reports.

  Financial reports allow you to see the forest and not just individual trees. They allow you to analyze your sales, your expenses and to see trends in your business. Again, the nature of your business will determine which types of reports are most valuable for you and how often you want to look. Comparing the results of two or more time periods can be a useful business tool.

  The three most common financial reports are the balance sheet, income statement and cash flow statement.

What is a balance sheet? *A balance sheet is often called a "snapshot" of the business's financial situation. It takes a look at the company at a certain point in time, often the end of a quarter or a year.*

The "balance" part of the balance sheet comes into play with the left side and the right side adding up to the same total at the bottom. On the left side are listed the assets of the company—the resources that it is using to do business. Beginning at the top with the most liquid item, cash, other categories might include inventory, accounts receivable (what is owed the business), equipment such as trucks or machinery and finally real estate.

On the right side of the balance sheet is a list of items that show how the assets were paid for. At the top are liabilities such as accounts payable, short term loans or notes, long-term bonds or other loans. Below the liabilities, the equity of the business is listed. Equity is the owner's contribution to the assets of the business, coming either from a contribution the owner made when the company was established or by earnings which were retained in the business and not paid out in any way.

What is an income statement? *An income statement shows how money has come into the business and been paid out over a period of time. At the top of the income statement is the revenue generated by sales. I*tems subtracted from revenue include the cost of goods sold, operating expenses and interest payments. Net profit (or loss) is the amount that is left after all expenses have been covered.

What is a cash flow statement? The cash flow statement is similar to the income statement, but it does not include noncash expenses like depreciation.

What are "cash" and "accrual" accounting methods? *Cash and accrual accounting methods treat time in two different ways.* The cash method is like a check book; revenue is recognized when it is received, and expenses are recognized when they are paid. Accrual accounting attempts to match the timing of revenue and expenses with their source. For example, if you purchased a 1-year magazine subscription on July 1, accrual accounting would recognize only half of the expense in the current year and the other half of the expense in the following year.

What is an "aging" report? *An aging report lists accounts that are owed by customers along with the length of time the debt has been outstanding.* This tool can help alert the business owner to show payers or changes in payment patterns that will require attention.

What is the difference between "inventory" and "cost of goods sold"? *Inventory and cost of goods sold are related. Inventory consists of the items your business is holding that you expect to sell to customers.* Cost of goods sold is the cost of your inventory once it has been sold to customers.

How long should I keep my financial records? *Hang on to your supporting paperwork—receipts, cancelled checks, etc.—for 7 years.* Tax returns should be kept for at least 7 years, ideally for the life of the business, as you may want them for information regarding retirement accounts.

What else should I keep forever? Financial statements, general ledgers, legal correspondence, contracts, real estate documents and corporate records should be kept in perpetuity.

Is there anything that I can eventually get rid of? *Bank statements and deposit slips, records of sales and employee-related records can be tossed after 6 years.* After 3 years, you can get rid of invoices that you have paid, payroll records, inventory records and cancelled checks.

If I do a good job of bookkeeping and can create my own reports, why do I need an accountant? *An accountant or accounting system may be needed for closing the books at the end of a quarter or year and to help prepare financial statements.* You may want financial statements every quarter, or even monthly.

Why else would I want to hire an accountant? *An accountant will be an expert in tax regulations, and you will most likely call on him or her to prepare your income tax* *returns.* An accountant also can help to make sure that you pay sales taxes, which are usually collected by local governments on a monthly basis. Maintaining payroll payments and records requires constant vigilance, and this is another area where an accountant can help keep you on track.

It can be helpful to have an outside perspective in understanding your finances, and a good accountant can be an excellent resource for information and advice.

TAXES

The two types of taxes to which you will devote most of your time are business income taxes and employment, or payroll, taxes.

INCOME TAXES

Most people do not find themselves staying up late at night reading the tax code with the eagerness that they would show for the latest page-turner. But if you develop a basic familiarity with business income tax rules, you just may find it interesting to see how you can manage your business with an eye toward minimizing taxes.

In general, you will find that the IRS gives a wide range of expenses that it allows as deductible. The term "ordinary and necessary" is operative here. If a deduction is "ordinary," or common to your industry, the odds are good that it will be allowed. The way your business is taxed will depend on the form of business you have selected.

The type of tax treatment and form you file will depend on the form of business entity that you have selected. This chart gives a quick overview.

Form of business	Tax treatment	IRS schedule to use
Proprietorship	Business does not pay the tax	Form 1040, Schedule C
Partnership	Business does not pay the tax	Form 1065
C Corporation	Corporation files return	Form 1120 or 1120-A
S Corporation	Business does not pay tax	Form 11-20 S
LLC	May file as sole practitioner (Form 1040, Schedule C), corporation (Form 1120 or 1120-A) or partnership (Form 1065)	

As indicated on the chart above, a proprietorship, partnership, S corporation and possibly an LLC will not pay taxes itself. The tax burden is passed along to the business owner, and the income is taxed at the individual's personal tax rate.

A corporation, which is treated as a separate entity or "person," pays taxes at a graduated rate. Currently, the first $50,000 of net income is taxed at a 15 percent rate. The next $25,000 of income is taxed at 25 percent. Rates for net income over $75,000 vary between 34 percent and 39 percent.

What about business tax deductions?
You can be fairly certain that just about any expense incurred to benefit your business will be deductible for tax purposes. Remember the "ordinary and necessary" guideline.

The IRS has been specific in its rulings regarding some types of deductions. Depreciation, travel expenses, meals and entertainment and auto expenses fall into that category. If it is ordinary or necessary to your industry, it normally will be deductible.

First, here are just a few deductions your business can take:

- interest payments
- rent
- office supplies
- fees and commissions
- insurance
- expenses for attorneys
- accounting services and other professional advisors
- repairs and maintenance of your equipment
- vehicles the business owns
- office supplies and expenses

Employee-related expenses can also be deducted, such as:

- wages
- payroll taxes
- benefits and retirement contributions
- pension and profit-sharing plans

Expenses related to selling your products are allowable deductions:

- marketing and advertising costs
- trade publications
- fees and commissions
- association memberships
- business conventions and trade shows

Health, dental and group life insurance are all allowable deductions, as are moving expenses. There are other qualified benefit plans which are deductible for the business. In addition, these benefits are not taxable to employees.

In general, the IRS wants to make sure that the business owner does not set up a business plan that benefits himself or herself more than his or her employees.

What do I need to know about depreciation?
Although depreciation is not a cash expense, it is deducted from income on your taxes and thus reduces your tax liability.

If you buy equipment or machinery that has a useful life of more than 1 year, you will most likely deduct the cost over a number of years. This rule recognizes that you will be using the asset for more than 1 year.

Can I buy a truck for my business and write it off right away? *This is where depreciation kicks in.* You will most likely have to depreciate it over a period of years.

How do you figure the amount of depreciation? There are two types of depreciation: "straight-line" and "accelerated."

Straight-line is the simplest. Divide the cost of the asset by the number of expected years of life.

Accelerated depreciation means that the tax deduction for a purchase is sped up; you are allowed to take a larger amount as a write-off in the first years after you have made the purchase.

So I can deduct the full cost of equipment when I buy it? Are there any exceptions? *The answer is yes. A small business is most likely to qualify.* You can choose to deduct up to $100,000 worth of depreciable assets in the year you make the purchase.

Of course there are exceptions. If you buy more than $400,000 of depreciable assets in the year, this rule does not apply; you will need to make adjustments to the $100,000 first year write-off as it phases out.

A second exception is that the amount you deduct cannot be greater than your taxable income for that year.

Can I deduct travel, meals and entertainment? *The IRS wants the business to distinguish between travel for business purposes and personal travel.* Deductions for business travel covers almost all expenses you would encounter on a business trip: any form of transportation that takes you to your destination, meals, lodging, cabs or limos from the airport or while in a city, tips, laundry and cleaning expenses.

If a trip is partly business and partly personal, you are allowed to deduct only the business portion.

As for meals and entertainment, the IRS allows a business to deduct only 50 percent of the expense. This applies to you and a guest that you might pay for—you can deduct half of each meal or entertainment.

If you are a sole proprietor paying taxes through your personal Form 1040, you will take the deduction on Schedule C. A corporation may reimburse its employee-owner or employee for 100 percent of the meal and entertainment expenses, but it will still only be able to deduct 50 percent for tax purposes.

Can I deduct my automobile expenses?
There are two ways to compute your automobile expenses.

Each year, the IRS states a per-mile allowance for deductions, and that might be the simplest way to calculate the expense. The alternate method is to keep track of all car-related expenses like gas and oil, tires and repairs and use the actual costs.

Can I deduct all of my automobile expenses?
As with business and personal travel, you will need to allocate expenses if you use your car for both business and personal reasons. Commuting expenses are not deductible, and neither are parking fees at your normal place of work; these are considered personal expenses.

Can I depreciate automobile expenses?
The business entity can depreciate an automobile that it has purchased.

Can I deduct software that comes separate from a computer?
Yes, you can deduct 100 percent of the software cost in the year you make the purchase.

EMPLOYMENT TAXES

Most of the employment taxes your business pays fit under the "payroll" category, although self-employment tax is closely related. In a sense, federal and local governments have asked you to be the tax collector, since you are required to withhold a number of taxes—income, Social Security, Medicare and unemployment, among others. It is vital to stay timely with your payments to the tax authorities, as penalties for delayed payment are steep.

What is a W-4?
Every employee that you hire will be asked to fill out a W-4 form, which helps calculate the amount of income tax your business will withhold. Geared to meet an employee's personal income tax obligation, the form includes the employee's marital status and how many exemptions he or she expects to claim. Using the frequency of the payroll period and the individual's wages, the IRS provides charts and other ways to calculate the appropriate amount to be withheld.

All but a handful of states and even a few cities have imposed their own income tax, and you will be responsible for withholding an appropriate amount for those taxes as well.

How much of my employees' Social Security and Medicare do I have to pay?
Social Security and Medicare taxes are shared equally by the employer and the employee. Unlike income tax, these taxes are calculated as a flat percent of wages. The Social Security portion has a ceiling of $90,000; there is no ceiling for Medicare.

The rate for Social Security is 6.2 percent of wages and for Medicare is 1.45 percent. This totals 7.65 percent; the employer pays 7.65 percent of total wages and withholds the employee's contribution of an additional 7.65 percent of wages.

In what situation will I need to pay unemployment tax?
You are responsible for a federal unemployment tax (FUTA) based on total wages you pay employees. This is not a withholding situation; the business pays the tax directly.

You will be liable for FUTA if you pay wages totaling $1,500 or more in a quarter, or if you have at least one employee during 20 "calendar weeks" in 1 year.

Currently, the tax is a flat rate of 6.2 percent on the first $7,000 that you pay each employee.

Do I not have to pay state unemployment insurance taxes too?
Yes, state unemployment insurance taxes fund programs for unemployed workers. Paying a state unemployment insurance tax may mean you can claim credits against the federal unemployment tax.

I am self-employed. What kind of employment taxes do I have to pay?
If you do not incorporate the business and thus do not pay yourself as an employee, you have a

special situation where you pay your own self-employment taxes. This process parallels paying employees with some exceptions.

First, you will not have income taxes withheld as an employee would. Instead you may need to make estimated tax payments to the IRS each quarter. Also, you effectively pay your own Social Security and Medicare taxes at the rate of 15.3 percent. You do not have an employer to pick up half the tab for this. Schedule SE is where you report your net self-employment income for Form 1040.

COLLECTIONS

In a perfect world, checks would arrive on time and for the right amount. A customer might even write "thank you" in the memo section.

Unfortunately, practical reality sets in and even the most careful businessperson will need to deal with late payments and deadbeats. (There is a school of thought that says, if you do not occasionally have trouble collecting, you are being overly cautious with the credit you extend.)

The first step in on-time collection is to do everything possible to ensure prompt payment. Once an account becomes seriously delinquent, there is another series of steps to take.

As you develop your credit policy, aim for one that ensures as much cash for your business as quickly as possible. You will, of course, be bound to practices within your industry and the characteristics of your customer base.

> **TIP:** Make your credit terms clear from the beginning, whether your customers are consumers or other businesses. Whenever possible, use a contract or letter agreement to specify terms including when payments will be due.

Credit terms may call for a down payment, the remainder payable in 30 days; final payment on delivery; or a discount for early payment.

How can I check when I get bad feeling about a customer? *If you have any doubts, get a credit check.* For retail transactions, check

with one of the three consumer credit bureaus. Dun and Bradstreet would be a way to investigate business customers.

How can I make sure I will get paid if my customer owes money to a lot of companies? *Become a secured creditor. As creditors line up to collect from a company, a secured creditor has a stronger claim than an unsecured creditor.* This status must be obtained in advance by filing the appropriate documents to restrain the customer from disposing of equipment they may have purchased from you.

What else can I do to ensure prompt payment? *If the type of your business warrants it, you may decide to accept credit cards.* For this, you will go to a bank and get a merchant account. The bank will charge a fee that ranges from 2.5 to 5.5 percent of sales.

> **TIP:** Send bills promptly. If invoices arrive weeks after your customer expects them, they may wonder if you are serious about collections. In fact, there is no rule that says you have to wait until the end of the month. If you have just finished a major project, why not get the invoice off while the work is still fresh in your customer's mind?

What can I do about overdue accounts? *Here are some steps you can take to collect once you have concluded that your debtor is stalling.* They are listed in order of increasing severity.

1. **DILIGENTLY MONITOR PAST-DUE ACCOUNTS**

    Good bookkeeping and preparation will pay off as you will not be surprised by an account that is 60 days late in paying. "Forewarned is forearmed," they say, and you will have time to plan your next steps.

2. **CONTACT YOUR DEBTOR REGULARLY**

    Once you are sure that you need to step up your collection efforts, begin with a series of phone calls and letters. The letters should be increasingly aggressive, although neither calls nor letters should step out of the boundaries of courtesy.

3. **MAINTAIN CONTACT RECORDS**

    Prepare for possible legal steps by keeping notes of details of conversations you have held with your debtor, alternatives you have discussed, dates of invoices sent and any other communications with the debtor.

4. **NEGOTIATE**

   Be ready to compromise. You may save time and energy by taking less than 100 percent on the dollar from a creditor.

5. **COLLECTION AGENCY**

   A collection agency will take a share of the amount received from your debtor, but it will free you up to pursue the growth of your business. For larger companies, a law called the Fair Debt Collection Practices Act regulates how agencies can contact debtors and ensures fair practices. It would be good to check with your collection agency to make sure their practices fall within the guidelines.

What about trying to make sure my customer does not sell the equipment I sold him or her? *You can put a lien on the equipment. A lien gives a creditor the right to take another's property if an obligation is not discharged. A mechanic's lien secures payment for work and materials in erecting or repairing a building or other structure.* Liens can impact the day-to-day operations of your creditor and have potential to be quite effective.

If I go to court and win, how do I collect? *You can go to court to collect your debt. If the court rules in your favor, the judgment can be enforced through a local sheriff who may take the property or record a lien against the property.* A sheriff can also arrange for the property to be sold.

RESOLVING DISPUTES

Mediation, arbitration and small claims courts are three ways small businesses can resolve disputes without resorting to the expense and time of a lawsuit.

Because an agreement arrived at through mediation does not have to be binding to the disputing parties, it is a more informal process that offers more potential for the parties to work together in the future. Arbitration does result in a legally binding decision; the arbitrator functions like a judge and the proceeding is more like a

traditional court case. However, like mediation, it does not involve the time and expense of a court case.

A third option is small claims court. Each state operates its own small claims court and sets its own limit on the dollar amount that can be awarded.

MEDIATION

If you are in a disagreement with a supplier or customer, mediation is a valuable step toward resolution. An obvious advantage is that it avoids the extended time frame and high cost of a court case; even more, its goal is to solve the problem, unlike a court of law where the thrust is to determine which party is in the wrong. With mediation, there is a chance that the business owner can regain a reasonable relationship with the other party.

The mediator cannot force a decision; he or she can only encourage a resolution to be made between the opposing parties. If an agreement has been made at the end of a mediation session, the two parties can go ahead and sign a contract or take the decision to a lawyer for review. If an agreement is not reached, going to court remains an option. Most mediations do result in a settlement, however.

How does mediation work? *The mediator who meets with you and the other party will most likely have had training in resolving conflicts.* The amount of training varies, which is why it is important to find a mediator you are comfortable with before you start the process.

Even though mediation is informal compared to a court proceeding, a process has been developed that should lead to an outcome that satisfies both parties. There are six stages to the process:

- ▶ **STAGE 1:** Mediator's opening statement, where the mediator makes introductions, explains the process and encourages everyone to be cooperative.
- ▶ **STAGE 2:** Disputants' opening statements, in which each party describes his or her concerns and the other party is not allowed to interrupt.

- **STAGE 3:** Joint discussion, in which the focus is on defining the issues that need to be resolved.

- **STAGE 4:** Private caucuses, the heart of the mediation. The mediator spends time with each party individually, sometimes alternating with the other, as aspects of the situation are reviewed and new solutions may emerge.

- **STAGE 5:** Joint negotiation, where the parties meet together for direct negotiation.

- **STAGE 6:** Closure, the end of the mediation. At this point, a written summary is created by the mediator. An agreement may or may not have been reached.

Can mediation be used to resolve any kind of disagreement? Mediation only works when both parties agree to the process, and it has historically been used to resolve disputes that involve small business issues such as contracts, leases and employment.

It does not work well if one party wants to use legal precedents or is looking for a large payment for some kind of wrongdoing. Mediation is not designed for many types of criminal cases.

Why would I want to use mediation rather than go to court? *Besides the advantages of lower cost and quicker resolution, you are not bound by legal precedent or a judge's biases.* Also, because mediation does not use the highly structured procedures that a court does, there is an opportunity to present all sides of the situation.

In mediation, you and the opposing party will work out a solution to your own dispute. Unless you freely agree, there will be no final resolution. And, although any kind of business dispute is likely to cause some personal tension, it is a more relaxed, friendlier process than a more formal legal situation.

ARBITRATION

Like mediation, arbitration is a faster and less expensive way to resolve a business disagreement. Unlike mediation, the decision of an arbitrator can be legally binding (although not always). Also, unlike mediation, the process of arbitration is similar to that of a court proceeding. Witnesses and evidence may be presented.

Arbitration has served as an effective business tool for decades. One study found that 90 percent of corporations surveyed had used mediation or arbitration and strongly preferred them to using lawsuits.

What are the most common types of business disputes that are resolved using arbitration? *Collective bargaining agreements have included arbitration clauses for many years.* Arbitration is frequently used in compensation and employment issues.

Can arbitration be specified in advance as a way or resolving a conflict? *Yes, almost any contract can include a clause stating that disagreements will be resolved by arbitration.* When you are drawing up a contract with a supplier or customer, you can specify arbitration as the way to resolve a disagreement.

SMALL CLAIMS COURT

Small claims court is one of the ways a business owner can pursue collections and resolve other disputes without the length and expense of litigation. It is particularly effective for collecting unpaid invoices as it circumvents the use of collection agencies or lawyers, whose fees will take a big bite out of any proceeds. In fact, even the threat of small claims court can encourage voluntary payment, since many debtors want to keep their credit strong.

Other business disputes can be resolved as well. If a contract issue arises—for example, nonpayment due to a claim of poor quality work performed—the parties can get an answer quickly and inexpensively.

The dollar limits of small claims courts have been increasing, although there is a huge range within the United States. Currently, Virginia and Georgia are the highest with a top limit of $15,000, and Kentucky is at the low end with a limit of $1,500.

What kinds of cases can be resolved in a small claims court? *Disputes revolving around money are one of the best uses of a small claims court.* And evictions can usually be handled through the small claims system.

You cannot sue the federal government or a federal agency. Divorce, guardianship and bankruptcy are also outside the sphere of a small claims court.

Where do I go to file in small claims court? *Generally, you will use the court that is closest to the person you are suing, either his or her residence or business office.* If the person or entity you are suing is located out of state or some distance from where you are, that may be a reason to pursue another path.

How do I know I will collect my money if I win in small claims court? *This is a legitimate concern. It may be that the person or business you have sued does not have the assets available to pay you. If you know your debtor has the resources to pay, you can garnish wages or look for another source of collection.* One advantage— these court judgments have a long life span, so if the person or business does acquire assets, you may be able to collect in the future.

What if I lose in small claims court? Is there an option to continue pursuing my case? *Your options will depend on where the case took place. In some states, the only ground for a trial is that the judge made a mistake from a legal perspective.* Other states allow an appeal within a fairly short period of time.

ENVIRONMENTAL ISSUES

"The totality of surrounding conditions" is how one dictionary defines environment. With such a broad, fuzzy definition, it is easy to see that the concept of environment covers a big territory. Focusing on the small-business owner, our topics cover environment in these conditions: buying and selling property, OSHA, management standards for environment and smoking in the workplace.

BUYING AND SELLING PROPERTY

When a potentially hazardous property is sold, both the buyer and seller have opportunities to protect themselves from liability for cleanup.

What is due diligence? *Once a buyer has a signed and accepted letter of intent, he or she has a period of time to perform due diligence on the business property. At this point, the buyer has a chance to review parts of the business that have previously remained private.* One of the areas the buyer will check is to make sure that he or she is clear on the company's environmental issues.

Owners and operators of properties that have been polluted with hazardous wastes are required by federal law to take care of cleaning them up, even if they were not responsible for the pollution in the first place. That is why a significant part of a pre-purchase due diligence process is ascertaining whether the buyer is going to inherit a hazardous waste cleanup and, if so, to determine the cost (usually enormous) of returning the property to a nonpolluted state.

This is not an easy liability to avoid. One potential defense against a government claim of hazardous waste is that the buyer must show he made a genuine effort to discover a hazardous condition and still did not know about it.

If I am buying or leasing a property for my business, how can I protect myself from the huge costs of cleaning up a polluted site? *At the time you sign a lease or purchase for a property, it is important to take any possible legal steps to avoid assuming responsibility for a hazardous waste liability.* For one thing, you can ask the owner or the landlord to indicate what the prior uses for the land were and whether they might have been the kinds of activities which would have caused environmental damage.

You can also request information about any governmental notices regarding the site. An independent inspection, called a Phase I or Phase II environmental audit, is also a possibility.

If I am selling my business property, how can I protect myself from the huge costs of cleanup if the site turns out to be polluted?
To make sure you are safe from claims after the sale, you will want to have a Phase I environmental audit performed. This protects you as a seller, since it attests to a clean condition at the time of the sale. It can support a claim that problems were caused by owners who followed. The audit must be conducted by environmental consultants who specialize in this activity.

What should I do as a seller before the sale of my business property?
If you are a seller who wants to make a quick, clean sale, be prepared to respond to your buyer's questions regarding environmental liabilities. In the event that problems turn up after the sale, former owners may be held accountable for some of the cost of cleanup. Some danger signals to look for include lead paint, leaking underground storage tanks or asbestos.

There is always the possibility that your buyer will create a hazardous waste problem and then later blame you as the former owner. A Phase I environmental audit, conducted by an outside consultant, can help you prove that the property was clean at the time of the sale.

What if problems turn up during the audit?
Then a Phase II environmental audit may be called for. This would provide more information about the problems and some determination as to how a cleanup should be implemented.

At this point, you may decide to reduce the asking price and sell the property "as is." Ignoring the problem is just not an option, as you will most likely be required to sign a disclosure statement at the closing.

OSHA

The mission of OSHA—the Occupational Safety and Health Administration—is to make sure that a workplace adheres to certain safety standards. Since there is such a wide range of workplace characteristics, many of OSHA's standards will not apply to your business. One of your first steps should be to find out which standards are appropriate to your workplace. The most direct way is to contact an OSHA office for help.

Categories of industry standards are organized based on materials used, chemicals used, the layout of the building (for emergencies, fires) and manufacturing operations. For each of the standards that seem to apply to your workplace, check the introduction. This is called scope and application. Scope will provide details to help you decide if the standards really do apply to your situation.

What kind of OSHA standards is my business subject to?
Offices typically are affected by these kinds of standards: walking and working surfaces, material handling and storage, health-related environmental control and fire protection. You are required to implement these standards in your workplace.

Can I get a variance from OSHA standards?
If it is difficult to meet a deadline, you can request an extension, or you can ask for a variance (similar to a zoning variance).

My business can hardly afford to comply with some of the OSHA standards. Where can I get some help?
To help meet OSHA standards, there is some financial help available. Loans to support implementation may be available to help you comply with the standards set by OSHA or standards set by your state.

Does the EPA offer support for my small business?
The Environmental Protection Agency offers a wealth of information and support for small businesses. A detailed document is available that covers EPA's small business-specific services. It lists state and local resources, compliance support, education

and training and can lead you to sources of information about specific environmental concerns (such as asbestos).

What is the ISO, and why should I care? *The International Standard for Organization is responsible for a series of international business standards.* Many businesses feel it is essential to meet these standards, often because they are required to do so by potential purchasers of their products.

The ISO 14000 series encourages organizations to manage the environmental impact of their activities. This is an international system which supports environmental responsibility and impacts a company's ability to participate in international trade. It identifies requirements for environmental management and sets a framework for an organization to control the environmental impact of its activities. Continual improvement is a primary objective.

Documentation for ISO 14000 includes activities such as environmental management systems and audits, labels and product life cycle assessment.

DESIGNATING SMOKING AREAS

It is getting more and more difficult to find a place to light up in the United States, and the workplace is no exception. There might be a state or local law to restrict smoking in your workplace, and even if there is not, there are many good reasons to disallow smoking in your business.

Where should I restrict smoking to in my business? *If smoking is restricted, management's most common response is to designate a spot for smoking: a specific break room, lobby or other specific part of the building.* Even if a separate smoking area is provided, it may still mean that other workers are affected by smoke in the air.

> **The Environmental Protection Agency counsels employers to limit smoking to areas with separate ventilation or to ban smoking altogether.**

Do I have to give my employees a smoking break? *Make sure employees know the timing of when they are permitted for a smoke break.* Issues can arise at this point because workflow can be interrupted, and nonsmoking employees want to feel that they are receiving equally fair treatment in terms of smokers' breaks. The Fair Labor Standards Act can come into play in such a situation.

Do I have to identify smoking and nonsmoking areas? *There may be requirements to identify smoking and nonsmoking sections of the workplace, including the use of the international no smoking sign.* States and local governments can also require that smoking policies be posted in common areas.

SELLING YOUR BUSINESS

If you intend to sell your business in addition to the real estate, you will need to determine the value not only of the real property but also of the business itself.

How do I determine the value of my business? *There are business appraisers available to assist in making the valuation determination and many are CPAs.* You may want to get the opinion of more than one appraiser. The appraiser's valuation report will provide credibility to potential buyers that the price you are asking is realistic.

To roughly estimate the value of your business on your own, consider:

- For an established business with steady revenue and strong market position and whose continued earnings are not dependent on an individual or specific management personnel: use a multiple of eight to ten times current profits.
- For an established business with good market position but with some competition and some variability to earnings and which requires continual management attention: use a multiple of five to seven times current profits.
- For an established business with no significant competitive advantages, strong competition, few hard assets and a heavy dependency on management's skills for success: use a multiple of two to four times current profits.

- For a small personal service business where the new owner will be the only, or one of the only, professional service providers: use a multiple of one times current profits.

What steps are there to selling my business and deciding on a buyer? Decide whether you want to sell your business as well as your property:

- Clarify what you will do with your life after the business sells.
- Discuss with legal counsel and an accounting professional the legal, tax and accounting ramifications of the sale.
- If you have a partner or shareholders, determine how a sale will impact them.
- Prepare a write-up covering the essential facts of your business and its likely future.

Valuing the business and deciding on a buyer:

- Carefully consider where you set the valuation of your business and the price you ask—overpricing your business will narrow the pool of potential buyers and may result in the deal falling apart.
- Make sure to include a figure for the goodwill you have built up in your company.
- Determine when the best time to sell will be.
- Investigate your potential buyer to determine the buyer's ability to finalize the sale, make promissory note payments and avoid a future default.

Preparing for the sale:

- Be available to answer questions and offer assistance to facilitate the sale and also to answer technical questions about your processes.
- The buyer likely will make the sale contingent on a thorough investigation of your financials, business practices and assets. Do not try to disguise or hide the problems of your business but do highlight all of its features.
- Consider your exit strategy and how it impacts the business and new owner.
- Understand the disclosures that you must make and when and how to disclose.

How can I decide whether to sell my business or pass it on to family members? *Some signs that it is time to sell, versus pass on, a family business include constant tension among family members and no plans for succession or retirement of the founder or leader*

of the business. If the "next in line" relative has no formal business training and other family members are not well-utilized in the business, then the family's ability to run the company may put it in jeopardy. Compensation to a family member may be unrealistic.

What are the major steps in closing the sale of a business? *First, a letter of intent is entered into that summarizes the price and terms that have been negotiated and provides for the confidentiality of the transaction and continuing investigation.* Conduct due diligence: the seller investigating the buyer's financial soundness and the buyer investigating the business. The buyer will need to obtain and coordinate financing.

Draft and finalize the purchase agreement together with any additional agreements, such as a noncompete agreement or consulting contract. Legal counsel will provide compliance with laws regarding notification to creditors, stockholder vote, tax payments and more.

Sign the purchase agreement and other contracts to transfer ownership and secure the deal including any promissory notes. The down payment is made, and possession of the business is then turned over and any third-party documentation, such as for lenders, is completed.

What tax consequences are there to selling my business? *The sale of business property may generate taxable capital gains or deductible losses. In addition, there may be other tax consequences, such as a depreciation deduction, from the sale.* Often, the sale of small business property may be reported on an individual's Form 1040. Consulting a tax attorney is advisable, as the attorney may help you minimize the taxes owed or may have methods to defer a portion of the tax payment.

> **TIP:** If you are selling rental property, see **www.irs.gov/faqs/faq11-4.html**—the IRS site discussing the tax ramifications for sales of rental properties, including which forms are required.

INDEPENDENT CONTRACTORS

As a businessperson, you may hire independent contractors—or you may be one. In fact, there is no reason why an independent contractor cannot hire a colleague who is also an independent contractor. This may seem confusing on the surface, but the rules for defining an independent contractor apply whether you are the one who is doing the hiring or the person who will actually perform the work.

Who is an independent contractor? *In the loosest terms, people who work on their own, often for multiple customers or clients, without a traditional paycheck (and all the deductions that go with it) or employee benefits, such as health care coverage, are independent contractors. These people are in business for themselves.* You can find them in a huge range of occupations from the professions (a lawyer, for instance), to the trades (such as a plumber or carpenter), to service occupations, (for example, a massage therapist or independent public relations person).

There are, however, tighter definitions of independent contractor, and they are important for legal and tax purposes. Even so, you will not find a single-purpose definition of the term. Agencies ranging from the IRS to state tax departments have come up with their own characteristics.

For the IRS, the primary consideration in differentiating between an employee and a contractor is the amount of control that the business exercises over the worker. "A general rule is that ... the payer [has] the right to control or direct only the result of the work done by an independent contractor, and not the means and methods of accomplishing the result," according to the IRS.

The amount of control and independence can be considered in light of the following three categories:

- Facts governing behavior control would demonstrate whether the business can direct and control work through instructions or training or similar actions.
- Financial control would relate to the extent to which a worker can realize a profit or incur a loss, the amount and kind of unreimbursed business expenses and how the business pays the worker.
- Examples demonstrating the type of relationship would be indicated by written contracts describing the relationship, the extent to which the worker could do similar work for other businesses and aspects of the permanency of the relationship.

What are the benefits of being an independent contractor? *Many workers would never consider giving up their lives as independent contractors.* They love being their own boss and feel they have more control over their destiny (and the amount of money they earn).

Independent contractors may pay lower taxes. Business-related expenses can be deducted, and there are several tax advantaged retirement plan options that allow saving for the future.

So what is the downside of being an independent contractor? *For one thing, there is no steady paycheck. The life of an independent contractor can be feast or famine—being buried in work one month and worrying about the mortgage payment the next.* And there are no employer-paid benefits; contractors have to cover their own payroll taxes, health insurance and give up income if they take a vacation. They also are not eligible for unemployment benefits.

Contractors are liable for any business debts they incur, and there is always the risk that a client or customer will not pay their bills.

What are the benefits of hiring an independent contractor versus an employee, especially if I ca not exert as much control over a contractor? *A company does not have to pay payroll taxes and benefits for an independent contractor, although an hourly rate for a contractor might be higher than what an employee would receive.* Also, a company can maintain flexibility with its workforce, not just in the number of workers, but also the skills that the business might need at a given time.

One of the most important benefits of hiring independent contractors is that the hirer does not assume tort (personal injury) liability for an independent contractor.

Do I need a contract to hire an independent contractor? *A written contract benefits both the contractor and the business because it defines the work relationship as well as the obligations of each party.* It shows government agencies that the intent is to create a relationship that meets the requirements for independent contractor status.

In the contract, address these topics: the amount, timing and conditions of payment; the actual work to be performed; who pays expenses and how reimbursable expenses will be handled; the length of the contract and how it can be terminated, as well as how disputes will be resolved. There should also be a section that addresses the independent contractor's status, such as licenses held and equipment he or she will provide.

Will I own the copyright to work I create as an independent contractor? *Maybe. If a business hires an independent contractor to create a work that could be subject to copyright law, the business does not own the copyright to the work.* To own the copyright, there must be an assignment of ownership in writing, which should be part of the hiring agreement.

In some cases of creative works, the concept of "work for hire" applies. That means, under the work for hire law, the hiring entity is legally considered to be the work's author and has copyright rights. Again, there must be a written agreement stating this.

The nine specific work for hire categories include translation, a test and its answers, contribution to a collective work (e.g., a magazine), an atlas, a compilation, an instructional text, a test, answer material for a test or a supplementary work (e.g., a foreword, chart, illustration, editorial note, bibliography, appendix, index).

What happens if I hire someone as an independent contractor, and later the IRS says I must classify that person as an employee? *The penalty for this mistake is pretty stiff.* Not only does the employer have to pay back taxes (and interest), there is a penalty of up to 35 percent of the tax owed.

It is also possible to get in trouble with your state, especially if a former contractor applies for unemployment compensation.

What are some tips on making sure independent contractor status is retained? *One tip is that a business should check on how the independent contractor has been functioning in the recent past.* That is, what recent work has he or she performed that could be deemed comparable? The contractor can be asked to fill out a questionnaire that will give the appropriate information.

Is freelance the same as independent contractor? *A freelance worker is one who works for himself or herself, for different employers and without a long-term contract.* Typically a writer or artist, a freelancer could also be an independent contractor.

Is a consultant the same as an independent contractor? *A consultant is defined as someone who gives expert or professional advice, and many consultants function as independent contractors.* However, there are many consultants who work for companies or partnerships, so in that case they would not be independent contractors.

HOME-BASED BUSINESSES

The nature of the business you are operating will be the major influence in your choice of location and the physical layout of your site. One option that continues to grow rapidly is a home-based business. Continually improving technology has fueled the trend. People are pursuing careers as everything from personal chefs to Web site designers, all based from a home office.

INSURANCE

As a home-based business owner, you will want to review the types of insurance that apply to a small-business owner. But you also want to make sure that you are prepared for the unique situations that can occur because you work from home.

Most important, make sure that the issuer of your homeowners' insurance knows your business is operated from home. If you have not planned for potential problems in advance, you might find that there is no coverage for a business-related accident that happens on your premises. Even fire insurance might not be valid if the insurance company was not made aware of your home-based business.

There are many options to adjusting your homeowners' policy to cover your specific business situation. In general, you will want to make sure that business equipment and furnishings are covered, ideally at the cost of replacement. And liability for business-related accidents should be taken into account. If you store inventory somewhere on your premises, that would be another area for discussion with the insurance agent or company representative.

The important point is to talk to your insurance agent or the company representative so that you are managing potential risk.

Are there any special insurance policies that cover both home and home-based business needs? *You can obtain riders to your homeowners' policy that cover many of the contingencies of your home-based business. And some companies have special policies that are designed for the purpose.* You can expect business property (including your computer) to be covered under those, as well as other liabilities.

What are the main considerations for insuring my home-based business? Here are a few topics to make sure you discuss with your insurance agent:

- ▶ **REPLACEMENT COST:** If a disaster destroys your business property, you want to be able to replace it without a loss. A replacement cost provision is designed to allow you to replace a used computer or used furniture with a comparable new item.
- ▶ **LIABILITY:** Business-related accidents that happen at your home—or away from your home if you have a business purpose—can be disallowed if you only have traditional homeowners' insurance.

ZONING AND PRIVATE LAND USE RESTRICTIONS

If your dream is to commute 10 feet down the hall to your home office, one of your first steps should be to make sure you understand your local zoning regulations. Since your town, city or county's role is to maintain the residential qualities of its neighborhoods, you may find unexpected rules and restrictions for your home business. And, if your residence is governed by a homeowners' association or you are a renter, there may be other limitations on how you can conduct your business.

What can be regulated? *You may encounter rules that govern whether you can hire employees to work with you from your home, or they may limit the number of employees that you are allowed.* Similarly, some cities limit the amount of space in a home that can be used for your business.

Environmental factors may be addressed in your regulations. The obvious ones—managing waste disposal, chemicals or other hazardous materials—could be addressed in local ordinances. A business that emits fumes or odors may be not allowed in your residential area. On a broader scale, rules are designed to keep all the neighbors happy. Parking or the types of commercial vehicles allowed on your street might be restricted.

> **TIP:** To find out about the ordinances in your locality, you can check the library for zoning rules, or you can inquire at your local zoning department.

Can my homeowners' association restrict my use of my home for business purposes? Besides town, county or state regulations, your home may be governed by a homeowners', condo or co-op association, or a lease agreement with your landlord may include additional restrictions.

Be sure to check your homeowners' association or lease documents to see if you can operate a business from your home. There might be specific limitations; for example, a condo association might allow a home-operated business as long as it does not involve a constant flow of patients or clients coming and going through the building.

What will happen if I am already running a home-based business, and I find out that it is illegal? In the worst case, you will be forced to move your home-based business, or even close it down, if you are found to be violating local zoning laws or private regulations.

On the other hand, you might be able to make changes which satisfy the concerns of your local government or neighbors. For instance, if your business means a steady stream of deliveries is an annoyance to neighbors, you might use a nearby mailbox drop service.

What if I do not think the local home-based business rules in my community are fair? *Home-based business rules and regulations are based on maintaining a quality of life within your neighborhood, and they are often overlooked if neighbors do not complain.* It is even possible that nearby families can see a positive, safety aspect to your presence in the area during the day.

This is an area where compromise and negotiation may be great tools in reaching your goal. After all, you live there too, and it may help if neighbors understand you have a personal interest in the quality of life there.

At the local level, you could apply for a zoning variance or even to effect a change in ordinances. The number of home-based businesses is growing each year, and local governments will feel a pressure to respond to the trend.

How do I proceed if I want to get a zoning variance or even a change in the local ordinances? You can deal with a zoning problem in three stages.

- First, negotiate with the staff of your town or city's zoning department. You might agree, for instance, to always park a truck used for your business in the garage, rather than leaving it on the street.
- Second, request a zoning variance from the city. Basically, you are asking for an exception to the ordinance, and you will want to be prepared with some solid reasons why the variance should be granted. If you have been

operating from home for the prior 5 years without complaint from neighbors, this is the kind of point that will help you accomplish your goal.

- Finally, you can get involved politically and try to change the regulations. If you are on the border of a commercial area, you could ask that the commercial area be extended to include your business. Or you could go even further and ask that the entire area be rezoned.

HOME OFFICE TAX DEDUCTIONS

Many expenses that you incur while working from home are tax deductible—even items that you do not specifically write checks for, such as depreciation.

You can think of these expenses that the IRS allows you to deduct as falling into two major categories. First, you can deduct expenses used in the course of your businesses—telephone, supplies, postage, etc.

Second, you may be able to deduct a portion of the costs of running your business from home. Beginning with rent or mortgage interest, you can potentially deduct utilities, insurance, real estate taxes in proportion to the amount of space your office uses in your home. Repairs and improvements that relate to the business can also be deductible.

Historically, the IRS had rigid rules that often eliminated home office deductions. The regulations have been relaxed somewhat in the past few years, but it is vital to meet the IRS's specific requirements. And, as they say on their Web site, "even then, your deduction may be limited."

To deduct expenses that apply to the business portion of your home, you must meet four requirements.

1. **EXCLUSIVE USE:** a space dedicated just to the business;

2. **REGULAR USE:** a consistent and continuing use of the work area;

3. **FOR YOUR TRADE OR BUSINESS;** and

4. **ONE OF THESE THREE OPTIONS:** your principal place of business, a place where you meet with clients or patients, or a separate, unattached structure that you use in connection with your trade or business.

What does the IRS mean by "exclusive use" in determining whether I can deduct my home office? *To the IRS, exclusive use means that a separate area of your home is used only for your trade or business.* It can be a separate room or a clearly identifiable space. The space does not have to be specifically marked off.

A key point is that you cannot use the area for personal purposes. That means you cannot, for example, use your work space to pursue a hobby of family history.

Is there an exception to the IRS "exclusive use" rule in determining whether I can deduct my home office? *Yes. If you consistently use a distinct part of your home to store inventory or product samples, and if your home is the only fixed location for your trade or business, you do not have to meet the exclusive use test.* Another exception is if you use part of your home for a day care business.

Can I deduct home office expenses even if I do not meet patients, clients or customers there as part of my business? *Meetings are just one of the ways to support deducting home office expenses.* In addition to meeting the exclusive, regular and for your trade or business requirements, the IRS says the business part of your home must meet just one of these:

- your principal place of business;
- a separate structure (not attached to your home) that you use to pursue your trade or business; or
- a meeting place.

In other words, you do not have to meet with others to satisfy the requirements if your home work space is your principal place of business, either in your home or in a separate structure.

Can I deduct a home office if I live in a condo or rent an apartment? You do not need to live in a house to qualify for a home office deduction, although you still need to meet the requirements set by the IRS.

If, for example, you are an interior designer and spend the majority of your time shopping for decorating products for your clients or meeting where they live, you may still qualify for the home office deduction. If you maintain your schedule and other records, have a primary telephone line and order products from your home office, you can be eligible to take the deduction.

What are some tips for meeting IRS requirements? As in any dealings with the IRS, you will benefit from maintaining records that support your case.

- Keep a calendar and a log of your business activities so that you can demonstrate how you spend your time. (Many consultants who bill by the hour already keep these detailed records.)
- Use a dedicated business phone line and make sure it, along with your address and business name, is included in your letterhead and other correspondence.
- Be ready to document your office space with layouts and possibly photos.

How do I determine the amount of home office expense I can deduct? *Once you are sure you meet the IRS regulations for a home office deduction, you will need to take two more steps.* First, compile your home-related expenses that will be eligible for the deduction. This includes a mortgage or rent payment, property tax, casualty losses and repairs. You will also calculate depreciation for the home.

Then you need to estimate the portion of the dwelling that is dedicated to your home business. This can be done by using square feet, dividing the number of square feet used by the home office by the home's total. Or you can use the proportionate number of rooms, assuming all rooms are about the same size.

You may have what the IRS calls "direct" expenses, meaning they apply only to the work area. The business can deduct the entire amount of a direct expense. Painting only the business area is an example of a direct expense.

Can I depreciate home office furniture and equipment? *Even if you do not qualify to deduct home office expenses, such as mortgage or rent, utilities and depreciation, you may be entitled to take depreciation for furniture and equipment.* This would apply whether you are the business owner or are working as a home-based employee.

Even if you may have paid cash for the whole amount of a business asset, for tax purposes you will take depreciation as an expense over a number of years that are roughly the same as the expected life of the asset. This "noncash" expense will help reduce the amount of income eligible for income tax; thus business owners want to take as much depreciation as allowed by the IRS.

The rules for depreciating business furniture and equipment depend on many factors. The IRS regulates depreciation based on the type of property, the percent of time it is used for business use versus personal use and whether it was purchased originally for business use or personal use.

How does depreciation work? *Let us start with an example. If you are a professional photographer, you might buy an expensive camera which you expect to use over many years.* You would like to be able to deduct this expense right away from your income tax.

But the IRS has other ideas. Since your equipment has a long expected life of use, you cannot deduct the entire expense in the first year. You are allowed to depreciate the expense over the approximate expected lifetime of the camera.

Each year, you can deduct a portion of the expense of the camera until you have reached the amount you paid for it.

How do I know how much depreciation expense I can take each year? *The simplest form of depreciation is called straight line.* Basically, you divide the cost of your asset by the number of years of expected life and take that equal amount each year until you have depreciated the entire cost.

Accelerated depreciation is favored by businesses because it allows bigger amounts of depreciation expense in the earlier years of the item's life.

For example, if our photographer paid $1,000 for his or her camera and expects a 5-year life for it, he or she would be able to expense $200 per year using straight line depreciation. With accelerated depreciation, he or she would take a larger amount of depreciation in the first years and a smaller amount in the later years, still totaling the $1,000 original cost of the camera.

Why does depreciation matter? *Depreciation is listed as an expense for tax and accounting purposes, but there is no actual cash outlay by the business.* Since the effect of depreciation is to conserve cash, it benefits cash flow. Stronger cash flow gives the business owner more flexibility in managing its finances and even for additional investment.

RETAIL: E-COMMERCE, CATALOG AND BRICKS-AND-MORTAR

Laws and regulations are lagging behind new forms of technology. Legislators and courts are being called on to adapt existing rules from nondigital sources—such as copyright laws or trade secrets—to the new uses that creative business minds have come up with. At the heart of new e-commerce directives are concepts aimed at the e-merchant's still-thriving predecessor, the catalog retailer.

What do I need to know about sales tax and the Internet? *As a shopper, one of the advantages of online buying is that sales tax is hardly ever part of the final price.* As an online merchant, what is your obligation to collect sales tax?

Each state sets its own sales tax policy and rates, and these differ across the United States Like the pre-Internet mail-order catalogers, the merchant collects sales tax only for states where it has a physical presence, like a warehouse or office. (There are five states that do not impose a sales tax.)

In theory, if sales tax is not collected by the seller, consumers are supposed to voluntarily pay what is called a "use tax" to the state where they live. This is not largely practiced, but states do pursue purchasers of big ticket items like boats or cars.

This situation has made at least two influential groups extremely unhappy. States are losing a large amount of revenue and are lobbying the national government for the right to tax Internet purchases. And traditional storefront merchants believe the Internet retailers have an unfair pricing edge, since consumers know that they will pay less for many products if there is no tax included.

The stakes in this battle are huge. And the states and traditional retailers will not give up. Until it is changed, the rule concerning sales tax remains whether there is a physical presence in a state.

If I have a storefront retail outlet, do I have to collect sales tax for every single sale that I make? *Every state has its own rules, but there some types of transactions that may be exempted. Certain items that are essential to subsistence, such as food or prescription drugs, might be exempted.* Nonprofits and charitable groups are often exempted from paying sales tax. Also, federal law prohibits states from taxing the government or agencies.

Sales made for resale are usually exempt. It is up to the seller to provide proof for this.

If I have a Web site and I want to include a URL link to another site, is there any legal reason why I should not? *The World Wide Web is an infinitely complex network of links to other sites and pages within sites.* So you would think that there should be no problem including a link, which is really just giving directions to another part of the Web. By and large, that is the case.

There may be exceptions, however, and courts are undecided on the issues. If, for instance, your link takes people to a part of a site that the site owners do not want the general public to see, you may be contributing to copyright infringement.

Which is it? E-mail marketing or spam? *There is just too much spam.* Not only are potentially productive hours wasted in deleting spam, but it slows down legitimate Internet traffic.

The CAN-SPAM Act of 2003 is the most potent weapon so far. It imposes penalties for spammers who use fraudulent or deceptive subject lines, do not have a working "unsubscribe system" or do not include a legitimate mailing address in the message. Sexually oriented emails must be clearly marked.

The Act applies to virtually any U.S. business that uses e-mail. If you want to use e-mail to market your products and services, the best strategy is to encourage potential buyers to "opt in" using a Web site or snail mail to sign up for sales information or a newsletter.

If I sell through a mail-order catalog, am I liable for including deceptive claims made by the manufacturer? *A merchant may be held responsible if he or she repeats untrue claims in his or her catalog or over the Web.* It is fair to ask manufacturers for proof to back up promises or guarantees that might be overblown. In any kind of ad copy or product description, claims should be supported.

Will a disclaimer keep me out of trouble? *A disclaimer might not be enough to counter a claim that is false or deceptive.* Any disclaimer must be understandable and easy to see and read.

INTERNATIONAL TRADE

Our world is getting smaller, and that opens up virtually infinite opportunities for businesses in the import/export field. The U.S. Department of Commerce reported that large companies are responsible for 4 percent of all exports. Simple subtraction would indicate that the vast majority of export business is being handled by smaller businesses.

What motivates international trade? Price is a significant driver, probably the most important. Also, consumers develop a taste for certain imports—German beer, for instance—and some items just cannot be found in the United States.

What countries are the biggest trade partners of the United States? In order of size, the U.S. Census Bureau reports the top ten are: Canada, Japan, Mexico, United Kingdom, Germany, China, Taiwan, France, South Korea and Singapore.

With all the concern about terrorism since 9/11, are importers not finding it more difficult to bring goods into the United States? *Some goods are getting a more intense look by the U.S. Customs Service.* As you might expect, these are products that could be tools of terrorism, such as chemicals or biological materials. Most importers reported delays right after 9/11 but have not experienced severe problems since then.

Who are some of the international trade participants? *As with any industry, there are countless variations in the way a business can participate.* Following are a few kinds of players.

1. **EXPORT MANAGEMENT COMPANY (EMC)**

   An EMC is a full-service manager hired by a U.S. company to sell its products overseas. Functions of the EMC include hiring and overseeing dealers, distribution, sales functions and shipping. You might find an EMC that specializes in certain products or parts of the world.

2. **EXPORT TRADING COMPANY (ETC)**

   An ETC works for foreign buyers who want to purchase U.S. products. The ETC finds suppliers who will export their goods.

3. **IMPORT/EXPORT MERCHANT**

   The international merchant may be more opportunistic (and takes on more risk) as the merchant does not work as an agent for others. In this business, the merchant purchases goods (either U.S. or foreign), then takes responsibility for shipping and selling them.

4. **FREIGHT FORWARDERS AND CUSTOMS BROKERS**

   Freight forwarders and customs brokers handle different sides of the same coin. A freight forwarder has the knowledge to move your products to their overseas destination. This takes more than simply a working knowledge of plane schedules. Freight forwarders know the best mode of transport for your particular goods, and they can get the proper paperwork handled for you.

   A good freight forwarder can help with packaging, warehousing and even financial details. He or she knows the important restrictions peculiar to each country.

On the other side, a customs broker will help get the goods into this country. It will pay off in the long run to work with a full-service broker who understands the intricacies of dealing with the many federal agencies who have an interest in the products that enter the United States. This is in addition to the countless laws that govern imports.

How is a letter of credit used in international trade? *A letter of credit is often used to facilitate international trade.* Once you have established credit with a bank, you can ask them to issue a letter of credit on your behalf. This will guarantee that the bank will pay your seller on the agreed-upon terms.

> **There is an international standard for letters of credit known as Uniform Customs and Practice for Commercial Documentary Credits which governs the details in transactions using letters of credit.**

Are there any government programs that provide funding for someone who wants to get into the import/export business?

The SBA has several programs to support businesses engaging in international trade. One is the International Trade Loan Program which goes to businesses that will help expand existing export markets or develop new ones.

Other SBA programs, such as the Section 7(a) loan guarantee program, can also be used for import/export businesses.

Where can I find more information on getting started in international trade? *If you need more information on import/export, here are a few organizations that will be able to help: Small Business Development Centers, Small Business Institutes and the U.S. Department of Commerce.* State and local governments usually have their own agencies to encourage trade, and there are many private and trade groups available as well.

What is the National Trade Data Bank (NTDB)? *The NTDB provides trade leads for businesses in the United States and abroad.* These are called Trade Opportunity Program Leads and United Nations Trade Leads.

How can I find out about regulations in foreign countries or even their customs for doing business? If you are not personally familiar with regulations and customs of a particular country, you might do best by working with a freight forwarder or customs broker.

11 TAXES & AUDITS

Both individuals and corporations must pay federal taxes on income and earnings. These taxes are the primary source of revenue for the federal government, with personal income taxes producing the bulk of the revenues. States rely mostly on sales and income taxes. Property taxes are the main source of revenue for local governments.

FEDERAL INCOME TAXES

What is an income tax? *Anyone who collects wages or earns money through investments and other income-producing vehicles must pay federal income taxes.* Taxes on wages are typically paid throughout the year through payroll withholding. Depending on your situation, you may receive a refund or owe the IRS.

> Not all income is taxed in the same way. For example, capital gains are taxed differently than income earned on money in a regular savings account.

What is meant by "withholding"? *Employers are responsible for paying payroll taxes from their employees' wages, which include Social Security taxes.* Payroll taxes are paid by "withholding" a sum of money from each employee's paycheck depending on her salary level and the number of dependants the employee claims. Payroll taxes keep a steady stream of revenue coming into the federal government. Additionally, withholding reduces the taxpayer's awareness of how much she is paying in federal income taxes, since the taxes are paid out gradually.

> **TIP:** To calculate how much you should have withheld from your paycheck, use the IRS withholding calculator located on the IRS Web site at: **www.irs.gov/individuals/article/0,,id=96196,00.html**.

What is a 1040? *The federal government keeps track of an individual's income and any taxes owed through tax returns know as a 1040, Form 1040, U.S. Individual Income Tax Return.* There are different varieties of 1040s depending on your income. The tax return is often accompanied by "schedules" – special forms filled out by the taxpayer detailing certain items on the tax return, such as business expenses.

Who has to pay federal income taxes? *Any citizen or resident of the United States who earns money during the year, including minors, is subject to income taxes.* This applies to aliens (noncitizens) living in the United States.

Who has to file a federal tax return? *Any citizen or resident of the United States earning a certain amount of income during the tax year must file a tax return.* For single filers, for example, anyone earning more than $7950 in 2004 had to file a return.

How do I know which form to fill out?

Typically, individuals or couples who do not have children, have an income less than $100,000 and are not itemizing deductions can use the 1040EZ form. Families and persons who itemize must file a longer version of the Form 1040.

> Taxpayers with income less than $100,000 that comes from wages only use Form 1040A. If you are receiving any income from sources other than employment, you must use Form 1040.

Do children have to pay taxes? *Yes. Laws do not exempt you from owing taxes because of your age.* However, if the child's earned income was less than $4,850 (for the 2004 tax year), he does not have to file a return. If the child is less than 14 years of age, the income may be included in the parents' income on the parents' tax return.

Is there one rate of taxation? *No. Tax rates are set by law according to income earned and reported on a taxpayer's tax return.* For every income level a certain percentage of those earnings must be paid to the federal government. This is a "progressive rate" of taxation. The basic rate is reduced by lowering or "adjusting" the taxpayer's gross income through a series of deductions and exemptions.

FILING STATUS

What is filing status and why is it important? *Because exemptions play a big part in reducing a taxpayer's gross income and, thus, her tax bill, filing status is crucial.* For example, a single woman gets one exemption; a married couple gets two exemptions; individuals with children claim additional exemptions and so on.

There are five filing statuses:

- Single
- Married Filing Jointly
- Married Filing Separately
- Head of Household
- Qualifying Widow(er) With Dependent Child

I am single because I am a widow, but I have child. Which filing status do I use?

If more than one filing status applies to you, choose the one that will give you the lowest tax. In your case, the qualifying widow status results in the lowest amount of tax.

My same-sex partner and I were married in Massachusetts. Can we file as a married couple? *No.* For tax filing purposes, the law defines marriage as a legal union between a man and a woman only as husband and wife.

I own my home and I'm not married. Why do I have to file as single instead head of household? *To qualify as "head of household," you must have a dependent.* The IRS defines a "head of household" as an unmarried person who maintains a household for the entire year for a dependent.

> Under IRS rules, a widow or widower can continue to file "jointly" for the two tax years after the year in which the spouse dies if he is maintaining a home for a dependent and meets certain other requirements. After 2 years, the spouse has head of household status until the dependant moves out.

Who claims head of household status if my girlfriend and I live together and have a child? Since the IRS allows only one of you to use the child to claim head of household status, the person who paid more than half the cost of keeping up the home during the year qualifies.

> If the cost of keeping up the house (rent, mortgage, utility bills) was split exactly in half, neither person can claim head of household status.

Which ex-spouse gets to claim head of household status if we share joint custody of our children? *The parent with whom the children spent more than half the year gets head of household status as long as you remained single and paid for more than half the cost of maintaining a home.* This allows your ex-spouse to claim the child as an exemption but still allows you to get head of household status (since only one of you gets an exemption for the child).

> **TIP:** Ex-spouses cannot both claim head of household status unless there is more than one child and each former spouse has different children living with her for more than half the year.

DEDUCTIONS, EXEMPTIONS AND CREDITS

What are deductions? *An individual's ultimate tax bill is based on the "ability to pay," rather than just the tax rate for his income level. In order to determine a taxpayer's ability to pay, there are rules in place that allow gross income to be reduced by claiming certain specific or "itemized" deductions.* For example, a taxpayer with children, a mortgage and high medical expenses has less ability to pay a portion of income to the federal government. By subtracting these expenses, the taxpayer can calculate his "adjusted income." His tax bill is then figured using the adjusted income.

> A taxpayer's income is reduced through the "standard" deduction. If the taxpayer's itemized deductions exceed the standard deduction, she uses the larger amount to calculate her taxable income.

Is an exemption the same as a deduction? *Similar to deductions, an "exemption" allows a taxpayer to subtract a set amount from his gross income for each allowable "exemption."* Every taxpayer gets to subtract an amount for himself. Married couples, for example, get two exemptions. Additionally, the taxpayer gets an exception for every child or legal dependent. Thus, those taxpayers with large families have a lower adjusted income since their ability to pay is much less than a childless couple.

> The Taxpayer Relief Act of 1997 gave certain taxpayers the ability to receive a per-child tax credit. The tax credit was $1,000 per child in 2004, but is slated to drop back down to $700 in 2005 unless Congress changes the amount.

> **TIP:** Because the per child tax credit is a credit, it is possible for taxpayers with very low incomes to not only owe zero taxes, but to get a refund.

Can I claim a child as a dependent who does not yet have Social Security number? *Yes.* If your child was born during the tax year, you can attach a copy of the child's birth certificate to your return.

> **TIP:** Parents in the process of a domestic or international adoption who do not have the child's Social Security number should request an adoption taxpayer identification number (ATIN) in order to claim the child as a dependent and (if eligible) to claim the child care credit. For more information call 800.829.3676 or visit the IRS Web site at **www.irs.gov/pub/irs-pdf/fw7a.pdf**.

What are dependants? *Every taxpayer may claim an exemption for her dependants.* A dependant is not necessarily a child. The IRS allows you to claim a dependent of any age as long as he meets five tests: relationship test, citizenship test, joint return test, gross income test and support test.

What is the relationship test? *A dependent is direct descendant–a child, grandchild, great-grandchild–whether living with you or not.* If the dependent is not a relative, the test requires her to live in the household for one year as "member of the household."

If there is no age limit on a dependent, can I claim my child as a dependent as long as I live? *Yes, in rare circumstances.* However, once your child is more than 19 years old and earns more than $3,100 per year, you cannot claim him. The exception is children still in school up until age 24. If you continue to support your child the rest of his life and he never earns an income more than $3,100 you can continue to claim him as a dependent.

Can my ex-husband and I split the dependency exemption? *No. The dependency exemption cannot be split.* The parent who provides more than half the support for the child gets the exemption. Generally, the custodial parent is assumed to have provided more than half of the child's support and gets the exemption. However, if the noncustodial provides more than half of the child's support, she may be entitled to the exemption.

What is a tax credit? *There are several types of credits available to taxpayers.* The credits are directly subtracted from the taxes owed. In 2004, available tax credits included education credits, child credits, earned income credits, credits for the elderly and disabled and dependent care credits.

How does my retirement account affect my income taxes? *Taxpayers can reduce their income for tax reporting purposes by contributing to certain retirement accounts.* Generally, these accounts are 401(k) and IRA accounts. For example, an individual can contribute up to $4,000 per year (as of 2005) to an IRA.

LATE RETURNS AND EXTENSIONS

Tax returns must be filed by April 15, every year, even if you owe no money and are not receiving a refund. If a taxpayer does owe taxes, the payment must be postmarked or paid by April 15, even if an extension for filing was granted.

Can I file my return late? *Yes.* The IRS permits the April 15 deadline to be extended.

How do I get an extension? *Your first extension is granted automatically by filing Form 4868 with the IRS.* The form can be filed by mail, electronically or over the telephone using the IRS telefile system.

> **TIP:** Go to the IRS Web site at **www.irs.gov/ taxtopics/tc304.html** for more information and directions.

How soon do I have to file an extension? You must file for an extension on or before April 15.

Does an extension extend the time for payment if I owe taxes? *No.* You must pay part or all of your estimated income tax due.

How long is the extension? The extension gives you an additional 4 months—until August 15.

PAYMENT AND PENALTIES

Any taxpayer who owes taxes is required to pay that amount to the IRS. Taxpayers who cannot pay may qualify for special plans that allow them to pay the taxes over time or settle the bill by paying a smaller amount. However, if the taxpayer has any assets at all, the IRS can seize and sell these to cover the taxes that are due.

I only sent a check for half the amount I owed when I filed my tax return. Will I hear from the IRS? *Yes.* Once the IRS determines your math is correct, that you owe a certain amount and that you did not pay all of it, you will receive a "Notice of Tax Due and Demand for Payment"—your tax bill.

> **Interest and penalties continue to accrue on the amount owed as long as it is not paid.**

> **TIP:** Once a taxpayer receives a bill, the IRS expects it to be paid by any means possible— credit card, a loan, money from a 401(k), etc.

I can't pay my tax bill. What do I do? *First, you must file a return even though you cannot pay.* Request that you be allowed to pay out the amount over time. The IRS permits taxpayers to pay taxes under installment agreement plans.

How do I set up an installment agreement? *You can file a special form requesting an installment agreement (IA).* Form 9465 is available online at www.irs.gov/pub/irs-pdf/f9465.pdf. You can also call the IRS at 800.829.1040. You should receive a response within 30 days.

> **TIP:** You will not receive tax refunds you might be eligible for in subsequent years while you are paying under an installment agreement. Any refunds that are owed to you will be applied to the debt.

> A taxpayer who owes less than $10,000 (and is not currently overdue for other years) has a right to pay out the amount under an IA, according to the IRS manual. To get more specific information about provisions and requirements, go to the IRS manual at **www.irs.gov/irm/part5/ch13s01.html**.

I cannot even afford to pay the taxes I owe under an installment agreement. What do I do?

You can request an Offer in Compromise or OIC. You must fill out an OIC package. You will calculate what amount, if any, you can offer to settle your tax bill. If you are facing economic hardship or other special circumstances and the IRS grants an OIC, you have no further tax liability (for that tax year).

> Only taxpayers who do not qualify for an installment agreement (typically those individuals whose total monthly income falls at or below income levels based on the Department of Health and Human Services poverty guidelines) are considered for an OIC.

> **TIP:** To get more detailed information on obtaining an OIC, go to the IRS's online guide at **www.irs.gov/pub/irs-pdf/p594.pdf**.

Will I have to pay a penalty if I do not pay my taxes on time?

Yes. Both interest and penalties are assessed against taxpayers who owe money to the IRS. The interest rate is tied to the federal short-term interest rate and is adjusted every 3 months. Additionally, taxpayers must pay a late payment penalty of one-half percent of the tax owed for each month the taxes are unpaid.

> **TIP:** Late penalties are explained in greater detail at **www.irs.gov/faqs/faq-kw136.html**.

FILING YOUR TAX RETURN

Filing a tax return is easier today because of software programs capable of calculating your adjusted income, deductions, exemptions, credits and so on. Taxpayers using these programs typically get their returns done much faster and do not put off or delay filing. Additionally, for many years the IRS has encouraged taxpayers to file their returns over the Internet, called e-filing.

What happens if I just don't file a tax return?

Eventually, the IRS will catch up with you and IRS employees will prepare the returns you did not file. You probably will not get credit for deductions and exemptions on the IRS-prepared returns. The IRS will then send a bill for the tax due, plus penalties and interest.

What is e-filing?

E-filing, or electronic filing, means your return is transmitted by an authorized service (an electronic return originator or ERO) directly to the IRS's computers.

Is there any advantage to e-filing my tax return?

Yes. If you are due a refund, you will get it in about 2 weeks (rather than the usual 10 week time frame) and it can be deposited directly into your bank account. There is also some data to suggest that e-filers may be audited less often. Additionally, since the data does not have to be entered by an actual person off a paper return, many human errors are avoided during the data entry process.

Who is eligible to e-file?

Anyone who must file a tax return is eligible to e-file unless:

- your return includes certain schedules;

> **TIP:** See IRS Publication 1345, Section 18 for list of schedules excluded from e-filing at **www.irs.gov/pub/irs-pdf/p1345a.pdf**.

- you are claiming miscellaneous tax credits;
- you are claiming a recapture of low income housing credit;
- you are claiming certain enterprise or rural empowerment zone income modifications; or
- you are claiming a resident credit with more than two states per taxpayer.

Is it secure to file my return electronically?

Yes. The return is encrypted and transmitted over secure phone lines to ensure safety, security and confidentiality.

How do I e-file my tax return?

You must have IRS approved software installed on your computer in order to e-file your return (such as TurboTax, Tax Basic or Quicken, to name a few). Your tax preparer, if you use one, can e-file from her office assuming she is an authorized ERO.

> A list of approved EROs is available on the IRS Web site at **www.irs.gov/efile/page/ 0,,id=10162,00.html**.

What does it cost to e-file? Although the IRS itself does not charge a fee for e-filing, EROs typically charge a fee of about $15 to transmit your return.

> **TIP:** Some software companies refund the fee if you use their tax software.

> Taxpayers who meet certain criteria may get free e-filing. To see if you qualify, go to the IRS's Web site at **www.irs.gov/efile/article/ 0,,id=118993,00.html#basics_3**.

Will I be notified if the IRS received my e-filed tax return? *Yes. The ERO will notify you by e-mail if your return has been accepted or rejected. If you return was rejected, you will be given the reason and asked to correct the error.* For example, you may have made a mistake typing in your spouse's Social Security number. Once you correct the mistake, the tax return is refiled—typically at no additional cost.

> When both federal and state returns are filed at the same time, the federal return is accepted or rejected first. Once the federal tax return is accepted by the IRS, the state return is then transmitted.

> **TIP:** An accepted tax return has an electronic confirmation number assigned to it. It is a good idea to print out the number in case a question is raised later about the return's transmission.

REFUNDS

By law, taxpayers who are due a refund and filed their tax return by April 15 must receive the refund from the IRS by June 1. Taxpayers who receive late refunds are entitled to interest on the amount of the refund.

Can the IRS withhold my refund? *In many cases, the IRS can legally withhold the refund check.* Taxpayers who owe child support, have defaulted on student loans or are paying back taxes under an installment plan can have their refund withheld to satisfy those outstanding debts.

IRS COLLECTION PROCESS

Under the law, the IRS has a variety of methods available to collect overdue taxes. Before the IRS begins its "collection process," a taxpayer is typically asked to pay voluntarily, either under an installment agreement or by working out some method of payment. Taxpayers who do not cooperate will probably have an IRS lien filed on their property and have property or wages levied (seized).

> Creditors are notified when the IRS files a lien and the liens are reflected on your credit report.

> **TIP:** The IRS publishes a pamphlet explaining its collection process in detail. It is available online at **www.irs.gov/pub/irs-pdf/p594.pdf**.

Can the IRS seize the funds in my retirement plan? *Yes. The IRS can seize property, such as retirement plans and 401(k)s, which are typically safe from debt collection.* The law allows the IRS to seize and sell any type of real or personal property that you own or have an interest in if you owe taxes.

Can I go to jail for failing to pay my taxes? *Yes. If you have violated criminal laws, you could be prosecuted and sent to jail.* However, just because you owe taxes, have not filed a return or are late filing a return does not necessarily mean you are under criminal investigation.

Are tax shelters legal? Although the term "tax shelter" implies some sort of tax loophole, in reality tax shelters are legal and available to many taxpayers.

EXAMPLE: A taxpayer's home is a type of tax shelter: mortgage interest is deductible, the profits from the sale of home (up to $500,000 per couple) are not taxed, and repairs from damage and theft may be deducted.

SOCIAL SECURITY AND MEDICARE TAXES

In addition to the basic income tax all wage earners must pay, the federal government collects a Social Security tax. Employers also pay Social Security tax. An employee pays 6.2 percent of his wage for Social Security taxes, which is withheld from his paycheck. The employer matches the employee's tax amount and the employer pays both portions to the federal government. These taxes go to support benefits paid out by the Social Security Administration.

Like Social Security taxes, Medicare taxes are withheld from an employee's wages, matched by the employer and remitted to the federal government to cover the cost of the Medicare program. The federal Medicare program pays the medical care of individuals more than 65 years of age, regardless of income.

> Medicare and Social Security taxes are often designated as "FICA" taxes on a paycheck after the Federal Income Contributions Act, which requires the deductions. FICA taxes are also called payroll taxes.

ESTATE AND GIFT TAXES

Taxes must be paid on estates and gifts above a certain value. The two subjects are intertwined because an individual may reduce the value of his estate by "gifting" (giving money and property) away every year.

> Congress has passed legislation phasing out the federal estate tax until it disappears altogether in 2010.

IRS rules allow an individual to "gift" another person up to $11,000 per year. Beyond that amount, the individual receiving the money must pay gift taxes on the excess. For example, gift taxes would be owed on $1,000 if the amount of the gift were $12,000.

For 2005, estates valued at less than $1.5 million are exempt, meaning they are not subject to the estate tax. The exemption amount rises to $2 million in 2006 and $3.5 million in 2009.

> Estates (or the portion of the estate) left to the surviving spouse are typically exempt from tax regardless of the value.

Estate and gift tax laws are complicated. It is highly recommended that you consult with a board certified tax and probate attorney if you have a large estate.

My mother gave me $10,000. Do I have to pay taxes on the money? *No.* Your mother may gift you up to $11,000 annually without either of you incurring any tax liability.

I have seven children. Can I gift more than $11,000 in one year? *Yes. You may gift the children $11,000 each (for a total of $77,000) if you wish.* There is no limit to the number of people that you can gift during the year or how much money you can gift during your lifetime.

My husband's mother gave him $20,000. Does he have to pay taxes on the amount over $11,000? *No. The extra $9000 can be allotted to you since you are his spouse.* You must fill out a "gift splitting" form with the IRS to report that you are splitting the gift and do not owe taxes on the money.

CAPITAL GAINS

A capital gain is the profit made when an asset is sold. For tax purposes, that profit counts as income. For individual taxpayers, typical capital gains include selling a home, real estate or stocks. Almost everything you own and use for personal purposes, pleasure or investment is a capital asset. When you sell a capital asset – such as stocks – the difference between the amounts you sell it for and what you paid for it is a capital gain or a capital loss.

Capital gains and losses are either long-term or short-term. If you hold an asset for more than one year, your capital gain or loss is long-term. If you hold the asset for one year or less, your capital gain or loss is short-term. Short-term capital gains are taxed at your current tax rate, while long-term capital gains are taxed anywhere between 5 and 28 percent.

My wife and I sold our house at a profit of $100,000. How much of this is taxed? None of the profit is taxed because you are not required to report capital gains less than $500,000 ($250,000 for a single taxpayer) for the sale of your personal residence.

> **TIP:** The loss on the sale of a personal residence is a nondeductible personal loss.

> **TIP:** A taxpayer can use the residential capital gains provision for only one property at a time and one sale every two years.

> **TIP:** For an extensive explanation of the residential exclusion and examples of several scenarios, go to IRS publication 523 at **www.irs.gov/publications/p523/ar02. html#doe1901**.

My wife and I bought and remodeled a home during the year. We made a $50,000 profit. Is the profit taxed? *Yes. The home does not qualify as a residence.* To avoid a capital gains tax for a residential sale you must have lived in the home for at least 2 years (out of the previous 5 years) as your main residence.

> **The length of time the taxpayer lives in the home is the ownership test. Whether or not the home was used as the taxpayer's primary residence (as opposed to a lake house), is the use test. Both tests must be met in order to avoid the capital gains tax.**

Can I deduct capital gains losses? *While the IRS requires you to report all capital gains, you can deduct only your capital losses on investment property, not personal property.*

Currently, you can deduct up to $3,000 of capital losses annually ($1,500 if married and filing separately).

STATE AND LOCAL TAXES

Aside from federal income taxes, there are a variety of state and local taxes that individuals must pay. All states have the right to impose taxes on their residents, including a state income tax.

State taxes go to pay for public services such as public schools, police protection, health and welfare benefits, and the operation of the state government.

STATE PERSONAL INCOME TAX

Most states require residents to pay a personal income tax and file a state income tax return. Income is taxed at either a flat or graduated rate. The following states do not have an income tax:

- Alaska
- Florida
- Nevada
- South Dakota
- Tennessee
- Texas
- Washington
- Wyoming

STATE SALES TAXES

States collect a great portion of their revenue from state sales taxes on the sale of goods and services. Typically, states impose three types of sales tax: the vendor tax, the consumer tax and the combination vendor-consumer tax.

1. Vendor tax–imposes a tax on the retailer or person in business. Retailers pay tax based on their revenues.

2. Consumer tax (sales tax)–is the sales tax that a person pays when she buys an item. The retailer collects the tax at the time of sale and sends the tax money to the state. Many states have set aside certain days as "tax-free," permitting consumers to make purchases without paying sales tax on certain items such as school supplies.

All persons, regardless of their income, pay the same rate of sales tax on their purchases. For this reason, some items of necessity are not taxed, such as food or prescription medicine, making those items more affordable for lower income individuals and families. Additionally, certain charitable and religious organizations are exempt from paying sales tax on their purchases.

3. Combination tax–is the amount the consumer pays when she makes a purchase; however, the amount includes the vendor's tax of his revenues. There is no difference to the consumer—in her mind, she is paying a sales tax.

> **Use taxes are imposed on certain transactions that are not subject to sales tax. One of the most common use taxes that states impose on residents is the use tax on vehicles leases and rentals.**

PROPERTY TAXES

All the states directly tax or permit certain property owned by residents to be taxed by local governments. Generally, local county and city governments tax real estate such as land, homes and other structures. Personal property is also taxed in some states. In those states, residents pay tax on vehicles, boats, equipment, furniture, and the like. The taxes are typically paid to the county, school district, college district or water district. Property tax revenue pays for local public services such as public schools, police and fire departments, garbage collection and salaries for local government officials.

INHERITANCE AND ESTATE TAXES

Although the federal government taxes estates, many states also impose estate taxes based on an estate's value. Additionally, beneficiaries may be required to pay a state inheritance tax when they receive property.

CORPORATE INCOME TAX

States collect taxes on income earned by a corporation operating in that state. The corporate tax varies from state to state. Many states have low corporate tax rates to encourage business, although tax revenue is subsequently decreased.

AUDITS

An audit is an official IRS examination of a federal tax return. Audits terrify taxpayers because it can seem as though the IRS has almost unlimited powers. To a certain extent, however, the IRS does have extremely broad authority.

> **TIP:** If you get a notice that you are being audited, consider following the rule that the taxpayer never directly speaks with the auditor. Get your CPA, lawyer or a tax advocate to represent you if it all possible.

What is an audit? *An IRS audit is a review of your tax return to confirm its accuracy.* Field and office audits typically include a taxpayer interview as well as an examination of documents.

What kinds of audits can the IRS perform? There are three different types of audits:

1. **CORRESPONDENCE AUDIT.** Most taxpayers are generally "audited" by getting a notice from the IRS regarding one or two items on their tax return. For example, the IRS may want to see documentation of your large noncash charitable donations. If you have receipts from the charity and have kept records of the items given, the IRS will probably be satisfied and the matter will be closed. Most taxpayers can competently handle their own correspondence audits.

2. **FIELD AUDIT.** The field audit is an on-site visit from an IRS auditor and typically occurs with businesses. The auditor examines the business records, bookkeeping methods and other accounting systems that are in place. For example, an auditor might come to a taxpayer's home to check the accuracy of his home office deductions—including measuring the square footage of the office.

3. **OFFICE AUDIT.** If you have been summoned to your local IRS office, the auditors have determined your tax return warrants an office audit. You must appear at the time and date requested in the notification, with the documents specified in the notice. Before you go, it is highly recommended you consult a tax lawyer to help you gather the documents the auditor has requested and only those

documents. Bringing documents relating to other matters only has the potential for broadening the subject matter of the audit.

Who gets audited?
Typically, three types of taxpayers are the most frequently audited by the IRS:

1. Those who take large and unusual deductions—donating a vehicle to charity, for example.

2. Pofessionals who bill for their services, set their rates, handle their own booking, etc., such as accountants, lawyers and doctors

3. Any cash business, or taxpayers receiving a substantial portion of their income from cash, such as bars, waiters, cosmetologists, etc.

What are the reasons for audits?
The IRS "scores" returns using a computer program and those tax returns that have a certain score are likely to be audited. The score is based on the probability that the tax return omitted income. Your tax return can also be audited if documents are missing, there is a questionable item (such as a deduction) or the IRS has received information that you may be committing tax fraud.

How can I avoid an audit?
Taxpayers who keep written records of their expenses and deductions can often deflect an audit. In other words, if the IRS is suspicious of your tax return's accuracy and begins by questioning your charitable donations, it may back off if you can provide impeccable documentation of the donations. Additionally, sloppy tax return preparation raises a red flag. Before filing a return, double-check and triple-check your numbers and math. Finally, if you are in one of the categories of taxpayers that the IRS frequently audits, set up a method of recording expenses and income.

EXAMPLE: A salesman's travel expenses should be documented by receipts, cancelled checks and credit card statements.

Can I be audited if my CPA prepared my return, handled all my records and receipts and decided what deductions should be taken?
Yes. The taxpayer is ultimately responsible (and liable) for her tax return
although someone else prepared it. If there are errors on the return, you are assessed back taxes, penalties and interest.

> **TIP:** Always keep the original records or a copy of any documents that back up your tax return's accuracy. You are responsible for maintaining records and if your preparer loses or misplaces documents, it will be impossible to defend an audit.

What is the best way to defend an audit?
The best way to defend an audit is to begin immediately organizing your records and finding all receipts and other paperwork that show deductions, expenses, mileage and charitable donations. If you speak with an IRS auditor, be calm, courteous and patient. A good attitude will greatly benefit you during the audit process.

A taxpayer should always have representation at any audit beyond the correspondence audit level since the taxpayer is typically interviewed. Tax professionals who aide taxpayers in defending audits may charge a fee of several thousand dollars for such representation. Taxpayers have the right to record the audit interview by giving 10 days' notice to the IRS of their intent to record.

> **TIP:** Individuals and small business owners can take out "audit protection insurance (API)." The insurance provides a certain level of coverage depending on amount of premium paid. Persons with a history of audits and those who do not have their returns professionally prepared may not be eligible for audit insurance.

Am I entitled to be represented during the audit?
Yes. You can be represented by an attorney, a certified public accountant, an enrolled agent (a person enrolled to practice before the IRS), an enrolled actuary or the person who prepared the return and signed it as the preparer.

> **TIP:** Former IRS employees often go into the business of representing taxpayers at audits.

I have been summoned to the IRS offices. Do I have the right to have the audit take place at my attorney's office? *No.* The IRS decides when, where and how the audit will take place.

> **TIP:** Taxpayers must be treated fairly and courteously. Make sure you are aware of your rights as a taxpayer when you are before the IRS. Some taxpayer rights include:
>
> - the right to representation at any IRS hearing;
> - the right to record interviews by IRS employees, auditors and agents;
> - the right to end the interview;
> - the right appeal the auditor's decisions; and
> - the right to obtain help from the Taxpayer Advocate's Office.
>
> Your rights are explained at **www.irs.gov/ newsroom/article/0,,id=105120,00.html**.

Can I appeal an audit? *A taxpayer has the right to formally agree or disagree with the auditor's conclusions.* By agreeing, the taxpayer concludes the audit; however he must pay any amounts due plus penalties that have been assessed against him.

Disagreeing with the audit puts the taxpayer into an appeals process. A supervisor in the IRS office may review the audit or the taxpayer can go directly to the IRS Appeals Office. From there, the appeal goes to U.S. Tax Court. Appeals from Tax Court are made to federal District Courts.

> **TIP:** If you cannot resolve the issue with a supervisor, you have the right contact the IRS Taxpayer Advocate Service. The Taxpayer Advocate Service is an independent organization within the IRS whose goal is to help taxpayers resolve problems with the IRS.

My audit is over and I won; however, my business has suffered irreparable damage as a result of the IRS's actions. Do I have any recourse? *Yes. Federal law allows you to sue the IRS for damages as a result of the agency's negligence.* Your recovery is limited to $100,000 plus attorney's fee and costs.

Can I be subject to criminal charges because of my tax filing? *Taxpayers who are suspected of "cheating" on their taxes or of being involved in fraudulent activities may find themselves under criminal investigation by IRS agents.* Tax fraud means that the taxpayer is willfully hiding or attempting to hide income from the IRS.

EXAMPLE: Typical crimes include tax evasion, failure to file or filing a false tax return.

Some of these individuals are nonfilers who are challenging the constitutionality of taxes, claims for fraudulent refunds, abusive trust schemes and unscrupulous tax return preparers.

The Socrates Practical Law Handbook: Solutions for Everyday Legal Questions

SPECIAL OFFER FOR BOOK BUYERS— SAVE 15% ON THESE ESSENTIAL PRODUCTS AT

Socrates.com/books/law-handbook.aspx

Socrates.com offers essential business, personal and real estate do-it-yourself products that can help you:

- Sell or lease a property
- Write a will or trust
- Start a business
- Get a divorce
- Hire a contractor
- Manage employees
- And much more

Business Legal Forms and Agreements Software (SS4323)

If you're tired of spending countless hours and money creating and filing business documents, this complete, convenient resource may be your solution. It contains **279 ready-to-use legal forms and agreements**, most of which can be customized to meet your needs to help you legally protect your business and make your life easier.

TOPICS COVERED INCLUDE:

- landlording
- lending and borrowing
- buying and selling agreements
- employment
- credit and collection letters and notices
- transfers and assignments
- insurance
- items for personal and family use

Incorporation Kit (K325)

INCLUDES CD, INSTRUCTION MANUAL AND 20 FORMS.

Protect your personal assets from your business' liabilities by incorporating. Decide which type of corporation is best for you and handle the incorporation yourself using this comprehensive kit.

Last Will & Testament Kit (K307)
INCLUDES INSTRUCTION MANUAL AND 17 FORMS.

Protect your loved ones, make your wishes known and award your assets as you desire. Contains the forms and instructions you need to plan your estate responsibly and affordably.

Living Will & Power of Attorney for Health Care Kit (K306)
INCLUDES INSTRUCTION MANUAL AND 14 FORMS.

Express your choice of when to discontinue treatment and life support and who should make that decision for you if you're permanently incapacitated. Free state-specific forms at Socrates.com.

Divorce Kit (K302)
INCLUDES INSTRUCTION MANUAL AND 13 FORMS.

Save time and costly legal fees by preparing yourself for a simple, uncontested divorce. This convenient Divorce Kit helps you and your partner come to an agreement early in the process.

Bankruptcy Kit (K300)
NEWLY UPDATED WITH OCTOBER 2005 LAW CHANGES. INCLUDES INSTRUCTION MANUAL AND 28 FORMS.

Obtain relief from debt and save on costly legal fees by preparing in advance for your bankruptcy proceedings. This comprehensive kit contains the legal forms and know-how you need to do it yourself.